ABA Criminal Justice Mental Health Standards

Albert J. Datz, Chairperson
ABA Criminal Justice Standards Committee

Terence F. MacCarthy, Chairperson
Section of Criminal Justice

* * *

Gerald T. Bennett, Reporter

Gerald M. Caplan, Reporter

William K. Carroll, Reporter

James W. Ellis, Reporter

Grant H. Morris, Reporter

Christopher Slobogin, Reporter

Elyce H. Zenoff, Reporter

B. James George, Jr., General Reporter

Approved by ABA House of Delegates
August, 1984

(Principles contained in Standards 7-6.1(a), 7–6.9(b), and 7–6.10(b) approved by ABA House of Delegates *February, 1983.*)

(Principles contained in Standards 7–5.5, 7–5.6 and 7–5.7 approved by ABA House of Delegates *August, 1987.*)

(Principles contained in Standards 7–5.8, 7–5.9 and 7–5.10 approved by ABA House of Delegates *August, 1988.*)

Library of Congress Catalog Card No. 89–83716
ISBN 0–89707–450–5

Project of the
American Bar Association
Criminal Justice Standards Committee
1800 M Street, NW
Washington, D.C. 20036

Supported by the John D. and
Catherine T. MacArthur Foundation
through the American Bar Association
Fund for Justice and Education

Printed in the United States of America

ABA CRIMINAL JUSTICE STANDARDS COMMITTEE

Albert J. Datz, *Chairperson*
Private practitioner, Datz, Jacobson & Lembcke, Jacksonville, Florida

Charles L. Becton
Judge, North Carolina Court of Appeals, Raleigh, North Carolina

Paul D. Borman
Chief Defender, Federal Defender Office, Detroit, Michigan

William P. Curran
County Attorney, Clark County, Las Vegas, Nevada

Arthur C. "Cappy" Eads
District Attorney, Belton, Texas

Steven H. Goldberg
Associate Dean, University of Minnesota School of Law, Minneapolis, Minnesota

Norman Lefstein
Dean, Indiana University School of Law, Indianapolis, Indiana

Patricia M. Wald
Chief Judge, U.S. Court of Appeals, District of Columbia Circuit, Washington, D.C.

Alexander H. Williams III
Judge, Superior Court, Los Angeles, California

* * *

Susan W. Shaffer
Director, Criminal Justice Standards Committee

* * *

Terence F. MacCarthy
Chairperson, Section of Criminal Justice

FORMER STANDING COMMITTEE ON ASSOCIATION STANDARDS FOR CRIMINAL JUSTICE*

William H. Erickson, *Chairman*
Justice, Supreme Court of Colorado, Denver, Colorado
Kenneth J. Hodson, *Vice Chairman*
Major General, United States Army (Retired); former Judge Advocate General of the Army, Washington, D.C.
Paul D. Borman
Chief Federal Defender, Detroit, Michigan
George J. Cotsirilos
Private practitioner, Cotsirilos & Crowley, Ltd., Chicago, Illinois
William P. Curran
County Attorney, Clark County, Las Vegas, Nevada
Norman S. Early, Jr.
District Attorney, Denver, Colorado
Robert M. Ervin
Private practitioner, Ervin, Varn, Jacobs, Odom & Kitchen, Tallahassee, Florida
Steven H. Goldberg
Associate Dean, University of Minnesota School of Law, Minneapolis, Minnesota
Michael J. Hemovich
Private practitioner, Hemovich & Nappi, Spokane, Washington

During much of the tenure of the Criminal Justice Mental Health Standards Project, *B. James George, Jr.*, Professor of Law, New York Law School, served as Chairman of the Standing Committee. During portions of this project the following persons also served as members of the Standing Committee: *William R. Beasley*, Judge, Michigan Court of Appeals, Southfield, Michigan; *Gerald T. Bennett*, Professor of Law, University of Florida; *Richard J. Brzeczek*, private practitioner, Chicago, Illinois; the late *Walter E. Craig*, Senior Judge, U.S. District Court, Phoenix, Arizona; *Albert J. Datz*, private practitioner, Jacksonville, Florida; *Corinne P. Grande*, Associate Justice, Superior Court, Providence, Rhode Island; *Francis B. Looney*, retired Deputy Police Commissioner, New York City, Farmingdale, New York; *Terence F. MacCarthy*, Executive Director, Federal Defender Program, Chicago, Illinois; and *Ben F. Overton*, Justice, Florida Supreme Court, Tallahassee, Florida.

* * *

---

* The listed titles of Committee members reflect positions held by members at the time the work of the Committee was undertaken.

ADVISORY COMMITTEE CRIMINAL JUSTICE MENTAL HEALTH STANDARDS PROJECT*

B. James George, Jr., *Chairman*
Professor of Law, New York Law School, New York, New York

Richard J. Bonnie
Professor of Law and Director, Institute of Law, Psychiatry & Public Policy, University of Virginia School of Law, Charlottesville, Virginia

Walter E. Craig †
Senior Judge, U.S. District Court, Phoenix, Arizona

Bernard Diamond
Professor of Law, Emeritus, University of California School of Law at Berkeley, and Clinical Professor of Psychiatry, University of California School of Medicine at San Francisco, Ross, California

Bruce J. Ennis
Private practitioner, Ennis, Friedman, Bersoff & Ewing, Washington, D.C.

Kenneth J. Hodson
Major General, United States Army (Retired); former Judge Advocate General of the Army, Washington, D.C.

Norval Morris
Julius Kreeger Professor of Law and Criminology, University of Chicago, Chicago, Illinois

McNeill Smith
Private practitioner, Smith Moore Smith Schell & Hunter, Greensboro, North Carolina

* The listed titles of Committee members reflect positions held by members at the time the work of the Committee was undertaken.

† Deceased

Contents

PART III. PRETRIAL EVALUATIONS AND EXPERT TESTIMONY 63

PART IV. COMPETENCE TO STAND TRIAL 157

PART V. COMPETENCE ON OTHER ISSUES 259

ADDITION TO PART V: COMPETENCE AND CAPITAL PUNISHMENT 284

ADDITION TO PART V: COMPETENCE AND CONFESSIONS 303

PART VI. NONRESPONSIBILITY FOR CRIME 321

PART VII. COMMITMENT OF NONRESPONSIBILITY ACQUITTEES 395

PART VIII. SPECIAL DISPOSITIONAL STATUTES 453

PART IX. SENTENCING MENTALLY ILL AND MENTALLY RETARDED OFFENDERS 463

PART X. MENTALLY ILL AND MENTALLY RETARDED PRISONERS 505

NOTE ON ABBREVIATIONS AND RELATED STANDARDS

References to related standards in text and footnotes are by initials or full name of the drafting organization, volume title (or title of the set of standards), and the number of the specific standard or, in the case of model or uniform codes or rules, the section or article number referred to: for example, NCCUSL, Uniform Rules of Criminal Procedure 421. References in text are to the version in effect at the time of the revision (unless otherwise indicated). For the convenience of the reader, a listing of the related standards with full name of the drafting organization and year of publication follows:

AAMD (American Association on Mental Deficiency), Classification in Mental Retardation (1983)

ABA (American Bar Association), (Standards Relating to) Appellate Courts (1977) (component volume of the Standards of Judicial Administration)

ABA, Code of Judicial Conduct (1978)

ABA, Code of Professional Responsibility (1978)

ABA, (Standards Relating to) Court Organization (1974) (component volume of the Standards of Judicial Administration)

ABA, Criminal Justice Mental Health Standards (Tentative Draft 1983)

ABA, Model Rules of Professional Conduct (1983)

ABA, Standards for Criminal Justice (1980)

ABA, (Standards Relating to) Trial Courts (1976) (component volume of the Standards of Judicial Administration)

ACA (American Correctional Association), Standards for Adult Correctional Institutions (2d ed. 1981)

ACA, Standards for Adult Local Detention Facilities (2d ed. 1981)

ALI (American Law Institute), Model Code of Pre-Arraignment Procedure (1975)

ALI, Model Penal Code (1962)

ALI, Model Penal Code (Permanent ed. & revised commentary 1985)

AMA (American Medical Association), Standards for Health Services in Jails (1981)

APA, American Psychiatric Association, Committee on Public Information, A Psychiatric Glossary (3d ed. 1969)

American Psychiatric Association, Diagnostic and Statistical Manual of Mental Disorders 367 (3d ed. 1980)

American Psychiatric Association, Model Statute (1982) [reprinted in Stromberg & Stone, A Model State Law on Civil Commitment of the Mentally Ill, 20 Harvard Journal on Legislation 275 (1983)]

American Psychiatric Association, The Principles of Medical Ethics with Annotations Especially Applicable to Psychiatry (1981)

American Psychiatric Association, Task Force on Clinical Aspects of the Violent Individual, Clinical Aspects of the Violent Individual (1974)

APA (American Psychological Association), Ethical Principles of Psychologists (1981)

American Psychological Association, Report of the Task Force on the Role of Psychology in the Criminal Justice System (1978)

American Psychological Association, Specialty Guidelines for the Delivery of Services by Clinical Psychologists (1981)

American Psychological Association, Specialty Guidelines for the Delivery of Services by Counseling Psychologists (1981)

American Psychological Association, Specialty Guidelines for the Delivery of Services by School Psychologists (1981)

American Psychological Association, Standards for Providers of Psychological Services (1981)

American Public Health Association, Standards for Health Services in Correctional Institutions (1976)

Bureau of Operations and Research of the International Association of Chiefs of Police, Inc., Training Key (1979)

Federal Standards for Prisons and Jails, U.S. Department of Justice Bureau of Prisons (1980)

IJA-ABA (Institute of Judicial Administration-American Bar Association), (Standards Relating to) Dispositions (1977) (component volume of the Juvenile Justice Standards Project)

MHLP (Mental Health Law Project), Model Statute: Civil Commitment [reprinted in 2 Mental Disability Law Reporter 64 (1977)]

MHLP, Model Statute: Insanity Defense [reprinted in 2 Mental Disability Law Reporter 71 (1977)]

MHLP, Model Statute: Mental Health Standards and Human Rights [reprinted in 2 Mental Disability Law Reporter 291 (1977)]

MHLP, Model Statute: Therapeutic Confidentiality [reprinted in 2 Mental Disability Law Reporter 337 (1977)]

Model Developmentally Disabled Offender Act [reprinted in Disabled Persons and the Law: State Legislative Issues 722-729 (B. Sales, D. Powell, R. Van Duizend *et al.* eds. 1982)]

Model Right/Consent Statute [reprinted in Disabled Persons and the Law: State Legislative Issues 425-452 (B. Sales, D. Powell, R. Van Duizend *et al.* eds. 1982)]

NAC (National Advisory Commission on Criminal Justice Standards and Goals), Community Crime Prevention (1973)

NAC, Corrections (1973)

NAC, Courts (1973)

NAC, Criminal Justice System (1973)

NAC, Disorders and Terrorism (1976)

NAC, Police (1973)

NAPSA (National Association of Pretrial Services Agencies), Performance Standards and Goals for Pretrial Release and Diversion (1978) (available from National Pretrial Services Resource Center, 918 F Street NW, Washington, D.C. 20004)

NCCD (National Council on Crime and Delinquency, Advisory Council of Judges of the), Model Sentencing Act (1963)

NCCUSL (National Conference of Commissioners on Uniform State Laws), Defense of Insanity Act (April 1984 draft)

NCCUSL, Defense of Insanity Act art. 1 (1983 draft)

NCCUSL, Model Public Defender Act (1970, amended 1974)

NCCUSL, Model Sentencing and Corrections Act (1978)

NCCUSL, Uniform Jury Selection and Service Act (1970)

NCCUSL, Uniform Post-Conviction Procedure Act (1966)

NCCUSL, Uniform Rules of Criminal Procedure (1974)

NDAA (National District Attorneys Association), National Prosecution Standards (1977)

NLADA (National Legal Aid and Defender Association), National Study Commission Recommendations (in NLADA, Guidelines for Legal Defense Systems in the United States: Final Report of the National Study Commission on Defense Services (1976))

NLADA, Standards for Defender Services (1976) (available from NLADA, 1625 K Street NW, Washington, D.C. 20036)

NMHA (National Mental Health Association), Myths and Realities: A Report of the National Commission on the Insanity Defense (1983)

Standards for Fellowship Programs in Forensic Psychiatry, 10 Bulletin of the American Academy of Psychiatry & Law 285 (1982)

PREFACE

The American Bar Association's Criminal Justice Mental Health Standards owe their existence to the generous financial support from the John D. and Catherine T. MacArthur Foundation, as well as to the significant contributions of the lawyers and mental health professionals who formed the seven interdisciplinary task forces and the special Advisory Committee which were responsible for the development of the Standards.

The majority of the Mental Health Standards were first published in 1986 as Chapter 7 of the *ABA Standards For Criminal Justice*, under the auspices of the ABA's former Standing Committee on Association Standards for Criminal Justice. The history of the Mental Health Standards Project is set out in the accompanying Introduction by the Former Standing Committee. Since then, the ABA Criminal Justice Section's Criminal Justice Standards Committee, under the chairmanship of Albert J. Datz, Esq., has assumed responsibility for the Standards and has overseen the addition of new standards on competence and capital punishment (August 1987) and competence and confessions (August 1988). Due to additional generous funding by the MacArthur Foundation, all of the Mental Health Standards are now being separately published and distributed in this soft-cover edition.

The ABA acknowledges with gratitude the immeasurable contributions of all of the participants in the Mental Health Standards Project, and particularly thanks the MacArthur Foundation for enabling this major effort to improve the administration of criminal justice.

INTRODUCTION

By Former Standing Committee On Association Standards For Criminal Justice

Mental disease, mental retardation, and the full range of abnormal conditions affecting mental and emotional processes should be familiar to all who administer the criminal justice system. Even persons untrained in such matters recognize the mental and emotional distress exhibited by many mentally ill or mentally retarded persons detained in police custody, arraigned and tried in criminal courts, or incarcerated in jails or prisons. No informed observer can fail to reflect upon the prevalence of significant mental abnormalities exhibited by detainees, defendants, and convicts. Many underprivileged persons caught up in the criminal process suffer the further disadvantages of mental affliction or retardation. This does not mean, however, that mental illness and retardation in any of their variegated forms are criminogenic. Nor does it suggest a demonstrable causal relationship between mental illness or retardation and criminal acts. Millions of law-abiding Americans suffer from and seek help for a wide range of mental and emotional problems.

How, then, can we account for the prevalence of psychic abnormality observed by police, prosecutors, jailors, judges, and clinicians involved with the administration of criminal justice? There is no certain explanation. Clearly the economically, educationally, and mentally disadvantaged are disproportionately represented at all stages of the criminal justice process; the rate of disproportionality appears to remain relatively constant.

The criminal law has confronted mental aberration for centuries. "Insanity" has long been the subject of legal scholarship. Ironically, however, the subject received scant attention during the twenty-year-long initial development of the American Bar Association's criminal justice standards. In the late 1970s, however, the ABA acknowledged its unfinished agenda. Although the issue of mental disease or defect was touched upon in chapter 18, Sentencing Alternatives and Procedures, at no point in the otherwise comprehensive second edition of the standards had the subject of mental health issues in the criminal law been canvassed in thorough fashion. Chapter 7, Criminal Justice Mental Health Standards, fills this lacuna. Its ninety-six black-letter standards were approved by the Association's House of Delegates on August 7, 1984.

The history of the development of this lengthy and comprehensive chapter may be of interest both to practitioners and to clinicians. Chapter 7 owes its existence to two principal factors: generous financial support from the John D. and Catherine T. MacArthur Foundation and remarkable *pro bono publico* contributions of the lawyers and mental health professionals who formed the six interdisciplinary task forces responsible for the development of standards proposals. A one-million-dollar grant from the MacArthur Foundation enabled the American Bar Association, through its Standing Committee on Association Standards for Criminal Justice, to establish the Criminal Justice Mental Health Standards Project. Under the direction of the Standing Committee, the Project began its planned four-year operation on February 1, 1981. In recognition of the fact that the subject matter was interdisciplinary, from their inauguration the expert task forces comprised mental health specialists as well as legal practitioners. During the early stages of the Project, forty-eight psychiatrists, psychologists, other mental health professionals, prosecutors, defense lawyers, judges, and legal academicians were involved. By mid-1982 the Project's six interdisciplinary task forces had been increased to involve seventy-nine nationally recognized experts in law and mental health. Moreover, to ensure adequate interdisciplinary involvement, the Project established formal liaisons with several nonlegal professional organizations. The American Psychiatric Association, the American Psychological Association, the American Orthopsychiatric Association, and the National Sheriffs' Association were invited to nominate official representatives to serve on one or more of the Project task forces. In addition, every effort was made to see that interested entities of the American Bar Association were represented during the developmental stages. The ABA Commission on the Mentally Disabled participated fully in the Project from its beginning. The Standing Committee acknowledges with gratitude the signal contributions of those who gave unstintingly of their time and abilities as members of the Project task forces and Advisory Committee. It also expresses its gratitude for the MacArthur Foundation's generosity which, in last analysis, enabled the committee to undertake this major effort to improve the administration of criminal justice.

Within our democratic society and under our system of law there are two principal avenues through which citizens may be deprived of their liberty. The usual basis for incarceration is arrest, trial, and conviction under the criminal law. However, the state's equally awesome police power also justifies the civil commitment of persons who, because of mental disease or defect, represent a danger to themselves or others. These two routes to restraint are separate, but not entirely so; there has for years been a growing interaction between them. When they mesh or become reciprocally confounded, problems result. Moreover, they represent areas in which the criminal justice system and civil legal institutions have interacted with not entirely satisfactory results. This chapter attempts to define clearly the limits of the state's criminal powers governing the mentally afflicted who become involved with the criminal law.

This century has seen noteworthy progress in the scientific understanding of mental illness in all its manifestations. Yet there seems to be general agreement among the most informed mental health and mental retardation experts that we are merely on the frontier of knowledge about the human mind. Nonetheless, relatively recent scientific achievements have been noteworthy. The development and wide-scale use of psychotropic medications has led to dramatic changes in the treatment of the severely mentally ill, particularly the movement toward deinstitutionalization. That movement, in turn, has had a profound effect on public attitudes toward mental illness and, indirectly, has affected the administration of criminal justice.

Psychiatrists and psychologists have played important roles within criminal justice institutions for many years. Yet the alliance between psychiatry and the law has not been a happy one. Partially because of their training, practitioners within these two great professions frequently hold diametrically opposite views. This is not, of course, always the case, but one may generalize by stating that the law teaches its practitioners to assess responsibility, while psychiatrists, psychologists, and other mental health professionals tend to be determinists who "explain" behavior rather than "blaming" persons for it. Thus, to a great extent these two major professions lack a common vocabulary and a common purpose. This is ironic inasmuch as both are, at heart, helping professions.

There seems to be little question that the criminal law will continue to rely upon medical and scientific judgments and upon the expert advice of psychiatrists, psychologists, and other mental health professionals. Moreover, mental health professionals will continue to be drawn to forensic practice. This continued reliance and interdependence suggest the need for cooperative, interprofessional programs designed, in their broadest sense, to generate understanding and cooperation and, in a narrower sense, to foster improved professional practice. The standards in this chapter address this overriding need and suggest specific ways through which the involved professions can foster mutual improvements in the practice of criminal law and the delivery of effective legal and forensic services. They make clear that such programs will further the interests of criminal justice litigants, the criminal justice system as an entity, and the public.

This chapter and its ninety-six standards are designed for the use of both lawyers and clinicians. The ABA expects that these standards will prove a valuable teaching resource for the legal and mental health professions. The ten parts of the chapter are organized for the most part to follow the route an offender would take from first police contact through release from incarceration. The coverage is as follows:

- Mental health, mental retardation, and criminal justice: general professional obligations;
- Police and custodial roles;
- Pretrial evaluations and expert testimony;
- Competence to stand trial;
- Competence on other issues;
- Nonresponsibility for crime;
- Commitment of nonresponsibility acquittees;
- Special dispositional statutes;
- Sentencing mentally ill and mentally retarded offenders;
- Mentally ill and mentally retarded prisoners.

The standards within this ten-part chapter address in specific terms each context in which better interprofessional communications can contribute to improved understanding and performance. Second, the standards recognize and address specifically the need to formulate uniform requirements and procedures for ordering, conducting, and reporting the results of mental examinations conducted after the initiation of criminal proceedings. From early in the Project's life the frequent inadequacy of existing mental evaluation reports was apparent. The empirical data gathered in the early phases of the Project supported the inescapable conclusion that judges, attorneys, and clinicians together can effect major improvements in the utilization of the mental health professions by criminal justice institutions.

This lengthy chapter reflects the past inattentiveness to the substantial interrelationships between mental health issues and the administration of the criminal law. More significantly, it represents a functional yet imaginative call for change. It examines anew the well-researched areas of the insanity defense and incorporates the cognitive "appreciation" test for insanity adopted by the Association's House of Delegates in February 1983. This new test eliminates ABA support for the volitional prong of the American Law Institute's Model Penal Code criteria. Thus, claims of inability to control or conform one's conduct to the requirements of law and claims of "irresistible impulse" are not grounds for exculpation under ABA policy.

In addition, chapter 7 urges an end to the use of the term *insanity* and recommends its replacement by the phrase *mental nonresponsibility*.[1] The Standing Committee heard substantial arguments favoring an end to the use of the term *insanity* as that term is currently employed within the criminal justice system. Proponents of this change argued that the word *insanity* is stigmatizing and conjures up visions from an earlier era. "Insanity," as that term is used today, is not a medical concept and the term has lost even its legal gloss, becoming instead a popularized lay diagnosis. Accordingly, these standards adopt the phrase *mental nonresponsibility* and by so doing avoid distorted connotations that no longer seem applicable. The substitution of "mental nonresponsibility" for "insanity" should assist lawyers and courts alike in focusing legal inquiries into mental state more directly on the issue of criminal responsibility.

Chapter 7 incorporates policies adopted by the House of Delegates in February 1983, establishing a formula for allocating the burden of proof in cases involving a defense of mental nonresponsibility [insanity] and opposing the enactment of statutes that would supplant or supplement a verdict of not guilty by reason of mental nonresponsibility [insanity] with a verdict of guilty but mentally ill. Next, the chapter focuses on the disposition of persons found not guility by reason of mental nonresponsibility. Here, the standards urge the adoption of special commitment procedures applicable to those defendants who were acquitted of very serious crimes of violence because of mental nonresponsibility. These special commitment procedures, which are to supplement existing civil commitment procedures, attempt to strike a fair and reasonable balance between the rights of acquittees and legitimate concerns about public safety. The chapter also focuses on the complex and often confusing area of competence to stand trial. It sets out detailed standards designed to bring order and coherence to the determination of competence to stand trial and addresses the disposition of persons found permanently incompetent to stand trial.

Within this ten-part chapter a special effort has been made to distinguish between mental illness and mental retardation to the extent that they create special and differentiated problems in the administration of

1. When individual black letter standards require the use of the term *mental nonresponsibility* they attempt to clarify that term for legal and historical purposes by following it with the bracketed term [*insanity*].

criminal justice. The standards stress the responsibilities of lawyers, judges, police, clinicians, and institutional officers or administrators in processing both mentally ill and mentally retarded suspects and offenders. Indeed, no major mental health or mental retardation issue in the criminal law has escaped examination. If the standards are vigorously implemented, they can do much to improve interprofessional practice, encourage effective mental health treatment, and enhance public safety.

Our debt to the John D. and Catherine T. MacArthur Foundation and to the professional volunteers who contributed so substantially to the development of these standards is acknowledged with gratitude. The full membership list for each of the task forces is set forth at the beginning of parts I through X. The members of the task forces devoted countless hours and gave wise counsel throughout the life of the Criminal Justice Mental Health Standards Project. A posthumous note of appreciation is extended in memory of Dr. Randolph A. Read, a young but highly experienced forensic psychiatrist who served enthusiastically as a member of one of the Project's task forces. Dr. Read's life ended tragically in April 1983. Many of his insightful contributions are reflected within the standards and commentary to parts I and III.

The Project benefited from the advice of a special Advisory Committee composed of Professor B. James George, Jr., General Kenneth J. Hodson, Judge Walter E. Craig, McNeill Smith, Bruce J. Ennis, Professor Richard J. Bonnie, Professor Norval Morris, and Dr. Bernard Diamond. All members of the Advisory Committee provided valuable advice and guidance. A special acknowledgment is due Dr. Diamond and Professor Bonnie for the extraordinary service and counsel they provided outside the formal task force and Advisory Committee structure. We add a special acknowledgment for the contributions made by the late Judge Walter E. Craig. Judge Craig died as these Criminal Justice Mental Health Standards were going to press. He was one of the principle actors in the Association's 23-year-old effort to develop comprehensive standards for the administration of criminal justice. It was during Judge Craig's tenure as president of the American Bar Association that work began in earnest on the ABA Standards for Criminal Justice.

Each of the Project's task forces benefited from the services of a law reporter: Professors Gerald T. Bennett, Gerald M. Caplan, William K. Carroll, James W. Ellis, Grant H. Morris, Christopher Slobogin, and Elyce Zenoff served in this capacity. Their legal research, drafting skills, and service to the task forces and Standing Committee proved invaluable.

Although the Criminal Justice Mental Health Standards Project began on February 1, 1981, its genesis dates back many years. The idea for the development of criminal justice mental health standards was nurtured by two lawyers in particular: Ephraim Gomberg, an active member of the Criminal Justice Section, and H. Lynn Edwards, former staff director of the Standing Committee. Their pioneering efforts were indispensable. As in any major undertaking, contributions came from a wide array of individuals and institutions. Many mental health professionals and lawyers contributed ideas and suggestions that proved most helpful. The Standing Committee acknowledges those otherwise unattributed contributions with gratitude. It also expresses its appreciation for the cooperation and support of several professional associations, including the American Psychiatric Association, the American Psychological Association, the American Orthopsychiatric Association, the National Sheriffs' Association, the National Mental Health Association, and the National Alliance for the Mentally Ill. Within the American Bar Association it thanks all interested entities and especially the Commission on the Mentally Disabled.

After the House of Delegates approved these standards, the Standing Committee undertook the final and painstaking task of updating and editing the lengthy commentary that illuminates these comprehensive guidelines for criminal justice reform. This task required legal research and editorial skills, provided by Professor B. James George, Jr. and his research assistant, Julie A. Interdonato, whose services are acknowledged gratefully.

This Project proved organizationally as well as substantively complex. These complexities were addressed wisely and efficiently, and the Standing Committee reserves a final and very special note of commendation for the highly professional performance of the Project's director, Richard P. Lynch, who was an active participant and contributor to every aspect of this major standards undertaking. He and Project Coordinator Sarah J. Applegate, Administrative Assistant Joan M. Flanegin, and the late Rosemarie Barto contributed immeasurably to the Project's success and to the standards which follow.

Part I

Mental Health, Mental Retardation, and Criminal Justice: General Professional Obligations

William H. Erickson, *Chairman*
Standing Committee on Association Standards for Criminal Justice

Albert J. Datz
Task Force Chairman

Grant H. Morris
Reporter

Task Force

Albert J. Datz, *Chairperson*
Private practitioner, Datz, Jacobson & Lembcke, Jacksonville, Florida

Richard J. Bonnie
Professor of Law and Director, Institute of Law, Psychiatry & Public Policy, University of Virginia School of Law, Charlottesville, Virginia

Thomas E. Bryant, M.D., J.D.
Chairman, Public Committee on Mental Health, Washington, D.C.

H. Lynn Edwards
Private practitioner, Annandale, Virginia

Sandra A. Garcia, Ph.D., J.D.
Associate Professor, Department of Psychology, University of South Florida, Tampa, Florida

Ephraim Gomberg
Private practitioner, Palm Springs, California

Ruth Nordenbrook
Assistant U.S. Attorney, Brooklyn, New York (representing ABA Section of Criminal Justice)

Randolph A. Read, M.D.*
Adjunct Professor of Law, University of San Diego; Assistant Professor of Psychiatry, University of California at San Diego, San Diego, California

Philip Roos, M.D.
Executive Director, Mothers Against Drunk Drivers, Hurst, Texas

Bruce D. Sales, Ph.D., J.D.
Professor, Psychology Department, University of Arizona, Tucson, Arizona (representing American Psychological Association)

Andrew S. Watson, M.D.
Psychiatrist, Professor of Law and Psychiatry, University of Michigan School of Law, Ann Arbor, Michigan

GRANT H. MORRIS, *Reporter*
Professor of Law, School of Law, University of San Diego

---

*Deceased

INTRODUCTION

For years psychiatrists, psychologists, and other mental health and mental retardation professionals have participated actively in the administration of criminal justice. Their roles and functions, however, seldom have been defined clearly. Although judges and lawyers repeatedly have called on the services of mental health and mental retardation professionals, far too often the professional alliance has been uneasy. Public confidence in the opinions of mental health and mental retardation professionals and in the criminal justice process itself has been eroded by the failure of the participants to understand the interdependent nature of their relationships.

Frequently mental health or mental retardation professionals have been asked to give expert opinions on matters not within their professional expertise. The law erroneously has masked moral assessments by posing questions that seem to call for clinical judgments. Attorneys often fail to grasp the limits of scientific understanding and the importance of protecting the integrity of forensic processes. Uninformed attorneys may attempt inappropriately to shape professional opinion by withholding information necessary to the evaluation process or by asking professionals to alter their clinical opinions. At trial, attorneys may ask professionals to respond to questions concerning which the latter lack special expertise. Mental health and mental retardation professionals often assume incorrectly that their general clinical training is sufficient to permit them to reach conclusions on legal issues. But without specialized training they lack both an understanding of legal matters and an appreciation of the significance of those matters to their forensic evaluations. Tensions existing in the relationship between mental health and mental retardation professionals and lawyers and judges can be reduced only if the obligations defining that relationship are clarified and understood by all participants in the criminal justice process.

The celebrated trial of John W. Hinckley, Jr. for the attempted assassination of President Reagan and his assaults on law enforcement officers resulted in increased scrutiny of the role of mental health and mental retardation professionals in the criminal process. Much criticism has been directed at professional testimony describing a defendant's mental state at some time in the past (for example, when defendants plead mental nonresponsibility (insanity)) or predicting a defendant's future dangerousness. The standards in part III of chapter 7 address these criticisms by articulating measures to improve the level of professional testimony.

In spite of these and other criticisms, mental health and mental retardation professionals contribute significantly to the criminal justice system in several contexts. Within these contexts their different roles must be identified and the obligations inherent in each role must be clarified if they are to function appropriately. Accordingly, the standards in part I delineate four specific roles played by mental health and mental retardation professionals in the criminal process — scientific, evaluative, consultative, and therapeutic. Although these roles generate ethical conflicts for mental health and mental retardation professionals, the standards outline the primary responsibilities of professionals in fulfilling their obligations within each role. They stress the importance of cooperation among legal, mental health, and mental retardation professional organizations to monitor performance, address ethical questions, and sponsor research. In addition, the standards establish a framework for basic and advanced education and training of judges, lawyers, and mental health and mental retardation professionals. The obligation to understand the role of these professionals in the criminal justice process should be borne not only by the professionals themselves, but by their coparticipants in the criminal process — judges and lawyers. The cooperative ventures and educational programs advocated in these standards should make all professionals sensitive to the roles and responsibilities of their coprofessionals within the criminal justice system.

Standard 7-1.1. Roles of mental health and mental retardation professionals in the criminal process

(a) Identification of appropriate roles. Mental health and mental retardation professionals serve the administration of criminal justice by offering expert opinions and testimony within their respective areas of expertise concerning present scientific or clinical knowledge; by evaluating and offering expert opinions and testimony on the mental condition of defendants and witnesses; by providing consultation to the prosecution or defense concerning the conduct of individual cases; and by providing treatment and habilitation for persons charged with or convicted of crimes. Because these roles involve differing and sometimes conflicting obligations and functions, these professionals as well as courts, attorneys, and criminal justice agen-

cies should clarify the nature and limitations of these respective roles. The professional's performance within these roles should be limited to the individual professional's area of expertise and should be consistent with that professional's ethical principles.

(b) Scientific and evaluative roles. In offering expert opinions and testimony concerning present scientific or clinical knowledge and in evaluating and offering expert opinions and testimony on the mental condition of criminal defendants, the mental health or mental retardation professional, no matter by whom retained, should function objectively within the professional's area of expertise. The qualifications of a mental health or mental retardation professional to offer expert testimony on present scientific or clinical knowledge are established in standard 7-3.13. In evaluating the mental condition of a defendant or witness, the professional has an obligation to make a thorough assessment based on sound evaluative methods and to reach an objective opinion on each specific matter referred for evaluation. Disclosure of information obtained during the evaluation is governed by limitations set forth in standards 7-3.2, 7-3.3(b), 7-3.4(b), and 7-3.8. The qualifications of a professional to serve as a court-appointed evaluator are established in standard 7-3.10. The qualifications of a professional to offer expert testimony about a person's mental condition are established in standard 7-3.11. Presentation of expert testimony is governed by standard 7-3.14.

(c) Consultative role. When providing consultation and advice to the prosecution or defense on the preparation or conduct of the case, the mental health or mental retardation professional has the same obligations and immunities as any member of the prosecution or defense team. Nevertheless, the prosecutor and defense counsel should respect the professional's ethical and professional standards. Any attempt by an attorney to compromise the professional's standards would constitute unprofessional conduct.

(d) Treatment and habilitation roles. When providing treatment or habilitation for a person charged with or convicted of a crime, the mental health or mental retardation professional's obligations to the person and to society derive primarily from those arising out of the treatment or habilitative relationship. Consistent with institutional security requirements, correctional and mental health or mental retardation facilities should not interfere with that traditional professional relationship. Any limitation on the professional relationship owing to the individual's involvement in the criminal pro-

cess or placement in an institutional setting should be precisely defined and explained to the individual at the time the professional relationship is established.

Commentary Introduction

Standard 7-1.1 defines the roles that mental health and mental retardation professionals play in the administration of criminal justice: scientist, evaluator, consultant, and therapist or habilitator. It explains the different obligations of mental health and mental retardation professionals performing each role and protects professional ethical obligations from possible compromise by prosecutors, defense attorneys, or the criminal justice system.

Related Standards

ABA, Model Rules of Professional Conduct 1.6, 3.8(d)

ABA, Standards for Criminal Justice 4-4.4, 7-3.5(b)

American Psychiatric Association, The Principles of Medical Ethics with Annotations Especially Applicable to Psychiatry §§2, 4, 7

American Psychological Association, Ethical Principles of Psychologists 1, 3, 6

American Psychological Association, Specialty Guidelines for the Delivery of Services by Clinical Psychologists 2.2.2, 2.3.5

American Psychological Association, Specialty Guidelines for the Delivery of Services by Counseling Psychologists 2.2.2, 2.3.5

American Psychological Association, Standards for Providers of Psychological Services 2.2.2, 2.3.5

Commentary

Ethical Concerns of Professionals in the Criminal Justice Process

Mental health professionals are individuals who have received extensive, formalized postgraduate education and training in human behavior. They include psychiatrists, psychologists, clinical social workers, psychiatric nurses, and other professionals licensed or certified to practice (if a jurisdiction requires licensure or certification for a particular discipline). Mental retardation professionals are individuals who have undergone extensive, formal postgraduate education and training in identifying specific functional deficits or habilitation needs of persons with mental retardation or a developmental disability. They include special education teachers, speech and language pathologists, audiologists, physical therapists, occupational therapists, as well as those psychiatrists, psychologists, clinical social workers, psychiatric nurses, and other mental health professionals who have received the necessary education and training in mental retardation matters. Mental retardation professionals must be licensed or certified to practice if licensure or certification is required.

The criminal justice system needs the expertise of mental health and mental retardation professionals.[1] Nevertheless, their ability to perform specific functions or tasks is dependent on their understanding of the role they are called on to perform and their qualifications to perform competently in that role. Standard 7-1.1(a) identifies the several roles played by mental health and mental retardation professionals as they participate in criminal justice administration. In deciding whether to participate in criminal justice processes, and in their actual participation, professionals should consider whether they are called on to perform tasks within their professional expertise[2] and to play a role consistent with the individual professional's ethical principles.

Mental health and mental retardation professional ethical standards encourage professionals to apply their expertise in judicial proceedings.[3] Nevertheless, professionals may decline to perform certain criminal justice roles because of personal ethical concerns. Generally mental health and mental retardation professional norms have been drafted to cover situations in which individual clients voluntarily seek professional services from private practitioners. Ethical difficulties arise for some professionals serving in the criminal justice system if a third party asserts a competing claim on professional loyalty.[4] For example, if patients are treated as a part of a legal disposition, professionals may decide that

1. It should be noted that the exclusion of qualified defense mental health or mental retardation expert witnesses on the issue of mental nonresponsibility [insanity] or diminished capacity denies due process of law. *See* Boykins v. Wainwright, 737 F.2d 1539, 1544 (11th Cir.), *reh'g denied,* 744 F.2d 97 (11th Cir. 1984), *cert. denied,* 105 S. Ct. 1775 (1985).

2. American Psychological Association, *Ethical Principles of Psychologists,* 36 Am. Psychologist 633 (1981) [hereinafter cited as APA *Ethical Principles*]. The Preamble to the Principles identifies competence and objectivity in the application of skills as two responsibilities of psychologists. *Ibid.*

3. American Psychiatric Association, Principles of Medical Ethics With Annotations Especially Applicable to Psychiatry §7, annots. 1, 2 (1981) [hereinafter cited as APA Medical Ethics].

4. American Psychological Association, *Report of the Task Force on the Role of Psychology in the Criminal Justice System,* 33 Am. Psychologist 1099, 1101 (1978) [hereinafter cited as APA *Task Force Report*]. *See Ethical Issues in the Practice of Forensic Psychiatry,* 10 J. Psychiatry & L. 7 (1982). The comments of Jonas Rappaport, M.D., are of particular interest. *Id.* at 19-25.

disclosure requirements imposed on them so severely compromise the therapist-patient relationship that they are unwilling to function as therapists under such circumstances. In like manner, professionals who believe that loyalty is owed exclusively to their patients may forgo forensic evaluations to avoid becoming "agents" of the criminal justice system. Moreover, even professionals who are willing to conduct some forensic evaluations may feel ethically constrained as to the kinds of cases in which they participate. For example, a mental health or mental retardation professional opposed to capital punishment as a matter of personal morality may refuse to conduct a forensic evaluation in a capital sentencing proceeding, thus avoiding an untenable situation in which his or her opinion might be used to support a death sentence.

Professionals as Evaluators

When mental health and mental retardation professionals serve as evaluators of a defendant's mental condition, the thrust of paragraph (b) is that they are obligated to function objectively. Although a professional may be retained by defense counsel or appointed by a court to conduct a prosecution-initiated evaluation, neither of these events should affect a professional evaluation or opinion. No matter who initiated the evaluation, an evaluator is expected to perform an objective evaluation and prepare an objective report. The evaluation process should not be viewed as a search for information helpful to only one party to litigation. Accordingly, referral sources should not influence evaluators or their processes or opinions.

Several standards in part III have been drafted to assist evaluators in achieving the goal of impartial and objective evaluations. Standard 7-3.5 asserts that professionals should be informed in writing about each specific matter to be addressed in an evaluation. An attorney initiating an evaluation should provide all records or information an evaluator regards as necessary for a thorough evaluation on each referred matter. Because defendants are the primary source of information about their mental condition, standard 7-3.11 stresses the need for personal interviews with them during the evaluation. To encourage a defendant's full cooperation, standard 7-3.8 precludes the prosecution from discovering evaluation reports containing information about a defendant's mental condition at the time of an alleged crime until after the defense has given notice of its intent to place the defendant's mental state in issue. In addition, standard

7-3.2 does not allow the prosecution to use incriminating disclosures made during an evaluation as evidence of guilt. To ensure that all evaluators have access to the same information and that a defendant's communications with a professional performing a prosecution-initiated evaluation are not unduly guarded or distorted, standard 7-3.4 authorizes a court to exclude professional testimony offered to support the position of an uncooperative defendant.

A mental health or mental retardation professional who accepts an evaluation referral from an attorney may feel a special obligation to formulate a professional opinion favorable to the referring attorney's case. Standard 7-1.1(b) clarifies that evaluators should harbor no such feelings. They are obliged to conduct only objective evaluations. No attorney, whether prosecutor or defense, should seek to influence an evaluator's opinion, and no evaluator should render other than an objective opinion. In short, an evaluator should remain free from all outside pressure and influence.

Mental health and mental retardation professionals who perform evaluations are frequently called as expert witnesses. Standards 3-3.3 and 4-4.4 provide that prosecutors and defense counsel who engage an expert to formulate an opinion are to respect the expert's independence and are not to try to influence the expert's professional opinion on the subject matter of the evaluation. An expert's independence also should be respected during the evaluation. An attorney should obtain a qualified evaluator who understands the scope and purpose of the forthcoming evaluation. To facilitate an objective evaluation, an attorney should explain clearly at the outset that the evaluator must function independently. No attorney should seek to influence a professional opinion or offer an excessive fee intended to promote a favorable opinion.

Statements of mental health and mental retardation professionals who have performed evaluations confirm that lawyers who engage evaluators need to act circumspectly. Although attorneys should ensure that evaluators understand fully the legal purposes for which an evaluation is conducted, attorneys in turn should understand and communicate to evaluators that evaluations are to be conducted in conformity with the ethical and performance requirements of the evaluator's professional discipline.

The mandate of standard 7-1.1(b) that evaluators act objectively is supported by the language of standard 7-3.5(b) urging that attorneys who initiate evaluations submit to evaluators all records and information necessary for a thorough professional evaluation on referred matters.[5] Attorneys who engage evaluators are not to withhold relevant information; legal ethics preclude counsel from advising clients to respond untruthfully to questions during prosecution-initiated evaluations. The counterpart to an attorney's responsibility to respect an evaluator's professional independence is, of course, the evaluator's obligation to perform objectively and to understand the need for objectivity.

Evaluators should not only avoid outside influences but be aware as well of the potentially distorting influences their internal value systems may exert on the evaluation process. For example, an evaluator's personal ethics, cultural background, gender, and personality may generate biases affecting the objectivity of data collection and interpretation. Moreover, an evaluator's professional orientation and training may create bias. Accordingly, evaluators should be aware of and attempt to neutralize the influence of conscious and unconscious biases or predispositions.[6]

Some mental health or mental retardation professionals limit their forensic practice to evaluations performed solely for the prosecution or solely for the defense. Such a limitation may engender or reflect bias or at least the appearance of bias. Some distinguished clinicians limit their forensic practice to one side of a case as a matter of personal conviction. For example, professionals who perform only defense-initiated evaluations believe their practice accords with the ethical obligation to help and not to harm. In contrast, however, other eminent clinicians are convinced that respect for the objectivity of professional evaluators and their evaluations is enhanced if professionals end their self-imposed limitations and willingly perform evaluations, no matter which party to litigation initiates them.

Evaluators have a special duty to explain to persons undergoing evaluation the objective nature of the evaluation process and the evaluator's role during an evaluation. This explanation should be given at the beginning of the evaluation because mentally ill or mentally retarded persons may inappropriately view an evaluator as a helping therapist rather than an objective assessor. Even though an evaluator should explain that state-

5. For a discussion of the need to afford evaluators maximum access to information about the subject and to facilitate objectivity in the interpretation of this information, *see generally* Bonnie & Slobogin, *The Role of Mental Health Professionals in the Criminal Process: The Case for Informed Speculation*, 66 VA. L. REV. 427, 496-522 (1980).

6. *Id.* at 512-514.

ments made by and information obtained from a defendant during a nontherapeutic evaluation will not be kept confidential, some mentally ill or mentally retarded defendants may not comprehend or may disregard those admonitions. They may become unduly trustful and even volunteer unsolicited information. Many skillful clinicians are able to generate trust in their patients. That ability ordinarily serves patient therapeutic needs, but during a forensic evaluation can create an ethical dilemma. Doctors Gutheil and Appelbaum have suggested as a means of resolving the dilemma that whenever a person undergoing evaluation appears to be developing a therapeutic mind-set in the course of a forensic evaluation, the evaluator should repeat the earlier admonitions stressing the nontherapeutic relationship and absence of confidentiality.[7]

The format of forensic evaluations usually differs greatly from that of clinical evaluations, which typically are open-ended and undirected. Patient complaints may fix the only boundaries on clinician inquiries. In contrast, forensic evaluations are directed toward the legal matters under consideration and thus are much more focused. Nonetheless, despite these differences forensic evaluators should utilize commonly accepted professional assessment methodologies in the course of examinations and should employ clinical skills that establish specialized knowledge and provide a basis for an expert opinion. In this way, evaluators can avoid serving inappropriately as investigators for referring attorneys.

Professionals as Consultants

Mental health and mental retardation specialists who serve as consultants to the prosecution or defense undertake a role of assisting that attorney. In that capacity, a consultant appropriately may assist at client interviews, probe for information helpful to counsel, assess client credibility, evaluate client ability to withstand cross-examination, and offer advice and suggest strategy and tactics on issues important to the litigation. For example, a consultant can apprise an attorney about the relative strengths and weaknesses of the consultant's opinion and the opinions of other professionals and can propose useful strategies to satisfy a factfinder that expert opinions supporting the attorney's case are valid.

Difficulties arise when professionals attempt to serve in the dual capacities of evaluator and consultant. Ideally, these roles should be sepa-

---

7. T. Gutheil & P. Appelbaum, Clinical Handbook of Psychiatry and the Law 289, 298 (1982).

rated so that the objectivity of an evaluation is not contaminated by a long-standing consultative relationship between a professional and an attorney or by a professional's hope that a referral for evaluation will generate future retainers for consultation.

As a practical matter, it may be impossible to preserve the distinction between the evaluative and consultative roles during interactions between attorneys and mental health or mental retardation professionals. Nevertheless, the functions inherent in each role must be separated carefully and the roles themselves need to be discharged sequentially. Thus, a professional who has been a defense or prosecution consultant in a given case ought not be called upon later to conduct an evaluation in that case. Under such circumstances, an objective evaluation would be impossible. In contrast, however, a professional who first performed an objective forensic evaluation, and who based professional conclusions and opinions on that evaluation, might properly serve thereafter as a consultant.

The conflicting obligations of evaluators and consultants might warrant an absolute bifurcation of these two roles. Bifurcation, however, is impractical; it is therefore essential that professionals understand clearly the obligations inherent in each role and clarify at the outset their relationship with counsel.

Professionals serving as consultants function as agents of the attorneys who call on them. Paragraph (c) stresses that consultant-professionals have duties identical to those imposed on other members of a prosecution or defense team. For example, a defense consultant assumes the same obligation as defense counsel under the ABA Model Rules of Professional Conduct to preserve client confidences except when disclosure is permitted by those rules.[8] A prosecution consultant shares the prosecuting attorney's obligation to disclose evidence to the defense supporting innocence or mitigating the offense.[9] The attorney-client privilege and the work-product doctrine govern consultant-professionals.[10] Consequently, confidential communications to and information obtained by professionals and professional opinions are not subject to discovery except as envisioned by standards 7-3.8 and 7-6.5. Although consultants

8. *See* Model Rules of Professional Conduct 1.6 (1983) and the discussion of its applicability in commentary to standard 7-3.2, notes 22-25 and accompanying text.

9. Model Rules of Professional Conduct 3.8(d).

10. *See* Saltzburg, *Privileges and Professionals: Lawyers and Psychiatrists*, 66 Va. L. Rev. 597, 625-629 (1980).

serve as agents of counsel, standard 7-1.1(c) nevertheless reminds attorneys that personal value systems and professional standards governing mental health and mental retardation professionals are not to be compromised in the course of consultations.

Professionals as Therapists or Habilitators — The Problem of Divided Loyalties

Mental health and mental retardation professionals serving as evaluators undertake professional obligations toward the referring party. Professional consultants, who serve as agents of the attorneys who retain them, should be loyal to those attorneys. When professionals function as either evaluators or consultants, they establish no therapeutic or habilitative relationships with defendants and thus owe them no loyalty. However, if a treatment or habilitative relationship commences, a professional owes loyalty to the person undergoing treatment or habilitation. The problem of divided professional loyalties emerges when a treatment or habilitative relationship is established as an incident of a judicial disposition of litigation or when incarcerated prisoners receive institution-based professional services.[11]

Paragraph (d) offers guidance to therapists or habilitators who experience conflicting loyalties while serving the criminal justice system. A treatment or habilitative relationship is the starting point in defining a professional's role. If therapists or habilitators are to play a helping role, their relationship with defendants should be structured as far as possible as if it were an ordinary therapist-patient or habilitator-client relationship. Thus, professional obligations to patients or clients undergoing treatment or habilitation within the criminal justice system should be, to the greatest extent possible, identical to those governing any treatment or habilitation relationship.[12] Confidentiality of patient or client communications made in the course of a therapeutic or habilitative relationship within the criminal justice system merits strict protection because mental

---

11. Divided loyalties are not unique to professionals who function within the criminal justice system. For example, professionals retained by employers may be asked to reveal information about employees in treatment. Therapists serving in the armed forces may be placed in a similar ethical bind. For other examples of therapeutic relationships that require the therapist to serve in a "double agent" role, *see* discussion and sources *cited in* R. Bonnie, Psychiatrists and the Legal Process: Diagnoses and Debate xiv-xxv (1977).

12. APA *Task Force Report, supra* note 4, at 1102, recommendation 2.

health and mental retardation professionals view confidentiality to be essential to treatment and habilitation outside that setting.[13] In neither setting, however, is confidentiality an absolute. A therapist is under both an ethical[14] and a legal[15] obligation to reveal confidential information necessary to protect either the patient or others from imminent danger.

A treating or habilitative relationship established with a patient as an incident to an adjudication or in an institutional setting carries with it disclosure requirements, imposed on the therapist or habilitator, that place added constraints on the confidentiality of patient communications. For example, a therapist treating an individual in the course of a pretrial diversion arrangement or under a condition of probation may be required to report to the authorizing or sentencing court periodically or at designated times, and to advise the court if an individual fails to cooperate in the treatment regimen, to keep appointments with the therapist, or to take medication resulting in a deterioration of the individual's mental condition, or engages in criminal behavior. In other respects, the duty to disclose may be more ambiguous. For example, it is far from clear that a therapist is obliged to report to a court that a patient smokes marijuana or has made threats but not acted on them. Although no bright line may always be clearly discerned, obligations toward a court that override claims of patient confidentiality should be predicated on the court's need for information to protect the integrity of the adjudicatory process.

Professionals providing treatment or habilitation in institutional settings also are likely to experience certain constraints limiting their ability to safeguard patient or client confidences. Such professionals typically

---

13. APA Medical Ethics, *supra* note 3, at §4, annotation 1; APA *Ethical Principles, supra* note 2, at 635-636, principle 5 (1981); American Psychological Association, Standards for Providers of Psychological Services 2.2.2, 2.3.5 (1981) [hereinafter cited as APA Psychological Services Standards]; American Psychological Association, *Speciality Guidelines for the Delivery of Services of Clinical Psychologists* 2.2.2, 2.3.5, 36 Am. Psychologist 640, 645-646 (1981) [hereinafter cited as APA *Clinical Psychologists' Guidelines*]; American Psychological Association, *Specialty Guidelines for the Delivery of Services by Counseling Psychologists* 2.2.2, 2.3.5, 36 Am. Psychologist 652, 657, 659 (1981) [hereinafter cited as APA *Counseling Psychologists' Guidelines*].

14. APA Medical Ethics, *supra* note 3, §4, annotation 8; APA *Ethical Principles, supra* note 2, at 636, principle 5.

15. The seminal case is Tarasoff v. Regents of the University of California, 17 Cal. 3d 425, 551 P.2d 334, 131 Cal. Rptr. 14 (1976). *See also* Jablouski by Pahls v. United States, 712 F.2d 391 (9th Cir. 1983); Lipari v. Sears, Roebuck & Co., 497 F. Supp. 185 (D. Neb. 1980); McIntosh v. Milano, 168 N.J. Super. 466, 403 A.2d 500 (1979). *See generally* Brakel, *Discharge and Transfer,* in The Mentally Disabled and the Law 203, 213-215 (S. Brakel, J. Parry & B. Weiner eds., 3d ed. 1985).

are under a duty to report escape plans, anticipated assaultive behavior, and possession of contraband. Obligations to institutional management that override patient confidentiality should be predicated only on institutional security requirements.[16]

All circumstances that generate dual loyalties restricting traditional treatment or habilitative relationships should be clearly identified for patient/clients at the outset of the relationship. Limits on confidentiality should be described as explicitly as possible to ensure mutual understanding between the individual and the therapist or habilitator and to promote the individual's informed consent at the outset of the relationship. Paragraph (d) recommends that professionals be required to explain to patients or clients the nature of limitations imposed by criminal justice considerations on a treatment or habilitative relationship, a requirement consistent with professional ethical obligations.[17]

Standard 7-1.2. Joint professional obligations for improving the administration of justice in criminal cases involving mental health or mental retardation issues

(a) National, state, and local judicial, legal, and mental health and mental retardation agencies and professional organizations have an obligation to work cooperatively to monitor the interdependent performance within the criminal process of their members and constituents and to improve the overall quality of the administration of justice in criminal cases involving mental health and mental retardation issues.

(b) Appropriate professional organizations and governmental agencies should establish programs, including peer review, for monitoring the performance of mental health and mental retardation professionals participating in the criminal process. Existing professional ethics boards and committees should develop specific criteria and

16. *See* standard 23-1.1.

17. APA Medical Ethics, *supra* note 3, at annotations 2, 6; APA *Task Force Report, supra* note 4, at 1102, recommendation 1; APA Ethical Principles, *supra* note 2, at 636, principle 6; APA Psychological Services Standards, *supra* note 13, at standard 2.3.5; APA *Clinical Psychologists' Guidelines, supra* note 13, at 646, guideline 2.3.5; APA *Counseling Psychologists' Guidelines, supra* note 13, at 659, guideline 2.3.5.

special review procedures designed to address the unique ethical questions that arise when mental health and mental retardation professionals participate in the criminal process.

(c) Appropriate professional, scientific, and governmental organizations should sponsor empirical research concerning:

(i) the validity and reliability of evaluations as relating to issues in criminal cases;

(ii) the development of standardized protocols for conducting mental evaluations in criminal cases;

(iii) the application and practical effect of substantive rules and procedures concerning mental illness and mental retardation in criminal law and procedure; and,

(iv) the quality and impact of participation by mental health and mental retardation professionals in the criminal process.

Commentary Introduction

Judicial, legal, and mental health and mental retardation professional organizations should embark on cooperative efforts on an array of shared concerns to ensure that competent mental health and mental retardation professional services are available to all persons and that all criminal defendants benefit from comprehensive mental health and mental retardation programs and services. Interdisciplinary efforts of this sort can also promote improvements in and expansions of such programs for offenders and ex-offenders at all levels of government — local, state, and national. Professional organizations in all disciplines (judicial-legal, mental health, and mental retardation) should initiate interaction with counterpart groups so that the required cooperative ventures can be launched.

Related Standards

ABA, Code of Judicial Conduct 4

ABA, Standards for Criminal Justice 3-1.4

American Psychiatric Association, The Principles of Medical Ethics with Annotations Especially Applicable to Psychiatry §1, annotation 3 and §7 (1981)

Commentary

The thrust of paragraphs (a) and (b) is that professional mental health and mental retardation organizations have the primary responsibility to evaluate and monitor the activities of their members, but that courts and the legal profession also have obligations concerning mental health and mental retardation professionals who participate in the criminal justice process. Those organizations indeed have declared their willingness to undertake that responsibility. The American Psychiatric Association has assented to peer review of psychiatrists' performance, at least in hospitals,[1] and an American Psychological Association task force has asserted that empirical evaluation of psychological services performed within the criminal justice system is an ethical mandate for the profession.[2] Standard 7-1.2(b) reflects the premise that professional ethics boards should address the special ethical problems that arise when mental health and mental retardation professionals function as part of the criminal process. Professional organizations should provide ongoing review of their members' professional competence and adherence to ethical standards.

Standard 7-1.2(c) recognizes that empirical research is needed on all issues relating to the criminal justice system that arise from activities of mental health and mental retardation professionals. Dr. Saleem Shah, Chief of the Center for Studies of Antisocial and Violent Behavior of the National Institutes of Mental Health, has identified several spheres of interaction requiring further research.[3] For example, he notes that relatively little research has been done to devise psycho-legal assessment instruments bearing on legally relevant capacities, such as capacity to form the requisite intent to commit various crimes.[4] More work should be done to improve the reliability and validity of predictions of behavior and to understand and clarify the decisional processes involved in making predictions.[5] Empirical studies are required to assess the validity of the behavioral and psychological assumptions underlying legal doctrines and policies.[6] Better channels must be developed to disseminate and utilize new research knowledge effectively.[7] All these specialized concerns have received inadequate attention in the past; only through adequate research can appropriate changes and improvements be achieved.

---

1. American Psychiatric Association, The Principles of Medical Ethics with Annotations Especially Applicable to Psychiatry §1, annot. 3 (1981).

2. American Psychological Association, *Report of the Task Force on the Role of Psychology in the Criminal Justice System*, 33 Am. Psychologist 1099, 1106 (1978).

3. Shah, *Legal and Mental Health Systems Interactions*, 4 Int'l J.L. & Psychiatry 219, 252-257 (1981).

4. *Id.* at 254.

5. *Id.* at 255.

6. *Id.* at 256.

7. *Id.* at 257.

Standard 7-1.3. Education and training

(a) Interdisciplinary cooperation. Judicial, legal, and mental health and mental retardation professional associations, organizations, and institutions at national, state, and local levels should cooperate in promoting, designing, and offering basic and advanced programs on the participation of mental health and mental retardation professionals in the criminal process to judges, attorneys, mental health and mental retardation professionals, and to students within these disciplines.

(b) Lawyers.

(i) Law schools should provide the opportunity for all students, as a part of their formal legal education, to become familiar with the issues involved in mental health and mental retardation law and mental health and mental retardation professional participation in the criminal process. When it is appropriate in view of the curricular framework, a law school should consider offering advanced courses on mental health and mental retardation law and mental health and mental retardation professional participation in the criminal process for students who desire to concentrate on criminal law practice.

(ii) Bar associations, law schools, and other organizations having responsibility for providing continuing legal education should develop and regularly conduct programs offering advanced instruction on mental health and mental retardation law and mental health and mental retardation professional participation in the criminal process. Prosecutors, public defenders, and other attorneys who specialize in, or regularly practice, criminal law should participate in these programs.

(c) Judges. Each jurisdiction's highest appellate tribunal or its judicial supervisory authority with responsibility for continuing judicial education should develop and regularly conduct programs on the participation of mental health and mental retardation professionals in the criminal process. Judges who preside over criminal trials should participate in these programs.

(d) Mental health and mental retardation professionals.

(i) Professional and graduate schools should afford the opportunity for the students of mental health and mental retardation disciplines, as a part of their formal education, to become familiar

with the issues concerning the participation of mental health and mental retardation professionals in the criminal process.

(ii) These professional and graduate schools should also provide advanced instruction for students of the mental health and mental retardation disciplines who desire to meet the minimum criteria established by standard 7-3.10 for qualifying as court-appointed evaluators and by standard 7-3.11 for qualifying as expert witnesses testifying about a person's mental condition.

(iii) Professional and graduate schools and other appropriate organizations, including governmental agencies having responsibility for continuing education for mental health and mental retardation professionals, should develop and regularly conduct programs offering instruction on the participation of such professionals in the criminal process designed to:

(A) enable those professionals to meet the minimum criteria established by standard 7-3.10 for qualifying as court appointed evaluators and by standard 7-3.11 for qualifying as expert witnesses testifying about a person's mental condition; and,

(B) inform all participants of significant new developments in law and criminal practice in order to improve the professional competence of those who play scientific, evaluative, consultative, treatment, or habilitation roles in the criminal process. Mental health and mental retardation professionals who participate in the criminal process should enroll in these programs.

Commentary Introduction

Standard 7-1.3 articulates a desirable level of education and training for lawyers, judges, and mental health and mental retardation professionals on issues of mental health and mental retardation law and participation by mental health and mental retardation professionals in criminal justice processes. The standard embodies a two-tiered approach: (1) a basic educational component designed to familiarize students in each discipline with these issues; and (2) an advanced educational component for professionals who anticipate participation in criminal justice activities. The educational requirements advocated in this standard should apply to law school and professional school students and to practitioners through professional continuing educational programs.

Related Standards

ABA, Code of Judicial Conduct §3A(1)

ABA, Model Rules of Professional Conduct §1.1

American Psychiatric Association, The Principles of Medical Ethics with Annotations Especially Applicable to Psychiatry §5

American Psychological Association, Ethical Principles of Psychologists 2

American Psychological Association, Specialty Guidelines for the Delivery of Services by Clinical Psychologists 1.5

American Psychological Association, Specialty Guidelines for the Delivery of Services by Counseling Psychologists 1.5

American Psychological Association, Standards for Providers of Psychological Services 1.5

Commentary

Professional ethical standards mandate that mental health and mental retardation professionals perform their services competently. For example, the American Psychiatric Association has stated that "a psychiatrist who regularly practices outside his/her area of professional competence should be considered unethical."[1] The American Psychological Association has declared, "The maintenance of high standards of competence is a responsibility shared by all psychologists in the interest of the public and the profession as a whole."[2] Professional education and training on matters in which the professional intends to practice are prerequisites to competent professional performance.[3] Professionals participating in the criminal justice process require specialized forensic knowledge because "[s]tandard mental status evaluations, assessments as to presence of or absence of a psychotic disorder, or other such clinical psychiatric or psychological considerations do not translate readily into the specific legal

1. American Psychiatric Association, The Principles of Medical Ethics with Annotations Especially Applicable to Psychiatry §2, annotation 3 (1981).

2. American Psychological Association, *Ethical Principles of Psychologists* 2, 36 Am. Psychologist 633, 634 (1981) [hereinafter cited as APA *Ethical Principles*].

3. American Psychological Association, *Report of the Task Force on the Role of Psychology in the Criminal Justice System*, 33 Am. Psychologist 1099, 1105 (1978); APA *Ethical Principles*, *supra* note 2; American Psychological Association, Standards for Providers of Psychological Services 1.5 (1981); American Psychological Association, *Specialty Guidelines for the Delivery of Services by Clinical Psychologists* 1.5, 36 Am. Psychologist 640, 644 (1981); American Psychological Association, *Specialty Guidelines for the Delivery of Services by Counseling Psychologists* 1.5, 36 Am. Psychologist 652, 656 (1981).

concerns."[4] Professional schools should therefore provide specialized training to ensure that students and professionals acquire the requisite forensic knowledge.

Judges and attorneys also have ethical responsibilities to understand the proper roles of mental health and mental retardation professionals and the limits of their technical knowledge when they testify in legal proceedings. The Association's *Code of Judicial Conduct* requires judges in the course of their judicial duties to maintain professional competence in the law.[5] Attorneys are required by the *Model Rules of Professional Conduct* to provide competent representation for their clients.[6] Because the law and not behavioral science governs the resolution of substantive issues at trial, as well as questions of evidence and procedure, judges and lawyers should not allow mental health and mental retardation professionals to exert undue influence on them through testimony exceeding the bounds of their expertise.[7] To avoid ethical difficulties, attorneys who appear in and judges who preside over criminal trials embracing issues of mental health or mental retardation law should have education and training necessary to understand the relevant issues and the proper uses of expert testimony.[8]

Law schools and mental health and mental retardation professional schools should provide their students with at least some opportunity to become familiar with cross-disciplinary issues. In addition, they should offer advanced instruction for attorneys specializing in criminal cases and for mental health and mental retardation professionals wishing to qualify for designation as evaluators or expert witnesses.

The language of standard 7-1.3 does not purport to dictate law school curricula. Nevertheless, it offers guidance for law schools desiring to offer advanced instruction in this field. Ideally, a curriculum should allow both classroom exploration of theoretical issues and clinical applications of theory in relation to (1) clients whose mental conditions present issues for resolution in the criminal process, and (2) mental health and mental retardation professionals who may perform evaluative, consultative, treatment, or habilitative roles in the criminal process.[9]

---

4. Shah, *Legal and Mental Health Systems Interactions,* 4 INT'L J.L. & PSYCHIATRY 219, 249 (1981) (emphasis omitted) [hereinafter cited as Shah].

5. CODE OF JUDICIAL CONDUCT CANON 3A(1).

6. MODEL RULES OF PROFESSIONAL CONDUCT 1.1 (1983).

7. Shah, *supra* note 4, at 251.

8. Shah, *Foreword* to NIMH, MENTAL HEALTH AND LAW: A SYSTEM IN TRANSITION ix (1974).

9. A three-credit course entitled "Law and Mental Disorder: Criminal Aspects," offered at the University of San Diego School of Law, presents a model for consideration. Psychi-

Advanced professional school training for mental health and mental retardation professionals desiring to qualify as court-appointed evaluators or expert witnesses should enable professionals to (1) understand the substantive, procedural, and evidence law doctrines bearing on the performance of evaluations or expert opinion testimony and (2) apply clinical skills relating to those legal doctrines. For example, advanced training programs for mental health and mental retardation professionals should include the following: a description of the judicial structure of the jurisdiction; basic elements of the adversary process and the roles of participants in that process; evaluation techniques; legal requirements governing written reports; the nature and limits of expert testimony; and coverage of other matters dealt with in part III of this chapter.[10]

Continuing professional educational programs within each discipline should be offered for practitioners who did not receive appropriate advanced instruction as undergraduate or graduate students. Programs of this nature should inform participants about new legal and practice developments, thus enhancing their level of professional competence. They should be available to criminal law practitioners, judges of courts with criminal jurisdiction, and mental health and mental retardation professionals functioning within the criminal justice system.

---

atrists and psychologists introduce students to topics like the theoretical perspectives of psychology and psychiatry; an overview of the current edition of the Diagnostic and Statistical Manual; mental status examinations; psychological testing; and psychological and psychiatric reports and medical records. Students observe videotaped patient interviews and actual interviews in nonforensic and forensic settings. Law professors instruct on concepts of mental illness; the role of mental health and mental retardation professionals in the criminal justice process; the defense of mental nonresponsibility [insanity] and procedures underlying that defense; commitment procedures for nonresponsibility acquittees; competency to stand trial and other competency issues; sentencing and sentencing reports; societal treatment of sex offenders; problems relating to alcoholism and drug addiction; and issues affecting mentally disordered convicts. Students participate in simulated exercises involving direct and cross-examination of psychiatrists and psychologists relating to the defense of mental nonresponsibility [insanity], competency to stand trial, and sentencing.

10. *See* standards 7-3.1 through 7-3.15 and commentary. Although the courses described in the commentary text may be offered in a residency or advanced training program, they may also constitute part of a separate fellowship program. The Joint Committee on Accreditation of Fellowship Programs in Forensic Psychiatry has suggested guidelines for a postresidency program in psychiatry. *Standards for Fellowship Programs in Forensic Psychiatry,* 10 Bull. Am. Academy of Psychiatry & L. 285 (1982).

Part II

Police and Custodial Roles

William H. Erickson, *Chairman*
Standing Committee on Association Standards for Criminal Justice

Richard J. Brzeczek
Task Force Chairman

Gerald M. Caplan
Reporter

Task Force

Richard J. Brzeczek, *Chairman*
Private practitioner, Chicago, Illinois

Patrick H. DeLeon, Ph.D., M.P.H., J.D.
U.S. Senate Staff, Washington, D.C. (representing American Psychological Association)

Robert S. Fertitta
Associate Dean, National College of District Attorneys, Houston, Texas (representing ABA Section of Criminal Justice)

Kenneth J. Hodson
Major General, United States Army (Retired); former Judge Advocate General of the Army, Washington, D.C.

M. Wayne Huggins
Sheriff, Fairfax County, Virginia (representing National Sheriffs' Association)

Francis B. Looney
Retired Deputy Police Commissioner, New York City; Past President, International Association of Chiefs of Police, Farmingdale, New York

Robert E. McKenna
Director, Division of Insurance Fraud, Office of Insurance Commissioner, State of Florida, Miami, Florida

Thomas F. A. Plaut, Ph.D.
Psychologist, National Institute of Mental Health, Rockville, Maryland

Martin Reiser, Ed.D.
Psychologist and Director, Behavioral Science Services, Los Angeles Police Department, Los Angeles, California

Douglas A. Sargent, M.D., J.D.
Assistant Professor of Psychiatry, Adjunct Professor of Law, Wayne State University, Detroit, Michigan (representing American Psychiatric Association)

Andrew Sonner
State's Attorney, Montgomery County, Maryland

Criminal Justice Mental Health Standards

Linda Teplin, Ph.D.
Assistant Professor of Psychiatry, Sociology & Urban Affairs, Department of Psychiatry & Behavioral Sciences, Northwestern University Medical School, Chicago, Illinois

H. Rutherford Turnbull III, J.D.
Professor, Special Education and Law, University of Kansas, Lawrence, Kansas

GERALD M. CAPLAN, *Reporter*
Professor of Law, National Law Center, George Washington University

INTRODUCTION

Police play an ill-defined and unenviable role in responding to a variety of public disturbances and other incidents involving mentally ill and mentally retarded persons; moreover, they often lack specialized training to handle such situations effectively. In large measure this reflects society's failure to establish and fund other public agencies more appropriate than the police to provide the services needed by mentally disordered persons. Historically, police officers have been reluctant to intervene in situations involving mentally ill or mentally retarded persons, unless at issue is the commission of a crime. This is so, in considerable measure, because of a legislative neglect in defining the proper functions of the police in noncriminal matters and in providing community resources for treatment and care to which officers can surrender mentally disabled persons taken into police custody.

Nevertheless, the standards must build on the existing social and political structure and not on an abstractly ideal organization of government. Accordingly, part II focuses on the appropriate roles of police and custodial personnel in interacting with mentally ill and mentally retarded persons in the community and in serving as a primary referral source to urban mental health centers responsible to initiate civil commitment proceedings. Clearly, however, the police can be effective only to the extent that society provides comprehensive, effective community mental health services to evaluate, treat, and habilitate the mentally disturbed people who inevitably will come to the attention of the police and require initial police custody. Under the standards, the police role is very limited and can be fulfilled effectively only with the support of other government agencies.

The Association position is that legislation should delineate narrowly the circumstances under which police officers can take designated classes of mentally disabled persons into emergency custody, *viz.*, circumstances indicating danger to those persons or others or suggesting an inability to provide life's basic necessities.[1] Police use of force should be limited to the need to protect mentally disabled persons and others from bodily harm.[2] The ensuing detention and transportation of persons taken into custody, other than persons arrested for felonies or serious crimes, should be solely for the purpose of obtaining suitable evaluation and treatment or habilitation.[3] This, of course, requires cooperation between police agencies and medical, mental health, and mental retardation facility administrators; principles governing such cooperation are embodied in joint guidelines and policies that have been disseminated widely to police officers and facility personnel.[4]

In many situations, mentally disabled persons have committed harmful or dangerous acts that are prima facie criminal, in which case they are processed as arrestees. In other instances, part II expresses a policy preference for a voluntary, noncriminal disposition of those who live with others and do not appear to be dangerous.[5] If a mentally disabled person has committed a felony or other serious crime, arresting officers should follow the usual procedures but should arrange for a mental health or mental retardation professional evaluation and necessary and appropriate treatment or habilitation.[6] The officers should also make sure that prosecuting attorneys and courts of criminal trial jurisdiction are apprised of the facts suggesting mental illness or mental retardation.[7]

Mentally disturbed arrestees often are suicidal or potentially assaultive. Police and custodial officers should be trained to recognize and control dangerous symptoms of mental illness or mental retardation,[8] particularly those reflecting suicidal tendencies.[9] Police are exposed to

1. *See* standard 7-2.1(a) and commentary.
2. *See* standard 7-2.4 and commentary.
3. *See* standards 7-2.1(b), 7-2.5(a) and commentary.
4. *See* standard 7-2.2 and commentary.
5. *See* standard 7-2.3 and commentary.
6. *See* standards 7-2.5(b), 7-2.6(c) and commentary.
7. *See* standard 7-2.5(c) and (d) and commentary.
8. *See* standards 7-2.6(a), 7-2.8(c) and commentary.
9. *See* standards 7-2.6(b), 7-2.8(c) and commentary.

inherent physical danger in responding to family disturbance calls; that danger is exacerbated if one or more family members are mentally disabled and the responding officers act or react inappropriately. Accordingly, the standards emphasize the need for police training focusing on street and home encounters with mentally ill and mentally retarded persons.[10] They recognize as well the desirability of relying on mental health or mental retardation professionals who join police officers in responding to emergency calls.[11]

Arrested persons who have been neither convicted nor civilly committed cannot be compelled to undergo treatment or habilitation,[12] except as required by court order or dictated by emergency circumstances.[13] If, however, an arrestee desires treatment or habilitation services while in pretrial detention, the police should cooperate in achieving a voluntary admission to a suitable mental health or mental retardation facility,[14] with appropriate notice to the detainee's counsel and the prosecuting attorney.[15]

Under part II, all police records of significant contacts with mentally disabled persons who are not charged with crimes should be kept separate from arrest records under strict confidentiality.[16] Access to or disclosure of the contents of records covering treatment of and habilitation services provided to persons detained in police facilities should be severely limited.[17]

The Association believes that its part II standards appropriately confirm the peacekeeping and community-safeguarding roles of police officers. The standards also achieve a harmonious balance between the claims, on the one hand, of mentally ill and mentally retarded persons to humane treatment and of the community, on the other, to protection against their harmful and, in particular, dangerous acts.

---

10. *See* standard 7-2.8(b) and commentary.
11. *See* standard 7-2.4(b) and commentary.
12. *See* standards 7-4.10 (persons committed as incompetent to undergo trial proceedings); 7-7.4(d) (special commitment following acquittal of charges of violent crime, based on mental nonresponsibility [insanity]); 7-9.11, 7-9.12 (special commitment of severely mentally ill or seriously mentally retarded convicted offenders); 7-10.8, 7-10.9 (severely mentally ill or seriously mentally retarded prisoners transferred to mental health or mental retardation facilities).
13. *See* standard 7-2.7(b) and commentary.
14. *See* standard 7-2.7(a) and commentary.
15. *See* standard 7-2.7(c) and commentary.
16. *See* standard 7-2.9(a) and commentary.
17. *See* standard 7-2.9(b) and (c) and commentary.

Standard 7-2.1. Classes of mentally ill and mentally retarded persons subject to police emergency detention

(a) Authority for the police to take mentally ill and mentally retarded persons into custody in emergency situations should be statutorily defined and limited to the following two classes of persons:

(i) those whose conduct represents a danger to themselves or others; and,

(ii) those who appear so gravely disabled as to be unable to provide themselves with the basic necessities of life.

(b) Detention is for the exclusive purpose of providing transportation to an appropriate facility where the detainee can be examined, and, if necessary, be provided appropriate evaluation, treatment, or habilitation. Wherever feasible, transportation should be to a mental health, mental retardation, or medical facility.

(c) Police agencies should promulgate written procedures to implement the emergency detention statute in their jurisdiction on behalf of the persons described in paragraph (a).

(d) The capacity of the police to implement the standards in this part is largely dependent upon the availability of comprehensive community mental health and mental retardation programs. This dependence is an explicit recognition of the fact that the police role in dealing with mentally ill and mentally retarded persons is a limited one.

Commentary Introduction

The standard recommends a statutory delineation of police authority to take specified classes of gravely disabled or dangerous mentally disabled persons into custody, to detain them, and to transport them to appropriate medical, mental health, or mental retardation facilities for examination and needed evaluation and treatment or habilitation services. Legislation should be implemented by written police agency procedures. The standard emphasizes that the police role in handling mentally ill and mentally retarded persons should be limited, and that an effective discharge of police responsibilities requires comprehensive community mental health and mental retardation programs.

Related Standards

ABA, Standards for Criminal Justice 1-3.4, 1-3.5, 7-10.5, 7-10.7

Commentary

Paragraph (a) recommends that the common law powers of the police to exercise emergency arrest powers over mentally disabled persons[1] be revised and incorporated into statutes; this builds on existing Association policy.[2] Police need for legislative guidance is pointed up by research demonstrating that police officers are involved in a majority of cases referred to urban mental health centers preliminary to involuntary civil commitment.[3] A statutory delineation of powers also is important to

1. In jurisdictions with no legislative provision (only Mississippi and Nebraska still lack clear legislative provisions for police detention of the mentally ill) common law police powers are neither "carefully defined nor commonly known." *See* 1•84, commentary to standard 1-3.4; *cf. Developments — Civil Commitment,* 87 HARV. L. REV. 1190, 1204 (1974). At common law, police officers apparently acted at their own peril in such situations: If they wrongfully detained a person, they might have been liable for civil damages even though they acted reasonably and in good faith. *See* Crawford v. Brown, 321 Ill. 305, 151 N.E. 911 (1926); Maxwell v. Maxwell, 189 Iowa 7, 177 N.W. 541 (1920); *cf.* A. MATTHEWS, MENTAL DISABILITY AND THE CRIMINAL LAW 170 (1970) [hereinafter cited as A. MATTHEWS]. Police are not liable on a nonfeasance theory unless they deliberately are indifferent to an affirmative duty to intervene based on statute or an established special relationship. Gilchrist v. City of Livonia, 599 F. Supp. 260, 262-264 (E.D. Mich. 1984) (federal Civil Rights Act suit, 42 U.S.C. §1983 (1982)).

Police can arrest individuals on emergency grounds more than once and take them to a mental health facility; judicial hearings can be conducted thereafter. McKinney v. George, 726 F.2d 1183, 1186-1189 (7th Cir. 1984).

2. *See* standard 1-3.4, which encourages legislatures to confer authority on law enforcement officers to respond to the self-destructive behavior of citizens "such as that engaged in by the mentally ill person."

3. On emergency detention generally, *see* Brakel, *Involuntary Institutionalization,* in THE MENTALLY DISABLED AND THE LAW 21, 51-52 (S. Brakel, J. Parry, & B. Weiner eds., 3d ed. 1985). Emergency detention legislation through October 1982 may be found in *id.* at 101-109, Table 2.4. *See also* Monahan, Caldeira & Friedlander, *Police and Mentally Ill: A Comparison of Committed and Arrested Persons,* 2 INT'L J.L. & PSYCHIATRY 509 (1979) [hereinafter cited as Monahan, Caldeira & Friedlander]; *cf.* Warren, *Involuntary Commitment for Mental Disorder: The Application of California's Lanterman-Petris-Short Act,* 11 LAW & SOC'Y REV. 629 (1977). *See also* American Psychiatric Ass'n Model State Law on Civil Commitment of the Mentally Ill, standard 4.A, 20 HARV. J. ON LEGIS. 276, 315-319 (1983); Durham, Carr & Pierce, *Police Involvement and Influence in Involuntary Civil Commitment,* 35 HOSPITAL & COMMUNITY PSYCHIATRY 580 (1984); Teplin, *Managing Disorder: Police Handling of the Mentally Ill,* in MENTAL HEALTH AND CRIMINAL JUSTICE 157 (L. Teplin ed. 1984).

shield officers from personal liability generated by unclear common law norms.[4]

Because in many instances police custody is the first official step leading to a civil commitment,[5] police emergency powers appropriately may be limited to circumstances supporting a reasonable belief on the part of officers that persons taken into custody meet the statutory criteria for compulsory commitment.[6] Paragraph (a) reflects the Association's position that only two categories of mentally disabled persons should be subject to police emergency custody:

1. Subparagraph (a)(i) incorporates a criterion of danger to mentally disabled persons themselves or to others, a universally recognized basis for civil commitment.[7]
2. Subparagraph (a)(ii) acknowledges the appropriateness of a norm of grave disability to provide for the basic necessities of life — food, clothing, and shelter. If, because of mental illness or mental retardation, persons cannot meet these basic needs,[8] police officers should be empowered to take them into protec-

4. *See generally* standard 1-3.4 and commentary. The standard does not cover expressly the substantial problem of police immunity when officers exercise statutory authority to take emergency custody of mentally ill or mentally retarded persons. The emphasis in paragraph (c) and other part II standards on the need for written departmental guidelines assumes a *de facto* immunity for officers who comply with lawful departmental guidelines. The topic of police immunity generally is covered in chapter 1, *Urban Police Function; see* standard 1-5.4. Ideally, immunity should be available whenever police officers act reasonably in good faith. That is the scope of police immunity under the federal Civil Rights Act, 42 U.S.C. §§1983-1985 (1982). *See* Pierson v. Ray, 386 U.S. 547 (1967).

5. *See* the authorities cited in note 4 *supra.*

6. *See* O'Connor v. Donaldson, 422 U.S. 563, 574-574 (1975) (constitutional criteria for commitment and continued confinement).

7. *See* Project, *Legal Issues in State Mental Health Care: Proposals for Change: Civil Commitment,* 2 Mental Disability L. Rptr. 57, 64 (1978).

8. For example, the standard contemplates the detention, preferably voluntary but forcibly if necessary, of homeless persons in immediate danger of starvation or hypothermia. In the past, there have been newspaper accounts of deaths of homeless persons which occurred because local authorities believed that they lacked the power to intervene lawfully. In one celebrated case, an elderly woman who had lived for eight months in a rug-covered cardboard box died after city officials failed in a ten-day effort to coax her into coming to a shelter or hospital. Herman, "Woman Refuses Aid, Dies in Carton on Street," N.Y. Times, Jan. 27, 1982, at A1. The woman, who had previously been diagnosed as schizophrenic, refused all help. A court order was sought and secured, but it arrived too late and the woman died from hypothermia. Herman, "One of New York City's Homeless Goes Home Again — In Death," N.Y. Times, Jan. 31, 1982, at 18.

> tive custody and transport them to suitable facilities for evaluation and, if necessary, for appropriate treatment or habilitation.[9]

In fact, a legislative adoption of these criteria will confirm the usual existing practice, which apparently has not proven destructive to the civil liberties of mentally disabled persons.[10] Note, however, that the standard does not envision police custody of confused and disoriented persons who, nevertheless, are able to meet their personal needs and who can decide for themselves whether to seek or receive treatment. The governmental interest in protecting individuals from harm does not override the right of individuals to manage their own lives.[11]

Legislation is not likely to provide for all the details of emergency custody and detention of mentally disabled persons meeting the paragraph (a) criteria. Therefore, paragraph (c) advocates the development and dissemination of written police departmental procedures to implement a jurisdiction's emergency detention statute.

The custody exercised under paragraph (a) is not a form of criminal

---

9. *See, e.g.,* Colyer v. Third Judicial Dist. Ct., 469 F. Supp. 424, 432 (D. Utah 1979).

10. In practice the police file petitions for emergency commitment in extreme situations in which a person has attempted suicide or appears violent, there are overt signs of serious mental disorder accompanied by idiosyncratic behavior like public nudity or bizarre posturing, a person is severely disabled and creating a public nuisance, or the police are summoned on an emergency basis by someone like an employer or personal physician who knows the person's condition. *See generally* Bittner, *Police Discretion in Emergency Apprehension of Mentally Ill Persons,* 14 Soc. Prob. 278 (1972) [hereinafter cited as Bittner]; Matthews, *Observations of Police Policy and Procedure for Emergency Detention of the Mentally Ill,* 61 J. Crim. L., Criminology & Police Sci. 283 (1970); Monahan, Caldeira & Friedlander, *supra* note 3, at 514. If the police characterize a person as "gravely disabled" (as opposed to "dangerous to self") it is likely that the person is severely disoriented as to time or place, incoherent or hallucinating, apparently starving, or severely mentally retarded. Monahan, Caldeira & Friedlander, *supra* note 3, at 514. Professor Bittner has concluded that police decisions to take persons to a hospital generally are based "on overwhelming conclusive evidence of illness." Bittner, *supra,* at 285. His conclusions have been confirmed more recently by Sheridan and Teplin who have described the "police-referred" patient as "seriously disturbed," typically "psychotic . . . and in need of hospitalization." Sheridan & Teplin, *Police-Referred Psychiatric Emergencies: Advantages of Community Treatment,* 9 J. Community Psychiatry 140, 145 (1981).

Part II endorses the practice of calling on mental health or mental retardation professionals, or persons with suitable mental health or mental retardation training, to assist police in effecting custody. *See* standard 7-2.4(b) and commentary.

11. *See* Colyer v. Third Judicial Dist. Ct., 469 F. Supp. 424, 432 (D. Utah 1979).

arrest.[12] Consequently, ensuing detention, according to paragraph (b), must be limited to transportation to an appropriate facility,[13] based on police evaluation of a mentally ill or mentally retarded individual as dangerous or severely disabled.[14] That in turn requires adequate procedural guidelines generated cooperatively by police officials and medical, mental health, and mental retardation facility administrators and disseminated to police officers and facility personnel.[15]

Legislation delineating police powers of emergency custody, detention, and transportation of mentally disabled persons is meaningless unless state and local legislative bodies provide suitable medical, mental health, and mental retardation facilities and programs into the custody of which police officers may surrender dangerously mentally ill or severely mentally disabled persons. If treatment, habilitation, or shelter facilities are lacking, the police apparatus cannot discharge its statutory obligations, and police officers are likely to become skeptical about intervening in noncriminal circumstances if no follow-up mental health or mental retardation services are available. Moreover, the inherent justification for police emergency custody and detention, with its inevitable restriction of personal freedom and potential for damage to civil liberties, is weakened or destroyed if overcrowded shelter-care facilities and hospitals turn away mentally disordered persons in police custody.[16] Police intervention

---

12. *See* standard 7-2.5(b) and commentary on the processing of persons arrested for felony or serious crime.

13. As determined under the jurisdiction's civil commitment legislation. *See* note 3 and accompanying text. "From the viewpoint of the person detained, there are corresponding virtues. He can be given medical attention and is held in an environment controlled by trained professionals rather than a jail." A. MATTHEWS, *supra* note 1, at 173.

14. One police department instructs officers, "Your job as a police officer is to get the disturbed person safely to a hospital where successful ways of treating and curing mental cases are available." Chicago Police Dep't, "Handling Abnormal People," Training Bull. No. 3-5 (1962). *See also* Manning, *Police Classification and the Mentally Ill*, in MENTAL HEALTH AND CRIMINAL JUSTICE 177 (L. Teplin ed. 1984).

15. *See* standard 7-2.2(a) and commentary.

16. The police should not have to depend on adult local detention facilities as holding facilities for mentally ill and mentally retarded persons. In some states, legislation prohibits confining such persons in jails or correctional institutions unless no other suitable place is available. *See, e.g.,* COLO. REV. STAT. §27-10-105(1.1) (1982); D.C. CODE ANN. §21-585 (1981). If mental health or mental retardation facilities are unavailable, police officers will be inclined to arrest mentally ill and mentally retarded persons for disorderly conduct as a legal basis for custody. R. ROCK, M. JACOBSEN & R. JANEPAUL, HOSPITALIZATION AND DISCHARGE OF THE MENTALLY ILL 90 (1968).

Emergency detention in county jails of persons awaiting involuntary civil commitment proceedings denies due process of law because it is not the least restrictive means of

proves largely a meaningless and wasted gesture under these circumstances.

Accordingly, paragraph (d) incorporates an Association admonition to legislatures that the legislation advocated in paragraph (a) will be largely meaningless unless comprehensive community mental health and mental retardation programs have been established (or if privately established, recognized) and funded. Only to the extent that such a supporting structure is effectively in place will the police be able to exercise competently, effectively, and humanely the powers conferred on them by legislatures under paragraphs (a) and (b).

Standard 7-2.2. Development of joint policy admitting persons detained by police for mental evaluation

(a) In every jurisdiction police officials and administrators of mental health, mental retardation, and medical facilities should cooperate in developing joint guidelines and policies regarding the admission of persons in police custody for appropriate evaluation, treatment, or habilitation. The joint guidelines should be widely disseminated to police, mental health, mental retardation, and medical facility personnel. The guidelines should provide for routine notification to police administrators and other appropriate officials when facility officials decline to accept a person in police custody for evaluation, treatment, or habilitation.

(b) Police officials and administrators of mental health, mental retardation, and medical facilities should periodically conduct a joint review of such guidelines and policies to evaluate performance and effect operational changes and improvements.

Commentary Introduction

The standard recommends the development, dissemination, and periodic review of joint guidelines and policies by police officials and medi-

---

furthering the governmental interest in preserving public safety. Lynch v. Baxley, 744 F.2d 1452, 1458-1459 (11th Cir. 1984). The court thought that the practice had led judges to combine probable cause hearings with final commitment hearings in order to shorten the period of incarceration, which impaired a respondent's opportunity to prepare for the hearing and thus violated procedural due process of law. *Id.* at 1461-1462.

cal, mental health, and mental retardation facility administrators. These guidelines are to govern the admission, evaluation, and treatment or habilitation of mentally disturbed persons taken into police emergency custody. They should also provide for routine notice to police and other designated officials when facility administrators decline to accept persons in police custody for evaluation, treatment, or habilitation.

Related Standards

ABA, Standards for Criminal Justice 7-1.2, 7-2.3, 7-2.5, 7-2.6

APA, Standards for Providers of Psychological Services 2.1.1, 2.1.2, 2.2.2, 2.3.3

Commentary

Traditionally, police have had little knowledge of and maintained few working relationships with social and medical agencies, whose work they have viewed as largely irrelevant to police functions.[1] Those attitudes have changed over the past two decades, however, and police officials have come to see the advantages in working cooperatively with medical, mental health, and mental retardation facility administrators to develop procedures and guidelines governing the disposition of mentally disabled persons taken into police custody.[2] Law enforcement officers generally are willing to relinquish custody under such circumstances only if they understand the admissions criteria invoked by personnel of community treatment or shelter-care facilities. If they view those criteria to be tedious, cumbersome, and erratically administered, they may hesitate to involve themselves in transfers of custody.[3] If facility administrators refuse to admit persons in police custody, law enforcement officers may consider that a callous response inimical to the police mission of protecting the community against violence and disorder; persons rejected as patients at times have caused substantial harm to themselves or others. In contrast, if the police and medical or psychiatric facility administrators have developed strong working relationships, police departments have

1. *See* Cumming, Cumming & Edell, *Policeman as Philosopher, Guide and Friend,* 12 Soc. Probs. 276, 285 (1965).

2. *See* A. Matthews, Mental Disability and the Criminal Law 170-178 (1970).

3. *See* Bittner, *Police Discretion in Emergency Apprehension of Mentally Ill Persons,* 14 Soc. Probs. 278, 281 (1966). *See also* commentary to standard 7-2.1, note 16 and accompanying text.

proven able to discharge their responsibilities to assist mentally ill and mentally retarded persons and to make effective use of available community mental health resources.[4]

Paragraph (a), therefore, advocates the development of joint guidelines covering the admission of persons in police emergency custody to medical, mental health, and mental retardation facilities for evaluation and needed treatment or habilitation. To be effective, the guidelines must truly be the product of cooperative action and decisions and must be disseminated to all police officers[5] and appropriate employees of medical, mental health, and mental retardation facilities. In only one aspect does the standard specify the contents of joint guidelines: They should always provide for routine notice to police administrators and other concerned agencies (for example, a prosecuting attorney's office) from medical, mental health, and mental retardation facilities whenever facility personnel have declined to accept persons in emergency police custody for evaluation, treatment, or habilitation. This is important, of course, from the standpoint of the completion of police departmental records concerning significant contacts with mentally ill or mentally retarded persons,[6] but it also should reduce the friction and lack of understanding between the two governmental organizations. Although the standard does not specify all details, it would seem desirable for facility personnel to indicate, without breaching confidentiality requirements,[7] the basis for their refusal to accept a mentally disabled person from the police.

Once joint guidelines have been put into place, all participating agencies should review them jointly from time to time, amending them if necessary in light of their utilization; that is the thrust of paragraph (b) of the standard. Ongoing evaluation also should highlight any needs to revise agency or individual practices to achieve improvements in the implementation of guidelines, otherwise apparently satisfactory in concept to those who apply them.

---

4. An example of a successful cooperative relationship between the Chicago Police Department and the Northwestern University Medical School is described in detail in Sheridan & Teplin, *Police-Referred Psychiatric Emergencies: Advantages of Community Treatment*, 9 J. Community Psychology 140 (1981).

5. The guidelines also should be a useful basis for police training. *See* standard 7-2.8(a) and commentary.

6. *See* standard 7-2.9(a) and commentary.

7. *Compare* standard 7-3.2 and commentary (use of disclosures or opinions derived from pretrial mental examinations).

Standard 7-2.3. Policy preference for voluntary police disposition

Even where the law authorizes custodial intervention for the purpose of transporting a person to a mental health, mental retardation, or medical facility, police departmental guidelines should nonetheless stress a preference for a voluntary disposition. Such guidelines should require police officers, whenever feasible, to negotiate a voluntary disposition, particularly when a mentally ill or mentally retarded person is living with others and does not appear to be dangerous. In some cases, police action to summon the assistance of the person's friends or relatives will be adequate. In others, referral to a community mental health, community mental retardation, or other appropriate community facility may be required.

Commentary Introduction

Under the standard the police should seek, whenever practicable, a voluntary disposition of mentally ill or mentally retarded persons who have been taken into emergency police custody, rather than pursuing further compulsory commitment measures.

Related Standards

ABA, Standards for Criminal Justice 1-3.1, 1-3.2, 7-2.5, 7-2.8
APA, Standards for Providers of Psychological Services 2.2.3

Commentary

Lawful custodial intervention by police involves a substantial infringement of personal liberty[1] even though it may be to the ultimate benefit of mentally ill or mentally retarded persons taken into emergency police custody. That curtailment of freedom is compounded if they are subjected to compulsory commitment proceedings. Accordingly, the standard encourages the adoption of police departmental guidelines that recognize and encourage a voluntary resolution of cases in which police officers have taken persons into emergency custody but in which no

---

1. *Compare* Robitscher, *Legal Standards and Their Implications Regarding Civil Commitment Procedures,* in DANGEROUS BEHAVIOR: A PROBLEM IN LAW AND MENTAL HEALTH 61 (C. Frederick ed. 1978) (general effect of civil commitment on personal liberty).

further involuntary custody or detention is involved. Such guidelines might recognize, for example, a surrender of custody of detained persons to friends or relatives, or police transportation to a residence or place of business. Informal resolution is especially desirable for persons already receiving professional care who have not committed criminal acts and do not appear to be dangerous.[2] Of course, police departmental screening or diversion, to be effective, requires that officers be familiar with suitable community mental health and mental retardation resources available as alternatives to emergency hospitalization.[3]

The standard recognizes, however, that voluntary dispositions are inappropriate whenever there is a perceived danger to mentally ill or mentally retarded persons or members of the community if controls no longer are exerted. Accordingly, emergency hospitalization is warranted, for example, in instances of street people whose mental condition exposes them to a risk of death from starvation, hypothermia, or other causes.[4]

Standard 7-2.4. Use of force in mental health emergency interventions

(a) Police departmental guidelines should stipulate that when custodial disposition is appropriate police should use only the force reasonably necessary to effect such custody, taking into consideration the obligation of the police to protect the mentally ill or mentally retarded person, themselves, and others from bodily harm.

(b) Whenever feasible police should utilize the services of persons with special mental health or mental retardation training, including mental health and mental retardation professionals, to assist them in effecting custody of mentally ill or mentally retarded persons in emergency situations.

Commentary Introduction

The standard confirms existing law and practice by limiting the use of force to the minimum necessary to exercise effective control over men-

2. *See* Bittner, *Police Discretion in Emergency Apprehension of Mentally Ill Persons,* 14 Soc. Probs. 278, 286-288 (1966).

3. *See generally* George, *Screening and Diversion in the United States,* 29 N.Y.L. Sch. L. Rev. 1, 4-5, 14-17 (1984).

4. *See* commentary to standard 7-2.1, note 8.

tally ill or mentally retarded persons. It encourages the police to utilize the assistance of persons with mental health or mental retardation experience, including professional training, in confronting emergencies created by or involving mentally ill or mentally retarded persons.

Related Standards

Bureau of Operations and Research of the International Association of Chiefs of Police, Inc., Training Key No. 274 (1979)

Commentary

As a matter of due process of law[1] as well as traditional law,[2] police may use only reasonable nondeadly force to reduce anyone to lawful control, unless they have reasonable grounds to believe that they or other persons present at the time are in danger of death or serious physical injury.[3] Paragraph (a) constitutes an adaptation of the basic rule in the context of emergency custody of mentally ill or mentally retarded persons who are dangerous to themselves or to others.[4] It rests on the reality that the opportunities for misunderstanding are greater in the context of mental health custody than in a typical arrest, because mentally ill or mentally retarded persons may well misapprehend police intentions and police officers may be relatively uncertain about appropriate responses to detainee conduct.[5] Nevertheless, the premise on which the standard rests is that force must be an appropriately measured response to the exigencies of each custodial episode and not a stereotyped or routine response in all mental health cases.

---

1. *See* Tennessee v. Garner, 105 S. Ct. 1694 (1985).
2. *See id.* at 1701-1703 (discussing precedent).
3. "Where the officer has probable cause to believe that the suspect poses a threat of serious physical harm, either to the officer or to others, it is not constitutionally unreasonable to prevent escape by using deadly force. Thus, if the suspect threatens the officer with a weapon or there is probable cause to believe that he has committed a crime involving the infliction or threatened infliction of serious physical harm, deadly force may be used if necessary to prevent escape, and if, where feasible, some warning has been given." *Id.* at 1701.
4. *See* standard 7-2.1(a)(i) and commentary.
5. The stereotype of mentally ill persons as "dangerous" has survived. *Cf.* D. Mechanic, Mental Health and Social Policy 143-145 (1969); Shah, *Dangerousness and Civil Commitment of the Mentally Ill: Some Public Considerations,* 132 Am. J. Psychiatry 501, 503-504 (1975). As a practical matter this affects police emotional and physical responses to mentally disturbed persons.

Consequently, police officers should attempt, to the extent practicable, to inform mentally disabled persons taken into custody that detention is for the sole purpose of transportation to a mental health, mental retardation, or shelter-care facility, and that any personal property impounded in the course of the transaction will be restored as swiftly as possible. If restraints are used, officers should do their best to indicate that they are following routine departmental policy and that the restraints will be removed swiftly.[6]

The standards advocate adequate training for law enforcement officers in identification of and appropriate responses to mentally disabled persons.[7] Nonetheless, few police acquire an advanced level of understanding and technique in the course of entry and in-service training that will enable them to handle all emergency interventions like professionally trained mental health or mental retardation specialists. Moreover, police officers have other duties to perform in emergencies, particularly those necessitating entries into premises.[8] Therefore, paragraph (b) recommends that, whenever feasible, police responding to emergency situations involving mentally disabled persons call for on-site assistance from mental health or mental retardation professionals or other persons with special mental health or mental retardation training.[9] This may well ease potentially explosive confrontations and should reduce the level of danger to both the police and mentally disturbed persons who are reduced to police control.

6. *See generally* R. Matthews & L. Rowland, How to Recognize and Handle Abnormal People: A Manual for the Police Officer 13-14 (1974).

7. *See* standard 7-2.8(a)-(b) and commentary.

8. In some instances the police may be notified by friends or family members that mentally disturbed persons are exhibiting dangerous behavior within their homes. Police officers lawfully may enter private residences and take into custody persons presenting a danger of bodily harm to themselves or others. *See* United States v. McKinney, 477 F.2d 1184 (D.C. Cir. 1973) (warrantless search held lawful after a person was seen to enter hotel room with sawed-off shotgun); United States v. Perez, 440 F. Supp. 272, 286 (N.D. Ohio 1977), *aff'd*, 571 F.2d 584 (6th Cir.), *cert. denied*, 435 U.S. 998 (1978) (warrantless search held lawful after defendant brought duffel bag with explosives from burning dwelling); State v. McCleary, 116 Ariz. 244, 568 P.2d 1142 (1977) (warrantless search for possible hostages held lawful). Mentally ill persons exhibiting dangerous behavior may be considered to create emergency situations during which law enforcement officers may exercise their general powers to minimize danger. However, officers should keep in mind that an entry into the residence of a mentally disturbed person may increase the latter's disorientation and the possibility of a violent response, and thus should enter with extreme care.

9. *See* standard 7-1.3(d)(ii) and commentary.

Standard 7-2.5. Custodial processing of mentally ill or mentally retarded persons

(a) When police custody of a mentally ill or mentally retarded person is based exclusively on either noncriminal behavior or minor criminal behavior, the police should either transport the person to an appropriate facility for evaluation or negotiate a voluntary disposition as provided for in standard 7-2.3.

(b) When a police officer has arrested a person for a felony or other serious crime, however, such person should be processed in the same manner as any other criminal suspect notwithstanding the fact that the arresting officer has reasonable grounds for believing that the person's behavior meets statutory and departmental guideline requirements for emergency detention for mental evaluation. In those cases, and as soon as possible following arrest, the police should arrange for a mental health or mental retardation professional to provide evaluation, treatment, or habilitation.

(c) Upon initial presentation to the prosecutor or the court, the arresting officer should reveal fully those facts which suggest that the arrestee is mentally ill or mentally retarded and in need of evaluation, treatment, or habilitation.

(d) At or after initial presentation to the prosecutor or the court, the arresting officer should record those facts which suggest that the arrestee is mentally ill or mentally retarded and in need of evaluation, treatment, or habilitation. This written record will preserve the arresting officer's observations for appropriate reference in conjunction with any future proceedings.

Commentary Introduction

The standard provides that mentally disturbed persons who have been taken into emergency police custody based on noncriminal or minor criminal behavior should be either transported to a medical, mental health, or mental retardation facility for evaluation, or be made the subject of a voluntary disposition.[1] Persons arrested for felonies or other serious crimes should be processed despite reasonable grounds for officers to believe they are candidates for emergency detention for mental evaluation.[2] However, police officers should arrange a mental evaluation

1. *See* standard 7-2.3 and commentary.
2. *See* standard 7-2.1(b) and commentary.

or needed treatment or habilitation services as swiftly as possible after arrest. When cases are forwarded for further official action, arresting officers are urged to apprise prosecuting attorneys and courts orally of facts indicating mental illness or mental retardation and a need for evaluation, treatment, or habilitation. They also are admonished to record in writing, for future reference, all facts suggesting mental disability appropriate for evaluation and treatment or habilitation.

Related Standards

ABA, Standards for Criminal Justice 1-3.2, 7-2.3, 7-2.3, 7-2.6, 7-4.1, 7-6.1, 10-2.2, 10-2.3, 10-3.1, 10-5.2, 10-5.4, 10-6.1, 11-2.3

ACA, Standards for Adult Correctional Institutions 2-4283

ACA, Standards for Adult Local Detention Facilities 2-5273, 2-5275, 2-5297, 2-5302

Commentary

Transactions in which law enforcement officers should be allowed to exercise emergency detention powers[3] do not always involve apparently criminal activity. Accordingly, mentally disturbed persons taken into police custody for noncriminal reasons, particularly an inability because of grave disability to provide themselves with life's basic necessities,[4] cannot be processed as criminal arrestees. Instead, they must either be taken to a suitable medical, mental health, or mental retardation facility for evaluation and necessary treatment or habilitation,[5] or be made the subject of a voluntary disposition.[6] The limited police responsibilities in such cases terminate swiftly. Paragraph (a) of the standard confirms that traditional concept.

Nevertheless, mentally disturbed persons by their actions frequently violate minor criminal legislation and thus are subject to criminal arrest. Indeed, as noted earlier,[7] police officers who are unclear about their authority to process mentally disturbed persons, or who are disillusioned about mental health and mental retardation facility inaction in such cases, are likely to ignore their emergency custodial powers and pursue

3. *See* standard 7-2.1(a) and commentary.
4. *See* standard 7-2.1(a)(ii) and commentary.
5. *See* standard 7-2.3 and commentary.
6. *See* standard 7-2.1(b) and commentary.
7. *See* commentary to standard 7-2.1, note 16 and accompanying text.

the criminal arrest procedures with which they are thoroughly familiar.[8] Paragraph (a) urges the abandonment of that practice whenever mentally disturbed persons have been arrested for "minor criminal conduct."[9] Those arrestees differ in no significant regard from mentally disturbed persons who have not committed crimes, and should be dealt with the same way, *viz.*, by either transportation to a medical, mental health, or mental retardation facility for evaluation, treatment, or habilitation, or a voluntary disposition.

If, however, mentally disturbed persons have committed felonies or serious crimes,[10] police officers should be entitled to process them like all other arrested persons, a premise confirmed in paragraph (b). Particularly in major felony cases like murder, manslaughter, rape, burglary, robbery, and life-endangering assaults, all of which manifest a serious threat to human life and safety, immediate and secure custody has to be the primary objective of the criminal justice system. Accordingly, arrested felons, even those reasonably believed by arresting officers to be within the legislative criteria for emergency mental health custody, should be transported securely to police facilities, booked, detained, and produced before judicial officers.[11] Under paragraph (b), police should try to arrange for mentally disturbed detainees to be evaluated and, if necessary, treated or habilitated appropriately by mental health or mental retardation professionals. Nevertheless, it should be stressed that this police responsibility is of relatively brief duration, because after a first appear-

---

8. *See* R. Rock, M. Jacobsen & R. Janepaul, Hospitalization and Discharge of the Mentally Ill 91, 93 (1968); Bittner, *Police Discretion in Emergency Apprehension of Mentally Ill Persons*, 14 Soc. Probs. 278 (1967); *but see* Gove, *The Labeling and Treatment of Mental Illness in Jails: A Theoretical Discussion*, in Mental Health Services in Local Jails 157 (C. Dunn & H. Steadman eds. 1982). Dr. Linda Teplin has examined the trend to "criminalize" mental disorder by handling minor problems within the criminal justice system instead of the mental health system. Teplin, *Criminalization of the Mentally Ill: Speculation in Search of Data*, 94 Psychological Bull. 1 (1983). *Cf.* Abramson, *The Criminalization of Mentally Disordered Behavior*, 24 Hospital & Community Psychiatry 105 (1972).

9. By intention, the standard does not define the term. However, a useful criterion is eligibility for mandatory issuance of a citation, *see* standard 10-2.2 and commentary, or a summons, *see* standard 10-3.2 and commentary, in lieu of arrest with or without warrant. Therefore, it might embrace violations ordinarily not punishable by confinement or misdemeanors punishable by brief periods of detention in an adult local detention facility.

10. The term is intended to embrace more serious misdemeanors, based either on a legislative classification, *e.g.*, class A and class B misdemeanors, *see, e.g.*, 18 U.S.C.A. §3559 (Supp. 1986); N.Y. Penal Law §55.05(1) (McKinney 1975), or ineligibility for a citation or summons, *see* standards 10-2.2, 10-2.3, 10-3.2 and commentary.

11. *See* standards 10-4.1, 10-4.2 and commentary.

ance all further detention, release, and provisions for treatment are authorized exclusively by judicial officers.[12]

Law enforcement investigation and processing of arrested mentally disturbed criminals must conform, of course, to constitutional and legal standards. In particular, officers should exercise extreme care in interrogating suspects in police custody, because abnormal mental condition or mental retardation bears strongly on the constitutional admissibility of confessions.[13]

Under paragraph (c), police officers who transmit cases involving mentally ill or mentally retarded persons to prosecuting attorneys' offices and the courts should advise the recipient officials of all the facts supporting

---

12. This might be in the form of conditional release, *see* standard 10-5.2 and commentary, preventive detention, *see* standard 10-5.4 and commentary, or (in cases not involving serious violence), conditional release pending diversion, *see* standard 10-6.1 and commentary.

13. Severe mental disability or serious mental retardation has been a strong, although not a controlling, factor in determining the voluntariness of confessions under due process of law. *See, e.g.,* Davis v. North Carolina, 384 U.S. 737, 742 (1966); Culombe v. Connecticut, 367 U.S. 568, 603, 625 (1961) (Frankfurter, J.); Blackburn v. Alabama, 361 U.S. 199, 207-208 (1960); Payne v. Arkansas, 356 U.S. 560, 567 (1958); Fikes v. Alabama, 352 U.S. 191, 196, 198, *reh'g denied,* 352 U.S. 1019 (1957); Vance v. Bordenkircher, 692 F.2d 978, 981 (4th Cir. 1982), *cert. denied,* 464 U.S. 833 (1983); People v. Connelly, 702 P.2d 722, 728 (Colo. 1985) (statement to officer at defendant's initiative held not to be voluntary); State v. Osborne, 174 Ga. App. 521, 521-522, 330 S.E.2d 447, 448-449 (1985); People v. Redmon, 127 Ill. App. 3d 342, 347-349, 350, 468 N.E.2d 1310, 1314, 1316 (1984); Finchum v. State, 463 N.E.2d 304, 309-310 (Ind. App. 1984). A confession by a seriously mentally disabled defendant is "highly suspect." Jurek v. Estelle, 623 F.2d 929, 938 (5th Cir. 1980), *cert. denied,* 450 U.S. 1001 (1981).

Mental disability likewise is a significant element in determining the validity of a waiver of rights under Miranda v. Arizona, 384 U.S. 436 (1966). *See, e.g.,* Corn v. Zant, 708 F.2d 549, 567 (11th Cir.), *reh'g denied,* 747 F.2d 159 (11th Cir. 1983), *cert. denied,* 104 S. Ct. 2670, *reh'g denied,* 105 S. Ct. 23 (1984); United States v. Glover, 596 F.2d 857, 865-866 (9th Cir.), *cert. denied sub nom.* Morrow v. United States, 444 U.S. 857; *cert. denied sub nom.* Glover v. United States, 444 U.S. 860 (1979); Cooper v. Griffin, 455 F.2d 1142, 1145-1146 (5th Cir. 1972); People v. Redmon, 127 Ill. App. 3d 342, 348, 468 N.E.2d 1310, 1314 (1984); People v. Ellison, 126 Ill. App. 3d 985, 992-994, 466 N.E.2d 1024, 1028 (1984).

The sixth amendment right to counsel governs interrogation of persons against whom adversary criminal proceedings have commenced, *see* Estelle v. Smith, 451 U.S. 454 (1981); Brewer v. Williams, 430 U.S. 387 (1977); *see also* commentary to standard 7-3.2, notes 12-16 and accompanying text, although the right to counsel can be waived. Mental condition affects the ability to do so. *See* Jurek v. Estelle, 623 F.2d 929, 940-941 (5th Cir. 1980), *cert. denied,* 450 U.S. 1001 (1981).

On the impact of mental retardation on confessions, *see* Ellis & Luckasson, *Mentally Retarded Criminal Defendants,* 53 Geo. Wash. L. Rev. 414, 445-452 (1985).

their belief that the defendants are mentally disabled and apparently in need of evaluation or interim treatment or habilitation services. For example, a police description might include signs of incoherence, disorientation, or bizarre behavior in an arrested or detained defendant. The standard envisions at this stage only a prompt oral account of police observations and experiences with detainees. Note that the police are not called upon and are not competent to indicate whether the observed data suggest incompetence to undergo further trial proceedings[14] or mental nonresponsibility [insanity].[15] They are simply neutral sources of possibly relevant information.

Quite soon after the control over mentally disturbed defendants has been surrendered to the courts, however, arresting officers under paragraph (d) should record in writing the facts and observations that they previously reported orally to judges or prosecuting officials. Paragraph (c) compliance should not be delayed while written records are prepared, but paragraph (d) fulfilment requires that the preparation of written records not be delayed long because contemporaneous records are likely to be the most accurate. If possible, a written report should be compiled by the time of a first appearance, but if necessary it can be accomplished as swiftly thereafter as possible.[16] The form and content of reports under paragraph (d) should be covered in police department regulations.

Standard 7-2.6. Postarrest obligations of police and custodial personnel

(a) It is the responsibility of custodial officials to ensure that mental health and mental retardation services are provided for detainees. To this end, and pursuant to the provisions of standard 7-2.8, training for all custodial personnel, and especially for personnel responsible for processing new admissions, should include instruction in the identification of symptoms and behavior indicative of mental illness and mental retardation.

(b) When arresting or custodial officers or other personnel observe

14. *See* standard 7-4.1 and commentary.

15. *See* standard 7-6.1 and commentary.

16. The standard does not cover discovery of police records generated in conformity with paragraph (d), a matter dealt with elsewhere in the standards. *See* standard 11-2.3 and commentary.

a detainee whose conduct or demeanor is indicative of mental illness or mental retardation, mental disturbance, disorientation or distress, or whose behavior is self-injurious or is indicative of the possibility of suicide, such officers or personnel have a duty to report those observations promptly to the official in charge of the detention or holding facility. Such official, after promptly confirming the need to do so, should summon a mental health or mental retardation professional to provide emergency evaluation, treatment, or habilitation. Arresting and custodial officers and other personnel are obliged to report these observations even in cases where the detainee's conduct, demeanor, or behavior does not fall within the classifications for emergency detention described in standard 7-2.1.

(c) When the mental health or mental retardation professional determines that a confined person requires immediate evaluation, treatment, or habilitation not available in the detention or holding facility, the detainee should promptly be transferred to a facility capable of providing such services.

Commentary Introduction

The standard confirms the constitutional duty to provide mentally disturbed detainees with adequate mental health and mental retardation services; it also urges training for police and custodial officers in the identification of symptoms and behavior indicative of mental illness or mental retardation. The standard further confirms the duty of custodial personnel to be alert for manifestations of suicidal behavior and to summon assistance from mental health or mental retardation specialists for the purposes of emergency evaluation, treatment, or, if necessary, habilitation in a medical, mental health, or mental retardation facility.

Related Standards

ABA, Standards for Criminal Justice 7-2.1(a), 7-2.8, 7-10.1 through 7-10.6, 23-5.1, 23-5.2, 23-5.3(a), 23-5.5, 23-6.9

ACA, Standards for Adult Correctional Institutions 2-4283, 2-4296

ACA, Standards for Adult Local Detention Facilities 2-5273, 2-5275, 2-5297, 2-5302

Federal Standards for Prisons and Jails 5.15

NAC, Criminal Justice Standards and Goals 9.4

Commentary

Custodial authorities have a constitutional duty to see that persons held in adult local detention facilities, like prisoners generally, receive adequate evaluation and care, including psychiatric treatment and habilitation.[1] Indeed, incarceration very well may intensify the need of mentally disturbed persons for mental health services.[2] Paragraph (a) makes specific the more general duty to provide mental health care reflected in other Association standards. An apparent increase in the number of mentally disordered prisoners in adult local detention facilities[3] has brought a correspondingly expanded need to augment the services available to those prisoners, a need difficult to meet if custodial personnel lack formal training in identifying the symptoms of mental illness and mental retardation.[4]

It is against this background that paragraph (a) recommends that all custodial personnel, particularly those responsible for processing newly received prisoners, should be given both entry and in-service[5] instruction on symptoms and behavior indicative of mental illness and mental retardation. The stress on facility intake or admissions staff training reflects the fact that mental disability should be identified, if possible, before new inmates are placed among the other prisoners in a facility. A routine mental health and mental retardation screening should be part of intake medical screening[6] and should include inquiries about earlier psychiatric care or hospitalization. Detainees with recognized significant mental disabilities should be given appropriate assignments within a facility, including secure custodial classifications if needed, and should be provided with necessary mental health or mental retardation professional evaluation and appropriate treatment or habilitation services during their

---

1. *See* standards 7-10.2, 2-5.1, 23-5.2 and commentary.

2. *See* AMERICAN PUBLIC HEALTH ASS'N REP., STANDARDS FOR HEALTH SERVICES IN CORRECTIONAL INSTITUTIONS 27 (1976).

3. *See* Lamb & Grant, *The Mentally Ill in an Urban County Jail,* 39 ARCH. GEN. PSYCHIATRY 17-22 (1982); Teplin, *Criminalization of the Mentally Ill: Speculation in Search of Data,* 94 PSYCHOLOGICAL BULL. 1 (1983).

4. *See* Megargee, *Psychological Assessment in Jails: Implementation of the Standards Recommended by the National Advisory Commission on Criminal Justice Standards,* in MENTAL HEALTH SERVICES IN LOCAL JAILS 100 (C. Dunn & H. Steadman eds. 1982). *Cf.* Timik, " 'Ding Tank' — Way Station for the Mentally Disturbed," Los Angeles Times, Dec. 13, 1982, at 3.

5. *See* standard 7-2.8(a) and commentary.

6. *See* standard 23-5.3(a) and commentary.

preadjudication incarceration.[7] If needed evaluation, treatment, or habilitation services are not available or cannot be provided effectively within a local detention facility, paragraph (d) confirms the responsibility of facility administrators to transfer mentally disabled prisoners to facilities capable of providing such services.[8]

The constitutional duty to provide a safe environment for prisoners includes an obligation to take reasonable measures to forestall suicide attempts[9] and assaultive behavior toward other inmates.[10] In support of that general principle, paragraph (b) of the standard delineates the duty of arresting officers, custodial personnel, and other law enforcement officials in contact with detainees to report immediately to the chief executive officer[11] of a facility all activities or demeanor[12] that indicates a risk of suicidal or assaultive behavior. A recipient official then should see that the necessary services for suicide prevention, crisis intervention, and the management of acute episodes are brought into play.

Paragraph (b), however, goes beyond a reporting requirement governing only potentially violent or suicidal inmates. All observations of conduct or demeanor suggestive of mental illness, mental retardation, mental disturbance, or disorientation also should be reported to facility administrators, for the purpose of avoiding unnecessary deterioration in a detainee's condition of mental health. Note that the observed activities or demeanor do not have to rise to the level of abnormality required for emergency custody and transportation;[13] in most instances, inmates have

7. Mentally ill or mentally retarded misdemeanants sentenced to imprisonment in adult local detention facilities should be processed under part X of the chapter.

8. This may be done, in the cases of preadjudication detainees, through a contractual arrangement with a hospital or other suitable facility. *See* standard 23-5.1(a) and commentary. Adjudicated misdemeanants should be transferred as prescribed in standards 7-10.3 through 7-10.5. If professional mental health or medical care is not available at a detention facility, a mentally disabled detainee should be transported in conformity with local law to the nearest mental health, mental retardation, or medical facility for treatment. Appropriate care should be exercised to protect the safety of the detainee and transporting officers. *See, e.g.*, Colo. Rev. Stat. §§27-10-105–27-10-111 (1982 & Supp. 1984).

9. *See* 23•105 note 6 and accompanying text.

10. *See* 23•104 note 5 and accompanying text.

11. *See* 23•7, glossary, for a definition of the term.

12. For example, a detainee's severe depression may be manifested by neglect of personal hygiene: hair and fingernails may be unkempt or fingertips may be burned and discolored from cigarettes. Although this passive behavior is less disturbing to the stability of a detention facility than aggressive and acting-out behavior of a detainee, it can be a significant indication of mental illness.

13. *See* standard 7-2.1(a) and commentary.

been taken into custody already through criminal arrest. Hence, paragraph (b) is not concerned with lawful bases for the detention of mentally abnormal inmates but with the implementation of the duty restated in paragraph (a) to provide them with needed evaluation, treatment, and habilitation services. An appropriate system response to a paragraph (b) report is a program of elective therapy and preventive services, if possible within the facility[14] or otherwise through a prompt transfer to another suitable facility under paragraph (c).

Standard 7-2.7. Treatment or habilitation of detainees; voluntary and involuntary transfer; notice to counsel

(a) A detainee who is able to make informed decisions regarding the need for treatment or habilitation and who requests or consents to such services may be treated in the detention or holding facility or may be transferred to a mental health, mental retardation, or other appropriate facility in conformity with the statutes or rules governing voluntary mental health treatment and hospitalization.

(b) A detainee who is unable to make the kind of informed decision set forth in paragraph (a), or who objects to treatment or habilitation, or who objects to transfer to a mental health, mental retardation, or other appropriate facility should not be transferred or required to accept treatment or habilitation services except:

(i) when required by court order; or,

(ii) when reasonably believed by the responsible professional to be necessary in an emergency to prevent death or serious physical injury to the detainee or others. An involuntary transfer hearing should be initiated not later than [forty-eight] hours after an emergency transfer is effected.

(c) The detainee's attorney and the prosecuting attorney should be notified whenever:

(i) custodial personnel observe or are otherwise informed that a detainee is exhibiting symptoms or behaviors indicative of significant mental disturbance;

---

14. *See* N.Y. City Dep't of Corrections, Minimum Standards for Mental Health Services 1 (March 15, 1982, unpublished); *see generally* Swank & Wener, *Occurrence of Psychiatric Disorder in a County Jail Population,* 133 Am. J. Psychiatry 11 (1976).

(ii) mental health or mental retardation professionals are summoned to provide treatment or habilitation or to determine the need for an emergency transfer to a mental health, mental retardation or medical facility; or,

(iii) the detainee is transferred to a mental health, mental retardation or medical facility. When possible, this notice should precede detainee's transfer.

Commentary Introduction

The standard confirms the propriety of facilitating consensual treatment or habilitation services for mentally disordered inmates of local detention facilities, or voluntary hospitalization for purposes of mental health treatment or mental retardation habilitation. Detainees who are incapable of consenting or refuse to accept treatment or habilitation should not be treated or habilitated, or transferred for treatment or habilitation services, unless a court authorizes it or an emergency transfer is made to prevent death or serious physical injury to the detainee or others. Provision is made for notice to prosecuting attorneys and defense counsel whenever (a) detainees exhibit symptoms or behavior indicative of significant mental disturbance, (b) mental health or mental retardation professionals are called to provide treatment or habilitation or to determine a need for an emergency transfer, or (c) a detainee is to be or has been transferred to a medical, mental health, or mental retardation facility.

Related Standards

ABA, Standards for Criminal Justice 4-2.1, 7-2.5, 7-2.6, 7-9.12, 7-10.5, 7-10.7, 7-10.9, 10-5.2, 10-6.1, 23-5.1, 23-5.2, 23-5.5

ACA, Standards for Adult Correctional Facilities 2-4296, 2-4297

ACA, Standards for Adult Local Detention Facilities 2-5275, 2-5284

Commentary

Voluntary treatment or habilitation for mentally disabled detainees entails the least constraints on individual civil liberties. Treating professionals prefer voluntary treatment or habilitation because it evidences a high degree of motivation to participate in and accept needed treatment.[1]

1. *See* R. Rock, Hospitalization and Discharge of the Mentally Ill 38 (1969).

Ideally, treatment or habilitation should occur in a mental health, mental retardation, or medical facility and not in a local detention facility.[2] This is not always possible, however; there may be no space in a hospital or mental health or mental retardation facility to accommodate a detainee, or a detainee may pose an excessive security risk in a minimum security facility. In that event, evaluation will have to be performed and necessary mental health treatment or mental retardation habilitation services must be provided in an adult local detention facility, in fulfilment of constitutional obligations to the detainee.[3] This is the thrust of paragraph (a).

The obverse of the ability of a sufficiently competent detainee to seek or consent to voluntary mental health treatment or mental retardation habilitation services is the basic ability to decline it;[4] that principle is recognized generally in this chapter.[5] Accordingly, paragraph (b) confirms the right of a sufficiently competent detainee to object to a transfer to a medical, mental health, or mental retardation facility and to treatment or habilitation services wherever provided.[6] There are only two exceptions to this principle:

1. A court order may be obtained in conformity with jurisdiction civil commitment or mental health or mental retardation statutes by authorized officials (who probably will not be detention facility officials); the recognition in subparagraph (b)(i) of that possibility reflects more general provisions elsewhere in the standards.[7]
2. A transfer is authorized by a responsible professional[8] on the basis of a reasonable belief that it is necessary in an emergency to forestall death or serious physical injury to the de-

2. *See* Singer, *Providing Mental Health Services to Jail Inmates: Legal Perspectives,* in MENTAL HEALTH SERVICES IN LOCAL JAILS 77 (C. Dunn & H. Steadman ed. 1982) [hereinafter cited as Singer].

3. *See* standards 7-10.2, 2-5.1, 23-5.2 and commentary.

4. "The prisoner's right to autonomy and privacy should be respected, and his body held inviolate, as it has been (except in emergencies) under the common law." Singer, *supra* note 2, at 77.

5. *See, e.g.,* standards 7-9.12, 7-10.9 and commentary.

6. *See* commentary to standard 7-9.12, notes 1-4 and accompanying text.

7. *See* standard 23-5.5(a) and commentary.

8. A "responsible professional" preferably should be a mental health or mental retardation professional or a medically trained person. However, this may not always be possible and, in fact, at times a police official or a correctional official in charge of an adult local detention facility will have to make the initial professional judgment.

tainee or others. The parallel for this is an emergency nonconsensual emergency transfer of prisoner/patients to mental health or mental retardation facilities outside the administrative jurisdiction of a department of prisons or corrections.[9] In that event, an involuntary transfer hearing should be initiated within a recommended forty-eight hours after an emergency transfer for treatment or habilitation has been accomplished.[10]

Paragraph (c) covers notification by detention facility authorities to a detainee's attorney and a prosecuting attorney whenever any of four circumstances appear:

1. Detainees have been observed to exhibit symptoms or behavior indicating a significant mental disturbance. Subparagraph (c)(i) envisions the same information that arresting officers should report to courts and prosecuting officials[11] and that custodial personnel should transmit to chief executive officers of adult local detention facilities.[12]
2. Mental health or mental retardation professionals have been called to provide treatment or habilitation services within a detention facility,[13] an alternative under subparagraph (c)(ii).
3. Mental health or mental retardation professionals have been invited to determine the need for an emergency transfer under subparagraph (b)(ii) to a medical, mental health, or mental retardation facility — the second alternative under subparagraph (c)(ii).
4. Detainees are transferred to a treatment facility, presumably because appropriate services are unavailable in a detention facility.[14] Subparagraph (c)(iii) expresses a clear preference for notice preceding rather than following a transfer, which is particularly important if a detainee's counsel wishes to contest a proposed transfer before it takes place.

---

9. *See* standard 7-10.7 and commentary.

10. The standard does not specify the form of the ensuing involuntary transfer proceedings, but standard 7-10.5 procedures are an appropriate pattern, particularly because they govern hearings after an emergency transfer under standard 7-10.7.

11. *See* standard 7-2.5(c)-(d) and commentary.

12. *See* standard 7-2.6(b) and commentary.

13. *See* standard 7-2.6(a) and commentary.

14. *See* standard 7-2.6(c) and commentary.

It should be stressed that the notice or advice under paragraph (c) should be transmitted whether or not detainees wish anyone else, including their counsel, to know they are receiving mental health treatment or mental retardation habilitation services. The important criminal justice system values, described below, underlying the notification requirement clearly outweigh a detainee's desire to keep secret information that is not confidential and therefore not subject to a legal privilege.

Multiple reasons underlie the requirement of notice to a detainee's attorney. The earlier that defense counsel can contemplate and begin to prepare submissions relating to competence to undergo criminal prosecution, mental nonresponsibility [insanity], or the want of a required culpability or *mens rea* element under a criminal statute, the more effective the defense preparation and presentation are likely to be. Counsel may be able to solicit judicial approval of conditional release[15] or conditional release pending diversion[16] for purposes of treatment or habilitation. Beyond that, counsel with awareness of a client's mental condition can marshal the support of friends and family members to improve the client's morale and help make incarceration more bearable; moreover, counsel may be able to obtain private medical or mental health care superior to that provided from government sources, if a client or the client's family has sufficient financial resources for the purpose.[17] Advance notice of a transfer to a treatment facility is, of course, indispensable to an effort to prevent a change of custodial circumstances but, as subparagraph (c)(iii) clearly recognizes, emergency conditions may well dictate an immediate transfer followed by later notification even though that makes possible only subsequent judicial review of the propriety of the transfer. In emergency transfer cases, notice should be given sufficiently in advance that a detainee's attorney can prepare for the forty-eight-hour involuntary transfer proceeding contemplated in subparagraph (b)(ii). In nonemergency cases, prompt notification is important so that defense counsel can communicate with and provide representation for a transferred inmate in the course of the underlying criminal proceedings.

The provision for notice to prosecuting authorities reflects, in part, the fact that they provide legal representation for county or local governmental units like sheriff's departments or municipal police departments. The

15. *See* standard 10-5.2 and commentary.
16. *See* standard 10-6.1 and commentary.
17. *See* 23•60 note 15 and accompanying text.

earlier that they are advised about any of the circumstances listed in paragraph (c), the better they can discharge their advisory, consultative, and representational functions as counsel to governmental units. In addition, early notice, particularly of the information described in subparagraph (c)(i), may facilitate the fulfilment of the due process-based duty of prosecutors to provide to defense counsel, without the requirement of a defense request or court order, with all potentially mitigating or exculpatory data.[18]

Standard 7-2.8. Specialized training

(a) All agencies should provide specialized training to their personnel to assist them in identifying and responding to incidents involving mentally ill or mentally retarded persons. Mental health and mental retardation professionals should be routinely consulted regarding curriculum preparation and training material selection. To the extent feasible police administrators should obtain qualified professionals to serve as instructors for recruit and in-service training programs.

(b) As an adjunct to training, all police agencies should promulgate written policies detailing department procedures for intervening in emergency situations involving the mentally ill and mentally retarded. In addition, promotional examinations should test each candidate's knowledge concerning the characteristics of such persons and the resolution of emergency situations.

(c) All custodial personnel, whether civilian or sworn, should receive training in identifying and responding to the symptoms and behaviors, including self-injurious behavior, associated with mental illness and mental retardation. Emphasis should be placed on those symptoms and behaviors that arise or are aggravated by the fact of incarceration, particularly as they relate to suicide prevention. Ex-

18. *See* United States v. Agurs, 427 U.S. 97 (1976); Brady v. Maryland, 373 U.S. 83 (1963). *See also* standard 11-2.1(c) and commentary. There is precedent indicating that prosecuting authorities are chargeable with knowledge of a detainee's behavior possessed by other governmental employees, even though they lack actual personal knowledge. *See, e.g.*, Barbee v. Warden, Maryland Penitentiary, 331 F.2d 842, 846 (4th Cir. 1964).

A prosecuting attorney also should be advised by custodial authorities whether notice has been given to defense counsel, because that affects the scope of the *Agurs-Brady* prosecutorial duty of disclosure under the circumstances of the particular case.

plicit guidelines for responding to emergency situations, providing first aid, and preventing individuals with suicidal tendencies from harming themselves should be published and made available to all facility personnel.

Commentary Introduction

The standard stresses the importance of providing entry and in-service training programs for law enforcement agency personnel to enable them to identify and respond appropriately in incidents involving mentally disabled persons. Law enforcement agencies should promulgate written policies covering procedures for emergency intervention in situations involving mentally ill and mentally retarded persons, disseminate them, and include their content in promotional examinations. Custodial personnel should be trained to recognize symptoms of mental illness or mental retardation indicative of suicidal and assaultive behavior, and be provided with detailed guidelines covering emergency responses, first aid, and suicide prevention.

Related Standards

ABA, Standards for Criminal Justice 1-7.3, 7-2.6
ACA, Standards for Adult Local Detention Facilities 2-5079, 2-5085 through 2-5088
AMA, Standards for Health Services in Jails 119, 120

Commentary

Paragraph (a) covers special training for law enforcement personnel to enable them to identify and respond to incidents involving mentally ill or mentally retarded individuals. That training should include entry-level education and continuing or in-service training and refresher courses.[1] Under paragraph (b), the contents of written departmental policies relating to emergency intervention in cases involving mentally disabled per-

1. A well-rounded training program should include role-playing scenarios as well as more traditional instruction based on lectures and the use of training keys and general orders. *See* R. Mathews & L. Rowland, How to Recognize and Handle Abnormal People: A Manual for the Police Officer (1974); H. Russell & A. Beigel, Understanding Human Behavior for Effective Police Work xii (1976); Anderson, *Handling of Mentally Disturbed Persons*, 45 Police Chief No. 2 (Feb. 1978), at 50.

sons should be disseminated (and perhaps supplemented through in-service training sessions[2]) and made a subject on promotional examinations (which require preparatory study by candidates for promotion). Lectures covering statutory provisions relating to police emergency intervention powers are not sufficient. Accordingly, police training administrators are urged in paragraph (a) to consult mental health and mental retardation professionals during the preparation of course outlines and training materials and to enlist their services in the classroom.

Emergency intervention is an especially difficult activity for law enforcement officers.[3] Paragraph (b) urges the development of written policies relating to emergency intervention in cases involving mentally disordered persons.[4] Although the thrust of the provision is the advancement of suitable entry-level and in-service training programs and an enforced understanding of the guidelines on the part of officers seeking promotion, written guidelines also are important to an awareness on the part of other criminal justice officials and members of the public about appropriate police responses under emergency conditions. As in the context of paragraph (a), mental health and mental retardation professionals should be called on to assist in the drafting of the guidelines.

Paragraph (c) implements the responsibility of custodial personnel to observe, report, and respond appropriately to symptoms and manifestations of mental illness and mental retardation, including self-injurious and self-destructive behavior.[5] It urges appropriate training for all custodial personnel of law enforcement agencies, whether they are sworn officers or civilian employees. Although custodial staff training, both entry-level and in-service,[6] should range as widely as possible over the

---

2. Some police agencies have found it useful to create a special cadre of highly trained officers to respond directly to emergency street situations or to assist other officers with less specialized training for such assignments. Where practicable, personnel from such special cadres should be utilized as adjunct instructors in the training programs recommended in paragraph (a).

3. *See* standard 7-2.4 and commentary.

4. In addition to delineating departmental rules governing specific police actions in these matters, these guidelines should give due consideration to, and reflect a concern for, the safety of the police officers, the safety and mental health condition of the persons who are the subject of police action, and the safety of other citizens including inmates within police lock-up or detention facilities.

5. *See* standard 7-7.6(b) and commentary. *See also* Gove, *The Labeling and Treatment of Mental Illness in Jails: A Theoretical Discussion*, in MENTAL HEALTH SERVICES IN LOCAL JAILS 157 (C. Dunn & H. Steadman ed. 1982).

6. All personnel periodically should receive instruction in identifying symptoms and behavior associated with self-mutilation and suicide, acute regressive states, and other

forms of mental disability likely to be manifested in a facility inmate population,[7] special attention should be paid to indications of suicidal or self-destructive tendencies that frequently are exacerbated by incarceration.[8]

Training directors should utilize medical, mental health, and mental retardation professionals in the development of courses, lesson outlines, and training materials and, if they are willing, use them as instructors. Paragraph (c) also calls for the preparation of explicit facility guidelines covering emergency response procedures, first-aid measures, and suicide prevention.[9] As in the counterpart coverage of paragraph (b), guidelines are critical to appropriate training and properly may be included in promotion examinations for detention facility personnel. However, because they are to be published other than in the form of training materials and disseminated throughout an agency, they will serve as official standards to regulate administrative and custodial practice and to inform inmate populations, other law enforcement agencies, and the public about appropriate and expected responses to the behavior of mentally disturbed inmates.

Standard 7-2.9. Police and custodial records of contacts with mentally ill or mentally retarded persons

(a) Records of significant contacts with mentally ill or mentally retarded persons who are not charged with crime should be filed separately from arrest records and should be subject to a high degree of confidentiality.

---

forms of severe mental disorientation. *See* AACP STANDARDS FOR PSYCHOLOGY SERVICES IN ADULT JAILS AND PRISONS 116-117 (1981); AMA STANDARDS FOR HEALTH SERVICES IN JAILS 119, 120 (1981).

7. Some forms of behavior or demeanor ordinarily associated with mental illness or mental retardation may not be viewed as abnormal by custodial officials. Indeed, because of the nature of detention institutions, otherwise classical signs of depression or withdrawal may be overlooked by custodial personnel more attuned to responding to overtly disruptive or destructive behavior. Moreover, disruptive behavior itself may be common and may routinely lead only to traditional disciplinary actions. *See generally* Ellis & Luckasson, *Mentally Retarded Criminal Defendants*, 53 GEO. WASH. L. REV. 414, 491-493 (1985).

8. *See* commentary to standard 7-2.6, note 12 and accompanying text.

9. Guidelines should prescribe rules and procedures for providing emergency intervention assistance and for restraining and isolating detainees with suicidal tendencies.

(b) Records of treatment and habilitation provided to the detainee by the mental health or mental retardation professional should be maintained separately from other records pertaining to the detainee, and access to them should be limited to professionals providing treatment or habilitation, detainee's attorney, and detainee except as otherwise provided. Custodial personnel, including supervisory personnel, may not examine these records without prior authorization of the detainee or the detainee's attorney. However, whenever a mental health or mental retardation professional concludes that the detainee presents an imminent risk of serious danger to another person, is imminently suicidal, or otherwise needs emergency treatment or habilitative intervention, the evaluator should notify the person in charge of the institution.

(c) Detainee's access to such treatment or habilitation records should be governed by rules similar to those applicable to patient access to public mental health institution treatment records.

Commentary Introduction

The standard advocates the segregated, highly confidential maintenance of law enforcement agency records concerning significant noncriminal contacts with mentally disturbed persons. Records of professional mental health or mental retardation treatment for detained persons should be kept separate from other facility records and should be available only to treating professionals, counsel for detainees, and custodial personnel authorized by detainees or their attorneys to gain access to them. Detainee perusal of personal treatment records should be governed by jurisdiction statutes or regulations governing patients in public mental health institutions. Treating or evaluating professionals, however, may notify facility chief administrators that a detainee presents an immediate risk of suicide or serious danger to others, or requires emergency treatment or habilitative intervention.

Related Standards

ABA, Standards for Criminal Justice 23-5.4, 23-6.11

ACA, Standards for Adult Local Detention Facilities 2-5290, 2-5291, 2-5292

AMA, Standards for Health Services in Jails 165

American Psychological Association, Specialty Guidelines for the Delivery of Services by Counseling Psychologists 2.3.5

American Psychological Association, Standards for Providers of Psychological Services 2.3.5

Federal Standards for Prisons and Jails 5.39, 5.40, 5.41

Standards for Psychology Services in Adult Jails and Prisons 47, 48, 49, 50, 51

Commentary

At the outset, it should be noted that standard 7-2.9 covers only two forms of law enforcement agency records: (1) records relating to significant contacts with mentally ill or mentally disturbed persons who are not charged with crimes, and (2) records concerning treatment or habilitation services provided to detainees by treating mental health or mental retardation specialists. Arrest records covering mentally disturbed persons taken into police custody because of contraventions of criminal statutes,[1] and other agency records governing their detention and transfer to the jurisdiction of courts or other governmental agencies, are subject to no special regulation under this part of the standards.

The fact that law enforcement officers have only limited powers to take seriously mentally disturbed persons into custody[2] does not mean they have no other lawful contacts with mentally ill or mentally retarded members of a community. Police officers should be required by departmental regulations to make contemporaneous records of all significant occurrences involving mentally disturbed people. Those contact reports are useful for several purposes: (1) They may provide useful data for evaluating or treating or habilitating professionals if mentally ill or mentally retarded persons are taken into emergency protective custody,[3] or arrested and either disposed of on a voluntary admissions basis[4] or detained pending further criminal proceedings.[5] (2) They can enable police agencies to detect repetitive patterns of conduct affecting the disposition of future cases arising from contacts, whether criminal or noncriminal,

1. *See* standard 7-2.5(a)-(b) and commentary.
2. *See* standard 7-2.1(a); commentary to standard 7-2.1, notes 1-11 and accompanying text.
3. *See* standards 7-2.1(a) (emergency detention), 7-2.5(c)-(d) (information and records concerning mental illness or mental retardation) and commentary.
4. *See* standards 7-2.3, 7-2.5(a) and commentary.
5. *See* standards 7-2.5(b), 7-2.7(a) and commentary.

with mentally disturbed persons. (3) They can help identify persons who might in the future commit dangerous acts against others.[6] (4) Their contents (with identifying data elided) can serve as valuable instructional aids on the recognition and evaluation of potentially dangerous abnormal behavior.[7]

Nevertheless, the subjects of significant contact records are not criminals and data on them should not be commingled with criminal arrest records. Accordingly, paragraph (a) admonishes law enforcement agencies to segregate strictly the two categories of records and to maintain significant contact records under a high level of security. Although the standard does not delineate access controls governing them, an appropriate analogy may well be ordinary medical records, because those to whom they relate are civil patients rather than criminal suspects or defendants. Police agencies should develop guidelines governing their dissemination, balancing the need for treating professionals, attorneys, and limited classes of law enforcement personnel[8] to know their contents against the privacy interests of the mentally ill and mentally retarded persons to whom they relate.

Paragraphs (b) and (c) relate to even more sensitive records reflecting mental health treatment and mental retardation habilitation services provided to detainees charged with crimes.[9] Treatment records may contain substantial amounts of confidential information, particularly if detainees have been evaluated, treated, or habilitated within a detention facility rather than transferred to a medical, mental health, or mental retardation facility,[10] that should not be disseminated routinely or casually.[11] Paragraph (b) envisions only four classes of persons who should be allowed access to facility treatment or habilitation records:

6. For example, routine law enforcement surveillance activities conducted during presidential visits may require law enforcement agencies to compile information regarding potentially dangerous persons, whether or not they have criminal records.

7. A training key for police officers in a large urban area instructs police to record emotional and physical responses indicating a mental disturbance such as hostility, resistance, passiveness, withdrawal, stupor, tearfulness, flight, fright and apprehension, as well as the identity of the person, and the location and time of the incident.

8. Dissemination should be allowed for appropriate police purposes, to attorneys for prehearing review and examination, to authorized personnel assisting in the diagnosis and treatment of mentally ill or mentally retarded persons, and pursuant to court process.

9. *See* standards 7-2.6(a), (c), 7-2.7(a)-(b) and commentary.

10. *See* standards 7-2.6(c), 7-2.7(a)-(b) and commentary.

11. *See generally* standard 7-3.2 and commentary. The standards, however, could not be implemented in certain states with sweeping freedom of information acts. *See, e.g.*, Fla. Stat. Ann. §§943.056-943.08 (West 1985).

1. Mental health or mental retardation professionals who evaluate, treat, or habilitate a detainee to whom facility records relate.
2. An attorney for the detainee.
3. The detainee, subject (under paragraph (c)) to the jurisdiction's statutes and regulations (applied by analogy) governing access by patients in public mental health institutions to their treatment records.[12]
4. Detention facility administrators and custodial personnel, provided they receive advance authorization from either the detainee to whom the file relates or the detainee's counsel.

Nevertheless, paragraph (b) recognizes an exception to the usual norm of confidentiality if a mental health or mental retardation professional concludes that a detainee meets one or more of three criteria:

1. The detainee presents an imminent risk of serious danger to another person. This is important to the protection of a reporting professional against civil liability to facility staff members or inmates who might be injured by an assaultive detainee,[13] as well as of the employing governmental entity that might be sued (if it has waived its sovereign immunity)[14] for a failure to provide a safe environment for detainees.[15]
2. The detainee appears to be imminently suicidal.[16] A prompt report of the danger will allow intervention and protective measures by facility personnel to forestall self-inflicted harm, which in turn is necessary if the employing governmental unit is to meet its constitutional responsibilities to safeguard the detainee against self-destructive acts.[17]

---

12. *See* Project, *Legal Issues in State Mental Health Care: Proposals for Change: Civil Commitment*, 2 Mental Disability L. Rptr. 57, 67 (1978).
13. *See* commentary to standard 7-3.2, notes 17-19 and accompanying text.
14. *See, e.g.*, Merchants National Bank and Trust Co. of Fargo v. United States, 272 F. Supp. 409 (D.N.D. 1967) (United States held liable for wrongful death of decedent owing to the negligent release of a mental patient known to be violent and dangerous); Thompson v. County of Alameda, 27 Cal. 3d 741, 614 P.2d 728, 167 Cal. Rptr. 70 (1980) (county was held statutorily immune from liability for release of juvenile offender who later killed another youth not readily identifiable from the offender's threats).
15. *See* 23•104 note 5 and accompanying text.
16. *See* standards 7-2.6(b), 7-2.7(b)(ii) and commentary.
17. *See* 23•105 note 6 and accompanying text.

3. Emergency treatment or habilitative intervention is indicated. When they have been alerted to the detainee's needs, facility administrators can base emergency treatment or involuntary transfers for treatment or habilitation[18] on the information supplied by treating professionals.

Note that the professionals who conclude that a detainee is dangerous are expected under paragraph (b) only to report their conclusions to the chief facility administrator, who then becomes responsible for an appropriate response on the part of facility administrators and personnel.

18. *See* standard 7-2.7(b)(ii) and commentary.

Part III

Pretrial Evaluations and Expert Testimony

William H. Erickson, *Chairman*
Standing Committee on Association Standards for Criminal Justice

Albert J. Datz
Task Force Chairman

Grant H. Morris
Reporter

Task Force

Albert J. Datz, *Chairperson*
Private practitioner, Datz, Jacobson & Lembcke, Jacksonville, Florida

Richard J. Bonnie
Professor of Law and Director, Institute of Law, Psychiatry & Public Policy, University of Virginia School of Law, Charlottesville, Virginia

Thomas E. Bryant, M.D., J.D.
Chairman, Public Committee on Mental Health, Washington, D.C.

H. Lynn Edwards
Private practitioner, Annandale, Virginia

Sandra A. Garcia, Ph.D., J.D.
Associate Professor, Department of Psychology University of South Florida, Tampa, Florida

Ephraim Gomberg
Private practitioner, Palm Springs, California

Ruth Nordenbrook
Assistant U.S. Attorney, Brooklyn, New York (representing ABA Section of Criminal Justice)

Randolph A. Read, M.D.*
Adjunct Professor of Law, University of San Diego; Assistant Professor of Psychiatry, University of California at San Diego, San Diego, California

Philip Roos, M.D.
Executive Director, Mothers Against Drunk Drivers, Hurst, Texas

Bruce D. Sales, Ph.D., J.D.
Professor, Psychology Department, University of Arizona, Tucson, Arizona (representing American Psychological Association)

Andrew S. Watson, M.D.
Psychiatrist, Professor of Law and Psychiatry, University of Michigan School of Law, Ann Arbor, Michigan

GRANT H. MORRIS, *Reporter*
Professor of Law, School of Law, University of San Diego

---

*Deceased

INTRODUCTION

The standards in part I identify the roles and responsibilities of mental health and mental retardation professionals in the criminal process. Those in part III articulate more specifically the principles governing mental health and mental retardation professional activity of two sorts: evaluation of mental condition and expert testimony.

The standards have several objectives. One is an assurance that mental health and mental retardation professionals perform thorough and competent evaluations consistent with the rights of defendants undergoing examination. A second is a delineation of the roles and functions of mental health and mental retardation professionals, lawyers, and judges at each stage of the criminal proceeding, bearing on every issue to which professional expertise is relevant. A third is promotion of a balance between prosecution and defense interests and concerns. Although some part III standards may favor the prosecution or defense on a particular issue, overall they balance an advantage given to one side with a corresponding advantage to the other at some stage in the justice process.

Standards 7-3.1 through 7-3.4 identify appropriate forms of mental evaluations and indicate who may obtain them. For example, standard 7-3.3 endorses the right of defense counsel to obtain a mental evaluation of a defendant's mental condition at the time of the alleged crime. The prosecuting attorney's countervailing right to obtain an evaluation on the same issue is provided for in standard 7-3.4. Although an evaluation initiated by the prosecution may be performed at approximately the same time as a defense-initiated evaluation, a report based on it is not available to the prosecutor until the defendant has given notice of an intention to utilize the testimony of a mental health or mental retardation professional to support a defense claim resting on the defendant's mental condition at the time of the alleged crime.

Standards 7-3.5 through 7-3.7 govern procedures to initiate, conduct, and report the results of mental evaluations. Standard 7-3.5 imposes on an attorney who initiates an evaluation a duty to provide the mental health or mental retardation professional with records and information necessary or helpful to the evaluation. Standard 7-3.6 imposes on an initiating attorney an additional obligation to ensure that the evaluator understands the legal and factual issues to be addressed, the rules governing disclosure, and the applicable evidentiary privileges. Both defense counsel and the mental health or mental retardation professional conducting an evaluation are obliged to explain to the defendant the purpose, nature, and consequences of the evaluation.

The presence of defense counsel during evaluation interviews poses a troubling issue that the courts have not resolved consistently. Standard 7-3.6(c) distinguishes between evaluations limited to present mental competency and all other evaluations. It permits defense counsel to attend of right only those evaluations limited to present mental competency, but it urges that all court-ordered evaluations initiated by the prosecution be recorded so that the defense attorney may learn later what transpired during evaluation interviews.

Standard 7-3.7 requires that mental health or mental retardation professionals prepare complete written reports concerning all evaluations not conducted at defense request. It details the contents of evaluation reports to ensure that evaluations for legal purposes are adequately performed. In this way, attorneys should be able to determine from them whether mental health and mental retardation professionals have acquired sufficient information on which to base expert conclusions.

Standards 7-3.9 through 7-3.15 cover expert testimony by mental health and mental retardation professionals. Standard 7-3.9 recognizes the admissibility of expert professional testimony on issues of present competency and past mental condition if it is based on specialized knowledge of the witness and will assist the trier of fact. The standard, however, opposes expert opinion testimony containing legal or moral conclusions properly reserved for a court or jury. Furthermore, because mental health and mental retardation professionals lack precise scientific criteria for predicting future dangerous conduct insofar as individual defendants are concerned, standard 7-3.9 severely restricts the settings where predictive expert testimony should be allowed.

Standards 7-3.10, 7-3.11, and 7-3.12 embody the premise that courts have an obligation to ensure the competence of court-appointed mental health and mental retardation evaluators and of expert witnesses, no matter who calls them, to offer expert opinions about mental condition. Eligibility to serve as a court-appointed evaluator should be based on sufficient clinical and forensic knowledge to ensure a competent professional evaluation on the issue being evaluated. To qualify as expert witnesses, mental health and mental retardation professionals (1) should have the requisite clinical and forensic knowledge, and (2) should have conducted personally an adequate evaluation on the legal and clinical matters about which the professional is called to testify. The qualifications of expert witnesses offering expert testimony on matters of contemporary scientific knowledge are the focus of standard 7-3.13.

Standard 7-3.14 covers the presentation of expert trial testimony. It urges that mental health and mental retardation professionals be required to explain the basis for and reasoning process underlying their expert opinions. Standard 7-3.15 identifies the judicial role in instructing juries concerning mental health and mental retardation professional expert testimony, and should assist courts in clarifying for juries the purpose of such testimony, the weight to be accorded expert opinions, and the jury's function in arriving at a result concerning the issues in a case.

Standard 7-3.1. Authority to obtain mental evaluations

(a) Evaluations of defendant's competency to stand trial are governed by part IV of this chapter. Evaluations of other present competency issues are governed by part V of this chapter.

(b) Defense-initiated evaluations of defendant's mental condition at the time of the alleged crime are governed by standard 7-3.3.

(c) Prosecution-initiated evaluations of defendant's mental condition at the time of the alleged crime may only be conducted when ordered by the court as provided by standard 7-3.4.

(d) Other pretrial mental evaluations. Law enforcement and prosecution authorities may not seek or obtain a pretrial mental health or mental retardation professional interview or mental evaluation of a person who is the subject of a criminal investigation but who has not yet been taken into custody or arrested. Law enforcement and prosecution authorities may seek and obtain a pretrial mental health or mental retardation professional interview or evaluation of a person who has been taken into custody or arrested only if such interview or evaluation is otherwise permitted under existing law and

(i) has been authorized by that person's attorney; or

(ii) has been ordered by a court pursuant to paragraphs (a) or (c); or,

(iii) is conducted either for the sole purpose of diverting the person from the criminal process or for the sole purpose of determining whether emergency mental health treatment or habilitation is warranted, in a situation in which law enforcement or prosecution authorities have reasonable, articulable grounds to believe that the person needs immediate mental health treatment or habilitation.

In all cases in which a pretrial mental health or mental retardation professional interview or mental evaluation is conducted pursuant to

paragraph (d), the person's attorney should be informed, whenever possible in advance, of the interview or evaluation and should receive a written report containing all information and opinions based on such interview or evaluation that were supplied orally or in writing to the law enforcement or prosecution authorities.

(e) Civil commitment of persons found not guilty by reason of mental nonresponsibility. Evaluations of the current mental condition of persons found not guilty by reason of mental nonresponsibility [insanity] are governed by standard 7-7.2.

(f) Presentence evaluations. Presentence evaluations of defendant's mental condition are governed by part IX of this chapter. An indigent offender's right to mental health or mental retardation professional assistance in the sentencing process is provided by standard 7-9.4. Evaluations of the current mental condition of offenders prior to or during a sentencing hearing to consider their commitment as mentally ill or mentally retarded offenders are governed by standard 7-9.8 of this chapter.

(g) Transfer of prisoners. Evaluations of the current mental condition of prisoners being considered for voluntary or involuntary transfer to mental health or mental retardation facilities are governed respectively by standards 7-10.3 and 7-10.4.

Commentary Introduction

Standard 7-3.1 identifies the forms of mental evaluations that may be performed on criminal defendants, principally through cross-references to more detailed provisions elsewhere in chapter 7. Paragraph (d) expresses ABA policy opposing the use by law enforcement and prosecution authorities of pretrial mental evaluations during criminal investigations or interrogation to obtain a confession or as a means to acquire evidence supporting the prosecution's case-in-chief against a defendant.

Related Standards

ABA, Standards for Criminal Justice 7-2.1, 7-7.2, 7-7.3, 7-7.4, 7-9.4, 7-9.8, 7-10.3, 7-10.4

American Psychiatric Association, The Principles of Medical Ethics with Annotations Especially Applicable to Psychiatry §4, annotation 13

Commentary

Paragraph (a) cross-refers to more detailed standards governing examinations to determine a defendant's competency; standard 7-3.1 thus is rendered specifically inapplicable to them. Paragraph (b) confirms as well that defense-initiated mental evaluations are governed solely by standard 7-3.3 and not the instant standard.

Prosecutors who believe that defendants may assert the defense of mental nonresponsibility [insanity] should be empowered to precipitate a mental evaluation soon after a defendant has been arrested. Nevertheless, the Association position embodied in paragraph (c) is that prosecuting attorneys at their own discretion should not have immediate access to arrestees or defendants for the purpose of evaluation. Instead, the standard rests on the premise that such examinations may be conducted only when authorized by court order under standard 7-3.4. Only in that way will a defendant's privilege against self-incrimination and right to counsel be safeguarded adequately.[1] To confirm that premise, paragraph (d) embodies a policy recommendation that law enforcement authorities should not be allowed, without court order, to obtain other evaluations from mental health or mental retardation professionals or to use such

1. In Estelle v. Smith, 451 U.S. 454 (1981), the United States Supreme Court ruled that a doctor's testimony at the death penalty phase of a first-degree murder prosecution violated the defendant's fifth amendment privilege against compelled self-incrimination. In *Smith*, the defendant was not advised of his rights by a prosecution-retained psychiatrist ostensibly conducting a court-authorized evaluation bearing on procedural competency. *Smith* appears to hold that a defendant's fifth amendment privilege is implicated in any prearraignment mental evaluation initiated by the police or prosecution.

Federal circuits are in disagreement over whether *Smith* is restricted to death penalty cases. *See* United States v. Chitty, 760 F.2d 425, 431-432 (2d Cir. 1985) (not so limited); Bauman v. United States, 692 F.2d 565, 576 (9th Cir. 1982) (limited to capital cases).

In Wainwright v. Greenfield, 106 S. Ct. 634 (1986), a state prosecutor had used a defendant's silence after *Miranda* warnings to support its position that the defendant (who had pleaded insanity) was in fact sane. The Florida Attorney General argued the vital importance of evidence of mental condition at the time of an offense and shortly thereafter. *Id.* at 640. The Court refused to depart from its holding in Doyle v. Ohio, 426 U.S. 610 (1976), that use of silence after *Miranda* warnings denies due process of law, and held that use of silence to rebut a mental nonresponsibility [insanity] defense violates the *Doyle* rule. However, it noted that the "State's legitimate interest in proving that the defendant's behavior appeared to be rational at the time of . . . arrest could have been served by carefully framed questions that avoided any mention of the defendant's exercise of [the] constitutional rights to remain silent and to consult counsel." *Id.*

professionals to assist them in the interrogation of suspects or defendants.[2]

The sixth amendment right to the assistance of counsel governs all "critical stages of the prosecutorial proceedings,"[3] at which counsel's presence is necessary to ensure a meaningful defense, including the right to meaningful cross-examination. The Supreme Court has indicated that counsel should be present when "potential substantial prejudice to defendant's rights inheres in [a] particular confrontation and the ability of counsel to help avoid that prejudice [exists]."[4] A pretrial evaluation conducted by a mental health or mental retardation professional selected by the prosecutor clearly constitutes such a "critical stage."[5]

The warnings mandated by *Miranda v. Arizona*[6] as a prerequisite to a valid waiver of a defendant's constitutional rights during custodial interrogation are inadequate safeguards in the context of a pretrial evaluation performed by a prosecution-retained mental health or mental retardation professional. First, a person in police custody is likely to be in a highly emotional, agitated, and even confused mental state. This condition may influence the individual's perceptions of the role of a mental health or mental retardation professional and the purposes of the evaluation. Second, persons undergoing evaluation often have already been subjected to hostile interrogation by police officers. The contrast between antagonistic police interviewers and seemingly compassionate mental health or mental retardation professional interviewers may bring defendants to speak unguardedly.[7] Finally, professionals in the behavioral sciences are sufficiently sophisticated in the use of interviewing techniques that their questions calling for seemingly innocuous answers may intentionally provoke legally damaging responses.[8] A professional's assessment also

---

2. *See* Goldzband, *Prearraignment Psychiatric Examination and Criminal Responsibility — A Personal Odyssey Through Law and Psychiatry West of the Pecos*, 4 J. PSYCHIATRY & LAW 447, 450-452 (1976) [hereinafter cited as Goldzband] for a discussion of abuses in prearraignment mental evaluations.

3. Maine v. Moulton, 106 S. Ct. 477, 484 (1985); Coleman v. Alabama, 399 U.S. 1, 9 (1970); United States v. Wade, 388 U.S. 218, 227 (1967).

4. United States v. Wade, 388 U.S. at 227.

5. Cape v. Francis, 741 F.2d 1287, 1297 (11th Cir. 1984), *reh'g denied en banc*, 760 F.2d 281 (11th Cir. 1985) (but not if the defense of mental nonresponsibility [insanity] ultimately is not pursued at trial); People v. Quirk, 129 Cal. App. 3d 618, 181 Cal. Rptr. 301 (1982).

6. 384 U.S. 436 (1966).

7. *See* Goldzband, *supra* note 2, at 450; Read, *Can a "Psychiatric* Miranda" *Work?: A California Perspective*, 14 RUTGERS L.J. 431, 433-434 (1983) [hereinafter cited as Read].

8. *See* Note, *Pre-Trial Mental Examination and Commitment: Some Procedural Problems in the District of Columbia*, 51 GEO. L.J. 143, 162 (1962).

may be influenced by (1) the way the person interviewed communicates, (2) the nature and appropriateness of the emotions displayed, (3) the degree of logicality in thinking, (4) relationships between patterns of thought and other data, and (5) even what is not communicated. The "process" of communication is far more basic to an interview than the mere content of responses to an evaluator's questions.[9]

Waivers of fundamental constitutional rights must be knowing and intelligent. A significant potential exists for waivers ostensibly tendered by persons who are confused about a professional's role in the interrogation process. In addition, courts find it difficult to evaluate later the adequacy of a waiver in an individual case. Accordingly, the position of the standards is that prosecution-initiated pretrial mental health or mental retardation professional evaluations, obtained without court approval, should be barred.

The American Psychiatric Association considers it a breach of professional ethics for a psychiatrist to conduct a psychiatric evaluation of an arrested person who has not yet had access to legal counsel.[10] Indeed, the APA has expressed its view that an examining psychiatrist must ensure "that the defendant has not only had access to counsel, but that counsel knows of the examination — including its time and place and the identity of the examining psychiatrist — and has agreed that the examination may proceed."[11] Because defendants are more likely to heed the warnings of their attorneys than of prosecution-retained psychiatrists, the latter are under an ethical obligation to refrain from examining defendants before they have consulted with defense counsel.[12] The policy advocated in paragraph (d) against prosecution-initiated evaluations, not authorized by court order, before defense counsel has been appointed or retained, therefore supports the ethical standards of mental health and mental

---

9. *See* Read, *supra* note 7, at 435-436.

10. American Psychiatric Association, The Principles of Medical Ethics with Annotations Especially Applicable to Psychiatry §4, annotation 13.

11. Amicus Curiae Brief for the American Psychiatric Association on Appellant's Petition for Rehearing at 9, Byers v. United States, No. 78-1451 (D.C. Cir., slip opinion, Dec. 24, 1980, as amended June 1, 1981) [hereinafter cited as APA Byers Brief].

In United States v. Garcia, 739 F.2d 440 (9th Cir. 1984), the court ruled that the sixth amendment requires that defense counsel be notified about a forthcoming prosecution-initiated psychiatric examination and be given an opportunity beforehand to consult with the client. Only in that way can a defendant be apprised of the consequences of cooperation or refusal to cooperate, the coverage of the privilege against self-incrimination, and the consequences of a waiver of privilege through responses to an examiner's questions. *Id.* at 442-443.

12. APA Byers Brief, *supra* note 11, at 9.

retardation professionals. Hence, paragraph (d) conforms to the principle of standard 7-1.1 that attorneys should not place such professionals in situations that would compromise their ethical obligations.

Paragraph (d) incorporates no policy inhibiting police and prosecution use of mental health and mental retardation professionals for purposes other than interviewing, interrogating, or evaluating suspects and defendants. For example, such professionals may train police officers in interrogation techniques. A professional appropriately may assist police in bringing about the release of hostages by observing the kidnapers and suggesting negotiating and rescue strategies. Although a professional's skills are being utilized to interpret a suspect's behavior, that professional is not dealing directly with the suspect by attempting to engage him or her in conversation. The fifth amendment right against compelled self-incrimination is not implicated and the potential for an inadequate waiver of that right does not arise unless the professional interacts with the individual. Thus, the restrictions reflected in paragraph (d) relate solely to mental health and mental retardation interviews and mental evaluations.

Law enforcement officials also act properly in obtaining mental evaluations for purposes of crisis intervention, emergency treatment or habilitation, or screening or diversion from the criminal process. In emergencies, police are authorized under standard 7-2.1 to transport mentally disturbed persons to mental health, mental retardation, or medical facilities. Standard 7-3.1(d) clearly legitimates evaluations performed exclusively to determine the need for such emergency treatment. Evaluations for the sole purpose of screening or diverting individuals from the criminal justice system are equally appropriate, provided they are not used to obtain incriminating evidence against defendants who are not diverted.

Standard 7-3.2. Uses of disclosures or opinions derived from pretrial mental evaluations

(a) Admissibility of disclosures or opinions in criminal proceedings. No statement made by or information obtained from a person, or evidence derived from such statement or information during the course of any pretrial mental health or mental retardation professional interview or mental evaluation, or during treatment or habilitation, and no opinion of a mental health or mental retardation

professional based on such statement, information, or evidence is admissible in any criminal proceeding in which that person is a defendant unless the disclosure or opinion is otherwise admissible under standard 7-3.9 and:

(i) relates solely to defendant's present mental competency and the use of such disclosure conforms to the requirements of standard 7-4.6; or,

(ii) is otherwise relevant to an issue raised by defendant concerning defendant's mental condition and defendant intends to introduce the testimony of a mental health or mental retardation professional to support the defense claim on this issue.

(b) Duty of evaluator to disclose information concerning defendant's present mental condition that was not the subject of the evaluation. If in the course of any evaluation, the mental health or mental retardation professional concludes that defendant may be mentally incompetent to stand trial, presents an imminent risk of serious danger to another person, is imminently suicidal, or otherwise needs emergency intervention, the evaluator should notify defendant's attorney. If the evaluation was initiated by the court or prosecution, the evaluator should also notify the court.

Commentary Introduction

Standard 7-3.2 restricts the use of (1) disclosures made by persons subjected to mental evaluations and (2) opinions formulated by mental health or mental retardation professionals who performed those evaluations. Disclosures and opinions are admissible in criminal proceedings only if they conform to admissibility requirements and are relevant either to present mental competency or to any issue regarding past or future mental condition that the defendant has raised and supported with professional testimony. The standard also clarifies the duty of professional evaluators to disclose information about a defendant's imminent dangerousness or emergency treatment or habilitation needs discovered in the course of an evaluation.

Related Standards

ABA, Model Rules of Professional Conduct 1.6

ABA, Standards for Criminal Justice 4-3.7(d), 7-4.6

American Psychiatric Association, The Principles of Medical Ethics with Annotations Especially Applicable to Psychiatry §4, annotation 8

American Psychological Association, Ethical Principles of Psychologists 5

American Psychological Association, Specialty Guidelines for the Delivery of Services by Clinical Psychologists 2.3.5

American Psychological Association, Specialty Guidelines for the Delivery of Services by Counseling Psychologists 2.3.5

American Psychological Association, Standards for Providers of Psychological Services 2.3.5

Commentary

Admissibility of Disclosures or Opinions

Paragraph (a) restricts the admissibility of defendant disclosures during a pretrial mental evaluation[1] and limits expert professional testimony based on the evaluation to the issues of present mental competency and past or future mental condition if any such issue has been raised by the defense and will be supported by expert opinion evidence. The standard thus harmonizes competing defense and prosecution interests by prohibiting affirmative prosecution use of incriminating data (such as proving the elements of the offense or any aggravating circumstances at a sentencing hearing), while promoting the easy availability of data bearing on mental condition at the time of an alleged crime when that issue is properly under consideration. Standard 7-3.2(a) rests on the premise that the fifth amendment privilege against compelled self-incrimination governs pretrial mental evaluations.

Nevertheless, if defense counsel obtains professional evaluations bearing on mental condition at the time of an alleged offense, fairness requires that the prosecution be able to obtain its own evaluation in order to respond after a defense notice of intent to use its evaluations. Accordingly, standard 7-3.4(a) provides for prosecution-initiated evaluations of defendants. Self-incrimination concerns are satisfied through standard 7-3.2(a) by limiting the admissibility of defendant disclosures or professional opinions derived from pretrial evaluations. At the same time, standard 7-3.4(c) ensures defendant cooperation in the course of court-authorized evaluations requested by the prosecution. Hence, disclosure

1. The term *pretrial mental evaluation* in standard 7-3.2 and subsequent standards in part III encompasses competency to stand trial and other evaluations of a defendant's present mental condition that may be performed during the course of trial.

of data resting on professional evaluations occurs under the standards only after the defense has made a strategic decision to place in issue the defendant's mental condition at the time of the crimes alleged against them; disclosure is limited to the matter of defendants' mental condition at the time of the alleged criminal acts.

The applicable federal rule rests on premises identical to those in standard 7-3.2: Federal courts can order psychiatric evaluations by government experts of defendants pleading the insanity [mental nonresponsibility] defense, but evidence thus obtained cannot be submitted on the issue of guilt.[2] Most federal courts implement that principle.[3] Commentators also advocate that "use of these disclosures to aid police investigation, prove the actus reus at trial, or impeach the defendant on issues other than mental state, should be prohibited."[4] Some jurisdictions have enacted statutes requiring a cautionary instruction to juries informing them that defendant statements at pretrial evaluation should not be misused by the jury to infer guilt.[5]

Courts generally have held that defendants who plead the mental nonresponsibility [insanity] issue waive the privilege against self-incrimination with respect to mental evaluations and expert opinions bearing on that issue alone.[6] Consequently, mental health and mental retardation professionals who have evaluated defendants at prosecution instance can

---

2. Fed. R. Crim. P. 12.2(c). In United States v. Whitlock, 663 F.2d 1094 (D.C. Cir. 1980), the court noted,

> Had this testimony [obtained in a compelled mental evaluation] been admitted for its tendency to buttress appellant's guilt, the self-incrimination question would generate grave concern. But the challenged testimony was elicited solely for the purpose of supporting the experts' conclusions that appellant was criminally responsible for her actions at the time of the offense.

Id. at 1107. In Cape v. Francis, 741 F.2d 1287, 1294-1296 (11th Cir. 1984), *reh'g denied en banc,* 760 F.2d 281 (11th Cir. 1985), the court found a *Smith* violation harmless error when Cape had not placed the issue of mental nonresponsibility [insanity] before the trier.

3. *See, e.g.,* Gibson v. Zahradnick, 581 F.2d 75 (4th Cir. 1978); United States v. Reifsteck, 535 F.2d 1030 (8th Cir. 1976); United States v. Alvarez, 519 F.2d 1036 (3d Cir. 1975); Collins v. Auger, 428 F. Supp. 1079 (S.D. Iowa 1977). *See also* State v. Lapham, 135 Vt. 393, 377 A.2d 249 (1977).

4. Slobogin, Estelle v. Smith: *The Constitutional Contours of the Forensic Evaluation,* 31 Emory L.J. 71, 107 (1982).

5. *See, e.g.,* Mo. Stat. Ann. §552.030(6) (Vernon 1983).

6. Estelle v. Smith, 451 U.S. 454 (1981); United States v. Cohen, 530 F.2d 43 (5th Cir.), *cert. denied,* 429 U.S. 855 (1976); United States v. Albright, 388 F.2d 719 (4th Cir. 1968). *See* United States v. Hinckley, 525 F. Supp. 1342 (1981) ("[I]n a case where a defendant puts his sanity in issue, he has waived his privilege with respect to the insanity question. . . ." *Id.* at 1349.). *See also* commentary to standard 7-3.4, notes 15-23 and accompanying text.

testify only with respect to mental condition at the time of crimes charged in indictments or informations, and for no other purpose.[7] The corresponding position embodied in the Model Penal Code[8] has been enacted in several states.[9]

The waiver theory has been invoked most frequently against defendants who have raised the mental nonresponsibility [insanity] defense and sought to use expert opinion in support of the plea, but who have resisted prosecution motions for court orders requiring them to submit to prosecution expert evaluations. Occasionally, however, defendants may inject the nonresponsibility issue without intending to use expert opinion testimony. Courts rarely have considered the question of whether in such instances the prosecution should be precluded from obtaining an expert evaluation and using expert opinion evidence at trial. The problem was analyzed by the United States Supreme Court in *Estelle v. Smith.*[10] The Court noted that if expert conclusions do not rest simply on observations of the defendant but rather on defendant's personal accounts of the crime — including statements and omitted details — the fifth amendment privilege governs.[11] *Smith* addressed the propriety of using, in the course of a capital sentencing hearing, information obtained during a court-ordered psychiatric competency evaluation performed at prosecution request. The Court precluded that use, in part because Smith had introduced no psychiatric testimony and indicated no purpose to do so.[12] The *Smith* majority concluded: "A criminal defendant, who neither initiates a psychiatric evaluation nor attempts to introduce any psychiatric evidence, may not be compelled to respond to a psychiatrist if his statements can be used against him. . . ."[13]

The Court distinguished the *Smith* facts from cases in which defendants offer expert professional witnesses in support of a defense of mental nonresponsibility [insanity]. Under those circumstances, the only

---

7. *See, e.g.*, United States v. Bennett, 460 F.2d 872 (D.C. Cir. 1972); Edmunds v. United States, 260 F.2d 474 (D.C. Cir. 1958), *cert. denied*, 362 U.S. 977 (1960).

8. ALI, Model Penal Code §4.09 (Permanent ed. & revised commentary 1985).

9. *See, e.g.*, Colo. Rev. Stat. §16-18-107 (1978); Ill. Ann. Stat. ch. 38, §115-6 (Smith-Hurd Supp. 1985); Mass. Gen. Laws Ann. ch. 233, §23B (West Supp. 1985).

10. 451 U.S. 454 (1981).

11. *Id.* at 464-465.

12. *Id.* at 466.

13. *Id.* at 468. A defendant who intends to introduce the testimony of a mental health or mental retardation professional to support a defense claim relating to defendant's mental condition at the time of the alleged crime is required to cooperate in a prosecution-initiated evaluation. *See* commentary to standard 7-3.4(c), notes 15-32 and accompanying text.

effective means for the prosecution to controvert the defense experts is through testimony by prosecution expert witnesses, who must have court-authorized access to the defendant if they are to give professionally competent evidence.[14]

Note that the word *information* in standard 7-3.2 includes nonverbal communications between defendants and mental health or mental retardation professionals.

Duty to Disclose Information Concerning Defendant's Present Mental Condition

In *Tarasoff v. Regents of University of California,*[15] the California Supreme Court held that psychotherapists have a duty to protect third parties from threats of serious danger posed by patients under their care. The American Psychiatric Association requires psychiatrists, as a matter of medical ethics, to reveal confidential information disclosed by a patient when necessary to protect either the patient or the community from imminent danger.[16] Principle 5 of the American Psychological Association Ethical Principles of Psychologists requires psychologists to reveal confidential information "in those unusual circumstances in which not to do so would result in clear danger to the person or to others."[17] The *Tarasoff* doctrine and the American Psychiatric Association and American Psychological Association principles address, however, a therapist-client therapeutic relationship and so are not directly relevant to pretrial mental evaluations. Nevertheless, mental health and mental retardation professionals may learn during the course of an evaluation that a defendant needs immediate treatment or habilitation or presents an imminent risk of harm to

14. Estelle v. Smith, 451 U.S. at 465.

15. 17 Cal. 3d 425, 551 P.2d 334, 131 Cal. Rptr. 14 (1976). *See also* Jablonski by Pahls v. United States, 712 F.2d 391 (9th Cir. 1983); Lipari v. Sears, Roebuck & Co., 497 F. Supp. 185 (D. Neb. 1980); McIntosh v. Milano, 168 N.J. Super. 466, 403 A.2d 500 (1979). *See generally* Laughran & Bakken, *The Psychotherapist's Responsibility Toward Third Parties Under Current California Law,* 12 West. St. L. Rev. 1 (1984); Meyers, *The Legal Perils of Psychotherapeutical Practice (Part II): Coping with* Hedlund *and* Jablonski, 12 J. Psychiatry & L. 39 (1984); Schorr & Quattrocchi, Tarasoff, *the Doctrine of Special Relationships and the Psychotherapist's Duty to Warn,* 12 J. Psychiatry & L. 13 (1984); Weiner, *Provider-Patient Relations: Confidentiality and Liability,* in The Mentally Disabled and the Law 559, 582-590 (S. Brakel, J. Parry & B. Weiner eds., 3d ed. 1985).

16. American Psychiatric Association, The Principles of Medical Ethics with Annotations Especially Applicable to Psychiatry §4, annotation 8 (1981).

17. American Psychological Association, *Ethical Principles of Psychologists* 5, 36 Am. Psychologist 633, 636 (1981).

another person. Paragraph (b) articulates a standard to guide evaluators under such circumstances:[18] They should notify defense counsel and, in instances of court-authorized evaluations, the court as well. Counsel or the court then may arrange suitable treatment or habilitation or take measures appropriate to forestall the reported danger.

Under paragraph (b), the duty to disclose information discovered in the course of a pretrial mental evaluation, indicating that a defendant presents an imminent risk of serious danger to another person, is identical to the disclosure duty incident to a treating or habilitative relationship. Compliance with the standard should serve to immunize professionals against civil, criminal, or administrative liability. Nevertheless, the standard does not foreclose additional ethically approved acts, for example, notification of potential victims of violence on the part of a defendant released pending trial, institution of civil commitment proceedings, and use of preventive detention proceedings against criminal defendants in pretrial detention or on pretrial release status.[19]

Disclosure to a defense attorney generates a problem of professional legal ethics. The Association Model Rules of Professional Conduct permits but does not require a lawyer to reveal information gained in the course of a confidential attorney-client relationship, "to the extent the lawyer reasonably believes [it] necessary to prevent the client from committing a criminal act that the lawyer believes is likely to result in imminent death or substantial bodily harm. . . ."[20] The commentary to rule 1.6 notes that an attorney's discretionary authority to reveal information reflects the difficulty of knowing whether a client actually will carry out the expressed purpose or abandon it.[21] A lawyer who learns of a client's dangerous propensities from a professional evaluator may disclose the information imparted by the evaluator under paragraph (b), because the lawyer's unsubstantiated personal judgment is not the sole support for the decision to reveal a client's dangerous propensities. Indeed, ethics opinions under the predecessor canons of ethics and Code of Profes-

18. American Psychological Association, Standards for Providers of Psychological Services 2.3.5, provides that if a psychologist is required by a statute, regulation, or court order to release confidential information, "the psychologist shall seek a resolution to the conflict that is both ethically and legally feasible and appropriate." Because ethical principle 5 requires a psychologist to reveal confidential information if the failure to do so would result in clear danger to the person or to others, psychologists can conform their conduct to the disclosure requirements of standard 7-3.2(b).

19. *See* standards 10-5.4, 10-5.8 and commentary.

20. ABA, Model Rules of Professional Conduct 1.6 (1983).

21. *Id.* at 26-27, comment to Rule 1.6.

sional Responsibility suggest a duty to reveal if counsel believes beyond a reasonable doubt that a client intends to commit a dangerous crime.[22] Thus, paragraph (b) disclosure from evaluator to counsel may generate a disclosure obligation if counsel concludes that the anticipated conduct will satisfy all the elements of a crime.

Standard 4-3.7(d) of the Standards for Criminal Justice reflects Association policy that defense attorneys must reveal the "expressed intention" of a client to commit a crime seriously endangering the life or safety of anyone if disclosure is necessary to prevent the crime. That duty to disclose, however, is not coextensive with the counterpart duty of disclosure on the part of mental health and mental retardation professionals incorporated in standard 7-3.2(b). Such professionals may rely on data other than a client's "expressed intention" in concluding that a client/defendant presents an imminent risk of serious danger to another.[23]

Standard 7-3.3. Evaluations initiated by defense

(a) Defense access to mental health or mental retardation professional assistance and evaluation. The right to defend oneself against criminal charges includes an adequate opportunity to explore, through a defense-initiated mental evaluation, the availability of any defense to the existence or grade of criminal liability relating to defendant's mental condition at the time of the alleged crime. Accordingly, each jurisdiction should make available funds in a reasonable amount to pay for a mental evaluation by a qualified mental health or mental retardation professional selected by defendant in any case involving a defendant financially unable to afford such an evalu-

---

22. *See, e.g.*, Los Angeles County Bar Ass'n Comm'n on Legal Ethics, Opinion No. 264 (1959), *reprinted in* 37 L.A.B. Bull. 389, 391 (1962); New Jersey Advisory Comm'n on Professional Ethics, No. 280 (Supp. 1974), *reprinted in* 97 N.J.L.J. 40 (1974). ABA, Comm'n on Professional Ethics, Formal Op. 314 (1965), suggests that counsel must disclose even the confidences of clients if "the facts in the attorney's possession indicate beyond reasonable doubt that a crime will be committed." ABA, Comm'n on Professional Ethics, Formal Op. 155 (1936), states that a communication by a client regarding future commission of an unlawful act is not privileged.

23. Consideration should be given by the Association to a revision of standard 4-3.7(d) to ensure that it adequately protects defense counsel. A defense attorney should be required to disclose information based on a belief that a client presents an imminent risk of serious danger to another person and that disclosure is necessary to prevent that risk from materializing.

ation. In such cases an attorney who believes that an evaluation could support a substantial legal defense should move for the appointment of a professional or professionals in an ex parte hearing. The court should grant the defense motion as a matter of course unless the court determines that the motion has no foundation. The court should promptly provide the prosecution with a copy of the order authorizing the evaluation. Assistance of mental health or mental retardation professionals during the sentencing process is governed by standard 7-9.4.

(b) Uses of disclosures. Whenever a mental health or mental retardation professional conducts an evaluation of defendant's mental condition upon the request or motion of the defense, all disclosures made by defendant or the attorney during the course of the evaluation are protected by the attorney-client privilege. As to that evaluation only, the privilege is waived to the extent that discovery is permitted by standard 7-3.8(b), if:

(i) defendant gives notice pursuant to standard 7-6.3 of an intention:

(A) to raise an issue concerning defendant's mental condition at the time of the alleged crime, and

(B) to introduce the testimony of the mental health or mental retardation professional who conducted the evaluation to support the defense claim on this issue; or,

(ii) defendant calls another mental health or mental retardation professional as an expert witness concerning defendant's mental condition at the time of the alleged crime, and the prosecution establishes, to the court's satisfaction, that in bad faith the defendant secured evaluations by all available qualified mental health or mental retardation professionals in the area thereby depriving the prosecution of the opportunity to obtain an adequate evaluation.

This standard does not preclude a mental health or mental retardation professional from disclosing the fact that the professional evaluated a named person upon defense request.

Commentary Introduction

Standard 7-3.3 covers defense access to mental health and mental retardation professional assistance and evaluation to explore the possibility of a defense based on the mental nonresponsibility [insanity] or other mental condition defense. The attorney-client privilege safeguards disclosures made during defense-initiated evaluations. That privilege is waived, however, to permit discovery of information revealed during an evaluation if a defendant has given notice of an intent to call a mental health or mental retardation professional as an expert witness concerning defendant's mental condition.

Related Standards

ABA, Standards for Criminal Justice 5-6.1, 7-3.8, 7-6.3, 7-9.3, 7-9.4, 11-3.2

Commentary

Defense Access to Mental Health and Mental Retardation Professional Assistance

In appropriate cases, the sixth amendment right to effective assistance of counsel requires access to a mental health or mental retardation professional to provide an adequate mental evaluation and to assist counsel in preparing and presenting a potential claim of mental nonresponsibility [insanity] or other mental condition defense. That almost certainly will be true of every serious homicide case, but even in other cases the circumstances of the commission of an alleged offense may suggest mental aberration. The relationship between a victim and a defendant or a defendant's prior history of mental impairment may also indicate that a professional evaluation will aid defense counsel. As one court noted, a mental health or mental retardation professional not only provides necessary testimony at trial supporting the defense of mental nonresponsibility [insanity], but also

> attunes the lay attorney to unfamiliar but central medical concepts and enables him, as an initial matter, to assess the soundness and advisability of offering the defense . . . and perhaps most importantly . . . permits a lawyer inexpert in the science of psychiatry to probe intelligently the foundations of adverse testimony.[1]

Another court characterized as "foolhardy" any lawyer who determines tactical and evidentiary strategy in a case involving psychiatric issues

1. State v. Pratt, 284 Md. 516, 398 A.2d 421, 423 (1979) (*quoting* United States v. Taylor, 437 F.2d 371, 377 n.9 (4th Cir. 1971)).

without the guidance and interpretation of psychiatrists and other behavioral experts.[2]

The Supreme Court of the United States has held, in *Ake v. Oklahoma,*[3] that if a defendant has made a preliminary showing that mental state at the time of the commission of an alleged offense is likely to be a significant factor at trial, due process requires the state to provide access to a psychiatrist if the defendant cannot afford the expense.[4] With that assistance, defendants have a fair chance "to present at least enough information to the jury, in a meaningful manner, as to permit it to make a sensible determination."[5] Although *Ake* considered the claim of a defendant in a capital case, the Court's rationale does not turn on that fact but rather on the need for psychiatric expert assistance.[6]

---

2. United States *ex rel.* Edney v. Smith, 425 F. Supp. 1038, 1047 (E.D.N.Y. 1976), *aff'd without opinion,* 556 F.2d 556 (2d Cir.), *cert. denied,* 431 U.S. 958 (1977).

3. 105 S. Ct. 1087 (1985). *See generally* Weiner, *Mental Disability and the Criminal Law,* in THE MENTALLY DISABLED AND THE LAW 693, 722-723 (S. Brakel, J. Parry & B. Weiner eds., 3d ed. 1985).

4. Ake v. Oklahoma, 105 S. Ct. at 1097.

5. *Id.* at 1096.

6. The Court in *Ake* stated,

> A defendant's mental condition is not necessarily at issue in every criminal proceeding, however, and it is unlikely that psychiatric assistance of the kind we have described would be of probable value in cases where it is not. The risk of error from denial of such assistance, as well as its probable value, are most predictably at their height when the defendant's mental condition is seriously in question. When the defendant is able to make an ex parte threshold showing to the trial court that his sanity is likely to be a significant factor in his defense, the need for the assistance of a psychiatrist is readily apparent. It is in such cases that a defense may be devastated by the absence of a psychiatric examination and testimony; with such assistance, the defendant might have a reasonable chance of success. In such a circumstance, where the potential accuracy of the jury's determination is so dramatically enhanced, and where the interests of the individual and the State in an accurate proceeding are substantial, the State's interest in its fisc must yield.

Id. at 1096-1097. The Court included within its doctrine the acquisition of defense expert data bearing on future dangerousness, an aggravating factor under the state's death penalty statute. *Id.* at 1097.

See also Blake v. Kemp, 758 F.2d 523 (11th Cir. 1985) (prosecution withholding of significant evidence bearing on the mental nonresponsibility [insanity] defense founded a presumption that defense counsel had been prevented from providing effective assistance, violating the sixth and fourteenth amendments).

In People v. Kinion, 97 Ill. 2d 322, 454 N.E.2d 625 (1983), the court held that a state statute imposing a ceiling of $250 on expert witness fees could not be considered as binding but simply as a legislative caution to trial courts that fees in excess of that amount might not be reasonable and therefore should be scrutinized carefully to avoid abuse.

The sixth amendment right to competent counsel, under the standards laid down by the Supreme Court,[7] can be abridged by counsel's failure to request the appointment or otherwise obtain the assistance of qualified mental health or mental rehabilitation professionals.[8]

Standard 7-3.3(a) embodies the principle derived from the Supreme Court's jurisprudence that financially unable defendants are entitled at public expense to the assistance of mental health and mental retardation professionals in preparing and presenting legal and factual defenses and claims resting on abnormal mental condition. This provision is consistent with standard 5-6.1, which supports the claim of financially unable defendants to "supporting services necessary to an adequate defense." The provision is also supported by court decisions[9] and statutes[10] authorizing the appointment of mental health and mental retardation professionals to effectuate the sixth amendment right to effective assistance of counsel.[11]

---

7. Strickland v. Washington, 466 U.S. 668 (1984); United States v. Cronic, 466 U.S. 648 (1984).

8. In Loe v. United States, 545 F. Supp. 662 (E.D. Va. 1982), the defendant had undergone nearly six weeks of observation and evaluation by government psychiatrists who thought him competent to stand trial and sane at the time of the alleged crime. Defendant's attorney, believing that an evaluation by another psychiatrist would merely confirm the government's evidence, did not request professional assistance. The court gave little credence to the attorney's lay belief and viewed the defendant's need for expert assistance to counteract the government's experts as "most acute." *Id.* at 672. Therefore, it ruled that the attorney's failure to pursue a request for assistance by an independent expert constituted a denial of the minimum level of representation guaranteed by the sixth amendment. *Id.*

See also Boykins v. Wainwright, 737 F.2d 1539 (11th Cir. 1984), *cert. denied,* 105 S. Ct. 1775 (1985) (defense counsel's failure to interview the state psychiatrists before trial, to collect lay evidence from friends and relatives, to demand a pretrial competency hearing, and to raise at trial the fact that the defendant was sedated at trial created a reasonable probability that the alleged inadequacies of counsel altered the outcome of the trial).

This assumes, however, that a defendant has established that counsel incompetence affected the resolution of the criminal litigation. *See* Strickland v. Washington, 466 U.S. at 693-696. *See also* Boykins v. Wainwright, 737 F.2d 1539, 1542-1543 (11th Cir. 1984), *cert. denied,* 105 S. Ct. 1775 (1985).

9. *See, e.g.,* United States *ex rel.* Edney v. Smith, 425 F. Supp. 1038 (1976); *In re* Ochse, 38 Cal. 2d 230, 238 P.2d 561 (1951); State v. Pratt, 284 Md. 516, 398 A.2d 421 (1979).

10. *See, e.g.,* Mich. Comp. Laws Ann. §768.20a(3) (1982); Tex. Crim. Proc. Code Ann. §46.03(3)(f) (Vernon Supp. 1985); Wash. Rev. Code Ann. §10.77.060(2) (1980). *See also* 18 U.S.C. §4247(b) (added by the Comprehensive Control Act of 1984, 98 Stat. 1976, §403(a)).

11. Standard 7-9.3 provides that evidence of mental illness or mental retardation should be available as a mitigating factor in sentencing a convicted offender, and it implements that right by confirming the claim of financially unable convicted defendants to the assistance of mental health and mental retardation professionals at sentencing proceedings. This is di-

Although professional assistance is needed to explore clinically based defenses and to assist in the context of sentencing, a financially unable defendant is not entitled to a government-funded professional to assist in jury selection. Courts have ruled that this function can be fulfilled adequately by defense counsel during voir dire.[12]

Counsel for a financially unable defendant must state affirmatively to the court that a request for appointment of a mental health or mental retardation professional is made in good faith; this is implicit in the standard and supported by precedent.[13] If that assurance is given, a trial court should not speculate about the nature of defenses that a professional evaluation might support.[14] If, in an unusual instance, defense counsel in supporting a request for appointment of a professional consultant must give the court information about the client's medical history, earlier or current mental state, or client admissions, paragraph (a) protects against premature disclosure of the defense case and breaches of the attorney-client privilege by providing for an ex parte hearing on the defense motion.[15] If the defense motion is granted the prosecution is to be given a copy of the authorizing court order, under paragraph (a), but this notification does not include access to information provided the court at the ex parte hearing.

Paragraph (a) states that "funds in a reasonable amount" should be made available to pay for the services of mental health and mental retardation professionals. This provision permits a defendant to choose from

---

rectly required by Ake v. Oklahoma, 105 S. Ct. at 1097. *See generally* Decker, *Expert Services in the Defense of Criminal Cases: The Constitutional and Statutory Rights of Indigents,* 51 Cin. L. Rev. 574, 580-599 (1982); Note, *An Indigent Criminal Defendant's Constitutional Right to a Psychiatric Expert,* 1984 U. Ill. L. Rev. 481 (discussions of pre-*Ake* decisions supporting the claim of financially unable defendants to expert services at public expense).

12. *See, e.g.,* United States v. Eagle, 586 F.2d 1193 (8th Cir. 1978) (denying the appointment of a sociologist); United States v. Harris, 542 F.2d 1283 (7th Cir. 1976) (denying the appointment of a psychologist).

13. *See* State v. Sahlie, 90 S.D. 682, 245 N.W.2d 476, 480 (1976).

14. "The trial judge should tend to rely on the judgment of the attorney, who has the primary duty of providing an adequate defense. Such reliance is recommended by the difficulty of requiring the trial judge to take an adversary view of the case." United States v. Theriault, 440 F.2d 713, 717 (5th Cir. 1971) (Wisdom, J., concurring). *See also* United States v. Walker, 537 F.2d 1192, 1195 (4th Cir. 1976); United States v. Taylor, 437 F.2d 371, 378 (4th Cir. 1971).

15. "The manifest purpose of requiring that the inquiry be ex parte is to insure that the defendant will not have to make a premature disclosure of his case." Marshall v. United States, 423 F.2d 1315, 1318 (10th Cir. 1970). *See also* United States v. Dolack, 484 F.2d 528 (10th Cir. 1973); United States v. Sutton, 464 F.2d 552 (5th Cir. 1972).

a pool of competent professionals but does not envision the selection of a particular nationally known professional whose fees may be unusually high. If possible, a mental health or mental retardation professional chosen by the defense should be appointed, but if that professional's evaluation proves unhelpful, the defendant should not be entitled at public expense to shop for another more "friendly" expert.[16]

Applicability of Attorney-Client Privilege

The attorney-client privilege covers defendant communications to a professional performing an evaluation to assist defense counsel in preparation for trial.[17] This privilege preserves maximum flexibility for counsel to explore tentative lines of defense, for if one professional consultant concludes that a defendant's mental condition at the time of the alleged criminal act does not comport with nonresponsibility or diminished responsibility, defense counsel should be free to turn to other experts for assistance. Consequently, defense counsel legally is able to silence experts whose opinions will not be called forth by the defense at trial.

Paragraph (b) restricts prosecuting attorney access to the results of a defense-initiated evaluation to instances in which the defense determines to call that specific professional evaluator at trial in support of the defense case; otherwise, the confidentiality of communications during other defense-initiated evaluations is protected. This position is consistent with standard 11-3.2: Prosecution discovery is permitted only of the opinions and reports of experts the defense intends to use at a hearing or trial.

Most courts that have considered the issue have ruled that defendants do not waive attorney-client privilege covering mental health and mental retardation professional consultants whose expert testimony will not be used at trial.[18] In *State v. Pratt,*[19] the court articulated several policy reasons justifying continued confidentiality:

16. This is supported by precedent. *See, e.g.,* Proctor v. Harris, 413 F.2d 383, 385-386 (D.C. Cir. 1969). *See also* McGarty v. O'Brien, 188 F.2d 151, 157 (1st Cir.), *cert. denied,* 341 U.S. 928 (1951).

17. *See, e.g.,* United States v. Alvarez, 519 F.2d 1036 (3d Cir. 1975); Houston v. State, 602 P.2d 784 (Alaska 1979); People v. Lines, 13 Cal. 3d 500, 531 P.2d 793, 119 Cal. Rptr. 225 (1975); State v. Pratt, 284 Md. 516, 398 A.2d 421 (1979); State v. Kociolek, 23 N.J. 400, 120 A.2d 417 (1957); Pouncey v. State, 353 So. 2d 640 (Fla. Dist. Ct. App. 1977).

18. *See, e.g.,* United States v. Alvarez, 519 F.2d 1036 (3d Cir. 1975); Houston v. State, 602 P.2d 784 (Alaska 1979); People v. Lines, 13 Cal. 3d 500, 531 P.2d 793, 119 Cal. Rptr. 225 (1975); State v. Pratt, 284 Md. 516, 398 A.2d 421 (1979); Pouncey v. State, 353 So. 2d 640 (Fla. Dist. Ct. App. 1977); People v. Hilliker, 29 Mich. App. 543, 185 N.W.2d 831 (1971).

19. 284 Md. 516, 398 A.2d 421 (1979).

1. Waiver of confidentiality would have a "chilling effect" upon a client's willingness to confide in counsel or defense consultants.
2. Inherent prejudice results if the trier of fact learns that a mental health or mental retardation professional originally was employed by the defense.
3. If waiver is recognized the defense in essence would assist the prosecution in discharging its burden of proof.
4. The defense would be inhibited from consulting mental health or mental retardation professionals with conflicting views for fear of generating prosecution witnesses.
5. The defense would be inhibited from consulting any mental health or mental retardation professionals even though consultation might be crucial to the case.[20]

---

20. *Id.* at 425-426. A position contrary to that in paragraph (b) is exemplified by People v. Edney, 39 N.Y.2d 620, 385 N.Y.S.2d 23, 350 N.E.2d 400 (1976). In *Edney,* the prosecution called a psychiatrist who had examined defendant at the request of defense counsel. The court affirmed a conviction, holding that the defense plea of insanity [mental nonresponsibility] waived any claim of privilege; it reasoned that a defendant who introduces psychiatric testimony in support of an insanity plea must submit to a prosecution-initiated mental evaluation during which he or she reveals the facts that would remain privileged under the majority rule. Therefore, a defendant is not harmed by a waiver because the prosecution will have obtained damaging facts in any event. If the defendant does not plead insanity the consultation remains privileged.

The *Edney* analysis is not persuasive. Although defendants who raise a defense of mental nonresponsibility [insanity] are vulnerable to prosecution-initiated mental health or mental retardation professional evaluations, the underlying factual basis for a defense evaluator's opinion may not always be revealed during the prosecution-initiated evaluation. If the prosecution is routinely allowed access to all defense evaluations, it may acquire information it otherwise would not have in a given case.

Moreover, there is a considerable difference between disclosure of otherwise privileged *facts* and disclosure of expert *opinion* based on those facts. Disclosure of the latter is potent prosecution evidence, while disclosed facts first must be interpreted by an evaluator for the prosecution. Under the *Edney* approach, defendants are prejudiced because waiver results in disclosure of a valued commodity — the opinion of the defense evaluator — that otherwise would not be obtainable even during a prosecution-initiated evaluation.

The *Edney* court also may have confused the physician-patient privilege with the attorney-client privilege. To support its premise that defendants who plead mental nonresponsibility [insanity] may be compelled to disclose facts to the prosecution, the *Edney* court relied upon a case, People v. Al-Kanani, 33 N.Y.2d 260, 351 N.Y.S.2d 969, 307 N.E.2d 43, *cert. denied,* 417 U.S. 916 (1973), that dealt solely with waiver of the physician-patient privilege. That privilege did not govern the consultations in the *Edney* case, however, because the defendant had not sought treatment; only the attorney-client privilege was invoked. *See* People v. Lines, 13 Cal. 3d 500, 531 P.2d 793, 119 Cal. Rptr. 225 (1975), in which the court

Limiting prosecutorial access to the results of defense-initiated evaluations should not deprive the prosecution of access to all available mental health and mental retardation professionals. Typically, defense counsel exploring a mental nonresponsibility [insanity] or diminished capacity defense will contact professionals before the prosecuting attorney is informed that the defense will be raised. Although the defense is entitled to evaluate the prospects of such a defense, the prosecution needs access to mental health or mental retardation professionals once the mental nonresponsibility [insanity] or a factual defense relating to *mens rea* or culpability has been asserted. Paragraph (b) forestalls unethical conduct by defense attorneys in freezing out from prosecution use all professionals: such conduct is made to be a waiver of the attorney-client privilege for excess evaluations on the basis of which the evaluator is not called as a defense witness.

Standard 7-3.4(a) authorizes prosecutors to obtain court-ordered evaluations of defendant mental condition at the time of an alleged crime almost simultaneously with defense-initiated evaluation interviews. The standard eliminates one of the justifications advanced by the New York Court of Appeals in *People v. Edney,*[21] in support of a contrary rule, namely, a concern that defense-initiated evaluations will produce more accurate results because they are performed closer in time to an alleged crime.

After a defendant has given notice[22] of an intent to raise an issue concerning mental condition at the time of the alleged crime and to introduce testimony of one or more mental health or mental retardation professionals in support of the defense claim, the prosecution is entitled

---

distinguished the psychotherapist-patient privilege from the attorney-client privilege; a patient-litigant waiver is inapplicable to the attorney-litigant relationship.

Nevertheless, despite these shortcomings, the *Edney* position has received some judicial support. *See, e.g.,* Noggle v. Marshall, 706 F.2d 1408 (6th Cir. 1983); Steve v. Carter, 641 S.W.2d 57 (Mo. 1982); State v. Dodis, 314 N.W.2d 233 (Minn. 1982); State v. Bonds, 98 Wash. 2d 1, 653 P.2d 1024 (1982). In Houston v. State, 602 P.2d 784 (Alaska 1979), the court ruled that generally no waiver occurs. However, after the defense psychiatrist had testified that he had relied on the report of a psychiatrist whom the defense had not called as a witness, the prosecution was permitted to call the uncalled psychiatrist as a rebuttal witness. *Id.* at 792.

The *Edney* rationale has received some scholarly endorsement. *See* Saltzburg, *Privileges and Professionals: Lawyers and Psychiatrists,* 66 VA. L. REV. 597 (1980) [hereinafter cited as Saltzburg].

21. *See* note 20 *supra.*

22. Notice is required pursuant to standard 7-6.3.

to discovery of written reports prepared by defense expert witnesses.[23] Although the defense notice may be viewed as a waiver of the attorney-client privilege, that waiver allows only prosecutor discovery unless cause is shown for denying, restricting, or deferring delivery of a report.[24] It does not legitimate prosecution use of the contents of a professional's evaluation report as affirmative evidence unless at trial the defense calls that professional as an expert witness.[25]

Standard 7-3.4. Court-ordered evaluations upon prosecution request

(a) Prosecution access to defendant for evaluation of mental condition at time of alleged crime. The defense attorney should notify the prosecution within [forty-eight] hours after a mental health or mental retardation professional begins a defense-initiated evaluation interview with defendant for the purpose of evaluating defendant's mental condition at the time of the alleged crime. If a defense attorney has obtained a court-ordered evaluation pursuant to standard 7-3.3, the requirement that the prosecution be provided with a copy of the court order satisfies the notification requirement of this standard. Upon motion of the prosecution after it receives notification, the court should order that defendant submit to an evaluation of defendant's mental condition to be performed by a qualified mental health or mental retardation professional acceptable to the prosecution. If the defense attorney fails to give the required notification, the court may impose sanctions appropriate to the degree of prejudice to the prosecution.

(b) Disposition of reports. A mental health or mental retardation professional who performs an evaluation initiated by the prosecutor pursuant to paragraph (a) should notify the prosecution and the defense in writing of the clinical findings and opinions reached in the evaluation. In this notification, the mental health or mental retardation professional should not refer to statements made by defendant or anyone else, identify the sources of information, or present the factual basis for the evaluator's clinical findings and opinions. The

23. Prosecution discovery is governed by standard 7-3.8(b)(ii).
24. *Ibid.*
25. *See* Saltzburg, *supra* note 20, at 647.

professional should also submit to the court a complete written report whose contents conform to the requirements of standard 7-3.7. The court should promptly provide the defendant with a copy of the report but should otherwise order that the report be sealed and that information contained in the report not be divulged. The court should not read the report prior to ordering it sealed. The report should remain sealed until such time as defendant gives notice, in accordance with standard 7-6.3, of an intention:

(i) to raise an issue concerning defendant's mental condition at the time of the alleged crime; and

(ii) to introduce the testimony of a mental health or mental retardation professional to support the defense claim on this issue.

Upon defendant's giving of the required notice, the court should promptly provide the prosecution with a copy of the mental health or mental retardation professional's report.

(c) Consequences of defendant's failure to cooperate in the evaluation. If the court determines that an adequate evaluation of defendant's mental condition at the time of the alleged crime has been precluded because defendant has refused to cooperate with the mental health or mental retardation professional, and that the refusal was not a result of defendant's mental illness or mental retardation, the court, in its discretion, may exclude the introduction at trial of testimony by a mental health or mental retardation professional offered by defendant concerning defendant's mental condition at the time of the alleged crime. Other proof of defendant's mental condition at the time of the alleged crime may be offered by defendant and, if otherwise competent, such evidence should be admissible. Sanctions for a defendant's refusal to cooperate in an evaluation of competency to stand trial are governed by standard 7-4.6.

Commentary Introduction

Standard 7-3.4 provides for court-ordered mental health and mental retardation evaluations initiated by the court or prosecution. It balances the legitimate need of the prosecution to have access to the defendant for an evaluation of his or her mental condition at the time the defendant obtains an evaluation against protection of the defendant's fifth amendment privilege against self-incrimination. Thus, neither an evaluation report nor information contained in it may be divulged to the prosecution until after the defendant has given notice of an intention to rely upon mental health or mental retardation professional testimony to support a defense claim concerning the defendant's mental condition at the time of the alleged crime. The standard imposes sanctions on a defendant who refuses to cooperate in a court-ordered evaluation.

Related Standards

ABA, Model Rules of Professional Conduct 1.4

ABA, Standards for Criminal Justice 3-5.5, 3-5.6(b), 3-5.8, 7-3.2, 7-3.3, 7-3.7, 7-4.6, 7-6.3, 7-6.4, 8-1.1(b)

Commentary

Court-Ordered Evaluation of Defendant

Traditionally, a prosecutor is entitled to a court-ordered evaluation only after the defendant has served an appropriate notice of an intention to rely upon a defense based on the defendant's mental condition at the time of the alleged crime.[1] Because many jurisdictions do not require such notice until shortly before trial, the prosecution may be seriously disadvantaged because a court-ordered evaluation may not be performed until several months following the alleged crime, after a defense evaluation already has been obtained. In some instances, an evaluation of a defendant's mental condition shortly after arrest may be most influential in determining defendant's mental condition at the time of the alleged crime, thus advancing a just determination in the case. Standard 7-3.4 balances the prosecution's need for a prompt evaluation against a defendant's fifth amendment interest and right to control the defense case. Paragraph (a) requires the defense to notify the prosecution that it has initiated an evaluation interview so that the prosecution promptly may obtain a court-ordered evaluation of the defendant. However, paragraph (b) precludes prosecution access to the results of the court-ordered evaluation unless and until defendant gives notice of an intention to introduce testimony of one or more mental health or mental retardation professionals to support a defense based on the defendant's mental condition at the time of the alleged crime. Thus, if the defense ultimately utilizes a clinically based defense, the prosecution evidence will be as current as that of the defense. If the defendant decides to forgo such a defense, the pros-

---

1. *See, e.g.,* Fed. R. Crim. P. 12.2(c); Cal. Penal Code §1027(a) (West Supp. 1985); N.Y. Crim. Proc. Law §250.10(3) (McKinney 1982).

ecution is not prejudiced, and prosecution access to defense evaluation results is precluded.[2]

The requirement that the defense notify the prosecution within forty-eight hours after a defense-initiated evaluation interview has commenced should not inhibit defense counsel from obtaining an evaluation. A defense request for a mental evaluation does not imply a belief that a mental condition defense could or should be presented at trial. Although the notice will alert the prosecution that defense counsel is considering a mental condition defense as one of several strategy options, the prosecution is precluded by these standards from misusing this information. For example, a prosecutor is subject to disciplinary action for making extrajudicial statements concerning the performance of a defense-initiated or prosecution-initiated evaluation.[3] Similarly, the prosecutor may not disclose to jurors that a defense-initiated evaluation did not result in a presentation of a mental condition defense;[4] a prosecution opening statement must be restricted to the issues in the case and to evidence the prosecution believes in good faith will be offered and admissible. It is unprofessional conduct for a prosecutor knowingly to offer inadmissible evidence.[5] Moreover, prosecution summation is restricted to reasonable inferences from evidence in the record:[6] "The most elementary rule governing the limits of argument is that it must be confined to the record evidence and the inferences that can reasonably and fairly be drawn therefrom."[7] A prosecution remark during closing argument that is not warranted by the evidence may result in a mistrial and a severe reprimand to the offending government attorney.[8]

Paragraph (a) provides that if the defense fails to give notice that a mental health or mental retardation professional has begun a defense-initiated evaluation interview, the court may impose sanctions appropriate to the degree of prejudice to the prosecution. In a typical case the court should order a continuance and may also note in its jury instructions that defense failure to give notice made it impossible for the prosecution to obtain an early evaluation. The court may discipline the

---

2. *See* Slobogin, Estelle v. Smith: *The Constitutional Contours of Forensic Evaluation*, 31 Emory L.J. 71, 96 n.102 (1982) [hereinafter cited as Slobogin].
3. ABA, Standards for Criminal Justice 8-1.1(b)(iii).
4. *Id.* standard 3-5.5.
5. *Id.* standard 3-5.6.
6. *Id.* standard 3-5.8.
7. *Id.* at 3•89, commentary to standard 3-5.8.
8. *See, e.g.*, People v. Brophy, 122 Cal. App. 2d 638, 265 P.2d 593 (1954).

defense counsel as well. However, a defense failure to give the notice required by paragraph (a) should not result in the exclusion of expert testimony by mental health or mental retardation professionals emanating from a defense-initiated evaluation. Such a sanction is inappropriate because it strikes at the defendant, not the offending defense attorney. Indeed, such a sanction might require a retrial premised on the constitutional inadequacy of counsel.[9]

It should be noted that the requirement of a defense notice as a prerequisite for a prosecution motion eliminates the problem of reciprocal notice to the defense concerning a prosecution-initiated mental examination.[10]

Paragraph (b) imposes special reporting requirements on evaluators who have conducted prosecution-initiated evaluations. Their clinical findings and opinions are to be reported in writing to both the prosecution and defense, but the bases for their professional conclusions are not to be included. The phrase *clinical findings and conclusions* is used so that a mental health or mental retardation professional may draw legally relevant inferences from an evaluation. For example, in addition to a diagnosis, the evaluator may express an opinion about whether a defendant's condition constitutes a mental disease or defect and whether the defendant was able to appreciate the wrongfulness of his or her conduct. Such an opinion, however, should not bear on a specific legal criterion or standard unless the opinion lies within the scope of the evaluator's spe-

9. *See* Strickland v. Washington, 466 U.S. 668 (1984); United States v. Cronic, 466 U.S. 648 (1984).

10. *See also* commentary to standard 7-3.1, notes 1-2 and accompanying text (limitations on pretrial mental evaluations at the instance of law enforcement and prosecution authorities). Federal circuits are in disagreement about the sixth amendment implications of a prosecution failure to give notice to defense counsel of an impending psychiatric examination of the defendant. *See, e.g.*, United States v. Garcia, 739 F.2d 440, 442-443 (9th Cir. 1985) (sixth amendment entitles a defendant to advance notice and opportunity to consult with counsel before an examination); Vardas v. Estelle, 715 F.2d 206, 210-212 (5th Cir. 1983), *cert. denied sub nom.* Vardas v. McKaskle, 465 U.S. 1104 (1984) (defense notice of intent to rely on the mental nonresponsibility [insanity] defense places the defendant on constructive notice that the state could and probably will conduct its own psychiatric evaluation of the defendant); *cf.* Cape v. Francis, 741 F.2d 1287, 1297 (11th Cir. 1984), *reh'g denied en banc,* 760 F.2d 281 (11th Cir. 1985) (psychiatric examination was not a critical stage of the proceeding under Coleman v. Alabama, 399 U.S. 1, 9 (1970), when the defense of mental nonresponsibility [insanity] was not pressed at trial; the court distinguished Estelle v. Smith, 451 U.S. 454 (1981), on the basis that in *Smith* the psychiatric testimony was critical to the state's burden of proving future dangerousness and thus was governed by sixth amendment considerations).

cialized knowledge. Although evaluator opinions sometimes may target ultimate legal issues about which the professional may not testify,[11] the instant standard governs only reports prepared before trial. Consequently, evaluators are not precluded from reporting their conclusions as long as the underlying bases are not divulged. Thus, the prosecution will know whether a professional evaluation supports the prosecution's case but will not have access to incriminating statements made by the defendant to an evaluator.

Evaluators also are expected under paragraph (b) to submit a complete written report to the authorizing court, which promptly is to provide a copy to the defense. The prosecution, however, obtains a copy only after the defense has given notice of an intent to utilize a clinically based defense utilizing the expert testimony of a mental health or mental retardation professional.

Some mental health and mental retardation professionals have asked whether only defense counsel will see their reports or whether defendants also will have access to them. They have noted that evaluators may be more circumspect in explaining their clinical findings and opinions if persons who are the subjects of professional evaluations will see them. The Association's Model Rules of Professional Conduct require lawyers to keep their clients reasonably informed, to comply promptly with reasonable requests for information, and to explain matters to the extent reasonably necessary to permit clients to make informed decisions.[12] Although full disclosure can be achieved in most situations, in some instances the commentary to the *Model Rules* recognizes that compliance may be impracticable.[13] Counsel may delay transmission of information if a client is likely to react imprudently to an immediate communication. Thus, defense counsel may withhold a psychiatric evaluation report whenever an evaluator indicates that disclosure may harm the defendant.[14]

Sanctions for Defendant Failure to Cooperate in a Court-Ordered Evaluation

Paragraph (c) covers the consequences of a defendant's refusal to cooperate in a court-ordered evaluation. Naturally, if such a refusal is a con-

---

11. Testimonial limitations are imposed by standard 7-3.9.
12. Model Rules of Professional Conduct 1.4 (1983).
13. *Id.* at 21, comment to Rule 1.4.
14. *Ibid.*

sequence of the defendant's mental disability, sanctions are inappropriate; they would inflict punishment without justification. In contrast, if a defendant can cooperate but chooses not to do so, sanctions are appropriate. Some courts have ruled that compelled cooperation violates the fifth amendment privilege against self-incrimination.[15] Most courts, however, require defendants to cooperate,[16] in some instances on the premise that defendants who raise a defense of mental nonresponsibility and offer mental health or mental retardation professional testimony on the issue have forfeited the right to remain silent.[17] Other precedent rests on concepts of fairness, in that the prosecution cannot adequately refute defense expert professional testimony supporting a clinically based defense without its own professional expert witnesses.[18] In *Estelle v. Smith*,[19] the Supreme Court in passing appears to have endorsed the "fairness" approach:

> When a defendant asserts the insanity defense and introduces supporting psychiatric testimony, his silence may deprive the state of the only effective means it has of controverting his proof on an issue that he interjected into the case. Accordingly, several courts of appeals have held that, under such circumstances, a defendant can be required to submit to a sanity examination conducted by the prosecution's psychiatrist.[20]

Paragraph (c) compels defendant cooperation. Nevertheless, a defendant's fifth amendment interests are adequately protected because his or

---

15. *See, e.g.*, French v. District Court, 153 Colo. 10, 384 P.2d 268 (1963).

16. *See, e.g.*, United States v. Greene, 497 F.2d 1068 (7th Cir. 1974), *cert. denied*, 420 U.S. 909 (1975); United States v. McCracken, 488 F.2d 406 (5th Cir. 1974); Winn v. United States, 270 F.2d 326 (D.C. Cir. 1959), *cert. denied*, 365 U.S. 848 (1961); People v. Spencer, 60 Cal. 2d 64, 383 P.2d 134, 31 Cal. Rptr. 782 (1963), *cert. denied*, 377 U.S. 1007 (1964); State v. Whitlow, 45 N.J. 3, 210 A.2d 763 (1965).

17. *See, e.g.*, Battie v. Estelle, 655 F.2d 692 (5th Cir. 1981); United States v. Baird, 414 F.2d 700 (2d Cir. 1969), *cert. denied*, 396 U.S. 1005 (1970); Pope v. United States, 372 F.2d 710 (8th Cir. 1967).

18. *See, e.g.*, United States v. Albright, 388 F.2d 719 (4th Cir. 1968); Alexander v. United States, 380 F.2d 33 (8th Cir. 1967); People v. Hayes, 421 Mich. 271, 364 N.W.2d 635 (1984); State v. Swinburne, 324 S.W.2d 746 (Mo. 1959). The harmless error rule can be invoked if the defense of mental nonresponsibility [insanity] ultimately is not pursued at trial. Cape v. Francis, 741 F.2d 1287, 1296 (11th Cir. 1984), *reh'g denied en banc*, 760 F.2d 281 (11th Cir. 1985). *See generally* Weiner, *Mental Disability and the Criminal Law*, in THE MENTALLY DISABLED AND THE LAW 693, 719-720 (S. Brakel, J. Parry & B. Weiner eds., 3d ed. 1985); Note, *The Fifth Amendment and Compelled Psychiatric Examinations: Implications of* Estelle v. Smith, 50 GEO. WASH. L. REV. 275 (1982).

19. 451 U.S. 454 (1981).

20. *Id.* at 465.

her disclosures are inadmissible unless the defendant's mental state is placed in issue at trial.[21] Moreover, the prosecution may call mental health or mental retardation professionals only in rebuttal on the responsibility or capacity issue.

An important premise on which paragraph (c) rests is that defendant participation in a court-ordered evaluation is not to be construed as a waiver of privilege against self-incrimination. Waiver, if present, flows from a decision to base a defense on the defendant's mental condition at the time of the alleged crime, using expert testimony of a mental health or mental retardation professional in support.[22] Because defense counsel retains full control over defense strategy, the standard strikes a fair balance between the individual and the state.[23]

Courts have imposed various sanctions against noncooperating defendants. Some have precluded all defense evidence, whether from mental health or mental retardation professionals or lay sources, to support a defense mental disability claim.[24] Most courts[25] and commentators,[26] however, have rejected that sanction as unjustifiably harsh. An alternative sanction is adverse comment to the jury, in the form of either a jury instruction[27] or prosecution final argument.[28] Either will inform a jury that a defendant has refused to cooperate with a court-designated professional evaluator and implies that defense evidence, including expert opinion evidence, is not credible. Nonetheless, the adverse comment sanction has been criticized as unfair to both the prosecution and the defense: The defendant is allowed to present expert testimony that cannot be effectively challenged by the prosecution, while the prosecution (or the court) is permitted to transmute a defendant's silence into adverse evidence.[29]

Paragraph (c) of the standard endorses an intermediate response. It does not bar noncooperating defendants from asserting defenses based on their mental condition at the time of an alleged crime, but instead allows courts to exclude mental health or mental retardation professional

---

21. Standard 7-3.2.
22. United States v. Malcolm, 475 F.2d 420 (9th Cir. 1973).
23. *See* Slobogin, *supra* note 2, at 95-103.
24. United States v. Wade, 489 F.2d 258 (9th Cir. 1973).
25. *See, e.g.*, Lee v. County Court, 27 N.Y.2d 432, 267 N.E.2d 452, 318 N.Y.S.2d 705, *cert. denied*, 404 U.S. 823 (1971); French v. District Court, 153 Colo. 10, 384 P.2d 268, 270 (1963).
26. *See, e.g.*, Slobogin, *supra* note 2, at 104.
27. Lee v. County Court, 27 N.Y.2d 432, 267 N.E.2d 452, 318 N.Y.S.2d 705, *cert. denied*, 404 U.S. 823 (1971).
28. Karstetter v. Cardwell, 526 F.2d 1144, 1146 (9th Cir. 1975).
29. *See* Slobogin, *supra* note 2, at 105.

testimony in support of the defense claim. This rule of reciprocity places in balance the prosecution and defense evidence, because a defendant's personal testimony, the testimony of lay witnesses, and other relevant nonexpert evidence may be used by either side to establish or refute the defense claim. Most appellate courts in fact have endorsed the reciprocity approach,[30] which has been incorporated in the Federal Rules of Criminal Procedure[31] and some state legislation.[32]

Nevertheless, a court should not impose the paragraph (c) sanction unless a defendant's noncooperation has precluded an adequate evaluation by the court-designated mental health or mental retardation professional evaluator. Moreover, the prosecution should be required to establish the fact of a defendant's noncooperation, that the noncooperation did not stem from the defendant's mental condition, and an actual adverse and unfair impact on the prosecution's ability to respond to the defense claim.

Standard 7-3.5. Procedures for initiating mental evaluations

(a) Specificity of request. Whoever initiates an evaluation of defendant's mental condition should inform the mental health or mental retardation professional in writing of each specific matter to be addressed in the evaluation.

(b) Attorney's duty to provide information. The attorney initiating an evaluation should take appropriate measures to obtain and submit to the evaluator any record or information that the mental health or mental retardation professional regards as necessary for conducting a thorough evaluation on the matter(s) referred. Ordinarily, such rec-

---

30. *See, e.g.,* Karstetter v. Cardwell, 526 F.2d 1144, 1145 (9th Cir. 1975); United States v. Handy, 454 F.2d 885, 888 (9th Cir. 1971), *cert. denied,* 409 U.S. 846 (1972); United States v. Baird, 414 F.2d 700, 707 (2d Cir. 1969); State v. Whitlow, 45 N.J. 3, 26, 210 A.2d 763, 775 (1965); Lee v. County Court, 27 N.Y.2d 432, 267 N.E.2d 452, 318 N.Y.S.2d 705, *cert. denied,* 404 U.S. 823 (1971). For a discussion of the various available sanctions, *see* Amicus Curiae Brief for the American Psychiatric Association on Appellant's Petition for Rehearing at 18-26, Byers v. United States, No. 78-1451 (D.C. Cir., slip opinion, Dec. 24, 1980, as amended June 1, 1981). *See also* Slobogin, *supra* note 2, at 103-106. Professor Slobogin favors the "reciprocity" option. *Ibid.*

31. FED. R. CRIM. P. 12.2(d).

32. *See, e.g.,* WIS. STAT. ANN. §971-16(3) (West 1985).

ords and information will include relevant medical and psychological records, police and other law enforcement reports, confessions or statements made by defendant, investigative reports, autopsy reports, toxicological studies, and transcripts of pretrial hearings. The attorney should also obtain and submit to the evaluator any other record or information that the attorney believes may be of assistance in facilitating a thorough evaluation on the matter(s) referred.

(c) Preference for single purpose evaluations. An evaluation of defendant's present mental competency should not be combined with an evaluation of defendant's mental condition at the time of the alleged crime, or with an evaluation for any other purpose, unless defendant so requests or, for good cause shown, the court so orders.

(d) Terms of court order. When an evaluation is conducted pursuant to court order, that order should:

(i) identify the initiating party;

(ii) identify the purpose or purposes of the evaluation;

(iii) describe the circumstances under which statements or other information obtained during the course of the evaluation, and any opinions of the mental health or mental retardation professional based on the evaluation, may be disclosed or used for any purpose in any criminal proceeding;

(iv) explain all applicable evidentiary privileges;

(v) specify whether the evaluator is required to prepare a written report, and, if so, delineate the scope, content, and disposition of the written report.

(e) Promulgation of standard court orders. Each jurisdiction should promulgate standard court orders designed to inform mental health and mental retardation professionals serving as evaluators of the laws and procedures within the jurisdiction applicable to such evaluations.

Commentary Introduction

Standard 7-3.5 promotes a "targeted" evaluation by requiring that an evaluator be informed in writing of the specific matter or matters that are the focus of the evaluation. An attorney who has initiated an evaluation is obliged to provide the evaluating mental health or mental retardation professional with any record or information necessary or of assistance to the evaluator. Special requirements govern court-ordered evaluations.

Related Standards

None

Commentary

A mental health or mental retardation professional who merely is asked to "evaluate" a defendant may well be confused about the purpose of the evaluation and the scope of the inquiry. Studies have documented that many evaluation referrals fail to identify clearly to a mental health or mental retardation professional the reason for a referral.[1] In some instances, no reason at all is stated.[2] To ensure that an evaluation will not focus on irrelevant matters, paragraph (a) requires that an evaluator be informed about the specific matters to be addressed in the evaluation.

Paragraph (b) imposes on an attorney who initiates an evaluation an obligation to provide the evaluator with records and information necessary to conduct the evaluation. Because an evaluator is expected to perform a competent, objective, and impartial evaluation, he or she requires access to documents that will enhance evaluator performance. In fact, without these needed materials, an evaluator may be unable to conduct or even begin the "thorough evaluation" required by the standard.

Studies have shown that evaluators, and even courts on occasion, confuse the criteria for competency to stand trial with those measuring criminal responsibility.[3] Moreover, a mental health or mental retardation evaluator's limited experience in conducting forensic examinations may cause the evaluator to expand the limited focus of a mental evaluation to embrace diagnostic, treatment/habilitation, and dangerousness issues.[4] To lessen the likelihood of that form of professional confusion, paragraph (c) expresses a preference for a single purpose evaluation.

Paragraph (d) imposes an obligation on an authorizing court to communicate to a mental health or mental retardation professional, through the authorizing order itself, information the professional will require to

1. Balcanoff & McGarry, *The Role of the Psychiatrist in Pretrial Evaluations,* 126 Am. J. Psychiatry 3 (1969).

2. Bendt, Balcanoff & Tragellis, *Psychiatric Evaluation of Alleged Offenders,* 58 A.B.A.J. 371, 373 (1972).

3. Harvard Medical School, Competency to Stand Trial and Mental Illness 1 (1973).

4. McGarry, *Demonstration and Research in Competency for Trial and Mental Illness: Review and Preview,* 49 B.U.L. Rev. 46, 50-53 (1969); Vann & Morganroth, *Psychiatrists and the Competence to Stand Trial,* 42 U. Det. L.J. 75, 81 (1964); Comment, *Commitment to Farview: Incompetency to Stand Trial in Pennsylvania,* 117 U. Pa. L. Rev. 1164, 1190 (1969).

perform an adequate evaluation. Specifically, this information includes the identity of the initiating party, the purpose(s) of the evaluation, the circumstances under which statements or other information obtained during an evaluation (and the professional's opinions based on that information) can be disclosed in the course of criminal proceedings and for what purposes, and the coverage of applicable evidentiary privileges. The court also is to indicate whether the evaluator is to submit a written report and the scope, contents, and disposition to be made of such a report if it is required.

Paragraph (e) urges the adoption of standardized forms for court orders that can assist and inform mental health and mental retardation professional evaluators. For example, such a form could clearly distinguish evaluations bearing on present mental competency from those relating to mental disability at the time of an alleged crime. Evaluators ordered to conduct evaluations of present mental competency should be informed that they are to test a defendant's ability to understand the nature of the proceedings and to assist and interact with defense counsel. Standard forms should be constructed on the framework of the items listed in paragraph (d).

Standard 7-3.6. Procedures for conducting mental evaluations

(a) Duty of attorney to explain nature of evaluation to evaluator. Whoever initiates the evaluation should inform the mental health or mental retardation professional conducting the evaluation and ensure that the professional understands:

(i) the specific legal and factual matters relevant to the evaluation;

(ii) the rules governing disclosure of statements or information obtained during the evaluation and governing disclosure of opinions based on such statements or information; and,

(iii) the applicable evidentiary privileges.

(b) Duties of defense attorney and evaluator to explain nature of evaluation to defendant. In any evaluation, whether initiated by the court, prosecution, or defense, the defendant's attorney and the mental health or mental retardation professional conducting the evaluation have independent obligations to explain to defendant and to ensure that defendant understands to the extent possible:

(i) the purpose and nature of the evaluation;

(ii) the potential uses of any disclosures made during the evaluation;

(iii) the conditions under which the prosecutor will have access to information obtained and reports prepared; and,

(iv) the consequences of defendant's refusal to cooperate in the evaluation as provided for in standard 7-3.4(c) and 7-4.6(b).

(c) Presence of attorney during evaluation.

(i) When the scope of the evaluation is limited to defendant's present mental competency, the defense attorney is entitled to be present at the evaluation but may actively participate only if requested to do so by the evaluator.

(ii) When the scope of the evaluation is not limited to defendant's present mental competency, the defense attorney may be present at the evaluation only with the evaluator's prior approval, and if present may actively participate only if requested to do so by the evaluator.

(iii) The prosecutor may not be present at any mental evaluation of defendant.

(d) Recording the evaluation. All court-ordered evaluations of defendant initiated by the prosecution should be recorded on audiotape or, if possible, on videotape, and a copy of the recording should be provided promptly to the defense attorney. The defense may use the recording for any evidentiary purpose permitted by the jurisdiction. If the defense intends to use the recording at trial, it should notify the court. Upon receiving notice, the court should promptly provide to the prosecution a copy of the recording. Upon defense motion, the court may enter a protective order redacting portions of the recording before it is forwarded to the prosecution.

(e) Joint evaluation. Joint evaluations should be encouraged. They should be permitted when agreed upon by the prosecutor and defense attorney. A joint evaluation involves either a simultaneous evaluation by two or more mental health or mental retardation professionals or a single evaluation by a mental health or mental retardation professional agreed on by both parties.

Commentary Introduction

Traditionally, attorneys and mental health or mental retardation professionals performing evaluations have not interacted well. Paragraph (a) advocates that attorneys be under an express duty to communicate to the evaluator and to provide detailed information necessary for mental health or mental retardation professionals to fulfill competently the role of evaluator. Paragraph (b) requires defense counsel and the professional alike to explain to a defendant both the evaluation objective and the evaluation process. Paragraph (c) addresses the issue of an attorney's presence during an evaluation interview with a defendant. It draws a distinction between evaluations limited to the issue of present mental competency and other evaluations. Even though defense counsel is not entitled by right to attend a prosecution-initiated evaluation interview bearing on a defendant's mental condition at the time of an alleged crime, paragraph (d) urges that the interview be recorded for later use by defense counsel. Paragraph (e) supports the use of joint evaluations to restrict the "gamesmanship" that occurs if attorneys attempt to manipulate evaluation results.

Related Standards

ABA, Standards for Criminal Justice 4-5.1(a), 7-3.2, 7-3.4(c)

American Psychiatric Association, The Principles of Medical Ethics with Annotations Especially Applicable to Psychiatry §4, annotation 2

American Psychological Association, Ethical Principles of Psychologists 5

American Psychological Association, Specialty Guidelines for the Delivery of Services by Clinical Psychologists 2.2.2, 2.3.5

American Psychological Association, Specialty Guidelines for the Delivery of Services by Counseling Psychologists 2.2.2, 2.3.5

American Psychological Association, Standards for Providers of Psychological Services 2.2.2, 2.3.5

Commentary

Duty of Attorney

Paragraph (a) addresses the problem of inadequate communication between attorneys and judges who initiate evaluations, on the one hand, and mental health or mental retardation professionals who perform evaluations, on the other. Because evaluations are authorized for specific purposes, a mere request that a professional perform an "evaluation" of a defendant will not suffice. In fact, mental health and mental retardation professionals themselves frequently assume they should not receive advance information bearing on an evaluation for fear it might contaminate the evaluation process. However, because an evaluation is appropriately targeted at a specific objective, barriers should be eliminated to communications between attorneys and mental health or mental retardation professionals. For example, if an evaluation is to be performed to reconstruct a defendant's mental condition at the time of an alleged crime, an evaluator needs to know the nature of that crime and the legal test for mental nonresponsibility [insanity] in the jurisdiction.

Duty to Explain Evaluation to Defendant

Paragraph (b) embodies the premise that both defense counsel and an evaluator have a duty to explain to a defendant the nature of the evaluation. An attorney's obligation to explain stems from the responsibility to advise an accused client about all aspects of the case.[1] A mental health or mental retardation professional's obligation flows, at least in part, from professional ethical standards. For example, the Principles of Medical Ethics require psychiatrists to describe fully "the nature and purpose and lack of confidentiality of the examination to the examinee at the beginning of the examination."[2] In an *amicus curiae* brief,[3] the American Psychiatric Association expressed the view that a psychiatrist examining a criminal defendant at the request of a court or prosecuting attorney should be even more explicit:

> Specifically, in describing the nature and purpose of the interview, a psychiatrist should explain that he is not the defendant's doctor and that the examination is not being conducted for therapeutic purposes. The psychiatrist should also state on whose behalf or at whose request — whether the prosecution or the court — he is examining the defendant. In addition, we think the defendant should be told that the psychiatrist may be called to testify for the prosecution at trial and that in such testimony the psychiatrist may relate statements made by the defendant during the psychiatric examination.[4]

1. ABA, Standards for Criminal Justice 4-5.1(a).
2. American Psychiatric Association, The Principles of Medical Ethics with Annotations Especially Applicable to Psychiatry §4, annotation 6 (1981).
3. Amicus Curiae Brief for American Psychiatric Association on Appellant's Petition for Rehearing at 6-7, Byers v. United States, No. 78-1451 (D.C. Cir., slip opinion, Dec. 24, 1980, as amended June 1, 1981) [hereinafter cited as APA Amicus Brief].
4. *Id.* at 7.

Psychologists are also required to inform defendants about legal limitations on confidentiality governing an evaluation.[5]

Paragraph (b) recognizes an obligation on the part of mental health or mental retardation professionals to provide defendants with sufficient information so that they can understand the nature of the evaluation. Specifically, at the outset a professional should explain the nature, purpose, and context of the evaluation[6] and should inform a defendant that the usual confidentiality inherent in a patient-therapist relationship does not govern disclosures made during this form of evaluation. An evaluator also should describe the evaluation techniques to be used. Without such a description, a defendant may not perceive that an evaluating professional will attempt to develop an overall impression of the defendant based on both nonverbal behavior and verbal responses to specific questions.[7] If both defense counsel and an evaluator endeavor in good faith to follow the pattern of client information set out in paragraph (b), a resulting evaluation should be useable in later court proceedings in accordance with the standards permitting such use. This should hold true even though the defendant's mental condition raises appropriate questions about informed consent.

If a mental health or mental retardation professional obtains information from another person in the course of an evaluation, he or she should inform the source about (1) the general nature of the inquiry, consistent with the defendant's privacy interests, (2) the fact that the information is sought for a mental evaluation, (3) the fact that a report will be prepared based on the evaluation, and (4) the fact that both the information given and the source of that information are not confidential and may be disclosed to the court, the prosecutor, and the defendant. The evaluator also should inform the defendant and defense counsel of the identity of persons from whom the evaluator has sought information about the defendant.

---

5. American Psychological Association, *Ethical Principles of Psychologists* 5, 36 Am. Psychologist 633, 636 (1981). *See also* American Psychological Association, Standards for Providers of Psychological Services 2.2.2, 2.3.5 (1981); American Psychological Association, *Specialty Guidelines for the Delivery of Services by Clinical Psychologists* 2.2.2, 2.3.5, 36 Am. Psychologist 640, 645-647 (1981); American Psychological Association, *Specialty Guidelines for the Delivery of Services by Counseling Psychologists* 2.2.2, 2.3.5, 36 Am. Psychologist 652, 657, 659 (1981).

6. Shah, *Legal and Mental Health System Interactions,* 4 Int'l J.L. & Psychiatry 219, 249-250 (1981).

7. *See* discussion in the commentary to standard 7-3.1, note 9 and accompanying text.

Presence of Defense Attorney at Evaluation Interview

Paragraph (c) addresses the difficult issue of whether a defendant's attorney should have a right to be present during a mental evaluation interview of a defendant. Two different types of evaluations must be distinguished in this context. The first is an evaluation limited to a consideration of defendant's present mental competency, which usually involves interaction between a defendant and defense counsel. Thus, an evaluation of present mental competency must explore whether the defendant is presently able to consult with counsel with a reasonable degree of rational understanding and has a rational and factual understanding of the proceeding.[8] A thorough evaluation may require that counsel be present at the interview to enable the evaluating professional to observe the attorney-client relationship. Counsel's attendance also may ensure that the clinician will receive needed information about the defense strategy in the case, although there may be differences of professional opinion on the point.

The second type of evaluation endeavors to reconstruct a defendant's mental state at the time of an alleged crime. Courts have divided as to whether a defendant's attorney has a right to be present at the evaluation interview. Many courts have commenced their analysis with *United States v. Wade,*[9] in which the Supreme Court stated that the sixth amendment requires counsel at any pretrial confrontation in which "the presence of counsel is necessary to preserve the defendant's basic right to a fair trial as affected by his right meaningfully to cross-examine the witnesses against him and to have effective assistance of counsel at the trial itself."[10]

Three factors govern whether a particular confrontation requires counsel: "First, the confrontation must pose potentially substantial adverse consequences for the defendant. . . . Second. . . . the nature of the confrontation must be such that its reconstruction at trial would prove difficult. . . . [T]hird. . . . the confrontation . . . must also inherently involve the risk of error."[11] In *Lee v. County Court,*[12] the New York Court of Appeals held that defense counsel is entitled to attend a pretrial mental

8. *See* standard 7-4.1(b).

9. 388 U.S. 218 (1967). *See also* Brewer v. Williams, 430 U.S. 387 (1977) (sixth amendment requires that counsel be present, or his or her presence be waived validly, during interrogation of a client against whom adversary criminal proceedings have commenced).

10. United States v. Wade, 388 U.S. at 227.

11. Slobogin, Estelle v. Smith: *The Constitutional Contours of the Forensic Evaluation,* 31 Emory L.J. 71, 117-118 (1982) [hereinafter cited as Slobogin].

12. 27 N.Y.2d 432, 267 N.E.2d 452, 318 N.Y.S.2d 705, *cert. denied,* 404 U.S. 823 (1971).

evaluation interview to enhance the prospects of effective defense cross-examination at trial. However, the court limited a defense attorney's role during an interview to that of a mere observer.[13] The *Lee* decision has been codified by the New York legislature.[14] The supreme courts of Oregon[15] and Alaska[16] have held that the presence of counsel is required by the sixth amendment. The Alaska Supreme Court also permitted a defense psychiatrist to attend a court-ordered mental evaluation interview conducted for the benefit of the prosecution.[17]

In light of the three criteria advanced in the *Wade* decision, many commentators believe that defendant interviews in the course of prosecution-initiated pretrial evaluations constitute a critical stage of the prosecution. Hence, they advocate a sixth amendment right to the presence of counsel.[18] Concern also has been expressed that a decision to exclude a defendant's attorney from a mental evaluation interview may encourage efforts to bar counsel in other situations, for example, when a defendant is interrogated by police or a prosecuting attorney.

Nevertheless, most courts have held that a defendant who pleads a defense based on mental condition at the time of an alleged crime legitimates a prosecution mental evaluation of the defendant, and that the sixth amendment right to counsel does not mandate defense counsel's presence at a prosecution-initiated evaluation interview of the defendant.[19] In *Estelle v. Smith*,[20] the United States Supreme Court held that a

---

13. Chief Justice Fuld, dissenting, would have allowed defense counsel to take an active role in order to provide effective assistance of counsel during an interview. *Id.* at 446-447, 267 N.E.2d at 460, 318 N.Y.S.2d at 717 (Fuld, C.J., dissenting in part).

14. N.Y. Crim. Proc. L. §250.10 (McKinney 1982).

15. State *ex rel.* Ott v. Cushing, 289 Or. 695, 617 P.2d 610 (1980).

16. Houston v. State, 602 P.2d 784 (Alaska 1979).

17. *Id.* at 795-796.

18. Slobogin, *supra* note 11, at 115-127; Comment, *The Right to Counsel During Court-Ordered Psychiatric Examinations of Criminal Defendants*, 26 Vill. L. Rev. 135 (1981).

19. *See, e.g.*, United States v. Cohen, 530 F.2d 43 (5th Cir.), *cert. denied*, 429 U.S. 855 (1976); United States v. Greene, 497 F.2d 1068 (7th Cir. 1974), *cert. denied*, 420 U.S. 909 (1975); United States v. Mattson, 469 F.2d 1234 (9th Cir. 1972), *cert. denied*, 410 U.S. 986 (1973); United States *ex rel.* Stukes v. Shovlin, 464 F.2d 1211 (3d Cir. 1972); United States v. Baird, 414 F.2d 700 (2d Cir. 1969); Thornton v. Corcoran, 407 F.2d 695 (D.C. Cir. 1969); United States v. Albright, 388 F.2d 719 (4th Cir. 1968); Presnell v. State, 241 Ga. 49, 243 S.E.2d 496 (1978); People v. Larsen, 74 Ill. 2d 348, 385 N.E.2d 679 (1979); People v. Martin, 386 Mich. 407, 192 N.W.2d 215 (1971), *cert. denied*, 408 U.S. 929 (1972); State v. Whitlow, 45 N.J. 3, 210 A.2d 763 (1965); State v. Wilson, 26 Ohio App. 2d 23, 268 N.E.2d 814 (1971). Presence of counsel at a sentencing evaluation has also been denied. Hollis v. Smith, 571 F.2d 685 (2d Cir. 1978).

20. 451 U.S. 454 (1981). *See also* United States v. Chitty, 760 F.2d 425, 431-432 (2d Cir.

defendant's sixth amendment right to the assistance of counsel is abridged if a defendant is denied an opportunity to consult with counsel before a psychiatric evaluation.[21] However, in an important footnote, the Court specifically reserved for later consideration the question of whether the sixth amendment permits defense counsel to be present during an evaluation interview.[22] The Court, quoting from the Fifth Circuit decision in *Smith,* noted that counsel's presence during an evaluation interview could contribute little to and might seriously disrupt the evaluation.[23] Other courts have also commented that a defense attorney's presence at a prosecution-initiated evaluation interview, even as an observer, may adversely affect an evaluator's ability to obtain information on which to base a professional opinion.[24] The American Psychiatric Association has expressed a belief that too little is known about the potentially disruptive effect of

> counsel's presence at the examination, or the use of other procedures, to confidently assess whether the perceived need for such safeguards outweighs their possible costs. . . . Although some psychiatrists may find that their examination is not disturbed or impaired by the use of certain procedures, other psychiatrists may find that the same procedures do interfere with the performance of a thorough and valid psychiatric evaluation.[25]

The Association's position expressed in paragraph (c) affords an evaluator maximum access to a defendant so that relevant, reliable information can be obtained about the defendant's mental condition at the time of an alleged crime. To achieve this result, defense counsel's presence at an evaluation interview is permitted only when the evaluation is directed solely at present mental competency or, in the context of other evaluations, if an evaluating mental health or mental retardation professional consents to counsel's presence. If counsel is not allowed to attend, a defendant's fifth amendment interest in avoiding self-incrimination and sixth amendment claim to adequate representation by counsel can be

---

1985); Cape v. Francis, 741 F.2d 1287, 1297 (11th Cir. 1984), *reh'g denied en banc,* 760 F.2d 281 (11th Cir. 1985).

21. Estelle v. Smith, 451 U.S. at 471.
22. *Id.* at 470 n.14.
23. *Ibid.*
24. *See, e.g.,* Gibson v. Zahradnick, 581 F.2d 75, 79 (4th Cir.), *cert. denied,* 439 U.S. 996 (1978); United States v. Baird, 414 F.2d 700, 711 (2d Cir. 1969); United States v. Albright, 388 F.2d 719, 726 (4th Cir. 1968).
25. APA Amicus Brief, *supra* note 3, at 30-31.

safeguarded in other ways. In particular, the instant standard encourages full disclosure by a defendant to a professional evaluator, but standard 7-3.2 restricts prosecution use of evaluation results, which are available only if relevant to a claim of mental nonresponsibility [insanity] or other mental condition defense at the time of an alleged crime, and on no other issue. Hence, defense counsel's presence at an evaluation interview would offer no protection of the defendant's fifth amendment interest beyond that already provided by restrictions on prosecution use of evaluation results.

The sixth amendment right to adequate representation by an attorney is protected under the standard by the requirement that all court-ordered evaluations initiated by the prosecution be recorded, preferably through videotaping, and by the further requirement that a copy of the recording be supplied to defense counsel. This promotes a monitoring of an evaluation interview that perhaps is more effective than the mere presence of counsel as an observer or participant.[26] The recording requirement reflects an appropriate compromise between positions advocated by those who assert that recording devices may substantially inhibit evaluation interviews[27] and those who maintain that recordings cannot convey the contextual variables at work during such interviews.[28]

Paragraph (c) entitles defense counsel to attend a single-issue evaluation interview of present mental competency. Because a defense attorney decides whether a defendant's *past* mental condition will be evaluated, defense counsel can ensure that a court-authorized or prosecution-initiated evaluation of present mental competency addresses that latter issue alone. However, if a defense attorney initiates an evaluation of a defendant's mental condition at the time of an alleged crime and thereby triggers the prosecution's right of access to the defendant, it is inefficient and clinically unrealistic to bifurcate the ensuing multiple issue evaluation interview. Instead, paragraph (d) takes the position that the

---

26. State v. Jackson, 298 S.E.2d 866, 872-873 (W. Va. 1982). *See* Bonnie & Slobogin, *The Role of Mental Health Professionals in the Criminal Process: The Case for Informed Speculation*, 66 Va. L. Rev. 427, 501-502 (1980). *See* United States v. Byers, 704 F.2d 1104, 1122-1123 (D.C. Cir. 1984) (plurality opinion) (even if it were an abuse of discretion not to have used judicial supervisory powers to order taping or recording of a psychiatric interview (which the plurality judges did not believe to be true), the examining expert's testimony would not be excluded or suppressed as an enforcement sanction against the district court).

27. APA Amicus Brief, *supra* note 3, at 30 n.16 (*citing* Tanney & Gelso, *Effect of Recording on Clients*, 19 J. Counseling Psychology 349 (1972).

28. Slobogin, *supra* note 11, at 126.

evaluation interview should be recorded, as a substitute for defense counsel's presence. This recording requirement, though, is not intended to enable a prosecuting attorney to obtain additional evidence, which would occur, for example, if a defense-initiated evaluation interview were recorded and a recording made available to the prosecution.

Note that paragraph (c)(iii) opposes the presence of a member of the prosecution staff at any evaluation interview with a defendant.[29]

Paragraph (d) permits the defense to use a recording of an evaluation interview with a defendant for any evidentiary purpose permitted by the jurisdiction. In a different context, the Supreme Court of California has allowed the use of audiotapes for witness impeachment.[30] If a defendant chooses to offer such a recording at trial, the prosecution should also be permitted to do so as well. In fact, recordings have been used frequently to illustrate the basis of expert mental health or mental retardation professional opinions.[31] However, recordings, like other evidence, must be excluded if their probative value is outweighed by a danger of undue prejudicial effect.[32]

Joint Evaluations

Paragraph (e) advocates the premise that a prosecuting attorney and defense counsel should consider joint evaluations and reports. This practice reduces the likelihood that trial tactics will be employed to confuse a jury as to the significance or weight of mental health and mental retardation professional testimony. As a leading proponent of the joint evaluation device has noted,

> Although different theories of interpretation may be utilized by the experts . . . , [the joint evaluation] procedure eliminates the "vast" discrepancies

29. *Compare* United States v. Stockwell, 743 F.2d 123, 127 (2d Cir. 1984) (the fact that an assistant United States Attorney listened to a recording of a psychiatric examination of the defendant did not as such infringe the fifth amendment privilege against self-incrimination or contravene Fed. R. Crim. P. 12.2(c), which limits the use of the results of such an examination to the issue of mental nonresponsibility [insanity]).

30. People v. Romo, 14 Cal. 3d 189, 534 P.2d 1015, 121 Cal. Rptr. 111 (1975).

31. *See, e.g.*, People v. Modesto, 59 Cal. 2d 722, 382 P.2d 33, 31 Cal. Rptr. 225 (1963) (audiotape); Pratt v. State, 39 Md. App. 442, 387 A.2d 779 (1978) (videotape). *See generally* Roesch, Jackson, Sollner, Eaves, Glackman & Webster, *The Fitness to Stand Trial Interview Test: How Four Professions Rate Videotaped Fitness Interviews*, 7 Int'l J.L. & Psychiatry 115 (1984).

32. *See, e.g.*, Eaton v. State, 394 A.2d 217 (Del. 1978); State v. Harris, 241 Or. 224, 405 P.2d 492 (1965).

that seem to exist between various observers. These discrepancies are far more likely to be related to trial tactics used by counsel than to differences in the psychiatric data.[33]

Standard 7-3.7. Preparation and contents of written reports of mental evaluations

(a) Requirement of written report. Promptly upon concluding the evaluation, the mental health or mental retardation professional should prepare a complete, written report. However, at the specific request of the defense attorney, a professional who conducted an evaluation initiated by the defense attorney may make only an oral report.

(b) Contents of written report.

(i) The written evaluation report should ordinarily:

(A) identify the specific matters referred for evaluation;

(B) describe the procedures, tests, and techniques used by the evaluator;

(C) state the evaluator's clinical findings and opinions on each matter referred for evaluation and indicate specifically those questions, if any, that could not be answered;

(D) identify the sources of information and present the factual basis for the evaluator's clinical findings and opinions; and,

(E) present the reasoning by which the evaluator utilized the information to reach the clinical findings and opinions. The evaluator should express an opinion on a specific legal criterion or standard only if the opinion is within the scope of the evaluator's specialized knowledge.

(ii) Except as limited by standard 7-3.8(a), the evaluator should include in the written report any statements or information that serve as necessary factual predicates for the clinical findings or opinions, even if the statements or information are of a personal or potentially incriminating nature.

(c) Clarification of written report. The attorney who requested the evaluation should not edit, modify, revise, or otherwise compromise the integrity of the report. However, after the report has been com-

33. Watson, *On the Preparation and Use of Psychiatric Expert Testimony: Some Suggestions in an Ongoing Controversy*, 6 Bull. Am. Academy Psychiatry & L. 226, 233 (1978).

pleted and submitted, the attorney may correspond in writing with the mental health or mental retardation professional in order to clarify the meaning or implications of the evaluator's findings or opinions. The report and any clarifying correspondence between the attorney and the evaluator should be disclosed at the time established for discovery of written reports.

(d) Promulgation of written guidelines. Each jurisdiction should promulgate written guidelines regarding the law and procedures within that jurisdiction governing the preparation of written reports in order to inform mental health and mental retardation professionals serving as evaluators.

Commentary Introduction

Standard 7-3.7 sets forth the requirements for written evaluation reports and specifies their contents. Those requirements should ensure that evaluation reports are adequate for legal purposes and should provide the necessary information for mental health or mental retardation professionals to form expert opinions.

Related Standards

ABA, Standards for Criminal Justice 4-4.4, 7-3.2(a), 7-3.3(b), 7-3.4, 7-3.8

Commentary

Although a written report normally should be prepared at the completion of an evaluation, defense counsel may request that only an oral report be made for any defense-initiated evaluation. Such a request is appropriate because, under standard 7-3.3(b), a mental health or mental retardation professional report becomes a part of the attorney's work product and is protected by the attorney-client privilege. The prosecution's need for an evaluation of a defendant is accommodated in standard 7-3.4. Although a defendant must cooperate in a prosecution-initiated evaluation, notwithstanding the fifth amendment privilege against self-incrimination,[1] standard 7-3.2(a) precludes the use of the results of a prosecution-initiated evaluation to support the prosecution's case-in-

1. *See* commentary to standard 7-3.4, notes 15-23 and accompanying text.

chief. Standard 7-3.7(a) urges the adoption of a requirement that evaluations initiated by prosecuting authorities always be reported in writing. Under standard 7-3.4(b), that type of report is to be submitted to the authorizing court, which in turn is to provide the defendant with a copy; otherwise the report should be sealed. An evaluation report may be discovered, pursuant to standard 7-3.8(b), only after a defendant gives notice of an intent to call a mental health or mental retardation professional to support a defense claim of mental nonresponsibility [insanity] or other mental condition defense. If defense counsel intends to use an expert witness who has not prepared a report earlier, standard 7-3.8(b) advocates that one be prepared and provided to the prosecution before the expert testifies.

Paragraph (b) lists the matters to be included in an evaluation report. An evaluator's report should (1) identify the specific matters referred for evaluation; (2) describe the procedures, tests, and techniques used in the evaluation; (3) state the evaluator's clinical findings and opinions on each referred matter and indicate whatever questions cannot be responded to; (4) identify the sources and nature of the information on which his or her clinical findings rest, so that defense counsel and the prosecuting attorney may pursue a follow-up investigation if they wish; and (5) set forth the reasoning by which the described information was used to formulate clinical findings and opinions. However, an evaluator should not express an opinion on a legal criterion or standard such as the test for mental nonresponsibility [insanity] at the time of an alleged crime, a matter not within the scope of the evaluator's expertise. Opinions may be included only if they fall within an evaluator's specialized knowledge.

Subparagraph (b)(ii) requires an evaluator to include statements and information constituting a necessary basis for clinical findings or opinions, even though they tend to incriminate the defendant. Nevertheless, an evaluator may omit potentially incriminating statements or information if he or she believes them to be irrelevant or extraneous to the formation of clinical findings or opinions on the issues referred for evaluation.

Under the standards,[2] a lawyer is not permitted to suggest "that the expert color an opinion to favor the interest of the client the lawyer represents." That standard justifies the premise embodied in standard 7-3.7(c) that reports of mental health and mental retardation professionals should not be edited by attorneys. Professional evaluators may not be

2. ABA, Standards for Criminal Justice 4-4.4

aware of the significance of changes in their reports requested by attorneys. If an evaluating professional is confused, the initial report will demonstrate the confusion and should be preserved without amendment. Later correspondence between a professional and an attorney can clarify the professional's opinion without compromising the integrity of the evaluation and the report; that correspondence, of course, must be disclosed to opposing counsel along with the underlying written report.

Paragraph (d) suggests that each jurisdiction should promulgate written guidelines, through either legislation or court rules, to assist mental health and mental retardation professionals in preparing written reports.

Standard 7-3.8. Discovery of written reports

(a) Discovery of reports concerning defendant's present mental competency. When the court has ordered a pretrial evaluation on any present mental competency issue, the evaluator should prepare a separate report on that issue even if other issues have also been referred for evaluation. The report should not contain information or opinions concerning either defendant's mental condition at the time of the alleged crime or any statements made by defendant regarding the alleged crime or any other crime. Upon satisfying itself that the report does not contain information or opinions that should have been excluded, the court should promptly provide copies to the prosecutor and to the defense attorney.

(b) Discovery of reports concerning defendant's mental condition at time of the alleged crime. When the defendant gives the notice specified in standard 7-6.3:

(i) the prosecution should promptly provide to the defense all written reports prepared by mental health or mental retardation professionals for the prosecution; and

(ii) the defense should promptly provide to the prosecution all written reports prepared by any mental health or mental retardation professional whom defendant intends to call as an expert witness on defendant's mental condition at the time of the alleged crime. Whenever defendant intends to call an expert witness who has not previously prepared a written report, a written report should be prepared and promptly provided to the prosecution. However, upon a showing of good cause by defendant, the court

may order that the delivery of a report or reports be denied, restricted, or deferred until a time certain before trial. The court may order defendant to promptly disclose to the prosecutor a list of the sources of information relied upon in any report whose delivery has been denied, restricted, or deferred.

(c) Promulgation of written guidelines. Each jurisdiction should establish, by statute or court rule, detailed guidelines governing discovery of written reports prepared by mental health or mental retardation professionals.

Commentary Introduction

Standard 7-3.8 governs the rules regarding discovery of written evaluation reports. To prevent misuse of data bearing on present mental competency evaluations, paragraph (a) recommends a requirement that a mental health or mental retardation professional prepare a separate report on present mental competency, even if other issues have been evaluated at the same time. Paragraph (b) establishes a balanced system of discovery of reports concerning a defendant's mental condition at the time of an alleged crime. Paragraph (c) advocates implementation of the standard through statute or court rule.

Related Standards

ABA, Standards for Criminal Justice 7-1.1, 7-3.3(b), 7-3.7(b), 7-6.3, 7-6.5, 11-1.1, 11-2.1, 11-2.2, 11-4.4, 11-4.5.

Commentary

A report relating to a defendant's mental competency to undergo criminal proceedings should not contain investigatory leads or information bearing on the defendant's mental condition at the time of an alleged crime. To forestall the misuse of competency evaluations as a source of prosecution information about unrelated matters,[1] paragraph (a) advocates a legal requirement that an independent report be prepared on the issue of present mental competency. Moreover, a recipient court should satisfy itself that unrelated data and professional opinions have been

1. *See* People v. Arcega, 32 Cal. 3d 504, 521-522, 651 P.2d 338, 346-347, 186 Cal. Rptr. 94, 102-103 (1982).

excised from such a report before copies are provided to the prosecuting attorney and defense counsel.[2]

Standard 7-6.3, reflecting legislation in many jurisdictions,[3] recommends that the defense be required to give notice of an intent to assert at trial the issue of mental nonresponsibility [insanity] or other mental condition defense at the time of an alleged crime. That notice triggers the discovery provisions of paragraph (b), and earlier discovery for the benefit of the prosecution is inappropriate. In the course of an evaluation, a mental health or mental retardation professional usually elicits statements from a defendant concerning the alleged crime. A defense assertion of innocence can be seriously prejudiced if the prosecution gains access to these statements.[4] Moreover, an evaluating professional rarely is trained to determine whether a defendant's statements are legally inconsequential or materially incriminating. A professional's function is to conduct a thorough and competent evaluation, not to screen out objectionable evidence. Only if a defendant's statements constitute necessary factual predicates for an evaluator's clinical finding or opinion should the evaluator include them in a written evaluation report, even though they may be incriminating.[5]

By precluding prosecutor discovery of reports before the defense gives notice of intent to claim mental nonresponsibility [insanity] or other mental condition defenses, paragraph (b) encourages defendants to be candid in responding to evaluator inquiries. Defendants are assured that their disclosures cannot be used to support the affirmative prosecution case or to provide the prosecution with investigative leads. Were the latter to occur, it might well exert a chilling effect on counsel's decision to seek a mental evaluation preliminary to a defense of mental nonresponsibility [insanity] or other mental condition defense. A defendant might be caused to forego a bona fide defense out of concern that he or she inadvertently might supply the prosecution with leads tipping the scales toward conviction.

---

2. ABA, Standards for Criminal Justice 11-4.5, it should be noted, permits a court to redact nondiscoverable information.

3. *See, e.g.*, Mich. Comp. Laws Ann. §768.20a (West 1982); N.Y. Crim. Proc. Law §250.10 (McKinney 1982); N.C. Gen. Stat. §15A-959 (1983); Pa. R. Crim. Proc. 305(C)(1)(b) (1985); Utah Code Ann. §77-14-3 (Supp. 1985). *See also* Fed. R. Crim. P. 12.2(a).

4. Amicus Curiae Brief for American Psychiatric Association on Appellant's Petition for Rehearing at 12, Byers v. United States, No. 78-1451 (D.C. Cir., slip opinion, Dec. 24, 1980, as amended June 1, 1981) [hereinafter cited as APA Amicus Brief].

5. *Id.* at 13. Standard 7-3.7(b)(ii) imposes this reporting requirement on an evaluator.

Standard 7-1.1 provides that mental health or mental retardation professionals should function independently and objectively in their role of evaluator. If investigative leads discovered in the course of an evaluation cannot be disseminated, evaluators will not be tempted to overreach to aid the prosecution and thus to abandon the independence and objectivity expected of them.

Of course, a defendant might spontaneously disclose an investigative lead in the course of a properly administered evaluation. Even in such an event, however, evaluators remain under an obligation to perform an independent and objective evaluation on the limited issue of a defendant's mental condition; they cannot be expected to determine statement by statement whether investigatory leads resulted from their own overreaching or were volunteered. Both considerations support a conclusion that no investigative leads should be reported to the prosecution. The American Psychiatric Association, because of its concern about the problem of investigative leads, has advocated the view that strict limitations should be placed on the use and dissemination of psychiatric evaluation reports.[6]

Before giving notice of an intent to rely on a mental condition defense, defense counsel may obtain discovery of material and information within the prosecutor's possession or control.[7] Association policy is that a defendant who has obtained discovery must disclose at prosecution request all expert reports the defense intends to use at trial.[8] Nevertheless, standard 7-3.8(b) approves prosecutor discovery only after a defense notice of an intent to rely on a mental condition defense. Thus, to protect fifth and sixth amendment interests and to encourage candor during the evaluation process, standard 7-3.8(b) should be considered an exception to the usual standards requirement.[9] Prosecutor discovery is delayed until defense counsel has given the notice of intent to rely on a mental condition defense envisioned in standard 7-6.3, even though the defense may have requested and received information from the prosecutor before such notice has been given.[10]

Once the notice required by standard 7-6.3 has been transmitted, the

---

6. APA Amicus Brief, *supra* note 4, at 11-12.

7. Prosecutorial disclosure to the accused is required by ABA, Standards for Criminal Justice 11-2.1.

8. *Id.*, standard 11-3.2(a).

9. *Ibid.*

10. For a further explanation of the relationship between standards 7-3.8(b) and 11-3.2(a), *see* commentary to standard 7-6.5.

ensuing discovery is broad, as embodied in the standards.[11] Thus, the prosecution must disclose to the defense all expert reports or statements, including the results of mental evaluations.[12] The prosecution's duty of disclosure is to be discharged "as soon as practicable. . . ."[13] Once the defense has requested and received discovery, at prosecution request it must disclose reports or statements, including mental evaluations, made by experts whom the defense intends to call as witnesses.[14] This disclosure requirement, however, does not embrace material prepared for the defense constituting a part of defense counsel's work product.[15] Thus, a report of a mental health or mental retardation professional employed as a defense consultant is protected against disclosure by the attorney-client privilege unless that professional will become an expert witness in support of a mental condition defense.[16]

After notice has been given under standard 7-6.3, standard 7-3.8(b) imposes on the defense an obligation to disclose even though no discovery requests have been made by either the prosecution or the defense. In this regard, paragraph (b) expands discovery beyond the basic scope of the standards[17] and the Federal Rules of Criminal Procedure.[18] Defense counsel in possession of an evaluation report strongly supportive of a mental condition defense should not be able to hide it from the prosecution simply by omitting to seek discovery of counterpart prosecution reports. Reciprocal discovery of evaluation reports without the necessity of a request clearly furthers the more general principle of full and free discovery proclaimed elsewhere in the standards.[19]

---

11. ABA, Standards for Criminal Justice ch. 11. *See id.*, standard 11-1.1(a)(iii) (procedures should permit thorough preparation for trial and minimize surprise at trial).
12. *Id.*, standard 11-2.1(a)(iv).
13. *Id.*, standard 11-2.2.
14. *Id.*, standard 11-3.2(a).
15. *Id.*, standard 11-3.2(b).
16. *See* standard 7-3.3(b)(i). Equivalent discovery limitations are embodied in Fed. R. Crim. P. 16. *See also* United States v. Stockwell, 743 F.2d 123, 125-127 (2d Cir. 1984) (government cross-examination of defendant, based on information revealed in a recording of a psychiatric interview, bore on the insanity [mental nonresponsibility] defense and thus was proper under Fed. R. Crim. P. 12.2(c)); United States v. Byers, 740 F.2d 1104, 1111 (D.C. Cir. 1984) (fifth amendment does not bar use of testimony by psychiatrist who examined defendant under court order after the defendant has introduced other psychiatric evidence on the insanity [mental nonresponsibility] issue).
17. ABA, Standards for Criminal Justice ch. 11. *See supra*, note 11.
18. Fed. R. Crim. P. 16.
19. ABA, Standards for Criminal Justice 11-1.1(b)(8).

Under subparagraph (b), a court may issue a protective order to prevent or limit disclosure of material in a report — for example, investigative leads — that may unduly prejudice the defense.[20] In fairness to the prosecution, however, if a protective order is issued, the court may require defense disclosure of the sources of information relied on in the report. Thus, if a mental health or mental retardation professional used police reports, preliminary examination transcripts, investigative reports and the like, the prosecution will know that and be able to investigate and verify the resources relied on by the evaluator. The likelihood of surprise at trial is significantly diminished.

Standard 7-3.8 should be implemented through statutes or court rules detailing discovery procedures governing mental health or mental retardation professional reports.

Standard 7-3.9. Admissibility of expert testimony concerning a person's mental condition or behavior

(a) Admissibility of expert testimony concerning a person's present or past mental condition. Expert testimony, in the form of an opinion or otherwise, concerning a person's present mental competency or mental condition at some time in the past should be admissible whenever the testimony is based on and is within the specialized knowledge of the witness and will assist the trier of fact. However, the expert witness should not express, or be permitted to express, an opinion on any question requiring a conclusion of law or a moral or social value judgment properly reserved to the court or the jury.

(b) Admissibility of expert testimony concerning a person's future mental condition or behavior. An expert opinion stating a conclusion that a particular person will or will not engage in dangerous behavior in the future should not be admissible in any criminal proceeding or in any special commitment hearing involving a person found not responsible under the criminal law. Expert testimony relating to the person's future mental condition or behavior should be admissible in any criminal proceeding or in any special commitment hearing

20. This provision is consistent with *id.*, standard 11-4.4 and FED. R. CRIM. P. 16(d)(1).

whenever the testimony is based on and is within the specialized knowledge of the witness and is limited to a description of:

(i) the clinical significance of the individual's personal history and proven past criminal act(s);

(ii) scientific studies involving the relationship between specific behaviors and variables that are objectively measurable and verifiable;

(iii) the possible psychological or behavioral effects of proposed therapeutic or habilitative interventions; or

(iv) the factors that tend to enhance or diminish the likelihood that specific types of behavior could occur in the future.

Commentary Introduction

Standard 7-3.9 addresses the admissibility in a criminal trial of mental health and mental retardation professional testimony. It permits such testimony relating to a defendant's present or past mental condition if the testimony is based on the witness's specialized knowledge. That knowledge, however, does not embrace value judgments reserved to a court or jury. Paragraph (b) limits expert testimony about future mental condition to clinical observations and behavioral data and precludes predictions about a given individual's future conduct.

Related Standards

ABA, Standards for Criminal Justice 7-4.5(a), 7-6.1, 7-6.6, 7-9.9(e), 7-10.5(b)

American Psychological Association, Ethical Principles of Psychologists

Commentary

Expertise of Mental Health and Mental Retardation Professionals on Issues of Present or Past Mental Condition

Although mental health and mental retardation professionals have testified frequently on matters of past, present, and future mental condition, their expertise to do so has been seriously questioned. Some commentators stress the lack of scientific verification of the operative theories underlying such purportedly scientific opinions; they argue that mental health and mental retardation professionals should not be allowed to testify about disputed theoretical matters or to state conclusions not based on firm scientific evidence.[1] The essential reliability of mental health and mental retardation professional testimony also has been questioned.[2] Accordingly, some commentators advocate an evidentiary rule that would limit expert witnesses to descriptions of behavior they actually have observed clinically.[3]

Notwithstanding such criticisms, the position embodied in standard 7-3.9(a) is that described by Professors Bonnie and Slobogin:

> According to the weight of authority, however, the fact that opinion testimony is uncertain does not by itself justify exclusion, as long as the evidence rises above mere conjecture or speculation. If it has any tendency to prove a fact, and is otherwise qualified as expert opinion, the evidence is admissible unless some overriding reason requires exclusion. The rationale for this position is that many observations, both scientific and lay, can be expressed only in terms of "probabilities" or "possibilities"; to deny the factfinder such evidence on this ground alone might deplete seriously the amount of information available.[4]

Mental health and mental retardation professionals obviously have more knowledge than jurors about mental and emotional processes and abnormal behavior, psychological aberrations, and criminal behavior. Their specialized knowledge, much of which appropriately may be called "informed speculation," should be available to assist factfinders. Consequently, the present standard, instead of advocating the exclusion of or severe limitations on expert testimony, endorses the use of such testimony as long as it is within the sphere of specialized knowledge of properly qualified experts. However, this and other standards in this part seek to ensure that factfinders are aware of the limitations inherent in

1. *See, e.g.*, J. Ziskin, Coping with Psychiatric and Psychological Testimony (2d ed. 1975); Morse, *Failed Explanations and Criminal Responsibility: Experts and the Unconscious*, 68 Va. L. Rev. 971 (1982) [hereinafter cited as Morse, *Failed Explanations*]; Morse, *Crazy Behavior, Morals, and Science: An Analysis of Mental Health Law*, 51 So. Cal. L. Rev. 527, 600-626 (1978) [hereinafter cited as Morse, *Crazy Behavior*]; Comment, *The Psychologist as Expert Witness: Science in the Courtroom?*, 38 Md. L. Rev. 539 (1979).

2. Morse, *Failed Explanations*, *supra* note 1, at 1018-1039.

3. Morse, *Crazy Behavior*, *supra* note 1, at 601.

4. Bonnie & Slobogin, *The Role of Mental Health Professionals in the Criminal Justice Process: The Case for Informed Speculation*, 66 Va. L. Rev. 427, 461-462 (1980) [hereinafter cited as Bonnie & Slobogin].

mental health and mental retardation professional testimony[5] and to improve the quality of expert opinion evidence.[6]

Paragraph (a), modeled after rule 702 of the Federal Rules of Evidence, permits a witness to offer an expert opinion concerning a subject not within common lay knowledge if the witness is qualified as an expert through knowledge, skill, experience, training, or education.[7] Even if critics of mental health and mental retardation professional opinion evidence are correct in asserting that the operating theories underlying psychiatry and psychology have not been verified scientifically, rule 702 does not limit "specialized knowledge" to scientific knowledge.[8] Generally, however, mental health and mental retardation professional testimony has been admitted as expert opinion evidence.

In *Frye v. United States,*[9] a leading case on the admissibility of scientific expert testimony, the court required that the scientific basis of the proposed testimony relied on by an expert "be sufficiently established to have gained general acceptance in the particular field in which it belongs."[10] The *Frye* test has been invoked frequently to determine the admissibility of proposed scientific testimony in many fields,[11] and specifically to the acceptability of mental health and mental retardation professional testimony.[12] In the latter context, courts focus on the scientific acceptability of the methodology relied upon rather than on the conclusions expressed by expert witnesses.[13]

---

5. *See* standard 7-3.15.

6. *See* standards 7-1.2, 7-1.3, 7-3.10 through 7-3.15.

7. *See, e.g.,* People v. Davis, 62 Cal. 2d 791, 800, 402 P.2d 142, 44 Cal. Rptr. 454 (1965).

8. "The fields of knowledge which may be drawn upon are not limited merely to the 'scientific' and 'technical' but extend to all 'specialized' knowledge.' " FED. R. EVID. 702, Notes of Advisory Committee on Proposed Rules.

9. 293 F. 1013 (D.C. Cir. 1923).

10. *Id.* at 1014.

11. *See, e.g.,* United States v. Kilgus, 571 F.2d 508 (9th Cir.), *cert. denied,* 412 U.S. 939 (1978) (use of infrared system of identification); People v. Kelly, 17 Cal. 3d 24, 549 P.2d 1240, 130 Cal. Rptr. 144 (1976) (voice analysis).

12. Hughes v. Mathews, 576 F.2d 1250, 1258 (7th Cir.), *cert. dismissed sub nom.* Israel v. Hughes, 439 U.S. 801 (1978) (psychiatric diagnosis satisfies the *Frye* test); State v. Marks, 231 Kan. 645, 647 P.2d 1292 (1982) (psychiatric testimony on "rape trauma syndrome" held admissible under *Frye* test); State v. Mulder, 29 Wash. App. 513, 629 P.2d 462 (1981) ("battered child syndrome" is generally accepted in the scientific community, and therefore expert testimony on the subject is admissible).

13. In two decisions regarding Patricia Hearst, the court admitted psychiatric testimony about the effect of kidnapping and incarceration on the defendant's mental state when she later committed a crime, United States v. Hearst, 412 F. Supp. 889 (N.D. Cal. 1976), but rejected psycholinguistics methodology as being insufficiently established in the scientific

Courts have not specified the extent to which mental health or mental retardation professional testimony qualifies as expert opinion. Instead, they usually have expressed their views in broad terms, allowing that form of testimony on issues of "insanity," "capacity to stand trial," "psychiatric diagnosis,"[14] and "mental condition."[15] Accordingly, a professional should be allowed to tender an expert opinion concerning a diagnosis of mental disorder or mental disability if it rests on one or more personal interviews with the subject of the opinion. The testimony lies within the witness's specialized knowledge and will assist the trier of fact in determining present mental competency or mental condition at the time of an alleged crime. Even though the test of mental nonresponsibility articulated in standard 7-6.1 conceives of "mental disease or defect" as a legal term not coextensive with diagnostic categories of "mental disorder" or "mental disability," a professional clinical diagnosis of mental disorder or mental disability is clearly relevant to the factfinder's determination whether a legally defined "mental disease or defect" exists.[16]

Most courts have ruled that mental health or mental retardation professional testimony is admissible concerning a defendant's state of mind when an underlying definition of crime requires proof of specific intent.[17] Expert opinion evidence from qualified professionals should be admissible on a *mens rea* issue even if a defendant has not pleaded a specific mental nonresponsibility [insanity] defense, as long as it is relevant to a determination of guilt, innocence, or level of culpability.

---

community to warrant admissibility. United States v. Hearst, 412 F. Supp. 893 (N.D. Cal. 1976), *aff'd*, 563 F.2d 1331 (9th Cir. 1977). *See also* Ibn-Tamas v. United States, 407 A.2d 626 (D.C. 1979).

14. Hughes v. Mathews, 576 F.2d 1250, 1258 (7th Cir.), *cert. dismissed sub nom.* Israel v. Hughes, 439 U.S. 801 (1978).

15. People v. Davis, 62 Cal. 2d 791, 800, 402 P.2d 142, 148, 44 Cal. Rptr. 454, 460 (1965).

16. *See* commentary to standard 7-6.1, notes 55-59 and accompanying text.

17. United States v. Brawner, 471 F.2d 969 (D.C. Cir. 1972); People v. Henderson, 60 Cal. 2d 482, 35 Cal. Rptr. 77, 386 P.2d 677 (1963); People v. Gorshen, 51 Cal. 2d 716, 336 P.2d 492 (1959); Becksted v. People, 133 Colo. 72, 80, 292 P.2d 189, 194 (1956); Leick v. People, 131 Colo. 353, 362, 281 P.2d 806, 811 (1955); Battalino v. People, 118 Colo. 587, 589, 199 P.2d 897, 899 (1948); Ingles v. People, 92 Colo. 518, 524, 22 P.2d 1109, 1112 (1933); State v. Gramenz, 256 Iowa 134, 126 N.W.2d 285 (1964); State v. DiPaolo, 34 N.J. 279, 168 A.2d 401, *cert. denied*, 368 U.S. 880 (1961), *modified* in State v. Sikora, 44 N.J. 453, 210 A.2d 193 (1965); State v. Padilla, 66 N.M. 289, 347 P.2d 312 (1959); People v. Moran, 249 N.Y. 179, 163 N.E. 553 (1928); People v. Colavecchio, 11 A.D. 2d 161, 202 N.Y.S.2d 119 (1960); Commonwealth v. Walzack, 468 Pa. 210, 360 A.2d 914, 915 (1976). *Contra*, Steele v. State, 97 Wis. 2d 72, 294 N.W.2d 2 (1980).

Testimony on Questions Requiring Conclusions of Law or Value Judgments

If the defense of mental nonresponsibility [insanity] has been asserted, mental health and mental retardation professionals are qualified to provide data and opinions about a defendant's mental status at the time of a professional evaluation, including diagnoses of mental disorder or mental disability. A professional may explain how a mental disorder or disability may have influenced a defendant's mental or emotional processes or behavior at the time of an alleged crime.[18] Typically, however, such expert witnesses are also invited to opine whether, according to the mental nonresponsibility [insanity] formulation employed in the jurisdiction, a defendant was legally nonresponsible at the time of the alleged crime. The practice of submitting conclusory opinions on legal issues has been criticized vehemently as a usurpation of a role and responsibility belonging to court and jury.[19] An arrogation of this function by mental health or mental retardation professionals is particularly inappropriate because their opinions of that character lie outside their training, experience, and theoretical constructs.[20]

Admittedly, rule 704 of the Federal Rules of Evidence permits experts to express opinions on ultimate issues to be decided by triers of fact, but standard 7-3.9(a) advocates the preclusion of such testimony. Such a position is warranted, in the Association's view, so that mental health and mental retardation professional testimony will be limited to matters within the scope of professional expertise, thus preventing juror confusion as to the limitations of that expertise and the role of the jury.

Although mental health or mental retardation professionals should not tender expert opinions on legal issues or value judgments such as criminal responsibility, they should be permitted to testify and offer opinions

18. S. Halleck, Law in the Practice of Psychiatry 213-214 (1980) [hereinafter cited as S. Halleck].

19. Shah, *Legal and Mental Health System Interactions*, 4 Int'l J.L. & Psychiatry 219, 248-249 (1981).

20. "Translating clinical data into opinions as to how mental illness makes a person legally insane and negates his responsibility for a criminal act is a task for which a psychiatrist has no training, no science, and no theories to guide him." S. Halleck, *supra* note 18, at 213. An American Psychological Association Task Force studying the role of psychology in the criminal justice system recommended: "Since it is not within the professional competence of psychologists to offer conclusions on matters of law, psychologists should resist pressure to offer such conclusions." American Psychological Association, *Report of the Task Force on the Role of Psychology in the Criminal Justice System*, recommendation 5, 33 Am. Psychologist 1099, 1105 (1978).

on matters transcending common lay knowledge. Professionals who have conducted adequate evaluations are competent to address a defendant's clinical state at the time of the evaluation. Beyond that, professionals may speculate retrospectively about a defendant's probable clinical state at the time of an alleged crime. In essence, they properly may address the probable impact of a given mental disorder on a person's functions and may tender an expert opinion about whether that disorder did or did not interfere with specific mental or emotional processes.

For example, suppose a hallucinating mother sees the angel of death who warns her of the forthcoming tortured dying of her beloved children in retribution for the mother's past sins. The angel offers her a transient opportunity to put them to death lovingly and peacefully, with God's blessing and the guarantee of a heavenly eternity, sparing them painful deaths and perpetual limbo. A mental health or mental retardation professional evaluator can confirm a diagnosis of chronic paranoid schizophrenia and testify about how the diagnosis was reached and the impact of the condition on rational thinking and judgment, especially in circumstances of stress. The expert then can tender a professional opinion about the effect of the particular defendant's condition on her reasoning and judgment at the time of the occurrence.

Paragraph (a) will require a substantial modification in traditional questions asked of mental health or mental retardation professionals. For example, under existing practice if a jurisdiction utilizes the test of mental nonresponsibility [insanity] paralleling that in standard 7-6.1, counsel might ask an expert witness: "Is it your opinion that, as a result of mental disease or defect, defendant was unable to appreciate the wrongfulness of her conduct?" Standard 7-3.9(a), if implemented within that jurisdiction, would render that form of questioning improper, thereby freeing an expert witness from the burden of transforming clinical observations into legal conclusions or moral judgments. Thus, under the paragraph (a) approach, more focused questions would be posed to the professional regarding the effect of a defendant's mental disorder on perception or understanding of reality, judgment, insight, and the like. The jury, not the professional, would make the moral assessment of whether the impairments described by the witness rendered the defendant unable to appreciate the wrongfulness of conduct.

The scope of expert testimony varies according to context; there are at least four such contexts. First, professional evaluators should be permitted to address issues of fact in language congruent with or identical to that embodied in law or used daily by laypersons. Those issues are proper subjects for expert testimony if the basis for an opinion is within an expert's specialized knowledge. Accordingly, an expert may testify whether a defendant perceived a certain aspect of reality, was aware of a certain circumstance, or had a particular conscious purpose or belief, for example, that he or she was in danger of being attacked.

Second, some situations call for value judgments or conclusions of law, concerning which expert witnesses should not be permitted to testify. For example, they should be precluded from testifying that a confession was "voluntary" or "involuntary," whether a defendant's belief was "reasonable" or "unreasonable," or whether a reasonable or ordinary person in the same situation would or would not have behaved as a defendant did. Similarly, standard 7-6.6 specifically opposes expert testimony directly bearing on mental nonresponsibility [insanity] at the time of an alleged crime.[21]

Third, statutory language in some contexts appears to rest on common usage but does not. For example, in many jurisdictions the word *premeditation* does not require advanced reflection, as common usage suggests or implies. Well-informed mental health or mental retardation professionals know the legal meaning of the word and will not use it incompatibly with the legal meaning. If an uninformed expert witness uses such a term, unaware of its legal meaning, a court should sustain an objection by opposing counsel because the witness's reliance on a legal term to convey a nonlegal meaning might mislead the jury.

Fourth, there are many situations in which a term does not fall clearly within a legal or nonlegal usage category, for example, the words *appreciate* and *mental disease* in the proposed mental nonresponsibility defense test of standard 7-6.1.[22] As another illustration, a strong argument can be made that "present mental competence" is a question of law requiring a value judgment. Therefore, professional witnesses arguably should limit their expert opinions to a defendant's understanding of criminal charges or ability to assist counsel. However, many courts and attorneys prefer that professional evaluators be permitted to state an opinion on the ultimate issue of competence. Although the standards in part IV do not specifically address the problem in the context of expert testimony, standard 7-4.5(a) takes the position that mental health or mental retardation professionals performing competency evaluations should reach a conclu-

---

21. The American Psychiatric Association is not opposed to a restriction on psychiatric testimony about ultimate legal issues concerning the defense of mental nonresponsibility [insanity]. AMERICAN PSYCHIATRIC ASSOCIATION STATEMENT ON THE INSANITY DEFENSE 18 (1982).

22. *See* commentary to standard 7-6.6, note 59 and accompanying text.

sion on that issue before addressing treatment or habilitation. Evaluators testifying at competency hearings should testify in a factual format most likely to provide courts with the clinical information necessary to a proper adjudication.[23] Because in almost all jurisdictions courts and not juries decide issues of present mental competency, there is little danger that expert opinion evidence on the ultimate issue will exert undue influence on its resolution by a trial judge. In the same way, a court may allow a mental health or mental retardation professional to express an opinion that an offender or prisoner is severely mentally disabled and requires treatment or habilitation in a mental health or mental retardation facility.[24]

Expertise of Mental Health and Mental Retardation Professionals on Future Mental Condition

Paragraph (b) advocates severe restrictions on the admissibility of mental health and mental retardation professional testimony on future mental condition or behavior. *Descriptive* data based on clinical observations and behavioral studies is admissible, but expert witnesses should not be permitted to predict an individual's future dangerousness.

In *Barefoot v. Estelle,*[25] the United States Supreme Court ruled that the Constitution does not preclude psychiatrists from testifying as expert witnesses and making predictions about defendants' potential future dangerousness at death penalty hearings. The *Barefoot* majority relied in part on existing rules of evidence that permit relevant evidence to be admitted, but that leave the determination of its weight to the factfinder in light of impeaching cross-examination and conflicting evidence presented by the opposing party.[26] Although in paragraph (b) the Association recommends the adoption of a more restrictive rule than the due process minimum embodied in the *Barefoot* decision, it conforms to and reflects a logical application of existing rules of evidence. It represents an application of the *Frye* test:[27] Because the relevant scientific community acknowledges the lack of a valid, reliable predictive technology, expert

23. *See* commentary to standard 7-4.8, notes 7-8 and accompanying text.

24. Standards 7-9.9(e) and 7-10.5(b) specifically permit such expert opinion testimony.

25. 463 U.S. 880 (1983).

26. *Id.* at 898-899.

27. *See supra,* notes 7-13 and accompanying text. *See also* Slobogin, *Dangerousness and Expertise,* 133 U. Pa. L. Rev. 97, 137-148 (1984). In United States v. Martin-Trigona, 767 F.2d 35 (2d Cir. 1985), the court held that the Bail Reform Act of 1984, 18 U.S.C.A. §3142(f) (Supp. 1986), does not allow a court to order a psychiatric examination to be performed on a defendant to formulate a prediction of future dangerousness.

testimony predicting a person's future mental condition or behavior should be inadmissible because it does not lie within the "specialized knowledge" of a mental health or mental retardation expert witness. The mental health and mental retardation professions themselves recognize the invalidity of predictions of long-term future dangerousness. In an American Psychiatric Association *amicus* brief submitted to the Supreme Court in the *Barefoot* case, the organization stated,

> Although psychiatric assessments may permit short-term predictions of violent or assaultive behavior, medical knowledge has simply not advanced to the point where long-term predictions — the type of testimony at issue in this case — may be made with even reasonable accuracy. The large body of research in this area indicates that, even under the best of conditions, psychiatric predictions of long-term future dangerousness are wrong in at least two out of every three cases.[28]

28. Amicus Curiae Brief for the American Psychiatric Association at 8-9, Barefoot v. Estelle, 463 U.S. 880 (1983) [hereinafter cited as APA *Barefoot* Amicus Brief].

The APA *amicus* brief cited a 1974 study conducted by an Association task force, which concluded that "judgments concerning the long-run potential for future violence and the 'dangerousness' of a given individual are 'fundamentally of very low reliability.' " *Id.* at 12 (citing American Psychiatric Association Task Force on Clinical Aspects of the Violent Individual, Clinical Aspects of the Violent Individual 23 (1974)). It also relied on a more recent study by Professor John Monahan reviewing all major research published in the 1970s. *Id.* at 13 (citing J. Monahan, The Clinical Prediction of Violent Behavior (1981) [hereinafter cited as J. Monahan]). Professor Monahan found that psychiatric procedures and techniques had not succeeded in reducing the high rate of "false positive" predictions, *i.e.*, affirmative predictions of future violent behavior that are subsequently proven erroneous. He concluded, "[T]he best clinical research currently in existence indicates that psychiatrists and psychologists are accurate in no more than one out of three predictions of violent behavior over a several-year period . . ." J. Monahan, *supra*, at 49.

On the ability of mental health and mental retardation professionals to make valid predictions of dangerousness, see Dix, *Expert Prediction Testimony in Capital Sentencing: Evidentiary and Constitutional Considerations*, 19 Am. Crim. L. Rev. 1 (1981) [hereinafter cited as Dix, *Expert Prediction Testimony*]; Dix, *Clinical Evaluation of the "Dangerousness" of "Normal" Criminal Defendants*, 66 Va. L. Rev. 523, 532-544 (1980) [hereinafter cited as Dix, *Clinical Evaluation*]; Schwitzgebel, *Prediction of Dangerousness and Its Implications for Treatment*, in W. Curran & C. Petty, Modern Legal Medicine, Psychiatry and Forensic Medicine 784 (1980). *See also* sources cited in Bonnie & Slobogin, *supra* note 4, at 431 n.6; Steadman & Cocozza, *Psychiatry, Dangerousness, and the Repetitively Violent Offender*, 69 J. Crim. L. & Criminology 226, 229-231 (1978); Ennis & Litwack, *Psychiatry and the Presumption of Expertise: Flipping Coins in the Courtroom*, 62 Calif. L. Rev. 693 (1974); Weiner, *Mental Disability and the Criminal Law*, in The Mentally Disabled and the Law 693, 735-736 (S. Brakel, J. Parry & B. Weiner eds., 3d ed. 1985) [hereinafter cited as Weiner]; Wenck, Robison & Smith, *Can Violence Be Predicted?*, 18 Crime & Delinq. 393 (1972).

Mental health and mental retardation professional testimony regarding the long-term dangerousness of a particular individual is not only of little or no probative value but also is highly prejudicial.[29]

The public erroneously believes that mental health and mental retardation professionals have a special expertise to predict dangerousness.[30] Because their testimony is offered as "expert" opinion, "an aura of scientific infallibility may shroud the evidence and thus lead the jury to accept it without critical scrutiny."[31] As Justice Blackmun commented in his

---

Justice Blackmun, dissenting in *Barefoot,* noted: "Neither the Court nor the State of Texas has cited a single reputable scientific source contradicting the *unanimous conclusion* of professionals in this field that psychiatric predictions of long-term future violence are wrong more often than they are right." Barefoot v. Estelle, 463 U.S. 880, 921 (1983) (Blackmun, J., dissenting) (emphasis added). Among the relevant "scientific" literature on prediction of behavior are JUDGMENT UNDER UNCERTAINTY: HEURISTICS AND BIASES (D. Kahneman, P. Slovic & A. Tversky eds. 1982); R. NISBETT & L. ROSS, HUMAN INFERENCES: STRATEGIES AND SHORTCOMINGS OF SOCIAL JUDGMENT (1980); I. JANIS & L. MANN, DECISION MAKING: A PSYCHOLOGICAL ANALYSIS OF CONFLICT, CHOICE, AND COMMITMENT (1977); P. MEEHL, CLINICAL VS. STATISTICAL PREDICTION (1955); Kahneman & Tversky, *On the Psychology of Prediction,* 80 PSYCHOLOGICAL REV. 237 (1973).

In 1980, the American Psychiatric Association concluded, "The professional literature uniformly establishes that such predictions are fundamentally of very low reliability, and that psychiatric testimony and expertise are irrelevant to such predictions. In view of these findings, psychiatric testimony on the issue of future criminal behavior only distorts the factfinding process." Amicus Curiae Brief for American Psychiatric Association on Appellant's Petition for Rehearing at 8, Byers v. United States, No. 78-1451 (D.C. Cir., slip opinion, Dec. 24, 1980, as amended June 1, 1981).

29. In People v. Murtishaw, 29 Cal. 3d 733, 631 P.2d 446, 175 Cal. Rptr. 738 (1981), the California Supreme Court excluded a psychopharmacologist's testimony regarding defendant's propensity for future violence. It noted,

> In view of the unreliability of that forecast, however, the probative value of that testimony is far outweighed by its prejudicial impact. One can imagine few matters more prejudicial at the penalty trial than testimony from an established and credentialed expert that defendant, if sentenced to life without possibility of parole, would be likely to kill again.

Id. at 773, 631 P.2d at 470, 175 Cal. Rptr. at 762 (footnote omitted).

30. Barefoot v. Estelle, 463 U.S. 880, 926-927 (1983) (Blackmun, J., dissenting).

31. Gianelli, *The Admissibility of Novel Scientific Evidence:* Frye v. United States, *A Half Century Later,* 80 COLUM. L. REV. 1197, 1237 (1980). *See also* Imwinkelried, *Evidence Law and Tactics for the Proponents of Scientific and Expert Evidence,* in SCIENTIFIC AND EXPERT EVIDENCE 33 (E. Imwinkelried ed. 1981).

The position of the American Psychiatric Association is as follows:

> [P]sychiatric predictions of violent conduct unduly facilitate a jury's finding of future dangerousness by providing a clinical explanation for what is, at best, only an

Barefoot dissent, defense cross-examination of expert witnesses and proffers of rebuttal witnesses are not adequate antidotes to the admission of professional "expert" opinion that a defendant is dangerous.[32] For example, a reputable defense expert can state only an opinion that all predictions of dangerousness are unreliable, but cannot predict with confidence that a defendant will *not* be violent.[33]

If a trier of fact is required by statute to determine an individual's future dangerousness, some courts have been reluctant to exclude mental health and mental retardation professional testimony on the issue. Thus, one court recharacterized the testimony of a professional on a defendant's "dangerousness" as a statement of *present* mental condition rather than a prediction of *future* propensity toward violence.[34] The characterization is, of course, dubious. It should be emphasized that the trier of fact will still have before it the best evidence available on the issue — the offender's earlier behavior and relevant data concerning factors found to have predictive significance in the scientific literature. It should be noted also that the evidentiary problems associated with predictions could be erased by eliminating future dangerousness as a statutory aggravating factor and by focusing instead on demonstrated dangerous activity in the

---

> assessment of statistical probabilities. A medical diagnosis of antisocial personality disorder is in essence a descriptive label for past aberrant behavior of a particular type. When stated to a jury, however, the term "sociopath" (or "antisocial personality disorder") conveys the erroneous impression of an endogenous disorder which bears a cause-and-effect relationship to similar, future behavior. Medical opinions in this area thus offer the jury a seductively facile — but wholly unfounded — explanation as to why a particular individual having the statistical "symptoms" of a recidivist will in fact be a recidivist. Psychiatrists testifying on the question of future dangerousness, in other words, tend to particularize actuarial data in a manner not permitted by the data themselves. The jury is told, in effect, that the defendant not only has the statistically relevant characteristics of persons who commit multiple criminal acts, but that he *is* such a person.

APA *Barefoot* Amicus Brief, *supra* note 28, at 17.

32. Barefoot v. Estelle, 463 U.S. 880, 930-931, 934 (1983) (Blackmun, J., dissenting).

33. "Given a choice between an expert who says that he can predict with a certainty that the defendant, whether confined in prison or free in society, will kill again, and an expert who says merely that no such prediction can be made, members of the jury charged by law with making the prediction surely will be tempted to opt for the expert who claims he can help them in performing their duty, and who predicts dire consequences if the defendant is not put to death." *Id.* at 934.

34. People v. Henderson, 107 Cal. App. 3d 475, 166 Cal. Rptr. 20 (1980).

past.[35] In this respect, however, the Association takes no position on the advisability of the death penalty or its predicates.[36]

Paragraph (b) neither affirms nor disclaims the propriety of descriptive expert testimony that a person was diagnosed as having a particular mental disorder or disability, as long as it is not coupled with a prediction of future dangerousness. Thus, an expert witness should not be allowed to testify that a defendant was diagnosed as having a particular mental disorder and that because of it he or she is dangerous.[37] However, for the circumscribed descriptive purposes permitted in paragraph (b), a professional expert should be permitted to use standard psychiatric and psychological nomenclature to delineate the clinical diagnosis, provided the testimony is relevant to the litigation.

---

35. The American Psychiatric Association listed the most reliable predictors of long-term future violent behavior as "an individual's past history of violent criminal behavior . . . ; age (a disproportionate amount of violent crime is committed by persons between ages fifteen and twenty); sex (nearly 90 percent of all persons arrested for violent crimes are male); and race (blacks account for 46 percent of all arrests for violent crime). Still other factors characteristic of criminal recidivists are a history of drug or alcohol addiction and persistent unemployment. Significantly, one factor which demonstrably *fails* to correlate with recurring criminal activity is mental illness." APA *Barefoot* Amicus Brief, *supra* note 28, at 14-15 (footnotes omitted) (emphasis in original). Paragraph (b) permits mental health and mental retardation professionals to inform the decisionmaker of the existence and findings of this research.

36. A decision to preclude mental health and mental retardation professional predictions of future dangerousness does not compel a reconsideration of the constitutional acceptability of "dangerousness" as a criterion for imposing the death penalty. In Jurek v. Texas, 428 U.S. 262 (1976), the Supreme Court ruled that a state may impose the death penalty upon a prediction of future dangerousness and that lay testimony may be sufficient to support the finding of dangerousness. If paragraph (b) is adopted, lay testimony can continue to be used to support these decisions. As Justice Blackmun commented in Barefoot v. Estelle, 463 U.S. 880, 922 (1983) (Blackmun, J., dissenting), "A layman with access to relevant statistics can do at least as well and possibly better [in predicting long-term future dangerousness]; psychiatric training is not relevant to the factors that validly can be employed to make such predictions, and psychiatrists consistently err on the side of overpredicting violence." On the impact of mental incompetency on administration of the death penalty, *see* Weiner, *supra* note 28, at 706-707.

37. The use of a clinical diagnosis to predict future dangerousness has been severely criticized. *See, e.g.*, Dix, *Clinical Evaluation*, *supra* note 29, at 550-573; Dix, *The Death Penalty, "Dangerousness," Psychiatric Testimony, and Professional Ethics*, 5 AM. J. CRIM. L. 151, 177-192 (1977). The American Psychiatric Association has concluded "that no mental illness or disorder — antisocial personality disorder included — is reliably predictive of future violent or assaultive behavior." APA *Barefoot* Amicus Brief, *supra* note 28, at 19 n.16.

Paragraph (b) opposes the use of expert testimony bearing on a particular defendant's future dangerousness in any sentencing hearing or other criminal proceeding and in special commitment hearings involving defendants found mentally nonresponsible [insane] under the criminal law.[38]

Standard 7-3.10. Evaluations of a person's mental condition: qualifications for court appointed evaluators

Evaluations by mental health and mental retardation professionals can contribute important information in cases that involve a person's mental condition. Accordingly, no professional should be appointed by the court to evaluate a person's mental condition unless the court determines that the professional's qualifications include:

(a) sufficient professional education and sufficient clinical training and experience to establish the clinical knowledge required for the specific type(s) of evaluation(s) being conducted; and,

(b) sufficient forensic knowledge, gained through specialized training or an acceptable substitute therefor, necessary for understanding the relevant legal matter(s) and for satisfying the specific purpose(s) for which the evaluation is being ordered.

Commentary Introduction

Standard 7-3.10 addresses the qualifications of mental health and mental retardation professionals to serve as court-appointed evaluators. To be a court-appointed evaluator, a professional should have both clinical and forensic knowledge necessary to perform an adequate evaluation.

38. Because a special commitment hearing requires the factfinder to predict dangerousness, the Standing Committee considered a proposal that would have permitted expert opinion on the issue if an expert specifically identified the factors tending to enhance or diminish the likelihood that dangerous behavior will occur. Nevertheless, the committee rejected even that restricted an opinion because such a prediction is not within the scope of expert specialized knowledge.

Related Standards

ABA, Standards for Criminal Justice 7-3.11, 7-3.12

Commentary

Standard 7-3.10 confirms a court's obligation to ensure that mental health and mental retardation professionals appointed to evaluate mental condition possess the expertise requisite for a competent evaluation. A court must be satisfied that an evaluator's professional education, training, and experience are sufficient to ensure a clinically sound evaluation. An evaluator also must be conversant with legal concepts on which an evaluation order rests and be able to formulate an opinion relevant to them. Thus, a prerequisite to appointment as a professional evaluator to assess a person's present mental condition must be an understanding of the jurisdiction's legal standard for present mental competency. Knowledge of the jurisdiction's test for mental nonresponsibility [insanity] is likewise indispensable to a court appointment to reconstruct a defendant's mental state at the time of an alleged offense. Ideally, evaluators will have acquired the requisite forensic knowledge through formalized training courses, but they can obtain it in other ways and yet qualify for court appointments.[1]

Standard 7-3.11. Expert witnesses: qualifications for testifying about a person's mental condition

(a) Qualifications. Expert opinion testimony about a person's mental condition is designed to assist the trial factfinder. Because such testimony often assumes extraordinary importance in cases that involve a person's mental condition, no witness should be qualified by the court to present expert opinion testimony on a person's mental condition unless the court determines that the witness:

1. The forensic knowledge requirement is discussed in greater detail at commentary to standard 7-3.11, notes 2-4 and accompanying text. Nonphysician mental health and mental retardation professionals who possess the requisite clinical and forensic knowledge may qualify for court appointment as evaluators of a person's mental condition. *See* commentary to standard 7-3.12, notes 4-6 and accompanying text.

(i) has sufficient professional education and sufficient clinical training and experience to establish the clinical knowledge required to formulate an expert opinion; and,

(ii) has either:

(A) acquired sufficient knowledge, through forensic training or an acceptable substitute therefor, relevant to conducting the specific type(s) of mental evaluation actually conducted in the case, and relevant to the substantive law concerning the specific matter(s) on which expert opinion is to be proffered; or,

(B) has had a professional therapeutic or habilitative relationship with the person whose mental condition is in question; and,

(iii) has performed an adequate evaluation, including a personal interview with the individual whose mental condition is in question, relevant to the legal and clinical matter(s) upon which the witness is being called to testify.

(b) Related standard. This standard refers only to qualifications for expert witnesses testifying about a person's mental condition. Qualifications for expert witnesses testifying on matters of present scientific or clinical knowledge are governed by standard 7-3.13.

Commentary Introduction

Standard 7-3.11 establishes the qualifications of mental health and mental retardation professionals to serve as expert witnesses testifying on mental condition. Three criteria must be met: (1) sufficient education and clinical training; (2) specialized knowledge regarding the professional and legal matters on which an expert will testify; and (3) performance of an adequate evaluation.

Related Standards

ABA, Standards for Criminal Justice 7-1.3(d), 7-3.10, 7-3.12

American Psychiatric Association, The Principles of Medical Ethics with Annotations Especially Applicable to Psychiatry §2, annotation 3; §7, annotations 3, 4

American Psychological Association, Standards for Providers of Psychological Services 1.5, 1.6, and definition of "Professional Psychologist"

American Psychological Association, Specialty Guidelines for the Delivery of Services by Clinical Psychologists 1.5, 1.6

American Psychological Association, Specialty Guidelines for the Delivery of Services by Counseling Psychologists 1.5, 1.6

American Psychological Association, Specialty Guidelines for the Delivery of Services by School Psychologists 1.5, 1.6

Commentary

The standard advocates changes in legal traditions governing the qualification of expert witnesses and court-appointed evaluators. Traditionally, only minimum educational qualifications have been expected of mental health or mental retardation professionals. However, "the scope of the training of the [mental health or mental retardation professional] is of critical importance [and] many factors other than academic degrees go to the admissibility and weight of the expert testimony."[1] Under standard 7-3.11 three criteria should be established by rule or statute before courts permit mental health or mental retardation professionals to testify as expert witnesses.

First, a professional should meet certain clinical educational and training requirements more stringent than an academic degree alone. Thus, a mental health professional whose training has been limited to evaluating mental illness should not be permitted to testify as an expert in a case involving a mentally retarded defendant.

Second, a professional should have acquired forensic knowledge on the substantive and procedural legal principles to which expert testimony will relate and should have acquired forensic knowledge in relation to them, based on education, training, and experience. To illustrate, a mental health or mental retardation professional expert witness, clinically trained to do a reconstructive evaluation of a person's mental condition at some time in the past, should have acquired sufficient training and experience regarding the legal test for mental nonresponsibility [insanity] in the jurisdiction.

Third, a mental health or mental retardation professional should have conducted a thorough evaluation, including a personal interview, with the subject of expert opinion evidence if he or she is to be considered qualified to testify as an expert.

1. Jenkins v. United States, 307 F.2d 637, 650 (D.C. Cir. 1962) (Burger, J., concurring).

Standard 7-3.11, if implemented, should ensure that only qualified mental health and mental retardation professionals are permitted to testify as expert witnesses. Although some commentators have responded to public concern over the quality of mental health and mental retardation professional testimony by recommending a comprehensive ban on that form of expert opinion evidence, standard 7-3.11 is premised on a belief that properly educated and trained mental health and mental retardation professionals can provide useful testimony in the course of criminal proceedings.

The Forensic Knowledge Requirement

It is unethical for psychiatrists to practice outside their area of expertise.[2] The American Psychological Association requires its members to maintain currency in developments directly related to the services they render[3] and to limit their practices to their demonstrated areas of professional competence.[4] If psychiatrists, psychologists, and other mental health or mental retardation professionals are to meet the ethical requirements of their professions as they serve as evaluators and expert witnesses, programs must be developed to ensure that they receive the necessary forensic knowledge. Professional and graduate schools are encouraged under standard 7-1.3(d)(ii) to provide advanced instruction to mental health and mental retardation professional students wishing to qualify as expert witnesses or court-appointed evaluators.[5] Regrettably,

2. American Psychiatric Association, Principles of Medical Ethics with Annotations Especially Applicable to Psychiatry §2, annotation 3 (1981).

3. American Psychological Association, Standards for Providers of Psychological Services 1.5 (1981); American Psychological Association, *Specialty Guidelines for the Delivery of Services by Clinical Psychologists* 1.5, 36 Am. Psychologist 640, 644 (1981); American Psychological Association, *Specialty Guidelines for the Delivery of Services by Counseling Psychologists* 1.5, 36 Am. Psychologist 652, 656 (1981); American Psychological Association, *Specialty Guidelines for the Delivery of Services by School Psychologists* 1.5, 36 Am. Psychologist 670, 674 (1981).

4. American Psychological Association, Standards for Providers of Psychological Services 1.6 (1981); American Psychological Association, *Specialty Guidelines for the Delivery of Services by Clinical Psychologists* 1.6, 36 Am. Psychologist 640, 644 (1981); American Psychological Association, *Specialty Guidelines for the Delivery of Services by Counseling Psychologists* 1.6, 36 Am. Psychologist 652, 656 (1981).

5. A recently conducted pilot project of the Forensic Evaluation Training and Research Center of the University of Virginia may well serve as an appropriate model for such programs. In the Virginia program, participants received thirty-one hours of instruction

specialized forensic training is not available today at most schools.[6] Therefore, although both standards 7-3.10(b) and 7-3.11(a)(ii)(A) advocate a requirement of professional forensic training, it need not be acquired solely through specialized forensic training offered by academic institutions.

Necessary forensic knowledge turns on the subject matter of an evaluation and the legal purpose for which an expert opinion is sought. For example, if a defendant has pleaded mental nonresponsibility [insanity], an expert requested only to discuss in clinical terms a diagnosis of mental disorder need know only the legal meaning of the term *mental disease or defect* in the test of mental nonresponsibility [insanity]. If, however, an evaluator is expected to relate the clinical diagnosis to other legal issues arising from the defense, greater forensic knowledge is required. If expert opinion does not relate to a person's mental condition, but is limited

---

devoted to the following topics: The Legal System: Sources of Law and Legal Procedure (2 hours); Application of the Fifth Amendment to the Forensic Process (1 hour); The Imprecision of the Behavioral Sciences: Implications for the Forensic Specialist (1 hour); Competency to Stand Trial: Legal and Clinical Considerations (6 hours); Mental State at the Time of the Offense: Insanity, Diminished Capacity and Automatism (6 hours); Evaluating Mental State at the Time of the Offense: The Screening Evaluation (2 hours); Comprehensive Evaluations: Information Gathering, Psychological Testing, Interview Technique (3 hours); Sentencing: Legal Considerations (1 hour); Amenability to Treatment and Predictions of Dangerousness (3 hours); Juvenile Courts (2 hours); Report Writing (1 hour); and Expert Testimony and Consultation with the Courts (3 hours). University of Virginia Institute of Law, Psychiatry and Public Policy, Annual Report of Forensic Evaluation Training and Research Center, Appendix 6, A-17 (June 30, 1982).

Four to eight weeks after completion of the program, trainees were examined through eighty multiple-choice questions divided equally among the following five topics: general forensic issues; competency to stand trial; mental state at the time of the offense; sentencing issues; and juvenile law. The mean score of trainees was significantly higher than that achieved by control subjects (who were comparable to the actual trainees except for their lack of specific training). *Id.* at 17. The examination, except for items covering Virginia law, was administered to fifty-three judges throughout the United States. Surprisingly, "[i]t was found that the trainees performed better than did the judges on each section of the examination. . . ." *Id.* at 18.

6. For example, a recent survey of graduate psychology departments revealed that only 23 percent offered at least one graduate level course in which at least half the content focused on the relationship between psychology and the law, legal system, or legal process. Grisso, Sales, & Bayless, *Law Related Courses and Programs in Graduate Psychology Departments*, 37 Am. Psychologist 267 (1982). Even when law-related training was offered, many of the courses did not discuss the defense of mental nonresponsibility [insanity], competency to stand trial, criminal procedure, or psychologists as expert witnesses. *Id.* at 276.

to an issue of present scientific or clinical knowledge, forensic experience is not required and the professional can qualify as an expert under standard 7-3.13.

As noted, professionals should be able to qualify as expert witnesses on the basis of requisite forensic knowledge under standard 7-3.11, whether or not such knowledge was acquired through specialized forensic training programs. A measure of flexibility in that respect should encourage broad participation by professionals in the criminal justice process and should forestall the creation of a guild of professional evaluators and expert witnesses.

A requirement of forensic knowledge should not govern if a professional treatment or habilitative relationship exists with a person whose mental condition is at issue. All the other requirements set forth in standard 7-3.11 should be fulfilled in such an instance, however.

The Requirement of a Personal Interview

The position of the Association expressed in subparagraph (a)(iii) is that a personal interview with the subject of expert testimony must be a prerequisite to qualification as a mental health or mental retardation expert witness. Implementation of the standard would work a major departure from existing practice. The commentary to rule 703 of the Federal Rules of Evidence states that expert opinions may be derived from three possible sources: firsthand observation by an expert witness, data presented at trial, and data provided to an expert outside of court.[7] Subparagraph (a)(iii) does not recognize presentation of data at trial as a sufficient basis alone for an expert opinion.

Two techniques have been recognized by courts as sufficient to generate an expert opinion despite the absence of a personal interview with the subject of expert testimony. The first is to allow hypothetical questions as a basis for mental health or mental retardation expert opinion; the lack of a personal interview with a defendant goes only to the weight and not the admissibility of opinion evidence.[8] The second is to permit expert testimony based on a witness's courtroom observations. The premise re-

7. Fed. R. Evid. 703, Notes of Advisory Committee on Proposed Rules.

8. *See, e.g.*, State v. Skaggs, 120 Ariz. 467, 586 P.2d 1279 (1978); People v. Bassett, 69 Cal. 2d 122, 443 P.2d 777, 70 Cal. Rptr. 193 (1968); People v. Phillips, 122 Cal. App. 3d 69, 175 Cal. Rptr. 703 (1981); People v. Ryan, 140 Cal. App. 2d 412, 295 P.2d 496 (1956); Commonwealth v. Burke, 376 Mass. 539, 382 N.E.2d 192 (1978); State v. Baker, 120 N.H. 773, 424 A.2d 171 (1980); State v. Edmon, 28 Wash. App. 98, 621 P.2d 1310 (1981).

flected in subparagraph (a)(iii) is that neither alternative provides an acceptable basis for expert opinion testimony; a personal interview is viewed as indispensable.[9] In adopting that premise, the Association endorses ethical principles recognized by the American Psychiatric Association.[10] In addition, under the *Frye* test for admissibility of scientific expert opinion evidence,[11] purported expert opinions based solely on hypothetical questions and courtroom observations, without earlier personal interviews, should be rejected because the data relied on to found such opinion testimony are of a type not relied on by mental health or mental retardation experts as a basis for a scientifically acceptable diagnosis or evaluation.[12]

---

9. As one court noted, "Expert testimony without personal knowledge is 'the weakest and most unreliable kind of evidence in respect to the sanity or insanity of the person inquired about.'" Zirt v. Pollack, 25 A.D.2d 920, 270 N.Y.S.2d 85, 87 (1966) (*quoting* Dobie v. Armstrong, 27 A.D. 520, 526-527, 50 N.Y.S. 801 (1898), *aff'd*, 160 N.Y. 584, 55 N.E. 302 (1899)).

10. Two annotations from the American Psychiatric Association Principles of Medical Ethics support the personal interview requirement of subparagraph (a)(iii). It is unethical for a psychiatrist to offer a professional opinion concerning a person who is "in the light of public attention," in the absence of a personal examination. American Psychiatric Association, Principles of Medical Ethics with Annotations Especially Applicable to Psychiatry §7, annotation 3 (1981). Arguably, every criminal defendant placed on trial fits that requirement. APA further expects a "personal examination" before a psychiatrist may certify a person for involuntary treatment. *Id.* at annotation 4. Although that standard was developed in the context of civil commitment, it should govern with equal or greater force decisions relating to criminal responsibility and involuntary confinement as an aftermath to acquittals based on mental nonresponsibility [insanity].

11. Frye v. United States, 293 F. 1013 (D.C. Cir. 1923). *See* commentary to standard 7-3.9, notes 9-13 and accompanying text.

12. In Barefoot v. Estelle, 463 U.S. 880, *reh'g denied*, 464 U.S. 874 (1983), two psychiatrists were permitted to express expert opinions that Barefoot suffered from "sociopathy" or an "antisocial personality disorder" based on hypothetical questions. In its *amicus* brief to the United States Supreme Court, the American Psychiatric Association stated,

> [S]uch a diagnosis simply cannot be made on the basis of a hypothetical question. Absent an in-depth psychiatric examination and evaluation, the psychiatrist cannot exclude alternative diagnoses; nor can he assure that the necessary criteria for making the diagnosis in question are met. As a result, he is unable to render a medical opinion with a reasonable degree of certainty.

Amicus Curiae Brief for the American Psychiatric Association at 9, Barefoot v. Estelle, 463 U.S. 880, *reh'g denied*, 464 U.S. 874 (1983). The diagnostic technique is essentially an inductive process in which a professional builds on answers to past questions in a search for crucial additional data confirming or excluding explanations for an individual's behavior. *Id.* at 20. Thus, APA concluded that deficiencies in psychiatric testimony

Although the Supreme Court has not imposed a constitutional barrier to the use of hypothetical questions on which expert opinions are based,[13] courts[14] and commentators[15] have recognized the desirability, if not the necessity, of a personal evaluation. The Association recommends in this standard a general adoption of that view: Hypothetical questions, observations of courtroom behavior and testimony, or perusals of interview records prepared by other mental health or mental retardation professionals are not adequate substitutes for personal evaluation.[16] Only through evaluations that include personal interviews can professionals

---

> will not be cured by improving or expanding on the hypothetical question format. . . . It is inconceivable that the record in a criminal case can contain the type of diagnostic data needed to construct a hypothetical that would allow the rendering of a valid psychiatric opinion concerning antisocial personality disorder or related illnesses.

Id. at 25.

13. Barefoot v. Estelle, 463 U.S. 880, 904-905, *reh'g denied*, 464 U.S. 874 (1983).

14. Chief Judge David L. Bazelon described a personal interview as "the basic tool of psychiatric study." Rollerson v. United States, 343 F.2d 269, 274 (D.C. Cir. 1964) (citing texts and articles). To reconstruct a defendant's mental condition at the time of an alleged crime, hours of interviewing, tests, and acquisition of other materials are required. *Ibid.* In United States v. Albright, 388 F.2d 719 (4th Cir. 1968), the court commented that "medical science . . . deems [courtroom observations and hypothetical questions] poor and unsatisfactory substitutes for testimony based upon prolonged and intimate interviews between the psychiatrist and the defendant." *Id.* at 725. The Hawaii Supreme Court noted that the needed rapport between an interviewer and an interviewed person cannot be achieved through viewing a defendant undergoing cross-examination. State v. Kim, 64 Haw. 598, 645 P.2d 1330 (1982).

15. Doctor Bernard Diamond and Professor David Louisell have characterized clinical testimony in response to hypothetical questions as "of doubtful worth and often of dubious ethical quality." Diamond & Louisell, *The Psychiatrist as an Expert Witness: Some Ruminations and Speculations*, 63 MICH. L. REV. 1335, 1347 (1965).

16. *See* Hyler, Williams & Spitzer, *Reliability in the DSM-III Field Trials*, 39 ARCHIVES GEN. PSYCHIATRY 1275 (1982). The study showed that the reliability of the major diagnostic classes of DSM-III was higher when diagnoses were made from live interviews than when they were based on case summaries.

The American Psychiatric Association has noted that hypothetical questions may be appropriate if an expert witness has conducted a personal interview with a person to whom expert opinion evidence relates, for purposes of clarifying the bases for expert testimony and testing the significance of altered assumed facts to the witness's expert conclusions. Attorneys arguably may use them also under standard 7-3.9(b)(ii), relating to scientific studies involving the relationship between specific behaviors and variables that are objectively measurable and verifiable. Letter from Robert Luskin, Esq. to Standing Committee Director (March 29, 1985) (presenting the APA view).

acquire the necessary basis to formulate expert opinions about defendants' mental condition.[17]

Standard 7-3.12. Establishing minimum professional education and clinical training requirements for evaluators and expert witnesses; recommended requirements

(a) Responsibility of jurisdictions to establish education and training requirements. Evaluators appointed under standard 7-3.10 and witnesses qualified under standard 7-3.11 play important roles in cases that involve a person's mental condition. The development of high and uniform education and training standards for professionals performing in these capacities will enhance the administration of justice. Accordingly, every jurisdiction should establish, by statute, regulation, or court rule, minimum professional education and clinical training requirements necessary to qualify persons for the performance of such roles. Forensic knowledge requirements are governed by standards 7-3.10 and 7-3.11.

(b) Factors to be considered in developing education and training requirements. In developing such minimum requirements, jurisdictions should take the following general factors into consideration:

(i) Necessary and desirable education and training requirements should differ according to the specific subject matter of the evaluation(s) being performed and the specific legal purpose(s) for which expert opinion is being solicited; and,

(ii) Sufficient flexibility should be provided to permit the courts to utilize persons who clearly demonstrate the requisite knowledge notwithstanding their lack of the formal education or training that may be specified in the requirements. However, experience in performing evaluations or in testifying as an expert should not, by itself, constitute a sufficient demonstration of the requisite clinical knowledge.

(c) Recommended education and training requirements. In establishing minimum professional education and clinical training re-

17. Bonnie & Slobogin, *The Role of Mental Health Professionals in the Criminal Process: The Case for Informed Speculation*, 66 Va. L. Rev. 427, 496 (1980).

quirements, each jurisdiction should strive for the highest possible qualifications and should adopt the following recommended minimum requirements or such higher requirements as may be feasible and appropriate:

(i) When an evaluation concerns a person's present mental competence, including issues governed by standard 7-4.9(a), or other matters concerning mental condition at the time of the evaluation, or a person's need for treatment or habilitation, evaluators and expert witnesses should be either:

(A) a licensed physician who has successfully completed at least two years of postdoctoral specialty training in a psychiatric residency program approved by the American Board of Psychiatry and Neurology (or one year of internship and one year of such residency training); or,

(B) a clinical, counseling, or school psychologist who has received a doctoral degree in psychology from an educational institution accredited by an organization recognized by the Council on Postsecondary Accreditation, and who is licensed or certified as a psychologist if the jurisdiction requires licensure or certification for that discipline; or,

(C) a clinical social worker who has received a master's degree in social work with an emphasis on clinical practice from an educational institution accredited by the Council on Social Work Education, and who has completed a minimum of two years or three thousand hours of postgraduate supervised clinical experience in the diagnosis, assessment, and treatment of mental disorders in an appropriate clinical setting, and who is licensed or certified as a social worker if the jurisdiction requires licensure or certification; or,

(D) a clinical specialist in psychiatric nursing or a psychiatric nurse, who has received a master's degree in psychiatric nursing from an educational institution accredited by an organization recognized by the National League of Nursing, and who is licensed or certified if the jurisdiction requires licensure or certification for the respective discipline.

(ii) When an evaluation concerns a person's mental condition at the time of an alleged crime, or a person's future mental condition or behavior when these issues arise within a sentencing proceeding or a special commitment proceeding held pursuant to standard

7-7.4 or standard 7-4.13, the evaluator or expert witness should be either:

(A) a licensed physician who has completed the postdoctoral specialty training in a psychiatric residency program approved by the American Board of Psychiatry and Neurology; or,

(B) a clinical or counseling psychologist who has received a doctoral degree in psychology from an educational institution accredited by an organization recognized by the Council on Postsecondary Accreditation, and who is licensed or certified as a psychologist if the jurisdiction requires licensure or certification.

(iii) A licensed physician who does not meet the requirements of specialty training in psychiatry established in this standard but who has completed the postdoctoral training requirements of another medical specialty, may, upon performing an adequate evaluation, qualify to testify as an expert witness regarding any physical condition or any organically based mental disability within the scope of the professional's specialized knowledge.

(iv) A certified special education teacher, speech or language pathologist, or an audiologist, who is licensed or certified if the jurisdiction requires licensure or certification for the respective discipline, may, upon performing an adequate evaluation, qualify to testify as an expert witness regarding a disability within the scope of the professional's specialized knowledge.

Commentary Introduction

Standard 7-3.12 urges the adoption of minimum clinical education and training requirements for expert witnesses and court-appointed evaluators, and offers a model for formulating those requirements.

Related Standards

ABA, Standards for Criminal Justice 7-3.10, 7-3.11, 7-4.8

Commentary

Paragraph (a) sets forth the principle that each jurisdiction should specify minimum professional education and clinical training requirements for persons serving as court-appointed evaluators and expert witnesses, applicable to criminal and criminal commitment proceedings governed by this chapter of the standards. Differing requirements, however, may be appropriate for such proceedings as sentencing hearings, depending on whether a court or jury makes the determination. The standard recognizes that education and training requirements cannot be uniform throughout the nation because the numbers and existing qualifications of mental health or mental retardation professionals vary widely; other factors such as urban and rural demography and geographical size of a jurisdiction also must be considered in setting standards for qualification.

Paragraph (b) recognizes that the subject matter of evaluations and the legal purposes for which expert opinions are solicited should be taken into account in formulating professional education and training requirements. Evaluations or expert opinions for one purpose may require different education and training than those for other purposes. Moreover, the standard advocates flexibility in administering education and training requirements, so that persons with demonstrably acceptable levels of knowledge are considered qualified even though they lack the formal education and training incorporated in statutes, regulations, or court rules.

Paragraph (c) presents an aspirational model of minimum requirements. The Association recognizes that formulating pattern statutes or codes is quite difficult, particularly in light of the diversity of American jurisdictions. Such proposals are vulnerable to criticism from the polar extremes of those who believe that too high a standard will result in a class of qualified professionals that will be unrealistically small and those who maintain that too low a standard will enable unqualified individuals to participate. The task of formulating criteria is complicated further if different education and training requirements govern separate types of evaluations. Nevertheless, despite these difficulties, the Association feels that the model incorporated in paragraph (c) is a proper starting point for implementation in various jurisdictions. The standards in part III can have a lasting impact only if courts and legislators acknowledge the inadequacy of existing standards governing professional evaluations and expert testimony and improve them as swiftly as possible.[1]

---

1. An earlier draft of this standard was reviewed by representatives of the American Psychiatric Association, American Academy of Psychiatry and the Law, National Mental Health Association, American Psychological Association, and National Federation of Societies for Clinical Social Work, Inc. Their comments on the preliminary draft were incorporated, to the extent the Standing Committee deemed them appropriate, in the Standards approved by the House of Delegates.

Traditionally, medically trained professionals have been responsible to diagnose and treat mental disorders; other mental health and mental retardation professionals have been required to function under the supervision of and to be answerable to physicians.[2] Dominance by the medical profession, however, has been challenged increasingly by psychologists and others who maintain that the judgments of nonphysician professionals ought not be subject to review and confirmation by medically trained professionals.[3] A constantly increasing number of courts have qualified psychologists and other nonphysicians as expert witnesses, reducing the legal barriers to nonmedical professional evaluations and expert testimony.[4] The recommended education and training requirements in paragraph (c) reflect the increasing status appropriately accorded nonmedically trained mental health and mental retardation professionals.[5]

Paragraph (c) assumes that assessments of competency or other issues of present mental condition may be made more easily than those requiring a reconstruction of mental condition at the time of an alleged crime

---

2. Dix & Poythress, *Propriety of Medical Dominance of Forensic Mental Health Practice: The Empirical Evidence,* 23 Ariz. L. Rev. 161, 962 (1981).

3. Dix and Poythress, after reviewing empirical evidence concerning educational background and demonstrated competence, concluded,

> The present state of the evidence confirms the desirability of changing existing legal barriers to encourage participation in forensic issues by nonphysician mental health professionals. The imposition of stringent limits upon nonphysician mental health professionals as expert witnesses and the limitation of the types of issues which they can address seem clearly unwarranted.

Id. at 987. The authors criticize legislation imposing lengthy experience requirements only on nonphysician professionals. *Ibid.*

4. The leading case is Jenkins v. United States, 307 F.2d 637 (D.C. Cir. 1962), in which the court ruled that the trial judge erred in refusing to qualify a psychologist as an expert witness solely on the ground that the witness was not medically trained. The appellate court reasoned that "a psychologist's competence to render an expert opinion based on his findings as to the presence or absence of mental disease or defect must depend upon the nature of his knowledge. It does not depend upon his claim to the title 'psychologist.' " *Id.* at 645. Because some psychologists have the necessary education and experience to advance an expert opinion of assistance to a jury, psychologists as a class cannot be automatically disqualified as expert witnesses. *Id.* at 646. *See generally* Perlin, *The Legal Status of the Psychologist in the Courtroom,* 4 Mental Disability L. Rptr. 194 (1980). "[L]egal barriers to testimony have virtually disappeared." *Id.* at 198. *But see* Morris & Sales, Psychological Testimony on the Insanity Defense: Report Prepared for the American Psychological Association Ad Hoc Committee on Legal Issues (1981) (based on statutes and case law, the status of psychologists in the courtroom is neither as secure nor as accepted as has been assumed).

5. *See generally* Ellis & Luckasson, *Mentally Retarded Criminal Defendants,* 53 Geo. Wash. L. Rev. 414, 484-491 (1985).

or a prediction of future mental condition or behavior. Therefore, it recommends fewer education and training requirements for assessments of present mental condition than for other evaluations, thereby enlarging the pool of potential evaluators and expert witnesses on competency questions. Evaluators qualified on these issues also may testify to the likelihood that a defendant will be restored to competence in the reasonably foreseeable future — an issue commonly addressed in competency evaluations.

Physicians performing present competency evaluations, according to paragraph (c), should have completed two years of postdoctoral specialty training in a psychiatric residency program. The first postdoctoral year, commonly known as the internship year, is insufficient to establish expertise for purposes of competency evaluations and expert opinion testimony because frequently it is focused on internal medicine. Clinical, counseling, and school psychologists with doctoral degrees should be considered qualified to perform competency evaluations,[6] which is the minimum professional qualification for independent practice. Clinical social workers and psychiatric nurses with master's degrees, which are generally accepted as the terminal degrees in those two professions, also should be viewed as qualified.

Only psychiatrists who have completed postdoctoral specialty training in a residency program approved by the American Board of Psychiatry and Neurology, and clinical or counseling psychologists with a doctorate in psychology from an educational institution accredited by an organization recognized by the Council on Post-Secondary Accreditation, should be considered competent as evaluators and expert witnesses on issues of past or future mental condition. The pool of experts thus is constituted by a small number of highly educated and professionally sophisticated individuals. The Association policy embodied in this restricted view of professional qualifications responds to criticisms levied against professionally inadequate expert opinion evidence on such important matters.

Paragraph (c) does not address specifically the qualifications of foreign-trained mental health and mental retardation professionals. Nevertheless, statutes or court rules might well allow foreign-trained professionals with education and training equivalent to those imparted through American programs to testify as experts on matters of present mental condition;

6. The American Psychological Association uses the words *professional psychologist* synonymously with *clinical, counseling, or school psychologist.* Although the terms are synonymous, the standard uses the more generally descriptive term for the benefit of those unfamiliar with APA terminology.

they may not, however, serve as experts on other mental health or mental retardation issues. Graduates of foreign programs may lack the cultural basis necessary to provide a competent evaluation of mental condition at the time of an alleged crime or a prognosis of future mental condition or behavior.

Subparagraph (c)(iii) recognizes that some physicians who do not specialize in mental health or mental retardation issues, for example, neurologists, nevertheless may testify on medical questions within their area of expertise. It should be noted as well that minimum educational requirements applicable to mental health and mental retardation professionals should not preclude attorneys from testifying on issues of competency. Defense counsel frequently is a very important witness on competency to stand trial.[7]

A special education teacher, a speech and language pathologist, or an audiologist may be quite helpful in evaluating a mentally retarded or potentially mentally retarded defendant's ability to communicate, understand, and learn. Professionals in these fields should be considered under subparagraph (c)(iv) as qualified to testify as expert witnesses in appropriate cases.[8]

Standard 7-3.13. Expert witnesses: qualifications for testifying on issues of present scientific or clinical knowledge

(a) Qualifications. Expert opinion testimony may involve issues of present scientific or clinical knowledge. Such testimony should be presented only by witnesses with demonstrable scientific or clinical qualifications. Accordingly, no witness should be qualified by the court to present expert opinion testimony on issues of present scientific or clinical knowledge unless the court determines that the witness:

(i) has a degree in an appropriate medical or scientific discipline; and,

(ii) has relevant clinical or research experience and demonstrated familiarity with current scientific or clinical information on the specific issue on which the witness is called to testify.

(b) Effect of credentials and general experience. Professional de-

7. *See* commentary to standard 7-4.8, notes 9-16 and accompanying text.
8. *See generally* Ellis & Luckasson, *supra* note 5.

gree credentials and general practical experience should not, in and of themselves, constitute a demonstration of expertise sufficient to warrant qualification as an expert witness on issues of present scientific or clinical knowledge.

(c) Related standard. The qualifications, including recommended education and training requirements, for any expert witness testifying about a person's mental condition are governed by the provisions of standards 7-3.11 and 7-3.12.

Commentary Introduction

Standard 7-3.13 recommends qualifications for mental health and mental retardation professionals testifying on matters of present scientific or clinical knowledge. Because they offer no opinions on individual mental condition or behavior, they need not satisfy the requirements of standards 7-3.9 and 7-3.10.

Related Standards

ABA, Standards for Criminal Justice 7-3.9, 7-3.10, 7-3.11, 7-3.12

Commentary

Expert opinion concerning matters of current scientific or clinical knowledge is admissible if it will assist the trier of fact to understand evidence more fully or to determine a disputed fact.[1] Consequently, although mental health and mental retardation professionals often are called as expert witnesses about mental condition, they are not limited to testimony on that issue. The competence of mental health and mental retardation professionals to give expert testimony on matters of scientific or clinical knowledge has been recognized in many contexts.[2] The

1. Fed. R. Evid. 702. *See, e.g.*, People v. Kelly, 17 Cal. 3d 24, 549 P.2d 1240, 130 Cal. Rptr. 144 (1976) (expert testimony concerning the scientific reliability of voiceprint analysis); Huntingdon v. Crowley, 64 Cal. 2d 647, 414 P.2d 382, 51 Cal. Rptr. 254 (1966) (expert medical testimony relating to the scientific validity of certain blood tests used to determine paternity); People v. Tanner, 13 Cal. App. 3d 596, 91 Cal. Rptr. 656 (1970) (expert testimony supporting the contention that males with an extra Y chromosome are likely to exhibit aggressive behavioral traits).

2. For example, the Supreme Court of Alaska held that the testimony of a psychologist regarding the "alcoholic blackout" phenomenon should have been admitted. Handley v. State, 615 P.2d 627 (Alaska 1980). The Florida Supreme Court ruled that a psychiatrist with

American Psychiatric Association recently has asserted that advances in psychiatric nosology and diagnosis now ensure a high level of diagnostic reliability in psychiatric expert opinion, provided the psychiatric testimony is restricted to medical and scientific issues.[3]

Courts must be satisfied that sources of expert opinion on matters of current scientific or clinical knowledge are qualified sources. Traditionally, the only qualification has been possession of a medical or other relevant professional degree. Deficiencies in experience or familiarity with current scientific or clinical knowledge about specific issues went only to weight and not admissibility. Standard 7-3.13 recommends the rejection of that practice. Courts should inquire into a proffered expert's professional qualifications to present relevant expert opinion evidence before allowing the expert to testify. Such an inquiry necessitates an evaluation of a proposed witness's clinical or research experience and familiarity with current scientific knowledge germane to the specific matter on which the witness has been called to testify.

An expert qualified under this standard, who will not give testimony concerning an individual's mental condition or behavior, need not satisfy in addition the requirements recommended in standards 7-3.9 and 7- 3.10. For example, an expert who offers only an opinion on the physiological effects of a neuroleptic medication need not conduct a personal interview with a defendant or determine in any way whether the defendant has taken that medication.

Standard 7-3.14. Presentation of expert testimony

(a) Attorney's duty to prepare expert for trial. An attorney intending to call an expert witness should assist the expert in preparing for trial.

(b) Presentation of data and reasoning upon which opinion is based.

(i) A mental health or mental retardation professional offering

---

substantial clinical experience regarding LSD should have been permitted to testify on the general psychological effects of that drug. Fouts v. State, 374 So. 2d 22 (Fla. 1979), *overruled on other grounds,* Parker v. State, 408 So. 2d 1037, 1038 (Fla. 1982). California Court of Appeal decisions have allowed psychiatric testimony on Munchausen's syndrome, People v. Phillips, 122 Cal. App. 3d 69, 175 Cal. Rptr. 703 (1981), and the general effects of hypnosis, People v. Marsh, 170 Cal. App. 2d 284, 338 P.2d 495 (1959).

3. American Psychiatric Association Statement on the Insanity Defense 9 (1982) (*citing* Spitzer, Forman & Nee, *DSM-III Field Trials: I. Initial Interrater Diagnostic Reliability*), 136 Am. J. Psychiatry 815-817 (1979).

an expert opinion should identify and explain the theoretical and factual basis for that opinion and the reasoning process through which the opinion was formulated.

(ii) An expert witness should not testify about defendant's statements, or about information obtained during or derived from an evaluation, or about other information that would not otherwise be admissible in evidence, unless those statements or information:

(A) are of a type that are customarily relied upon by mental health or mental retardation professionals in formulating their opinions; and

(B) are relevant to serve as the factual basis for the expert's opinion; and

(C) the court determines that the probative value of the statements or information outweigh their tendency to prejudice or confuse the trier of fact.

(c) Promulgation of written guidelines. Every jurisdiction should promulgate written guidelines designed to inform and advise mental health and mental retardation professionals called to testify as expert witnesses about all aspects of the law and procedure within that jurisdiction applicable to the effective presentation of expert opinions.

Commentary Introduction

Standard 7-3.14 promotes improved mental health and mental retardation professional expert testimony through adequate witness preparation for trial and full explanations by the witness at trial of the underlying bases for expert opinion evidence. Attorneys who intend to call qualified mental health and mental retardation professionals as expert witnesses are obligated to prepare them for direct examination and cross-examination. Expert witnesses also should be responsible to explain their data and the rationales underlying their professional conclusions and opinions if triers of fact are appropriately to evaluate their testimony and resolve fact issues.

Related Standards

ABA, Standards for Criminal Justice 3-3.3(a), 4-4.4(a), 7-3.9, 7-3.10, 7-3.11, 7-3.12, 7-3.13

American Psychiatric Association, The Principles of Medical Ethics with Annotations Especially Applicable to Psychiatry §2, annotation 3

American Psychological Association, Ethical Principles of Psychologists 2

American Psychological Association, Specialty Guidelines for the Delivery of Services by Clinical Psychologists 1.6

American Psychological Association, Specialty Guidelines for the Delivery of Services by Counseling Psychologists 1.6

American Psychological Association, Standards for Providers of Psychological Services 1.6

Commentary

Preparing Expert Witnesses for Trial

Standard 7-3.14(a) confirms the responsibility of attorneys who anticipate using mental health or mental retardation professionals as expert witnesses to prepare them to present direct testimony and respond to cross-examination. If counsel and a professional have worked together in the past, a telephone conference may suffice, but otherwise a face-to-face pretrial meeting almost always will be required. In that conference, the attorney should explain the legal implications of the expert's clinical observations, so that the expert can use terminology understandable by laypersons. Counsel should apprise the witness of evidentiary privileges that may affect the scope of testimony, such as the attorney-client privilege, work-product privilege, and professional-patient/client privilege. The conference coverage should also embrace the qualification requirements of standards 7-3.9 through 7-3.13. As a consequence of the conference, at trial a professional should understand the requirements for qualifying as an expert[1] and presenting the data and reasoning on which an expert opinion is based,[2] the prohibition against offering opinions on questions requiring a conclusion of law or a judgment properly reserved to the court or jury[3] and the limitations on expert testimony concerning future mental condition.[4]

Ethical standards require that mental health or mental retardation professionals prepare themselves adequately to testify at trial.[5] Otherwise,

1. *See* standards 7-3.10 through 7-3.13.
2. Standard 7-3.14(b).
3. Standard 7-3.9(a).
4. Standard 7-3.9(b).
5. American Psychiatric Association, Principles of Medical Ethics with Annotations Especially Applicable to Psychiatry §2, annotation 3 (1981); American Psychological Association, Standards for Providers of Psychological Services 1.6 (1981); American Psychological Association, *Specialty Guidelines for the Delivery of Services by Clinical Psychologists* 1.6, 36

they will be practicing outside the scope of their professional competence. The Standards for Criminal Justice impose on prosecuting attorneys and defense counsel an obligation to "explain to the expert his or her role in the trial as an impartial expert called to aid the factfinders and the manner in which the examination of witnesses is conducted."[6] An attorney's unexplained failure to adequately prepare a mental health or mental retardation professional witness may constitute ineffective assistance of counsel[7] and subject the attorney to professional discipline.

Mental health or mental retardation professionals, like other expert witnesses, serve as impartial sources of information for and assistance to triers of fact. Therefore, their expert opinions should rest on impartial, objective evaluations and reflect clinical findings derived impartially and objectively. Evaluations, clinical findings, and mental health or mental retardation expert opinions should not be affected or modified according to the partisan needs of the attorneys who elicit them at trial.

Expert witnesses, however, are not disabled from presenting their professional opinions vigorously. They should be able to articulate and defend their conclusions based on their evaluations and clinical findings. In doing so, they should testify clearly and coherently for the benefit of court and jury. Therefore, notwithstanding the fact that they may be advocates or proponents of the opinions they express, they are properly to be characterized as impartial witnesses as long as they perform their evaluations impartially and objectively. Stated thus, the professional role of expert witness occupies a middle ground between an adversary witness and a wholly impartial and disinterested source of data. As Dr. Bernard Diamond has noted, because an expert's testimony in fact supports one party's position, the expert necessarily identifies with that side:[8]

Am. Psychologist 640, 644 (1981); American Psychological Association, *Specialty Guidelines for the Delivery of Services by Counseling Psychologists* 1.6, 36 Am. Psychologist 652, 656 (1981).

6. *See* Standards for Criminal Justice 3-3.3(a), 4-4.4(a). The commentary to those standards clarifies the requirement by stating that the prosecutor and defense attorney "should explain the workings of the adversary system and the expert witness' role within it as an independent and impartial expert." *Id.* at 3•44, commentary to standard 3-3.3; 4•61, commentary to standard 4-4.4.

7. *See* Boykins v. Wainwright, 737 F.2d 1539, 1541-1542 (11th Cir.), *reh'g denied,* 744 F.2d 97 (11th Cir. 1985), *cert. denied,* 105 S. Ct. 1775 (1985); Tillery v. United States, 419 A.2d 970 (D.C. 1980).

8. Diamond, *The Fallacy of the Impartial Expert,* 3 Archives of Criminal Psychodynamics 221 (1959), *reprinted in* Readings in Law & Psychiatry 217 (R. Allen, E. Ferster & J. Rubin

> It is absurd to pretend that the psychiatric expert remains neutral under [the process of cross-examination]. For the sake of his own ego integrity, he must identify himself with his own opinions and become the advocate of those opinions. But in proportion as those opinions favor one side or the other, the witness loses his hypothetical impartiality.[9]

Dr. Seymour Halleck's position is diametrically opposite to Diamond's. He asserts that a mental health or mental retardation professional who becomes a witness should view this role not as an adversarial one but one of service to the court:

> . . . When he takes the witness stand the psychiatrist becomes a person committed to the process of truth seeking no matter how the truth may conflict with his own ideologies. . . .
>
> The psychiatrist's abandonment of the adversarial role when taking the witness stand should put him in a very comfortable position. Once the thought of "winning the case" is temporarily dissociated from his consciousness, the psychiatrist has no duty other than that of telling what he knows as clearly as possible. He emerges as a sincere and honorable witness. He is not likely to be riled by vigorous cross-examination, but rather can view such interrogation as a welcome technique for bringing out the strengths and shortcomings of his testimony.[10]

Presenting Bases for Expert Opinions

Under subparagraph (b)(i) mental health or mental retardation professionals should explain during their testimony the theoretical and factual bases for their opinions and the reasoning process through which they arrived at those opinions. Adherence to the standard will preclude expert testimony couched solely in conclusory terms. Factfinders must be given an opportunity fully to evaluate the credibility of an expert's opinion. They can do so only if the theoretical and factual predicates for and rationale underlying the opinion are explained to them. A suitable explication of the theoretical basis for an opinion relating to mental condition should embrace (1) a description of a conceptual model and procedural guidelines generally accepted within the professional's discipline and (2)

---

eds., rev. ed. 1975) [hereinafter cited as Diamond]. *See also* Diamond & Louisell, *The Psychiatrist as an Expert Witness: Some Ruminations and Speculations,* 63 Mich. L. Rev. 1335, 1344-1345 (1965); Diamond, *The Psychiatrist as Advocate,* 1 J. Psychiatry & L. 5 (1973).

9. Diamond, *supra* note 8, at 223, Readings in Law & Psychiatry at 218.

10. S. Halleck, Law in the Practice of Psychiatry 199 (1980).

the applicability of both to the expert's clinical findings on the subject matter of the evaluation and of the testimony relating to it. One should note that, although the Federal Rules of Evidence permit experts to testify without disclosing the facts or data underlying their expert opinions,[11] many authorities and decisions support the contrary position espoused in subparagraph (b)(i).[12]

Expert Opinion Based on Hearsay or Otherwise Inadmissible Evidence

Mental health or mental retardation professionals frequently utilize hearsay data, *e.g.*, nurses' notes, in formulating opinions. Standard 7-3.14(b)(ii) endorses the admissibility of expert opinion evidence based in part on third-party information if (1) the information customarily is

---

11. FED. R. EVID. 705.

12. In Carter v. United States, 252 F.2d 608 (D.C. Cir. 1957), the court stated,

> The chief value of an expert's testimony in this field, as in all other fields, rests upon the material from which his opinion is fashioned and the reasoning by which he progresses from his material to his conclusion; in the explanation of the disease and its dynamics, that is, how it occurred, developed, and affected the mental and emotional processes of the defendant; it does not lie in his mere expression of conclusion.

Id. at 617.

In United States v. Brawner, 471 F.2d 969 (D.C. Cir. 1972), Chief Judge Bazelon characterized conclusory opinions as "the experts' stranglehold on the process." *Id.* at 1011 (Bazelon, C.J., concurring and dissenting). The process of cross-examination is thwarted because conclusory statements make it difficult to discern both the inadequacies of an evaluation on which expert testimony was based and limitations on professional knowledge generally. *Id. See also* Bazelon, *The Role of the Psychiatrist in the Criminal Justice System*, 6 BULL. AM. ACAD. PSYCHIATRY & LAW 139, 146 (1978).

The Supreme Court of California characterized conclusory mental health and mental retardation professional testimony as "a medieval trial by oath." People v. Bassett, 69 Cal. 2d 122, 140, 443 P.2d 777, 789, 70 Cal. Rptr. 193, 205 (1968). In our system of justice, a person's life should not be dependent "on whether or not the witnesses against him correctly recite by rote a certain ritual formula." *Ibid.* Expert testimony "is valuable only in regard to the proof of the *facts* and the validity of the *reasons* advanced for the conclusions." *Id.* at 141, 443 P.2d at 789, 70 Cal. Rptr. at 205 (*quoting* People v. Martin, 87 Cal. App. 2d 581, 584, 197 P.2d 379, 380 (1948)) (emphasis in original). Other judicial decisions involving psychiatric testimony have expressed a similar viewpoint both on the issue of competency to stand trial, *see, e.g.*, People v. Williams, 87 Ill. App. 3d 860, 409 N.E.2d 439 (1980) ("[T]he conclusions of experts are only as valid as the bases or reasons for them." *Id.* at 864, 409 N.E.2d at 441), and mental condition at the time of the alleged crime. *See* People v. Cruz, 26 Cal. 3d 233, 605 P.2d 830, 162 Cal. Rptr. 1 (1980) ("[T]he value of a psychiatric expert's conclusions on diminished capacity lies in the material on which they are based and the reasoning by which they are reached." *Id.* at 247, 605 P.2d at 837, 162 Cal. Rptr. at 7).

relied on by other qualified professionals in the expert witness's profession to formulate opinions, and (2) the court determines the probative value of the evidence to outweigh its prejudicial effect. The principle of allowing expert testimony based in part on otherwise inadmissible data is supported by the Federal Rules of Evidence[13] and several judicial opinions.[14] Nevertheless, limitations have been placed on the use of inadmissible statements or information as a basis for the expert's opinion. Accordingly, the standard assumes that the data will be of a type customarily relied on by professionals in formulating their opinions.[15] The fact that the data are customarily utilized by professionals in formulating their opinions usually has led courts to attribute to them a high degree of reliability.[16]

The use of inadmissible data as a supporting basis for expert testimony is limited further by the requirement of standard 7-3.11(a)(iii) that expert witnesses have performed adequate evaluations, including personal interviews with the persons whose mental condition is in issue, on the specific matters about which they are summoned to testify. Consequently, expert opinion may not be based *entirely* on hearsay or other inadmissible statements or information.

Finally, a trial court may exclude testimony the probative value of which is outweighed by a tendency to prejudice or confuse a trier of fact. For example, an expert witness presenting the factual basis for a professional opinion may wish to refer to immoral or illegal acts, other than those directly incorporated in the indictment or information on which a defendant is on trial, recounted by the defendant during an evaluation

13. Fed. R. Evid. 703.

14. In France v. State, 179 Ind. 659, 387 N.E.2d 66 (1979), the court ruled that the testimony of a psychiatric expert is not inadmissible simply because the expert's opinion rests in part on reports from mental hospitals or other psychiatrists. *Id.*, 387 N.E.2d at 69. In State v. DeGregory, 285 N.C. 122, 203 S.E.2d 794 (1974), a psychiatrist was permitted to testify regarding the defendant's sanity based on a personal examination and inadmissible hospital records prepared by others. *Id.*, 203 S.E.2d at 802.

15. In Jenkins v. United States, 307 F.2d 637 (D.C. Cir. 1962), the court adopted the "customary reliance" test to determine the propriety of expert testimony: "[W]e agree with the leading commentators that the better reasoned authorities admit opinion testimony based, in part, upon reports of others which are not in evidence but which the expert customarily relies upon in the practice of his profession." *Id.* at 641 (footnotes omitted).

16. *See* People v. Ward, 61 Ill. 2d 559, 568, 338 N.E.2d 171, 177 (1975) (dictum). *See also* Jenkins v. United States, 307 F.2d 637 (D.C. Cir. 1962) (courts should accept that which "is relied on by mankind generally in matters that involve the health and may involve the life of their families and of themselves. . . ." *Id.* at 641 (*quoting* Sundquist v. Madison Ry., 197 Wis. 83, 221 N.W. 392, 393 (1928)).

interview. Because jurors may equate earlier bad acts to those with which a defendant stands charged, testimony of that nature may well work substantial prejudice to the defendant.[17]

Standard 7-3.15. Jury instructions

(a) The court should instruct the jury concerning the functions and limitations of mental health and mental retardation professional expert testimony. As provided for in standard 15-3.6(e), preliminary instructions should be given prior to the introduction of the expert testimony. The jury should be informed that the purpose of such testimony is to identify for the trier of fact the clinical factors relevant to the issues of past, present, and future mental condition or behavior that are under consideration.

(b) Jurors also should be informed that they are not asked or expected to become experts in medicine, psychology, or other behavioral sciences and that their task is to decide whether the explanation offered by a mental health or mental retardation professional is persuasive. In evaluating the weight to be given an expert's opinion, the jury should consider the qualifications of the witness, the theoretical and factual basis for the expert's opinion, and the reasoning process by which the information available to the expert was utilized to formulate the opinion. In reaching its decisions on the ultimate questions in the trial, the jury is not bound by the opinions of expert witnesses. The testimony of each witness should be considered in connection with the other evidence in the case and given such weight as the jury believes it is fairly entitled to receive.

Commentary Introduction

Standard 7-3.15 delineates the appropriate scope of jury instructions relating to the relevance and limitations on the use of mental health and mental retardation professional expert testimony, so that jurors do not rely excessively on it. They also should be reminded of their role in the trial process.

---

17. *See, e.q.,* People v. Quicke, 71 Cal. 2d 502, 455 Cal. 2d 502, 455 P.2d 787, 78 Cal. Rptr. 683 (1969) (when psychiatrist at penalty trial related defendant's revelations of earlier crimes and immoral acts, the court committed prejudicial error by failing to give a limiting jury instruction).

Related Standard

ABA, Standards for Criminal Justice 15-3.6(e)

Commentary

Jurors require guidance concerning the nature of mental health and mental retardation professional testimony. They should be given preliminary instructions for their guidance immediately before professional expert testimony is offered,[1] telling them that it will identify clinically reasonable possibilities to explain human behavior. As Professors Bonnie and Slobogin have noted,

> Although explanatory clinical formulations by careful forensic specialists are hardly "scientific facts," they do represent something more than idiosyncratic "guesses." Such witnesses offer "informed speculation," essentially in the following form:
>
> > I cannot assure you that this is what happened, and I cannot measure for you the impact that these intrapsychic variables had on the defendant's behavior under the circumstances which existed at the time of the offense. Nonetheless, based on our operating theories of psychology, which we employ in our everyday clinical practice, and on my own study of the relevant literature concerning this type of psychological functioning and this type of criminal behavior, I think the following explanation(s) are possible (or probable).
>
> These explanatory formulations can assist the factfinder, who must speculate in any event, by identifying "clinically reasonable" possibilities that otherwise may not occur to him. Appropriately instructed, the jury will know that these explanations are only possibilities and will not be misled.
>
> Expert opinion can offer valuable assistance not only by suggesting explanations for puzzling behavior, but also by gathering and marshalling information that otherwise might appear random or of questionable significance. The expert may suggest a conceptual framework that, if accepted by the factfinder, can serve as an organizational and interpretational tool that neither the factfinder nor counsel could have supplied.[2]

1. Standard 15-3.6(e).
2. Bonnie & Slobogin, *The Role of Mental Health Professionals in the Criminal Process: The Case for Informed Speculation*, 66 Va. L. Rev. 427, 488 (1980).

Appropriate instructions should cover the jury's role in evaluating mental health and mental retardation professional expert testimony, reassuring jurors that they are to determine the ultimate facts and not become experts in psychology. They decide the ultimate credibility of all evidence, including expert opinion testimony.[3] They may find some experts more credible than others[4] and may even reject a unanimous conclusion of experts in favor of lay-witness opinion evidence contradicting the experts.[5] Indeed, a jury may reject all opinion evidence, whether lay or expert, and rely on basic presumptions embodied in judicial instructions.[6]

3. Mayes v. State, 440 N.E.2d 678, 681 (Ind. 1982).
4. State v. Carlson, 328 N.W.2d 690, 694 (Minn. 1982).
5. Taylor v. State, 440 N.E.2d 1109, 1110 (Ind. 1982).
6. Brooks v. State, 247 Ga. 744, 279 S.E.2d 649 (1981).

Part IV

Competence to Stand Trial

William H. Erickson, *Chairman*
Standing Committee on Association
Standards for Criminal Justice

Ben F. Overton
Task Force Chairman

Gerald T. Bennett
Reporter

Task Force

Ben F. Overton, *Chairman*
Justice, Supreme Court of Florida, Tallahassee, Florida

Joseph J. Balliro
Private practitioner, Balliro, Mandano & Balliro, Boston, Massachusetts (representing ABA Section of Criminal Justice)

Bruce E. Bennett, Ph.D.
Psychologist, Northbrook, Illinois (representing American Psychological Association)

Bruce J. Ennis
Private practitioner, Ennis, Friedman, Bersoff & Ewing, Washington, D.C.; Chairman, ABA Commission on the Mentally Disabled

D. Lowell Jensen
Judge, U.S. District Court, San Francisco, California; former Deputy Attorney General, U.S. Department of Justice

Murray Levine, Ph.D.
Professor; Director, Clinical/Community Graduate Program, Department of Psychology, State University of New York at Buffalo, Buffalo, New York (representing American Orthopsychiatric Association)

Ruth Luckasson, J.D.
Department of Special Education, University of New Mexico, Albuquerque, New Mexico

Mary M. McCormick
Private practitioner, Senior Lecturer and Director, Legal Clinic, Law Faculty, University of Papua, New Guinea

Donald Paull, Ph.D., J.D.
Attorney and Psychologist; Chief, Mental Health Law Division, Cook County Public Defenders Office, Chicago, Illinois

Ralph Slovenko
Professor of Law and Psychiatry, Wayne State University Law School, Detroit, Michigan

Henry C. Weinstein, M.D., J.D.
Director, Forensic Psychiatric Services, New York University Medical Center/ Bellevue Hospital Center, New York, New York

GERALD T. BENNETT, *Reporter*
Professor of Law, University of Florida College of Law

INTRODUCTION

Perhaps the mental health concepts most frequently misunderstood by the lay public, as well as by many attorneys, judges, and mental health or mental retardation professionals, are the doctrine of mental nonresponsibility [insanity] at the time of an alleged offense as a defense to criminal charges and the doctrine establishing the nontriability of defendants found mentally incompetent to undergo proceedings. The confusion of these concepts has not been alleviated by the continued use of traditional but archaic references to the defense of mental nonresponsibility as "insanity at the time of the offense" and to incompetence to stand trial as "insanity at time of trial."[1] At least in this century, however, it has become quite clear that the doctrines should be distinguished as to purpose, governing tests, procedural aspects of raising and determining relevant issues, and disposition of defendants found incompetent or mentally nonresponsible. The defense of mental nonresponsibility [insanity] is an affirmative defense to criminal charges that, if established, negates the culpability requisite to a finding of guilt. The doctrine of incompetence to stand trial, in contrast, has no bearing on guilt or innocence; it sounds, not in substantive determination, but in procedural fairness. It sets parameters under which society may proceed against defendants who may be unable because of mental condition to defend themselves, and it establishes the premise that those who because of mental illness or mental retardation cannot understand the nature of the proceedings or who are unable to assist in their defense may not properly be put to trial. In jurisprudential analysis, the doctrine of nonresponsibility for crime as a substantive defense is most important in that it establishes the param-

1. Massey v. Moore, 348 U.S. 105 (1954). *See, e.g.*, Fla. Stat. §917.01 (1955 (repealed)).

eters of society's right to punish those whose actions are not rational and therefore distinguishes those who are not blameworthy human beings. In pragmatic terms, however, the doctrine of incompetence to stand trial or to proceed has far greater impact. Despite the emotional appeal and controversial character of issues relating to mental nonresponsibility [insanity] as an affirmative defense, in purely quantitative terms the determination of incompetence affects a far larger number of criminal defendants than the substantive law defense.[2] One survey, for example, showed that some 52 percent of all persons in mental institutions were confined because of incompetence to stand trial, in contrast to a mere 4 percent committed as not guilty by reason of mental nonresponsibility [insanity].[3] Another commentator estimated that for each defendant found not guilty by reason of insanity or mental nonresponsibility, at least 100 are determined incompetent to stand trial.[4]

Development of Incompetence to Stand Trial Doctrine

The doctrine that defendants should not be tried while mentally incompetent had its origins in the common law, dating at least to mid-seventeenth-century England. Blackstone noted that a defendant should neither plead nor be tried if mentally defective.[5] Although English courts did not articulate specific criteria establishing the "madness" necessary to avoid trial, the common law seemed to emphasize as determinative the inability of defendants to defend themselves at trial. Common law judges in the eighteenth century were, in retrospect, "surprisingly sophisti-

2. *See* Steadman & Hartstone, *Defendants Incompetent to Stand Trial*, in MENTALLY DISORDERED OFFENDERS: PERSPECTIVES FROM LAW AND SOCIAL SCIENCE 40-42 (J. Monahan & H. Steadman eds. 1983) [hereinafter cited as Steadman & Hartstone].

3. SCHEIDEMENDEL & KANNO, THE MENTALLY ILL OFFENDER: A SURVEY OF TREATMENT PROGRAMS, XIV 20, Table IV (1969) (*cited in* Brakel, *Presumption, Bias and Incompetency in the Criminal Process*, 1974 WIS. L. REV. 1105, 1105 n.3).

4. Bacon, *Incompetency to Stand Trial: Commitment to an Inclusive Test*, 42 S. CAL. L. REV. 444, 444 (1969). More recent research seems to indicate that the number of persons committed for incompetence was overstated, however, since the data included those being evaluated as well as those committed. Steadman & Hartstone, *supra* note 2, at 40.

5. ". . . [I]f a man in his sound memory commits a capital offence, and before arraignment for it, he becomes mad, he ought not to be arraigned for it; because he is not able to plead to it with that advice and caution that he ought. And if, after he has pleaded, the prisoner becomes mad, he shall not be tried: for how can he make his defence?" 4 W. BLACKSTONE, COMMENTARIES *24 [hereinafter cited as W. BLACKSTONE].

cated"[6] in the evidence they received to adjudge the issues of incompetence: they considered many of the factors still used today to determine competence, including the defendant's medical history, military and social background, behavior and appearance at trial, and testimony from lay and professional witnesses who knew or had observed the defendant. The issue then was whether these factors so affected a defendant's cognitive processes[7] that the resultant "insanity" rendered the defendant unable properly to defend himself or herself. The cases expressed two philosophical bases for the doctrine: (1) conviction and punishment of a lunatic would not deter future criminal acts; and (2) it was fundamentally unfair to try a mentally incompetent defendant who might be unable because of mental incapacity to present evidence in defense.[8]

The British common law rules preventing trial of mentally incompetent defendants were transposed virtually intact into early nineteenth-century United States jurisprudence, as demonstrated by *United States v. Lawrence*[9] (a case which adopted the principles of *Hadfield's Case*[10]) and *Youtsey v. United States.*[11] The *Youtsey* court, citing common law authorities, indicated that "it is not due process of law to subject an insane person to trial upon an indictment involving liberty or life," and initially placed upon the trial judge the duty to investigate and decide the issue once "tendered" by counsel.[12] Seven years after *Youtsey,* the decision in *United States v. Chisholm* further defined the applicable standard in terms of whether ". . . the mental impairment of the prisoner's mind . . . disables him . . . from fairly presenting his defense."[13] Following *Chis-*

---

6. Mickenberg, *Competency to Stand Trial and the Mentally Retarded Defendant: The Need for a Multi-Disciplinary Solution to a Multi-Disciplinary Problem,* 17 Cal. W.L. Rev. 365, 368 (1981) [hereinafter cited as Mickenberg].

7. Blackstone referred to the "deficiency of will" which arises from "defective or vitiated understanding." W. Blackstone, *supra* note 5, at *24.

8. Frith's Case, 22 Howell's St. Trials 1281 (1800); Mickenberg, *supra* note 6, at 369. Blackstone emphasized two additional points in his commentary: (1) that "whether the party be compos or not, this shall be tried by jury;" and (2) that ". . . in the case of absolute madmen, as they are not answerable for their actions, they should not be permitted the liberty of acting unless under proper control; and, in particular, they ought not be suffered to go loose, to the terror of the king's subjects." W. Blackstone, *supra* note 5, at 25.

9. F. Cas. No. 15,577, 26 F. Cas. 887, 889-891 (D.C. Cir. 1835).

10. 27 How. St. Tr. 1281 (K.B. 1800).

11. 97 F. 937 (6th Cir. 1899).

12. The case further emphasized that the record show affirmatively the "exercise of judicial judgment and discretion." Youtsey v. United States, *id.* at 944, 947.

13. 149 F. 284, 289 (S.D. Ala. 1906).

holm, and throughout the first half of the twentieth century, most jurisdictions gradually modified the common law doctrine, affirming the need to inquire into a defendant's understanding of the trial process and ability to assist in the defense. However, as the medical discipline of psychiatry became increasingly sophisticated, courts inquired more frequently into the effects of specific medical disorders on a defendant's competence to be tried.[14]

In 1960, the United States Supreme Court entered the incompetence arena with its landmark decision in *Dusky v. United States*,[15] which established the fundamental test for incompetence to stand trial:

> [T]he test must be whether [a defendant] has sufficient present ability to consult with his lawyer with a reasonable degree of rational understanding — and whether he has a rational as well as factual understanding of the proceedings against him.[16]

Three cases since *Dusky* have elaborated the current parameters of incompetence doctrine. In *Pate v. Robinson*,[17] the Court apparently accepted the doctrine that trial of a person incompetent to stand trial violates the due process clauses of the Constitution.[18] A hearing on procedural incompetence is mandated whenever the "evidence raises a bona fide doubt as to the defendant's competence to stand trial."[19] The case of *Drope v. Missouri*[20] reiterated the *Robinson* due process standard, explicitly

---

14. United States v. Gundelfinger, 98 F. Supp. 630 (W.D. Pa. 1951); United States v. Chandler, 72 F. Supp. 230 (D. Mass. 1947); United States v. Harriman, 4 F. Supp. 186 (S.D.N.Y. 1933); United States v. Boylen, 41 F. Supp. 724 (D. Or. 1941); People *ex rel.* Berstein v. McNeill, 48 N.Y.S.2d 764 (N.Y. Sup. Ct. 1944); Mickenberg, *supra* note 6, at 371-372. In the words of one commentator, "[t]he historical development of the competency doctrine can thus be viewed as a progression from a rough concept of basic fairness to a complex issue requiring expert medical and legal judgment." Mickenberg, *supra* note 6, at 375.

15. 362 U.S. 402 (1960).

16. *Id.* at 402. *See generally* Weiner, *Mental Disability and the Criminal Law*, in The Mentally Disabled and the Law 693, 694-696 (S. Brakel, J. Parry & B. Weiner eds., 3d ed. 1985).

17. 383 U.S. 375 (1966). *See* commentary to standard 7-4.1, notes 3-4 and accompanying text; commentary to standard 7-4.2, notes 1-5 and accompanying text; commentary to standard 7-4.13, note 2.

18. U.S. Const. amends. V, XIV.

19. Pate v. Robinson, 383 U.S. at 385.

20. 420 U.S. 162 (1974). *See* commentary to standard 7-4.1, notes 1-2, 8-12 and accompanying text; commentary to standard 7-4.13, note 2.

recognizing a trial judge's constitutional obligations to resolve competence issues and to be alert before and during trial to evidence suggesting possible incompetence of a defendant.[21] The third of the trilogy, *Jackson v. Indiana*,[22] discussed the equal protection and due process issues attendant on commitment of an incompetent defendant for treatment to restore procedural competence, holding that the Constitution permits such confinement solely for the purpose of treatment that reasonably may result in attainment of competence in the foreseeable future.[23]

Misuse of the Incompetence Process

A number of commentators in recent years have decried instances of abuse of the incompetence procedures by all actors in the criminal process. Defense counsel allegedly have used it for other purposes than the determination of procedural competence, because a psychiatric examination ordered in relation to triability also affords the defense information useful in plea negotiations, mitigation of sentence, or a later proceeding to determine mental nonresponsibility.[24] In some instances, a commitment for treatment based on incompetence has been considered more in a defendant's best interests than a substantive determination of guilt or innocence.[25] Even if invocation of the incompetence to stand trial procedure does not result in eventual withdrawal of criminal charges, it may delay the proceedings to avoid media or societal pressure for immediate and harsh treatment of a defendant.[26] Prosecutors, who are legally empowered to inject the issue of procedural incompetence, have viewed the process as a mechanism to remove from society defendants against whom they might have a weak case or "as a means of curbing anticipated violent behavior; as a form of 'preventive detention' or legal strategy; and, finally, as a way of dealing with individuals when there seems to be

21. Drope v. Missouri, 420 U.S. at 181.

22. 406 U.S. 715 (1972). *See* commentary to standard 7-4.5, notes 8-9 and accompanying text; commentary to standard 7-4.9, notes 3-5, 8 and accompanying text; commentary to standard 7-4.13, notes 1-8 and accompanying text.

23. Jackson v. Indiana, 406 U.S. at 738.

24. *See* commentary to standard 7-4.2, notes 24-29 and accompanying text.

25. A defense mechanism described by one commentator as "medical immunity." Slovenko, *The Developing Law on Competency to Stand Trial*, 5 J. Psychiatry & L. 167 (1977).

26. Cooke, Johnston & Pogany, *Factors Affecting Referral to Determine Competency to Stand Trial*, 130 Am. J. Psychiatry 870, 874 (1973).

no other legal recourse."[27] Whether the abuses cataloged are as pervasive and intentional as some commentators suggest or flow instead from an inadequate comprehension of the doctrine, it is clear that the concepts surrounding mental incompetence to stand trial are often misunderstood and misapplied to the detriment of all involved in the criminal justice system.

The Standards: Issues and Answers

Part IV of the standards addresses the several issues, manifest throughout the historical development of the legal doctrine of incompetence to stand trial, that still affect the legal system.[28] The standards first address the definitional criteria for a finding of incompetence, incorporating almost without change the test set forth in the case of *Dusky v. United States.*[29] Adoption of a general standard to determine incompetence does not solve the pragmatic questions of the extent to which expert testimony should be available to help resolve this complex legal determination, nor does it endeavor to define the ways in which diagnoses properly may be translated into judicial findings. The standards do point out clearly that the issue of competence is a legal one, and that mental incompetence may result from causes other than mental illness; mental retardation,[30] developmental disability, or even hearing impairment may produce present incompetence. Standard 7-4.2 addresses several complex issues bearing on the responsibility of counsel and courts to raise incompetence issues. It adopts the Supreme Court's reasoning in *Pate v. Robinson*[31] and *Drope v. Missouri,*[32] first enunciated in *Youtsey v. United States,*[33] that the primary obligation to raise and alleviate doubts about competence falls upon trial courts. The standard further rests on the premise that incom-

27. Geller & Lister, *The Process of Criminal Commitment for Pre-trial Psychiatric Examination and Evaluation,* 135 Am. J. Psychiatry 53 (1978). The studies by Roesch and Golding in North Carolina revealed uses of incompetence procedures for purposes other than strictly a determination of incompetence to stand trial by defense counsel, prosecutors and judges. R. Roesch & S. Golding, Competency to Stand Trial (1980). *See* standard 7-4.2 and commentary.

28. *See generally* Bennett, *A Guided Tour Through Selected ABA Standards Relating to Incompetence to Stand Trial,* 53 Geo. Wash. L. Rev. 375 (1985).

29. 362 U.S. 402 (1960). *See* standard 7-4.1 and commentary.

30. *See generally* Ellis & Luckasson, *Mentally Retarded Criminal Defendants,* 53 Geo. Wash. L. Rev. 414, 452-460 (1985).

31. 383 U.S. 375 (1966). *See supra,* notes 17-19 and accompanying text.

32. 420 U.S. 162 (1974). *See supra,* notes 20-21 and accompanying text.

33. 97 F. 937 (6th Cir. 1899). *See supra,* notes 11-12 and accompanying text.

petency procedures exist for a single purpose — the determination of competence — and that it is improper for either a prosecuting attorney or defense counsel to use them for unrelated purposes. It then addresses the ethical problems that arise when defense counsel believes a client to be incompetent but the client objects to raising the competency question. The standard stresses a lawyer's duty to the court as the paramount obligation in such an instance, and hence expects an attorney to advance the issue even over a client's objection.

Issues of confidentiality and privileged communications recur throughout the standards. The standards emphasize that attorney-client privilege and privileges relating to confidential communications should not be breached by defense counsel, whether through motions for mental examinations or permitted or required proffers of testimony. Problems relating to disclosure of defendant communications also arise with respect to court-ordered evaluations requiring defendant cooperation in the form of communications with appointed examiners. The standards embody the premises that defendants may not refuse a court-ordered examination but that their statements to court-appointed examiners should be confidential and within the protection of fifth amendment privilege against self-incrimination. Consequently such communications should be used to help determine present mental competence and for no other purposes.

Standard 7-4.3 addresses the issue of commitment for treatment in relation to a defendant's claim to pretrial release. It condemns the traditional practice of automatic commitment for evaluation of competence whenever the issue of incompetence has been asserted. Instead, commitment of incompetent defendants should occur only if necessary and not merely convenient, or if mandated under pretrial release principles applicable to all criminal defendants. The standards in later parts covering commitment for treatment adopt the same philosophy, namely, that commitment for treatment should occur only when necessary and that the least restrictive alternative treatment is preferred.[34] Consistent with the principle that incompetency procedures should be used only to ascertain competence and related treatment or habilitation needs, the standards caution that determinations of pretrial release or detention not be subsumed under competence to stand trial processes, but instead should be disposed of as separate and distinct issues.

The standards address the necessity for hearings at the time the issue

34. *See* standards 7-7.4(d), 7-9.9(d), 7-9.10(b), 7-10.5(b).

of incompetence is first raised and for purposes of periodic review of determinations of incompetence. They consider the possibility of waiver of hearings, the evidence that should be adduced at hearings, and applicable burdens of persuasion (proof). An especially troubling issue is the propriety of testimony by defense counsel at an incompetency hearing. Counsel is perhaps the most knowledgeable witness concerning that branch of the incompetence doctrine focusing on a criminal defendant's ability to communicate with counsel. Nevertheless, traditional standards of attorney-client confidentiality generally have forestalled testimony of this sort. Despite this tradition, the instant standards take the position that a defense attorney properly may elect to testify or be required to respond to pertinent questions by a court.[35] The standards further track the decisional law in most jurisdictions that jury trial of incompetence issues should not be required.[36] However, if a hearing may result in a defendant's involuntary commitment for treatment in a jurisdiction where jury trial is mandated for civil commitment, an equivalent jury trial should be available to resolve the issues of treatment and commitment.[37]

Two particularly difficult issues are addressed by the standards, *viz.*, the right to treatment and the right to refuse treatment. Standard 7-4.10 advocates that defendants committed for treatment or ordered to report for treatment be afforded treatment appropriate to restore competence and that courts be obliged to monitor that treatment. It advances a requirement that professionals responsible for treatment develop a treatment plan for submission to an authorizing court to facilitate judicial monitoring. The standards incorporate only a quite limited right to refuse treatment appropriate to restore procedural competence, a right limited to treatment methods that are particularly hazardous or experimental or that pose an unreasonable risk of irreversible or serious side effects.

Several other important issues are covered by the standards. One of the most perplexing is the disposition to be made of defendants determined to be permanently incapacitated to undergo criminal proceedings. Courts have not developed a satisfactory alternative response to this phenomenon. Under current constitutional principles, defendants cannot be tried while they remain incompetent. Because by definition permanently incompetent defendants will always remain incompetent, they cannot be committed for treatment to restore competence in the foreseeable future.

35. *Ibid.*
36. *See* standard 7-4.8(b).
37. *Ibid.*

If they are not committable under laws governing civil involuntary hospitalization, they must be released even though they may have committed serious offenses. Standard 7-4.13 proposes that permanently incompetent defendants charged with felonies causing or seriously threatening serious bodily harm be subjected to a hearing to determine factual guilt. If guilt is not established, or if any other less serious offense underlies pending criminal charges, the defendant should be discharged and could be hospitalized only on the basis of independent civil commitment proceedings. If factual guilt of a requisite felony is determined, then the special commitment proceedings envisioned for dangerous persons acquitted of criminal charges because of mental nonresponsibility [insanity] may be invoked.[38]

A final issue addressed by the standards is the validity of a trial of a defendant on psychotropic medication. Rejecting the "absolute bar" rule followed by many courts, which automatically prohibits the trial of defendants whose competence depends upon continuous psychotropic medication, the standards look to the ultimate issue to be resolved: a defendant's actual competence or incompetence. A defendant who is competent — whether through psychotropic medication or otherwise — is triable.[39] If a medication adversely affects trial processes, for example, through distorting a defendant's demeanor either in the courtroom or on the witness stand, a court must take appropriate steps to correct the distortion, perhaps through testimony about the medication and its effects or through appropriate jury instructions.[40]

Standard 7-4.1. Mental incompetence to stand trial; rules and definitions

(a) No defendant shall be tried while mentally incompetent to stand trial.

(b) The test for determining mental competence to stand trial should be whether the defendant has sufficient present ability to consult with defendant's lawyer with a reasonable degree of rational understanding and otherwise to assist in the defense, and whether

38. *See* standard 7-7.4.
39. Standard 7-4.4(a).
40. Standard 7-4.4(b).

the defendant has a rational as well as factual understanding of the proceedings.

(c) The terms *competence* and *incompetence* as used within Part IV of this chapter refer to mental competence or mental incompetence. A finding of mental incompetence to stand trial may arise from mental illness, physical illness, or disability; mental retardation or other developmental disability; or other etiology so long as it results in a defendant's inability to consult with defense counsel or to understand the proceedings.

Commentary Introduction

The issue of triability of defendants determined to be mentally incompetent or "insane at time of trial" was one of the earliest criminal mental health issues addressed in both English and American common law jurisprudence, probably second only in historical importance to that of mental nonresponsibility [insanity] at the time of an offense. Today the issue of present mental incompetency, quantitatively speaking, is the single most important issue in the criminal mental health field, based on the frequency of present mental incompetency cases in comparison to those involving the defense of mental nonresponsibility [insanity], and the statistical prevalence of mental illness and mental retardation among inmates of penal institutions. Standard 7-4.1 addresses the two most fundamental issues of the consideration of incompetence: (1) the basic rule of nontriability of mentally incompetent defendants and (2) the legal criteria for determining when incompetence exists. The standard clarifies the definition of mental incompetency, thus demonstrating by design that it is a matter of legal and not medical or psychological definition and indicating that incompetence is to be determined according to functional rather than diagnostic criteria.

Related Standards

ABA, Standards for Criminal Justice 7-4.13, 7-4.14, 7-5.1, 7-5.2, 7-5.3
ALI, Model Penal Code 4.04

Commentary

Standard 7-4.1 reflects the fundamental constitutional principle prohibiting trial of defendants determined to be mentally incompetent to stand trial. This principle of nontriability conforms to the apparent conclusion of the Supreme Court that the prohibition is absolute: One determined to be incompetent to stand trial cannot be tried. In *Drope v. Missouri,*[1] the Court analyzed its rule in terms of due process and characterized it as "fundamental to an adversary system of justice."[2] In *Pate v. Robinson,*[3] the Court noted and apparently concurred with the government's stipulation ". . . that the conviction of an accused person [who] is legally incompetent violates due process . . . and that state procedures must be adequate to protect this right."[4]

In *Jackson v. Indiana,*[5] the Court delineated procedures permissible "despite the defendant's incompetency," but notably omitted a reference to a possible substantive determination of the ultimate factual issue of guilt. The pragmatic consequences resulting from the adoption of a rule of absolute nontriability are not entirely satisfactory. Nonetheless, the standards accept that position as constitutionally mandated by *Robinson, Drope,* and *Jackson.*[6]

Standard 7-4.1(b) sets forth a test for incompetence to stand trial taken virtually verbatim from the decisions in *Dusky v. United States*[7] and *Drope v. Missouri.*[8] In *Dusky,* the Court established the standard in these terms:

> . . . [The] test must be whether [a defendant] has sufficient present ability to consult with his lawyer with a reasonable degree of rational understanding — and . . . a rational as well as factual understanding of the proceedings against him.[9]

---

1. 420 U.S. 162 (1974).
2. *Id.* at 172.

> It has long been accepted that a person whose mental condition is such that he lacks the capacity to understand the nature and object of the proceedings against him, to consult with counsel, and to assist in preparing his defense may not be subjected to a trial.

Id. at 171.

3. 383 U.S. 375 (1966).
4. *Id.* at 378. The Court concluded that the trial judge's failure to make sufficient inquiry into the issue "deprived Robinson of his constitutional right to a fair trial." *Id.* at 385.
5. 406 U.S. 715, 740 (1972). *See* standards 7-4.12 and 7-4.13 and commentary for a more complete discussion of procedures that might be available despite a defendant's incompetence.
6. *See* commentary to standard 7-4.13, notes 9-20 and accompanying text, for a discussion of various alternatives suggested by commentators and adopted by some states.
7. 362 U.S. 402 (1960).
8. 420 U.S. 162 (1974).
9. Dusky v. United States, 383 U.S. at 402.

Standard 7-4.1(b) combines with the *Dusky* formulation language taken from *Drope v. Missouri* that a defendant be able to "assist in his defense."[10] Decisional law and commentators consider the *Dusky* test adequate to meet the policy demands undergirding the incompetence to stand trial doctrine. Because the fundamental purpose of the rule is to promote accurate factual determinations of guilt or innocence by enabling counsel to evaluate and present available defenses to factfinders, defendants should have at least the intellectual capacity necessary to consult with a defense attorney about factual occurrences giving rise to criminal charges. Obviously, to accomplish that, defendants require a minimal understanding of the nature of criminal proceedings, the importance of presenting available defenses, and the possible consequences of either conviction or acquittal. The incompetence rule serves, as well, a broader societal interest in maintaining a certain dignity in the administration of criminal justice.[11] It rests on the assumption that a defendant will be a conscious participant in presenting the defense case; the trial of one incapable of fulfilling that expectation does not reflect "a reasoned interaction between an individual and his community" but societal "invective against an insensible object."[12]

Utilization of the basic *Dusky* language as the criterion to determine procedural competence hardly terminates consideration of the issue. Indeed, a careful reading of the language of the test shows three separate factors to be requisite. Defendants must be able (1) to consult with defense counsel, (2) to "otherwise assist with [their] defense," and (3) to have both a rational and factual understanding of the proceedings. The interpretation of these discrete elements of the *Dusky* test has been the subject of much scholarly and decisional analysis; while all concede the general language of the test, few agree on its more specific applications. Some jurisdictions have attempted with varying results to codify more particularly the test for incompetence. Illustrations are found in the extensive criteria adopted by statute in New Jersey[13] and a decision of the United States District Court for the Western District of Missouri:[14]

10. Drope v. Missouri, 420 U.S. at 171. *See* Weiner, *Mental Disability and the Criminal Law*, in The Mentally Disabled and the Law 693, 694-696 (S. Brakel, J. Parry & B. Weiner eds., 3d ed. 1985). State legislation as of October 1982 may be found in *id.* at 744-754, Table 12.1.

11. *See* Winick, *Incompetency to Stand Trial: Developments in the Law, Mentally Disordered Offenders*, in Mentally Disordered Offenders: Perspectives from Law and Social Science 3 (J. Monahan & H. Steadman eds. 1983) [hereinafter cited as Winick].

12. *Id.* at 5; Note, *Incompetency to Stand Trial*, 81 Harv. L. Rev. 454, 458 (1967) [hereinafter cited as Harvard Note].

13. N.J. Stat. Ann. §2C:4-4 (West 1982).

14. Wieter v. Settle, 193 F. Supp. 318, 321-322 (W.D. Mo. 1961).

1. A defendant must have the mental capacity to appreciate his or her presence in relation to time, place, and things.
2. A defendant's elementary mental processes must be adequate to comprehend (a) that the defendant is in a court of justice charged with a criminal offense; (b) that a judge is on the bench; (c) that a prosecutor is present who will seek to convict the defendant of a criminal charge; (d) that the defendant has a lawyer who will undertake to defend against that charge; (e) that the defendant is under no duty to testify in personal defense but that, if he or she chooses to testify, the defendant will be expected to relate to the best of his or her mental ability the surrounding facts at the time and place of the alleged criminal violation; and (f) that there will or may be a jury present to pass upon evidence adduced as to guilt or innocence of the charge.
3. A defendant must have the mental capacity to participate in an adequate presentation of his or her defense.
4. A defendant electing to enter into plea negotiations or plead guilty must comprehend the consequences of a guilty plea and be able knowingly, intelligently, and voluntarily to waive rights that legally are no longer applicable upon entry of a guilty plea.

Mental health professionals at the Harvard Medical School Laboratory of Community Psychiatry produced a list of thirteen "quantifiable clinical criteria" to assess competence[15] that, slightly paraphrased, were adopted by court rule in Florida.[16] The Nebraska Supreme Court proposed yet another list of twenty similar yet differing criteria.[17] Arizona, in endeavoring to codify the *Dusky* rule, has directed examining experts to file with trial courts reports addressing seven specific matters.[18]

Lists of this sort, replete with factors more specific than, but as ambiguous as, those in *Dusky,* appear to establish objective criteria. In fact, however, they fail to address two fundamental issues: (1) the standard by which to assess defendants' rational assessments of the criminal trial

---

15. Harvard Medical School Laboratory of Community Psychiatry Final Report, Competency to Stand Trial and Mental Illness (1973) [hereinafter cited as Laboratory of Community Psychiatry Report].

16. Fla. R. Crim. Proc. 3.211 (1980).

17. State v. Guatney, 207 Neb. 501, 299 N.W.2d 538 (1980).

18. Ariz. Rev. Stat. Ann. §13-1621(A) (1970) (abrogated by Ariz. R. Crim. P. 11.1 (1973) (utilizing the *Dusky* test)). The Arizona codification was couched in somewhat conclusory language, requiring that an evaluator determine such facts as "the defendant's ability to assist in his own defense" and "whether the defendant's ability to reason or to control his conduct is substantially impaired." Wexler, Scoville, *et al., The Administration of Psychiatric Justice: Theory and Practice in Arizona,* 13 Ariz. L. Rev. 1, 163-164 (1971) [hereinafter cited as Wexler *et al.*].

process; and (2) the assistance to be required from them. An inquiry whether a defendant "comprehends . . . that there is a judge on the bench" is certainly insufficient. A nonbinding compilation of many specific factfindings corresponding to a lengthy list of suggested criteria may limn an overall picture of a defendant's mental state and give significant aid to a court in making a final determination of competence. However, to crystallize such a list in the form of a statute or rule requirement proves counterproductive because it causes courts to substitute particularized judgments on discrete and superficial aspects of defendant's mental state for a far more important ultimate conclusion of competence. Standard 7-4.1(b), rather than formulating specific criteria to be addressed by courts and evaluators, recognizes that the Supreme Court in *Dusky* and *Drope* has established a basic norm, understandably and necessarily imprecise, that permits individual judges to evaluate each case in the light of an individual defendant's level of functioning in relation to the complexity of that case.[19]

The *Dusky* test, accepted as legally adequate by judges and attorneys, has proven far less satisfactory to professional evaluators who try to apply it to individual defendants. In the course of their efforts to translate clinical diagnostic findings into the legal conclusions required by the test for legal competence, mental health and mental retardation professionals usually have taken one of two roads. They have either translated clinical diagnostic labels into conclusions couched in legal terms or have attempted to construct their own diagnostic criteria to permit application of clinical findings to legal requirements.[20] Another difficulty experienced by professional examiners arises from a confusion of the issues of competence and sanity. For want of guidance from appointing or authorizing courts, examining experts often have confused criteria governing present mental incompetence with those defining mental nonresponsibility [in-

---

19. *See* Slovenko, *The Developing Law on Competency to Stand Trial,* 5 J. PSYCHIATRY & L. 165 (1977) [hereinafter cited as Slovenko].

20. Roesch and Golding, for example, pointed out that their study had uncovered a significant relationship between clinical diagnoses and determinations of competence: "Those defendants considered incompetent by hospital staff received labels of either psychosis or mental retardation, while competent defendants were viewed as being without psychosis." Roesch, *A Brief, Immediate Screening Interview to Determine Competency to Stand Trial,* 5 CRIM. JUST. & BEHAV. 241 (1978). Geller and Lister related that, despite specific instructions to examiners to report on the issues of competence and sanity, the majority of reports submitted to courts made no mention of either issue. Geller & Lister, *The Process of Criminal Commitment for Pre-Trial Psychiatric Examination and Evaluation,* 135 AM. J. PSYCHIATRY 53 (1978).

sanity].[21] The most widely known checklist of diagnostic criteria designed to promote accurate clinical assessment of competence is that developed by the Harvard Medical School Laboratory of Community Psychiatry.[22] The Laboratory staff developed two instruments to test competence, the Competency Screening Test and the Competency Assessment Instrument. The creators of those instruments have been criticized severely, chiefly because they allegedly injected their own political and philosophical beliefs into what they proposed as devices to attain objective assessments: competence to stand trial was equated with an understanding and acceptance of an idealistic view of the criminal justice system that might well not be shared by defendants brought into the process.[23] More recently, critics have acknowledged that the Laboratory's instruments probably can effectively screen out defendants who are competent to stand trial but are less effective in determining actual incompetence.[24] Whatever the particular value of test instruments of this sort, they exemplify the difficulties inherent in attempting to translate the nuances of legal definitions into specific, objective diagnostic criteria.

A review and analysis of precedent and commentary from legal and mental health or mental retardation professionals reveals a general trend toward certain categories of analysis to determine competence. Most commentators feel that criteria to determine competency under the general *Dusky* formulation should be "functional," in that they require an evaluation of a particular defendant's skills rather than a general determination of that defendant's mental condition.[25] An evaluation should touch on at least five different areas:

1. Defendants should have a perception of the process not distorted by mental illness or disability. Whether phrased in terms of (a) an ability to perceive rationally and without dis-

---

21. Hess & Thomas, *Incompetency to Stand Trial: Procedures, Results, and Problems,* 119 Am. J. Psychiatry 713 (1963); Robey, *Criteria for Competency to Stand Trial: A Checklist for Psychiatrists,* 122 Am. J. Psychiatry 616 (1965) [hereinafter cited as Robey].

22. *See generally* Laboratory of Community Psychiatry Report, *supra* note 15.

23. *See* Brakel, *Presumption, Bias and Incompetency in the Criminal Process,* 1974 Wis. L. Rev. 1105, 1109-1110, 1128.

24. Nottingham & Mattson, *A Validation Study of the Competency Screening Test,* 5 Law & Hum. Behav. 329 (1981).

25. Bennett, *Comment: Competency to Stand Trial: A Call for Reform,* 59 J. Crim. L.C. & P.S. 569 (1968); Mickenberg, *Competency to Stand Trial and the Mentally Retarded Defendant: The Need for a Multi-Disciplinary Solution to a Multi-Disciplinary Problem,* 17 Cal. W.L. Rev. 365 (1981) [hereinafter cited as Mickenberg].

tortion,[26] (b) an "understanding" of the process,[27] or (c) an "awareness" of the charge and possible verdicts,[28] or (d) couched in a codified requirement that defendants understand that there is a judge on the bench, a prosecutor who will try to convict, and defense counsel who will defend against criminal charges, the thrust of the requirement is that defendants understand the nature of the process and their functions as participants within that process free from undue perceptual distortion.

2. Defendants require a capacity to maintain the attorney-client relationship, embracing an ability to discuss the facts of a case with counsel "without paranoid distrust,"[29] to advise and accept advice from counsel, to elect an appropriate plea, and to approve the legal strategy of the trial. The relationship requires an ability to consult rationally about a pending case which is something more than a superficial capacity to converse with others.[30]
3. A third requirement, somewhat akin to the second, bears on the ability to recall and relate factual information. If a primary purpose of the prohibition against trying incompetent defendants is to preserve accuracy in factfinding, then defendants must be able to recall and relate factual occurrences. If they are not, they cannot reveal exonerating circumstances to their attorneys.[31] This requirement has been variously phrased: that a defendant have "sufficient memory to relate answers to questions posed" to him or her, that "he [or she] can follow the testimony reasonably well," and that there be a "capacity

---

26. Mickenberg, *supra* note 25, at 382.

27. H. Steadman, Beating a Rap?: Defendants Found Incompetent to Stand Trial 113 (1979).

28. Robey, *supra* note 21, at 619.

29. *Ibid.*

30. Mickenberg, *supra* note 25, at 385. This requirement has been expressed in terms of (1) defendants' ability "both [to] give and receive advice from [their] attorneys" and to "confer coherently with some appreciation of the proceedings," State v. Guatney, 207 Neb. 501, 299 N.W.2d 538, 545 (1980) (Krivosha, C. J., concurring), (2) their capacity to "relate to the attorney" and to "assist the attorney in planning [a] defense." Fla. R. Crim. P. 3.211 (1980).

31. Harvard Note, *supra* note 12, at 457. This criterion should include the ability to listen to witnesses and to "inform [a] lawyer of distortions or misstatements." Robey, *supra* note 21, at 619.

to realistically challenge prosecution witnesses." Without that capacity, defendants realistically are unable to exercise the rights to consult with counsel, testify in personal defense, and confront accusers.[32]

4. Defendants should be capable of testifying in personal defense if that should prove appropriate.[33]
5. A final factor is a defendant's abilities to meet the competency criteria in the setting of the particular charges, the extent of the defendant's needed participation in trial proceedings, and the complexity of the case. Therefore, an evaluator should consider a defendant's mental ability in relation to the severity of the charge and the complexity of the case.[34]

Standard 7-4.1(c) establishes a clear dichotomy between mental health or mental retardation concepts and legal principles governing present mental competency. If defendants are capable of meeting the articulated requirements for competence, the presence or absence of mental illness is irrelevant. Conversely, defendants may not be mentally ill yet may be incompetent to stand trial. Legal criteria, not medical or psychological diagnostic categories, govern competency. Hence, the presence or absence of mental illness, while certainly significant in evaluating defendant competence, is by no means conclusive.[35] Even though a defendant in a criminal case may be severely psychotic, "if the patient is able to comprehend those aspects of the court procedure listed, and able to work with his lawyer in conducting a defense, he should go back to trial."[36] The standard, therefore, clearly adopts the position that a finding of incompetence does not depend on a preliminary diagnosis of mental illness. A determination of competence or incompetence is functional in nature, context-dependent and pragmatic in orientation, and should be viewed as such by both courts and mental health and mental retardation professionals.

---

32. Harvard Note, *supra* note 12, at 458.

33. This criterion has been couched in varying ways, *e.g.*, "defendant's capacity to testify relevantly," FLA. R. CRIM. P. 3.211 (West Supp. 1985), and an expectation that defendants will be expected to tell to the best of their mental ability the facts surrounding them at the time and place of an alleged violation. *See* LABORATORY OF COMMUNITY PSYCHIATRY REPORT, *supra* note 15, at 103.

34. *See* Robey, *supra* note 21, at 620.

35. B. ENNIS & R. EMERY, THE RIGHTS OF MENTAL PATIENTS 100 (1978).

36. Robey, *supra* note 21, at 617.

Standard 7-4.2. Responsibility for raising the issue of incompetence to stand trial

(a) The court has a continuing obligation, separate and apart from that of counsel for each of the parties, to raise the issue of incompetence to stand trial at any time the court has a good faith doubt as to the defendant's competence, and may raise the issue at any stage of the proceedings on its own motion.

(b) The prosecutor should move for evaluation of defendant's competence to stand trial whenever the prosecutor has a good faith doubt as to the defendant's competence. The prosecutor should further advise defense counsel and the court of any information that has come to the prosecution's attention relative to defendant's incompetence to stand trial.

(c) Defense counsel should move for evaluation of the defendant's competence to stand trial whenever the defense counsel has a good faith doubt as to the defendant's competence. If the client objects to such a motion being made, counsel may move for evaluation over the client's objection. In any event, counsel should make known to the court and to the prosecutor those facts known to counsel which raise the good faith doubt of competence.

(d) A motion for evaluation should be in writing and contain a certificate of counsel indicating that the motion is based on a good faith doubt that the defendant is competent to stand trial and that it is not filed for purposes of delay. The motion should also set forth the specific facts that have formed the basis for the motion.

(e) In the absence of good faith doubt that the defendant is competent to stand trial it is improper for either party to move for evaluation. It is improper for either party to use the incompetence process for purposes unrelated to incompetence to stand trial such as to obtain information for mitigation of sentence, to obtain favorable plea negotiation, or to delay the proceedings against the defendant.

(f) In making any motion for evaluation, or, in the absence of a motion, in making known to the court information raising a good faith doubt of defendant's competence, the defense counsel should not divulge confidential communications or communications protected by the attorney-client privilege.

Commentary Introduction

Standard 7-4.2 addresses the relative obligations of courts, prosecuting attorneys, and defense counsel to raise the issue of a defendant's possible incompetence to stand trial, and it sets forth the appropriate procedure to do so. It recognizes that trial courts have the primary and fundamental responsibility to ensure that criminal proceedings are both valid and fundamentally fair to defendants. Therefore, whether or not counsel for either party moves, a trial court is obliged to raise and resolve the competency issue whenever a good faith doubt about competence arises. A prosecuting attorney has a twofold obligation. After generating a good faith doubt about a defendant's competence, he or she has an obligation to move for an evaluation. Alternatively, a prosecutor with information about a defendant's mental state that does not support the requisite level of doubt, but that might assist defense counsel in evaluating the client's competence, must make it available to defense counsel. Defense counsel, who has an independent professional responsibility toward the court and the fair administration of justice, as well as an allegiance to the client, also should move for an evaluation whenever a good faith doubt arises about a defendant's competence to stand trial, notwithstanding defense counsel's doubt as to what is in the defendant's legal best interests. Should the client oppose such a motion, the standards urge that a defense attorney be given two options. One is to move for an evaluation over the client's opposition. If, however, that might deleteriously affect the attorney-client relationship, the second option is to elect not to submit a formal motion but simply to advise the trial court about the information that generated counsel's doubt about the client's competence. This may require, of course, that an attorney seek judicial permission to withdraw as defense counsel because of a conflict of interest.[1] The standard specifies the contents of a motion for an evaluation to determine competence and addresses the ethical issue of proper and improper uses of such a motion.

Related Standards

ABA, Standards for Criminal Justice 6-2.5, 7-1.2, 7-2.3

Commentary

Standard 7-4.2(a) reflects the common law obligation of trial courts to respond to indications that defendants might not be competent to stand trial, an obligation expressly reaffirmed by the United States Supreme

1. Model Rules of Professional Responsibility 1.7 (1983).

Court in *Pate v. Robinson*[2] and *Drope v. Missouri.*[3] In each, a judgment of guilt was reversed because of a trial court's failure to order an evaluation of the defendant's competence to stand trial after being confronted with evidence sufficient to raise a doubt about that competence.[4] Standard 7-4.2(a) adopts "good faith doubt" as the prerequisite criterion for initiating an evaluation of a defendant's competence to stand trial; this is intended as an equivalent to the "bona fide doubt" standard of *Robinson* and *Drope.* Whether the good faith doubt about competence arises from a motion by a prosecuting or defense counsel or from any other source, a court must order a competence evaluation and decide the issue of procedural competence. It need not be convinced that a defendant is incompetent to stand trial before ordering an evaluation, because that is the objective of an evaluation.[5] Admittedly, the quantum of doubt a trial court, defense attorney, or prosecuting attorney must achieve before injecting the competence issue is difficult to define.[6]

Standard 7-4.2(b) urges recognition of a twofold obligation on prosecuting attorneys: (1) to move for an evaluation of a defendant's competence based on a good faith doubt about competence; and (2) to advise defense counsel when information in their possession does not generate the necessary doubt but might not be available to defense counsel. The wisdom of permitting the prosecution to move for a competence evaluation that may require an extended commitment has been seriously questioned because of its potential for abuse[7] and because of the actual or apparent unfairness of a procedure allowing the prosecution to initiate

2. 383 U.S. 375 (1966).

3. 420 U.S. 162 (1975).

4. In Pate v. Robinson, 383 U.S. at 384, the Court referred to the evidence presented as being sufficient to raise a "good faith doubt," a reference specifically noted in Drope v. Missouri. 420 U.S. at 180. The *Drope* language did not refer specifically to a "good faith doubt," but noted instead that "the information . . . created a sufficient doubt of [Drope's] competence to stand trial to require further inquiry on the question." *Id.* at 181.

5. *See* Mitchell v. United States, 316 F.2d 354 (D.C. Cir. 1963): "It cannot reasonably be supposed that Congress intended to require the accused to produce, in order to get a mental examination, enough evidence to prove that he is incompetent or irresponsible. . . . If the accused already had such evidence, there would be little need for the examination." *Id.* at 360.

6. As the Supreme Court noted in *Drope,* "[t]here are, of course, no fixed or immutable signs which invariably indicate the need for further inquiry to determine fitness to proceed; the question is often a difficult one in which a wide range of manifestations and subtle nuances are implicated." 420 U.S. at 162.

7. *See* Weiner, *Mental Disability and the Criminal Law,* in The Mentally Disabled and the Law 693, 696 (S. Brakel, J. Parry & B. Weiner eds., 3d ed. 1985); Note, *Incompetence to Stand Trial on Criminal Charges,* 2 Mental Disability L. Rep. 617, 620 (1978).

a process that compels a defendant, over objection, to discuss with someone other than defense counsel otherwise confidential information that may become accessible to the prosecution.[8] The primary support for the premise that prosecuting attorneys should be empowered to submit such motions arises from the view that prosecuting authorities are advocates of justice whose interests must go beyond mere criminal convictions and so owe a special duty to courts to ensure fair and proper criminal proceedings.[9]

A prosecuting attorney's duty to disclose information indicating incompetence flows not to a court but to counsel if the information appears not already to be in counsel's possession. The duty to disclose reflects a prosecutor's obligation to seek justice rather than solely to convict and may well be required by the Constitution.[10]

Standard 7-4.2(c) resolves an apparent conflict between the obligations of defense counsel (1) effectively to represent a client's best interests and (2) to reflect candor toward the tribunal.[11] Because of the sometimes severe consequences traditionally attendant upon a determination of incompetence, defense counsel may conclude that it is better for a technically incompetent defendant to proceed to trial. This may be so for several reasons. An involuntary commitment for treatment to restore competence may extend well beyond the maximum sentence imposable for a relatively minor offense. A defendant could view the stigma flowing from a finding of mental illness as more opprobrious than that generated by a criminal conviction. An evaluation may force a defendant to reveal to a court-appointed expert information the defendant would prefer to keep secret. If the probable criminal penalty in a pending criminal matter is a relatively minor fine, inception of a cumbersome incompetence

8. *See* commentary to standard 7-4.8, notes 16-17 and accompanying text, for a discussion of the confidentiality of matters related to an examining expert.

9. *See* standard 3-1.1 and commentary.

10. In a series of decisions beginning with Brady v. Maryland, 373 U.S. 83 (1963), the Supreme Court has required the prosecution to furnish defense counsel with material that might be exculpatory. *See* United States v. Agurs, 427 U.S. 97 (1976); Giles v. Maryland, 386 U.S. 66 (1967). *See also* Evans v. Kropp, 254 F. Supp. 218 (E.D. Mich. 1966) (reversing a conviction based on a guilty plea because of a prosecutor's failure to disclose information indicating the defendant's possible incompetence). At least one commentator has argued that to withhold information of possible incompetence to stand trial more directly affects the fairness of proceedings than to withhold exculpatory material, which was the conduct condemned in *Brady*. Pizzi, *Competency to Stand Trial in Federal Courts: Conceptual and Constitutional Problems,* 45 U. Chi. L. Rev. 21, 25 (1977) [hereinafter cited as Pizzi]. *See also* standard 11-2.1.

11. Bennett, *Competency to Stand Trial: A Call for Reform,* 59 J. Crim. L.C. & P.S. 569, 571 (1968) [hereinafter cited as Bennett].

evaluation may precipitate an unnecessary expenditure of scarce public resources. A defendant might even prefer to be punished through imprisonment than to experience commitment to a mental hospital for treatment, given the marginal conditions in many public mental institutions.[12] If the prosecution case against a defendant is weak, or if a defendant's assistance is not actually required during trial, defense counsel may believe that an acquittal is likely even though defendant is incompetent.[13]

Moreover, the due process violation inherent in and presumed from the trial of an incompetent defendant cannot be waived, if for no other reason than the incompetence itself.[14] Once incompetence proceedings have been initiated, the defense thereafter is foreclosed from halting the requisite evaluation and commitment for restoration to competence. Consequently, some commentators have contended that defense counsel not only is permitted, but in some instances is required, to decline to raise the issue of a client's possible incompetence if it seems to be in the client's best interests to forgo that procedure. They argue that any duty to a court to protect the integrity of criminal proceedings justly must be subordinated to the client's interest, granted the pragmatic shortcomings of the system and the potentially greater hardship and injustice to a defendant stemming from an incompetency commitment.[15]

Nonetheless, the arguments asserting defense counsel's duty to raise the issue are equally compelling. Because the trial of an incompetent defendant necessarily is invalid as a violation of due process, a defense lawyer's duty to maintain the integrity of judicial proceedings requires that a trial court be advised of the defendant's possible incompetence.[16] Ultimately, this requirement provides protections for criminal defendants. In addition, to permit defense counsel to proceed to trial with incompetent clients deprives defendants of their personal right to partici-

---

12. Chernoff & Sadler, *Defending the Mentally Ill: Ethical Quicksand,* 10 Am. Crim. L. Rev. 505, 519 (1972) [hereinafter cited as Chernoff & Sadler].

13. *See* standard 7-4.15 and commentary.

14. *See* Comment, *Incompetency to Stand Trial,* 81 Harv. L. Rev. 454, 467, 468 (1967). One commentator, analogizing the issue of incompetence to that of mental nonresponsibility [insanity], and relying on the Supreme Court opinion in Lynch v. Overholzer, 369 U.S. 705 (1962), has characterized the procedure as existing for the benefit of a defendant. Therefore, if initiating the process appears more detrimental to a client than failure to do so, it should be considered improper to require the defense to inject the issue. Bennett, *supra* note 11, at 578.

15. *See* Model Rules of Professional Conduct 3.3(a)(1) ("A lawyer shall not knowingly . . . make a false statement of material fact or law to a tribunal").

16. Pizzi, *supra* note 10, at 30. *Compare* Faretta v. California, 422 U.S. 806 (1975) (sixth amendment guarantees a competent defendant the right to conduct a personal defense).

pate in and to control the thrust of their defense.[17] It further assumes that defense attorneys properly determine the best interests of their clients.[18] Criminal defendants, even though represented by trial counsel, have the exclusive right to make certain critical decisions, *e.g.*, to waive or demand jury trial, to decide whether or not to testify in personal defense, and to decide the plea to be entered.[19] Obviously, incompetent defendants cannot make these decisions and they may not be made by their attorneys.[20]

Standard 7-4.2(c) recommends a clear requirement that defense counsel raise the issue of a defendant's present mental incompetence whenever counsel has a good faith doubt about competence. It resolves the difficult conflict of concerns inherent in such circumstances, discussed above, in favor of counsel's obligation to the court. The conflict, if it exists, arises from a perceived pragmatic failure of the criminal justice system to live up to its promise, in that the deficiencies in the system of incompetence evaluation and treatment implicitly threaten excessive or inappropriate sanctions against defendants. The standard takes the position that, if such problems exist, the thrust should be to correct the problems not to permit a pragmatic but philosophically unsound mechanism to avoid them.[21] If elements of unfairness are eliminated from the system, defendants will have little reason to prefer a pragmatic avoidance of the competence issue in favor of trial on the merits.[22]

---

17. The statement by the Supreme Court in *Robinson* seems compelling: "[I]t is contradictory to argue that a defendant may be incompetent, and yet knowingly or intelligently 'waive' his right to have the court determine his capacity to stand trial." Pate v. Robinson, 383 U.S. at 384.

18. *See* standard 4-5.2.

19. *Ibid.*

20. For example, one of the unspoken sanctions applied to defendants raising possible incompetence has been automatic incarceration until the issue of competence is resolved. That problem is addressed by standard 7-4.3, which provides that defendants in that situation should be eligible for appropriate pretrial release. Another implicit detriment is the fact that defendants may be committed for treatment and then, after restoration of competence, tried and sentenced for the crime, which precipitates a second deprivation of liberty. This problem is addressed by standard 7-4.15, which provides that convicted defendants should receive credit against sentence for earlier hospitalization based on incompetency.

21. *See* Chernoff & Sadler, *supra* note 12, at 530: "In large measure counsel's difficulties merely reflect failures elsewhere in the system and his problems could be considerably alleviated by conforming the law in practice to the law in theory."

22. Hess and Thomas, based on observations that crimes repeatedly associated with incompetence proceedings were generally "heinous," "revolting," or "pointless," and the defendants "pitiable or puzzling," suggest that the procedure be used as a means of pragmatic disposition of offenders for whom there is "no other recourse under the law." Hess & Thomas, *Incompetency to Stand Trial: Procedures, Results and Problems*, 119 AM. J. PSYCHIATRY 713 (1963).

Paragraphs (d) and (e) establish the scope of proper and improper uses of competency evaluation procedures. Researchers examining the competence evaluation process have concluded that often it has been invoked improperly to achieve aims unrelated to a determination of competence or incompetence.[23] Incompetence evaluations have been misused to "short-circuit" more complex civil commitment proceedings,[24] to avoid prolonged trial, or to obtain information to support a later defense of mental nonresponsibility [insanity].[25] Prosecutors allegedly have invoked the incompetence process improperly to avoid possible acquittals based on that defense,[26] to forestall trial in cases in which they lack sufficient evidence to convict,[27] or to achieve pretrial detention of defendants whom they wish to remove from the streets pending trial.[28] Defense attorneys have misused the incompetence process to gain additional time for preparation, to weaken the prosecution's case because of the passage of time, or to precipitate a competence evaluation that may produce expert data of aid to them on matters other than procedural competence, for example, pleas in mitigation, plea negotiations, or recommendations concerning dispositional alternatives to prison.[29]

Paragraphs (d) and (e) expressly condemn use of the incompetence evaluation process for any purpose other than determining competence to stand trial, and state clearly that it is improper conduct for either a prosecuting or defense attorney to move for evaluation for any unacceptable reason. The only valid basis for a motion for evaluation is a good-faith doubt about a defendant's present mental competence. To ensure that motions are properly submitted, standard 7-4.2(d) urges that attorneys submitting such motions be required to (1) represent specifically to recipient courts that they are made in good faith and (2) set forth the facts giving rise to the requisite doubt. Standard 7-4.2(e) then lists purposes for which the incompetence evaluation may not be used.

---

23. Eisenstat, *Mental Incompetency to Stand Trial*, 4 Harv. C.R.-C.L.L. Rev. 379 (1968).

24. Cooke, Johnston & Pogany, *Factors Affecting Referral to Determine Competency to Stand Trial*, 130 Am. J. Psychiatry 870, 874 (1973).

25. Bennett, *supra* note 11, at 572.

26. H. Steadman, Beating a Rap?: Defendants Found Incompetent to Stand Trial 88-89, 92 (1979); Chernoff & Sadler, *supra* note 12, at 515, 516.

27. B. Ennis & R. Emery, Rights of Mental Patients 102 (1978).

28. *See* Wexler, *Incompetency to Stand Trial*, 13 Ariz. L. Rev. 160, 162 (1971) (based on a study of the incompetence process in Arizona).

29. Roesch, *A Brief, Immediate Screening Interview to Determine Competency to Stand Trial*, 5 Crim. Just. & Behav. 241 (1978); Slovenko, *The Developing Law on Competency to Stand Trial*, 5 J. Psychiatry & L. 165, 166 (1977).

Standard 7-4.2(f) circumscribes somewhat the factual allegations required of or permitted from defense counsel by prohibiting disclosures of confidential communications, including those protected by attorney-client privilege.[30]

Standard 7-4.3. Pretrial release of a defendant pending competence examination

(a) A defendant otherwise entitled to pretrial release should not be involuntarily confined or taken into custody solely because the issue of the defendant's competence to stand trial has been raised and an evaluation has been ordered unless confinement is necessary for any personal examination that may be necessary for the evaluation process.

(b) If a defendant has been released from custody under any pretrial release provision, the court may order the defendant to appear at a designated time and place for outpatient examination and such appearance may be made a condition of pretrial release.

(c) If the court determines that a defendant will not submit to outpatient examination as a condition of pretrial release, that the defendant refuses to appear for examination, or that adequate examination is impossible without the confinement of the defendant, the court may order that the defendant be involuntarily confined until the examination is made.

(d) If a defendant who is on pretrial release is subsequently involuntarily confined or otherwise taken into custody for examination, such confinement should be in the least restrictive setting and for the minimum amount of time necessary to complete the examination. Immediately upon completion of the examination the defendant should be returned to pretrial release status.

(e) A defendant otherwise entitled to a judicial determination of eligibility for pretrial release should not have the determination postponed because of the pendency of proceedings to determine competence to stand trial.

30. *See* commentary to standard 7-4.8, notes 14-16 and accompanying text, for a more complete discussion of the applicability of principles of confidentiality and attorney-client privilege.

Commentary Introduction

Standard 7-4.3 rejects the historically common practice of routinely committing for evaluation defendants whose competence to stand trial has been put at issue. The standard distinguishes decisions regarding pretrial release or detention from those concerning commitment for evaluation, treatment, or habilitation; it emphasizes that separate issues are involved and that an independent decision must be made on each. Commitment based on incompetence to stand trial should be authorized only when shown to be necessary to permit an evaluating expert properly to examine a defendant. Pretrial custody to determine procedural incompetence should never be automatic and should be authorized only if necessary to a clinically valid evaluation. If it is not, a defendant whose competence is under professional scrutiny should be released or detained on the same basis as other defendants.

Related Standards

ABA, Standards for Criminal Justice 7-4.10; Chapter 10

Commentary

Standard 7-4.3 addresses the traditional practice of automatically arresting and committing for evaluation defendants whose competence to stand trial is questioned.[1] The rationales advanced to justify mandatory detention are that incompetence to stand trial is integrally related to severe mental illness, and that mentally ill defendants should be afforded special treatment administered outside the criminal process; a generally pervasive fear that mentally ill persons are, by virtue of their illnesses, dangerous also has been a major factor.[2]

---

1. *See* A. Stone, Mental Health and Law: A System in Transition 208 (1975) [hereinafter cited as A. Stone]; Weiner, *Mental Disability and the Criminal Law*, in The Mentally Disabled and the Law 693, 701 (S. Brakel, J. Parry & B. Weiner eds., 3d ed. 1985) [hereinafter cited as Weiner].

2. *See* Note, *Incompetency to Stand Trial*, 81 Harv. L. Rev. 454, 460 (1967); Kaufman, *Evaluating Competency: Are Constitutional Deprivations Necessary?*, 10 Am. Crim. L. Rev. 465, 475 (1972) [hereinafter cited as Kaufman].

Blackstone, after noting that if a defendant ". . . becomes mad, he shall not be tried, for how can he make his defence?," states:

> Yet, in the case of absolute madmen, as they are not answerable for their actions, they should not be permitted the liberty of acting unless under proper control; and,

Although the constitutional status of a right to bail is a matter of debate and controversy,[3] constitutional limits on pretrial detention[4] protect the weighty liberty interest of defendants awaiting trial.[5] Commentators have attacked on both procedural and constitutional grounds a denial of pretrial release solely on grounds of questioned competency to stand trial.[6] At a minimum, procedural due process claims almost certainly are compromised if defendants undergoing a competency evaluation are committed without an appropriate hearing on the relationship between their apparent mental illness or mental retardation on future flight or danger to other persons or the community.[7]

The denial of pretrial release, for whatever objective, constitutes a severe restriction on fundamental rights justifiable solely on the basis of a compelling state interest. Moreover, if alternative means exist to accomplish the same objective, the one least restrictive of a defendant's liberty should be employed. Obviously, the government interest in an accurate resolution of competency issues (which defendants share) is compelling enough to justify commitments reasonably necessary to professional assessments of competency. However, most writers agree that

---

> in particular, they ought not to be suffered to go loose, to the terror of the king's subjects. It was the doctrine of our auncient law, that persons deprived of their reason might be confined till they recovered their senses without waiting for the forms of a commission or other special authority from the crown: and now, by the vagrant acts, a method is chalked out for imprisoning, chaining, and sending them to their proper homes.

4 Blackstone Commentaries *24-25.

3. The Supreme Court has never ruled that the eighth amendment prohibition against excessive bail carries with it a right to bail. *Compare* Stack v. Boyle, 342 U.S. 1, 4, 5 (1951) ("Unless this right to bail before trial is preserved, the presumption of innocence secured only after centuries of struggle, would lose its meaning . . . [; b]ail set at a figure higher than an amount reasonably calculated to fulfill this purpose is 'excessive' under the Eighth Amendment"), *with* Carlson v. Landon, 342 U.S. 524, 545, *reh'g denied,* 343 U.S. 988 (1952) (the English Bill of Rights "has never been thought to accord a right to bail in all cases, but merely to provide that bail shall not be excessive in those cases where it is proper to grant bail . . . [; t]he Eighth Amendment has not prevented Congress from defining the class of cases in which bail shall be allowed in this country. . . .").

4. The sole constitutional control over preadjudication detention appears to be the fourth amendment; probable cause based on an ex parte showing suffices. *See* Schall v. Martin, 467 U.S. 253 (1984); Gerstein v. Pugh, 420 U.S. 103, 114 (1975). *See generally* Introduction to chapter 10 of the standards.

5. *See* Gobert, *Competency to Stand Trial: A Pre- and Post-*Jackson *Analysis,* 40 Tenn. L. Rev. 659, 671 (1973).

6. *See* Kaufman, *supra* note 2, at 469, 472-473; Weiner, *supra* note 1, at 696.

7. *See* standard 10-5.4 (criteria), 10-5.9 (procedural requirements).

confinement for examination is not always necessary and that outpatient examinations are often as effective as, and certainly less restrictive than, examinations conducted in hospitals.[8]

The standards strongly express the Association's policy that motions for incompetency examinations should not be used under any circumstances to achieve unrelated objectives.[9] The practice of automatic commitment based on such motions has proven the source of much of the well-documented abuse of incompetency evaluation procedures, for example, through preventive detention, threats of confinement in a mental institution as a bargaining tool, delay in judicial proceedings, and incarceration of unconvicted defendants against whom the prosecution case is weak.

Standard 7-4.3(a) explicitly condemns the practice of automatic commitments of defendants whose competence to stand trial has been questioned and thereby reinforces a fundamental principle in this part that incompetency procedures must be focused exclusively on determination of incompetency issues.[10] Consequently, defendants should be committed for professional evaluation only if confinement for examination is indispensable to a clinically valid diagnosis and report. The criterion of necessity precludes detention solely for the convenience of an examining expert. Through this approach, the standard recognizes that the state interest in accurate determinations of procedural competency is substantial enough to outweigh defendants' liberty interests, but that the state's interest cannot be peripheral; confinement may be ordered only if necessary for a personal examination. No other ground is sufficient to warrant a deprivation of liberty.

The standard emphasizes throughout the dichotomy between issues of confinement for competency evaluation and pretrial release. Although

---

8. *See* A. Stone, *supra* note 1, at 209; Project, *Legal Issues in State Mental Health Care: Proposals for Change,* 2 Mental Disability L. Rep. 617, 619 (1978). As one commentator has suggested,

> The amount of time spent in the hospital for evaluation (up to 60 days in the past and currently about 17 days) may not add to the decision-making ability of the evaluators, since the information obtained during the hospitalization has little influence on the judgments about competency. In terms of decision-making, the deprivation of liberty and expense of hospitalization may well be unnecessary.

Roesch, *Determining Competency to Stand Trial: An Examination of Evaluation Procedures in an Institutional Setting,* 47 J. Consulting & Clinical Psychology 542, 548 (1979).

9. *See* standard 7-4.2(d)-(e) and commentary, notes 22-30 and accompanying text.

10. *See supra,* note 9 and accompanying text.

the two issues are sometimes intertwined, courts should consider and rule on them separately. Pretrial release or detention should be determined in accordance with the principles elaborated in chapter 10, unaffected by concurrently pending motions for competency evaluations — a principle focused upon by standard 7-4.3. Paragraph (e) confirms that principle by cautioning against delay in reaching pretrial release or detention decisions because of the pendency of proceedings to determine present mental competence. Paragraph (b) provides that courts may condition pretrial release[11] on appearance for competency evaluations separately authorized in response to motions under standard 7-4.2, paragraphs (a) through (c). Premised on the least-restrictive alternative principle, however, confinement for examination should be authorized only if a pretrial release condition that a defendant report for outpatient examination is likely to fail in its implementation. It should be emphasized that the standard does not affect the fundamental pretrial release decision. It does not specify pretrial release or detention criteria,[12] other than to declare the irrelevancy of a defendant's possible incompetence to undergo criminal proceedings, which is a determination separate and independent from a release or detention decision.[13]

Standard 7-4.3(c) delineates the bases on which defendants, otherwise eligible for pretrial release, may be confined pending a competency evaluation. Courts should not authorize detention for the purpose unless they have determined that (1) a defendant will not submit to outpatient examination on which pretrial release has been conditioned, (2) a defendant has refused to appear at a designated time and place for outpatient examination, or (3) it is impossible[14] to conduct an adequate examination unless a defendant has been confined. The standard further stresses that decisions to confine must rest on specific determinations of fact and not entered routinely or automatically.

Standard 7-4.3(d), which likewise is bottomed on the least restrictive alternative principle, urges that restraint for purposes of competency examinations be in the least-restrictive setting suitable for the purpose and

---

11. *See* standard 10-5.3.

12. *See* standard 10-5.4(b) and commentary.

13. Note the premise of paragraph (d) that pretrial release and detention determinations should not be delayed because of pending competency evaluations.

14. The term *impossible* stresses that confinement is not to be ordered unless it is imperative for the examination; the mere preference of the examiner for examination in an institutional setting or the examiner's convenience is insufficient. *See* Marcey v. Harris, 400 F.2d 772, 774 (D.C. Cir. 1968).

limited to the minimum time necessary to complete them. Once an examination has been completed, a defendant should be returned immediately to the pretrial release or detention status independently ordered by a trial court.

Standard 7-4.4. Judicial order for competence evaluation

(a) Whenever, at any stage of the proceedings, a good faith doubt is raised as to the defendant's competence to stand trial, the court should order an evaluation and conduct a hearing into the competence of the defendant to stand trial. The court should follow this procedure whether the doubt arises from a motion of counsel, from information supplied by counsel, from the court's own observation of the defendant, or from any information otherwise known to the court.

(i) An evaluation of defendant's competence to stand trial should not be ordered by the court before there has been a judicial determination of probable cause for criminal prosecution unless the early evaluation is requested by defense counsel. If the court finds that the requisite probable cause for criminal prosecution does not exist, there should be no further inquiry into the defendant's competence to stand trial.

(ii) An evaluation to determine competence to stand trial should not be ordered before the defendant is represented by counsel who has had an opportunity to consult with the defendant and to be heard by the court.

(iii) The evaluator(s) appointed to perform the evaluation of the defendant's competence to stand trial should be persons qualified by training and experience to offer testimony to the court on matters affecting competence. A mental health or mental retardation professional who is appointed as an evaluator should have the qualifications set forth in standard 7-3.10.

(b) The order for evaluation should specify the nature of the evaluation to be conducted and should specify the legal criteria to be addressed by the evaluator in accordance with the requirements set forth in standard 7-3.5(d). Unless a joint evaluation has been requested by the defendant or for good cause shown in accordance

with standard 7-3.5(c), the evaluation should not include an evaluation into the defendant's sanity at the time of the offense, civil commitment, or other matters collateral to the issues of competence to stand trial.

(c) Each jurisdiction should establish time periods by which the evaluation should be concluded and a report returned to the court. Such periods normally should not exceed [seven] days in the case of a defendant in custody nor [fourteen] days in the case of a defendant at liberty. For good cause, the time periods might be extended but should never exceed [thirty] days.

Commentary Introduction

Standard 7-4.4 invokes concepts more fully explored in other standards and commentary. It articulates the necessity for a judicial determination of procedural competence after a reasonable doubt has emerged about its existence, a concept more fully discussed in standard 7-4.2. It incorporates a strong preference in all instances for competency hearings according to the criteria of standard 7-4.7 and addresses in detail two significant prerequisites to judicial orders for a competence evaluation. No evaluation should be ordered without a preliminary probable cause finding that a defendant committed an alleged offense. This requirement rests on the fact that a valid criminal prosecution must underlie an examination into competence in which a defendant can be compelled to cooperate. Because competency examinations are performed primarily for the benefit of the system rather than defendants, they should not be conducted without a preliminary determination of probable cause. The right to representation by counsel attaches at critical stages of a criminal prosecution at which important rights may be adversely affected. Standard 7-4.4 is premised on a judgment that a competence evaluation is such a stage and that both constitutional norms and professional ethical standards dictate representation by counsel by the time an examination is authorized.

Related Standards

ABA, Standards for Criminal Justice 4-2.1, 4-3.6, 4-5.1, 5-4.1, 5-4.2, 5-5.1, 6-2.5

Commentary

The obligation of trial courts to resolve doubts about defendants' procedural competence has long been established in federal practice[1] and is incorporated in due process of law.[2] Standard 7-4.4 acknowledges the existence of that duty whether or not counsel formally has asserted incompetence, by reiterating and condensing the more extensive coverage of standard 7-4.2.

Standard 7-4.4(a)(i) embodies Association policy that, because competency procedures seriously affect defendant liberty and ensuing defense presentations at trial, a finding of probable cause that a defendant has committed an alleged offense must precede judicial action to resolve the question of competence to stand trial. To elaborate, an assertion of a doubt concerning procedural competence to stand trial almost always generates a partial restriction of liberty when defendants are required to undergo outpatient evaluation or treatment; it may result in protracted pretrial deprivation of liberty during treatment to restore competence.[3] Ordinary and reasonable treatment, although it may not be refused, may cause unwanted side effects or affect the manner in which the defense case is later presented to a jury.[4]

The probable cause criterion in subparagraph (a)(i) is derived from the Supreme Court holding in *Gerstein v. Pugh*[5] that an adversary hearing is unnecessary to determine the probable cause that under the fourth amendment must underlie pretrial detention or a "significant restraint on

---

1. *See* Youtsey v. United States, 97 F. 937 (6th Cir. 1899).

> Assuming, as we shall, that no duty rested upon the court to impanel a jury to inquire whether the accused was in truth incapable of understanding the proceedings, and intelligently advising with his counsel as to his defense, and that it was optional with the court to call a jury, or to resort to any other special mode of aiding his judgment, it was nevertheless his duty to consider and determine the matter judicially; and the record should show affirmatively that upon this issue there has been the exercise of judicial judgment and discretion.

Id. at 946-947. *See also* introduction to part IV, notes 11-12 and accompanying text.

2. Drope v. Missouri, 420 U.S. 162 (1975); Pate v. Robinson, 383 U.S. 375 (1966). *See* commentary to standard 7-4.2, notes 1-5 and accompanying text, for a more extended discussion of the constitutional doctrine and dimensions of judicial responsibilities when doubts are suggested about defendants' procedural competence.

3. *See* standard 7-4.10 and commentary for a discussion of the treatment incompetent defendants may be required to undergo.

4. *See* standards 7-4.10, 7-4.14 and commentary.

5. 420 U.S. 103 (1975).

liberty."[6] The latter accurately characterizes the aftermath to an interjection of the issue of a defendant's competence to stand trial, which embraces compelled treatment to restore competency either as an outpatient or during involuntary hospitalization; in extreme cases, a defendant may even be confined in jail for treatment.[7] Appropriate treatment regimens may include medication affecting mental functioning or generating serious side effects. In addition, the single fact that defendants undergoing evaluation are required to reveal confidences to examining evaluators is sufficiently intrusive to justify a requirement of a preliminary determination of probable cause for criminal prosecution.

A competency decision is fundamentally unlike resolution of the affirmative defense of mental nonresponsibility [insanity]. The issue of incompetency can be injected in a criminal proceeding by either a court or prosecuting attorney over defense objection, unlike the substantive penal law defense that can be asserted only by defendants.[8] Treatment of incompetent defendants is restricted to attainment of competence and not restoration of mental health; it thus is inherently for the benefit of the criminal justice system and not for defendants.[9] Accordingly, the validity of the underlying criminal charges appropriately should be tested, at least to the modest extent reflected in a probable cause standard. The suitable mechanism for the purpose is the nonadversarial probable-cause determination mandated by *Pugh.* If the requisite probable cause cannot be established, no further action ought to be taken with respect to a competence evaluation, although civil hospitalization proceedings might be initiated in a given case.[10]

Standard 7-4.4(a)(ii) advocates a second requirement to be met before a competency evaluation may be ordered: A defendant should be represented by counsel before being required to submit to evaluation. In *Coleman v. Alabama,*[11] the Supreme Court established the principle that counsel is required at any "critical stage" of the proceedings, defined as any part of the proceedings at which important rights might be affected.[12] The standard equates a judicial order authorizing a competence evalu-

6. *Id.* at 114.
7. *See* standard 7-4.10 and commentary.
8. *See* standard 7-6.3.
9. *See* standard 7-4.10 and commentary.
10. *See* State v. McCredden, 33 Wis. 2d 661, 148 N.W.2d 33 (1967).
11. 399 U.S. 1 (1970).
12. *Id.* at 9.

ation to a "critical stage" of the proceedings, because important rights are involved. The first of these obviously is the right to liberty, which may be curtailed for the benefit of the system whenever a defendant is committed for evaluation and perhaps subsequent treatment or, to a lesser extent, circumscribed if a defendant is ordered to submit to outpatient treatment. A second right inheres in the requirement that defendants, in conversing with professional evaluators, reveal confidential or incriminating information; the advice of counsel is very important under such circumstances. A third relates to the core element in a competency inquiry, namely, a client's ability to assist counsel.[13] It is critical that defense counsel have an early opportunity to assess a defendant's competency in that regard.[14] Standard 7-4.4 rests on Association policy, reflected elsewhere in the standards,[15] that defendants ought to be represented at the earliest possible stage of criminal prosecutions and proceedings collateral to them, including determinations of competence to stand trial. It also is consistent with professional ethical standards governing psychiatrists.[16]

Standard 7-4.4(a)(iii) confirms that evaluators should be professionally qualified to conduct diagnostic examinations[17] and testify as expert witnesses.[18] Under paragraph (b), an appointing court should specify the nature of the evaluation to be conducted and the legal criteria to be addressed by the evaluator.[19] The same paragraph confirms the premise that competency evaluations should not extend to collateral matters unless a defendant has requested a multipurpose examination or cause has been shown for one.[20]

The important liberty interest of defendants implicated by compelled evaluations bearing on competency[21] dictates that evaluations should be promptly concluded and reported to the appointing court. Paragraph (c) advocates adoption of restricted time limitations governing competency

---

13. *See* commentary to standard 7-4.1, notes 29-32 and accompanying text.
14. *See* standards 7-4.1, 7-4.8 and commentary.
15. *See* standards 5-4.2, 5-5.1 and commentary.
16. The American Psychiatric Association position is that the ethics of the profession "preclude the psychiatric evaluation of any adult charged with criminal acts prior to access to, or availability of, legal counsel." Principle 4, annotation 13 (1981 ed.). *See* Amicus Curiae Brief of American Psychiatric Association, Byers v. United States, No. 78-1451 (D.C. Cir. 1981).
17. *See* standard 7-3.10.
18. *See* standard 7-3.13.
19. *See* standard 7-3.5(d).
20. *See* standard 7-3.5(c).
21. *See supra,* notes 5-10 and accompanying text.

evaluations of defendants in custody (a recommended seven-day maximum period) or at liberty (a recommended fourteen-day maximum). Extensions based on cause shown should never exceed a recommended thirty days beyond the base period.

Standard 7-4.5. Report of evaluator

(a) The first matter to be addressed in the report should be the assessment of the defendant's competence to stand trial. If it is determined that the defendant is competent to stand trial, issues relating to treatment or habilitation should not be addressed. If it is determined that the defendant is incompetent to stand trial, or that the defendant is competent to stand trial but that continued competence is dependent upon maintenance of treatment or habilitation, the evaluator should then report on the treatment or habilitation necessary for the defendant to attain or maintain competence.

(b) If it is determined that treatment or habilitation is necessary for the defendant to attain or maintain competence, the report should address the following issues:

(i) the condition causing the incompetence;

(ii) the treatment or habilitation required for the defendant to attain or maintain competence and an explanation of appropriate treatment alternatives in order of choice;

(iii) the availability of the various types of acceptable treatment or habilitation in the local geographical area. The evaluator should indicate the agencies or settings in which such treatment or habilitation might be obtained. Whenever the treatment or habilitation would be available in an outpatient setting, the evaluating expert should make such fact clear in the report;

(iv) the likelihood of the defendant's attaining competence under the treatment or habilitation and the probable duration of the treatment or habilitation.

(c) If the evaluating expert determines that the only appropriate treatment or habilitation would require that the defendant be taken into custody or involuntarily committed, then the report should include the following:

(i) an analysis of whether the defendant, because of the condition causing mental incompetence, meets the criteria for involuntary civil commitment or placement set forth by law;

(ii) whether there is a substantial probability that the defendant will attain competence to stand trial within the reasonably foreseeable future;

(iii) the nature and probable duration of the treatment or habilitation required for the defendant to attain competence;

(iv) alternatives other than involuntary confinement which were considered by the evaluator and the reasons for the rejection of such alternatives.

Commentary Introduction

Standard 7-4.5 outlines the information necessary to judicial determinations of competence to be contained in reports from court-appointed evaluators. It is to be read in conjunction with standard 7-4.9, governing judicial orders for treatment, and the more general criteria for evaluator reports in standard 7-3.7. The standard establishes a dichotomy between the issues of competence and treatment; they should not be confused and evaluating professionals ought not address treatment concerns until they have resolved the question of incompetence. Standard 7-4.9 establishes a like sequence for judicial determinations of procedural competency. Competency evaluation reports should contain adequate information about treatment that courts can use in discharging their supervisory role over treatment or habilitation to achieve defendant procedural capacity. This is particularly important if treatment may entail involuntary hospitalization or commitment; committing courts must be able to ascertain, based at least in part on information contained in competency evaluation reports, that treatment under court order will generate competence within the reasonably foreseeable future.

Related Standards

ABA, Standards for Criminal Justice 7-1.1, 7-3.3, 7-3.7, 7-3.8, 7-4.6, 7-4.8, 7-4.9, 7-4.10, 7-4.13, 7-4.14

Commentary

Accurate communication between judges and lawyers, on the one hand, and mental health and mental retardation professionals, on the other, has been a problem in the interaction of the legal discipline and the behavioral sciences. It is nowhere more evident than in the context of determining present mental competence, particularly in the nature of evaluation reports on competency submitted by examining professionals to the courts that authorized an evaluation. The most frequent block to effective communication has been a confusion of competence with mental illness or psychosis, dangerousness, mental nonresponsibility [insanity] at the time of an alleged offense, or even a defendant's treatment needs based on mental illness or mental retardation.[1] In fact, issues of mental illness and present mental competence clearly are not of necessity interdependent; defendants can be incompetent to undergo criminal proceedings and yet not be mentally ill or mentally retarded,[2] or they can be competent to stand trial despite severe mental illness.[3] As a corollary, treatment appropriate to achieve present mental competence may not necessarily be congruent with that appropriate to cure or remit an underlying mental illness or mental retardation.[4]

Standard 7-4.5(a) addresses evaluation reports bearing on present mental competence and treatment or habilitation appropriate to achieve it, and should be read in context with the more general chapter 7 standards governing mental evaluation reports.[5] The format for information to be supplied in evaluation reports corresponds to and in effect establishes the sequence of judicial determinations leading to a decision concerning present mental competence.[6] The standard cautions evaluators first to address the issue of competence and then to consider treatment or

---

1. Geller & Lister, *The Process of Criminal Commitment for Pre-trial Psychiatric Examination and Evaluation*, 135 Am. J. Psychiatry 53, 58 (1978); Mickenberg, *Competency to Stand Trial and the Mentally Retarded Defendant: The Need for a Multi-Disciplinary Solution to a Multi-Disciplinary Problem*, 17 Cal. W.L. Rev. 365 (1981); Roesch & Golding, *Legal and Judicial Interpretation of Competency to Stand Trial Statutes and Procedures*, 16 Criminology 420 (1978); Note, *Incompetency to Stand Trial*, 81 Harv. L. Rev. 454 (1967).

2. One of the most telling examples of the dichotomy is the case of People v. Lang, 76 Ill. 2d 311, 391 N.E.2d 350, *cert. denied sub nom.* Lang v. Illinois, 444 U.S. 954 (1979), and *cert. denied sub nom.* De Vito v. Lang, 444 U.S. 1045 (1980), in which a deaf defendant was held incompetent to stand trial but could not be treated because he was not "mentally ill" as defined by the statute.

3. *See* B. Ennis & R. Emery, The Rights of Mental Patients 101 (1978); Pizzi, *Competency to Stand Trial in Federal Courts: Conceptual and Constitutional Problems*, 45 U. Chi. L. Rev. 21 (1977).

4. Rosenberg, *Competency for Trial: A Problem in Interdisciplinary Communication*, 53 Judicature 316 (1970). Throughout this commentary, references to "treatment" are generic; the term includes aspects of habilitation, education, and training appropriate to achieve competence to stand trial.

5. *See* standards 7-3.7, 7-3.8 and commentary.

6. *See* standard 7-4.9 and commentary.

habilitation needs only if defendants appear to be incompetent. This should forestall confusion on the part of both professional evaluators and judges between treatment suitable to achieve present mental competency and treatment or habilitation dictated by mental illness or mental retardation unrelated to competence. Standards 7-4.8 and 7-4.9 note the correlative responsibility of trial courts to determine the two issues separately; judges, like professional evaluators, should not consider mandates for treatment until they have found defendants incompetent to stand trial and not only mentally ill or mentally retarded.[7]

Standard 7-4.5(b) delineates the appropriate contents of evaluation reports bearing on treatment or habilitation to achieve competence. The listed information is either necessary or useful to recipient courts in supervising the treatment or habilitation regimens authorized in their orders and in safeguarding defendants' rights to treatment or habilitation through the least-restrictive available methodology. It may not be clear as a matter of constitutional doctrine whether judicial overview of treatment or habilitation to achieve competency is directive or merely an aspect of judicial review. It is evident, however, that courts have a constitutional responsibility to see that treatment is authorized and provided solely and appropriately to achieve competence and for no other purpose, at least if defendants are involuntarily committed for treatment or habilitation.

In *Jackson v. Indiana,*[8] the Supreme Court enunciated the principle that defendants committed to undergo treatment or habilitation to restore or achieve competence to stand trial may be held only for the

> reasonable period of time necessary to determine whether there is a substantial probability that [they] will attain that capacity in the foreseeable future. . . . Furthermore, even if it is determined that the defendant probably soon will be able to stand trial, . . . continued commitment must be justified by progress toward that goal.[9]

A committing court, therefore, must be informed, both at the outset of treatment or habilitation and periodically thereafter, about the nature of the treatment or habilitation regimen and a defendant's progress under it.

The policy reflected in the standard is consistent with the position of the American Psychiatric Association that the onus should be placed on mental health or mental retardation professionals and not the courts to ensure that "all possibilities for securing adequate treatment should be

7. *See* standards 7-4.8, 7-4.9 and commentary.
8. 406 U.S. 715 (1972).
9. *Id.* at 738.

explored. . . ."[10] Standard 7-4.5(b) anticipates the expectation in standard 7-4.9 that judicial orders authorizing treatment or habilitation to restore or achieve procedural competence should envision ongoing judicial overview of treatment in conformity with the least restrictive alternative principle.[11] Under the standards, trial courts clearly are not considered as equivalents of treating professionals; they do not prescribe or administer treatment or select from among different treatment methodologies equally suitable to effect competence.[12] Nonetheless, they are under a general duty to monitor the appropriateness of court-authorized treatment or habilitation and to require specific information from professional evaluators to enable them to discharge that duty. The information to be contained in evaluation reports under standard 7-4.5(b) is, therefore, essential to an ensuing judicial order for treatment or habilitation to achieve competence, whether or not commitment is necessary.

Standard 7-4.5(c)(i) expresses the principle that defendants should not be involuntarily committed for treatment or habilitation unless they meet a jurisdiction's statutory criteria for involuntary civil commitment; professional evaluators should report their findings and conclusions bearing on those criteria. Subparagraphs (ii) and (iii) have been drawn to meet the stringent requirements of *Jackson v. Indiana*[13] that courts monitor the treatment or habilitation of defendants committed for the purpose of attaining competence. Accordingly, they incorporate the standard of "substantial probability" that committed defendants will attain competence within the foreseeable future, as well as a judicial specification of the nature and probable duration of treatment or habilitation required for the purpose. The final dimension, set out in subparagraph (iv), is an indication by evaluators of other less-restrictive treatment alternatives than involuntary confinement that they considered and the reasons for rejecting them. In this way, recipient courts can meet the constitutional responsibility to select the least-restrictive suitable treatment or habilitation methodology for each defendant.

---

10. American Psychiatric Association, *Position Statement on the Question of Adequacy of Treatment*, 123 Am. J. Psychiatry 1458 (1967); American Bar Association, *Summary of Action of the House of Delegates*, 1978 Annual Meeting 19.

The ABA endorsed the recommendation of the President's Commission on Mental Health that state mental health laws should provide ". . . (b) a right to treatment in the least restrictive setting." *Ibid.*

Standard 7-4.5(b) and (c)(iv) utilize the concept of least restrictive or least drastic alternative first articulated in Lake v. Cameron, 364 F.2d 657 (D.C. Cir. 1966).

11. *See* standard 7-4.9 and commentary.
12. *See* standard 7-4.10 and commentary.
13. 406 U.S. 715 (1972). *See supra*, notes 8-9 and accompanying text.

Standard 7-4.6. Use of reports; defendant remaining mute

(a) Any information or testimony elicited from the defendant at any hearing or examination on competence or contained in any motion filed by the defendant or any information furnished by the defendant to the court or to any person evaluating or providing mental health or mental retardation services, and any information derived therefrom and any testimony of experts or others based on information elicited from the defendant, should be considered privileged information and should be used only in a proceeding to determine the defendant's competence to stand trial and related treatment or habilitation issues. The defendant may waive use of information contained in a report evaluating competence to stand trial by using the report or parts thereof for any other purpose. The defendant's use of the evaluation report for a purpose other than the determination of competence to stand trial should be considered a waiver of any privilege of nondisclosure, and the prosecutor should be permitted to use the report or any part of the report, subject only to the applicable rules of evidence.

(b) The court should have the authority to confine involuntarily, for observation to determine the issue of competence to stand trial, a defendant who refuses to cooperate or to provide sufficient information to permit a determination of competence.

(i) The confinement may continue for such time as is necessary for the evaluation to determine competence, but should last no longer than [fourteen] days under the initial order with such extensions as may be necessary to determine competence.

(ii) At the expiration of [sixty] days, however, the court must hold a hearing at which the burden shall be on the prosecutor to show justification for further confinement.

Commentary Introduction

Standard 7-4.6 recognizes the principle that defendants must cooperate with evaluators in the course of a court-ordered competence examination, whether the competence issue has been asserted by defendant, prosecuting attorney, or court. It rests on the premise that, because trial of incompetent defendants denies due process of law, courts are obligated to determine defendant competency to ensure the constitutional validity of ensuing criminal proceedings. Because competency evaluations seldom can be accomplished without a defendant's cooperation, courts must have the power to compel that cooperation, even though it entails a risk of incriminating admissions in response to appropriate evaluator inquiries. Uncooperative defendants should be involuntarily committed, based on their refusal alone, to enable professional evaluators to observe them and reach a professional conclusion about their competence. Privilege against self-incrimination is safeguarded through stringent limitations on prosecution use of information obtained through a defendant's compelled cooperation with an evaluator.

Related Standards

ABA, Standards for Criminal Justice 6-2.5, 7-3.3, 7-3.4, 7-3.6, 7-3.8, 7-3.13, 7-4.2, 7-4.3, 7-4.8

Commentary

Standard 7-4.6 harmonizes the conflict between the judicial system's need to compel defendant cooperation in court-ordered competency evaluations and defendants' privilege against self-incrimination. If a court has a good-faith doubt about a defendant's present mental competence, it is obliged to resolve the issue promptly.[1] That in turn requires an accurate professional assessment of mental condition that must rest, at least in part, on information supplied by a defendant, some or all of which may be incriminating because it relates to an alleged offense.[2] Indeed, granted the nature of the techniques commonly used by qualified evaluators, a more serious infringement of self-incrimination protections

1. *See* standard 7-4.2 and commentary for a general discussion of the judicial responsibility to determine competence whenever a good faith doubt about competence is raised.

2. The court in Blaisdell v. Commonwealth, 372 Mass. 753, 759-760, 364 N.E.2d 191, 197 (1977), pointed out that

> [n]ot only may a defendant in such an examination be called on to recite his life history, emotions, feelings, thoughts and views as to relations with others, but, more importantly, to render the examination completely effective, he may have to talk about the crime charged itself as well as acts, events and emotions relative to its commission. From this it is clear that any order that a defendant fully cooperate with the psychiatrist may well result in disclosure of significant information which will constitute either a full confession of the acts charged in the indictment or result in admissions which may be probative as to those acts. . . .

may ensue than in the stationhouse interrogation severely restricted by the Supreme Court in *Miranda v. Arizona:*[3] Because evaluators occupy a somewhat ambivalent position, defendants may see them as a "helper, healer or sympathizer,"[4] even though they discharge an objective professional role on behalf of appointing or authorizing courts. Consequently, they often obtain information that defendants would conceal from investigators whom they recognize as adversaries.[5] To require defendants to cooperate in interviews of this sort might well infringe privilege against self-incrimination unless suitable safeguards are established.[6] Standard 7-4.6 delineates those safeguards.

Courts, on varying grounds, generally have sustained the constitutionality of legal requirements that defendants undergo compelled psychiatric examinations. At times, the rationale has been that interviews of that nature are not as inherently coercive as other forms of custodial interrogation,[7] while in other precedent[8] the results have been viewed as "real" or "physical," and thus not as "testimony," compulsion of which is prohibited by the self-incrimination clause.[9] The latter position is premised on the assumption that defendant statements are usable only as a basis for an evaluator's opinion, so that their truth or falsity is irrelevant.[10]

The Supreme Court addressed the matter in *Estelle v. Smith,*[11] which arose from prosecution use, at the capital-penalty phase of a murder

---

3. 384 U.S. 436 (1966). *See also* Estelle v. Smith, 451 U.S. 454 (1981), *discussed infra,* notes 11-13 and accompanying text.

4. *See* commentary to standard 7-3.1, note 9 and accompanying text.

5. Diamond & Louisell, *The Psychiatrist as Expert Witness: Some Ruminations and Speculations,* 63 Mich. L. Rev. 1335, 1349 (1965).

6. *See generally* Bennett, *A Guided Tour Through Selected ABA Standards Relating to Incompetence to Stand Trial,* 53 Geo. Wash. L. Rev. 375, 392-396 (1985). *See also* standard 7-3.4 for a general discussion of evaluation reports and their use. For an excellent overview of the problems caused by the interface between compelled examinations and privilege, *see* Meister, *Miranda on the Couch: An Approach to Problems of Self-Incrimination, Right to Counsel, and Miranda Warnings in Pre-Trial Psychiatric Examinations of Criminal Defendants,* 11 Col. J.L. & Soc. Probs. 414 (1975); Weiner, *Mental Disability and the Criminal Law,* in The Mentally Disabled and the Law 693, 701-702 (S. Brakel, J. Parry & B. Weiner eds., 3d ed. 1985).

7. United States v. Cohen, 530 F.2d 43 (5th Cir.), *cert. denied,* 429 U.S. 855 (1976).

8. *See, e.g.,* United States v. Baird, 414 F.2d 700, 709 (2d Cir. 1969), *cert. denied,* 396 U.S. 1005 (1970).

9. *See* Mincey v. Arizona, 437 U.S. 385 (1978) (defendant's confession, obtained under coercion, was inadmissible for any purpose including impeachment of trial testimony). *See also* South Dakota v. Neville, 459 U.S. 553 (1983) (refusal to take an intoxication test was not compelled according to fifth amendment criteria).

10. *See* State v. Whitlow, 45 N.J. 3, 210 A.2d 763 (1965).

11. 451 U.S. 454 (1981).

prosecution, of statements made by Smith to a prosecution-retained psychiatrist who interviewed Smith under court order to evaluate Smith's competency to stand trial. The Court ruled that use of Smith's incriminating statements to support the prosecution's case-in-chief on the death penalty issue infringed privilege against self-incrimination.[12] It refused to characterize defendant admissions under such circumstances as nontestimonial in character.[13]

Standard 7-4.6(a) provides the *quid pro quo* for compelled cooperation on the part of defendants in the form of a strict prohibition against prosecution or judicial use of incriminating admissions for any purpose other than a determination of competency, unless they waive the privilege by word or procedural activity before or during trial. The bar embraces defendant disclosures made concerning incompetency or treatment or habilitation of the underlying mental infirmity, including testimony and derivative evidence, the existence or location of which is revealed by a defendant in the course of a compelled evaluation; the constitutional privilege against self-incrimination embraces derivative as well as direct evidence.[14] Only if a defendant determines to submit an evaluating professional's expert testimony or report on some issue other than present mental competence will privilege be waived, thereby opening up the contents and evidence derived from them to prosecution use (as permitted by the evidence and procedure law of the jurisdiction). In this way,

---

12. The Court also invalidated the psychiatrist's testimony on the basis of its rule that interrogation of defendants against whom adversary criminal proceedings have commenced cannot be conducted in the absence of counsel or a valid waiver of counsel's attendance, based on the sixth amendment right to counsel. *See id.* at 470-471; United States v. Henry, 447 U.S. 264 (1980); Brewer v. Williams, 430 U.S. 387, *reh'g denied,* 431 U.S. 925 (1977).

13. The *Smith* Court summarized its position as follows:

> A criminal defendant, who neither initiates a psychiatric examination nor attempts to introduce any psychiatric evidence, may not be compelled to respond to a psychiatrist if his statements can be used against him at a capital sentencing proceeding. . . . If, upon being adequately warned, respondent had indicated that he would not answer [the psychiatrist's] questions, the validly ordered competency examination nevertheless could have proceeded upon the condition that the results would be applied solely for that purpose. In such circumstances, the proper conduct and use of competency and sanity examinations are not frustrated, but the State must make its case on dangerousness in some other way.

451 U.S. at 468.

14. *See* Kastigar v. United States, 406 U.S. 441, *reh'g denied,* 408 U.S. 931 (1972); Blaisdell v. Commonwealth, 372 Mass. 753, 762, 364 N.E.2d 191, 198 (1977). It is not clear whether the inevitable discovery doctrine of Nix v. Williams, 467 U.S. 431 (1984), governs fifth amendment compulsion cases as well as fourth and sixth amendment violations.

the protection envisioned in the standard is coextensive with privilege against self-incrimination.[15]

Standard 7-4.6(b) is bottomed on the reasoning of *Estelle v. Smith.*[16] It assumes the obligation of defendants to assist in resolving the issue of their present mental competence through submission to competency evaluations. It focuses on the very difficult matter of appropriate judicial responses to defendants who refuse to cooperate even though their self-incrimination rights are adequately protected under standard 7-4.6(a). It is evident that courts cannot punish, through contempt of court or otherwise, defendants whose present mental competency is at issue, based on a court's good-faith doubt about their competency; noncooperation probably cannot be characterized as willful and therefore contumacious.[17] Accordingly, standard 7-4.6(b) recommends no direct enforcement mechanism in such instances. Nevertheless, the overriding judicial interest in an accurate resolution of the incompetency issue should permit a court immediately to order the commitment of an uncooperative defendant, based on the lack of cooperation alone, for whatever limited period is necessary to allow professional evaluators to reach expert conclusions concerning triability,[18] despite the want of defendant's cooperation.

Standard 7-4.7. Necessity for hearing on competence to stand trial

(a) In every case in which a good faith doubt of the defendant's competence to stand trial has been raised and as soon as practicable after receipt of the reports of the evaluators, the court should conduct a hearing on the issue of competence to stand trial unless all parties stipulate that no hearing is necessary and the court concurs. If the defendant has been confined for examination, the hearing should be

15. *See* New Jersey v. Portash, 440 U.S. 450 (1979).

16. 451 U.S. 454 (1981). *See supra,* notes 11-13 and accompanying text.

17. While the standard does not specifically delineate sanctions to be applied for willful failure to obey a lawful court order, it is apparent that a court lawfully may punish defendants who competently and intentionally fail to comply with a valid court order, usually in the form of criminal or civil contempt proceedings.

18. However, one should keep in mind McNeil v. Director, Patuxent Institution, 407 U.S. 245 (1972), which held that a person could not be indefinitely maintained in diagnostic status under a defective delinquency statute based on his failure to cooperate with examiners (and in *McNeil,* not longer than the individual could have been imprisoned following conviction of the criminal charges that gave way to the defective delinquency diagnostic commitment).

held within [seven] days of the receipt of the report of the evaluators; if the defendant is at liberty it should be held within [thirty] days.

(b) If the parties agree on the issue of competence to stand trial or issues related to treatment or habilitation, a stipulation containing the factual basis for the agreement may be accepted by the court and the court, after review of the factual basis for the stipulation, should enter the appropriate order on the basis of the stipulation. In the absence of stipulation by the parties and concurrence by the court, a hearing on the issues should be mandatory in all cases.

(c) Trial by jury should not be required for the hearing on the issues of competence to stand trial and issues related to treatment or habilitation, provided that in those jurisdictions which authorize trial by jury for determination of issues of involuntary civil commitment, jury trial should be available to a defendant to determine issues of competence to stand trial and of involuntary confinement for treatment or habilitation to effect competence.

Commentary Introduction

Standard 7-4.7 recommends that a court, prosecuting attorney, and defendant whose competence is at issue be accorded an absolute right to a hearing after an evaluation report has been submitted to an authorizing court; it recommends that the court specifically ascertain competency. Nevertheless, to forestall unnecessary expenditure of limited resources, the standard recognizes that an evidentiary hearing can be waived under specified circumstances, provided a trial court reviews the facts contained in an evaluation report and counsel for both the prosecution and defense stipulate as uncontroverted the facts establishing competence or its lack. The Association policy expressed in the standard is that the jury trial right need not extend to competency proceedings, which may be conducted in the form of bench trial.

Related Standards

ABA, Standards for Criminal Justice 3-3.3, 4-4.4, 7-1.1, 7-1.3, 7-1.5, 7-1.13, 7-4.8, 7-4.9

Commentary

Courts historically have appeared reluctant to question the reported conclusions of professional evaluators relating to defendants' present mental competence, have accepted unsubstantiated conclusions at face value, and have based competency rulings solely on them.[1] In some jurisdictions, hearings have been required only if evaluators report that defendants are incompetent but not if they find defendants competent; in the latter event, defendants have been returned immediately for trial.[2] Yet it is in precisely the latter context that defendants' rights are most seriously threatened, because incompetent defendants may be forced to trial, an event clearly prohibited under the due process clauses as interpreted by *Pate v. Robinson*[3] and *Drope v. Missouri.*[4]

Standard 7-4.7(a) rests on the premise that either the prosecuting attorney or defendant should have an absolute right to a competency hearing.[5] Although the full implications of the Supreme Court's *Robinson* decision are unclear, and it may be limited to its somewhat peculiar facts, its language, particularly as explained in the later *Drope* decision, supports a conclusion that a hearing is constitutionally required if a good faith doubt about competency has precipitated a competency evaluation.[6]

---

1. A study of competence proceedings in North Carolina revealed that 59 percent of the judges interviewed never held hearings on issues of incompetence to stand trial but relied solely on evaluator reports. Thirty-five percent indicated that they never disagreed with conclusions in the reports while the other 65 percent said they seldom disagreed. Roesch & Golding, *Legal and Judicial Interpretation of Competency to Stand Trial Statutes and Procedures,* 16 CRIMINOLOGY 420 (1978). The North Carolina experience is not atypical. Another author reported that courts conducted bench trial of competency issues, adopted conclusions in evaluator reports without question, and processed defendants with "astonishing speed." Bacon, *Incompetency to Stand Trial: Commitment to an Inclusive Test,* 42 S. CAL. L. REV. 444 (1969). Still another investigator pointed out that hearings on incompetence in New York were of three kinds: so-called confirmation hearings at which all participants agreed with the report, hearings at which only the defendant disagreed, and those at which the prosecution disagreed with the conclusions of the report. The "confirmation" hearings, which constituted the bulk of the competence determinations, were generally completed within three minutes. "Thus, most of the confirmations which comprised 64 percent of the 129 hearings were two- or three-minute rubber stampings of the psychiatric reports. There was no serious dialogue on the legal and medical issues." H. STEADMAN, BEATING A RAP?, DEFENDANTS FOUND INCOMPETENT TO STAND TRIAL 46 (1979) [hereinafter cited as H. STEADMAN].
2. *See* H. STEADMAN, *supra* note 1, at 39.
3. 383 U.S. 375 (1966). *See* introduction to part IV, notes 17-19 and accompanying text.
4. 420 U.S. 162 (1974). *See* introduction to part IV, notes 20-21 and accompanying text.
5. *See generally* Bennett, *A Guided Tour Through Selected ABA Standards Relating to Incompetence to Stand Trial,* 53 GEO. WASH. L. REV. 375, 396-398 (1985); Weiner, *Mental Disability and the Criminal Law,* in THE MENTALLY DISABLED AND THE LAW 693, 702 (S. Brakel, J. Parry & B. Weiner eds., 3d ed. 1985).
6. "We believe that the evidence introduced on Robinson's behalf entitled him to a hearing on the issue. The court's failure to make such inquiry thus deprived Robinson of his constitutional right to a fair trial." Pate v. Robinson, 383 U.S. at 385.

Judicial failure to afford a formal hearing, standing alone, may be viewed to infringe the "meaningful opportunity to be heard" on the issue of present mental competency, required by due process as a prerequisite to a judicial determination of the matter.[7]

Compelling policy grounds support the conclusion that courts and prosecuting attorneys, as well as defendants under the mandates of the due process clauses, should have an opportunity to contest conclusions contained in evaluation reports. First, competence is a legal, not a medical or psychological determination, based on legal and not medical or psychological criteria.[8] As has been noted throughout this part, mental illness or mental retardation may or may not be relevant to present mental competence: some defendants may be severely mentally ill or mentally retarded and yet be competent to undergo proceedings, while others may be incompetent despite the want of a discernable mental illness.[9] Moreover, the primary interests of courts and lawyers, on the one hand, and mental health and mental retardation professionals, on the other, may well be divergent. The latter are principally concerned with diagnosing and treating mental abnormalities, and therefore may not be attuned to the legal dimensions of present mental competence. Courts, in contrast, focus on triability as delineated by constitutional precedents; treatment or habilitation is significant only to the extent that it may achieve triability of an incompetent defendant within the reasonably foreseeable future. Moreover, although evaluation reports are helpful to the extent they recount evaluator observations and descriptions of observed data in relation to diagnosable mental conditions, they diminish in value when evaluators attempt to translate their observations into legal conclusions.[10] The standard, therefore, takes the position that both parties must have the right to have a hearing on the report, to question evaluator conclu-

7. State *ex rel.* Matalik v. Schubert, 57 Wis. 2d 315, 204 N.W.2d 13, 18 (1973) (*citing* Boddie v. Connecticut, 401 U.S. 371 (1971)).

8. *See* commentary to standard 7-4.1, notes 20-34 and accompanying text.

9. *See* commentary to standard 7-4.1, notes 35-36 and accompanying text.

10. Pizzi, *Competency to Stand Trial in Federal Courts: Conceptual and Constitutional Problems,* 45 U. Chi. L. Rev. 21 (1977) [hereinafter cited as Pizzi]. In fact, researchers discovered that many evaluation reports were couched only in conclusory legal terms and sometimes confused the tests for incompetence and mental nonresponsibility [insanity] to the extent that, at least in one study, the researchers labeled the majority of such reports "empty and meaningless, and yet they were accepted and acted upon by the courts as if they contained information which could be construed as evidence and, as such, decided." Hess & Thomas, *Incompetency to Stand Trial: Procedures, Results, and Problems,* 119 Am. J. Psychiatry, 713, 715 (1963). *See* commentary to standard 7-4.1, notes 20-21 and accompanying text.

sions, and to require judicial findings on the issues of competence and treatment or habilitation.

Standard 7-4.7(b) outlines the circumstances in which a competency hearing should be considered waivable. Commentators have differed on the availability of waiver. Some have condemned waiver under any circumstances; courts have a responsibility to adjudicate competence that cannot be avoided even through stipulation.[11] In effect, judicial action without a hearing constitutes a delegation of the judicial decisionmaking authority to professional evaluators.[12] Other authors, basing their conclusions on more pragmatic considerations, have argued that a hearing, although available to the parties, should be waivable in certain instances.[13] Standard 7-4.7(b) adopts essentially the second position by recognizing at least a limited possibility for waiver.

However, the requirements for waiver are strict. Both the prosecution and defense counsel must agree on waiver and the court independently must determine that adjudication of competency without a hearing is proper. In effect, all must agree that a competency hearing will be merely a waste of time and resources. Under the standard, either party has an absolute right to a hearing on request or, in the absence of a request, one must be held if the court deems it proper despite absence of demand by the parties. Even if neither party requests a hearing on the issues raised by an evaluation report, the hearing may be waived only after the court independently has reviewed the report and adopted its findings. A court cannot abdicate its responsibilities to an evaluating professional by rubber-stamping an evaluation report and either ordering a defendant to proceed to trial or requiring a defendant to undergo treatment or habilitation to attain competency. Instead, it must review the report and stipulations of counsel and reach an independent conclusion that no issue of fact need be litigated. In sum, the judicial decision must be based on the undisputed and reported facts, but it must be a decision independently reached by the trial court.

---

11. Pizzi, *supra* note 10, at 52-53.

12. Gobert, *Competency to Stand Trial: A Pre- and Post-*Jackson *Analysis,* 40 Tenn. L. Rev. 659, 661 (1973).

13. The pragmatic considerations listed include matters of judicial economy and the unnecessary expenditure of prosecutorial, defense, treatment, and judicial resources resulting from the requirement of a hearing in instances in which all participants know the outcome in advance. *See* Wexler, *The Waivability of Recommitment Hearings,* 20 Ariz. L. Rev. 175 (1978).

Standard 7-4.7(c) takes the position that a jury determination of procedural competence is not constitutionally required even though a deprivation of liberty may be involved.[14] A defendant's triability is a matter peculiarly within the province of a court, which has a special responsibility to resolve it. However, in some jurisdictions, involuntary hospitalization for treatment has been considered a matter appropriate for jury determination. In those jurisdictions, it would deny equal protection to mandate a nonjury determination of cognate issues because of the pendency of a criminal charge.[15] Therefore, under those circumstances the jury trial right must be implemented in proceedings resulting in involuntary commitment for treatment or habilitation to attain present mental competence.

Standard 7-4.8. Hearing on competence; defendant's rights, evidence, and priority of issues

(a) Fundamental constitutional rights afforded a defendant in criminal cases should apply to the hearing on competence to stand trial.

(i) In all cases, the defendant should have the right to be present at the hearing, to confront and fully cross-examine witnesses, to call independent expert witnesses, to have compulsory process for the attendance of witnesses, and to have a transcript of the proceedings. Either party should have the authority to call and to examine as a court witness any person designated by the evaluators as a source of information for preparation of the evaluative report other than the defendant or the defense attorney.

(ii) The defendant should have the right to adequate notice and time to prepare for the hearing, including timely disclosure of the report of appointed evaluators and, if necessary, opportunity to interview or to depose the evaluators before the hearing.

14. *See* McKiever v. Pennsylvania, 403 U.S. 528 (1971) (fundamental fairness does not require jury trial in juvenile cases).

15. As the Court said in *Jackson:* "If criminal conviction and imposition of sentence are insufficient to justify less procedural and substantive protection against indefinite commitment than that generally available to all others, the mere filing of criminal charges surely cannot suffice." Jackson v. Indiana, 406 U.S. 715, 724 (1972).

(b) Evidence presented at the hearing should conform to rules of evidence applicable to criminal cases within that jurisdiction. The evaluators, whether called by the court or by either party, should be considered court witnesses and be subject to examination as such by either party.

(i) Defense counsel may elect to relate to the court personal observations of and conversations with the defendant to the extent that counsel does not disclose confidential communications or violate the attorney-client privilege; counsel so electing may be cross-examined to that extent.

(ii) The court may properly inquire of defense counsel about the professional attorney-client relationship and the client's ability to communicate effectively with counsel. The defense counsel, however, should not be required to divulge the substance of confidential communications or those that are protected by the attorney-client privilege. Defense counsel responding to inquiry by the court on its own motion should not be subject to cross-examination by the prosecutor.

(c) At the hearing, the court should consider separately each discrete issue raised and should first consider the issue of the defendant's competence to stand trial.

(i) The party raising the issue of incompetence should have the burden of going forward with the evidence to show incompetence. If the defendant has moved for evaluation then the defense should have the burden of going forward; if the prosecutor or the court on its own motion or on information supplied by the prosecutor has raised the issue, then the prosecutor should have the burden of going forward.

(ii) If the court, after hearing the evidence, finds by the greater weight of the evidence that the defendant is competent to stand trial the matter should proceed to trial; if not, the court should proceed to issues of treatment or habilitation to effect competence.

Commentary Introduction

Standard 7-4.8 covers the procedural rights available to defendants undergoing competency hearings, which essentially are those governing other stages of criminal proceedings. The standard urges the applicability of the usual rules of evidence applicable at criminal trials, and in particular it advocates a requirement that evaluating professionals be called as expert witnesses unless both the prosecution and defense stipulate to the contents of an evaluation report and the defendant waives the right to confront and cross-examine an evaluator. Standard 7-4.8(b) addresses the impact of professional ethical rules on defense counsel's availability to testify at a competency hearing; it approves such testimony as long as confidential communications are not disclosed or other breaches of attorney-client privilege do not occur. It places the burden of going forward on the defense if it moved for a competency evaluation and on the prosecution in all other instances. Standard 7-4.8(c)(ii) states the level of persuasion (proof) as the preponderance (greater weight) of the evidence. Trial courts are admonished to consider and decide the matter of present mental competence before addressing treatment and habilitation needs to attain competence.

Related Standards

ABA, Model Rules of Professional Conduct 1.7, 3.7(a)
ABA, Standards for Criminal Justice 4-5.2, 6-2.5, 7-1.3, 7-1.4, 7-1.5, 7-4.2, 7-4.7
ALI, Model Penal Code 4.07

Commentary

The baseline of standard 7-4.8(a) is that all rights afforded criminal defendants in the course of criminal proceedings apply to competency hearings,[1] which can result in significant deprivations of or restrictions on liberty in the form of commitments for treatment or habilitation to attain competence or orders to report involuntarily for outpatient treatment.[2] The delineated rights include adequate advance notice to facilitate preparation for hearings, discovery of evaluation reports and depositions of court-appointed evaluators, representation by counsel, compulsory process for witnesses including evaluating professionals, confrontation and

1. *See In re* Gault, 387 U.S. 1 (1967); Lessard v. Schmidt, 349 F. Supp. 1078 (E.D. Wis. 1972), *vacated,* 414 U.S. 473, *on remand,* 379 F. Supp. 1376 (E.D. Wis. 1974), *vacated,* 421 U.S. 957 (1975), *on remand,* 413 F. Supp. 1318 (E.D. Wis. 1976). This does not include jury trial. *See* commentary to standard 7-4.7(c), notes 13-14 and accompanying text.

2. *See* standard 7-4.3 and commentary.

cross-examination, and transcripts of competency hearings.[3] The catalog of rights in the standard does not dictate that competency hearings be adversarial, but it recognizes that they may become so.[4]

Standard 7-4.8(b) focuses on two discrete aspects of evidence law in the setting of competency hearings. The first is the general applicability of the rules of evidence; the premise in standard 7-4.8(b) is that the usual rules should govern this phase of a criminal proceeding. This principle is generally accepted, though with one exception: Some have contended that the hearsay rule should be relaxed so that evaluator reports are admissible even though the experts who prepared them do not appear at competency hearings. The standard rejects that position because it allows evaluator conclusions to stand without an effective opportunity to cross-examine,[5] a premise consistent with the standards' position that competency hearings are the norm.[6]

Another reason for confirming the governance of confrontation principles where evaluator expert testimony is concerned is that competency is a legal determination, not a medical or psychological diagnosis. Traditionally, evaluation reports have been couched in legal conclusory terms

3. Appeal is not listed because interlocutory appeal should not be available if defendants are found competent (the issue can be preserved for posttrial motions and appeal following conviction), and habeas corpus or other extraordinary process can be used to contest commitment or compelled outpatient treatment. There is no due process right to an appeal against a competency determination. Vardas v. Estelle, 715 F.2d 206, 208 (5th Cir. 1983), *cert. denied sub nom.* Vardas v. McKaskle, 104 S. Ct. 1603 (1984).

4. Some commentators contend that hearings should always be nonadversarial because competency determinations do not necessarily impel the prosecution and defense to take opposing positions. Indeed, both sides might agree to an appropriate disposition. Moreover, the usual roles may be reversed if a prosecuting attorney asserts incompetence and defense counsel competence. Even though defense counsel might seek to waive a client's procedural rights in such an instance, the usual adversary tools should be available to the defense if it opposes the prosecution position. How extensive the panoply of rights asserted in each case will be turns, of course, on its facts and circumstances. *See* Pizzi, *Competency to Stand Trial in Federal Courts: Conceptual and Constitutional Problems,* 45 U. Chi. L. Rev. 21 (1977) [hereinafter cited as Pizzi].

5. In at least one state it has been held a violation of a defendant's rights of confrontation and cross-examination to proceed on the basis of a report alone. State *ex rel.* Hawks v. Lazaro, 157 W. Va. 417, 202 S.E.2d 109 (1974). In the federal system, it has been ruled a violation of due process to commit a defendant for treatment for incompetence to stand trial solely on the basis of conclusory medical reports. Miller v. Blalock, 411 F.2d 548 (4th Cir. 1969).

6. *See* standard 7-4.7. If it is improper to proceed on the basis of the report of the evaluator without hearing, it is equally improper to hold a hearing that merely "rubber stamps" the report without meaningful testimony by the evaluator.

and not the language of clinical observations and diagnoses, and courts too frequently have accepted them uncritically.[7] Hence, the standard rests on the principle that evaluators must be present to testify to the observations and diagnoses underlying a professional conclusion of competence or incompetence tendered to aid courts in adjudicating present mental competence.[8] In this context, one should note that standard 7-4.8(a)(ii) contemplates timely disclosure to the defense of evaluation reports from court-appointed experts and opportunity to interview them or take their depositions.

An inflexible requirement that, in order to satisfy the hearsay rule, evaluating professionals must appear in court to lay foundation for introduction of the contents of their reports would, of course, be counterproductive under some circumstances. Therefore, the prosecution and defense need the option of stipulating to the contents of an evaluation report and dispensing with the attendance at a hearing of its source. That is appropriate, for example, if incompetency is conceded and a suitable treatment or habilitation program obvious. The parties, in other words, should not be placed in the position of having to waive a hearing entirely or undergo a fullblown hearing. To illustrate further, a defense attorney who accepts a client's lack of present mental competence, but who is dissatisfied with the treatment or habilitation recommended by an evaluator, should have the ability not only to stipulate to the evaluation report as far as it bears on competence but also to have the examiner present for examination and cross-examination on the matter of disposition. However, if counsel for either side or the court wants an evaluator to testify in person, the position of the standard is that the evaluator must appear.

The ability of defendants to consult and interact appropriately with their defense attorneys lies at the heart of the incompetency standard.[9] The premise on which standard 7-4.8(b)(i) rests is that defense counsel may well be the single most important witness on that dimension of incompetency.[10] A defense attorney not only is in close and continuing communication with a client, but he or she also knows the extent to which presentation of substantive and factual defenses may turn on the

---

7. *See* commentary to standard 7-4.5, notes 5-7 and accompanying text.

8. *See* part III in general and standards 7-3.9 and 7-3.2 and commentary in particular for a more complete discussion of the admissibility and scope of expert testimony by mental health and mental retardation professional evaluators.

9. *See* commentary to standard 7-4.1, notes 29-32 and accompanying text.

10. *See ibid.*

client's ability to understand them and assist counsel in advancing them.[11] Under the standard, defense counsel, whose testimony may be as important as, or even more important than that of an expert witness,[12] should not be precluded automatically from appearing as a witness at a competency hearing.

The decision to appear on behalf of the client is exclusively that of defense counsel under the standard, however. Accordingly, a prosecuting attorney should be disabled from summoning a defense attorney as a prosecution witness on the incompetency issue. Moreover, counsel's initial submission might properly be informal in nature, usually in the form of an unsworn submission to the court with the same effect as sworn testimony. Whatever the form of counsel's submission, however, standard 7-4.8(b)(i) recognizes that the prosecution must have the opportunity to cross-examine defense counsel concerning the contents. In addition, under standard 7-4.8(b)(ii), a hearing court can inquire of a defense attorney about the relationships between the attorney and client and the client's ability to communicate with counsel. This reflects a court's basic responsibility to resolve competency issues,[13] and defense counsel must be responsible to assist the court in discharging this duty. The standard is express, however, that a prosecuting attorney should not be allowed to cross-examine counsel concerning statements elicited by the court.

Standard 7-4.8(b) assumes that the provisions of the Model Rules of Professional Conduct governing conflicts of interest[14] and attorneys as witnesses in litigation in which they appear as counsel[15] do not govern testimony by defense attorneys concerning clients' procedural competence. The inapplicability of the Model Rules is a defensible assumption

---

11. The demands on a client are greater, of course, if he or she will have to testify in support of one or more defense theories, and hence will be exposed to the rigors of prosecution cross-examination. Ennis & Hansen, *Memorandum of Law: Competency to Stand Trial,* J. Psychiatry & L. 491 (1976).

12. Because of this proximity to client and case, "counsel's firsthand evaluation of a defendant's ability to consult on his case and to understand the charges against him may be as valuable as expert psychiatric opinion on his competency." United States v. David, 511 F.2d 355, 360 (D.C. Cir. 1975). One commentator has suggested that in a given case, "not only might the testimony of the defense counsel be admissible on the issues of competence, it might well be essential." Mickenberg, *Competency to Stand Trial and the Mentally-Retarded Defendant: The Need for a Multi-Disciplinary Solution to a Multi-Disciplinary Problem,* 17 Cal. W.L. Rev. 365, 386 (1981).

13. For a discussion of the responsibility of the court to resolve the competence issues, *see* commentary to standard 7-4.2, notes 1-4 and accompanying text.

14. Rule 1.7.

15. Rule 3.7(a).

in this narrow competency context, because evidence of that sort is not directed at the substantive merits of the case and counsel does not serve in an adversary role with respect to other litigants or witnesses. Nevertheless, the ethically permissible act of becoming a witness is not lightly to be engaged in, particularly because of the strain it might place on the attorney-client relationship if a defendant observes defense counsel apparently testifying against the client's best interests as the client perceives them.[16] Defense counsel's autonomous role should be preserved intact whenever possible.

Important as counsel data may be bearing on client competency, they cannot be offered to or demanded by a court if they rest on or are derived from confidential communications under the protective umbrella of the attorney-client privilege. Standard 7-4.8(b) expressly reflects this traditional limitation on otherwise ethical conduct on the part of defense counsel who testify at competency hearings. Nevertheless, an attorney may relate nonconfidential conversations with a client if the client did not intend them to be private or privileged. Counsel also may describe such nontestimonial matters as the defendant's physical characteristics, demeanor, and the coherence of defendant's communications (provided that their substance is not disclosed). The limitations recommended in the standard, while probably dictated by professional ethics and traditional concepts of evidence law, may be considered undesirable by trial judges who want access to all information bearing on defendant competency. Nevertheless, the Association believes that the important traditional interest in protecting the confidentiality of counsel-client communications strongly outweighs any immediate advantages to trial courts in resolving competency issues.

Standard 7-4.8(c) cautions courts that they should consider separately the issues of competence and treatment or habilitation in response to incompetency, the same dichotomy that informs evaluation reports.[17] That is, of course, important to an appropriate dispositional order under standard 7-4.9. It is even more significant to concerns of burden of going forward and burdens of persuasion.

Standard 7-4.8(c)(i) covers the responsibilities of the prosecution and defense to go forward with evidence to show incompetence. If defense counsel moved at an earlier time for a competency examination,[18] the burden of going forward also rests on the defense; if it advances no data

16. *See* Pizzi, *supra* note 4, at 63.
17. *See* commentary to standard 7-4.5, notes 5-7 and accompanying text.
18. *See* standard 7-3.3 and commentary.

in support of a finding of incompetency, presumably the court must find the defendant competent and proceed to trial. If the original motion for an evaluation was tendered by the prosecuting attorney, or if made by the court on its own motion (whether or not based on information supplied by the prosecuting attorney), then the burden of going forward rests on the prosecuting attorney.

Standard 7-4.8(c)(ii) addresses the allocation of the burden of persuasion (proof) at a competency hearing. Precedent and commentators reflect three separate positions on the matter, none of which is entirely satisfactory. The first is that the party alleging incompetence bears the burden of persuasion (proof), apparently based on a general presumption of competence and sanity; the party attacking the presumption should carry the burden of proof to sustain its attack.[19] A second places on a defendant who has raised the issue of incompetence the burden to demonstrate that incompetence.[20] Both positions have been criticized on the basis that the burden to establish either competence or incompetence cannot be allocated validly to a defendant concerning whose competence a good faith doubt exists.[21] The third position, which rests on such criticisms, holds that the prosecution always should bear the burden of proving a premise adverse to a defendant.

Standard 7-4.8(c)(ii) in effect resolves the controversy by suggesting no assignment of the burden of persuasion (proof).[22] In contrast to most issues arising in the course of adversarial criminal proceedings, the responsibility to pursue and resolve the competence issue, once a good faith doubt about it has been expressed, rests primarily on a trial court. Moreover, no consistent pattern of advocacy is discernable in this con-

---

19. For a more complete discussion of this position regarding allocation of burden of proof, *see* Weiner, *Mental Disability and the Criminal Law*, in THE MENTALLY DISABLED AND THE LAW 693, 703 (S. Brakel, J. Parry & B. Weiner eds., 3d ed. 1985); Project, *Legal Issues in Mental Health Care: Proposals for Change*, 2 MENTAL DISABILITY L. REP. 624 (1978). The position is based, in part, on the proposals of HARVARD MEDICAL SCHOOL LABORATORY OF COMMUNITY PSYCHIATRY, COMPETENCY TO STAND TRIAL AND MENTAL ILLNESS 4 (DHEW Pub. No. (HSM) 73-9105, Rockville, Md., National Institute of Mental Health, Center for Studies of Crime and Delinquency, 1973).

20. *See* State v. Aumann, 265 N.W.2d 316, *reh'g denied*, 268 N.W.2d 228 (Iowa 1978).

21. People v. Binder, 20 Ill. 2d 45, 53-54, 169 N.E.2d 328, 332 (1960):

> It would be a strange rule, indeed, to impose upon [the defendant] the burden of proving his own incompetence where the very disability which he would be seeking to prove renders him incapable, either logically or legally, of sustaining the burden of proof.

22. *See generally* Bennett, *A Guided Tour Through Selected ABA Standards Relating to Incompetence to Stand Trial*, 53 GEO. WASH. L. REV. 375, 398-399 (1985).

text. Although frequently the prosecution asserts competence and defense counsel incompetence, the posture of the parties may become inverted. In the latter event, an arbitrary placement on the prosecution of a burden to prove competence would be singularly inappropriate. Furthermore, the prosecution may be in the least effective position to acquire needed information bearing on competency, particularly with reference to a defendant's ability to consult with and to assist defense counsel.[23] Indeed, a prosecutor may concur in allegations of defendant incompetence.[24]

Consequently, the only recommendation in standard 7-4.8(c)(ii) is that a hearing court should find affirmatively that the greater weight of the evidence supports the court's competency determination; that renders a burden of persuasion (proof), as contrasted with a burden of going forward, irrelevant. Nevertheless, as a procedural matter, a party who alleged a certain fact may well labor in fact under a burden of producing evidence in support of its existence. A failure to do so may generate an adverse ruling, not because of a formal failure to discharge a burden of persuasion (proof), but because the preponderance of the evidence before the court supports a contrary position. In other words, and to illustrate, a failure of the defense to advance evidence showing incompetency would not of itself legitimate a judicial determination of competency; the latter should rest on independent data supporting a finding of competence by the greater weight of the evidence.

Standard 7-4.9. Hearing on competence; dispositional issues

(a) Once the court has found that the defendant is incompetent to stand trial or that competence depends on continuation of treatment or habilitation, the court should consider issues relating to treatment or habilitation to effect competence, including its appropriateness, its availability in the geographic area, its probable duration, the likelihood of restoration to competence in the reasonably foreseeable fu-

23. *See* Pizzi, *supra* note 4, at 56.

24. Because of these possible inconsistencies in position, one commentator has recommended that a trial judge conduct and control the hearing, "mandated by the court's ultimate responsibility for the proper determination of the competency issue." *Id.* at 63.

ture, and the availability of the least restrictive treatment alternative.

(i) A defendant may be ordered to undergo treatment if the court finds that the defendant is in need of such services and that such services are available. The court may make outpatient treatment or habilitation a condition of the defendant's pretrial release. When the defendant is in custody the court may order treatment or habilitation services to be administered at the custodial facility or may order defendant's transfer to another facility for treatment or habilitation or may order outpatient treatment services.

(ii) A defendant on pretrial release should not be involuntarily confined in a residential facility to restore competence unless the court determines by clear and convincing evidence that:

(A) there is substantial probability that defendant's incompetence will respond to treatment or habilitation and defendant will attain or maintain competence in the reasonably foreseeable future;

(B) treatment or habilitation appropriate for the defendant to attain or maintain competence is available in a residential facility; and

(C) no appropriate treatment or habilitation alternative is available less restrictive than that requiring involuntary hospitalization.

(b) At the conclusion of the hearing the court should enter its written order for treatment to effect competence. The order should contain the following:

(i) written findings of fact setting forth separately and distinctly the findings of the court on the issues of competence, treatment or habilitation, and involuntary confinement;

(ii) copies of supporting evaluative information sufficient for a professional involved in providing treatment or habilitation to ascertain the charge against the defendant and the nature of the condition causing the incompetence;

(iii) a finding that the institution to which the defendant is to be committed is sufficiently staffed and equipped to meet that defendant's treatment or habilitation needs;

(iv) the time at which reports will be required from the professionals providing treatment or habilitation.

(c) An order adjudicating the defendant incompetent to stand trial should be an appealable order.

Commentary Introduction

Standard 7-4.9 addresses procedures leading to the commitment of mentally incompetent defendants who need appropriate treatment[1] to attain competence. The standard rejects a practice of automatic commitments for treatment based on a determination of present mental incompetence; treatment and confinement are separate issues requiring discrete adjudications. In recognition of a presumption in favor of pretrial liberty, the standards provide that courts should consider first the feasibility of outpatient treatment, so that defendants otherwise eligible for pretrial release on condition[2] should be compulsorily hospitalized only if treatment cannot be accomplished under appropriate pretrial release conditions. The standard further urges that court orders authorizing confinement for treatment be in writing and contain specified information to assist treating professionals.

Related Standards

ABA, Standards for Criminal Justice 10-1.1 *et seq.*, 7-4.3

Commentary

Standard 7-4.9 adopts the position that courts should address separately the issues of present mental competence and the circumstances of treatment, including involuntary confinement, of incompetent defendants. Although the Supreme Court in *Jackson v. Indiana*[3] did not expressly mandate a hearing and findings relating to treatment, it did require that treatment "bear a reasonable relation to the purpose for which the individual is committed . . ." and that there be a "substantial probability" that it will result in restoration of competence in the "foreseeable future."[4] That language implies that trial courts are responsible

1. For uniformity throughout the commentary in part IV, the term *treatment* is used generically to encompass appropriate aspects of medical or psychological treatment, habilitation, education, or social training.
2. *See* standards 10-5.2, 10-5.3 and commentary.
3. 406 U.S. 715 (1972).
4. *Id.* at 738. *See* Weiner, *Mental Disability and the Criminal Law,* in The Mentally Disabled and the Law 693, 703-704 (S. Brakel, J. Parry & B. Weiner 3d ed. 1985) [hereinafter cited as Weiner].

to ensure that such a relationship exists, which they cannot accomplish unless they are informed adequately about the nature of the condition underlying incompetence, the treatment most appropriate to restore competence, and the resources available to provide it on either an inpatient or outpatient basis.[5]

In the past, courts too frequently have used commitments ostensibly for the purpose of treating present mental incompetence as devices to confine, pending trial, dangerous mentally ill defendants or defendants charged with serious felonies. In many states, legislation has authorized the immediate arrest and confinement of defendants whose present mental competence has been placed at issue.[6] If they were found to be incompetent to undergo criminal trial proceedings, they were automatically committed to mental hospitals, often for the so-called criminally insane, until their competence had been restored, without regard to the question of whether treatment or habilitation was available there appropriate to that objective.[7] Clearly, automatic confinement has been considered the normative dispositional response to incompetent defendants; courts have given little or no consideration to the relationship between that form of

5. *See* Ennis & Hansen, *Memorandum of Law: Competency to Stand Trial,* 4 J. PSYCHIATRY & L. 491 (1976) [hereinafter cited as Ennis & Hansen].

6. *See* commentary to standard 7-4.3, notes 12-15 and accompanying text, for a discussion of pretrial release during competence evaluations.

7. Professors Wexler and Scoville, reviewing such commitment procedures in Arizona, found them to be mandated by legislation. Wexler, Scoville *et al., The Administration of Psychiatric Justice: Theory and Practice in Arizona,* 13 ARIZ. L. REV. 1, 167-168 (1971). Paull, in evaluating the since-repealed Illinois statutes, observed that a finding of incompetence alone sufficed for commitment to a mental hospital; factors such as a defendant's "amenability to treatment, the nature of the mental disorder, the availability of treatment, the probable duration of the person's stay in a mental hospital, or whether the defendant met the legal criteria for civil commitment" were not considered. Paull, *S.B. 133: The Near Resolution of a Major Problem: Fitness in the Criminal Law,* 56 CHI.-KENT L. REV. 1107, 1108 (1980). Roesch and Golding, in their study of judicial attitudes toward incompetent defendants, reported that almost one-half of the judges responding to their survey believed that commitment should be routinely ordered after defendants were found incompetent; 60 percent of them advocated automatic commitment of incompetent defendants charged with violent felonies and three-quarters approved the practice for presently mental incompetents charged with nonviolent felonies. Another facet of their study showed that one-half the judges believed that "dangerousness" rather than necessity for treatment was the single most important criterion for committing presently incompetent defendants. Roesch & Golding, *Legal and Judicial Interpretation of Competency to Stand Trial Statutes and Procedures,* 16 CRIMINOLOGY 420, 423-424 (1978).

confinement and attainment of present mental competence, or even to the incapacitation of dangerous offenders.

The standard reflects the axiomatic philosophy that hearings to determine present mental competence may eventuate in compulsory commitments solely for the purpose of achieving triability and not for tangential and possibly unconstitutional objectives like pretrial detention of dangerous defendants charged with serious crimes. A determination of incompetence does not necessarily impel a commitment. Indeed, the Supreme Court in *Jackson* made it quite clear that confinement for treatment is constitutional only after courts have determined that: (1) a defendant is both presently incompetent and treatable; (2) commitment bears a reasonable relationship to the treatment; and (3) the treatment is likely to achieve competence in the foreseeable future.[8] Consequently, hearings bearing on present mental condition must focus on: (1) a defendant's present mental competency; (2) the availability of treatment to attain competence if a defendant is not mentally competent; and (3) the situs most appropriate for that treatment. Compelled hospitalization is acceptable only if it is shown to be indispensable to successful treatment or habilitation because outpatient treatment is unavailable or likely to prove ineffective. Concerns about flight or nonappearance, or danger to other persons or the community,[9] must be addressed in completely independent proceedings.

A court's responsibility under the standard is not to select one from among two or more medically acceptable treatment alternatives, but rather to determine the least restrictive mode appropriate to attain present mental competence[10] and to supervise its implementation. In most instances, the preferred treatment will be psychotropic medication that requires no hospitalization or at most a relatively brief involuntary confinement.[11] It needs also to be kept in the forefront that treatment to attain present mental competence is not primarily to benefit the defend-

---

8. *See* Ennis & Hansen, *supra* note 5, at 502. *See also supra,* note 1, for the meaning of "treatment."

9. *See* standards 7-4.3, 10-5.4, 10-5.9 and commentary.

10. American Bar Association, *Summary of Action of the House of Delegates,* 1978 Annual Meeting 19, states expressly that mental health laws should provide for ". . . b) a right to treatment in the least restrictive setting." *See also* Weiner, *supra* note 4, at 704.

11. Daniels, *Post-Traumatic Stress Disorder and Competence to Stand Trial,* 12 J. Psychiatry & L. 5 (1984); Roesch & Golding, *Treatment and Disposition of Defendants Found Incompetent to Stand Trial: A Review and a Proposal,* 2 Int'l J.L. & Psychiatry 349 (1979).

ant/patient (as that incident to compulsory civil hospitalization would be); rather it is to benefit the criminal justice system by achieving a mental competence compatible with continued criminal proceedings.[12] Consequently, treatment methods appropriate for persons civilly committed may be excessive if applied to criminal defendants incompetent to undergo criminal trial.[13]

Paragraph (b) delineates the contents of written commitment orders based on present mental incompetence:

1. Factual findings supporting the court's determination of the issues of competence, treatment, and involuntary confinement.
2. Appended copies of professional evaluative information suitable to apprise treating professionals of the basis for the commitment order and the limited objectives of the treatment they are to provide; often, treating professionals will not have performed initial evaluations.[14] Indeed, the two functions ought to be considered as separate and distinct.[15] Hence, they may be unaware of the information relied on by a committing court or of the objectives of the treatment for which defendants have been referred to them.[16]

---

12. *See* Shah, *Some Interactions of Law and Mental Health in the Handling of Social Deviance,* 23 Cath. U.L. Rev. 674, 696 (1974) [hereinafter cited as Shah] (*citing* Wilder, Levin & Zwerling, *A Two-Year Follow-Up Evaluation of Acute Psychotic Patients Treated in a Day Hospital,* 122 Am. J. Psychiatry 1095 (1966); Herz, Endicott *et al., Day Versus Inpatient Hospitalization: A Controlled Study,* 127 Am. J. Psychiatry 1371 (1968) [hereinafter cited as Herz, Endicott]).

One 1968 study concluded that the data ". . . showed that by virtually every measure used to evaluate progress and outcome there was clear indication of the superiority of day treatment." Herz, Endicott, *supra,* at 1379. *See also* Gobert, *Competency to Stand Trial: A Pre- and Post-Jackson Analysis,* 40 Tenn. L. Rev. 659, 663 (1973); Morse, *A Preference for Liberty: The Case Against Involuntary Commitment of the Mentally Disordered,* 70 Cal. L. Rev. 54 (1982). Indeed, inpatient treatment may be counterproductive. McGarry and Bendt found that commitment of persons for treatment of the condition causing incompetence was often antitherapeutic. McGarry & Bendt, *Criminal v. Civil Commitment of Psychotic Offenders: A Seven-Year Follow-Up,* 125 Am. J. Psychiatry 1387 (1969).

13. *See* Note, *Incompetency to Stand Trial,* 81 Harv. L. Rev. 454, 462-463 (1967).

14. *See* Shah, *supra* note 12, at 676.

15. Available empirical data indicate that outpatient or community-based treatment is at least as effective as hospitalization, if not more effective. *See also* commentary to standard 7-4.5, notes 8-9, 13 and accompanying text.

16. *See* Hess & Thomas, *Incompetency to Stand Trial: Procedures, Results, and Problems,* 119 Am. J. Psychiatry 713, 716 (1963).

3. A finding that an institution to which a defendant is to be committed is adequately staffed and equipped to provide treatment appropriate to achieve present mental competence.
4. The times at which treating professionals are to report their progress in treating a committed defendant.

Under paragraph (c), an adjudication of present mental incompetence should be an appealable order. If defendants wish to contest findings of present mental competence, they must await a guilty verdict and then appeal on the basis of indications in the trial record that they did not meet the constitutional criteria for triability.[17]

Standard 7-4.10. Right to treatment or habilitation and to refuse

(a) A defendant determined to be incompetent to stand trial has a right to prompt and adequate treatment or habilitation to effect competence and a right to have such services administered by competent and qualified professionals.

(b) Within [fourteen] days after entry of an order detaining or committing a defendant for treatment or habilitation or directing that a defendant report for treatment or habilitation on an outpatient basis, the professional providing such services should develop and file with the court, copies being made available to both parties, an individualized plan of treatment or habilitation. Each treatment plan should contain the following:

(i) a statement of the specific causes of defendant's incompetence including, where appropriate, diagnosis and description of any physical or mental illness, mental retardation or physical disability, and reference to any other factors causing the incompetence to stand trial;

(ii) a statement of the planned treatment or habilitation, whether medical, psychological, educational, or social, appropriate to effect competence;

---

17. *See* commentary to standard 7-4.1, notes 7-12 and accompanying text. There is no federal constitutional right to an appeal against a finding of competency. *See* Vardas v. Estelle, 715 F.2d 206, 208 (5th Cir. 1983), *cert. denied sub nom.* Vardas v. McKaskle, 465 U.S. 1104 (1984).

(iii) a statement setting forth any restrictions to be placed on the defendant and the reasons for imposing such restrictions;

(iv) a statement of the expected duration of treatment or habilitation required to effect the defendant's competence.

(c) A defendant has a right to treatment or habilitation in the least restrictive setting appropriate to effect competence to stand trial.

(i) If necessary for treatment or habilitation persons may be treated or habilitated in facilities established for that purpose or in sections of general treatment or habilitation facilities which are specifically set apart and designated for treatment or habilitation of persons under criminal charges.

(ii) Whenever a defendant who is incompetent to stand trial has been denied pretrial release or is unable to meet the release conditions imposed, that defendant may be detained in jail only if adequate treatment or habilitation to effect competence is provided in that setting.

(d) A person determined to be incompetent to stand trial and detained or committed for treatment or habilitation or ordered to appear for outpatient treatment or habilitation should have no right to refuse ordinary and reasonable treatment or habilitation designed to effect competence. However, a defendant should have the right to refuse any treatment or habilitation which may impair the defendant's ability to prepare a defense to the charge, which is experimental, or which has an unreasonable risk of serious, hazardous, or irreversible side effects.

Commentary Introduction

Standard 7-4.10 governs the treatment[1] of defendants found incompetent to stand trial. It confirms in paragraph (a) the right to treatment both

1. Throughout the commentary, the term *treatment* is used in its broadest sense to refer to aspects of medical treatment, habilitation, education, or training appropriate to restore a criminal defendant's competence to stand trial. *See also* subparagraph (b)(ii).

The American Psychiatric Association believes that antipsychotic medication has been proven to be a highly effective and often essential treatment for patients requiring involuntary psychiatric hospitalization and that it ought to be regarded as "ordinary and reasonable treatment" within the meaning of the standard. Naturally, as standard 7-4.14 and commentary reflect, the goals of the criminal justice system may forestall the use of medication that impairs a defendant's ability to defend against criminal charges. Letter from Robert Luskin, Esq., to Standing Committee Director (March 29, 1985).

for those committed involuntarily and for those allowed to remain in the community on pretrial release status pending attainment of present mental competence. Paragraph (b) urges that treating professionals be required to file a treatment plan with the court that ordered inpatient or outpatient treatment, so that the court and counsel are apprised of the treatment regimen to be followed and can monitor a defendant's progress under it; on that basis they can, if necessary, intervene if treatment proves ineffective or inappropriately intrusive. Paragraph (c) confirms the governance of the least restrictive alternative principle throughout the commitment, so that defendants should be jailed only when that is consonant with adequate treatment. They may, however, be accomodated in facilities specially designated for the treatment or habilitation of persons under criminal charges. Paragraph (d) rests on the premise, manifest elsewhere in this part,[2] that treatment is for the benefit of the criminal justice system (in the form of present mental competence achieved through treatment), and not solely for a defendant/patient's benefit. Accordingly, defendants ordered to undergo inpatient or outpatient treatment to achieve triability cannot refuse ordinary and reasonable treatment aimed at attaining competence to undergo criminal proceedings, as long as it (1) will not impair a defendant's ability to present or support a factual or legal defense, (2) is not experimental,[3] or (3) poses no unreasonable risk of serious, hazardous, or irreversible side effects.

Related Standards

ABA, Standards for Criminal Justice 7-4.14, 10-5.4, 23-5.8

Commentary

Standard 7-4.10(a) rests on the premise, established in judicial precedent, that persons found presently mentally incompetent have a right to treatment and, as paragraph (d) attests, are under a duty to undergo either inpatient or outpatient treatment to achieve a mental state com-

2. *See* commentary to standard 7-4.4, notes 8-10 and accompanying text; commentary to standard 7-4.7; notes 7-9 and accompanying text; commentary to standard 7-4.9, notes 8-9 and accompanying text.

3. *Compare* standard 23-5.8 (nontherapeutic experimentation using prisoners should never be allowed; therapeutic medical programs not available generally to free-world patients may be used only if directly beneficial to a prisoner/patient, based on either a full, voluntary, and informed consent or a court order when appropriate).

patible with triability. In that respect, treatment necessitated by incompetence to undergo criminal proceedings differs markedly from treatment required for persons civilly committed. The latter traditionally has been justified on two theories: (1) as an exercise of the police power to protect society from dangerously mentally ill persons; and (2) as a manifestation of the *parens patriae* obligation of the state as "the guardian of all infants, idiots and lunatics."[4] The second of these two theories increasingly has been asserted to require adequate mental health care as the *quid pro quo* for the deprivation of liberty suffered by involuntarily committed mental patients,[5] a principle that courts,[6] including the United States Supreme Court,[7] have come to recognize.

Nevertheless, commitment of criminal defendants because of present mental incompetence differs fundamentally from compulsory civil commitment of free persons for mental health treatment under a *parens patriae* theory. The first benefits primarily the state, in that the treatment incident to inpatient or outpatient status is intended to achieve a mental condition compatible with triability, a boon to the prosecution legitimating even a pretrial deprivation of liberty for treatment.[8] The second is

4. *See generally* Wyatt v. Aderholt, 503 F.2d 1305 (5th Cir. 1974); Brakel, *Involuntary Institutionalization,* in The Mentally Disabled and the Law 21, 24-25 (S. Brakel, J. Parry & B. Weiner eds., 3d ed. 1985).

5. *See* Birnbaum, *The Right to Treatment,* 46 A.B.A.J. 499 (1960). Dr. Morton Birnbaum, a practicing physician and attorney, asserted that if, to achieve a proper purpose, the state deprives one of liberty it then must make every reasonable effort to effectuate that purpose, as the *quid pro quo* for a restraint of liberty. Accordingly, persons civilly committed because of mental illness are owed a duty of treatment that the state cannot neglect or ignore.

6. The leading case is Rouse v. Cameron, 373 F.2d 451 (D.C. Cir. 1966). Although the court relied chiefly on District of Columbia legislation requiring treatment, it noted the probability of an equivalent constitutional right, so that a failure to treat might generate either due process or equal protection violations. *See also* Wyatt v. Stickney, 325 F. Supp. 781 (M.D. Ala. 1971), 344 F. Supp. 373 (M.D. Ala. 1972), *aff'd sub nom.* Wyatt v. Aderholt, 503 F.2d 1305 (5th Cir. 1974).

7. *See* O'Connor v. Donaldson, 422 U.S. 563 (1975). Although the *Donaldson* Court appeared to ignore the *quid pro quo* rationale of the earlier federal court of appeals precedent, it noted that a nondangerous mentally ill individual, capable of surviving safely in freedom, may not be validly confined "without more." *Id.* at 575. However, the Court did not address the issue of involuntary confinement of those considered dangerous.

8. Jackson v. Indiana, 406 U.S. 715 (1972), impliedly reflects the *quid pro quo* doctrine, namely, that a deprivation of liberty may not occur unless the benefit to the state is reasonably to be achieved, through its holding that presently mentally incompetent criminal defendants may be committed for treatment only as long as commitment is justified by progress toward attainment of competence. *Id.* at 738. That appears to imply that appropriate treatment must be available if a defendant is to be committed for the purpose. *Ibid.*

principally for the benefit of civilly committed patients to restore them sufficiently to health that they can function safely within the community; the police power or protective function is only of secondary significance. Paragraphs (a) and (d) are bottomed on the principle, demonstrated in *Jackson v. Indiana,* that defendants found not presently mentally competent are to receive appropriate treatment to achieve competence, on either an outpatient or an inpatient basis as the least restrictive alternative theory dictates, and that they have a duty to submit as long as a treatment regimen is not inappropriate or excessive as defined in paragraph (d). This, in the Association's view, reflects the fact that both defendants and prosecuting authorities have important stakes in the speedy termination of criminal proceedings, so that the state must treat and a defendant must accept treatment aimed at achieving a mental condition appropriate to triability.

Paragraph (a) is broadly phrased to embrace not only medical but also psychological, educational, or social treatment. It includes habilitation appropriate to restore or attain mental competence and may, for example, include special training focused exclusively on imparting communication skills.[9] In other words, treatment or habilitation is appropriate if it restores triability, no matter its category for other purposes.

Paragraph (b) advocates a duty on the part of treating professionals to develop and file with committing courts an individualized treatment plan for each defendant ordered to undergo treatment or habilitation to attain present mental competence. A plan must include: (1) the specific causes of a defendant's incompetence, including a diagnosis and description of physical or mental illness, retardation, physical disability, or other factors accounting for nontriability; (2) a delineation of a recommended treatment or habilitation plan; (3) a description of restrictions that need to be imposed on a defendant and the reasons for them; and (4) the anticipated duration of treatment or habilitation to attain competence.

The requirement that a treatment plan be submitted promptly (within a recommended fourteen days) has four objectives. First, treating professionals will be impelled to tailor treatment plans to the sole objective for the commitment, and not a broader purpose of restoring mental health to

9. *See also* subparagraph (b)(ii). For example, in the oft-cited case of Donald Lang, the treatment appropriate to attain present competence of a mentally retarded deaf defendant was training in sign language as a communication device. People v. Lang, 76 Ill. 2d 311, 391 N.E.2d 350, *cert. denied sub nom.* Lang v. Illinois, 444 U.S. 954 (1979), and *cert. denied sub nom.* De Vito v. Lang, 444 U.S. 1045 (1980) (court refers to "sign language instruction"). For later litigation involving Lang, *see* People v. Lang, 127 Ill. App. 3d 313, 468 N.E.2d 1303 (1984).

a patient. The conflicting objective of the courts, on the one hand, which is restored or attained competence to undergo criminal proceedings, and that of treating professionals, on the other, who wish to restore mental health,[10] should be resolved in favor of accomplishing the judicial purpose, since that offers the sole legal basis for this form of commitment or treatment order.

Second, courts may use individualized treatment plans as a background for the required judicial review of the nature and objectives of treatment regimens under standard 7-4.11, their suitability to restore or attain present mental competence, and the time requisite for the purpose. Although courts may not have been allotted by legislation a direct control over the administration of treatment to attain competence, *Jackson v. Indiana*[11] laid down a constitutional requirement that they review the progress of treatment periodically. That should imply a power to direct or control treating professionals exercisable only against the criterion of an adequate treatment plan for each defendant/patient.

Third, because copies of treatment plans submitted under paragraph (b) are to be provided to prosecuting attorneys and defense counsel, either can monitor independently the fulfilment of the obligation to treat or habilitate. Similarly, either can call to a court's attention failures to treat appropriately or deviations from treatment plans suggesting that treating professionals are addressing patient mental health needs generally and not restoration of triability. Naturally, treatment plans should be viewed as presumptively valid and put immediately into effect unless either a prosecuting attorney or defense counsel objects. Moreover, courts are not to convert themselves into treating professionals and should not enmesh themselves in the specifics of treatment plans and their effectuation. Consistent with the doctrine expounded in *Wyatt v. Stickney*,[12] treatment plans provide courts with an overview of treatment, treatment objectives, and probable duration of treatment, but judicial fiat cannot supplant therapeutic assessments.

Fourth, treatment plans enable courts and attorneys to generate appro-

---

10. *See* Hess & Thomas, *Incompetency to Stand Trial: Procedures, Results and Problems*, 119 Am. J. Psychiatry 713 (1963) [hereinafter cited as Hess & Thomas]. *See* commentary to standard 7-4.1, notes 35-36 and accompanying text; commentary to standard 7-4.5, notes 1-4 and accompanying text.

11. 406 U.S. 715, 738 (1972).

12. 325 F. Supp. 781 (M.D. Ala. 1971), 344 F. Supp. 373 (M.D. Ala. 1972), *aff'd sub nom.* Wyatt v. Aderholt, 503 F.2d 1305 (5th Cir. 1974), *discussed supra*, note 6 and accompanying text.

priate responses if defendants refuse to cooperate with treatment consonant with the restrictions in paragraph (d).

Paragraph (c) addresses the situs of treatment to attain present mental competence. Some commentators have urged that defendants who are incompetent to stand trial should have the same status as those civilly committed and be hospitalized with them.[13] Others assert that criminal defendants, though incompetent to undergo criminal proceedings, are different from civilly committed patients who have not been charged with crime and that they cannot be intermingled without serious detrimental consequences to both groups. Treating professionals frequently are confused about the differing treatment goals and methods pertaining to the two groups;[14] because they view criminal defendants as a distinct class, they often treat them more harshly and less adequately than civilly committed patients.[15] The latter group also may suffer because of their fear of the consequences of a forced association with criminal defendants. On the other hand, an intermingling of incompetent defendants, only some of whom may be truly dangerous, with former defendants found not guilty because of mental nonresponsibility [insanity] and convicted prisoners transferred because of their severe mental illness[16] may adversely affect treatment or habilitation to attain competence[17] and arguably denies equal protection as well.[18]

13. The case for commitment of incompetent defendants to facilities used for civil committees reflects the fact that separate facilities for commitment to attain or restore competence often have been far worse than those for treatment of civil patients, exposing criminal defendants to the "worst of both possible worlds." *See* H. Steadman, Beating a Rap? Defendants Found Incompetent to Stand Trial (1979) [hereinafter cited as H. Steadman]; Ennis & Hansen, *Memorandum of Law: Competency to Stand Trial,* 4 J. Psychiatry & L. 491 (1976). This especially has proven true if a treatment facility for incompetent defendants is administered by a department of corrections rather than a state mental health or mental retardation agency. *See* H. Steadman, *supra,* at 57-83. Because about the same level of treatment or habilitation is offered in either institution, some authors have concluded that extended confinement is used more to punish or incapacitate than to restore or attain competence. *See generally* Hess & Thomas, *supra* note 10, at 714-715.

14. *See supra,* notes 4-8 and accompanying text (discussing the contrasting purposes of treatment for incompetent criminal defendants and civil committees).

15. *See* Hess & Thomas, *supra* note 10.

16. *See* standard 7-10.5 and commentary.

17. *See* Gobert, *Competency to Stand Trial: A Pre- and Post-*Jackson *Analysis,* 40 Tenn. L. Rev. 659, 664 (1973).

18. *See* Jackson v. Indiana, 406 U.S. 715, 724 (1972) (Court indicated that filing of criminal charges does not warrant treating a defendant differently from civil committees).

An appropriate resolution of such diametrically opposed concerns is not simple to accomplish. Nevertheless, paragraph (c) incorporates a premise that security and treatment constitute dual goals of the criminal justice system and that neither is subordinate to the other. Separate facilities can prove advantageous for several reasons. Treating professionals on the staff of specialized institutions probably will not be confused about the purposes of treatment or habilitation offered there and will focus their professional activities on restoration or attainment of competence. They can standardize their reports, based on their specialized experience, thereby providing trial courts with compatible data on which consistent adjudications can be based. Subparagraph (c)(i), by recognizing the appropriateness of separate facilities or sections of facilities devoted to the treatment or habilitation of incompetent criminal defendants, accommodates an array of concerns by reiterating the right to treatment or habilitation in the least-restrictive suitable facility; it permits, however, otherwise appropriate treatment programs in segregated settings.

Subparagraph (c)(ii) envisions treatment in detention facilities for defendants preventively detained or otherwise unable to achieve pretrial release and, indeed, may be read to require their transfer to a special facility under subparagraph (c)(i) or to a general mental health or mental retardation facility if suitable treatment or habilitation is not or cannot be provided in a jail or local detention facility. Note that under standard 7-4.11(a), a committing or authorizing court is under a duty to monitor treatment or habilitation to achieve competence, whatever the setting in which it is offered. Proper discharge of that duty is especially imperative if defendants are held in jail, because the danger that custodial personnel will interfere with or obstruct treatment is significantly greater there than in instances of confinement in mental health or mental retardation facilities.

Paragraph (d) delineates the extent of an incompetent defendant's obligation to accept treatment or habilitation authorized to restore or achieve triability. Judicial decisions have recognized the right of civilly committed patients to refuse treatment under at least some circumstances,[19] even though they have not defined clearly the balance appropriately to be struck between the competing interests of patients and the

19. *See* Rennie v. Klein, 462 F. Supp. 1131 (D.N.J. 1978); Rogers v. Okin, 634 F.2d 650 (1st Cir. 1980), *remanded sub nom.* Mills v. Rogers, 457 U.S. 291 (1982). Grounds have included the first amendment guarantee of freedom of religion, Scott v. Plante, 532 F.2d 939 (3d Cir. 1976); Winters v. Miller, 446 F.2d 65 (2d Cir. 1971), *cert. denied,* 404 U.S. 985 (1971), the eighth amendment prohibition against cruel and unusual punishment, Scott v. Plante, 532

state that has compulsorily hospitalized them. In the context of part IV, however, the interest of the criminal justice system in achieving triability through treatment or habilitation is stronger, perhaps, than the state's general concern to restore dangerous civilly committed patients to acceptable levels of mental health. Although the standard does not endeavor to anticipate or preempt the development of constitutional principles respecting the scope of a right to refuse treatment, it does express a clear legislative judgment that criminal defendants are obliged to undergo generally accepted treatment or habilitation appropriate to restore or achieve triability.

Nevertheless, a defendant/patient's obligation to submit is not absolute. Defendants and their counsel have a constitutionally protected interest in preserving defendant mental processes requisite to an adequate factual or legal defense.[20] Paragraph (d) expressly recognizes the right to refuse treatment or habilitation that may impair that ability. Note, however, that this right to withhold consent to treatment does not extend to medications that might alter demeanor or jury perception of a defendant; the state's interest in achieving triability outweighs a defense preference to present a different facade to jurors.[21] Defendants likewise should have the same right as any other person to reject experimental treatment[22] or treatment posing an unreasonable risk of serious, hazardous, or irreversible side effects.[23]

F.2d 939 (3d Cir. 1976); Welsch v. Likins, 373 F. Supp. 487 (D. Minn. 1974), *aff'd in part, vacated and remanded,* 550 F.2d 1122 (8th Cir. 1977), and a developing first amendment-based right to privacy or personal autonomy. Rennie v. Klein, 462 F. Supp. at 1144. *See generally* Weiner, *Treatment Rights,* in The Mentally Disabled and the Law 327, 341-351 (S. Brakel, J. Parry & B. Weiner eds., 3d ed. 1985) [hereinafter cited as Weiner].

20. There is some claim, for example, that the administration of electroconvulsive therapy impairs short-term memory. If this were so, that form of treatment could affect adversely a defendant's ability to present a defense and should not be permitted if the defense objects.

21. *See* standard 7-4.14 and commentary for a discussion of the trial of defendants on psychotropic medication. *See also* Gutheil & Appelbaum, *"Mind Control," "Synthetic Sanity," "Artificial Competence," and Genuine Confusion: Legally Relevant Effects of Antipsychotic Medication,* 12 Hofstra L. Rev. 77 (1983).

22. *See also* standard 23-5.8 (nontherapeutic experimentation using prisoners should never be allowed; therapeutic medical programs not available generally to free-world patients may be used only if directly beneficial to a prisoner/patient, based on either a full, voluntary, and informed consent or a court order when appropriate).

23. For a general description of various therapies and their attendant side effects *see* Brooks, *The Constitutional Right to Refuse Antipsychotic Medications,* 8 Bull. Am. Acad. of Psychiatry & L. 179, 183-186 (1980); Weiner, *supra* note 19, at 327-330; Winick, *Psychotropic Medication and Competence to Stand Trial,* 1977 Am. B. Found. Research J. 769 (1977).

Standard 7-4.11. Periodic redetermination of incompetence

(a) Defendant's continuing incompetence to stand trial should be periodically redetermined by the court without the necessity of motion by either party. The facility or person responsible for treatment or habilitation should therefore be required periodically to file with the court a report on the defendant's current status, with copies to the prosecutor and defense counsel and with notice to the defendant. The report should be filed:

(i) at any time when the treating facility or person responsible for treatment or habilitation believes that the defendant has attained competence to stand trial;

(ii) at any time the treating facility or person responsible for treatment or habilitation believes that there is not a substantial probability that the defendant will attain competence within the foreseeable future; or,

(iii) at intervals not to exceed [ninety] days.

(b) The report should contain the following:

(i) a reevaluation of those issues required by standard 7-4.5 to be contained in the initial report to the court;

(ii) a description of the treatment or habilitation administered to the defendant;

(iii) an evaluation of the defendant's continued progress toward attaining competence within the reasonably foreseeable future, if the report concludes that the defendant remains incompetent to stand trial.

(c) Either party should have the right to contest the report or any issues addressed in the report within such time as is established in that jurisdiction and have the right to demand a hearing on the issues contested.

(i) Before the hearing, upon motion of either party and upon cause shown, the court should order that the defendant be evaluated by independent evaluators and that reports be submitted;

(ii) Each party should have the right to present evidence at the hearing. At the conclusion of the hearing the court should enter its written order setting forth separately and distinctly the findings of the court on the issues of competence, treatment or habilitation, and involuntary confinement.

(d) If neither party contests the report within the time set, the court should then independently review the report and:

(i) if the court concurs in the report's recommendations the court should enter an order accepting the report and continuing the defendant's treatment or habilitation or setting the case for trial, as appropriate;

(ii) if the court does not concur in the report's conclusions the court, if appropriate, should order an independent reevaluation of the defendant and should hold a hearing on the issues addressed in the report.

(e) Notwithstanding the availability of periodic redeterminations by the court, either party should, upon good cause to believe that a defendant has attained competence to stand trial, be able to initiate a redetermination of the defendant's competence.

(i) The prosecutor or the defense counsel, upon a showing of good cause, should be able to make a motion for reevaluation of a defendant by independent experts or for rehearing by the court of the issue of the defendant's continuing incompetence. For good cause shown, the court should be empowered to order such reevaluation or rehearing at any time.

(ii) Defense counsel should be permitted to have the defendant reevaluated at defense expense at any time, and the treating institution should be mandated to make the defendant available to the evaluator for reexamination. All records necessary to independent evaluation should be available to the prosecutor or defense counsel at any time.

Commentary Introduction

Standard 7-4.11 envisions continuing judicial oversight and periodic redetermination of continuing incompetence to undergo criminal proceedings of defendants committed as incompetent. Review should be accomplished if: (1) treating professionals conclude that a defendant has attained competence; (2) they report no substantial probability that competence can be achieved within the foreseeable future; or (3) a recommended ninety days have passed since the original order or an ensuing review. In addition, either a prosecuting attorney or defense counsel can contest an evaluator report or demand a hearing to redetermine competence and the need for treatment or confinement for treatment. A committing trial court is responsible to review a defendant/patient's status after receipt of a treating professional's report or at a contested hearing. In either case, the court should redetermine the need for continued treatment or confinement for treatment.

Related Standards

ABA, Standards for Criminal Justice 7-1.3, 7-4.7, 7-4.13, 7-4.14, 23-5.4, 23-6.2, 23-6.11

Commentary

Under the standard, courts should review issues of incompetence, treatment, and confinement for treatment at relatively frequent intervals. Until recently, few legislatures mandated periodic review of commitments based on present mental incompetence;[1] for the most part, incompetent defendants were committed to a suitable institution until its staff notified a committing court that competence had been restored.[2] The consequent abuse of the commitment process resulted more from disinterest than from malevolent misuse.[3] The standard reflects the funda-

1. For a review of the statutory restrictions on length of commitment for treatment in the various states, *see* Roesch & Golding, *Treatment and Disposition of Defendants Found Incompetent to Stand Trial: A Review and a Proposal,* 2 INT'L J.L. & PSYCHIATRY 349 (1979) [hereinafter cited as Roesch & Golding]. *See also* Weiner, *Mental Disability and the Criminal Law* 693, in THE MENTALLY DISABLED AND THE LAW 705 (S. Brakel, J. Parry & B. Weiner eds., 3d ed. 1985).

2. *See* commentary to standard 7-4.9, notes 6-9 and accompanying text. For some unfortunate defendants, commitment for treatment to restore competence in effect resulted in commitment for life. Dr. Thomas Szasz recounts a series of cases in which the process obviously was misused. T. SZASZ, PSYCHIATRIC JUSTICE (1965). Two telling examples in reported cases are United States *ex rel.* Von Wolfersdorf v. Johnston, 317 F. Supp. 66 (S.D.N.Y. 1970), a case in which an 86-year-old defendant had been committed for twenty years as incompetent to stand trial on kidnapping charges, and United States v. Barnes, 175 F. Supp. 60 (S.D. Cal. 1959), in which a defendant was held unable to move for dismissal of a case on speedy trial grounds because he had been held incompetent to stand trial.

3. *See* commentary to standard 7-4.2, notes 6-8 and accompanying text, for a discussion of improper uses of the evaluation process. Some researchers observed misuse of incompetence commitments as a method to dispose of difficult cases to avoid trial on the merits. Hess & Thomas, *Incompetency to Stand Trial: Procedures, Results, and Problems,* 119 AM. J. PSYCHIATRY 713 (1963) [hereinafter cited as Hess & Thomas]. One early study reported that courts virtually ignored and manifested a "total lack of interest" in defendants after they had been committed. *See* Hess & Thomas, *supra,* at 716. A study of Bridgewater, Massachusetts commitments showed that in many instances the length of commitment for treatment

mental premise that courts cannot abdicate to treating institutions or professionals their responsibility to monitor the continued commitment of incompetent defendants, and it rejects the notion that defendant-initiated review is sufficient. As the Supreme Court recognized in *Jackson v. Indiana,*[4] commitment for treatment to restore competence can be justified only by progress toward that goal.[5] By committing a defendant on this basis, a court becomes responsible to monitor the progress of treatment that offers the sole legal justification for continued commitment.

Paragraph (a) reflects a correlative obligation on treating professionals to furnish periodic treatment reports as a prerequisite to effective judicial monitoring.[6] Reports should be filed when any of three conditions are met: (1) a treating professional or a staff member of a facility required by court order to provide treatment believes that present mental competence

---

to restore competence to stand trial far exceeded the length of correlative civil commitment of mentally ill patients for treatment. McGarry & Bendt, *Criminal Versus Civil Commitment of Psychotic Offenders: A Seven Year Follow-Up,* 125 Am. J. Psychiatry 1387 (1969) [hereinafter cited as McGarry & Bendt]. McGarry's later study confirmed those findings and added a telling indictment of the system: After finding that 56 defendants who could be returned for trial as competent had been committed for an average of 4.3 years, McGarry noted somewhat wryly that ". . . prior to 1960 more of this type of patient had left Bridgewater by dying than by all other avenues combined." McGarry, *The Fate of Psychotic Offenders Returned for Trial,* 127 Am. J. Psychiatry 1181 (1971). Wexler's study of the Arizona commitment practice revealed "the uncomfortable fact that several Arizona defendants have spent considerable periods of time, often in the maximum security ward, purportedly awaiting trial on criminal charges." Wexler, Scoville *et al., The Administration of Psychiatric Justice: Theory and Practice in Arizona,* 13 Ariz. L. Rev. 1, 160 (1971). The commitment process apparently was treated by some courts as a substitute for criminal prosecution; after defendants were finally released from commitment for treatment, criminal charges were often dismissed, sometimes because the actual duration of pretrial commitment had far exceeded the maximum sentence possible for the criminal offense charged. *See* McGarry & Bendt, *supra,* at 1391.

4. Jackson v. Indiana, 406 U.S. 715 (1972).

5. *Id.* at 738.

6. Imposition of this obligation on a treating professional is consistent with the position of the American Psychiatric Association, which has proposed in the context of involuntary hospitalization of mentally ill persons that ". . . if and after the patient is hospitalized, frequent and periodic reports of his condition, treatment, and progress be made to the committing court or to its agency, to the patient's attorney, and to all of the examining physicians. . . ." American Psychiatric Association, *Position Statement on Involuntary Hospitalization of the Mentally Ill,* 128 Am. J. Psychiatry 1480 (1972). It is not inappropriate to extend that philosophy to those undergoing court-ordered treatment for present mental incompetence.

has been achieved;[7] (2) a treating professional or staff member believes there is no substantial probability that an incompetent defendant will attain competence within the foreseeable future;[8] or (3) an interval not to exceed a recommended ninety days has passed since the original commitment or an earlier periodic review.[9]

Paragraph (b) outlines the contents of periodic reports from treating professionals. In general, they should address and update the matters inquired into by the original professional evaluators.[10] Moreover, under subparagraph (b)(ii) they must describe the treatment or habilitation provided to the date of the report and, under subparagraph (b)(iii), a prognosis of continued progress to restore or attain competence within the reasonably foreseeable future.[11] If competence turns on the continued administration of psychotropic medication, a report should identify it and its effects on the defendant, since a trial court may need to authorize continued medication after the defendant has been returned for trial in order that competence can be maintained.[12] Similarly, a description of side effects from chemotherapy is important to a judicial imposition of conditions or restrictions to ensure that such side effects will not affect a defendant adversely during trial.

Paragraph (a) contemplates that a treating professional or staff member who files a report will provide copies to the prosecuting attorney and defense counsel in the case, and notify the defendant personally that a

7. Given the effectiveness of psychotropic medication, it is generally accepted that restoration of competence in cases treatable in that manner will be accomplished in a relatively short time, *see* Roesch & Golding, *supra* note 1, at 355, if it occurs at all, *see* Hess & Thomas, *supra* note 3, at 717-718.

8. This incorporates specifically the rule of Jackson v. Indiana, 406 U.S. 715, 738 (1972). *See supra,* notes 4-5 and accompanying text.

9. While the ninety-day interval envisioned in the standard is somewhat arbitrary, it has been adopted in some states, apparently without undue difficulty. *See, e.g., In re* Davis, 8 Cal. 3d 798, 505 P.2d 1018, 106 Cal. Rptr. 178 (1973); N.Y. Crim. Proc. Law §730.50(1) (1971). No number of civil commitment hearings can suffice to justify an indefinite commitment based on incompetence to stand trial. People v. Lang, 127 Ill. App. 3d 313, 456 N.E.2d 1301, 1307-1309 (1984) (court ordered reinstatement of criminal charges to allow for a hearing, following review hearing three years earlier).

10. *See* standard 7-4.5(b)-(c) and commentary for a description of the contents of an original evaluation report.

11. Although Jackson v. Indiana, 406 U.S. at 738, dealt only with continued commitment for treatment, which can be justified only by progress toward attainment of competence, it is not inappropriate to extend its reasoning to embrace any court-ordered treatment, whether necessitating confinement or not.

12. *See* standard 7-4.14 and commentary for a discussion of the trial of defendants whose competence is maintained by psychotropic medication.

report has been filed. That does not mean, however, that a formal hearing must ensue. Under paragraph (d), if neither party demands a hearing within a time period set by legislation or court rule, a recipient court may exercise its review responsibilities on the basis of the written report(s). The converse, of course, is the confirmation in paragraph (c) of the right of either the prosecution or defense counsel to contest a report and demand a hearing on the parts of the report that are not considered satisfactory. This contrasts by design with the procedures to be followed at the time of an initial commitment under standard 7-4.7, namely, that a hearing always must be held unless both parties stipulate to the underlying facts and the court accepts the stipulation.[13] Under standard 7-4.11(c), a formal hearing will not be held unless counsel for one of the parties demands it. Regardless of whether a report is contested or uncontested, however, it must be stressed that there is no difference in the nature of a trial court's duty to determine a valid basis for a finding of present mental incompetence and the appropriateness of treatment and confinement for treatment.

The power of an attorney for either the state or a defendant to seek a review of a commitment is not dependent on the submission of a periodic report by a treating professional or institutional staff member. If counsel for either side has good cause to believe that a defendant has become incompetent, he or she can move for a reevaluation by independent experts, request a rehearing on the issue of present mental competence, or both. In addition, subparagraph (e)(ii) confirms the right of defense counsel to have a defendant reexamined at any time, although not at state expense; treating institution staff members should be required to make the defendant/patient available for the purpose, subject, it may be assumed, to reasonable restrictions on time and duration.[14] Records appropriate to an independent evaluation also should be available at any time to either the prosecuting attorney or defense counsel.[15] If neither party has demanded a hearing, a court to which a report has been submitted can order one if it is not satisfied with the data or conclusions in the report. In that event, and before continuing in effect an existing order for treatment or confinement for treatment, the court may order an

---

13. *See* commentary to standard 7-4.7, notes 10-12 and accompanying text.

14. *Compare* the visitation rights for prisoners under standard 23-6.2(e) ("Visits with attorneys, clergy, and public officials . . . should be unlimited except as to time and duration.")

15. *Compare* standard 23-5.4(b) (confidentiality of prisoner medical records); standard 23-6.11(b) (confidentiality of prisoner records generally).

independent reevaluation and report by one or more mental health or mental retardation professionals.

Should a hearing be held at the demand of either attorney or on the court's initiative, both parties have the confirmed right under subparagraph (c)(ii) to present evidence concerning any of the matters on which the court must render a ruling.

If a court is not requested or does not decide to conduct a hearing on the sufficiency of a periodic report, under subparagraph (d)(i) it should enter an order accepting the report and find either that: (1) the defendant has been restored to triability so that criminal proceedings may continue; (2) the defendant continues mentally incompetent and should be treated under the same or an altered regimen and in the same or a less-restrictive or a more-restrictive setting; or (3) the defendant cannot be restored to triability within the reasonably foreseeable future.[16] Otherwise, the requisite findings are to be entered on the basis of all evaluation reports and other data adduced at a hearing. Subparagraph (c)(ii) envisions separate judicial findings on each contested matter.

Standard 7-4.12. Defense motions; proceedings while defendant remains incompetent

The fact that the defendant has been determined to be incompetent to stand trial should not preclude further judicial action, defense motions, or discovery proceedings which may fairly be conducted without the personal participation of the defendant.

Commentary Introduction

Standard 7-4.12 opposes the erection of an inflexible barrier against the completion of pretrial procedures that do not require a defendant's personal participation,[1] such as suppression hearings, motions posing legal rather than factual issues, and some discovery procedures, if they can be carried through fairly despite a defendant's present incompetence to stand trial.

16. The disposition of permanently incompetent defendants is discussed in standard 7-4.13 and commentary.

1. *See* commentary to standard 7-4.13 for the origins of the rule in relation to a factual determination of guilt or innocence.

Related Standards

ABA, Standards for Criminal Justice 7-4.4, 7-4.13
ALI, Model Penal Code §4.06

Commentary

The standard 7-4.12 rejects a premise that no proceedings of any kind can take place during a time of mental incompetence, whether or not a defendant could benefit from their early completion. Although that may have been the operative premise in common law criminal procedure,[2] the Supreme Court in *Jackson v. Indiana*[3] envisioned and apparently approved of the completion of certain preliminary procedures without regard to a defendant's present mental competence.[4] The standard allies itself with the Model Penal Code[5] and legislation in several states[6] by allowing certain pretrial procedures to be accomplished despite a defendant's current nontriability.

The standard rests on the assumption that a number of pretrial matters can be disposed of without any possible prejudice to defendants and that a refusal to allow them to take place might work affirmatively to deny

2. From the mid-seventeenth century, the common law rule was that criminal defendants could not be required to plead to an indictment or stand trial if they were mentally disordered enough to be unable to develop a "rational" defense. Slovenko, *The Developing Law on Competency to Stand Trial,* 5 J. Psychiatry & L. 165, 166 (1977).

3. 406 U.S. 715 (1972).

4. The Court stated,

> Both courts and commentators have noted the desirability of permitting some proceedings to go forward despite the defendant's incompetency. . . . Some states have statutory provisions permitting pretrial motions to be made or even allowing the incompetent defendant a trial at which to establish his innocence, without permitting a conviction. We do not read this Court's previous decisions to preclude the states from allowing, at a minimum, an incompetent defendant to raise certain defenses such as insufficiency of the indictment, or make certain pretrial motions through counsel.

Id. at 740-741.

5. ALI, Model Penal Code §4.06 (Permanent ed. with revised commentary 1985): "The fact that the defendant is unfit to proceed does not preclude any legal objection to the prosecution which is susceptible of fair determination prior to trial and without the personal participation of the defendant."

6. In some states, a case may proceed through an "innocent only" trial or "discharge hearing" at which the state is required to try the defendant but with only the possibility of an acquittal. *See* commentary to standard 7-4.13 for a discussion of the various procedures permitted in various jurisdictions. For example, the applicable Illinois statute, Ill. Ann.

fair proceedings.[7] Proceedings that might validly be permitted include motions to suppress illegally seized evidence[8] or possibly a motion to dismiss a prosecution based on entrapment, if the defendant's personal testimony is not needed to resolve factual issues.[9] Motions attacking an indictment or information on exclusively legal grounds, for example, double jeopardy, denial of speedy trial, or expiration of a statute of limitations, clearly fall within the standard.

Moreover, prompt discovery procedures for both the prosecution and the defense, in an appropriate case, may alleviate some of the effects of delayed proceedings while defendants are treated to achieve competence.[10] For example, depositions to perpetuate witness testimony might well minimize the risk that witnesses will become unavailable or that

---

STAT. ch. 38, §104-23 (Smith-Hurd Supp. 1985), provides that after a finding of a want of a substantial probability that a defendant will become competent within one year from the original finding of incompetence, the defendant may file for a discharge hearing. *See* Paull, *S.B.133: The Near Resolution of a Major Problem: Fitness in the Criminal Law,* 56 CHI.-KENT L. REV. 1107, 1119 (1980). This hearing takes the form of a full bench trial at which the prosecution must prove guilt beyond a reasonable doubt. If the defendant is found not guilty, the charges are dismissed; if the hearing does not result in a not-guilty finding, the defendant is remanded for additional treatment to attain present mental competence.

7. United States v. Barnes, 175 F. Supp. 60 (S.D. Cal. 1959), demonstrates the systemic frustration that can result from a mandatory suspension of all proceedings because of a defendant's incompetence. In *Barnes,* four defendants were charged with the murder of a fellow military prisoner ten years after the occurrence of the event. The trial court dismissed the indictment of three of the defendants on the grounds that their constitutional right to a speedy trial had been compromised. The fourth defendant, however, had been held incompetent to stand trial. Applying the rule that all proceedings for and against an incompetent had to be suspended, the Court refused to consider the speedy trial defense and committed the defendant until he should be restored to competence, at which point, one assumes, the motion would automatically have been granted. The absurdity of disallowing the solely procedural defense because of the defendant's incompetence is obvious.

8. Motions to suppress based on the invalidity of a search warrant or the insufficiency of the affidavit on which the warrant was issued, *see* Massachusetts v. Upton, 104 S. Ct. 2085 (1984); Illinois v. Gates, 462 U.S. 213 (1983), also could appropriately be dealt with under standard 7-4.12, because defendant testimony is unlikely to be necessary or useful in resolving fourth amendment issues.

9. *See* Bacon, *Incompetency to Stand Trial: Commitment to an Inclusive Test,* 42 S. CAL. L. REV. 444, 448 (1969).

10. *See* standards 11-1.1 through 11-3.3 for the discovery procedures that ought to be available to both the prosecution and the defense under standard 7-4.12. *See also* Weiner, *Mental Disability and the Criminal Law,* in THE MENTALLY DISABLED AND THE LAW 693, 704-705 (S. Brakel, J. Parry & B. Weiner eds., 3d ed. 1985).

their memories will fade through passage of time.[11] Accordingly, courts should be free to authorize deposition proceedings participated in by defense counsel only, unless the defendant's participation would enhance the effectiveness of direct or cross-examination.

Standard 7-4.13. Disposition of permanently incompetent defendants

(a) A defendant may be adjudged permanently incompetent to stand trial if the defendant has previously been adjudged incompetent and there is no substantial probability that the defendant will become mentally competent to stand trial within the foreseeable future.

(i) The court should hold a hearing to determine permanent incompetence to stand trial whenever the issue has been raised by the report of the professional providing treatment or habilitation, at the expiration of the maximum time of sentence for the crime charged or [twelve/eighteen] months from the date of adjudication of incompetence to stand trial, whichever first occurs.

(ii) If the defendant has been found permanently incompetent to stand trial and has been charged with a felony causing or seriously threatening serious bodily harm, then the defendant may be subject to hearing on factual guilt and special commitment as set forth in paragraph (b) below.

(iii) If the defendant has been found permanently incompetent to stand trial and has not been charged with the crimes set forth in paragraph (a)(ii), then the defendant should be released from any detention or commitment for treatment or habilitation to attain or restore competence. If the defendant meets the criteria for involuntary civil commitment, the court may order such commitment.

(b) At such time as a defendant charged with a felony causing or seriously threatening serious bodily harm has been adjudged perma-

11. *See* Bennett, *Competency to Stand Trial: A Call for Reform,* 59 J. Crim. L., Criminology & Police Sci. 569, 570-571 (1968): "Delay makes it more difficult for the accused to present his defense upon regaining his capacity. For example, by the time of trial, witnesses may forget important facts, or they may disappear from the jurisdiction or even be deceased."

nently incompetent to stand trial, or, upon motion of the state or the defense counsel at any time after the expiration of [twelve/eighteen] months from the date the defendant was first adjudicated incompetent to stand trial, the court should hold a hearing to determine the factual guilt of the defendant.

(i) The following principles should apply at the hearing:

(A) The hearing should be an adversary hearing.

(B) Rules of evidence applicable to criminal cases in that jurisdiction should apply at the hearing.

(C) Constitutional rights generally applicable to defendants at criminal trials, other than the right not to be tried while incompetent, should apply at the hearing. Such rights would include the privilege against self-incrimination, exclusion of evidence unlawfully obtained, and the right to call witnesses on the defendant's behalf and to confront and cross-examine witnesses against the defendant.

(D) The prosecution should have the burden of proof, beyond a reasonable doubt, of each element of the offense charged.

(E) Evidence adduced at such hearing should be recorded.

(F) The court should make specific findings of the extent to which the defendant's incompetence affected the outcome of the case, including its effect on the defendant's ability to consult with and assist the defense counsel, to testify in the defendant's behalf, the extent to which the evidence could be reconstructed without the assistance of the defendant, and the strength of the prosecution's case.

(G) The defendant should have a right to jury determination of the issues raised at the hearing.

(ii) If the finder of fact determines that the prosecution has failed to establish, beyond a reasonable doubt, any element of the offense charged or that the prosecution has failed to carry its burden under the law of the jurisdiction of disproving any affirmative defense raised by the defendant, the defendant shall be acquitted of the crime. If the finder of fact determines that the prosecution has established, beyond a reasonable doubt, all elements of the offense and that the prosecution has met its burden under the law of the jurisdiction of disproving any affirmative defense raised by the defendant, then the defendant may be subject to the special commitment procedures set forth in part VII.

Commentary Introduction

Standard 7-4.13 addresses the disposition to be made of pending criminal prosecutions against defendants incompetent to undergo criminal proceedings who will not attain competence within the reasonably foreseeable future. It recommends an innovative procedure similar to a "discharge hearing" or a "not-guilty-only trial," followed by a special commitment proceeding for defendants proven to have committed violent criminal acts. Commitment in that form provides greater protection for society than an ordinary civil commitment, and at the same time it protects incompetent defendants against unfair criminal convictions.

Related Standards

ABA, Standards for Criminal Justice chapter 10, 7-4.1, 7-4.3, 7-7.3 to 7-7.11

ALI, Model Penal Code §§4.04, 4.06, 210.0(3)

Commentary

Background: The Genesis of the Problem

Under the rule of *Jackson v. Indiana,*[1] defendants who are presently mentally incompetent and therefore nontriable under the due process clause[2] cannot be committed or otherwise ordered to undergo treatment or habilitation if there is no "substantial probability that [they] will attain that capacity in the near future."[3] If they can be neither tried nor committed for treatment to achieve present mental competence, the only

1. 406 U.S. 715 (1972).

2. *See* Drope v. Missouri, 420 U.S. 162 (1975); Pate v. Robinson, 383 U.S. 375 (1966). Using the due process clause of the Constitution, the Court in *Robinson* and *Drope* appears to have enunciated an irrebuttable presumption that incompetent defendants cannot receive a fair trial comporting with due process of law. In *Robinson,* 383 U.S. at 378, the Court in dictum indicated that the "conviction of an accused person while he is legally incompetent violates due process," *citing* Bishop v. United States, 350 U.S. 961 (1956), while in *Drope,* 420 U.S. at 171, the Court reaffirmed the common law principle that a person whose mental condition is such that he or she lacks the capacity to understand the nature and object of the proceedings, to consult with counsel, and to assist in preparing a defense may not be subjected to trial.

3. Jackson v. Indiana, 406 U.S. at 738.

alternatives are ordinary civil commitment proceedings[4] or release into the community.[5] Those alternatives are unsatisfactory from the viewpoints of the criminal justice system, defendants, and society.[6]

Accordingly, the Association believes strongly that a procedural mechanism must be provided to determine factual guilt or innocence of nontriable defendants, in fairness to them, and to commit to compelled hospitalization dangerous former criminal defendants, in fairness to society. Indeed, *Jackson v. Indiana*[7] recognized in passing that alternatives to its basic rule of disposition might be devised consistent with constitu-

4. It has been predicted that the more likely result of a strict application of *Jackson* will be an unjustified extension of civil commitment statutes to keep incompetent defendants in custody. "Most civil commitment statutes lend themselves readily to this purpose; substantive standards are vague; factfinding processes are haphazard; and no effective time limits on commitment are assured." Burt & Morris, *A Proposal for the Abolition of the Incompetency Plea*, 40 U. Chi. L. Rev. 66, 71 (1972) [hereinafter cited as Burt & Morris].

5. *See* Jackson v. Indiana, 406 U.S. at 738. Paradoxically, the Supreme Court's very insistence on protecting defendants' due process rights may deprive them of due process of law. For an extended discussion of the applicability of the enumerated rights to the permanent incompetent, *see* Gobert, *Competency to Stand Trial: A Pre- and Post-*Jackson *Analysis*, 40 Tenn. L. Rev. 659, 667-673 (1973) [hereinafter cited as Gobert]. The Court's apparent absolute prohibition against the trial of incompetents furthermore fails to recognize that present mental incompetence may be totally irrelevant to a legal or factual defense, for example, entrapment or suppression motions based on the fourth amendment concerning which their testimony may be unneeded, *see* Bacon, *Incompetency to Stand Trial: Commitment to an Inclusive Test*, 42 S. Cal. L. Rev. 444, 448 (1969), or alibi based entirely on the testimony of witnesses other than a defendant. *See* Gobert, *supra*, at 664. The refusal to try an incompetent may even result in a denial of the sixth amendment right to a speedy trial. *See id.* at 669.

Even if defendants are released, there is no mandate that the criminal charges be dismissed. Consequently, their inability to remove the stigma of unresolved allegations of criminal conduct may be more unfair to them than the completion of criminal proceedings while they are incompetent. Specifically, they may never have their day in court, and thus may lose the benefits of, *e.g.*, jury trial, confrontation, compulsory process for defense witnesses, the presentation of personal testimony in defense, and an adjudication of either innocence or guilt beyond a reasonable doubt.

6. One writer has described the resultant problem as a "three-horned dilemma":

> [I]f [the state] tries and punishes the defendant despite his lack of competency to stand trial, he has been denied due process; if it commits him until he is competent to stand trial, which, if he is permanently incompetent, he will never be, he has in effect been punished without trial; and if it finds him incompetent to stand trial yet is not allowed to commit him, he may as a practical matter have been given carte blanche to commit other crimes.

Gobert, *supra* note 5, at 659-660.

7. 406 U.S. at 740-741.

tional criteria.[8] In the years since *Jackson,* several separate forms of proceedings have been advocated as consistent with its dictum.

Procedural Responses to *Jackson*

One response is based on the fundamental holding of *Jackson v. Indiana:* If defendants are determined to be permanently incompetent, they should be released immediately from commitment to achieve competence to undergo trial and either discharged from custody or subjected to ordinary civil commitment proceedings. During the development of chapter 7, the Standing Committee included this response as one of three alternatives under standard 7-4.13;[9] it seemed the most pragmatic response and certainly the most clearly constitutional.

For the most part, however, some form of procedure beyond the limited *Jackson* alternatives has been urged by scholars and commentators. Four principal alternative procedures have been offered as solutions to the *Jackson* dilemma: (1) Incompetence might be ignored[10] except as a basis for a brief continuance; thereafter, a "super-fair" trial would be

---

8. The Court, *id.*, cited People *ex rel.* Myers v. Briggs, 46 Ill. 2d 281, 263 N.E.2d 109 (1970), as an example of a judicially approved conditional trial on the merits; an aquittal would terminate the matter, while a trial court could vacate a judgment of guilt if it appeared that a defendant was prejudiced at trial through inability to understand the proceedings or communicate with court or counsel.

9. The following Alternative A was included in the Standing Committee's First Tentative Draft of the Standards in July 1983, but was withdrawn from the proposals submitted to the House of Delegates in August 1984:

> [(a) A defendant may be adjudged permanently incompetent to stand trial if the defendant has previously been adjudged incompetent and there is no substantial probability that the defendant will become mentally competent to stand trial within the foreseeable future. The court should hold a hearing to determine permanent incompetence to stand trial whenever the issue has been raised by the report of the treating professional, at the expiration of the maximum time of sentence for the crime charged or five years from the date of adjudication of incompetence to stand trial, whichever first occurs.
>
> [(b) If the court should at any time determine that the defendant is permanently incompetent, the defendant should be released from any detention or commitment for treatment to restore competence. If the defendant meets the criteria for involuntary civil commitment, the court may order such commitment.]

ABA, Criminal Justice Mental Health Standards 7•227-7•228, standard 7-4.13, Alternative A (Tent. Draft No. 1, 1983).

10. Whether this would be constitutional is doubtful, unless the Supreme Court withdrew or drastically altered its *Robinson* and *Drope* doctrine of nontriability — a relatively unlikely event. *See supra* note 2.

held to resolve once and for all a defendant's guilt or innocence.[11] (2) Defendants might be tried in an "innocent only" proceeding[12] that could result in a termination of criminal proceedings but not in a conviction. The "innocent only" procedure was included as one of three alternatives during developmental work on chapter 7,[13] even though substantial criti-

11. *See* Burt & Morris, *supra* note 4, at 77. The authors proposed abolition of the traditional doctrine barring trial of incompetent defendants, substituting for it a claim to a continuance for a six-month period during which efforts would be made to attain competence. If defendants continued incompetent beyond that period, the prosecution would be required either to dismiss the pending charges or to carry the matter to trial using special procedures to compensate for a given defendant's incapacities. Such a "super-fairness" trial might embrace expanded pretrial discovery, a higher burden of proof, special requirements of corroboration in some cases, special instructions to juries, and less stringent postconviction relief procedures. Acquitted defendants would be protected by double jeopardy principles against retrial, and a conviction might be reversed based on evidence unavailable at the original trial because of a defendant's incompetence, if it might have generated a reasonable doubt about the defendant's guilt.

12. Illinois has adopted a "discharge hearing." ILL. ANN. STAT. ch. 38, §104-23 (Smith-Hurd Supp. 1985).

> [The discharge hearing] is a full bench trial, at which the state bears the burden of proof beyond a reasonable doubt. If the defendant is found not guilty, this trial completes the criminal process and renders to the defendant the constitutional protections of the double jeopardy clause, although he may be subject to civil commitment if the legal tests for that disposition are met. If the discharge hearing does not result in a not guilty finding, the defendant is remanded for extended periods of treatment. . . . If the defendant is found fit at the end of the extended treatment period or at any time within it, the criminal charges against him are handled within the criminal justice system. However, if the defendant remains unfit at the end of the extended treatment period, the court is required to order a civil commitment hearing; if the defendant is committed, charges are to be dismissed with leave to reinstate.

Paull, *S.B.133: The Near Resolution of a Major Problem: Fitness in the Criminal Law,* 56 CHI.-KENT L. REV. 1107, 1118-1119 (1980).

13. The following Alternative B was included in the Standing Committee's First Tentative Draft of the Standards in July 1983, but was withdrawn from the proposals submitted to the House of Delegates in August 1984:

> [(a) A defendant may be adjudged permanently incompetent to stand trial if the defendant has previously been adjudged incompetent and there is no substantial probability that the defendant will become mentally competent to stand trial within the foreseeable future. The court should hold a hearing to determine permanent incompetence to stand trial whenever the issue has been raised by the report of the treating professional, at the expiration of the maximum time of sentence for the crime charged or five years from the date of adjudication of incompetence to stand trial, whichever first occurs.

cisms have been levied against it.[14] (3) Resolution of the competency

---

[(b) If the court should at any time determine that the defendant is permanently incompetent, the defendant should be released from any detention or commitment for treatment to restore competence. If the defendant meets the criteria for involuntary civil commitment, the court may order such commitment.

[(c) The charges against the defendant shall be dismissed at the expiration of the maximum time of sentence for the crime charged or [twelve/eighteen] months from the date of adjudication of incompetence to stand trial, whichever first occurs.

[(d) At such time as a defendant charged with a felony causing or seriously threatening serious bodily harm has been adjudged permanently incompetent to stand trial, or, upon motion of the state or the defense at any time after the expiration of [twelve/eighteen] months from the date the defendant was first adjudicated incompetent to stand trial, the court should hold a hearing to determine the factual guilt of the defendant.

[(i) The following principles should apply at the hearing:

[(A) The hearing should be an adversary hearing.

[(B) Rules of evidence applicable to criminal cases in that jurisdiction should apply at the hearing.

[(C) Constitutional rights generally applicable to defendants at criminal trials, other than the right not to be tried while incompetent, should apply at the hearing. Such rights would include the privilege against self-incrimination, exclusion of evidence unlawfully obtained, the right to call witnesses on the defendant's behalf and to confront and cross-examine witnesses against the defendant.

[(D) The prosecution should have the burden of proof, beyond a reasonable doubt, of each element of the offense charged.

[(E) The court should make specific findings of the extent to which the defendant's incompetence affected the outcome of the case, including its effect on the defendant's ability to consult with and assist the defense counsel, to testify in the defendant's behalf, the extent to which the evidence could be reconstructed without the assistance of the defendant, and the strength of the prosecution's case.

[(F) The defendant should have a right to jury determination of the issues raised at the hearing.

[(ii) At the conclusion of the hearing, if the evidence does not prove the defendant guilty beyond a reasonable doubt, the court should enter a judgment of acquittal.

[(e) Whenever a person who has been judged permanently incompetent is civilly committed or certified and is determined to be a danger to others, that person may be placed in any appropriate secure facility.]

ABA Criminal Justice Mental Health Standards 7•228-7•229, standard 7-4.13, Alternative B (Tent. Draft No. 1, 1983).

14. *See* Burt & Morris, *supra* note 4, at 77. Defense counsel may view the "not-guilty-only trial" or "discharge hearing" as a mechanism to determine guilt that otherwise will remain unadjudicated, while prosecuting authorities may view it as a burden on already overstrained public resources. Most prosecutors have opposed it because they have little to gain from establishing factual guilt but much to lose if a jury acquits a defendant. Its principal advantage lies in the fact that defendants can avoid pending jeopardy in cases in which a substantive defense can be established or the prosecution case is too weak to support a

question might be deferred until trial has been completed.[15] An acquittal would render further inquiry unnecessary, while a conviction would necessitate a targeted inquiry into whether the defendant had proven incompetent during the course of the proceeding. If so, the verdict would be set aside.[16] This appears to be constitutionally acceptable, judging by dicta in *Drope v. Missouri*[17] and *Jackson v. Indiana.*[18] (4) The decision on present mental competency could be deferred until after acquittal or conviction; in the latter event, a determination of incompetency would impel a vacation of a verdict only if as a consequence the trial was fundamentally unfair and prejudicial to a defendant.[19] The advantages of this alternative, like the third, may outweigh its disadvantages.[20]

---

conviction. At the same time, they cannot be subjected to fundamentally unfair determinations of guilt because of their present mental incompetence. The principal prosecution counterarguments to the defense position are that the process is a "one-way street": An acquittal is final, while a determination of factual guilt is not dispositive if a defendant later becomes competent; in the latter event the government will have to waste its judicial and prosecutorial resources while guilt once more is established in a new criminal trial.

15. *See* Ennis & Hansen, *Memorandum of Law: Competency to Stand Trial,* 4 J. PSYCHIATRY & L. 491, 509 (1976).

16. *See id.* at 510.

17. In *Drope,* the Court noted that a deferral of a competence hearing "may have advantages." Drope v. Missouri, 420 U.S. at 182.

18. In *Jackson,* the Court appeared to approve a trial court resolution of pretrial matters not requiring a defendant's personal participation. 406 U.S. at 740-741. It cited in a footnote, *id.* at 741 n.30, an English case, Regina v. Roberts, [1953] 3 W.L.R. 178, [1953] 2 All E.R. 340 (Devlin, J.) (*see also* Regina v. Southey, 4 F. & F. 862 (1865) (Mellor, J.)), that had approved the practice, although English courts have been less than enthusiastic in endorsing the method. *See, e.g.,* Regina v. Beynon, [1957] 2 All E.R. 513 (Byrne, J.).

19. *See* Wilson v. United States, 391 F.2d 460 (D.C. Cir. 1968), which outlined in some detail a system of after-the-fact review:

> A prediction of the amnesic defendant's ability to perform these functions must, of course, be made before trial at the competency hearing. But where the case is allowed to go to trial, at its conclusion the trial judge should determine whether in fact the defendant has been able to perform these functions. He should before imposing sentence, make detailed written findings, after taking any additional evidence deemed necessary, concerning the effect of the amnesia on the fairness of the trial. In making these findings the court should consider the following factors:
>
> (1) The extent to which the amnesia affected the defendant's ability to consult with and assist his lawyer.
>
> (2) The extent to which the amnesia affected the defendant's ability to testify in his own behalf.
>
> (3) The extent to which the evidence in suit could be extrinsically reconstructed in view of the defendant's amnesia. Such evidence would include evidence relating to the crime itself as well as any reasonably possible alibi.
>
> (4) The extent to which the government assisted the defendant and his counsel in that reconstruction.

Analysis of the Standard

Standard 7-4.13 incorporates a solution to the problems created by *Drope v. Missouri*[21] and *Jackson v. Indiana*[22] that borrows selectively from several of the proposals canvassed above.[23] Paragraph (a) sets out a two-part definition of permanent incompetence:

1. A defendant has already been adjudged incompetent. The intent of the standard is that some period of time must have elapsed between an initial determination of present mental incompetence and the ensuing procedures contemplated under the standard.
2. There is no substantial probability that the defendant will become mentally competent to undergo trial proceedings within the foreseeable future. This restates the constitutional criterion of *Jackson v. Indiana* and is not intended to embrace a medical prognosis of incurability of the mental illness, mental retardation, or other condition underlying a state of nontriability.

Subparagraph (a)(ii) envisions three alternative events that may bring about a determination of permanent incompetence to stand trial. However, the first of the three to occur creates a judicial obligation to conduct a hearing to establish whether permanent incompetence exists.

---

(5) The strength of the prosecution's case. Most important here will be whether the government's case is such as to negate all reasonable hypotheses of innocence. If there is any substantial possibility that the accused could, but for his amnesia, establish an alibi or other defense, it should be presumed that he would have been able to do so.

(6) Any other facts and circumstances which would indicate whether or not the defendant had a fair trial.

Id. at 463.

20. A practical objection to the procedure outlined in *Wilson* is the possibility that a lengthy and expensive proceeding, carried to verdict, will come to nothing. Nonetheless, the procedure has merit. Even if a conviction must be vacated, the prosecution has been forced to advance a sufficient weight of evidence to justify a continuation of pending charges. It also provides the most ample body of data on which to base an accurate assessment of the impact of a defendant's present mental incompetence on fairness of trial.

21. 420 U.S. 162 (1975).

22. 406 U.S. 715 (1972).

23. *See* Bennett, *A Guided Tour Through Selected ABA Standards Relating to Incompetence to Stand Trial,* 53 Geo. Wash. L. Rev. 375, 407-408 (1985).

The first event is a report from a treating mental health or mental retardation professional to whose custody an incompetent defendant has been committed for treatment to attain present mental competence. Although the intent of the standard is to disapprove a determination of permanent incompetence entered contemporaneously with the initial judicial finding of nontriability and order of commitment for treatment,[24] there is no minimum time that must elapse between a commitment order and submission of a report from a treating professional suggesting permanent incompetence.

The second event is the expiration of the maximum period of imprisonment to which a defendant would be subject should the pending criminal charges have been carried to a judgment of conviction. This is not intended to indicate that commitment for purposes of treatment to achieve triability is a form of punishment; this is prohibited by the doctrine of *Jackson v. Indiana.* Instead, it rests on a concept of fairness — the duration of compelled hospitalization, as a significant form of restraint on personal liberty, should not extend longer than the maximum period of incarceration possible under a jurisdiction's penal laws.[25]

The third event is the passage of a specified period[26] following an initial adjudication of incompetence, during which a defendant has not been restored to a condition of triability.

When the first of the three alternative events has occurred, subparagraph (a)(i) contemplates that a judicial hearing on permanent incompetence should ensue; this is the counterpart to the judicial obligation under standard 7-4.7 to determine present mental competence, but without any of the procedural shortcuts envisioned there;[27] in this context a hearing is indispensable to a finding of permanent incompetence. Although no specific reference is made, the intent of the standard is to incorporate the provisions of standard 7-4.8 to govern a permanent incompetency determination. A hearing under subparagraph (a)(i) will result in one of five dispositions.

---

24. *See* standard 7-4.9 and commentary.

25. *See* standard 7-7.7 and commentary, containing a similar limitation on the period of special commitment following an acquittal by reason of mental nonresponsibility [insanity].

26. The bracketed material in subparagraph (a)(i) suggests a period of from twelve to eighteen months as appropriate for legislative consideration.

27. *See* commentary to standard 7-4.7, notes 10-13 and accompanying text.

1. A defendant might be found to be competent to undergo further proceedings. Although this is relatively unlikely, a hitherto undetected failure on the part of treating professionals to report a significant change of condition under standard 7-4.11(a) could come to light in the course of a hearing under subparagraph (a)(i), which would justify the same disposition that would have been made under standard 7-4.11(d)(i).
2. The court might find that continued treatment or habilitation may result in restored or attained mental competence within the foreseeable future. This would be unlikely if the event precipitating the hearing is a report from a treating professional that a defendant is permanently incompetent, but conceivably might occur if either of the other alternatives is met. In that event, a recommitment for treatment for a relatively brief additional period may be possible, depending on the length of time elapsed since an original determination of present mental incompetence.[28]
3. If the defendant meets the criteria for permanent nontriability, under subparagraph (a)(iii) he or she should be released into the community, free of any continued duty to submit to hospitalization or undergo treatment or habilitation, unless one of the following two dispositional procedures is pursued.[29]
4. If the defendant meets the legislative standards for civil commitment, the court might order compulsory hospitalization as provided for under the jurisdiction's civil commitment statutes — a disposition also contemplated in subparagraph (a)(iii). Adherence to the procedural criteria advocated in stan-

---

28. Jackson v. Indiana, 406 U.S. 715 (1972), did not establish a precise maximum constitutional limit on commitments for incompetency treatment or habilitation, but held that to detain Jackson for three and one-half years during which his condition remained unchanged was excessive. *Id.* at 738-739. There may also be a speedy trial problem if trial is too long delayed because of present mental incompetence. *Id.* at 740. The leading Supreme Court case delineating the effect of delay is Barker v. Wingo, 407 U.S. 514 (1972) (establishing the parameters of the right to speedy trial); *see also* United States v. Lovasco, 431 U.S. 783, *reh'g denied,* 434 U.S. 881 (1977) (due process effects of delayed arrest or initiation of criminal proceedings).

29. Until pending criminal charges have been dismissed, a defendant released from a treatment facility should still be subject to conditional pretrial release or preventive detention, if governing criteria are satisfied. *See* standards 10-5.2, 10-5.4 and commentary.

dard 7-4.8 should forestall due process or equal protection objections to such a commitment ancillary to a criminal prosecution.[30] This is the ultimate resolution for defendants who were not charged with felonies of causing or threatening serious bodily injury.

5. If a permanently incompetent defendant was charged with a felony based on causing or seriously threatening serious bodily harm,[31] subparagraph (a)(ii) envisions that a court may transform the matter into a special commitment hearing that may result in an order for special commitment.

A special dispositional hearing may also occur under the provisions of paragraph (b) if a set period of time[32] has elapsed from the initial adjudication of present mental incompetency and either the prosecuting attorney or defense counsel moves for such a proceeding.

Paragraph (b) advances a catalog of procedural rights governing "factual guilt" hearings that conforms substantially to the usual attributes of a criminal trial: (a) Subparagraph (b)(i)(A) confirms that the hearing must be adversarial; *ex parte* proceedings to determine factual guilt are unacceptable. (b) Under subparagraph (b)(i)(B), the usual rules of evidence governing criminal trials must be followed. This is, of course, consonant with the premise embodied in standard 7-4.8(b), governing original incompetency hearings. (c) Subparagraph (b)(i)(C), like standard 7-4.8(a), incorporates an array of constitutional criminal procedural rights, including protection against self-incrimination, exclusion of unconstitutionally obtained or derived evidence, the right of compulsory process, and the right of confrontation and cross-examination; subparagraph (b)(i)(G) also envisions jury trial as the norm. (d) Since the factual guilt hearing under standard 7-4.13 is a functional counterpart to a criminal trial, the burden of persuasion (proof) beyond a reasonable doubt, according to subparagraph (b)(i)(D), has to rest on the prosecution concerning every element of the offense. (e) Granted that appellate review lies against the court's

30. *See* Baxstrom v. Herold, 383 U.S. 107 (1966); standard 7-9.16 and commentary; standard 7-10.12 and commentary.

31. The standard does not assay a definition of the term. *Cf.* ALI, Model Penal Code §210.0(3) (Permanent ed. with revised commentary, 1985) ("'serious bodily injury' means bodily injury which creates a substantial risk of death or which causes serious, permanent disfigurement, or protracted loss or impairment of the function of any bodily member or organ"). The term is intended to include homicide charges.

32. The bracketed material in subparagraph (a)(i) suggests a period of from twelve to eighteen months as appropriate for legislative consideration.

judgment at the conclusion of a factual guilt hearing and entry of a commitment order,[33] subparagraph (b)(i)(E) contemplates that evidence introduced at the hearing should be recorded.[34] (f) Under subparagraph (b)(i)(D), a court should enter special findings (if under subparagraph (b)(i)(G) a jury returns a special verdict of factual guilt) concerning issues germane to the constitutional norms governing triability: (i) the extent to which, as a whole, a defendant's incompetence appeared to have affected the outcome of the case; (ii) the effect of the defendant's condition on the ability to consult with and assist defense counsel; (iii) the defendant's ability to testify in personal defense; (iv) the extent to which the underlying events could be reconstructed without the defendant's assistance; and (v) the strength of the prosecution's case (presumably, in light of all the evidence including whatever has been adduced by the defense).

The consequences of a hearing turn on the nature of the findings. Under subparagraph (b)(ii), a judgment of acquittal is to be entered if a jury (or the court, should jury trial validly have been waived) determines that (a) the defendant's guilt has not been established beyond a reasonable doubt concerning every element of a charged crime of violence, or (b) the prosecution has not met a burden established under jurisdiction law to disprove an affirmative defense advanced by the defendant. That should bar further criminal proceedings against the defendant concerning the matter.[35]

On the other hand, if the trier of fact determines beyond a reasonable doubt the existence of all elements of the offense and the prosecution has disproved applicable affirmative defenses, the court should proceed to the same special commitment procedure that follows an acquittal based on mental nonresponsibility [insanity].[36] That form of commitment may not be punitive as a constitutional matter, even though factual guilt has been determined, but instead is intended to precipitate the incapacitation, treatment, and ultimate release of a person whose mental condition poses

---

33. If the trier determines a want of factual guilt, arguably the "penumbra" of the fifth amendment prohibition against double jeopardy should prevent prosecution appeal. *Compare* Sanabria v. United States, 437 U.S. 54 (1978); Burks v. United States, 437 U.S. 1 (1978); United States v. Martin Linen Supply Co., 430 U.S. 564 (1977). However, by design the standard leaves the issue to federal constitutional litigation.

34. This parallels 7-4.8(a)(i) governing an original competency hearing.

35. *See supra* note 33. The ideal would be transactional immunity, although it might prove to be the "same offense" protection traditionally associated with double jeopardy. *See* Simpson v. United States, 435 U.S. 6 (1978); Brown v. Ohio, 432 U.S. 161, 166 (1977); Blockburger v. United States, 284 U.S. 299, 304 (1932).

36. *See* standards 7-7.3 through 7-7.5.

a danger to the community, precisely congruent with the consequences under part VII of a finding of mental nonresponsibility [insanity].

The Association is confident that adoption of the standard 7-4.13 approach to disposing of cases against permanently incompetent criminal defendants will achieve an appropriate balance between the needs of the criminal justice system and criminal defendants for the prompt disposition of criminal cases, the need of society to be protected against dangerous untried defendants, and the claim of defendants to have a procedurally fair trial unaffected by their present mental incompetence.

Standard 7-4.14. Trial of defendants on medication

(a) A defendant should not be considered incompetent to stand trial because the defendant's present mental competence is dependent upon continuation of treatment or habilitation which includes medication, nor should a defendant be prohibited from standing trial or entering a plea solely because that defendant is being provided such services under professional supervision.

(b) If the defendant proceeds to trial with the aid of treatment or habilitation which may affect demeanor, either party should have the right to introduce evidence regarding the treatment or habilitation and its effects and the jury should be instructed accordingly.

Commentary Introduction

Psychotropic medications to control serious mental illnesses have allowed mental patients, including presently mentally incompetent defendants, to be treated and supervised in the community rather than in mental institutions; these medications have freed many such patients from lifelong compulsory hospitalization. Courts, however, have differed over the triability of defendants whose present mental competence rests on continued medication during trial. While the standard assumes the propriety of proceeding in instances in which defendants are competent because of ongoing medication, it recommends procedures to safeguard the fairness of trial proceedings under such circumstances.

Related Standards

ABA, Standards for Criminal Justice 7-4.1, 7-4.13

Commentary

The discovery that "major tranquilizer" drugs can control symptoms of severe mental illness has made such psychotropic medications the treatment of choice,[1] releasing mental patients from what often had been lifelong imprisonment[2] into the community where outpatient or community mental health center supervision and aftercare could provide ongoing treatment while patients lead otherwise normal and productive lives.[3] Because psychotropic medication of this sort does not cure but only alleviates symptoms, discontinuance of the medication quickly leads to "disabling symptoms or varying degrees of personality disorganization."[4]

Some courts reacted strongly against "synthetic sanity" or "chemical competence," and invoked an automatic bar rule[5] forbidding the trial of defendants whose competence rests solely on continued psychotropic medication. That inevitably created a revolving-door effect: Defendants incompetent to undergo trial were hospitalized and given tranquilizing drugs that stabilized their condition; after their return to court, judges ordered discontinuance of medication pending trial, which rendered the defendants nontriable and again commitable.[6] Such a cycle might continue indefinitely.[7]

Two principal grounds underlay a judicial refusal to allow defendants to be tried while on medication. The first rested on a distrust of criminal trials in the course of which the defendants' normal mental functions were affected by medications. Many tranquilizing drugs produce sedation and drowsiness,[8] and patients complain that their normal mental

1. Crane, *Clinical Psychopharmacology in Its 20th Year*, 181 Sci. 124 (1973). Thorazine, or chlorpromazine, discovered in 1953, has been the prototype medication. *Ibid.*

2. *See* Hess & Thomas, *Incompetency to Stand Trial: Procedures, Results, and Problems*, 119 Am. J. Psychiatry 713, 717-718 (1963) (". . . well over one-half of the individuals committed as incompetent will spend the rest of their lives confined to the hospital").

3. Davis & Cole, *Antipsychotic Drugs*, in II A. Freedman, H. Kaplan & B. Sadock, Comprehensive Textbook of Psychiatry 955, 1821-1822 (2d ed. 1975); Gutheil & Appelbaum, *"Mind Control," "Synthetic Sanity," "Artificial Competence," and Genuine Confusion: Legally Relevant Effects of Antipsychotic Medication*, 12 Hofstra L. Rev. 77 (1983); Scrignar, *Tranquilizers and the Psychotic Defendant*, 53 A.B.A.J. 41 (1967).

4. Buschman & Reed, *Tranquilizers and Competency to Stand Trial*, 54 A.B.A.J. 284 (1968).

5. Winick, *Psychotropic Medication and Competence to Stand Trial*, 3 Am. B. Found. Research J. 769 (1977) [hereinafter cited as Winick].

6. *Id.* at 773.

7. Professor Winick discovered that the "automatic bar rule" appeared to exist in at least thirteen states although, because of lack of response, the data were incomplete. *Id.* at 775.

8. *Id.* at 789. Defendants may experience side effects like "excessive salivation, tremors of the hands, a mask-like facial appearance and a shuffling gait." United States *ex rel.* Bornholdt v. Ternullo, 402 F. Supp. 374, 376 (S.D.N.Y. 1975).

processes are slowed.[9] Side effects of this sort have been viewed as incompatible with the constitutional norm for triability[10] and therefore unacceptable.[11] Some courts, however, have rejected this kind of analysis as overly simplistic and have argued that the focus should be on procedural competence and not on the mere fact of continuing medication.[12] Under this view, if chemotherapy restores triability then proceedings may continue. If, on the other hand, a defendant continues nontriable in spite or because of medication, the court should order continued alternative forms of treatment or authorize other arrangements effective to overcome a drug-generated disability.[13]

The second ground advanced to support a freeze on trying psychotropically medicated defendants is that due process of law will be denied if their demeanor in the courtroom and, more particularly, on the witness stand may be so affected that juries reach erroneous conclusions about a defendant's functioning in an unmedicated state. This might occur in two ways: (1) A jury may view the medicated state of a defendant who has asserted mental nonresponsibility [insanity] as his or her normal state and discount the claim of nonresponsibility.[14] (2) A jury may find the

---

9. Mental patients frequently advance that as a reason for discontinuance of the medication if they are not under medical supervision.

10. *See* standard 7-4.1 and commentary.

11. A corollary argument decries the possibility that if the prosecution is permitted, "during the time of trial, to administer drugs to a defendant, contrary to [a defendant's] will, it is able to affect the judgment and capacity of its own adversary." State v. Maryott, 6 Wash. App. 96, 98, 492 P.2d 239, 241 (1971).

12. *See* State v. Jojola, 89 N.M. 489, 553 P.2d 1296 (1976), in which the court found that the medication, rather than blunting the defendant's mental acuity, simply permitted the mind to function normally as if there were not some illness affecting the mind. Under such circumstances, a rule automatically prohibiting trial because of medication is counterproductive, thwarting the very result it purports to achieve. It would "mean that an individual with a mental disorder which could be controlled by medical science could not be tried for a criminal offense regardless of [an] ability to comprehend the nature of the proceedings and to assist counsel in [personal] defense." Mines v. State, 390 So. 2d 332, 335 (Fla. 1980), *cert. denied sub nom.* Mines v. Florida, 451 U.S. 916 (1981).

13. Professor Winick pointed out in his study that most symptoms of drowsiness and the like occur immediately after initiating treatment or shortly after the ingestion of a dose of the medication. By scheduling administration of the medication properly, by taking frequent breaks, or even by scheduling court sessions during the morning only, a defendant in most cases instances can remain alert during the proceedings. Winick, *supra* note 4, at 789.

14. A picture of a docile defendant seated at counsel table undermines a defense argument that the defendant was mentally nonresponsible [insane] at the time of the offense. Some defendants fear that the glassy-eyed, vacant stare caused by the dulling of affect from some medications presents an equally unappealing picture to the jury. Slovenko, *The Devel-*

testimony of a medicated defendant not credible because tranquilizers have rendered the defendant's demeanor and mode of response apparently inappropriate to the occasion.[15] Weighty as those concerns may be, a number of courts have permitted trial of or testimony by medicated defendants if jurors are told of the fact of medication and given a description of the specific side effects of that medication on the individual defendant.[16] This should enable jurors to assess accurately the defendant's unmedicated mental state, despite the altered appearance and demeanor of the medicated defendant as observed in the courtroom.

Paragraph (a) of the standard aligns the Association with the judicial precedent rejecting the automatic bar rule[17] and accepts the premise that defendants whose medicated state is compatible with triability[18] may be placed on trial at their own instance or that of prosecuting authorities.[19] The only operative concern is triability, not the source or cause of present mental competence. The standard applies also to competence to enter a guilty or nolo contendere plea. It should be noted, however, that psychotropic medications prescribed for the purpose of maintaining a defen-

---

oping Law on Competency to Stand Trial, 5 J. Psychiatry & L. 165, 182 (1977) [hereinafter cited as Slovenko]. The tremors, mask-like appearance, and shuffling gait of the defendant in the *Bornholdt* case, United States *ex rel.* Bornholdt v. Ternullo, 402 F. Supp. 374 (S.D.N.Y. 1975), must have had some impact on the jurors' perception of Bornholdt as a person.

15. Witness demeanor, and in particular the effect of subliminal "demeanor testimony," are important to juror evaluation of veracity. A defendant whose emotions are dulled, and whose responses are not appropriate to the emotional message conveyed by the defendant's testimony, may create a false impression concerning veracity on the part of observing jurors. Therefore, it has been asserted that due process is violated because the defendant cannot "through conduct or mode of testifying demonstrate to a jury the irrationality or lack of control under pressure. . . . " George, *Emerging Constitutional Rights of the Mentally Ill,* 2 J. Crim. Def. 35, 38 (1976).

16. *See* Slovenko, *supra* note 14, at 182; State v. Jojola, 89 N.M. 489, 553 P.2d 1296 (1976); State v. Hayes, 118 N.H. 458, 389 A.2d 1379 (1978), *In re* Pray, 133 Vt. 253, 336 A.2d 174 (1975). A description of the effects of medication should include an explanation of the type and dosage of the medication and its effect on a defendant's mental state, including "appearance, attitude and verbal style." Project, *Legal Issues in State Mental Health Care: Proposals for Change,* 2 Mental Disability L. Rep. 613, 627 (1978).

17. *See generally* Weiner, *Mental Disability and the Criminal Law,* in The Mentally Disabled and the Law 693, 700-701 (S. Brakel, J. Parry & B. Weiner eds., 3d ed. 1985). Professor Winick demonstrated a number of ways in which the absolute bar rule might be challenged by a defendant who wishes to go to trial: equal protection, procedural due process, substantive due process, speedy trial, and cruel and unusual punishment. *See* Winick, *supra* note 5, at 793-807.

18. *See* standard 7-4.1.

19. *See* Bennett, *A Guided Tour Through Selected ABA Standards Relating to Incompetence to Stand Trial,* 53 Geo. Wash. L. Rev. 375, 408-412 (1985).

dant's competence to be tried must be administered under medical supervision; adult local detention facility personnel or defense counsel cannot administer tranquilizers to a defendant on their personal initiative.

If any regimen of treatment or habilitation, whether or not it utilizes psychotropic medication, can affect a defendant's demeanor, under paragraph (b) either the prosecuting attorney[20] or defense counsel should have a right to introduce evidence about the medication or the treatment or habilitation regimen, its direct and side effects in general, and its impact on the individual defendant's appearance, demeanor, and conduct at trial. A trial court then should be under a duty to instruct or explain to jurors the appropriate use of this evidence in deciding criminality or nonresponsibility. This, too, comports with the Association's rejection of the automatic bar precedent.

Standard 7-4.15. Credit for time served

A defendant who has been detained or committed for examination of competence to stand trial or treatment or habilitation to effect competence to stand trial should receive credit against any sentence ultimately imposed for the time of such pretrial confinement.

Commentary Introduction

Custody for treatment to restore or attain present mental competence is a consequence of a criminal prosecution and is more for the benefit of the criminal process than for defendants' welfare. The standard incorporates Association policy that formerly incompetent defendants convicted after trial should receive credit against sentence for pretrial confinement for evaluation and treatment or habilitation.

Related Standards

ABA, Standards for Criminal Justice 7-4.1, 7-4.5, 7-4.10, 7-4.11, 10-5.13

20. For example, a prosecuting attorney may wish to argue that a defendant would be vicious and uncontrollable except for the medication that presents the defendant to the jury in an unusually benign state.

Commentary

The overwhelming weight of precedent[1] denies credit against sentence for periods of confinement necessitated by evaluation and treatment or habilitation for present mental incompetence, usually on the premise that compulsory hospitalization is for the benefit of mentally ill defendants[2] and therefore is not to be likened to pretrial preventive detention[3] or detention because of inability to comply with pretrial release conditions.[4] Nonetheless, some states have legislated credit against sentence for periods spent undergoing treatment for mental illness.[5]

Part IV of the standards rests on the premise that treatment to attain present mental competence primarily benefits the system by restoring or attaining triability; benefit to defendants is incidental.[6] That accounts as well for defendants' inability to refuse to cooperate with evaluators[7] or to resist appropriate, reasonable, and ordinary treatment or habilitation.[8] Consequently, because defendants are restrained during the pendency of criminal proceedings for the benefit of the criminal justice system and not for the primary purpose of cure or habilitation, standard 7-4.15 advocates that they be given the same credit against a later sentence of imprisonment that they would have had they been preventively detained or otherwise subjected to detention pending adjudication.[9] The credit em-

---

1. The Supreme Court has not addressed the issue.
2. *See, e.g.*, Makal v. Arizona, 544 F.2d 1030, 1035 (9th Cir. 1976), *cert. denied*, 430 U.S. 936 (1977) (". . . [T]here was no custody related to his guilt for which he need be given credit unless for some reason the state provided it in its own system."). In State v. Enebak, 272 N.W.2d 27 (Minn. 1978), after characterizing the confinement as "not criminal in nature," 272 N.W.2d at 30, the court denied the defendant credit for time spent undergoing treatment before trial.
3. *See* standard 10-5.4 and commentary.
4. *See* standards 10-5.2 and 10-5.3 and commentary.
5. *See* Ill. Ann. Stat. ch. 38, §104-26(5) (Smith-Hurd Supp. 1985), People v. Williams, 23 Ill. App. 3d 127, 318 N.E.2d 692 (1974); Ohio Rev. Code Ann. §5120.17 (Page 1981), State v. Abner, 43 Ohio App. 2d 141, 334 N.E.2d 530 (1974).
6. Recall that the criteria for determining present mental incompetence need not rest on mental illness, mental retardation, or developmental disability, but relate strictly to a defendant's ability to undergo a criminal prosecution. *See* commentary to standard 7-4.1, notes 35-36 and accompanying text. Medical or psychological diagnoses may be irrelevant to that determination, as medical or psychological treatment may be. *See* commentary to standard 7-4.10, note 9 and accompanying text.
7. *See* standard 7-4.6 and commentary.
8. *See* standard 7-4.10(d) and commentary.
9. *See* standard 10-5.13 and commentary.

braces both detention for evaluation and compulsory hospitalization. However, a presently mentally incompetent defendant who was evaluated or treated as an outpatient was not detained within the meaning of the standard, and therefore should no more be entitled to credit against sentence than a defendant allowed to remain in the community on conditional release pending completion of criminal proceedings.

Part V

Competence on Other Issues

William H. Erickson, *Chairman*
Standing Committee on Association
Standards for Criminal Justice

Ben F. Overton
Task Force Chairman

Gerald T. Bennett
Reporter

Task Force

Ben F. Overton, *Chairman*
Justice, Supreme Court of Florida, Tallahassee, Florida

Joseph J. Balliro
Private practitioner, Balliro, Mandano & Balliro, Boston, Massachusetts (representing ABA Section of Criminal Justice)

Bruce E. Bennett, Ph.D.
Psychologist, Northbrook, Illinois (representing American Psychological Association)

Bruce J. Ennis
Private practitioner, Washington, D.C.; Chairman, ABA Commission on the Mentally Disabled

D. Lowell Jensen
Judge, U.S. District Court, San Francisco, California, former Deputy Attorney General, U.S. Department of Justice

Murray Levine, Ph.D.
Professor; Director, Clinical/Community Graduate Program, Department of Psychology, State University of New York at Buffalo, Buffalo, New York (representing American Orthopsychiatric Association)

Ruth Luckasson, J.D.
Department of Special Education, University of New Mexico, Albuquerque, New Mexico

Mary M. McCormick
Private practitioner, Senior Lecturer and Director, Legal Clinic, Law Faculty, University of Papua, New Guinea

Donald Paull, Ph.D., J.D.
Attorney and Psychologist; Chief, Mental Health Law Division, Cook County Public Defenders Office, Chicago, Illinois

Ralph Slovenko
Professor of Law and Psychiatry, Wayne State University Law School, Detroit, Michigan

Henry C. Weinstein, M.D., J.D.
Director, Forensic Psychiatric Services, New York University Medical Center/ Bellevue Hospital Center, New York, New York

GERALD T. BENNETT, *Reporter*
Professor of Law, University of Florida College of Law

INTRODUCTION

Mental competence to participate in the full range of criminal proceedings involves issues broader than more general determinations of present mental competence to be tried, and the criteria governing these determinations in other phases of criminal proceedings differ from those governing trial.[1] For example, a decision to exercise the sixth amendment right of self-representation[2] or to submit a guilty or nolo contendere plea, with its attendant relinquishment of a broad array of procedural rights,[3] requires a more sophisticated understanding than is required to undergo trial represented by counsel. Whether or not the criteria for determining mental competence in these special procedural contexts are higher than those governing trial competence, they are different and therefore warrant special coverage in these standards.

The consequences of present mental incompetence differ, although in varying degrees, depending on the procedural context. It is as much a violation of due process fairness to accept pleas from incompetent defendants as it is to require them to undergo trial. In either event, an ensuing criminal conviction should be vacated. In contrast, however, defendants as a general rule have only a minimal role to play in the course of appellate procedures, so that mental incompetence should not require a suspension of appellate court activities. Sentencing proceedings that con-

1. *See* standard 7-4.1 and commentary. An illustration of a competency context not frequently enough presented to warrant special treatment in a standard is participation in an extradition hearing. *See* Pruett v. Barry, 696 P.2d 789, 792-794 (Colo. 1985) (following the *Dusky* rule and the plea competency criteria of standards 7-5.1(a)(ii), 7-5.2(a)(8), 7-5.4(a)).

2. Faretta v. California, 422 U.S. 806 (1975).

3. *See* standard 7-5.1 and commentary.

form to the provisions of part IX of this chapter and to the provisions of chapter 18, Sentencing Alternatives and Procedures,[4] should not be delayed automatically because a defendant is presently mentally incompetent; indeed, delay might very well work an unfair hardship on the defendant because it will postpone the commencement of service of sentence.

Consequently, part V contains a sequence of standards focused on special problems of competency to plead guilty or nolo contendere, to exercise the right of self-representation at trial, to be sentenced in noncapital cases, and to appeal noncapital convictions. Each is addressed in sufficient detail to offer guidance to legislatures, courts, and rulemakers.

Standard 7-5.1 advances a standard for present mental competence to tender a plea of guilty or nolo contendere corresponding essentially to that governing triability[5] but with greater emphasis on the ability to recognize the consequences of the acceptance of such a plea. On the basis of a good faith doubt about competence to plead guilty or nolo contendere, a court should follow the same procedures laid down to ascertain competence to undergo trial proceedings.[6] While competent defendants should be allowed to plead, the consequences of a finding of present mental incompetence during the plea process are identical to those affecting nontriable defendants.[7]

Competence to undergo sentencing after conviction, under standard 7-5.2, comports generally with that for triability or pleading guilty or nolo contendere, but has no effect other than to legitimate a resentencing hearing after a defendant attains competence. At such a hearing the defendant's right of allocution can be implemented and mitigating factors, hitherto unavailable because of the defendant's incompetence, can be considered by the court as a basis to modify the original sentence. A convicted defendant who is incompetent when sentenced to incarceration or when otherwise significantly restricted in personal liberty ought to receive treatment or habilitation to restore or attain competence.

Standard 7-5.3 delineates a special test for competency to waive representation by counsel, a test that focuses on the special constitutional concern that criminal defendants not be deprived of functional representation. Accordingly, a judicial decision to accept a tendered waiver of counsel should be postponed until the defendant has been evaluated for

4. *See* standards 18-6.1 and 18-6.9 and commentary.
5. *See* standard 7-4.1 and commentary.
6. *See* standards 7-4.3 through 7-4.9 and commentary.
7. *See* standards 7-4.10 through 7-4.12 and commentary.

competency. A competent defendant must, of course, be allowed to exercise the right of self-representation under *Faretta v. California.*[8] A defendant who cannot waive counsel may prove triable with counsel, of course, under the basic constitutional test.[9]

The fundamental criterion for triability also governs appeals under standard 7-5.4. However, because represented defendants typically do not participate personally in appellate hearings, present mental incompetence has no impact on the continuation of an appeal under standard 7-5.4. Instead, appellate counsel may advance all issues germane to an appeal, whether or not a convicted defendant is able to approve them in advance. Nevertheless, either counsel should make known on the appellate record a good faith doubt about a defendant/appellant's present mental competence. After a defendant/appellant regains or attains competence, the standard advocates that matters adequate to support a reversal, not advanced because of earlier mental incompetence, be considered in postconviction review proceedings without regard to otherwise applicable procedural bars against the consideration of issues not posed earlier in the course of regular appeal.

Standard 7-5.1. Mental competence to plead guilty or nolo contendere

(a) No plea of guilty or nolo contendere should be accepted from a defendant who is mentally incompetent to enter a plea of guilty.

(i) Ordinarily, absent additional information bearing on defendant's competence, a finding made that the defendant is competent to stand trial should be sufficient to establish the defendant's competence to plead guilty.

(ii) The test for determining mental competence to plead guilty should be whether the defendant has sufficient present ability to consult with defendant's lawyer with a reasonable degree of rational understanding and whether, given the nature and complexity of the charges and the potential consequences of a conviction, the defendant has a rational as well as factual understanding of the proceedings relating to entry of a plea of guilty.

(b) If, at the time entry of a plea of guilty is proposed by the

8. 422 U.S. 806 (1975).
9. *See* standard 7-4.1 and commentary.

defendant, the court should have a good faith doubt as to the defendant's competence to enter such plea, whether the doubt arises from motion of the prosecutor or the defense attorney, or from the court's own observations, the court should not accept such proferred plea, but should order an evaluation of the defendant's competence to plead guilty and competence to stand trial according to the procedures set forth in part IV of these standards.

(c) If, at the time a plea of guilty is proferred by a defendant, the prosecutor or the defense counsel should have a good faith doubt as to the competence of the defendant to plead guilty, the attorney having such doubt should so advise the court and move for evaluation according to the procedures established by standard 7-4.2.

(d) If, after evaluation and report returned to the court, the defendant is determined to be competent to enter a plea of guilty, the court should proceed to accept the plea in accordance with the principles set forth in chapter 14, Pleas of Guilty, otherwise the court should proceed to those issues of treatment and habilitation as set forth in part IV.

Commentary Introduction

The test for present mental competence to plead guilty or nolo contendere, although resembling substantially that for triability,[1] differs fundamentally in application. Standard 7-5.1 reiterates the elements of present mental competence as embracing the ability to consult with counsel and the possession of a rational and factual understanding of plea proceedings. The latter element, however, does not correspond precisely to lay knowledge expected of defendants undergoing trial, but extends to matters like the constitutional rights relinquished through a plea, the process of admitting guilt, and the exercise of free will inherent in tendering a voluntary plea. In all other significant aspects, however, the standard mirrors the procedures for determining present mental competency and the procedures to be followed after a finding of present mental competence.

Related Standards

ABA, Standards for Criminal Justice 7-4.1, 7-4.2 through 7-4.13, 14-1.4, 14-1.5

1. *See* standard 7-4.1 and commentary.

Commentary

Common law criminal procedure recognized that defendants had to be competent to submit pleas of guilty as well as to undergo trial.[2] That tradition is vested today in the due process clauses of the Constitution, which bar the entry of a judgment of conviction based on a plea of guilty or nolo contendere tendered by a mentally incompetent defendant.[3] Although courts agree generally about the basic doctrine, they have not been in accord about the contents of the test. Many judges have applied routinely the basic test of *Dusky v. United States,*[4] abbreviated to a norm of ability to understand and assist counsel.[5]

Nevertheless, within the guilty plea context the *Dusky* test has been criticized as a governing standard because it emphasizes a defendant's ability to consult counsel[6] but places less emphasis on the defendant's present reasoning ability.[7] Defendants, by pleading guilty or nolo con-

---

2. "If a man in his sound memory commits a capital offence, and before arraignment for it, he becomes mad, he ought not to be arraigned for it: because he is not able to plead to it with that advice and caution that he ought." 4 W. BLACKSTONE, COMMENTARIES *24.

3. *See* Drope v. Missouri, 420 U.S. 162, 172 (1975).

4. 362 U.S. 402, 402 (1960) (a defendant must have a "sufficient present ability to consult with his lawyer with a reasonable degree of rational understanding, and . . . a rational as well as factual understanding of the proceedings against him"). *See* commentary to standard 7-4.1, notes 7-14. *See generally* Note, *Competence to Plead Guilty: A New Standard,* 1974 DUKE L.J. 149 [hereinafter cited as *New Standard*]. It is not enough that a defendant is oriented to time and place and has some recollection of events. Dusky v. United States, 362 U.S. at 402 ("sufficient present ability to consult with [the defense] lawyer with a reasonable degree of rational understanding").

5. Dusky v. United States, 362 U.S. at 402.

6. Courts in determining competence to stand trial are concerned primarily with a defendant's capacity to provide information to defense counsel, who then makes needed strategic and tactical decisions on behalf of the client.

7. Sieling v. Eyman, 478 F.2d 211, 214 (9th Cir. 1973) ("Where the question of the defendant's lack of mental capacity lurks in the background, however, the same inquiry, while still necessary, fails to completely resolve the question of whether the defendant can properly be said to have had a 'rational as well as factual understanding.' "). *See also* Weiner, *Mental Disability and the Criminal Law,* in THE MENTALLY DISABLED AND THE LAW 693, 696-697 (S. Brakel, J. Parry & B. Weiner eds., 3d ed. 1985) [hereinafter cited as Weiner]; Note, *Competence to Plead and the Retarded Defendant: United States v. Masther, 539 F.2d 721 (D.C. Cir. 1976),* 9 CONN. L. REV. 176 (1976); *New Standard, supra* note 4, at 168 (explaining that the understand and assist test only looks to (1) adequate recall, (2) present lucidity, and (3) some reasoning ability).

In Allard v. Helgemoe, 572 F.2d 1 (1st Cir.), *cert. denied,* 439 U.S. 858 (1978), for example, the defendant was given all necessary information about the charge, but claimed an inability to assess that information adequately against the background of the elements of the offense and his own divergent view of the facts. He claimed that the "lack of understanding reduced his capacity to make the decision as to whether or not to go to trial." *Id.* at 3. The

tendere, forgo many important rights[8] and are subject to severe sanctions inherent in entry of a criminal conviction.[9] In addition, the norm governing trial competence fails to consider a defendant's volitional powers, powers that may be significantly affected by mental illness[10] or mental retardation.[11] Accordingly, there is significant support for an independent test for determining present mental competency to plead guilty or nolo contendere; such a test would focus on the ability to make a reasoned choice among described alternatives and to understand the nature and consequences of a plea.[12] Despite the counter-criticisms lodged by proponents of the *Dusky* test against a special plea-related standard of competency,[13] standard 7-5.1 embodies the Association's judgment that a special norm ought to govern plea proceedings.

---

court rejected his claim on the basis that he had to rely heavily on the advice of counsel in evaluating the possibility of success at trial. *Id.* at 6.

8. *E.g.*, the rights against compulsory self-incrimination, to trial by jury, and to confront accusers. *See* Boykin v. Alabama, 395 U.S. 238, 243 (1969).

9. *See* Kercheval v. United States, 274 U.S. 220 (1927).

10. *See New Standard, supra* note 4, at 155. For example, a depressed defendant might be so overwhelmed by feelings of guilt caused not by any rational assessment of fault, but by mental illness, that a guilty plea could appear as the only means of expiating guilt. A plea should not be accepted if it rests on mental illness and not a voluntary personal assessment of guilt.

11. *See generally* Ellis & Luckasson, *Mentally Retarded Criminal Defendants*, 53 Geo. Wash. L. Rev. 414, 460-466 (1985). Mentally retarded defendants present a particular difficulty because very little psychological research has been conducted on their ability to understand guilt, the procedural rights relinquished through tender of a guilty plea, and a court's functions and powers in the course of plea proceedings. *See* Tarjan, *Mental Retardation and Clinical Psychiatry*, 1 Care & Intervention 401 (1977); Weiner, *supra* note 7, at 699. It seems very likely, however, that mentally retarded individuals are highly suggestible. *See* United States v. Masther, 539 F.2d 721 (D.C. Cir. 1976).

12. *See* Sieling v. Eyman, 478 F.2d 211, 214 (9th Cir. 1973). Support for the separate test rationale may be found in the United States Supreme Court opinion in Westbrook v. Arizona, 384 U.S. 150 (1966), in which the defendant had been afforded a hearing on competence to stand trial and found competent. Westbrook later waived counsel, stood trial, and was convicted. The Court held that the hearing on the issue of competence to stand trial was insufficient to resolve the issue of competence to waive the constitutional right to assistance of counsel. *Ibid.* Because a guilty plea necessarily works a waiver of several constitutional rights, the *Sieling* court likened the entry of a guilty plea to the *Westbrook* waiver of counsel, and accordingly set forth an independent test for competency to plead guilty. Sieling v. Eyman, 478 F.2d at 214. Nevertheless, *Westbrook* may well apply only to waiver of counsel and be limited to its facts. The reasoning that a separate test for competence is required for waiver of counsel can be distinguished from determinations to tender guilty or nolo contendere pleas on the advice of competent counsel. *See* White Hawk v. Solem, 693 F.2d 825 (8th Cir. 1982), *cert. denied*, 460 U.S. 1054 (1983).

13. The "reasoned choice" test may be unnecessary because a court before accepting a

Paragraph (a) reiterates the traditional doctrine that mentally incompetent defendants should not be allowed to plead guilty or nolo contendere, but in subparagraph (a)(i) the Association recommends that defendants determined competent to undergo trial proceedings be considered competent to plead guilty unless their incompetence to do so is properly questioned. If it is, then subparagraph (a)(ii) stresses that the test for plea competency should embrace two elements. The first element relates to a defendant's present ability to consult with defense counsel with a reasonable degree of rational understanding. This does not differ in any significant way from the counterpart dimension of the standard to determine competence to undergo trial proceedings.[14] The second element addresses a defendant's rational and factual understanding of (1) the nature and complexity of the pending charges (and particularly those concerning which a guilty plea will be tendered), (2) the consequences of a judgment of conviction based on a guilty or nolo contendere plea, and (3) the procedures according to which a tendered plea may be accepted by the court. This branch of the competency criteria is intended to embrace an ability to understand and relinquish constitutional rights governing criminal trials, to admit guilt, and to make a voluntary decision to plead to criminal charges.[15] As in the context of the *Dusky* test for triability, the criteria are not crystallized absolutes but rather are existential concerns

---

guilty or nolo contendere plea must determine that it is made knowingly, intelligently, and voluntarily. *See* Johnson v. Zerbst, 304 U.S. 458 (1938); Fed. R. Crim. P. 11; standards 14-1.4, 14-1.5. Consequently, the court has to determine reasoning ability, which renders a separate "reasoned choice" test for competence to plead guilty unnecessary. *See* United States *ex rel.* McGough v. Hewitt, 528 F.2d 339, 343 n.2 (3d Cir. 1975). It is evident that the "reasoned choice" test has come under significant attack, *see* Curry v. Estelle, 531 F.2d 766, 767 (5th Cir. 1976); Sailer v. Gunn, 387 F. Supp. 1367 (C.D. Cal. 1974), *rev'd on other grounds,* 545 F.2d 271 (9th Cir. 1974), most frequently because it could create a class of defendants competent to stand trial under the "easier" *Dusky* test, but incompetent to plead guilty according to the more stringent "reasoned choice" standard. *See* Suggs v. LaVallee, 570 F.2d 1092, 1118 n.65 (2d Cir.), *cert. denied,* 439 U.S. 915 (1978); Malinauskas v. United States, 505 F.2d 649 (5th Cir. 1979); United States *ex rel.* Heral v. Franzen, 667 F.2d 633 (7th Cir. 1981); White Hawk v. Solem, 693 F.2d 825, 829 n.7 (8th Cir. 1982), *cert. denied,* 460 U.S. 1054 (1983). Members of the latter class thus would be precluded from negotiating whatever benefits might accrue from entry of a guilty or nolo contendere plea, even though that would be in their best interests. (There is, of course, no absolute right to have a tendered guilty plea accepted. United States v. Jackson, 390 U.S. 570, 584 (1968); Lynch v. Overholzer, 369 U.S. 705, 719 (1962).) A further criticism of the "reasoned choice" test rests on concerns about judicial economy: defendants competent to stand trial would have to undergo a second evaluation and hearing to determine competency to plead under a separate, more stringent standard.

14. *See* commentary to standard 7-4.1, notes 10-14 and accompanying text.

15. *See* Boykin v. Alabama, 395 U.S. 238, 243 (1969); standards 14-1.4, 14-1.5.

that bear on the complexity of issues in a given case and the degree of participation to be expected of a defendant.[16]

Paragraph (c) envisions that the prosecuting attorney and defense counsel have equal responsibility for voicing a good faith doubt about and for moving for an evaluation of a defendant's competence to plead guilty or nolo contendere whenever a defendant's present mental competency to undergo trial is doubtful.[17] If such a motion is made, or if a court *sua sponte* raises a good faith doubt about competency, paragraph (b) contemplates that the court will defer plea proceedings and order a competency evaluation, following the same procedures applicable to evaluations to determine trial competency.[18] After evaluation reports have been submitted, the court should conduct a hearing to determine competency to plead[19] under the test established in subparagraph (a)(ii).

If the court concludes that the defendant is competent to enter a plea, then plea-acceptance proceedings can proceed according to the usual procedural statutes or rules.[20] If the defendant is not competent in light of the criteria in subparagraph (a)(ii), the standard envisions three alternatives. One is to commit the defendant for treatment or habilitation to restore or attain competence to plead.[21] This probably is the disposition of choice for defendants who would manifestly benefit from a guilty plea[22] (although a court should weigh the ultimate benefits inherent in an accepted guilty or nolo plea against the inherent prejudice in postponement of plea proceedings for purposes of treatment or habilitation to restore or attain competence). A second is to determine whether the defendant is competent to undergo trial even if not to plead. A prompt trial might well be more advantageous to a defendant than deferred plea

16. *See* commentary to standard 7-4.1, note 19 and accompanying text. Slovenko, *The Developing Law on Competency to Stand Trial*, 5 J. Psychiatry & L. 165, 189-190 (1977).

17. *See* standard 7-4.2 and commentary.

18. *See* standards 7-4.4 through 7-4.6 and commentary. In Willis v. United States, 468 A.2d 1320 (D.C. 1983), the court refused to allow the defendant to withdraw a plea of guilty on grounds that no separate hearing had been held to determine competence to plead, following an earlier determination that defendant was competent to undergo trial; no new factual issues had been advanced to suggest that Willis was competent to stand trial but not to plead guilty under the criteria discussed *supra* note 7. The *Willis* court relied on Alfano v. United States, 326 F. Supp. 792 (D. Conn. 1971), to the same effect in equivalent circumstances.

19. *See* standards 7-4.7 and 7-4.8 and commentary.

20. *See, e.g.*, Fed. R. Crim. P. 11; chapter 14 of the standards.

21. *See* standards 7-4.9 through 7-4.11 and commentary. There should be no objection to the use of psychotropic medication to restore or attain competence to plead. *See* standard 7-4.14 and commentary.

22. *See supra* note 13.

proceedings. A third alternative, related to the second, is to find that the defendant is competent neither to plead guilty or nolo contendere nor to undergo trial. In that event, the defendant should be committed for treatment or habilitation to restore or attain competency.[23]

Standard 7-5.2. Competence at time of sentence: noncapital cases

(a) Although a defendant may be incompetent at time of sentence, the court, in a noncapital case, may proceed to provisionally sentence such incompetent defendant.

(i) The test for determining competence at time of sentence should be whether the defendant has the sufficient present ability to consult with the defendant's attorney with a reasonable degree of rational understanding and whether the defendant has a rational as well as factual understanding of the sentence proceedings.

(ii) If, at time of sentence, a good faith doubt is raised as to the defendant's mental competence, the court has an obligation to determine the defendant's competence at time of sentence and, before imposing sentence, should order a presentence mental evaluation of the defendant according to the procedures set forth in part IV of these standards.

(iii) If the evaluators determine that the defendant is incompetent at the time of sentence, the court should make a specific finding, on the record, of the nature of the incompetence and the extent to which the sentencing proceeding has been affected by the incompetence of the defendant.

(b) A defendant who has been sentenced while incompetent at time of sentence should have the right, upon regaining competence, to exercise the right of allocution and to present to the court at a hearing matters of mitigation which were not presented to the court at the sentencing proceeding because of the defendant's incompetence at that time. The judge should reconsider the sentence imposed in the light of such matters.

---

23. *See* standards 7-4.9 through 7-4.11 and commentary. In this event, the special procedures under standards 7-4.12 and 7-4.13 should be available if competency proves impossible to achieve. Credit against sentence, of course, should be granted if a defendant, originally incompetent to plead, regains competency, pleads guilty or nolo contendere, and is sentenced to imprisonment. *See* standard 7-4.15 and commentary.

(c) If the sentence imposed is one involving incarceration or other significant restraint on liberty, the defendant should receive adequate treatment or habilitation to restore competence during the time the defendant is serving the sentence, pursuant to standard 23-5.1.

Commentary Introduction

Standard 7-5.2 rejects the traditional view that convicted defendants who are mentally incompetent at the time of sentencing cannot be sentenced. This view is rejected because all, or almost all, relevant sentencing data are acquired through exhaustive presentence investigations and reports, thus minimizing a defendant's actual role at sentencing. The standard adopts the view that a court can sentence a mentally incompetent convicted defendant but provides that an incarcerated defendant should receive adequate treatment or habilitation to overcome the cause of incompetency. If mental competence is restored or attained, a new sentencing hearing should be available at which the defendant's right of allocution will be implemented and mitigating data, not earlier tendered because of the defendant's mental condition, can be offered for judicial consideration.

Related Standards

ABA, Standards for Criminal Justice 3-6.1, 3-6.2, 4-8.1, 18-5.1 through 18-6.9

Commentary

The right of allocution, *i.e.*, to speak on one's behalf following conviction but before imposition of sentence, is a recognized right in most jurisdictions[1] even though it probably is not of constitutional weight.[2] It was of particular importance in earlier times when parties to litigation

1. Jurisdictions differ as to the nature of the right. For example, although some states require that sentencing courts ask defendants if they wish to say anything before sentence is pronounced, *see* Saddler v. United States, 531 F.2d 83 (2d Cir. 1976); 18•459, commentary to standard 18-6.4(a)(iii), others mandate only that an opportunity be afforded before sentencing for defendants and their counsel to make whatever statements they wish. *See* Berry v. State, 345 So. 2d 613 (Miss. 1977).

2. *See* Hill v. United States, 368 U.S. 424, 428, *reh'g denied*, 369 U.S. 808 (1962) (a failure to offer the opportunity "is not a fundamental defect which inherently results in a complete miscarriage of justice").

routinely were barred as witnesses, and a defendant's sole opportunity to address a court arose at sentencing.[3] Today the standards view it to be essential to fundamentally fair sentencing proceedings.[4]

A logical corollary to the rule requiring defendant allocution at sentencing is that incompetent defendants may not be sentenced during the period of their incompetency,[5] particularly if they are unable personally to address the sentencing court.[6] If, however, the right is not recognized as an absolute, there is no need to suspend sentencing proceedings for a

---

3. *See* Cross on Evidence 166-167 (2d Australian ed., J. Gobbo, D. Byrne & J. Heydon eds. 1979); C. McCormack, Handbook of the Law of Evidence 142 (2d ed. 1980).

Jurisdictions differ over the details of the right of allocution. Some require courts to address defendants personally, *see* United States v. Byars, 290 F.2d 515 (6th Cir.), *cert. denied,* 368 U.S. 905 (1961), while others hold that statements by defense counsel are sufficient. *See* Cunningham v. State, 94 Nev. 128, 575 P.2d 936 (1978). Some jurisdictions recognize the right only in some classes of cases. *See* Colombus v. Herrell, 18 Ohio App. 2d 149, 247 N.E.2d 770 (1969) (allocution applicable to misdemeanor convictions); Brogan v. Banmiller, 184 Pa. Super. 552, 136 A.2d 141 (1957) (allocution applicable only to murder); *see also* Barrett, *Allocution,* 9 Mo. L. Rev. 115, 116 (1944). Others hold it unavailable following convictions based on guilty or nolo contendere pleas. Goodloe v. State, 486 S.W.2d 430 (Mo. 1972). Courts differ as to the consequences of denials of the right. All agree that resentencing is the sole functional remedy, but some require a showing of actual prejudice at the time of the original sentencing proceeding as a condition to resentencing. *See* annot., 96 A.L.R.2d 1292, 1296 (1964); ALR Later Case Service 164, 174-176 (1983).

The rule prohibiting sentencing of mentally incompetent defendants was recognized at English common law: "If, after he [the prisoner] be tried and found guilty, he loses his senses before judgment, judgment shall not be pronounced; . . ." 4 W. Blackstone, Commentaries *24.

4. *See* standard 18-6.4(a)(iii) and commentary.

5. *See, e.g.,* Cameron v. Fisher, 320 F.2d 731 (D.C. Cir. 1976); State v. Hehman, 110 Ariz. 459, 520 P.2d 507 (1974); State v. Denton, 101 Ariz. 455, 420 P.2d 930 (1966); People v. Williams, 84 Ill. App. 3d 247, 405 N.E.2d 358 (1980); People v. Mitchell, 57 Ill. App. 2d 238, 205 N.E.2d 655 (1965); State v. Dyer, 371 A.2d 1079 (Me. 1977); State v. Saxon, 187 Neb. 854, 190 N.W.2d 854 (1971); Commonwealth v. Robinson, 494 Pa. 372, 431 A.2d 901 (1981); Commonwealth v. Maroney, 424 Pa. 493, 227 A.2d 159 (1967).

In many jurisdictions, the suspension of imposition of sentence is mandated by statute or court rule. In others, courts have required it as a matter of procedural fairness, because incompetent defendants cannot properly exercise the right of allocution perpetuated from the common law. *See generally* Weiner, *Mental Disability and the Criminal Law,* in The Mentally Disabled and the Criminal Law 693, 705-706 (S. Brakel, J. Parry & B. Weiner eds., 3d ed. 1985).

6. *See* Green v. United States, 365 U.S. 301, 304, *reh'g denied,* 365 U.S. 890 (1961) ("The most persuasive counsel may not be able to speak for a defendant as the defendant might, with halting eloquence, speak for himself."). The court in Wojtowicz v. United States, 550 F.2d 786 (2d Cir.), *cert. denied,* 431 U.S. 972 (1977), assumed that mental incompetence at time of sentencing the "Dog Day Afternoon" robber, if shown at an evidentiary hearing, would be sufficient to require the vacation of sentence, and remanded the case for the purpose.

convicted defendant represented by counsel, particularly if a thorough presentence report has been prepared and presented to the sentencing court.[7] The Association endorses the latter position in standard 7-5.2. If defense counsel is afforded an opportunity to contest the contents of a presentence report and to advance data omitted from it, the chances are relatively slight that a defendant's incompetence will frustrate the submission and consideration of information useful to a sentencing decision. Moreover, deferred sentencing may be significantly more oppressive to a defendant, particularly if coupled with commitment for treatment or habilitation to restore or attain competence, than imposition of a sentence during the enforcement of which the defendant may receive appropriate treatment or habilitation.

Accordingly, paragraph (a) recommends that courts be authorized to proceed to sentence incompetent defendants provisionally. The test for incompetency under subparagraph (a)(i) incorporates the basic components of standard 7-4.1:[8] (1) a sufficient present ability to consult with defense counsel with a reasonable degree of rational understanding; and (2) a rational and factual understanding of sentencing proceedings. If a defendant is competent under those criteria there is, of course, no inherent defect in sentencing proceedings. As in instances of nontriability because of present mental incompetence,[9] if counsel for either party moves for a competency evaluation based on a good faith doubt about competency, or the court from its own observations generates its own good faith

---

7. *See* standards 18-5.1 through 18-5.5 and commentary.

8. *See* commentary to standard 7-4.1, notes 7-14 and accompanying text.

The presence of mental illness alone is insufficient to establish incompetence; it must affect a defendant's understanding of sentencing proceedings. Hall v. United States, 410 F.2d 653 (4th Cir.), *cert. denied,* 396 U.S. 970 (1969); State v. Saxon, 187 Neb. 338, 190 N.W.2d 854 (1971). A number of jurisdictions have adopted the test in Dusky v. United States, 362 U.S. 402 (1960), *and see* standard 7-4.1 and commentary, as the criterion for determining competence at time of sentence, although others require only a factual and rational understanding of what is occurring, on the basis that the "ability to assist counsel" facet of the *Dusky* test is not relevant to allocution. *See* Saddler v. United States, 531 F.2d 83 (2d Cir. 1976); Cameron v. Fisher, 320 F.2d 731 (D.C. Cir. 1963); State v. Denton, 101 Ariz. 455, 420 P.2d 930 (1966); People v. Willis, 64 Ill. App. 3d 737, 381 N.E.2d 799 (1978); People v. Mitchell, 57 Ill. App. 2d 238, 205 N.E.2d 655 (1965); Commonwealth v. Robinson, 494 Pa. 372, 431 A.2d 901 (1981). Examples of the more limited version of the *Dusky* rationale are Barksdale v. Ricketts, 233 Ga. 60, 209 S.E.2d 631 (1974); State v. Dyer, 371 A.2d 1079 (Me. 1977); State v. Saxon, 187 Neb. 338, 190 N.W.2d 854 (1971). Wojtowicz v. United States, 550 F.2d 786 (2d Cir.), *cert. denied,* 431 U.S. 972 (1977), adopted a two-pronged test: whether a defendant was able "meaningfully [to] exercise [the] right of allocution or rationally [to] comprehend the nature of the proceedings." *Id.* at 790.

9. *See* standards 7-4.2, 7-4.4 and commentary.

doubt, under subparagraph (a)(ii) the court should order a competency evaluation and report. If the evaluators believe the defendant to be incompetent, the sentencing court should enter specific findings on the record, under subparagraph (a)(iii), concerning the nature of the incompetency and the impact it may have on the sentencing proceeding. Beyond that entry on the trial court record, however, incompetency for the moment has no further effect on the validity of the sentencing proceedings.

Paragraph (c) governs the treatment or habilitation for persons incompetent at the time of sentencing. In contrast to defendants incompetent to undergo trial or to plead guilty or nolo contendere, persons incompetent for purposes of standard 7-5.2 are not committed for treatment or habilitation, and sentencing occurs as if a defendant were fully competent. If the sentence is probation,[10] then presumably the court can condition it on appropriate outpatient treatment or, if necessary under a least restrictive alternative analysis, on a "voluntary" commitment to a mental institution. In unusual instances, a civil commitment might be in order. A convicted defendant sentenced to imprisonment, according to paragraph (c), has a claim to adequate treatment or habilitation directed at restoring or attaining competence to undergo renewed sentencing proceedings.[11] The only time limits governing this form of treatment or habilitation are those inherent in the criminal sentence itself, because sentencing proceedings have not been postponed for the purpose.

Under paragraph (b), a sentenced defendant who becomes competent to undergo sentencing proceedings should have a right to a repeated sentencing hearing at which the right to allocution can be exercised. In addition, the defendant should have an opportunity to present mitigating data to the court if the defendant's earlier incompetence had made it impossible to do so at the original sentencing hearing. The court then should reconsider the sentence originally imposed, but is not required to alter it simply because the defendant has allocuted.[12]

Standard 7-5.3. Competence to waive counsel and to proceed without assistance of counsel

(a) A defendant who is mentally incompetent to waive counsel or to defend himself or herself at trial without the assistance of counsel

10. *See* standard 18-2.3(f) and commentary at 18•97-18•99.

11. This should be accomplished under standards 7-10.2 through 7-10.11, *and see* standard 23-5.1.

12. *See* standards 18-4.9, 18-7.1 and commentary.

should not be permitted to stand trial without the assistance of counsel.

(b) The test for determining the competence to waive counsel and to represent oneself at trial should be whether the defendant has the present ability to knowingly, voluntarily, and intelligently waive the constitutional right to counsel, to appreciate the consequences of the decision to proceed without representation by counsel, to comprehend the nature of the charge and proceedings, the range of applicable punishments, and any additional matters essential to a general understanding of the case.

(c) If, after explaining the availability of a lawyer and making sufficient inquiry of a defendant professing a desire to waive counsel and represent himself or herself, the trial judge has a good faith doubt of the mental competence of the defendant to waive counsel or to represent himself or herself the judge should order a pretrial mental evaluation of the defendant according to the procedures set forth in part IV of this chapter.

(d) After obtaining the report of the evaluators, the court should hold a hearing on the issues raised according to the procedures set forth in part IV of this chapter.

(i) If, after hearing, the court determines that the defendant is competent to waive counsel and to represent himself or herself, the court should proceed with the case. The court in any such case should consider the appointment of standby counsel in accordance with standard 6-3.7 to assist the defendant or, if it should prove necessary, to assume representation of the defendant.

(ii) If, after hearing, the court should determine that the defendant is incompetent to waive counsel and is incompetent to stand trial or to plead, the court should proceed to issues of treatment and habilitation in accordance with part IV of this chapter.

(iii) If, after hearing, the court should determine that the defendant is competent to stand trial but is incompetent to waive counsel and to proceed without assistance of counsel, the court should appoint counsel to represent the defendant and should proceed to trial of the case.

Commentary Introduction

Standard 7-5.3 incorporates a special criterion for determining a defendant's mental competence to relinquish the sixth amendment right to counsel and to exercise the correlative constitutional right of self-representation. It incorporates a judgment that the criterion governing these important rights must be more stringent than that governing triability, because defendants must be able to recognize the dangers of self-representation and to select intelligently between self-representation and representation by counsel. It also reflects the judgment that a defendant incompetent to waive counsel but otherwise competent to undergo trial must be represented by retained or appointed counsel.

Related Standards

ABA, Standards for Criminal Justice 5-7.2, 6-3.6, 7-4.1 to 7-4.15

Commentary

The sixth amendment right to counsel is perhaps the single most important constitutional right for the protection of state and federal criminal defendants.[1] That right, however, has two dimensions: (1) counsel must be provided for financially unable criminal defendants who desire representation; and (2) competent defendants who wish to represent themselves, and who meet minimum criteria for lay understanding of criminal pretrial and trial procedure, must be allowed to represent themselves.[2] The choice must be a defendant's, not a choice made ostensibly on a defendant's behalf by someone else.[3] The selection of one of these rights, however, clearly constitutes a relinquishment of the other.

1. The leading case is Gideon v. Wainwright, 372 U.S. 335 (1963), which established the right to assigned counsel as fundamental to a fair trial. Earlier decisions include Johnson v. Zerbst, 304 U.S. 458 (1938), which provided for mandatory appointment of counsel for indigent defendants in federal criminal cases, and Chandler v. Fretag, 348 U.S. 3 (1954), in which the Court referred to the right to retained counsel as "unqualified." *Id.* at 9. The right extends to misdemeanor cases in which a defendant actually is imprisoned. Scott v. Illinois, 440 U.S. 367 (1979); Argersinger v. Hamlin, 407 U.S. 25, 36-37 (1972) (even relatively minor cases "often require the presence of counsel to ensure the accused a fair trial").

2. Faretta v. California, 422 U.S. 806 (1975). *See also* McKaskle v. Wiggins, 465 U.S. 168, *reh'g denied,* 465 U.S. 1112 (1984) (proper functions of standby counsel); Singer v. United States, 380 U.S. 24 (1965) (a defendant who waived the right to trial by jury did not have the right to insist on a bench trial); United States v. Powers, 622 F.2d 317 (8th Cir.), *cert. denied,* 449 U.S. 837 (1980) (the right to a public trial does not accord an unqualified right to insist that the public be excluded). Some courts have held that an improper denial of the right of self-representation is reversible error without a need to show prejudice. *See, e.g.,* United States v. Price, 474 F.2d 1223, *reh'g denied,* 484 F.2d 485 (9th Cir. 1973); United States v. Dougherty, 473 F.2d 1113 (D.C. Cir. 1972).

3. *See* Faretta v. California, 422 U.S. at 834 ("It is the defendant, therefore, who must be free personally to decide whether in his particular case counsel is to his advantage.").

Defendants must be mentally competent to exercise an election between self-representation and representation by counsel. Arguably, a decision to exercise the right of self-representation requires a greater degree of mental competency than a decision to seek trial representation by counsel; much more is at stake in the former decision,[4] even though some courts have been content to apply a single competency criterion to both decisions.[5] In this context, a focused test for competency comprises three elements: (1) competence to stand trial, (2) competence to comprehend the proceedings, and (3) competence knowingly and voluntarily to waive a constitutional right.

The first element, competence to stand trial with the assistance of counsel,[6] does not suffice for self-representation, although it is the threshold to a proper determination of the second element of competency. Defendants must be able to appreciate the consequences of a decision to conduct their own defense, and courts are responsible under *Faretta v. California*[7] to determine that defendants are competent to do so.[8]

---

4. In *Faretta,* for example, the Supreme Court pointed out that many of the "traditional benefits" associated with representation by counsel are lost through self-representation. Therefore, a defendant must make a "free choice" "knowingly and intelligently" to forgo those benefits. Faretta v. California, 422 U.S. at 836 (*citing* Johnson v. Zerbst, 304 U.S. at 464-465). The trial court record must establish that a defendant " 'knows what he is doing and his choice is made with eyes open.' " *Ibid.* (*citing* Adams v. United States *ex rel.* McCann, 317 U.S. 269, 279 (1942), *reh'g denied,* 317 U.S. 713 (1943)). In Westbrook v. Arizona, 384 U.S. 150 (1966), the Court noted that a trial court is under a special "protecting duty" to ensure "an intelligent and competent waiver by the accused" of assistance by counsel. *Id.* at 150 (*citing* Johnson v. Zerbst, 304 U.S. at 465). These decisions support a higher measure of competence to exercise the right of pro se representation than to stand trial with the assistance of counsel.

5. *See* United States v. Odom, 423 F.2d 875 (9th Cir. 1970); People v. Reason, 37 N.Y.2d 351, 334 N.E.2d 572, 372 N.Y.S.2d 614 (1975); Silten & Tullis, *Mental Competency in Criminal Proceedings,* 28 Hastings L.J. 1053 (1977) [hereinafter cited as Silten & Tullis]. *See generally* Weiner, *Mental Disability and the Criminal Law,* in The Mentally Disabled and the Law 693, 697 (S. Brakel, J. Parry & B. Weiner eds., 3d ed. 1985).

6. *See* standard 6-3.6 and commentary; standard 7-4.1 and related commentary for a discussion of the criteria governing competence to stand trial.

7. 422 U.S. 806 (1975).

8. One commentator has suggested a greater functional ability is required to represent one's self than to undergo trial while represented, entailing not merely a selection from alternatives posed by counsel, but the necessity of conceiving, developing, and implementing defense strategies. Note, *The Identification of Incompetent Defendants: Separating Those Unfit for Adversary Combat from Those Who Are,* 66 Ky. L.J. 666 (1978). Other writers have suggested that unrepresented defendants need the mental capacity to make tactical decisions during trial unaided by counsel, and that ". . . the higher standard of *Westbrook* necessarily involves an assessment of the defendant's ability to conduct his own defense." Silten &

This in turn requires that judges adequately warn defendants about the dangers of self-representation and reassure themselves that defendants understand and appreciate those dangers sufficiently to make a reasoned choice between constitutional alternatives.[9] The third element relates to a defendant's ability "knowingly and intelligently" to relinquish the sixth amendment right to representation by counsel.[10]

Tullis, *supra* note 5, at 1068. The Supreme Court, however, has never imposed such a requirement. Other courts consider the issue one of competence to make a valid choice, not competence to function in the capacity of a lawyer: "The significant issue, then, is the sufficiency of the trial court's inquiry into petitioner's capacity to make an intelligent choice." United States *ex rel.* Konigsberg v. Vincent, 388 F. Supp. 221, 226 (S.D.N.Y.), *aff'd* 526 F.2d 131 (2d Cir. 1975), *cert. denied,* 426 U.S. 937 (1976). *See also* United States v. Spencer, 439 F.2d 1047 (2d Cir. 1971); Minor v. United States, 375 F.2d 170, *cert. denied,* 389 U.S. 882 (1967); People v. Teron, 23 Cal. 3d 103, 588 P.2d 733, 151 Cal. Rptr. 633 (1979), *and see* People v. Wolozon, 138 Cal. App. 3d 456, 188 Cal. Rptr. 35 (1982). Accordingly, trial courts should not substitute their views of the wisdom of self-representation for those of defendants; the latter must accept the unpleasant consequences of their bad decisions. Minor v. United States, 375 F.2d 170 (1967); People v. Teron, 23 Cal. 3d 103, 588 P.2d 733, 151 Cal. Rptr. 633 (1979); Goode v. State, 403 So. 2d 931 (Fla. 1979). On the other hand, the capacity for pro se representation is not to be determined on the basis of a given defendant's technical knowledge or strategic disadvantages flowing from a decision to forgo representation by counsel.

9. The exact limits of what trial courts must ascertain are unclear. The plurality opinion in Von Moltke v. Gillies, 332 U.S. 708 (1948), indicates that courts must determine that a defendant understands:

1. the nature of the charges,
2. the statutory offenses included within those charges,
3. the range of allowable punishments if convicted,
4. possible defenses to the charge, and circumstances in mitigation thereof,
5. all other facts essential to a broad understanding of the matter.

Id. at 724.

However, the litigation concerned the validity of a guilty plea from an uncounseled defendant, so that the decision may have melded concerns over waiver of counsel for purposes of a plea hearing with exercise of the right of self-representation at trial. For example, the plurality opinion in *Von Moltke* suggested that a court should familiarize itself with the facts of the case, including all defenses to the pending charges, in order to advise a defendant. That would be proper for purposes of considering a tendered guilty plea but most inappropriate if a defendant will undergo trial. Clearly, however, a court should advise a defendant about the dangers of pro se representation and satisfy itself that the defendant has the understanding delineated in standard 6-3.6(a).

10. Edwards v. Arizona, 451 U.S. 477, *reh'g denied,* 452 U.S. 973 (1981) (a "reasoned judgment and a deliberate choice based upon adequate knowledge of what that fundamental right encompasses"); Johnson v. Zerbst, 304 U.S. 458 (1938) (an "intentional relin-

Paragraph (a) of the standard establishes unequivocally that defendants who are mentally incompetent either to waive representation by counsel or to represent themselves during a criminal trial should not be allowed to undergo trial without retained or assigned counsel. If defense counsel, the prosecuting attorney, or the court has a good faith doubt about the defendant's competency to undergo trial while represented, the appropriate measures should be taken under part IV. Paragraph (b) sets out the more precise criteria to ascertain competency to waive counsel, based on a present ability: (1) knowingly, voluntarily, and intelligently to relinquish the right to representation by an attorney; (2) to understand and appreciate the consequences of a decision to represent one's self; and (3) to understand and comprehend the nature of the charge, criminal proceedings, applicable sanctions, and anything else essential to a general understanding of the case. By intent, the criteria are phrased broadly so that ad hoc evaluations can be made of defendants' mental capacity to perform the functions to be expected of them at trial.

As provided elsewhere in the standards,[11] a court faced with a defendant desirous of exercising the right of self-representation is obliged to apprise the defendant of the right to representation by and assignment of counsel. The court also must ascertain that the defendant has the intelligence and capacity to understand the consequences of a decision to relinquish representation by counsel, the nature of the charges and proceedings, the range of permissible punishments, and anything else requisite to a broad understanding of the criminal case. If in the course of that colloquy, the court generates a good faith doubt about the defendant's present mental competence as delineated in paragraph (b), it should order a pretrial mental evaluation under paragraph (c), under the same procedures that govern mental evaluations to determine competency to undergo trial while represented by counsel.[12]

After evaluation reports have been transmitted to the court, it should

---

quishment or abandonment of a known right or privilege"); *see also* United States *ex rel.* Brown v. Fay, 242 F. Supp. 273 (S.D.N.Y. 1965). *See* Westbrook v. Arizona, 384 U.S. 150 (1966): "This protecting duty imposes the serious and weighty responsibility upon the trial judge of determining whether there is an intelligent and competent waiver by the accused." *Id.* at 150 (*citing* Johnson v. Zerbst, 304 U.S. 458, 465 (1983)). *See also* United States *ex rel.* Konigsberg v. Vincent, 388 F. Supp. 221 (S.D.N.Y.), *aff'd,* 526 F.2d 131 (2d Cir. 1975), *cert. denied,* 426 U.S. 937 (1976). A court, therefore, must consider directly whether a tendered waiver of representation by counsel is submitted intelligently and competently, an issue that cannot be resolved incidentally to a decision concerning competence to undergo trial while represented by counsel. Westbrook v. Arizona, 384 U.S. 150 (1966).

11. *See* standard 6-3.6(a) and commentary.

12. *See* standards 7-4.4 through 7-4.6 and commentary.

conduct a hearing in the usual form[13] to ascertain the defendant's competence. One of three alternative determinations of the matter may ensue. The first, covered by subparagraph (d)(i), is a finding that the defendant is competent according to the criteria in paragraph (b). In that event, trial may proceed,[14] although the court should consider appointment of standby counsel[15] to assist the defendant or to take over the conduct of the case if the defendant proves incapable of conducting a defense personally.

A second finding would be that the defendant is both incompetent to elect self-representation and to stand trial or plead guilty or nolo contendere. In that event, according to subparagraph (d)(ii), the court should determine the need for treatment or habilitation and enter an appropriate order.[16]

A third finding would be that the defendant is incompetent to waive representation by counsel, but otherwise is competent to undergo trial while represented by an attorney. In that event, under subparagraph (d)(iii), the court should see that the defendant has retained counsel or, if financially unable, receives appointed counsel.[17]

Although the approach embodied in standard 7-5.3 is not duplicated precisely in any jurisdiction at the present time, it clarifies for legislative consideration the procedures mandated by *Faretta v. California* and the appropriate system responses to mental incompetency in its several forms.

---

13. *See* standards 7-4.7 through 7-4.9 and commentary.

14. *See* standard 6-3.6(b): "When a litigant undertakes to represent himself or herself, the court should take whatever measures may be reasonable and necessary to ensure a fair trial."

15. *See* standard 6-3.7; McKaskle v. Wiggins, 465 U.S. 168, *reh'g denied,* 465 U.S. 1112 (1984).

16. *See* standards 7-4.9 through 7-4.11 and commentary. The same special procedures and dispositional measures under standards 7-4.12 and 7-4.13 should be available in this context as in cases of nontriable defendants. It may be proper to use psychotropic medications in treating defendants incompetent to waive counsel, if the procedural safeguards described in standard 7-4.14 are observed. *See* Bennett, *A Guide Through Selected ABA Standards Relating to Incompetence to Stand Trial,* 53 Geo. Wash. L. Rev. 375, 408-412 (1985). Credit against sentence for periods of involuntary commitment must be given. *See* standard 7-4.15 and commentary.

17. Although standards 5-6.1 and 5-6.2 assume that counsel should be provided only for defendants wholly or partially unable to afford counsel, implementation of subparagraph (d)(iii) may require appointment of counsel for funded defendants who refuse to retain counsel. In that event, reimbursement of the government for the cost of assigned counsel might be achieved through a liberal application of standard 5-6.2.

Standard 7-5.4. Mental incompetence at time of noncapital appeal

(a) A defendant is incompetent at the time of appeal in a noncapital case if the defendant does not have sufficient present ability to consult with defendant's lawyer with a reasonable degree of rational understanding, or if the defendant does not have a rational as well as factual understanding appropriate to the nature of the proceedings.

(b) Mental incompetence of the defendant at time of appeal from conviction in a criminal case should not prohibit the continuation of such appeal as to matters deemed by counsel or by the court to be appropriate.

(i) If, following the conviction of the defendant in a criminal case, there should arise a good faith doubt about the mental competence of the defendant during the time of appeal, counsel for the state or the defendant should make such doubt known to the court and include it in the record.

(ii) Counsel for the defendant should proceed to prosecute the appeal on behalf of the defendant despite the defendant's incompetence and should raise on such appeal all issues deemed by counsel to be appropriate.

(c) Mental incompetence of the defendant during the time of appeal shall be considered adequate cause, upon a showing of prejudice, to permit the defendant to raise, in a later appeal or action for postconviction relief, any matter not raised on the initial appeal because of the defendant's incompetence.

Commentary Introduction

Standard 7-5.4 covers the effect of mental incompetence on appeals and other postconviction review procedures. Because convicted defendants, like parties to appellate litigation in general, do not participate in appeal proceedings, mental incompetence rarely affects the fairness or accuracy of appellate decisions. Therefore, the standard envisions that appellate or postconviction review procedures will be carried to completion despite an appellant's mental incompetence, provided it later appears that matters important to review could not be presented because of mental incompetence, they should be considered in postconviction review proceedings.

Related Standards

ABA, Standards for Criminal Justice 4-8.2, 21-2.2, 21-2.5, 21-3.2, 22-2.2

Commentary

Convicted defendants do not participate directly in appellate proceedings because review is based exclusively on trial court records and appellate courts do not redetermine fact issues. Although, in theory, financially unable defendants might have a right to represent themselves before appellate courts,[1] the position of the standards is that trial or appellate counsel should present criminal appeals.[2] Hence, concerns about mental competency to undergo trial[3] or to plead guilty or nolo contendere[4] have no close counterpart as far as appellate proceedings are concerned.

Nevertheless, the decision to lodge an appeal is that of defendants and not their attorneys,[5] and defendants must have at least some ability to discuss with appellate counsel their desires concerning points to be advanced, even though counsel are not bound by the Constitution to follow their clients' demands.[6] Accordingly, the question of competency during

---

1. It is not clear that the right to self-representation under Faretta v. California, 422 U.S. 806 (1975) (*see also* commentary to standard 7-5.3, notes 1-4 and accompanying text) applies to appellate proceedings. However, the right to counsel extends to appeals of right. *See* Ross v. Moffitt, 417 U.S. 600, 618-619 (1974). Perhaps the matter is best resolved through a determination of competence to waive counsel under standard 7-5.3.
2. *See* standards 20-2.2(c), 21-2.2(a) and commentary.
3. *See* standard 7-4.3 and commentary.
4. *See* standard 7-5.1 and commentary.
5. The ABA position is that defendants decide whether to appeal, standard 21-2.2(b), as they do whether to plead guilty, standard 4-8.2.
6. In Jones v. Barnes, 463 U.S. 745 (1983), the Supreme Court considered the extent to which a defendant can insist that appellate counsel press nonfrivolous issues that impress counsel less than the client. Because attorneys are better able to evaluate the significance of points of error than laypersons, and should be encouraged to "go for the jugular," *id.* at 753 (quoting Davis, *The Argument of an Appeal,* 26 A.B.A.J. 895, 897 (1940)), rather than to press every potentially valid issue, the Court held that a defendant is bound by the strategic decision of counsel as to the most effective points on appeal. Therefore, counsel can press some points and abandon others that a client believes are more important. *Id.* at 752.

The ABA's position, however, is that clients and not their attorneys lodge appeals. Therefore, although counsel can exercise professional judgment and endeavor to dissuade clients from pressing unpromising points, the final determinations should be made by clients. *See* standard 21-3.2 and commentary.

appeals and, by extension, postconviction review proceedings generally, cannot be ignored.

Paragraph (a) of the standard sets forth an adapted version of the basic incompetency norm: Appellants should be viewed as incompetent if they lack (1) a present ability to consult with appellate counsel with a reasonable degree of rational understanding, or (2) a rational and factual understanding appropriate to their role as appellants. The standard does not go into the details of procedures to advance questions about appellants' present mental competency, other than in subparagraph (b)(i) to authorize appellate counsel for either side to spread on the record a good faith doubt about competency. That doubt might rest on a competency evaluation by mental health or mental retardation professionals; standard 7-5.4 does not envision orders for evaluation, evaluation reports, evaluation hearings, and dispositional orders as a responsibility of appellate courts.[7]

Incompetency should not be a ground to stay appellate proceedings, according to subparagraph (b)(ii), and appellate counsel may advance or withhold points on appeal in the exercise of good professional judgment.[8] This resolution of the problem assumes that appellants generally wish appeals to go forward expeditiously and are required to rely on their counsel's strategic and tactical decisions.

Nevertheless, it is theoretically possible that an appellant's mental incompetence might prevent counsel from acquiring information or learning of a client's concerns important to a proper disposition of an appeal. Paragraph (c) accommodates instances of that sort by recommending the availability of postconviction review, after a defendant attains competence, concerning matters that were not raised during an earlier appeal because of incompetence.[9] This form of postconviction review is not

7. However, because competency to stand trial extends through postconviction motions in a trial court, *see* standard 7-4.2(a) ("offer at any stage of the proceeding"), either attorney or the court under standard 7-4.2 can generate a competency inquiry under part IV, with the usual consequences.

8. Subparagraph (b)(ii) thus incorporates the constitutional doctrine of Jones v. Barnes, 463 U.S. 745 (1983); *see* note 6.

9. This is the basis under subparagraph (b)(i) for the expectation that an appellant's counsel who believes a defendant/appellant to be mentally incompetent during an appeal should advise the appellate court of the perceived incompetence and include the submission in the appellate record. This will be important at a later time if a second appellate court is to determine that one or more matters not advanced during regular appeal or earlier postconviction review proceedings were withheld because of an appellant's mental incompetence.

automatic; a defendant/appellant must make a threshold showing of prejudice related to mental incompetence[10] before omitted issues are considered by an appellate court.

10. *See* Wainwright v. Sykes, 433 U.S. 72 (1977); Holcomb v. Murphy, 701 F.2d 1307 (10th Cir.), *cert. denied*, 463 U.S. 1211 (1983). In federal habeas corpus proceedings under 28 U.S.C. §2241(c)(3) (1982), a showing of incompetence at time of regular appeal might excuse a failure to pursue a point in state court, and thus a failure to exhaust state remedies under *id.* §2254(b). *See* Engle v. Isaac, 456 U.S. 107 (1982). It would not excuse, however, a failure to utilize available state postconviction review proceedings after competency was restored or attained.

ADDITION TO PART V: *Competence and Capital Punishment*

Albert J. Datz, Chairperson
ABA Criminal Justice Standards Committee

Steven H. Goldberg
Task Force Chairperson

Norman Lefstein
Chairperson, Section of Criminal Justice

John M. Greacen
Chairperson-Elect, Section of Criminal Justice

James W. Ellis
Reporter

August, 1987

ABA Criminal Justice Standards Committee

Albert J. Datz, *Chairperson*
Private practitioner, Datz, Jacobson & Lembcke, Jacksonville, Florida

Paul D. Borman
Chief Defender, Federal Defender Office, Detroit, Michigan

George J. Cotsirilos
Private practitioner, Cotsirilos, Crowley, Stephenson, Tighe & Streicker, Ltd., Chicago, Illinois

William P. Curran
County Attorney, Clark County, Las Vegas, Nevada

Steven H. Goldberg
Associate Dean, University of Minnesota School of Law, Minneapolis, Minnesota

Michael J. Hemovich
Private practitioner, Hemovich, Nappi & Oreskovich, Spokane, Washington

Richard H. Kuh
Private practitioner, Warshaw, Burstein, Cohen, Schlesinger & Kuh, New York City, New York

Patricia M. Wald
Chief Judge, U.S. Court of Appeals, District of Columbia Circuit, Washington, DC

Alexander H. Williams III
Judge, Superior Court, Los Angeles, California

****

William A. Geller
American Bar Foundation Liaison

August, 1987

Task Force: Competence and Capital Punishment

Steven H. Goldberg, *Chairperson*
Associate Dean, University of Minnesota School of Law, Minneapolis, Minnesota

Richard J. Bonnie
Director, Institute of Law, Psychiatry & Public Policy, John S. Battle Professor of Law, University of Virginia School of Law, Charlottesville, Virginia

Bernard L. Diamond, M.D.
Professor of Law, Emeritus, University of California School of Law, Berkeley, California; Clinical Professor of Psychiatry, University of California School of Medicine, San Francisco, California

Judith H. Friedman
Special Assistant to the Assistant Attorney General, Criminal Division, U.S. Department of Justice, Washington, DC

Howard Janssen
Private practitioner, Crosby, Heafey, Roach & May, Oakland, California

Donald Paull
Chief, Mental Health Law Division, Cook County Public Defenders Office, Chicago, Illinois

Phillip J. Resnick, M.D.
Associate Professor of Psychiatry and Director, Division of Forensic Psychiatry, Case Western Reserve University Medical School, Cleveland, Ohio

Henry C. Weinstein, M.D. (*ex-officio*)
Director, Forensic Psychiatric Services, New York University Medical Center, Bellevue Hospital Center, New York, New York

---

James W. Ellis, *Reporter*
Professor of Law, School of Law, University of New Mexico

****

Gerald T. Bennett
Professor of Law, University of Florida, Gainesville, Florida, served as Chairperson of the Task Force during a substantial portion of the Task Force's work.

INTRODUCTION

Few issues in criminal justice are as controversial as capital punishment. Both the death penalty itself and the procedures for its implementation produce arguments of emotional and intellectual intensity. The debates on this issue have dominated much of the discussion concerning the criminal justice system, both among the general public and within the legal profession, since the Supreme Court declined to abolish the penalty in 1976.[1]

The American Bar Association has not taken a general position either approving or opposing the imposition of the death penalty; the following Standards do not represent such a position, and neither approval nor disapproval of capital punishment should be inferred from them. But the fact that a substantial majority of the states have reenacted death penalty statutes, and the additional fact that there are more than 1,700 prisoners on death row,[2] mean that the procedural issues surrounding its application in cases involving mentally ill and mentally retarded convicts are extremely important.

The United States Supreme Court has recently addressed some of these issues. In *Ford v. Wainwright*,[3] the Court held that the Constitution's prohibition on cruel and unusual punishment forbids the execution of convicts who are "insane." Although the Justices did not agree on a single rationale for their ruling,[4] a majority concluded that the common-law doctrine that prohibited execution of insane convicts was incorporated in the Eighth Amendment.[5]

The Court also found unconstitutional Florida's procedures for ascertaining whether a condemned convict was insane. Florida law placed the responsibility for determining whether the inmate was insane in the hands

1. *See* Gregg v. Georgia, 428 U.S. 153 (1976).

2. Ward, *Competency for Execution: Problems in Law and Psychiatry*, 14 FLA. ST. U.L. REV. 35, 37 (1986).

3. 106 S. Ct. 2595 (1986).

4. "As is often true of common-law principles, . . . the reasons for the rule are less sure and less uniform than the rule itself." 106 S. Ct. at 2601.

5. On this issue, Justice Marshall wrote for a majority that included Justices Brennan, Blackmun, Stevens and Powell.

of the Governor, who was to be advised by a commission of three psychiatrists. As Justice Marshall's opinion noted, "[t]he procedure is conducted wholly within the executive branch, *ex parte*, and provides the exclusive means for determining sanity."[6] The Justices reached a variety of conclusions regarding the precise nature of the Constitution's procedural requirements for ascertaining a convict's current mental condition, but seven Justices agreed that Florida's procedures were constitutionally inadequate.[7]

Procedures in the various states for ascertaining the mental condition of prisoners who face execution vary widely.[8] In response to the *Ford* decision, many states will be examining and reevaluating their procedures. The Court has given substantial latitude to the states in designing procedures that are both fair and practical. The following Standards include procedures somewhat more painstaking than what appears to be the constitutionally acceptable minimum under *Ford*. However they represent an attempt to balance the interests of both the convict and society in preventing the execution of any individual who is currently incompetent, with the interest of the criminal justice system in fair and expeditious resolution of disputes about the convict's current mental condition.

6. 106 S. Ct. at 2603.

7. Justices Marshall, Brennan, Blackmun, and Stevens stated that the Florida procedures were unconstitutional because they excluded from consideration evidence offered by the convict or counsel, and because they failed to afford any right to challenge the testimony of adverse witnesses. Justice Powell's concurring opinion found fewer procedural requirements in the Constitution than did the plurality opinion, but concluded that "[t]he State should provide an impartial officer or board that can receive evidence and argument from the prisoner's counsel, including expert psychiatric evidence that may differ from the state's own psychiatric examination. Beyond these basic requirements, the States should have substantial leeway to determine what process best balances the various interests at stake." 106 S. Ct. at 2611. Justices O'Connor and White, while concluding that the Eighth Amendment did not prohibit the execution of insane prisoners, found that Florida had created a liberty interest and violated due process by failing to give the prisoner an opportunity to be heard. "[D]ue process at the very least requires that the decisionmaker consider the prisoner's written submissions." 106 S. Ct. at 2613. Justice Rehnquist and Chief Justice Burger dissented.

8. *See* Ward, *supra* note 2, at 73-76.

Standard 7-5.5. Postconviction determination of mental competence in capital cases

Standard 18-1.1 makes it clear that the American Bar Association Standards for Criminal Justice do not deal with whether the death penalty should be an available sentencing alternative. Like Standard 18-1.1., Standards 7-5.6 and 7-5.7 establish no policy on the death penalty itself. Their sole purpose is to address complex issues dealing with postconviction determinations of mental competence in capital cases.

Commentary Introduction

Standard 7-5.5 makes clear that the Standards on Competence and Capital Punishment do not constitute a general position of the American Bar Association on the death penalty.

Related Standards

ABA Standards for Criminal Justice 7-5.6, 7-5.7, 18-1.1.

Commentary

The American Bar Association has taken no general position on the adoption of statutes imposing the death penalty. But the lack of such a general position on the overall issue does not preclude the ABA from speaking to important issues of implementation in those jurisdictions that choose to adopt capital punishment. Standards 7-5.6 and 7-5.7 are not the first such positions to be adopted by the Association; the ABA has positions opposing the imposition of the death penalty for acts committed while the defendant was a juvenile, and calling on all jurisdictions to provide counsel for all death row inmates to pursue appeals and collateral matters. The following Standards on currently incompetent death row inmates address a similarly crucial issue. The decision by the United States Supreme Court in *Ford v. Wainwright*[1] calls into question the constitutionality of the procedures of many states for evaluating the current mental condition of death row inmates. The ABA can offer assistance to such states in drafting appropriate, constitutional procedures without addressing the overall desirability of the death penalty itself.

Standard 7-5.6 Currently incompetent condemned convicts; stay of execution

(a) Convicts who have been sentenced to death should not be executed if they are currently mentally incompetent. If it is determined that a condemned convict is currently mentally incompetent, execution should be stayed.

(b) A convict is incompetent to be executed if, as a result of mental illness or mental retardation, the convict cannot understand the nature of the pending proceedings, what he or she was tried for, the reason for the punishment, or the nature of the punishment. A convict is also incompetent if, as a result of mental illness or mental retardation, the convict lacks sufficient capacity to recognize or understand any fact which might exist which would make the punishment unjust or unlawful, or lacks the ability to convey such information to counsel or to the court.

Commentary Introduction

Standard 7-5.6 provides that currently incompetent defendants should not be executed and provides a definition of incomptence to be executed.

Related Standards

ABA Standards for Criminal Justice 7-4.1, 7-5.2.

1. 106 S. Ct. 2595 (1986).

Commentary

The common-law prohibition on the execution of defendants who are currently mentally incompetent has received substantial attention from commentators,[1] but while various rationales have been offered in support of the prohibition, none has achieved universal agreement.[2] Nevertheless, none of the states that retain the death penalty has abandoned the common-law rule.[3] The common law's prohibition has recently been held in *Ford v. Wainwright* to be required by the Constitution's prohibition on cruel and unusual punishment.[4]

Paragraph (a) of this Standard reflects the constitutional and common-law prohibition against executing defendants who are currently incompetent. The principal reason for the Standard is the belief that the integrity of the criminal justice system is eroded by the execution of a defendant who is incapable of understanding the penalty that is about to be imposed or who is unable to communicate exculpatory or mitigating information that might affect the decision regarding capital punishment. The rule rests less on sympathy for the sentenced convict than on concern for the integrity of the criminal justice system.

Paragraph (b) of the Standard recommends a formulation for the test of current competence to be executed. The elements of this test have been selected to reflect the substantive concern that individuals should not be executed while they lack the capacity for rational understanding of the nature of the proceedings or of the penalty that is about to be imposed, or while they are unable to communicate possibly exculpatory or mitigating information to their lawyers or to the court. (The language of the test is

---

1. *See, e.g.*, Ward, *Competency for Execution: Problems in Law and Psychiatry*, 14 FLA. ST. U. L. REV. 35, 37 (1986); Hazard & Louisell, *Death, the State, and the Insane: Stay of Execution*, 9 U.C.L.A. L. REV. 381 (1962); Note, *The Eighth Amendment and the Execution of the Presently Incompetent*, 32 STAN. L. REV. 765 (1980); Note, *Insanity of the Condemned*, 88 YALE L.J. 533 (1979); Radelet & Barnard, *Ethics and the Psychiatric Determination of Competency to be Executed*, 14 BULL. AM. ACAD. PSYCHIATRY & LAW 37 (1986).

2. "Unanimity of rationale, therefore, we do not find." Ford v. Wainwright, 106 S. Ct. at 2601. *See* Ward, *supra* note 1 at 49-57.

3. Ford v. Wainwright, 106 S. Ct. at 2601 n.2; S. BRAKEL, J. PARRY & B. WEINER, THE MENTALLY DISABLED AND THE LAW 706 (3d ed. 1985).

4. 106 S. Ct. at 2602 ("...the restriction finds enforcement in the Eighth Amendment.").

adapted from that of Justice Frankfurter in his dissenting opinion in *Solesbee v. Balkcom*.[5]) This test involves a very substantial degree of disability,[6] but such disability may be caused by either mental illness or mental retardation.[7]

---

5. 339 U.S. 9, 20 n.3 (1950) (Frankfurter, J. dissenting). The language in the Standard is also similar to that in the statutes of some states. *See, e.g.*, MO. ANN. STAT. § 552.060 (Vern. Supp. 1986) ("As a result of mental disease or defect he lacks capacity to understand the nature and purpose of the punishment about to be imposed upon him or matters in extenuation, arguments for executive clemency or reasons why the sentence should not be carried out."). *See also In re* Smith, 25 N.M. 48, 59, 176 P. 819, 823 (1918) ("If the prisoner has not at the present time, from the defects of his faculties, sufficient intelligence to understand the nature of the proceedings against him, what he was tried for, the purpose of his punishment, the impending fate which awaits him, a sufficient understanding to know any fact which might exist which would make his punishment unjust or unlawful, and the intelligence requisite to convey such information to his attorneys or the court. . .").

6. It should also be noted that a lesser degree of disability or other manifestations of mental illness or mental retardation, while not constituting incompetence for these purposes, may be relevant for consideration in evaluating proposals for clemency.

7. The definition of "insanity" for purposes of competence to be executed was not decided by the Supreme Court in *Ford*. Only Justice Powell, in his concurring opinion, offered a view as to the constitutional requirements for such a definition. "I would hold that the Eighth Amendment forbids the execution only of those who are unaware of the punishment they are about to suffer and why they are to suffer it." 106 S. Ct. at 2609. Justice Powell declined to find a constitutional requirement that inability to assist and communicate with counsel be included in this definition. Justice Powell did not include this element because he viewed it as unlikely "that a defendant today could go to his death with knowledge of undiscovered trial error that might set him free." 106 S. Ct. at 2608. The Standard reflects a different viewpoint. This parallels the Standards' two-pronged test for incompetence to stand trial, addressing both ability to understand the proceedings and ability to assist counsel. *See* Standard 7-4.1. The possibility that a defendant could be executed because of inability to communicate information that could be relevant to the decision whether to carry out the death sentence is equally unacceptable as executing someone who could not understand the penalty. (It need not, of course, be information that would "set him free" to be relevant.) Mental retardation or illness that has persisted for a considerable period of time is more likely to constitute such an impairment of the convict's ability to recollect relevant facts and assist counsel than, for example, mental illness that occurs in a previously nondisabled convict only as the execution becomes imminent. (Mental disability of late onset will be sufficient to constitute incompetence, of course, if it impairs the convict's ability to understand the nature of the penalty.)

The Standard also emphasizes that any incompetence should be sufficient to stay the execution, not just incompetence that developed subsequent to sentencing. *See* Standard 7-5.7, Commentary at note 22. The possibility of a defendant having a severe mental

Although the Supreme Court's decision in *Ford* and the statutes of several states discuss the prohibition on executions in terms of whether the convict is "insane," the Standards employ the term "incompetent." Use of the term "insanity" in the context of mental condition at the time of execution may result in substantial misunderstanding, and resulting confusion for the criminal justice system. The Association's Standards have already rejected the use of the term "insanity" in its more customary context of the criminal defense of mental nonresponsibility. It was rejected, in part, because it "conjure[s] up visions of beastlike derangement," and because confusion results from its use in common language as a "lay diagnosis."[8] The term also creates confusion because of ambiguity about whether it includes mental retardation as well as mental illness.[9] The use of the term "insanity" is even more confusing in the context of mental condition at the time of execution of a death sentence, since it may lead some to conclude incorrectly that the appropriate inquiry is identical to that involved in determining criminal responsibility.

Standard 7-5.7 Evaluation and adjudication of competence to be executed; stay of execution; restoration of competence

(a) Whenever a correctional official, other state official, the prosecution, or counsel for the convict have reason to believe that a convict who has been sentenced to death may be currently incompetent, such person should petition the court for an order requiring an evaluation of the convict's current mental condition. If the court concludes that the information in the petition indicates reasonable cause to believe that the convict may be incompetent, it should order an evaluation. Unless counsel for the defendant is the petitioner, counsel should be notified that such an evaluation is to be conducted. If the convict is not represented by counsel, the court should

---

disability that was not detected or correctly evaluated at trial also suggests the importance of including the second (recollection and assistance of counsel) element in the definition of competence to be executed.

8. ABA Standards, Introduction to Part VI at 7.287.

9. Ellis & Luckasson, *Mentally Retarded Criminal Defendants,* 53 Geo. Wash. L. Rev. 414, 457-59 (1985).

appoint counsel at the same time it orders the evaluation.

(b) Any interested person who has reason to believe that the convict may be currently incompetent may petition the court for an order requiring an evaluation of the convict's current mental condition. If the court concludes that the information in the petition indicates reasonable cause to believe that the convict may be incompetent, it should order an evaluation, and, if the convict is not represented by counsel, appoint counsel for the convict.

(c) In the absence of a petition, if the court obtains information that indicates reasonable cause to believe that the convict may be incompetent, it should order an evaluation *sua sponte*. If the convict is not represented by counsel, the court should appoint counsel at the same time it orders the evaluation.

(d) All evaluations of a convict's current mental condition for purpose of determining the issue of competence to be executed should be conducted by mental health and/or mental retardation professionals whose qualifications meet the requirements of Standards 7-3.10 and 7-3.12(c)(ii). The convict should be entitled to an evaluation by a qualified professional or professionals who should present the results of their evaluation to the convict's counsel. If the convict is indigent, the court should appoint an appropriate professional evaluator or evaluators for the convict, and such evaluators should be compensated at public expense. The state should be permitted to have its own qualified professional or professionals conduct an evaluation as well.

(e) If, after receiving the reports of the evaluation or evaluations, counsel for the convict believes that the convict is currently incompetent, counsel should move for a hearing on the issue of competence. Upon receiving such a motion, the court should order a hearing.

(f) Following the hearing, if the court finds, by a preponderance of the evidence, that the convict is currently incompetent, it should stay the order of execution for the duration of the convict's incompetence. The court's finding on the issue of competence should be considered a final, appealable order.

(g) If evaluations or proceedings under this standard cannot be accomplished before the scheduled date of the convict's execution, the court should order a stay of execution until the proceedings on the issue of competence are completed.

(h) In the absence of good faith doubt about the convict's current competence, it is improper for an attorney to move for an evaluation pursuant to paragraph (a) or (b) of this Standard. It is improper to use proceedings on the issue of current mental condition solely for the purpose of delay.

(i) When the appropriate state official has reason to believe that a condemned convict who has been found incompetent pursuant to paragraph (f) of this Standard has been restored to competence, the official may petition the court for an order recognizing the restoration to competence and lifting the stay of execution. Upon receipt of such a petition, the court should order the convict's current mental condition reevaluated under the provisions of paragraph (d) of this Standard. Counsel for the defendant should be notified that such an evaluation is to be conducted. Following the reevaluation, the court should hold a hearing on the convict's current mental condition. The convict should be represented by counsel at the hearing. Following the hearing, the court should lift the stay of execution if it finds, by a preponderance of the evidence, that the convict is no longer incompetent. The court's finding on the issue of competence should be considered a final, appealable order.

Commentary Introduction

Standard 7-5.7 provides procedures for evaluating a convict's current mental condition and ascertaining the convict's competence, as defined in Standard 7-5.6. It also establishes the appropriate level of training and expertise for mental health and mental retardation professionals conducting an evaluation. The Standard also provides procedures for cases in which the convict is restored to competence.

Related Standards

ABA Standards for Criminal Justice 7-3.10, 7-3.12, 7-4.2, 7-4.4, 7-5.6.

Commentary

The procedures currently employed by the states for determining whether a condemned prisoner is incompetent to be executed vary widely.[1] The United States Supreme Court's decision in *Ford v. Wainwright* calls into question the constitutionality of some of these procedures. In *Ford,* the Court invalidated a Florida statute because it deprived the condemned prisoner of an opportunity to receive a fair hearing on the issue of his current mental condition.

This Standard reflects the view that the consequence of executing a defendant who is currently mentally incompetent are so substantial that principles of fundamental fairness require great care in the adjudication of this question.[2] The Standard also reflects concern that the issue of incompetence to be executed should not become a mere tool for delay.[3] The procedures in this Standard represent a balance of the needs of the criminal justice system for a resolution of the issue that is both fair and expeditious.

Paragraph (a) provides that correctional officials and other state officials have an obligation to inform the court if they have reason to believe that a condemned prisoner is currently incompetent. Because of the importance of the issue, it is unacceptable to allow these officials to decline to convey to the court relevant information on the convict's mental condition which might indicate incompetence. The Standard does not specify the procedures by which correctional officials should monitor the mental condition of condemned prisoners. One appropriate mechanism would be regular periodic review by qualified mental health and mental retardation professionals. But whether it comes from such reviews or any other source, information that indicates current incompetence must be communicated to the court.

---

1. The various procedures are described in Table 12.4 of S. Brakel, J. Parry & B. Weiner, The Mentally Disabled and the Law 765-68 (3d ed. 1985).

2. The fact that mental disability, particularly mental illness, can be variable in its manifestations and symptoms emphasizes the importance of a careful evaluation of a defendant's current mental condition, even if there was a thorough evaluation at the time of trial.

3. The United States Supreme Court was previously of the view that it might be impossible to provide a fair adversarial hearing on the issue of incompetence before a judicial forum without introducing unreasonable delays in the execution of death sentences. Nobles v. Georgia, 168 U.S. 398, 409 (1897); Solesbee v. Balkcom, 339 U.S. 9, 12 (1950). Similar concerns were expressed by some of the Justices in *Ford*. 106 S. Ct. at 2612 (Justices O'Connor and White, concurring and dissenting); 106 S. Ct. at 2615 (Justice Rehnquist and Chief Justice Burger, dissenting). The majority in *Ford* disagreed, as does the Standard. *See, e.g.*, paragraph (h) of the Standard.

Although attorneys for the state are less likely than correctional officials to be aware of the current mental condition of death row inmates, the same principle requires that prosecutors and attorneys general inform the court if they have reason to believe that the convict may be currently incompetent.[4]

Paragraph (a) also provides that counsel for a condemned prisoner is under a similar obligation to petition for an evaluation if there is reason to believe that the convict is currently incompetent. A number of states provide that only correctional officials are authorized to raise the issue of current incompetence.[5] Fundamental fairness requires that counsel for the convict should have the opportunity to present evidence regarding current incompetence to a neutral factfinder. The Court in *Ford* held this to be a constitutional requirement.[6]

Paragraph (b) provides that any interested person can present evidence of current incompetence. If the information provided is sufficient, the Standard requires the court to order an evaluation. If the convict is unrepresented, the Standard requires the appointment of counsel. If the convict is represented by counsel, the interested party should attempt to seek an evaluation through a petition from the convict's attorney. Only if the attorney declines to make such a petition to the court would it be appropriate for the interested party to petition the court directly.

Paragraph (c) provides that the court is obligated to order an evaluation of the convict's mental condition *sua sponte* when it obtains evidence indicating reasonable cause to believe that the convict may be incompetent.[7]

Some death row inmates are not represented by counsel. The ABA previously has taken the position that every death row inmate is entitled to

---

4. *Cf.* Standard 7-4.2(b), requiring prosecutors to initiate an evaluation "whenever the prosecutor has a good faith doubt as to the defendant's competence" to stand trial.

5. *See* Introduction, note 7.

6. "[A]ny procedure that precludes the prisoner or his counsel from presenting material relevant to his sanity or bars consideration of that material by the fact finder is necessarily inadequate." 106 S. Ct. at 2604 (Marshall, J. for plurality). "The States should provide an impartial officer or board that can receive evidence and argument from the prisoner's counsel, including expert psychiatric evidence that may differ from the state's own psychiatric examination." 106 S. Ct. at 2611 (Powell, J. concurring).

7. *Cf.* Standard 7-4.2(a): "The court has a continuing obligation, separate and apart from that of counsel for each of the parties, to raise the issue of incompetence to stand trial at any time the court has a good faith doubt as to the defendant's competence, and may raise the issue at any stage of the proceedings on its own motion."

counsel. Not every state has adopted this recommendation. However, in every case where there is substantial reason to believe that the inmate may be currently mentally incompetent, the needs of the judicial system require that the inmate be represented by counsel. The prospect of an incompetent defendant litigating the issue of his or her own competence *pro se* does not afford sufficient assurance of a fair adjudication. Therefore, even in jurisdictions that do not routinely provide appointed counsel for all death row inmates, the Standard requires the appointment of counsel whenever information from correctional or other state officials[8] or third parties suggests incompetence, or when the court orders an evaluation *sua sponte*.

Due process may also require the appointment of counsel under such circumstances. In the terms of the *Mathews v. Eldridge*[9] balancing test, the individual interest in an accurate determination of his or her current mental condition is extremely high, while the state's interest in avoiding the appointment of counsel is relatively small. Equally importantly, the risk of erroneous determination when the inmate is not represented is very high, and the likelihood that counsel will reduce the risk of error is substantial.[10]

Paragraph (d) outlines the procedures for evaluating the inmate's current mental condition. It provides that all evaluations should be conducted by mental health and/or mental retardation professionals whose qualifications meet the requirements of Standards 7-3.10 and 7-3.12(c)(ii). The latter is the Standard that applies in other cases to evaluations of an individual's previous or future mental condition. Although the evaluation covered by this Standard involves current mental condition, the experts' qualifications should be set at the higher level because of the importance of this issue involved in death penalty cases.[11]

The evaluation under the Standard adopts the adversarial model of *Ake v. Oklahoma*,[12] which provides the defendant with the assistance of his or

8. *See* Standard 7-5.7(a).

9. 424 U.S. 319 (1976).

10. In Lassiter v. Department of Social Services, 452 U.S. 18 (1981), the Supreme Court stated that there was a presumption against the appointment of counsel in cases that involved deprivations of liberty less serious than incarceration. It would be implausible to suggest that such a presumption also applied to cases in which the deprivation proposed is of life itself.

11. The other requirements of Part III of Chapter 7 of the Standards should also be satisfied, such as the requirement of a personal interview specified in Standard 7-3.11(a)(iii).

12. 105 S. Ct. 1087 (1985).

her own mental health or mental retardation expert. Even if the assistance of a mental disability expert is not constitutionally guaranteed in capital punishment competence cases (as it is in trials involving the insanity defense[13]), the Standard adopts the position that it is necessary to assure a fair hearing on the issue of current mental condition. The Standard selects the *Ake* model instead of the single-evaluator model used in cases involving competence to stand trial[14] because competence to be executed—unlike competence to stand trial—is an issue on which the adversarial positions of the parties are clearly established.

Another reason for the selection of the *Ake* model is the concern that a system involving only one mental disability professional would transform that professional into a *de facto* decisionmaker on the issue of current incompetence. If the court is confronted with the opinion of only one expert, the temptation merely to defer to that expert's opinion would be substantial. It is noteworthy on this point that both the American Psychological Association and the American Psychiatric Association have concluded that the decision on competence should be made by the court and that an adversarial system of expert witnesses is essential to fundamental fairness.[15] The Standard is in accord and provides that a court[16] should be

---

13. *Id.* In *Ford v. Wainwright*, Justice Marshall, writing for a plurality of the Court, cites *Ake* and appears to require a roughly comparable hearing on the issue of competence at the time of execution. 106 S. Ct. at 2604. Justice Powell's concurring opinion, while noting that the Court was not required to "determine the precise limits that due process imposes in this area," suggested that the Constitution could be satisfied with proceedings less formal than *Ake* required. "In general, . . . my view is that a constitutionally acceptable procedure may be far less formal than a trial. . . . Beyond [the basic requirements of due process], the States should have substantial leeway to determine what process best balances the various interests at stake." 106 S. Ct. at 2611. But it is noteworthy that one of the elements of due process that Justice Powell mentioned was the right to present "expert psychiatric evidence that may differ from the state's own psychiatric examination." *Id.*

14. *See* Standard 7-4.4.

15. *Amici Curiae* Brief of American Psychological Association and Florida Psychological Association, Ford v. Wainwright, U.S. Sup. Ct. No. 85-5542 (filed January 1986); *Amicus Curiae* Brief of American Psychiatric Association, *id.*

16. The Standard does not take a position on which court should be given jurisdiction over these cases. Somes states may choose to assign the task to the trial court that heard the criminal trial. Others may prefer that venue in which the inmate's prison is located. Logistical considerations, especially in large states, may favor the latter approach.

the ultimate decisionmaker on the issue of competence.[17] Therefore, both the convict and the state are entitled to evaluations by their own qualified mental disability professionals.

Justice Marshall's opinion for a plurality in *Ford* noted that "legitimate pragmatic considerations" may affect "the procedural safeguards that feasibly can be provided."[18] In particular, Justice Marshall suggested that:

> It may be that some high-threshold showing on behalf of the prisoner will be found a necessary means to control the number of nonmeritorious or repetitive claims of insanity. *Cf. Pate v. Robinson,* 383 U.S. 375, 387 (1966) (hearing on competency to stand trial required if "sufficient doubt" of competency exists).[19]

The Standard incorporates such a threshold requirement. Any person seeking an evaluation of a prisoner's current mental condition must have "reason to believe" that the individual is currently incompetent,[20] and the court is directed to order an evaluation upon motion by the convict's counsel or a third party only if it finds "reasonable cause to believe" that the individual is incompetent.[21]

Paragraph (f) provides that following the hearing (at which the inmate should be entitled to procedural protections such as confrontation and cross-examination), the court should stay the execution of the sentence if it concludes, by a preponderance of the evidence, that the convict is currently incompetent under the test established in Standard 7-5.5(b).[22] Thus

---

17. The Standard also explicitly rejects the system employed in several states under which the Governor or other political officials make the decision whether an inmate is currently competent. Such officials are insufficiently insulated from political pressures and are an inappropriate forum for resolution of this issue. *See* Ford v. Wainwright, 106 S. Ct. at 2605 (plurality opinion) ("The commander of the State's corps of prosecutors cannot be said to have the neutrality that is necessary for reliability in the fact-finding proceeding.").

18. 106 S. Ct. at 2606.

19. *Id.*

20. Standard 7-5.7(a) and (b).

21. Standard 7-5.7(a), (b) and (c). *See also* Standard 7-5.7(h).

22. It should be noted that neither this Standard nor Standard 7-5.6 requires that the convict's incompetence have arisen since the trial. Some states have ruled otherwise. A convict who is currently incompetent should not be executed, regardless of when the condition began. The fact that, in a particular case, the trial process failed to detect the defendant's disability, or failed to assess accurately its severity and impact on the defendant's ability to function, should not require a postsentencing court to ignore the effect of that disability on a condemned prisoner's current competence. *See generally* Ellis &

there is a presumption of competence, and the burden of demonstrating incompetence must be carried by counsel for the inmate. The court's finding on the issue of competence is a final, appealable order. States may wish to consider providing for expedited hearings for appeals from such orders.

Paragraph (g) authorizes the court to order such stays of execution as may be necessary to conduct evaluations and hearings under this Standard. However, the delays involved in adjudicating this issue should not be excessive, and paragraph (h) emphasizes that it is improper for counsel to use the provisions of this Standard solely for the purpose of delay.[23]

Paragraph (i) provides procedures for adjudicating the inmate's restoration to competence. The state may, when it has reason to believe that the prisoner is no longer incompetent, petition for an order lifting the stay of execution. The filing of such a petition is discretionary. Upon receiving the petition, the court is directed to order a reevaluation of the prisoner's current mental condition under the procedures of paragraph (d) of this Standard. Therefore, the prisoner is entitled to an expert mental health or mental retardation professional to assist the defense. If, following the hearing, the court finds by a preponderance of the evidence that the prisoner is no longer incompetent under the terms of Standard 7-5.6(b), it may lift the stay of execution.

The Standard does not address the issue of possible therapeutic or habilitative efforts to restore the competence of a condemned prisoner. Such efforts raise profoundly troubling ethical issues for mental disability professionals.[24] The extent of the state's ability to force unwanted treatment on

---

Luckasson, *Mentally Retarded Criminal Defendants*, 53 GEO. WASH. L. REV. 414, 457-59 (1985) (discussing the possibility that the incompetence of many mentally retarded defendants to stand trial may not be detected).

23. *See* note 3, *supra*. *Cf.* Standard 7-4.2(e): "In the absence of good faith doubt that the defendant is competent to stand trial it is improper for either party to move for evaluation. It is improper for either party to use the incompetence process for purposes unrelated to incompetence to stand trial such as to obtain information for mitigation of sentence, to obtain favorable plea negotiation or to delay the proceedings against the defendant."

24. *See* Appelbaum, *Competence to be Executed: Another Conundrum for Mental Health Professionals*, 37 HOSPITAL & COMMUNITY PSYCHIATRY 682 (1986); Appelbaum, *Psychiatrists' Role in the Death Penalty*, 32 HOSPITAL & COMMUNITY PSYCHIATRY 761 (1981); Ward, *Competency for Execution: Problems in Law and Psychiatry*, 14 FLA. ST. U. L. REV. 35, 90-95 (1986).

such a prisoner is also unclear.[25] The Standard leaves to the discretion of the states the issue of whether to seek restoration of competence and whether to attempt to persuade the court to lift the stay of execution. Although it is beyond the scope of these Standards, it is important for states to address the issues raised by permanently incompetent convicts on death row.

25. *See* Ward, *supra* note 24 at 95-99.

ADDITION TO PART V: *Competence and Confessions*

Albert J. Datz, Chairperson
ABA Criminal Justice Standards Committee

Steven H. Goldberg
Task Force Chairperson

John M. Greacen
Chairperson, Section of Criminal Justice

Terence F. MacCarthy
Chairperson-Elect, Section of Criminal Justice

James W. Ellis
Reporter

August, 1988

ABA Criminal Justice Standards Committee

Albert J. Datz, *Chairperson*
Private practitioner, Datz, Jacobson & Lembcke, Jacksonville, Florida

Paul D. Borman
Chief Defender, Federal Defender Office, Detroit, Michigan

George J. Cotsirilos
Private practitioner, Cotsirilos, Crowley, Stephenson, Tighe & Streicker, Ltd., Chicago, Illinois

William P. Curran
County Attorney, Clark County, Las Vegas, Nevada

Steven H. Goldberg
Associate Dean, University of Minnesota School of Law, Minneapolis, Minnesota

Richard H. Kuh
Private practitioner, Warshaw, Burstein, Cohen, Schlesinger & Kuh, New York, New York

Norman Lefstein
Dean, Indiana University School of Law, Indianapolis, Indiana

Patricia M. Wald
Chief Judge, U.S. Court of Appeals, District of Columbia Circuit, Washington, DC

Alexander H. Williams III
Judge, Superior Court, Los Angeles, California

August, 1988

Task Force: Competence and Confessions

Steven H. Goldberg, *Chairperson*
Associate Dean, University of Minnesota School of Law, Minneapolis, Minnesota

Richard J. Bonnie
Director, Institute of Law, Psychiatry & Public Policy, John S. Battle Professor of Law, University of Virginia School of Law, Charlottesville, Virginia

Bernard L. Diamond, M.D.
Professor of Law, Emeritus, University of California School of Law, Berkeley, California; Clinical Professor of Psychiatry, University of California School of Medicine, San Francisco, California

Judith H. Friedman
Special Assistant to the Assistant Attorney General, Criminal Division, U.S. Department of Justice, Washington, DC

Howard Janssen
Private practitioner, Crosby, Heafey, Roach & May, Oakland, California

Donald Paull
Chief, Mental Health Law Division, Cook County Public Defenders Office, Chicago, Illinois

Phillip J. Resnick, M.D.
Associate Professor of Psychiatry and Director, Division of Forensic Psychiatry, Case Western Reserve University Medical School, Cleveland, Ohio

Henry C. Weinstein, M.D. (ex-officio)
Director, Forensic Psychiatric Services, New York University Medical Center, Bellevue Hospital Center, New York, New York

---

James W. Ellis, Reporter
Professor of Law, School of Law, University of New Mexico

****

Gerald T. Bennett
Professor of Law, University of Florida, Gainesville, Florida, served as Chairperson of the Task Force during a substantial portion of the Task Force's work.

INTRODUCTION

The mental disability of a suspect can affect a confession or other inculpatory statement[1] in a number of ways. The reliability of such a statement can be affected by mental illness or mental retardation.[2] Disability may impair the suspect's ability to understand his or her rights, and may therefore invalidate any waiver of those rights. Mental disability can render a suspect vulnerable to forms of persuasion and coercion which would have no effect on a nondisabled individual. Mental illness or mental retardation may make it more likely that some suspects will be willing to make a confession.

Each of these effects require extraordinary care on the part of lawyers, courts, and law enforcement officers[3] in handling cases that involve statements by suspects who may be mentally ill or mentally retarded. The following Standards offer guidelines for these circumstances.

Standard 7-5.8 Statements by mentally ill or mentally retarded persons

(a) Mental illness or mental retardation can affect the reliability

1. The previous distinctions in law between confessions and other forms of statements by suspects which tend to prove guilt have diminished over the years. McCormick on Evidence 361-63 (E. Cleary 3d ed. 1984). The terms "confession" and "statement" will be used interchangeably in these Standards and the Commentary to describe all such statements.

2. Either mental illness or mental retardation can produce the problems described in these Standards. Those problems are compounded when the suspect is both mentally ill and mentally retarded. *See* Luckasson, *The Dually Diagnosed Client in the Criminal Justice System*, in MENTAL RETARDATION AND MENTAL HEALTH: CLASSIFICATION, DIAGNOSIS, TREATMENT, SERVICES 54 (J. Stark, F. Menolascino, M. Albarelli & V. Gray eds. 1988).

3. Although these Standards are proposed for Part V dealing with competence issues, they are of particular importance to police and other law enforcement officials, and therefore should be emphatically cross-referenced in Part II of Chapter 7, dealing with police and custodial roles.

of statements. Where the court finds that the reliability of such a statement has been significantly impaired by a person's mental illness or mental retardation, it should exclude the statement from evidence. Where the statement has not been excluded, the court should permit evidence to be presented to the trier of fact regarding the effect of the defendant's mental illness or mental retardation on the reliability of the statement.

(b) Mental illness or mental retardation can affect the voluntariness of statements. Official conduct that does not constitute impermissible coercion when employed with nondisabled persons may impair the voluntariness of the statements of persons who are mentally ill or mentally retarded. Where such impairment of voluntariness is significant, the court should exclude the statement from evidence. However, in the absence of any such impermissibly coercive official conduct, such statement should not be excluded from evidence solely because it was the product of the person's mental illness or mental retardation, unless it is found unreliable pursuant to standard 7-5.8(a).

Commentary Introduction

Standard 7-5.8 addresses the reliability and voluntariness of statements by mentally disabled individuals. It provides that some such statements should be held inadmissible, and that in other cases the trier of fact should receive evidence on the effect of the mental disability on the statement's reliability. Paragraph (b) provides that statements should be inadmissible when their voluntariness has been significantly impaired by the effect of mental disability. However, it also provides that a statement should be considered involuntary only when it was induced by impermissible official conduct.

Related Standards

ABA Standards for Criminal Justice 7-2.8, 7-5.9, 7-5.10

Commentary

This Standard addresses the reliability and voluntariness of confessions, whether they are made in custody or in noncustodial settings. Such statements can be affected, and even motivated, by the effects of mental illness or mental retardation. Evidentiary questions about the admissibility of such statements present difficult issues for the courts.

Reliability. Paragraph (a) of the Standard recognizes that even in the absence of any coercion by the police, admissions and confessions by mentally ill or mentally retarded individuals may be of questionable reliability. Its provisions seek to assure that mentally disabled defendants are not convicted on the basis of confessions that are not credible.

The common law has long recognized the potential problems of unreliability inherent in confessions. Concern for the trustworthiness of such statements by defendants and suspects was the original reason for the requirements of corroboration and independent proof of the *corpus delicti.*[1] The perceived unreliability of coerced statements was also a principal reason for the common-law (and later constitutional) requirement of voluntariness for confessions.[2] The issue of a statement's possible unreliability is no less troubling when its questionable truthfulness results from the suspect's mental disability rather than from the effects of official misconduct. As Justice Brennan has observed, "Because the admission of a confession so strongly tips the balance against the defendant in the adversarial process, we must be especially careful about a confession's reliability."[3]

1. McCormick on Evidence 365-71 (E. Cleary 3d ed. 1984). *See* Opper v. United States, 348 U.S. 84, 89-90 (1954) ("In our country the doubt persists that the zeal of the agencies of prosecution to protect the peace, the self-interest of the accomplice, the maliciousness of an enemy or the aberration or weakness of the accused under the strain of suspicion may tinge or warp the facts of the confession").

2. The King v. Warickshall, 168 Eng. Rep. 234, 1 Leach 263 (1783); Hopt v. Utah, 110 U.S. 574 (1884); Brown v. Mississippi, 297 U.S. 278 (1936); W. LaFave & J. Israel, Criminal Procedure 264-65 (1985); McCormick on Evidence 372-73 (E. Cleary 3d ed. 1984).

3. Colorado v. Connelly, 107 S.Ct. 515, 530 (1986) (Brennan, J. dissenting). Justice Brennan would have based a requirement of reliability on the due process clause. "To hold otherwise allows the State to imprison and possibly to execute a mentally ill defendant based solely upon an inherently unreliable confession." 107 S.Ct. at 531. The majority of the Court entrusted the matter to the evidence laws of the states. "A statement rendered by one in the condition of respondent [mentally ill] might be proved to be quite

The reliability of statements by persons who are mentally disabled is particularly suspect. For example, a mentally ill individual may make a false or inaccurate confession because of a delusional belief. Similarly, a person with mental retardation may make such a statement because of a mistaken understanding of the facts of an incident or the nature of criminal responsibility.[4] Therefore substantial skepticism is warranted regarding the use of confessions by mentally disabled suspects in criminal proceedings.

The Standard provides for evidence on the issue of the reliability of a mentally disabled defendant's statements to be admissible before the trier of fact. Such evidence, as well as responding evidence which may be presented by the prosecution, may include the expert testimony of mental disability professionals.[5] This allows the trier of fact to determine how much weight to assign to a statement whose reliability is called into question because of the effects of the defendant's mental disability, and to give the statement less credence if the evidence so warrants.[6] An admonitory instruction from the court on this issue may also be appropriate.

Although expert and lay testimony on a statement's reliability will ordinarily suffice to inform the trier of fact about the appropriate weight to assign to a confession, some statements by mentally disabled suspects are so clearly unreliable that they should not be admitted as evidence. Some such statements are simply unworthy of belief, and the prejudicial impact of their introduction would clearly outweigh their negligible probative

---

unreliable, but this is a matter to be governed by the evidentiary laws of the forum, . . . and not by the Due Process Clause of the Fourteenth Amendment." 107 S.Ct. at 502.

The Standard constitutes a recommendation to the states regarding reliability as an evidentiary matter. Some state courts may also choose to address this as an issue of state constitutional law. *See generally* Perlin, *State Constitutions and Statutes as Sources of Rights for the Mentally Disabled: The Last Frontier?* 20 LOYOLA L.A. L. REV. 1249 (1987); Meisel, *The Rights of the Mentally Ill Under State Constitutions,* 45 LAW & CONTEMP. PROBS. 7 (Summer 1982).

4. *See, e.g.,* Ellis & Luckasson, *Mentally Retarded Criminal Defendants,* 53 GEO. WASH. L. REV. 414, 466 n. 286 (1985) (describing a mildly mentally retarded defendant who entered a guilty plea because he regretted that he had not prevented the commission of a criminal act by another person and therefore believed himself to be "guilty" of the offense).

5. *See* Standard 7-5.10.

6. The evidence may also involve the circumstances under which the statement was made. As Justice O'Connor recently observed for a unanimous Court, "evidence about the manner in which a confession was obtained is often highly relevant to its reliability and credibility." Crane v. Kentucky, 106 S.Ct. 2142, 2147 (1986).

value.[7] Fundamental fairness requires that obviously unreliable statements by mentally disabled suspects, like other forms of inherently untrustworthy evidence, be excluded from consideration by the trier of fact.

The Standard calls for the exclusion from evidence of statements whose reliability has been substantially impaired by the effects of the suspect's mental disability.[8] But the Standard also recognizes that such instances will be rare, and that most statements by mentally disabled suspects will not be so clearly unreliable as to require their exclusion. In many cases, despite the fact that the court admits the statement into evidence, questions will remain about the reliability of a disabled suspect's statement. The Standard provides that evidence, including expert testimony from mental health or mental retardation professionals, should be permitted to allow the trier of fact to determine the extent to which the individual's mental disability may have undermined the credibility of the statement. The trier of fact can then decide how much credence to give to the statement.

Voluntariness. Paragraph (b) of the Standard recognizes that mental disability may also impair the voluntariness of a suspect's confession or statement.

Involuntary confessions have long been excluded from evidence by the courts. As the Supreme Court has noted, "a complex of values underlies the stricture against the use by the state of confessions which, by way of convenient shorthand, this Court terms involuntary."[9] These include both the fact that involuntary confessions are likely to be factually unreliable and concerns about the acceptability of police practices used to produce involuntary statements.[10] The increasing focus of the courts on the waiver of rights under *Miranda v. Arizona*[11] has reduced the attention paid to the

7. Such a clearly unreliable statement by a mentally disabled suspect can be analogized to the exclusion of testimony by a child who is found to be too young to give competent testimony. *See generally* Christiansen, *The Testimony of Child Witnesses,* 62 WASH. L. REV. 705 (1987); T. GRISSO, JUVENILES' WAIVER OF RIGHTS: LEGAL AND PSYCHOLOGICAL COMPETENCE (1981).

8. The question of whether the reliability of a statement by a mentally disabled suspect has been significantly impaired by mental retardation or mental illness can be determined by the court in a pretrial hearing. *Cf.* Jackson v. Denno, 378 U.S. 368 (1964). The court should admit testimony at such a hearing on the issue of the impact of the suspect's mental disability on the reliability of the statement. *See* Standard 7-5.10.

9. Blackburn v. Alabama, 361 U.S. 199 (1960).

10. MCCORMICK ON EVIDENCE 373-74 (E. Cleary 3d ed. 1984).

11. 384 U.S. 486 (1966). *Cf.* Standard 7-5.9.

voluntariness doctrine, but it remains clear that due process forbids the admission of an involuntary statement, whether the statement is made in custody or a noncustodial setting.

The focus of modern cases involving the voluntariness of confessions is the extent to which the suspect's will was overborne by governmental conduct. In this context, the Supreme Court has consistently observed that "certain interrogation techniques, either in isolation or *as applied to the unique characteristics of a particular suspect,* are so offensive to a civilized system of justice that they must be condemned."[12]

Paragraph (b) of the Standard reflects this rule by providing that interrogation techniques that would not constitute unacceptable coercion in cases involving nondisabled suspects may impair the voluntariness of a confession of a suspect who is mentally ill or mentally retarded.[13] The increased vulnerability of a mentally disabled suspect, and his or her naivete, ignorance, confusion, suggestibility, delusional beliefs, extraordinary susceptibility to pressure, and similar considerations may make it possible for law enforcement officers to induce an involuntary statement by using techniques that would be acceptable in cases involving mentally typical suspects. Where such a showing is made, typically at a suppression hearing, the Standard provides that the statement should be excluded.[14]

---

12. Miller v. Fenton, 106 S.Ct. 445, 449 (1985) (emphasis supplied).

13. The majority in *Connelly* noted that "mental condition is surely relevant to an individual's susceptibility to police coercion...." Colorado v. Connelly, 107 S.Ct. 515, 521 (1986). *See also* Blackburn v. Alabama, 361 U.S. 199 (1960) (mental illness); Columbe v. Connecticut, 367 U.S. 568 (1961) (mental retardation).

14. Defendants are constitutionally entitled to have the voluntariness of their confession determined by the court at a suppression hearing outside of the presence of the jury. Jackson v. Denno, 378 U.S. 368 (1964). The majority of states follow the so-called "orthodox rule," under which the court's determination on voluntariness is not reviewed by the jury. Other states follow the so-called "Massachusetts rule," under which a judge's ruling that a statement admitted into evidence was voluntary can be reviewed independently by the jury. McCORMICK ON EVIDENCE 465-66 (E. Cleary 3d ed. 1984). The Standard makes no recommendation about the relative desirability of these two rules, and is compatible with either. In jurisdictions employing the orthodox rule, the judge at the suppression hearing should exclude any statement where the suspect's voluntariness was significantly impaired. In states using the Massachusetts rule, the same criteria would apply, but in addition, where the judge has declined to exclude the statement as involuntary, the parties should be permitted to introduce evidence to the jury about the factors, including the effect of the suspect's mental disability, that touch upon the voluntariness of the statement.

Involuntary confessions, within the meaning of this Standard, involve suspects who make a statement in the context of some form of unacceptable official conduct designed to elicit a statement. The United States Supreme Court has rejected the invitation to extend this constitutional rule[15] to those statements which are "involuntary" in the sense that they are the product of the suspect's mental disability, but which involve no police attempts to elicit a confession. In *Colorado v. Connelly*,[16] the Court held that a confession was admissible despite the fact that it was a product of the "command hallucinations" caused by defendant's mental illness. The majority concluded that a confession could not be considered "involuntary" as a constitutional matter without some form of coercive police activity.

The final sentence of paragraph (b) of the Standard addresses the admissibility of statements made by mentally ill or mentally retarded individuals who are not in custody and who are not the subjects of official attempts to elicit a confession. Such statements may be influenced — indeed, may be motivated or "caused" — by the individual's disability. For example, a mentally ill person may feel compelled by delusional beliefs or hallucinatory instructions to tell law enforcement officials that he committed a crime. The Standard recommends that such statements, if otherwise acceptable, be considered admissible evidence when they occur outside of police custody and in the absence of any official coercion. The Standard thus adopts the holding of *Connelly* that official conduct is a prerequisite to finding a statement involuntary.

It has been argued that such statements should be excluded on the theory that they are not "voluntary."[17] As a semantic matter, this position has some attraction. Statements blurted out by an individual as a result of mental disability may not involve the same kind of volition as statements

---

15. The Court's majority concluded that any inquiry about voluntariness beyond the scope of official coercion is more appropriately "resolved by state laws governing the admission of evidence. . . ." Colorado v. Connelly, 107 S.Ct. 515, 522 (1986). The Standard makes no recommendation about expanding the rights of suspects beyond the due process clause's protection against official coercion. If subsequent constitutional caselaw provides inadequate recognition of the extraordinary vulnerability of mentally disabled suspects, courts are urged to use their authority over evidentiary matters, and perhaps in interpreting state constitutions, to implement the recommendations of this Standard. See note 3, *supra*.

16. 107 S.Ct. 515 (1986).

17. *See, e.g.*, Colorado v. Connelly, 107 S.Ct. 515, 525 (1986) (Brennan, J. dissenting).

volunteered by nondisabled individuals. But the Standard takes the position that "voluntariness" in the context of confessions refers more appropriately to the absence of state coercion. To exclude a reliable statement that involves no official misconduct serves no purpose sufficient to outweigh the cost of losing probative evidence. Therefore the Standard holds that a statement made in the absence of any opportunity for official coercion should not be excluded from evidence on the grounds that it is "involuntary." Such a statement, of course, may still be inadmissible for other reasons, such as lack of reliability.

Confessions produced by the effects of mental disability but without official coercion may also be argued to be inadmissible because the individual lacked the ability to make a legally valid waiver of the right to remain silent and the privilege against self-incrimination. It is true that some individuals who make inculpatory statements as a result of mental disability would not meet the test for voluntary relinquishment of rights as expressed in *Johnson v. Zerbst.*[18] But the Standard reflects the position that no such waiver is involved in the absence of any official attempt to elicit information, because no constitutional right has attached. The right at issue regarding the voluntariness of confessions is the right not to be forced by the state to make self-incriminating statements, not an abstract right not to make the statements at all. Similarly, "the right to remain silent" as announced in *Miranda*[19] is a right within the context of custodial interrogation.[20] Where the courts can be certain that no coercion was involved in obtaining the statement, the individual has not waived any constitutional rights within the meaning of *Miranda* or *Johnson v. Zerbst.*

Standard 7-5.9 Waiver of rights by mentally ill or mentally retarded persons

(a) Custodial confessions by persons who are mentally ill or mentally retarded should be admissible only if the person has made a

18. 304 U.S. 458 (1938).

19. Miranda v. Arizona, 384 U.S. 486 (1966).

20. "The sole concern of the Fifth Amendment, on which *Miranda* was based, is governmental coercion. Indeed, the Fifth Amendment privilege is not concerned 'with moral and psychological pressures to confess emanating from sources other than official coercion.'" Colorado v. Connelly, 107 S.Ct. at 523 (citations omitted).

knowing, intelligent, and voluntary waiver of rights. A person's mental disability can affect and impair each element of an otherwise valid waiver.

(b) Law enforcement officials should be alert to the possibility that a person may be mentally ill or mentally retarded. Mental illness or mental retardation may impair the disabled person's ability to understand the rights explained by officials, thereby invalidating any waiver and subsequent statement. Official conduct that does not constitute impermissible coercion when employed with nondisabled persons may invalidate the waiver of rights by persons who are mentally ill or mentally retarded.

Commentary Introduction

Standard 7-5.9 provides that mental disability may impair each element of a suspect's waiver of rights concerning a custodial statement. Law enforcement officials should be alert to the possible effect of mental disability on the suspect's ability to understand explanations of rights, and to the fact that a suspect's disability may affect the determination of what constitutes acceptable official conduct in eliciting statements.

Related Standards

ABA Standards for Criminal Justice 1-7.3, 7-2.8, 7-5.8, 7-5.10.

Commentary

In addition to the potential problems of reliability and voluntariness of confessions discussed in Standard 7-5.8, statements made in the context of custodial interrogation may be rendered inadmissible by the effects of mental illness or mental retardation because the disabled suspect may be unable to give an effective waiver of his right to counsel and right to refrain from answering questions. Although the holding of *Miranda v. Arizona*[1]

1. 384 U.S. 436 (1966).

remains controversial,[2] the Supreme Court has made clear that it is settled constitutional law.[3] Its teaching, and the policies which underlie it, apply with special emphasis to cases involving mentally disabled suspects.

Paragraph (a) of Standard 7-5.9 recognizes that the admissibility of any custodial confession requires a valid waiver of the suspect's constitutional rights, and that any waiver must be knowingly, intelligently, and voluntarily made.[4] These three elements parallel the requirements for legally valid consent in other areas of mental disability law, and as is true in those other areas, each of the elements is rendered problematic by the effects of mental disability.[5]

The requisite knowledge for an effective waiver may be negated by either mental illness or mental retardation. The standard *Miranda* warning may not be sufficient to overcome the knowledge deficits a mentally disabled defendant may have. A mentally retarded defendant is unlikely to understand the terminology in the standard warning, and may not understand the basic concepts involved in the idea of adversarial proceedings and of rights and their voluntary relinquishment.[6] Similarly, a mentally ill defendant may misperceive the roles of the police or defense counsel and the

---

2. *See, e.g.,* Caplan, *Questioning Miranda,* 38 VAND. L. REV. 1417 (1985); White, *Defending Miranda: A Reply to Professor Caplan,* 39 VAND. L. REV. 2 (1986). *See generally* L. BAKER, MIRANDA: CRIME, LAW AND POLITICS (1983); Y. KAMISAR, POLICE INTERROGATION AND CONFESSIONS: ESSAYS IN LAW AND POLICY (1980).

3. As Justice O'Connor recently observed for the Court's majority, "the [*Miranda*] decision as written strikes the proper balance between society's legitimate law enforcement interests and the protection of the defendant's Fifth Amendment rights...." Moran v. Burbine, 475 U.S. 412, 424 (1986).

4. The United States Supreme Court has recently summarized the requirements of *Miranda*:

> First the relinquishment of the right must have been voluntary in the sense that it was the product of a free and deliberate choice rather than intimidation, coercion or deception. Second, the waiver must have been made with a full awareness both of the nature of the right being abandoned and the consequences of the decision to abandon it. Only if the "totality of the circumstances surrounding the interrogation" reveals an uncoerced choice and the requisite level of comprehension may a court properly conclude that the Miranda rights have been waived.

Moran v. Burbine, 475 U.S. 412, 421 (1986).

5. *See* AMERICAN ASSOCIATION ON MENTAL DEFICIENCY, CONSENT HANDBOOK (H. Turnbull ed. 1977).

6. Ellis & Luckasson, *Mentally Retarded Criminal Defendants,* 53 GEO. WASH. L. REV. 414, 447-50 (1985).

nature of the transaction to which he is being asked to agree.

Similarly, the requirement that a valid waiver be "intelligent" may be negated when the disabled defendant fails to understand and appreciate the nature of his relinquishment of rights. The Supreme Court has held, in a case involving a nondisabled defendant, that it is not necessary for the suspect to fully and completely understand and appreciate every aspect of the consequences of his action.[7] But for any waiver to be valid, a suspect must understand clearly that his or her rights include the right to counsel, the right to refrain from answering questions, and the fact that the voluntary relinquishment of these rights may produce evidence that can be used to obtain a conviction. A mentally ill or mentally retarded individual's level of understanding will sometimes be so deficient that a valid waiver is impossible.[8]

Perhaps the most difficult problems arise from the requirement that a waiver of constitutional rights must be voluntary. This rule parallels, but is not identical to, the inquiry into whether a confession is voluntary.[9] Here the inquiry is whether the suspect's decision to give up the right to counsel and the right to remain silent was voluntarily made. Where that decision was the product of unacceptable official coercion, the waiver is invalid, and any resulting statement is inadmissible.[10]

As paragraph (b) of the Standard notes, techniques of interrogation that would be acceptable to the courts for nondisabled suspects may be unacceptably coercive in cases involving mental disability. Just as such techniques may lead a court to conclude that a disabled suspect's statement

---

7. Oregon v. Elstad, 470 U.S. 298, 316 (1985).

8. *See, e.g.*, Smith v. Kemp, 664 F. Supp. 500 (M.D. Ga. 1987).

9. *See* Standard 7-5.8(b) and accompanying Commentary.

10. This conclusion is not affected by the United States Supreme Court's decision in Colorado v. Connelly, 107 S.Ct. 515 (1986). In that case, the Court's majority held that a waiver of *Miranda* rights was not "involuntary" where it was the product of effects of his psychotic mental illness. The Court cautioned against "importing ... notions of 'free will' " into the area of *Miranda* waivers. 107 S.Ct. at 523. But the Court's admonition went only to rejecting the possibility of finding involuntariness in waivers which involved no police coercion. *Connelly* certainly does not stand for the proposition that courts need not inquire into the voluntariness of the waivers of mentally disabled defendants, not does it indicate that suspect's mental disability is irrelevant to the issue of whether psychological pressure or other interrogation tactics constitute overreaching in a particular case. The test remains whether, given the totality of the circumstances, the mentally disabled suspect made a free choice to give up rights that he fully understood.

was not voluntary because of his exceptional vulnerability, similar techniques may invalidate a mentally ill or mentally retarded suspect's waiver of rights.[11] The suggestibility of mentally retarded individuals and their extraordinary susceptibility to the perceived wishes of authority figures have been well documented,[12] and therefore the vulnerability of mentally retarded suspects to nonphysical coercion has been long recognized.[13] Similarly, police techniques that seek to take advantage of extraordinary vulnerability caused by a suspect's mental illness may also invalidate a waiver.[14]

Paragraph (b) of the Standard admonishes law enforcement officials, in particular, to be alert to the possibility that a suspect may be mentally disabled. While Standard 7-2.5(b) addresses the responsibility of the police to obtain evaluation of a disabled suspect who may meet the legal criteria for emergency detention and treatment, this Standard focuses on the need to ascertain whether a suspect's disability may affect the admissibility of any statement that might be made.

This will require careful attention, since some forms of mental disability are not clearly visible or readily apparent. Although mentally ill individuals who are violent, irrational, or engaging in bizarre behavior often will be

---

11. A majority of the United States Supreme Court has accepted waivers of rights from nondisabled suspects in circumstances involving some level of deception or withholding of relevant information. *See, e.g.*, Moran v. Burbine, 475 U.S. 412 (1986); Connecticut v. Barrett, 107 S.Ct. 828 (1987). "Mild" deception or a withholding of information that would not invalidate a waiver by a nondisabled suspect could be a form of unacceptable coercion when viewed in the totality of the circumstances of a mentally ill or mentally retarded suspect's confession.

12. *See, e.g.*, Harter, *Mental Age, IQ and Motivational Factors in the Discrimination Learning Set Performance of Normal and Retarded Children*, 5 J. EXPERIMENTAL CHILD PSYCHOLOGY 123, 137-38 (1967) (retarded individuals seek approval from authority figures even when it requires giving an answer they know to be incorrect); Sigelman, Budd, Stankel & Schoenrock, *When in Doubt, Say Yes: Acquiescence in Interviews with Mentally Retarded Persons*, 19 MENTAL RETARDATION 53 (1980). *See generally* DeVellis, *Learned Helplessness in Institutions*, 15 MENTAL RETARDATION 10 (1977).

13. *See, e.g.*, Jurek v. Estelle, 623 F.2d 929, 938 (5th Cir. 1980) (en banc), *cert. denied* 450 U.S. 1001 (1981) ("The concern in a case involving a defendant of subnormal intelligence is one of suggestibility"); Hamilton v. State, 77 Miss. 675, 27 So. 606 (1900); Peck v. State, 147 Ala. 100, 41 So. 759 (1906); United States v. Hull, 441 F.2d 308 (7th Cir. 1971); United States v. Blocker, 354 F. Supp. 1195 (D.D.C. 1973), *aff'd*, 509 F.2d 538 (D.C. Cir. 1975).

14. *See generally* Brewer v. Williams, 430 U.S. 387 (1977), where the fact that the suspect was an escaped mental patient was one of the considerations in evaluating the validity of his purported waiver.

easy to detect, many other disabled suspects will present no such apparent manifestations of their illness or retardation. A mentally ill individual whose principal symptom is clinical depression may present few overt signs of his illness, and many mildly and moderately mentally retarded individuals have learned to devote a considerable amount of effort to hiding their disability.[15] Failure to identify the possibility that a suspect is disabled may result in a confession or statement that later proves inadmissible because of the lack of a valid waiver, and this can imperil the prosecution of the case. The significance of this matter emphasizes the importance of the recommendation in Standard 7-2.8 that law enforcement agencies should provide their personnel with specialized training in the basic elements and manifestations of mental illness and mental retardation.

Standard 7-5.10 Expert testimony

The court should admit into evidence expert testimony by qualified mental health or mental retardation professionals bearing on the effect of a person's disability on the reliability and voluntariness of a statement and the validity of any waiver of rights that preceded such a statement.

Commentary Introduction

Standard 7-5.10 provides for the admission of expert testimony bearing on the effect of mental disability on the reliability and voluntariness of statements and on the validity of waivers of rights.

Related Standards

ABA Standards for Criminal Justice 7-3.9, 7-3.11, 7-3.12, 7-5.8, 7-5.9.

---

15. *See* R. EDGERTON, THE CLOAK OF COMPETENCE: STIGMA IN THE LIVES OF THE MENTALLY RETARDED (1967); Ellis & Luckasson, *supra* note 6 at 430-31. A mentally retarded defendant who is illiterate may pretend to "read over" the written version of his statement prepared by the police in order to avoid detection of his disability. Morrow, *A Legal Framework: An Insider's Perspective*, in REHABILITATION AND THE RETARDED OFFENDER 60-61 (P. Browning ed. 1976).

Commentary

This Standard emphasizes that expert testimony by mental health or mental retardation professionals may often be appropriate and necessary in evaluating a particular confession under the provisions of Standards 7-5.8 and 7-5.9.[1] This is consistent with the overall view expressed in the Criminal Justice Mental Health Standards that courts should make use of the expertise of professionals in the various disciplines that address the problems of mental disability.[2] Courts will require the assistance of qualified mental disability experts, both at trials on the issue of the reliability of a defendant's statement, and at suppression hearings on the issue of the reliability or voluntariness of a statement or the validity of a waiver of *Miranda* rights. The qualifications of experts to address the question of the effect of an individual's mental illness or mental retardation on the issues addressed in these Standards should meet the requirements of Standards 7-3.11 and 7-3.12.

Standard 7-5.10 does not address the issue of whether mental disability experts should be permitted to express an opinion on questions requiring a conclusion of law. However, the Criminal Justice Mental Health Standards already contain a general prohibition on "ultimate issue" testimony in Standard 7-3.9(a), which provides, in part, that "the expert witness should not express, or be permitted to express, an opinion on any question requiring a conclusion of law or a moral or social value judgment properly reserved to the court or jury." Indeed, the commentary to Standard 7-3.9 suggests the applicability of this general principle to the issues surrounding confessions:

> some situations call for value judgments or conclusions of law, concerning which expert witnesses should not be permitted to testify. For example, they should be precluded from testifying that a confession was "voluntary" or "involuntary". . . .[3]

Mental health or mental retardation professionals can give the court or

1. The provisions regarding expert testimony do not, of course, preclude the use of competent lay testimony on these issues where that is appropriate.

2. *See generally* George, *The American Bar Association's Mental Health Standards: An Overview*, 53 GEO. WASH. L. REV. 338 (1985).

3. Commentary to Standard 7-3.9, at page 7.124.

jury the benefit of their expertise in the field of mental disability, as well as observations about the particular defendant, without directly commenting upon the issue properly reserved to judicial decision-makers.

Part VI

Nonresponsibility for Crime

William H. Erickson, *Chairman*
Standing Committee on Association
Standards for Criminal Justice

Terence F. MacCarthy
Task Force Chairman

Christopher Slobogin
Reporter

Task Force

Terence F. MacCarthy, *Chairman*
Executive Director, Federal Defender Program, Chicago, Illinois

Constance L. Belfiore
Special Assistant to the U.S. Attorney for the District of Columbia, Washington, D.C. (representing ABA Young Lawyers Division)

William H. Erickson
Justice, Supreme Court of Colorado, Denver, Colorado

Lawrence Zelic Freedman, M.D.
Chairman, Institute of Social & Behavioral Pathology, University of Chicago, Chicago, Illinois

Robinsue Frohboese, Ph.D., J.D.
Attorney and Psychologist, Washington, D.C. (representing American Psychological Association)

Michael Kindred
Professor of Law, Ohio State University, Columbus, Ohio

Norman Lefstein
Professor of Law, University of North Carolina School of Law, Chapel Hill, North Carolina (representing ABA Section of Criminal Justice)

Michael Mantell, Ph.D.
Chief Psychologist, San Diego Police Department, San Diego, California (representing American Orthopsychiatric Association)

E. Michael McCann
District Attorney, Milwaukee County, Milwaukee, Wisconsin

Alan A. Stone, M.D.
Professor of Law and Psychiatry, Harvard University Law School, Cambridge, Massachusetts (representing American Psychiatric Association)

Russell E. Webb
Private practitioner, Idaho Falls, Idaho

CHRISTOPHER SLOBOGIN, *Reporter*
Professor of Law, University of Florida College of Law

INTRODUCTION

Almost 150 years ago, Daniel M'Naghten was acquitted "by reason of insanity" on charges of murdering the private secretary of Prime Minister Robert Peel. The verdict caused an uproar in England and moved the House of Lords to scrutinize carefully the grounds on which mentally disordered persons should be excused from crime. Since that time, probably no other area of the criminal law has attracted as much professional or public attention as the doctrine these standards refer to as the defense of mental nonresponsibility.* The amount of scholarly, judicial, and legislative energy expended on this subject in the Anglo-American legal community has been prodigious and, some would say, excessive. The best evidence suggests that the mental nonresponsibility [insanity] defense is raised in less than 1 percent of all felony cases in the United States and is successful in about a fourth of those.[1] In terms of its inci-

---

*As noted in the Introduction to this chapter, "mental nonresponsibility" is used instead of "insanity" throughout these standards. Terms like *insanity* and *the criminally insane* conjure up visions of beastlike derangement; however accurate that perception may have been when the words were applied to "mad" individuals centuries ago, to perpetuate it today when symptoms of mental affliction often can be eliminated entirely though medication and other modern treatments is both offensive and stigmatizing. Moreover, the word *insanity* has lost its legal flavor and has become almost a "lay diagnosis." Use of the phrase *mental nonresponsibility* avoids distorted connotations and forces one to focus on the moral nature of the inquiry into whether a person should be exculpated for his or her acts. Accordingly, these standards will use the latter term other than when "insanity" appears in quoted remarks or the context makes its use necessary. In the latter instances, it will be placed in quotation marks or brackets.

1. NAT'L MENTAL HEALTH ASS'N, MYTHS AND REALITIES: A REPORT OF THE NATIONAL COMMISSION ON THE INSANITY DEFENSE 14-15 (1983) [hereinafter cited as MYTHS AND REALITIES]; Steadman, Keitner, Braff & Arvanites, *Factors Associated with a Successful Insanity Defense,* 140 AM. J. PSYCHIATRY 401 (1983).

In 1978, there were approximately 1600 defendants acquitted by reason of mental nonresponsibility nationwide, an average of thirty-two per state. *See* Steadman, Monahan, Hartstone, Davis & Robbins, *Mentally Disordered Offenders: A National Survey of Patients and Facilities,* 6 LAW & HUM. BEHAV. 31, 33 (1982). In 1978, only 1625 federal defendants — 0.10 percent of the total — pleaded the defense, and relatively few prevailed. *See generally* Steadman & Braff, *Defendants Not Guilty by Reason of Insanity,* in MENTALLY DISORDERED OFFENDERS: PERSPECTIVES FROM LAW AND SOCIAL SCIENCE 109, 110, 117-118, 123-124 (J. Monahan & H. Steadman ed. 1983) (summarizing statistical studies in several states, showing a low rate of pleading and acquittals based on mental nonresponsibility [insanity]); Weiner, *Mental Disability and the Criminal Law,* in THE MENTALLY DISABLED AND THE LAW 693, 720 (S. Brakel, J. Parry & B. Weiner eds., 3d ed. 1985) [hereinafter cited as Weiner].

dence, the defense occupies a very small nook of the criminal justice system.

Yet it continues to command a large portion of our attention. In 1981, the attempted assassination of President Reagan by John W. Hinckley, Jr., resulted in a new round of controversy over the defense rivaling the *M'Naghten* experience. Hinckley's subsequent acquittal by reason of insanity certainly was a strong factor in the enactment in 1984 of the Insanity Defense Reform Act,[2] which contains an appreciation test[3] approximating that in standard 7-6.1(a). State legislatures have been active as well.[4] The hostile public mood that sparked this flurry of legislative activity echoed the reaction of Queen Victoria (herself once the target of a gunman later acquitted on "insanity" grounds) upon hearing the outcome of the *M'Naghten* case: "The law may be perfect, but how is it that whenever a case for its application arises, it proves to be of no avail?"[5]

As the standards in this part make clear, the American Bar Association opposes abolition of the mental nonresponsibility [insanity] defense.[6] Judge Bazelon succinctly has answered those who question the purpose of a defense that excuses a person for otherwise criminal conduct: "Our collective conscience does not allow punishment where it cannot impose blame."[7] The basis for the nonresponsibility defense is a moral one; its jurisprudential underpinnings reach back to the origins of Western ethical and legal thought.[8] At least as early as 1300, records show that English kings pardoned murders because their crimes were committed "while

2. Comprehensive Crime Control Act of 1984, Pub. L. No. 98-473, §402, 98 Stat. 1976 (1984).

3. 18 U.S.C.A. §20 (Supp. 1986).

4. *See* commentary to standard 7-6.1, notes 23-26 and accompanying text.

5. Quoted in Becker, *Durham Revisited: Psychiatry and the Problem of Crime*, in DIAGNOSIS AND DEBATE 49 (R. Bonnie ed. 1977) [hereinafter cited as Becker].

6. *See* commentary to standard 7-6.1, notes 28-30 and accompanying text. *See generally* Weiner, *supra* note 1, at 716-717.

7. Durham v. United States, 214 F.2d 862, 876 (D.C. Cir. 1954), *overruled by* United States v. Brawner, 471 F.2d 969 (D.C. Cir. 1972).

8. As early as the sixth century B.C., commentary on the Hebrew scriptures distinguished between harmful acts traceable to fault and those that occur without fault. To these ancient scholars, the paradigm of the latter type of act was one committed by a child, who was seen as incapable of weighing the moral implications of personal behavior, even when willful; retarded and insane persons were likened to children. *See* Platt & Diamond, *The Origins and Development of the "Wild Beast" Concept of Mental Illness and Its Relation to Theories of Criminal Responsibility*, 1 J. HIST. BEHAV. SCI. 355, 366 (1965) [hereinafter cited as Platt & Diamond]. The Greek moral philosophers, at least as far back as the fifth century B.C., considered the distinction between a culpable and nonculpable act to be among the "unwritten laws of nature supported by the universal moral sense of mankind." B. JONES, THE LAW AND LEGAL

suffering from madness."[9] The first recorded jury acquittal by reason of insanity was in 1505.[10] Sir Matthew Hale, the eminent seventeenth-century jurist, summarized centuries of thought thus: "The consent of the will is that which renders human actions either commendable or culpable. . . . And because the liberty or choice of the will presupposeth an act of understanding to know the thing or action chosen by the will, it follows that where there is a total defect of the understanding there is no free act of the will."[11]

The Lords responsible for the *M'Naghten* rule undoubtedly understood this precept even if they were not familiar with Hale's formulation of it; despite severe public and royal displeasure over M'Naghten's acquittal, they did not question the continuing validity of a defense based on mental nonresponsibility. In the face of the most recent onslaught on the doctrine, the United States Congress likewise has refused to abolish the defense or enact alternative pleas.[12] The ABA, as described in more detail below, has adopted a series of resolutions favoring the retention of the defense and opposing the enactment of so-called guilty but mentally ill statutes that would supplement or replace the mental nonresponsibility verdict.[13]

If one assumes that morally blameless persons should not be punished as criminals, it becomes necessary to define the class of morally blame-

---

THEORY OF THE GREEKS 264 (1956). The same view pervaded Roman law and appeared in the teaching of the early Christian theologians. It emerged in Anglo-Saxon law no later than the twelfth century, the result of the "mutual influences and interaction of Christian theology and Anglo-Saxon law." Levitt, *The Origin of the Doctrine of Mens Rea*, 17 ILL. L. REV. 117, 136 (1922). The idea was reinforced in England after the Norman invasion brought with it continental legal thought, itself strongly influenced by Christian ethics and canon law, which had already absorbed Jewish ethical teachings, classical philosophy, and Roman law. *See* Platt & Diamond, *supra*, at 356.

9. *See* Becker, *supra* note 5, at 43.

10. *See* N. WALKER, CRIME AND INSANITY IN ENGLAND 26 (1968).

11. 1 M. HALE, HISTORY OF PLEAS OF THE CROWN *14-15.

12. See notes 2 and 3 and accompanying text.

13. This view is shared by the American Psychiatric Association, the National Mental Health Association, and the National Conference of Commissioners on Uniform State Laws (in its draft Defense of Insanity Act), as well as the weight of scholarly opinion. *See* AMERICAN PSYCHIATRIC ASS'N, STATEMENT ON THE INSANITY DEFENSE 8 (Dec. 1982); MYTHS & REALITIES, *supra* note 1, at 30; NAT'L CONFERENCE OF COMMISSIONERS ON UNIFORM STATE LAWS, DEFENSE OF INSANITY ACT art. 1 (1983 draft); Bonnie, *The Moral Basis of the Insanity Defense*, 69 A.B.A.J. 194 (1983); Diamond, *With Malice Aforethought*, 2 ARCHIVES CRIM. PSYCHOLOGY 1 (1957); Hart, *The Aims of the Criminal Law*, 23 LAW & CONTEMP. PROBS. 401 (1958); Packer, *Mens Rea and the Supreme Court*, 1962 SUP. CT. REV. 107. *But see* N. MORRIS, MADNESS AND THE CRIMINAL LAW 61 (1982).

less criminal defendants, to prescribe procedures to be followed in evaluating and adjudicating defendants who assert the defense, and to dispose appropriately of those determined to lack responsibility. The first issue is discussed in this part; the second is considered both in this part and part III of this chapter; the third issue is the province of part VII of this chapter. To grasp the thrust of the ABA's proposals concerning the mental nonresponsibility defense, all three parts must be read together.

The History of Part VI

At the time the *Hinckley* verdict was announced in June 1982,[14] the Standing Committee on Association Standards for Criminal Justice, in carrying on its Criminal Justice Mental Health Standards Project,[15] had had under consideration for close to a year and a half a number of mental health law and criminal justice issues, including the nonresponsibility defense. Although the Project's standards were not scheduled for formal presentation to the Association's House of Delegates until the 1984 Annual Meeting, the events triggered by the *Hinckley* case suggested that early House of Delegates' consideration of certain key issues would be helpful to Congress, state legislatures, and the public.

Accordingly, in February 1983, the Standing Committee presented to the House of Delegates three recommendations, all of which the House adopted as official ABA policy. The first resolution approved a defense of nonresponsibility for crime focusing solely on a defendant's appreciation of the wrongfulness of his or her conduct and rejecting the volitional prong of the American Law Institute Model Penal Code test for nonresponsibility[16] as well as the so-called irresistible impulse tests.[17] The sec-

14. *See* United States v. Hinckley, 525 F. Supp. 1342 (D.D.C. 1981), *clarified*, 529 F. Supp. 520, *aff'd*, 672 F.2d 115 (D.C. Cir. 1982); Crim. Case No. 81-306 (D.C. Cir. 1982) (jury instruction); L. Caplan, The Insanity Defense and the Trial of John W. Hinckley, Jr. 33-47, 59-100 (1984); Wexler, *Redefining the Insanity Problem*, 53 Geo. Wash. L. Rev. 528, 528-531, 537-540 (1985).

15. *See* XV, introduction to chapter 7.

16. ALI Model Penal Code §4.01 (Permanent ed. with rev. commentary 1985). It should be noted that the interdisciplinary task force that worked on this part recommended retention of the ALI test for mental nonresponsibility and advocated placing the burden of disproving nonresponsibility under this test on the prosecution beyond a reasonable doubt. These recommendations were considered but not accepted by the Standing Committee which, joined by the ABA Commission on the Mentally Disabled, recommended the positions eventually adopted by the House of Delegates.

17. *See* commentary to standard 7-6.1, notes 8-9 and accompanying text.

ond adopted the principle that the prosecution should be legally required to disprove a defense claim of mental nonresponsibility [insanity] beyond a reasonable doubt in jurisdictions using the Association's preferred test, but that the defense should have the burden to establish nonresponsibility, by a preponderance of the evidence, in jurisdictions using a test with a volitional prong as one of its elements. The third resolution opposed the enactment of statutes that supplant or supplement a verdict of not guilty by reason of mental nonresponsibility [insanity] with a verdict of guilty but mentally ill. Thus, three different subparagraphs of the standards in this part[18] were already official ABA policy before the project was completed.

Principal Features of Part VI

The first two standards in part VI cover substantive criminal law doctrines that may necessitate participation by mental health and mental retardation professionals in the criminal process. As already noted, standard 7-6.1 incorporates the ABA's test for mental nonresponsibility [insanity] that tracks closely, with some modifications, what this commentary calls the "cognitive-affective" or "appreciation" prong of the ALI test for criminal responsibility. The standard also provides a definition of the term *mental disease or defect* designed to make clear that the threshold for the ABA nonresponsibility test is much narrower than the myriad conditions that might colloquially be called "mental disease." Standard 7-6.2 permits the introduction of expert testimony regarding mental condition when it is relevant to the *mens rea* or culpability element of a charged offense. This evidentiary rule, wrongly labelled the "diminished capacity" doctrine, is conceptually distinct from the defense of mental nonresponsibility [insanity]. The commentary to this standard attempts to clear up misconceptions about expert testimony on *mens rea* and suggests that rulings excluding such testimony are constitutionally infirm.

The next three standards address a number of matters, many of which are also alluded to in part III, relating to the pretrial administration of defenses based on mental condition. All three standards attempt to ensure a fair adjudication of these defenses by affording both sides as much access to relevant information as is constitutionally permissible. Standard 7-6.3(a) requires defense counsel to give notice to the prosecution once a

18. *See* standards 7-6.1(a), 7-6.9(b)(i)-(ii), 7-6.10(b) and commentary.

decision to assert a defense based on mental abnormality has been reached; the standard should be read in conjunction with standard 7-3.4(a) directing the defense attorney to apprise the prosecuting attorney of the fact a defense-requested evaluation has taken place. Both forms of notice trigger a number of other provisions in standards 7-6.4 and 7-6.5 designed to promote disclosure of information about mental condition. Standard 7-6.3(b) ensures that this disclosure normally will take place *only* after receipt of defense notice by the prosecution; it provides that neither a prosecuting attorney nor a court may raise *sua sponte* the nonresponsibility or *mens rea* issue, unless a defendant is incompetent to make a decision about these defenses.

Assuming notice has been given,[19] standard 7-6.4 provides for a prosecution-requested evaluation, and describes the manner in which it should be conducted, echoing similar standards in part III.[20] The standards in both parts facilitate full disclosure from defendants by: (1) permitting courts to sanction defendants who fail to cooperate in the course of a prosecution-initiated examination; (2) prohibiting defense counsel from participating in such an examination unless requested to attend by the examiner; (3) expressing a preference for single rather than multiple issue examinations; (4) providing for the recording of evaluations; and (5) assuring defendants and defense counsel that no statement made by a defendant during a prosecution-initiated evaluation will be admissible at trial except on issues concerning mental condition which already have been advanced by the defense. The standard also takes the position that only a defendant, or a prosecuting attorney in response to a defense notice, should be able to obtain a pretrial evaluation of the defendant's mental state at the time of the offense; again, permitting *sua sponte* judicial motions infringes unduly upon the right of defendants to control the character of their defense presentation.

Standard 7-6.5 provides that once notice has been given under standard 7-6.3(a), the prosecution is required to disclose information bearing on the defendant's mental condition. This issue has analogs in other criminal justice contexts and, therefore, necessitates a cross-reference to chapter 11 of the standards, Discovery and Procedure Before Trial, covering generally the prosecutorial duty to disclose such data fully and timely before trial.

The final five standards in this part relate to the conduct of trials at which evidence of abnormal mental condition is presented. Standard 7-

19. Under either standard 7-3.4(a) or standard 7-6.3(a).

20. *See* standards 7-3.5 through 7-3.7 and commentary.

6.6 addresses the difficult and vexing issue of the form in which testimony by mental health and mental retardation professionals should be phrased so as to avoid incursions into the legal domain. The problem may seem trivial, but in fact it is symbolically and practically significant. A central emphasis in part VI is the fact that "mental nonresponsibility" is a jurisprudential, not a medical, concept. This standard in particular attempts to reconcile the need for full and active participation in the criminal process by representatives of mental health disciplines with the fact that the decisionmaking function in criminal trials properly falls to jury and judge. Contrary to the current trend, it bars expert testimony on issues of "criminal responsibility." Standard 7-6.7 tackles the question of when, if ever, a trial in which evidence of nonresponsibility is to be introduced should be bifurcated. The standard takes the position that mandatory bifurcation is inappropriate and that a unitary trial is preferable unless a defendant would be prejudiced substantially by it.

Standards 7-6.8 through 7-6.10 address the conduct of jury trials on the mental nonresponsibility [insanity] issue. Standard 7-6.8 incorporates a recommendation running counter to the law in most states that juries be instructed about the dispositional consequences of a verdict of not guilty by reason of mental nonresponsibility [insanity], on the premise that such information will promote more appropriate jury determinations. As already mentioned, standard 7-6.9 incorporates the ABA stance on the burden of persuasion and standard of proof in nonresponsibility cases. For jurisdictions using the ABA test set forth in standard 7-6.1 or any other test focusing solely on a defendant's ability to understand or appreciate the significance of personal conduct, the standard endorses the principle that triers of fact should find defendants not guilty by reason of mental nonresponsibility [insanity] if the prosecution fails to disprove the defense claim of nonresponsibility beyond a reasonable doubt. In jurisdictions using the ALI test, the Association prefers that a factfinder be required to find a defendant not criminally responsible only if the defendant can prove the elements of the mental nonresponsibility [insanity] defense by a preponderance of the evidence. This dichotomy recognizes the differing proof problems presented by tests that focus on a defendant's lack of control and tests that focus on a lack of appreciation or understanding. Finally, standard 7-6.10 incorporates Association policy that a jury in a trial at which mental nonresponsibility [insanity] is an issue should be given only three verdict options: guilty, not guilty, or not guilty by reason of mental nonresponsibility [insanity]. It restates the ABA policy, previously alluded to, opposing the enactment of statutes providing for guilty but mentally ill verdicts. It also recommends a procedural requirement that juries find beyond a reasonable doubt that defendants committed the conduct or *actus reus* elements of a charged offense before they can return a verdict of not guilty by reason of mental nonresponsibility [insanity]. This latter provision is an important predicate to the part VII standards covering the disposition of defendants found to be criminally nonresponsible. Persons acquitted by reason of mental nonresponsibility [insanity] should not be punished as criminals; they should be confined only upon a showing that they are dangerous, as evidenced by clear and convincing proof they have committed violent acts and are mentally disordered.

Standard 7-6.1. The defense of mental nonresponsibility [insanity]

(a) A person is not responsible for criminal conduct if, at the time of such conduct, and as a result of mental disease or defect, that person was unable to appreciate the wrongfulness of such conduct.

(b) When used as a legal term in this standard *mental disease or defect* refers to:

(i) impairments of mind, whether enduring or transitory; or,

(ii) mental retardation,

either of which substantially affected the mental or emotional processes of the defendant at the time of the alleged offense.

Commentary Introduction

The standard restates Association policy favoring a test for mental nonresponsibility [insanity] based on inability, because of mental disease or defect, to appreciate the wrongfulness of otherwise criminal conduct. It defines the legal term *mental disease or defect* to require conditions that substantially affected mental or emotional processes at the time of an alleged criminal offense.

Related Standards

ABA, Standards for Criminal Justice 7-6.9, 7-6.10(b), 7-7.4
ALI, Model Penal Code 4.01
APA, Statement on the Insanity Defense 12
NCCUSL, Defense of the Insanity Act, art. 1, §2 (April 1984 draft)
NMHA, Myths and Realities, recommendations 1, 5

Commentary

Historical Development of Mental Nonresponsibility [Insanity] Defenses

A survey of even relatively recent Anglo-American jurisprudence reveals several different formulations of the mental nonresponsibility [insanity] defense. Writing in the early seventeenth century, Sir Edward Coke commented that the "idiot," "lunatic," and a person who "wholly loseth his memory and understanding" should be considered among the insane.[1] Later in the same century, Sir Matthew Hale concluded that the "best measure" for determining "insanity" was whether the accused had "as great understanding as ordinarily a child of fourteen hath."[2] In 1723, Justice Tracey instructed a jury that to be found nonresponsible "a man must be totally deprived of his understanding and memory so as not to know what he is doing, no more than an infant, brute or a wild beast."[3] At about the same time, other English courts were excusing those who lacked the capacity to distinguish "good from evil" or "right from wrong."[4]

This latter approach, in slightly modified form, became the "*M'Naghten* test of insanity" as announced by the House of Lords in 1843: "[I]t must be clearly proved that, at the time of the committing of the act, the party accused was laboring under such a defect of reason, from disease of the mind, as not to know the nature and quality of the act he was doing; or if he did know it, that he did not know what he was doing was wrong."[5] Although this was the first time an appellate court in either England or the United States had declared a rule for determining mental nonresponsibility, the *M'Naghten* test became the accepted standard in both countries within a short period of time.

The rule also came under immediate attack. Some of the most strenuous criticism came from the medical community which, far from wanting to do away with the defense, argued that it needed to be recast in light of contemporary understanding about human behavior. Dr. Isaac Ray, an

---

1. *See* 2 E. Coke, The First Part of the Institutes of the Laws of England *247.a. (discussing testamentary capacity).

2. 1 M. Hale, History of Pleas of the Crown *30.

3. Rex v. Arnold, 16 How. St. Tr. 695, 766 (1723).

4. *See generally* Becker, Durham *Revisited: Psychiatry and the Problem of Crime,* in Diagnosis and Debate 43-44 (R. Bonnie ed. 1977) [hereinafter cited as Becker]; Platt & Diamond, *The Origins of the "Right and Wrong" Test of Criminal Responsibility,* 54 Calif. L. Rev. 1227, 1236-1237 (1966).

5. M'Naghten's Case, 10 Cl. & F. 200, 8 Eng. Rep. 718 (H.L. 1843). *See* Weiner, *Mental Disability and the Criminal Law,* in The Mentally Disabled and the Law 693, 709-710 (S. Brakel, J. Parry & B. Weiner eds., 3d ed. 1985) [hereinafter cited as Weiner].

American physician who was one of the most prominent spokesmen for this point of view, felt that the law's emphasis on a defendant's ability to distinguish good from evil failed to recognize "those nice shades of the disease" that could render a person blameless for antisocial conduct. He felt that the defense should turn instead on whether "the mental unsoundness . . . embraced the act within the sphere of its influence."[6]

In 1870, the New Hampshire Supreme Court, apparently influenced by Ray, adopted a rule commonly known as the "product" test:

> No man shall be held accountable, criminally, for an act which was the offspring and product of mental disease. . . . No argument is needed to show that to hold a man may be punished for what is the offspring of disease would be to hold that he may be punished for disease. Any rule which makes that possible cannot be law.[7]

No other court at the time followed the New Hampshire lead. Toward the end of the century, however, several courts, apparently persuaded by the contention that the *M'Naghten* defense of mental nonresponsibility [insanity] was too narrow, supplemented it with a rule focusing on volitional impairment.[8] This so-called irresistible impulse doctrine posited that persons who could not control their actions should not be held criminally responsible for them.[9]

By the turn of the century, about one-third of the states had nonresponsibility tests consisting of *M'Naghten* and the irresistible impulse rule; one state, New Hampshire, had the product rule; and the rest adhered to the *M'Naghten* test alone. This state of affairs remained "essentially unchanged" until the 1950s.[10]

---

6. I. Ray, A Treatise on the Medical Jurisprudence of Insanity 21 (1838). *See also* Tighe, *Francis Wharton and the Nineteenth-Century Insanity Defense: The Origins of a Reform Tradition*, 27 Am. J. Leg. Hist. 223 (1983).

7. State v. Jones, 50 N.H. 369, 394 (1871).

8. *See* 2 J. Stephen, A History of the Criminal Law of England 168 (1883).

9. In 1886, the first American court to adopt such a test stated it thus:

> [A defendant is not] legally responsible if the two following conditions concur: (1) [i]f, by reason of the duress of such mental disease, he had so far lost the power to choose between the right and wrong, and to avoid doing the act in question, as that his free agency was at the time destroyed; (2) and if, at the same time, the alleged crime was so connected with such mental disease, in the relation of cause and effect, as to have been the product of it solely.

Parsons v. State, 81 Ala. 577, 596, 2 So. 854, 866-867 (1886).

10. P. Low, J. Jeffries & R. Bonnie, Criminal Law, Cases and Materials 658 (1982) [hereinafter cited as P. Low].

In that decade, in response to the continuing attacks by psychiatrists and legal academicians against the rigidity of existing formulations, two important events occurred. The first was *Durham v. United States,*[11] a 1954 decision in which the United States Court of Appeals for the District of Columbia adopted a modernized version of the "product" test. Although followed by only two other jurisdictions,[12] *Durham* stimulated rich judicial and scholarly debates about the complexities of the defense.[13] The second significant event was the American Law Institute's promulgation of the Model Penal Code test for mental nonresponsibility in 1955:

> A person is not responsible for criminal conduct if at the time of such conduct as a result of mental disease or defect he lacks substantial capacity either to appreciate the criminality [wrongfulness] of his conduct or to conform his conduct to the requirements of the law.[14]

This language combined the notions underlying both the *M'Naghten* and irresistible impulse formulations, but also made it clear that a defendant's cognitive or volitional impairment at the time of the offense need only be "substantial," rather than total, in order to merit a nonresponsibility defense. The ALI test proved a popular one; over the next two decades a majority of the country's jurisdictions adopted it.[15] Nonethe-

---

11. 214 F.2d 862 (D.C. Cir. 1954).

12. Me. Rev. Stat. Ann. tit. 15, §102 (1964); V.I. Code Ann. tit. 14, §14(4) (1964). The Maine legislature later repealed its "product" statute and adopted a modified version of the ALI test. Me. Rev. Stat. Ann. tit. 17A, §39(1) (1983).

13. *See, e.g.,* McDonald v. United States, 312 F.2d 847 (D.C. Cir. 1962); Blocker v. United States, 274 F.2d 572 (D.C. Cir. 1959); Carter v. United States, 252 F.2d 608 (D.C. Cir. 1957); Stone, *Psychiatry and the Law,* 1 Psychiatric Ann. 31 (1971).

14. American Law Institute Model Penal Code §4.01 (Permanent ed. with revised commentary 1985). *See also* Weiner, *supra* note 5, at 710-711.

15. At the present time, the ALI test is used in just over half the states and, excepting the Fifth Circuit, *see* United States v. Lyons, 731 F.2d 243 (5th Cir.), *cert. denied,* 105 S. Ct. 323 (1984), was used in all federal courts (including the District of Columbia Circuit, which overruled *Durham* in 1972, *see* United States v. Brawner, 471 F.2d 969 (D.C. Cir. 1972)) until Congress replaced it by legislation. *See* notes 18-22 and accompanying text. Some variation of *M'Naghten* is still the exclusive test of mental nonresponsibility in about one-third of the states. About five states have the irresistible impulse standard together with some version of the cognitive test. New Hampshire continues to use the "product" test, Rhode Island relies on the "justly responsible" formulation, and three states, Montana, Idaho, and Utah, have abolished the defense. The Montana statute was sustained as constitutional in State v. Korell, 690 P.2d 992, 1000 (Mont. 1984). For a complete list of state and federal rules as of 1981, *see* Favole, *Mental Disability in the American Criminal Process: A Four Issue Survey,* in Mentally Disordered Offenders: Perspectives from Law and Social Science 257-269 (J.

less, some critics inveighed against the test because it continued to rely on the so-called medical model of mental nonresponsibility.[16] A final version of the test came from the Rhode Island Supreme Court which, in 1979, held that persons should be excused from criminal liability if they are "so substantially impaired" that they cannot "justly be held responsible."[17]

The Federal Insanity Defense Reform Act of 1984

As early as 1971, Congress considered the enactment of a single mental nonresponsibility [insanity] defense to replace the judicial tests in the various federal circuits, as part of a comprehensive federal criminal code.[18] In 1984, noting changes in attitude toward the ALI test,[19] and undoubtedly influenced by the *Hinckley* case,[20] it enacted the Insanity Defense Reform Act of 1984 containing the following standard for mental nonresponsibility [insanity] governing all federal crimes:

> It is an affirmative defense to a prosecution under any Federal statute that, at the time of the commission of the acts constituting the offense, the

---

Monahan & H. Steadman eds. 1983) [hereinafter cited as Favole], and as of October 1982, *see* Weiner, *supra* note 5, at 712, 769-777, Table 12.5, col. 7. *See also* MacBain, *The Insanity Defense: Conceptual Confusion and the Erosion of Fairness,* 67 MARQUETTE L. REV. 1 (1983).

The insanity defense was held inapplicable to probation revocation proceedings in People v. Allegri, 127 Ill. App. 3d 1041, 469 N.E.2d 1126 (1984).

16. United States v. Brawner, 471 F.2d 969, 1027-1030 (D.C. Cir. 1972) (Bazelon, J., concurring); Morse, *Crazy Behavior, Morals, and Science: An Analysis of Mental Health Law,* 51 S. CAL. L. REV. 527, 640-645 (1978).

17. State v. Johnson, 121 R.I. 254, 267, 399 A.2d 469, 476 (1979). This test incorporates the position adopted in 1953 by the British Royal Commission on Capital Punishment (REPORT OF THE ROYAL COMMISSION ON CAPITAL PUNISHMENT 116 (1953)), which took the view that the question of criminal responsibility is not amenable to categorization and should be left entirely to jury discretion.

18. The original submission by the National Commission on Reform of Federal Criminal Laws incorporated the ALI test. *See* U.S. NAT'L COMM'N ON REFORM OF FEDERAL CRIMINAL LAWS FINAL REPORT §503 (1971). The Senate bill that came closest to enactment, S. 1, 94th Cong., 1st Sess. (Jan. 15, 1975), §522, incorporated a purely *mens rea* test. By 1981, S. 1630, 97th Cong., 1st Sess. (Sept. 9, 1981), Congress had abandoned the effort to define a mental nonresponsibility [insanity] test. Thus, the 1984 legislation manifested a significant change in direction on the part of Congress.

19. *See* REPORT OF THE COMMITTEE ON THE JUDICIARY, UNITED STATES SENATE, ON THE COMPREHENSIVE CRIME CONTROL ACT OF 1983, S.1762, Report No. 98-225, 98th Cong., 1st Sess. (1983), at 227-228 [hereinafter cited as REPORT No. 98-225].

20. *See* introduction to part VI, note 14 and accompanying text.

> defendant, as a result of a severe mental disease or defect, was unable to appreciate the nature and quality or the wrongfulness of his acts. Mental disease or defect does not otherwise constitute a defense.[21]

The qualifier *severe* was intended to rule out "mere emotional processes" that impair appreciation of the nature and quality or wrongfulness of otherwise criminal activities.[22] Congress did not provide a definition for the term *mental disease or defect*.

Nature of the Standard 7-6.1(a) Test

The test for nonresponsibility set out in paragraph (a) of this standard is similar to the tests enacted by Congress[23] and legislated in New York,[24] North Dakota,[25] and Texas,[26] and is almost identical to the proposal advanced by the American Psychiatric Association.[27] As noted in the introduction to this part,[28] the standard[29] reflects the 1983 resolution adopted by the ABA's House of Delegates:

> The ABA approves, in principle, a defense of nonresponsibility for crime which focuses solely on whether the defendant as a result of mental disease

21. 18 U.S.C.A. §20(a) (Supp. 1986) (effective Oct. 12, 1984).

22. *See* Report No. 98-225, *supra* note 19, at 229. The Department of Justice opposes defense counsel efforts to establish a lack of appreciation based on emotional or subjective factors. *See* Handbook on the Comprehensive Crime Control Act of 1984 and Other Criminal Statutes Enacted by the 98th Congress 59-60 (1984).

23. *See* notes 21-22 and accompanying text.

24. N.Y. Penal Law §40.15 (McKinney Supp. 1986).

25. N.D. Cent. Code §12.1-04-03 (1976).

26. Tex. Penal Code §8.01(a) (Vernon Supp. 1986). *See* Farabee & Spearly, *The New Insanity Law in Texas: Reliable Testimony and Judicial Review of Release,* 24 S. Tex. L.J. 671, 677-678 (1983).

27. American Psychiatric Ass'n, Statement on the Insanity Defense 12 (Dec. 1982) [hereinafter cited as APA Statement].

28. *See* notes 16-17 and accompanying text.

29. The Standing Committee and the Reporter to this part acknowledge the substantial assistance of Professor Richard J. Bonnie, of the University of Virginia Law School, in formulating the position endorsed in this standard. Many of the ideas expressed in the Standing Committee's report to the ABA House of Delegates in February 1983 and in the commentary to this standard are drawn from Professor Bonnie's testimony before the Senate Judiciary Committee in August 1982, *see* Report No. 98-225, *supra* note 19, at 226-227, and the National Commission on the Insanity Defense that same month, and from his article, Bonnie, *The Moral Basis of the Insanity Defense,* 69 A.B.A.J. 194 (1983) [hereinafter cited as Bonnie].

or defect was unable to appreciate the wrongfulness of his or her conduct at the time of the offense charged.[30]

The Rationale for the ABA's Formulation

Judge Kaufman has written that "[a]cquittals by reason of insanity in highly publicized cases such as the Hinckley affair tend to undermine the public's faith in the courts' ability to respond to crime in a rational fashion."[31] The aim of this part of the Standards and its associated parts is to respect the moral basis[32] of the mental nonresponsibility [insanity] defense while avoiding the creation of a framework that leaves the public distrustful of its institutions.

In reexamining the defense, the options run the gamut from its abolition to the product test and Rhode Island's "justly responsible" standard.[33] The introduction to this part has already noted that the Association considers the abolition option indefensible.[34] The moral basis of the mental nonresponsibility defense is undeniable and has been reaffirmed throughout the history of western civilization.

The Mens Rea *Limitation*

However, before leaving this point and as a means of emphasizing it, mention must be made of one currently popular "alternative" proposal to the defense. This approach, which would permit evidence of mental condition bearing on the requisite mental or culpability element of the crime but eliminate mental nonresponsibility [insanity] as an independent, exculpatory doctrine, was considered for a time by Congress[35] and was adopted in Idaho, Montana, and Utah.[36] The ABA has rejected it out of

30. ABA, Summary of Action of the House of Delegates, 1983 Midyear Meeting 3.

31. Kaufman, "The Insanity Plea on Trial," N.Y. Times Magazine, Aug. 8, 1982, at 16-17. *See also* Hermann, Morrison, Sor, Norman & Neff, People of the State of Illinois vs. John Gacy: *The Functioning of the Insanity Defense at the Limits of the Criminal Law,* 86 W. Va. L. Rev. 1169 (1984); Morse, *Excusing the Crazy: The Insanity Defense Reconsidered,* 58 S. Cal. L. Rev. 777, 780-795 (1985) [hereinafter cited as Morse]; Rappeport, *The Insanity Plea Scapegoating the Mentally Ill — Much Ado About Nothing?,* 24 S. Tex. L.J. 687 (1983); Wexler, *Redefining the Insanity Problem,* 53 Geo. Wash. L. Rev. 528, 537-540 (1985) [hereinafter cited as Wexler].

32. *See* Morse, *supra* note 31, at 806-821.

33. *See supra* notes 12-15 and accompanying text.

34. *See* notes 12, 13, 16 and accompanying text.

35. *See supra* note 18 and accompanying text.

36. Idaho Code §18-207 (1982); Mont. Code Ann. §46-14-102 (1981); Utah Code Ann. §76-2-305(1) (1983). *See* Singer, *Essay: Abolition of the Insanity Defense: Madness and the Criminal Law,* 4 Cardozo L. Rev. 683 (1983); Weiner, *supra* note 5, at 716-717.

hand. Such a jarring reversal of hundreds of years of moral and legal history would constitute an unfortunate and unwarranted overreaction to the problems typified by the *Hinckley* verdict.

Historically, it is true, sanity was related organically to the concept of *mens rea,* which originally was regarded as a generalized requirement of moral blameworthiness required for criminal liability. In the twentieth century, however, *mens rea* terminology has come to refer to the specific state of mind required for the conviction of particular criminal offenses. Thus, today, if there were no independent nonresponsibility [insanity] defense, defendants could be convicted of crimes as long as they knew what they were doing at the time of an offense and possessed the intent to commit it.

The issue of criminal blameworthiness merits deeper inquiry because it implies a certain *quality* of knowledge and intent transcending a minimal awareness and purposefulness. Otherwise, for example, a defendant who knowingly and intentionally killed his son under the psychotic delusion that he was the biblical Abraham, and his son the biblical Isaac, could be held criminally responsible. The Montana, Idaho, and Utah enactments, on their face, would deny a defense to such a defendant.[37]

Because the *mens rea* approach asks those who administer and apply the law to condemn as criminal the acts of mentally ill defendants who are grossly out of touch with reality, an argument could be made that it violates the due process and cruel-and-unusual-punishment clauses of the Constitution.[38] But constitutional support for the position endorsed in

37. However, compare the position of Professor Morris concerning the *Hadfield Case,* 27 How. St. Tr. 1281 (K.B. 1800). Hadfield had suffered a severe head wound during the Napoleonic wars. "There was no doubt of Hadfield's brain damage nor of his gross psychological disturbance. He did, however, clearly intend to kill the king. He had the insane *mens rea* for murder and treason. I do not regard the phrase 'insane *mens rea*' as a contradiction in terms." Morris, *Psychiatry and the Dangerous Criminal,* 41 S. Cal. L. Rev. 514, 521 (1968).

38. Early in this century, three state supreme courts, relying on either due process, equal protection, or eighth amendment grounds, or a combination thereof, overturned statutes that directly or indirectly abolished the defense of mental nonresponsibility [insanity]. Sinclair v. State, 161 Miss. 142, 132 So. 581 (1931); State v. Lange, 168 La. 958, 123 So. 639 (1929); State v. Strasbourg, 60 Wash. 106, 110 P. 1020 (1910). However, unlike statutes implementing the *mens rea* approach, the statutes held unconstitutional in those cases did not replace the defense with any defense or doctrine that would have permitted consideration of mental abnormality. Thus, the precedential value of these early cases is suspect.

Constitutional arguments in support of the nonresponsibility defense nonetheless can be made. More recent United States Supreme Court decisions imply that the fairness concerns underlying "substantive" due process and the proportionality idea associated with the cruel-and-unusual-punishment clause require that criminal liability be predicated on an act that is blameworthy. Robinson v. California, 370 U.S. 660, *reh'g denied,* 372 U.S. 905 (1962);

this standard is not necessary. As Professor Bonnie has pointed out,[39] the *mens rea* limitation forces judges and juries confronted with defendants who are uncontrovertibly psychotic either to return morally obtuse convictions or to acquit in outright defiance of the law. Neither alternative is palatable. The abolitionist approach as embodied in the *mens rea* limitation inhibits if not prevents the exercise of humane judgment that has distinguished our criminal law heritage. For this reason the Association has rejected the *mens rea* approach.

Selection of a Mental Nonresponsibility Test

Having concluded that a defense of mental nonresponsibility [insanity] is necessary to the fair administration of criminal justice, the ABA considered carefully the various formulations of the defense to determine which most successfully responds to that moral imperative. The early tests, *viz.*, the *M'Naghten* and irresistible impulse rules, are couched in arcane language that on its face accepts the outmoded view that a bright line exists between the responsible and the nonresponsible.[40] As Professor Wechsler wrote in explaining the rationale underlying the ALI formulation,

> [N]o test is workable that calls for complete impairment of ability to know or to control. . . . Disorientation, we were told, might be extreme and still might not be total; what clinical experience revealed was closer to a graded scale with marks along the way.[41]

Professor Goldstein has demonstrated that both the *M'Naghten* and irresistible impulse rules have been liberally construed, at least in some jurisdictions, and that they seldom have prevented juries from hearing or considering evidence of mental condition.[42] But it makes no sense to

---

Lambert v. California, 355 U.S. 225 (1957), *reh'g denied*, 355 U.S. 937 (1958). *See* Jeffries & Stephen, *Defense, Presumptions and Burden of Proof in the Criminal Law*, 88 YALE L.J. 1325, 1370-1379 (1979). Given the Court's wary use of due process and proportionality analysis, it is not clear whether future cases will provide a firmer ground for linking these notions to arguments favoring the defense of mental nonresponsibility.

39. *See* Bonnie, *supra* note 29, at 193; Wexler, *supra* note 31, at 540-546.

40. Because of its focus on volitional impairment, the irresistible impulse rule is also infirm for other reasons, discussed *infra* notes 48-50 and accompanying text.

41. Wechsler, *Codification of the Criminal Law in the United States: The Model Penal Code*, 68 COLUM. L. REV. 1425, 1443 (1968).

42. A. GOLDSTEIN, THE INSANITY DEFENSE 45-79 (1967) [hereinafter cited as A. GOLDSTEIN].

depend upon courts or juries to interpret rules against their plain meaning when broader, more sensible language has been devised.

The tests at the other end of the spectrum go too far, however. The "justly responsible" test was first proposed in 1972 by Judge Bazelon, who believed that "the boundary of a legal concept — criminal responsibility — should [not] be marked by medical concepts, especially when the validity of the 'medical model' is seriously questioned by some eminent psychiatrists."[43] He thus rejected a requirement of "mental disease or defect" as a threshold determination on the nonresponsibility issue. But the law has an obligation to structure a responsibility inquiry. The "justly responsible" test leaves juries with no direction but their own whim in deciding the forms of impairment sufficient to relieve defendants from criminal liability. Reliance on the so-called medical model, whatever its exact scope, permits consideration of a wide panoply of behavior at the same time that it protects the law from unbounded determinism.[44]

The product test adheres to the medical model but still fails to give factfinders adequate guidance about the appropriate limits of criminal responsibility. The history of the *Durham* decision attests to the problems, at both the trial and appellate levels, generated in the administration of such an ill-defined formulation.[45]

This reasoning process leaves a choice between the ALI test and some variation of it. The eventual selection of the standard 7-6.1(a) test was based on two underlying propositions: first, that the "appreciation of wrongfulness" formula is sufficiently broad to take into account the morally significant effects of severe mental disorder; and second, that any independent volitional inquiry involves a significant risk of "moral mis-

---

43. Brawner v. United States, 471 F.2d 969, 1029 (D.C. Cir. 1972) (Bazelon, J., concurring).

44. *See* State v. Sikora, 44 N.J. 453, 474-479, 210 A.2d 193, 205-207 (1965) (Weintraub, C.J., concurring).

45. *See* Becker, *supra* note 4, at 53-73. Ironically, in the eighteen years it remained the law in the District of Columbia Circuit, the *Durham* test accumulated a judicial gloss that came to approximate the ALI test. For instance, in McDonald v. United States, 312 F.2d 847, 850-851 (D.C. Cir. 1962), the court defined "mental disease or defect" in the product test to mean "any abnormal condition of the mind which substantially affects mental or emotional processes and substantially impairs behavior controls." When inserted in the product test ("an accused is not criminally responsible if his unlawful act was the product of a mental disease or mental defect") the language is not far removed from the ALI test. In United States v. Brawner, 471 F.2d 969 (D.C. Cir. 1972), the court of appeals finally declared the product test a failure and replaced it with the ALI test.

takes" in the adjudication of criminal responsibility. In short, the standard rests on a policy judgment that "morally correct" results are likely to be achieved more often under a circumscribed test that does not include a volitional criterion than under a broader test that does.

The principal problem with a continued utilization of the volitional or "control" test is that it is often combined with vague or broad interpretations of the term *mental disease.* The mixing of these two imprecise notions results in expert opinions regarding the psychological causes of criminal behavior which strain public credulity and offend moral sentiments, especially in cases involving defendants with personality disorders, impulse disorders, or some other diagnosable abnormality short of a clinically recognized psychosis. One approach to this problem is to restrict the types of mental disorder that can serve as a basis for a nonresponsibility defense. For instance, the American Psychiatric Association has proposed that mental disease and mental retardation be defined, for purposes of the mental nonresponsibility [insanity] defense, as "conditions that grossly and demonstrably impair a person's perception or understanding of reality."[46] While this definition restricts the mental disease or defect threshold, it also makes the volitional prong unnecessary. Anyone whose mental state "grossly impairs perception or understanding" at the time of the offense presumably would be found nonresponsible under the "appreciation" formulation alone. In sum, the control tests cannot be circumscribed so as to avoid moral mistakes without at the same time rendering them irrelevant; the preferable approach is to rely solely on the "appreciation" or "cognitive-affective" test which, as defined below,[47] should encompass all defendants who merit exculpation because of severe mental disorder.

The questionable morality of excusing defendants who can convince juries that their acts were significantly "determined" by even a severe mental disorder is exacerbated by the difficulty of defining the class of defendants who should be disposed of in that manner. The inclusion in the ALI test of a volitional element reflected a wave of clinical optimism that scientific knowledge concerning psychopathology had progressed substantially enough to permit informed judgments about the causes of abnormal behavior. Unfortunately, subsequent experience has not borne out that optimism. Behavioral science has not yielded clinical tools to

46. APA Statement, *supra* note 27, at 12. The APA proposal also explicitly eliminates the volitional prong. *Id.* at 11.

47. *See* note 55 and accompanying text.

calibrate impairments of behavior controls. There is, in short, no objective basis to distinguish between offenders who were undeterrable and those who remained undeterred, impulses that were irresistible and those not resisted, between "substantial" impairment of capacity and some lesser impairment. Whatever the precise terms of the volitional test, the question is unanswerable, or at best can be answered only by "moral guesses."[48] Consequently, as the American Psychiatric Association has pointed out,[49] testimony under the cognitive test is much more likely to be based on a solid scientific foundation than testimony under a volitional criterion. Clinicians can be more precise and arrive at more reliable conclusions about awareness, perceptions, and understanding of an event than about the "causes" of a person's behavior, especially when the determinants of behavior are felt to be unconscious.[50]

---

48. *See* Bonnie, *supra* note 29. *See generally* Morse, *Failed Explanation and Criminal Responsibility: Experts and the Unconscious,* 68 VA. L. REV. 971 (1982). As Lady Wooten has argued,

> It is clear that in certain circumstances the limits of a man's knowledge and understanding can be convincingly demonstrated. Thus, if I am asked to translate a passage from Japanese into English it is indisputable that this is beyond my powers: everyone knows that merely trying harder will not make me any more successful. But if I assert that I have an uncontrollable impulse to break windows, in the nature of the case no proof of uncontrollability can be adduced. All that is known is that the impulse was not in fact controlled; and it is perfectly legitimate to hold the opinion that, had I tried a little harder, I might have conquered it. It is indeed apparent that some people, such as sadistic sexual perverts, suffer from temptations from which others are immune. But the fact that an impulse is unusual is no proof that it is irresistible. In short, it is not only difficult to devise a test of volitional competence the validity of which can be objectively established: it is impossible.

Wooton, Book Review, 77 YALE L.J. 1019, 1026-1027 (1968) (reviewing A. GOLDSTEIN, THE INSANITY DEFENSE (1967)).

49. In its December 1982 Statement on the Insanity Defense, the American Psychiatric Association commented on "volition" by stating that,

> Many psychiatrists . . . believe that psychiatric information relevant to determining whether a defendant understood the nature of his act, and whether he appreciated its wrongfulness, is more reliable and has a stronger scientific basis than, for example, does psychiatric information relevant to whether a defendant was able to control his behavior. The line between an irresistible impulse and an impulse not resisted is probably no sharper than that between twilight and dusk. Psychiatry is a deterministic discipline that views all human behavior as, to a good extent, "caused." The concept of volition is the subject of some disagreement among psychiatrists. Many psychiatrists therefore believe that psychiatric testimony (particularly that of a conclusory nature) about volition is more likely to produce confusion for jurors than is psychiatric testimony relevant to a defendant's appreciation or understanding.

APA STATEMENT, *supra* note 27, at 11.

50. *See generally* Morse, *supra* note 31.

It should be emphasized that a preference for a narrow test of mental nonresponsibility is not based on the view that the defense is now systematically abused. The empirical evidence is to the contrary: Of those pleas that are successful, most are the result of plea bargain arrangements and many more are resolved at uncontested bench trials,[51] meaning that consensus on the nonresponsibility issue is commonplace and that the maligned "battle of the experts" before "impressionable" juries is an extremely rare occurrence. Rather, the rejection of the "control" prong is based in large part on the observation that there are occasional mistakes, most likely to be associated with the volitional criterion. These observations cannot be documented with findings from systematic empirical investigation. No scientific studies have addressed the issue, and the imposing methodological difficulties of conducting such research are readily apparent. In the absence of empirical investigation, it seems sensible to rely on the informed observation of forensic practitioners and scholars, such as those in the American Psychiatric Association.

By doing away with the volitional inquiry and focusing on the extent to which defendants could "appreciate" the wrongfulness of their conduct, the standard is in concert with current clinical expertise and theoretical possibility.[52] The approach endorsed by the Association should help psychiatrists, counsel, and courts focus on the more objective psychiatric factors that should be taken into consideration in determining responsibility for crime. Accordingly, it should reduce expert speculation and offer a more realistic basis to evaluate the exculpatory weight of psychiatric testimony while at the same time preserving the moral imperative of blameworthiness as a predicate for criminal punishment.

---

51. Smith & Hall, *Evaluating Michigan's Guilty but Mentally Ill Verdict: An Empirical Study*, 16 U. MICH. J.L. REF. 77, 94 (1982) (90 percent of defendants found NGRI were adjudicated in nonjury trials, often through a quasi-plea-bargaining process); "Characteristics of Persons Committed to Oregon's Psychiatric Security Review Board," paper presented by Rogers & Bloom, American Academy of Psychiatry & Law Annual Meeting, in San Diego, California (Oct. 1981) (70 percent of Oregon's NGRIs are result of a "plea bargain").

52. It is noteworthy that the APA has endorsed a test for mental nonresponsibility similar to that found in the standard, APA STATEMENT, *supra* note 27, at 12, and that several states have refused to adopt a volitional prong to the defense. *See, e.g.*, State v. Levier, 226 Kan. 461, 601 P.2d 1116 (1979); Hill v. State, 339 So. 2d 1382 (Miss.), *cert. denied*, 430 U.S. 987 (1976); State v. Jacobs, 190 Neb. 4, 205 N.W.2d 662, *cert. denied sub nom.* Jacobs v. Nebraska, 414 U.S. 860 (1973); Comm'r v. Woodhouse, 401 Pa. 242, 259, 164 A.2d 98, 106 (1960); Sollars v. State, 73 Nev. 248, 316 P.2d 917, 920, *reh'g denied*, 73 Nev. 343, 319 P.2d 139 (1957); People v. Wood, 12 N.Y.2d 44, 187 N.E.2d 116, 236 N.Y.S.2d 44 (1962); State v. Law, 270 S.C. 664, 244 S.E.2d 302 (1978).

The Language of the Standard

The claim has been made that once the issue of mental nonresponsibility [insanity] has been placed in front of a jury, the precise language used to guide its deliberations has little or no effect on the outcome.[53] If one looks merely at the effect of certain phrases on the jury treatment of a given amount and type of evidence, as the principal studies of the issue do,[54] one might reasonably conclude that the impact of variations in the substantive test for mental nonresponsibility [insanity] is noticeable only in the most marginal cases. But the impact of particular language on decisions made *before* a jury retires to deliberate also must be considered — the decisions of experts whether or not to testify and, if so, the formulation of their testimony; the strategic decisions by defense counsel relating to the mental nonresponsibility [insanity] defense, direct and cross-examination, and summation; and trial court rulings on the legal sufficiency of the evidence to raise a jury question. Given this constellation of decision points, the cumulative effect of given normative language on a case from the time a nonresponsibility defense is contemplated to the moment the jury reaches a verdict is probably not insubstantial. This would seem particularly true if the choice is between a volitional and cognitive approach; even if the alternatives are *M'Naghten* and one of the appreciation formulations, the precise phrasing could have a significant influence on the resolution of the issue.

With this in mind, several explanatory comments should be made about the wording in paragraph (a). First, the standard uses the word *appreciation* for the same reason it was included within the "cognitive" prong of the ALI test. The drafters of the ALI test discarded the term *know*, which had been used by the House of Lords in the original formulation of the *M'Naghten* test, because the focus of the inquiry into criminal responsibility should not be limited, as the term *know* might suggest, to a defendant's superficial intellectual awareness of the law or prevailing social morality. Instead, the nonresponsibility test should take into account all aspects of a defendant's mental and emotional functioning relating to an ability to recognize and understand the significance of personal actions.[55] The language of the standard allows a proper latitude for ex-

53. *See, e.g.*, A. Goldstein, *supra* note 42, at 213-214.

54. *See, e.g.*, R. Simon, The Jury and the Defense of Insanity (1967).

55. Consider, for example, a woman who shoots her already wounded aunt to "end the suffering," knowing who her victim is and that it is wrong to shoot another, but lacking, because of psychotic regression, the insight necessary to appreciate the actual consequences of her act. *See* Bonnie, *supra* note 29. *See generally* P. Low, *supra* note 10, at 660-669, 675-681.

perts to testify fully concerning the defendant's mental and emotional condition and for juries to consider this testimony in deliberating on the issue of mental nonresponsibility.

A second important feature of the language of paragraph (a) is the use of "wrongfulness" rather than "criminality," both of which are options under the ALI test as originally formulated. Courts have been divided on the appropriate definition of "wrong" under both the *M'Naghten* and the ALI tests. Some courts hold that mentally disordered defendants should be exculpated only if their misunderstanding of reality disabled them from recognizing the illegality of their conduct. Others recognize a broader, essentially moral, criterion.[56] The standard adopts the latter view. Use of the term *criminality* suggests to triers of fact that they ignore even the most florid effects of delusions and hallucinations in any case in which a defendant's conduct would still be criminal had the delusions been true or the hallucinations real.[57] The term *wrongfulness,* which focuses on the extent to which the convictions on the part of actors about their acts were influenced by their mental disorders, is therefore necessary to accommodate adequately the morally significant effects of severe mental illness.[58]

Finally, it should be pointed out that the standard employs the term *unable* to replace the "substantial capacity" language of the ALI test. This has been done both to simplify the formulation and to reduce the risk that juries will interpret the test too loosely. By using the "substantial capacity" language, the drafters of the ALI standard tried to avoid the rigidity implicit in a *M'Naghten* formulation. They correctly recognized

---

56. A leading case in this group of precedents is People v. Schmidt, 216 N.Y. 324, 110 N.E. 945 (1915), *reh'g denied,* 216 N.Y. 762, 111 N.E. 1075 (1916), involving a defendant who claimed that he killed a woman after hearing the voice of God calling upon him to do so as a sacrifice and atonement. In an opinion by Judge Cardozo, the Court of Appeals held that "there are times and circumstances in which the word 'wrong' . . . ought not to be limited to legal wrong." *Id.* at 339, 110 N.E. at 949. In particular, if a person has "an insane delusion that God appeared to [him] and ordained the commission of a crime, we think it cannot be said of the offender that he knows that act to be wrong." *Id.* at 340, 110 N.E. at 949.

57. On the *Schmidt* facts, for instance, the narrow view would focus on whether religious penance is a legal justification for homicide; since it is not, the defendant should be found, despite his psychosis, to appreciate the "criminality" of his act. This result fails to recognize that severely mentally ill persons may become so detached from reality that they are unable to apprehend why their conduct is wrong, and in fact may feel, because of their disorder, that it is morally justified despite its "illegality."

58. A majority of states using the ALI test have adopted this view. Of the twenty-six states that rely on the test, roughly two-thirds use the "wrongfulness" language. *See* Favole, *supra* note 15, at 257-269.

that it is rarely possible to say that mentally disordered persons were totally unable to "know" what they were doing or to "know" that it was wrong; even psychotic persons typically retain some grasp of reality. However, it is unnecessary to retain the phrase *substantial capacity* in order to take into account these clinical realities. Sufficient flexibility is provided by the term *appreciate,* as defined earlier.

Paragraph (b) of the standard defines "mental disease or defect." Only if the inability of defendants to appreciate the wrongfulness of their conduct is attributable to mental disease or defect should they be entitled to exculpation on grounds of mental nonresponsibility [insanity]. As used in this standard, the phrase *mental disease or defect* purposely has been given a legal and not a medical or scientific meaning.[59] It does not refer to and is not coextensive with concepts of "mental disorder" or "mental disability" as those terms are used by mental health or mental retardation professionals for diagnostic and therapeutic purposes. Those concepts are much broader than the categories of psychopathology or disability that ought to cross the threshold of legal significance for purposes of the exculpatory doctrine of mental nonresponsibility [insanity].

On the other hand, the standard does not tie the concept of mental disease or defect to any narrow collection of diagnostic entities. Although it clearly embraces all severe mental disorders which clinicians classify as psychoses, it is *not* limited to them. In a similar vein, it is not possible to state in the abstract that a certain level of retardation (*e.g.,* severe as opposed to moderate or mild) does or does not cross the legal threshold.[60] To impose such limitations would take insufficient account of both the continuing imprecision of the diagnostic process and the unique features of each individual's disorder. Instead, the language of the standard refers to a generic criterion — an abnormal condition that substantially affects mental or emotional processes. Such an effect may be associated with an "impairment" of ordinary functioning (mental disease) or with deficient or retarded development (mental defect).

Simply put, the "impairment of mind" referred to in subparagraph (b)(i) should not be equated with any particular diagnostic category but must be attributable to a substantial process of functional or organic impairment. Mere defects of character or strong passion, if legally rel-

59. *But see* United States v. Smeaton, 762 F.2d 796, 798 (9th Cir. 1985) (definition of mental illness or defect is a "factual medical question, not a legal issue"). *See generally* Slovenko, *The Meaning of Mental Illness in Criminal Responsibility,* 5 J. Leg. Med. 1 (1984).

60. *See* Ellis & Luckasson, *Mentally Retarded Criminal Defendants,* 53 Geo. Wash. L. Rev. 414, 432-444 (1985).

evant in any sense, should be considered only at sentencing. Were it otherwise, the defense would have no threshold at all; every abnormal defendant, and every normal defendant who became abnormally impassioned, could be said to have a "mental disease." It should also be emphasized, however, that the substantial process of functional or organic impairment need not be chronic or enduring; an "acute" psychotic break is a mental disease even in the absence of an underlying psychotic disorder.

Finally, it must be remembered that a mental disease or defect is without exculpatory significance, no matter how severe, unless it resulted in an inability to appreciate the wrongfulness of the conduct at the time of the offense.

The Involuntary Act and Intoxication Doctrines

This standard relates only to the defense of mental nonresponsibility [insanity]; no position is taken that would modify any other commonly accepted rule dealing with criminal responsibility. For example, elimination of the volitional prong of the nonresponsibility test is not meant to modify the traditional "involuntary act doctrine" codified in the Model Penal Code.[61] Under this doctrine, persons do not commit the *actus reus* of a criminal offense if they have no conscious physical control over their behavior at the time of the offense. Thus, for instance, courts have held that physical movements during states of impaired consciousness such as sleep, concussion, or epileptic seizures are not "voluntary acts."[62] Elimination of the volitional prong, which deals with conscious behavior that was not consciously willed, would and should have no effect on this doctrine.

61. ALI MODEL PENAL CODE §4.01 (Permanent ed. with revised commentary 1985).

62. The leading cases include Fain v. Comm'r, 78 Ky. 183 (1879); Polston v. State, 685 P.2d 1, 6 (Wyo. 1984); Regina v. Wakefield, 75 W.N. 66 (New South Wales 1957). *See generally* H. HART, PUNISHMENT AND RESPONSIBILITY 90-92 (1968).

Efforts to establish a compulsion to gamble as a defense to charges of theft have proven consistently unsuccessful. *See, e.g.,* United States v. Davis, 772 F.2d 1339 (7th Cir. 1985); United States v. Gould, 741 F.2d 45, 50-51 (4th Cir. 1984); United States v. Torniero, 735 F.2d 725, 731-732 (2d Cir. 1984), *cert. denied,* 105 S. Ct. 788 (1985); United States v. Llewellyn, 723 F.2d 615, 619 (8th Cir. 1983). *See also* Skeen, *The Genetically Defective Offender,* 9 WM. MITCHELL L. REV. 217 (1983) (chromosone abnormality in relation to the mental nonresponsibility [insanity] defense); Note, *Criminal Law: Premenstrual Syndrome in the Courts?,* 24 WASHBURN L.J. 54 (1984).

Another area of existing law that would remain unchanged concerns the relationship between intoxication and mental nonresponsibility [insanity]. Under traditional rules, impairments associated with voluntary intoxication, no matter how severe or unanticipated, usually do not have exculpatory significance.[63] The only exceptions concern cases lying on the moral border between risks that are and are not voluntarily assumed, when drug use precipitates psychotic deterioration in a predisposed person,[64] chronic alcohol use results in organic brain pathology,[65] or a person has an excessive (or "pathological") reaction to a small amount of alcohol insufficient to induce intoxication in most people.[66] These conditions may result in exculpation either through an interpretation of the nonresponsibility defense or through a parallel interpretation of the involuntary intoxication doctrine. Finally, if persons become intoxicated "involuntarily" (*e.g.*, because someone puts LSD in their coffee), it is clear that the resulting impairment can have exculpatory significance, either because they lack the *mens rea* required in the definition of the offense, their intoxication was "involuntary," or their incapacity was equivalent to that required for the nonresponsibility defense.[67]

Standard 7-6.2. Admissibility of other evidence of mental condition

Evidence, including expert testimony, concerning the defendant's mental condition at the time of the alleged offense which tends to show the defendant did or did not have the mental state required for the offense charged should be admissible.

63. *See* 1 M. Hale, The History of the Pleas of the Crown *32. *See, e.g.*, Linehan v. State, 442 So. 2d 244, 254 (Fla. Dist. Ct. App. 1983), *approved*, 476 So. 2d 1262 (Fla. 1985) (if voluntary intoxication is not a defense to a general intent crime of arson, it is likewise not a defense to a felony murder charge predicated on the arson).

64. People v. Kelly, 10 Cal. 3d 565, 516 P.2d 875, 111 Cal. Rptr. 171 (1973); State v. Maik, 60 N.J. 203, 287 A.2d 715 (1972), *overruled on other grounds*, State v. Krol, 68 N.J. 236, 344 A.2d 289 (1975). *See also* Mandiberg, *Protecting Society and Defendants Too: The Constitutional Dilemma of Mental Abnormality and Intoxication Defenses*, 53 Fordham L. Rev. 221 (1984).

65. Beasley v. State, 50 Ala. 149 (1874).

66. Leggett v. State, 21 Tex. App. 382, 17 S.W. 159 (1887); ALI Model Penal Code §2.08(4) (Permanent ed. with revised commentary 1985).

67. *See* Minneapolis v. Altimus, 306 Minn. 462, 238 N.W.2d 851 (1976). For a full discussion of the concepts covered in this paragraph, *see* P. Low, *supra* note 10, at 713-726.

Commentary Introduction

The standard favors the admissibility of evidence, including expert evidence, bearing on the existence *vel non* of the culpability or *mens rea* required by the statute upon which criminal charges are based, as distinguished from the defense of mental nonresponsibility [insanity].

Related Standards

ABA, Standards for Criminal Justice 7-3.9, 7-6.1, 7-6.3, 7-6.4, 7-6.6, 7-6.9(c), 11-3.3, 18-5.1, 18-6.5
ALI, Model Penal Code §4.02
Federal Rules of Criminal Procedure 12.2
NCCUSL, Defense of Insanity Act, art. 1, §5 (April 1984 draft)

Commentary

This standard makes evidence of abnormal mental condition admissible to the extent it bears on the mental state required for the offense charged. It differs from the mental nonresponsibility [insanity] test proposed in standard 7-6.1 in two respects. First, it focuses solely on the extent to which a defendant intended to commit alleged criminal conduct; it does not permit inquiry into the emotional and intellectual "appreciation" of the consequences of personal conduct. Second, the standard in another sense is broader than the nonresponsibility rule, because it places no "mental disease or defect" restriction on the relevant condition of mind.[1] In taking this position, the Association has allied itself with a substantial number of states,[2] many of which have followed

1. Standard 11-3.3, which also addresses the issue, is equally nonrestrictive. It refers to mental disease, defect or "other condition" bearing upon a defendant's mental state at the time of an offense.

2. Eleven states (Alaska, Arkansas, California, Colorado, Hawaii, Idaho, Maine, Missouri, Montana, New Jersey, Oregon) have adopted provisions, based on the Model Penal Code, providing for admissibility of evidence of mental condition whenever it is relevant to prove any subjectively defined mental state. Several other states (Connecticut, Kentucky, New York, Pennsylvania, Texas, Utah, and Washington), with culpability structures derived from the Model Penal Code (purpose or intent, knowledge, recklessness, negligence), have adopted the rule by judicial decision. Texas limits such evidence to homicide cases. *See generally* Weiner, *Mental Disability and the Criminal Law*, in THE MENTALLY DISABLED AND THE LAW 693, 711 (S. Brakel, J. Parry & B. Weiner eds., 3d ed. 1985).

In jurisdictions employing common law *mens rea* concepts (specific and general intent), at least ten (Iowa, Kansas, Michigan, Nebraska, Nevada, New Mexico, Rhode Island, Utah,

the lead of the Model Penal Code,[3] and has rejected the position reflected in current federal legislation.[4]

Standard 7-6.2 incorporates a simple evidentiary principle based on a rule of "logical relevance." Except in strict liability cases, criminal adjudication always involves determining whether a defendant possessed the *mens rea* for an offense. Therefore, evidence, including properly qualified expert testimony, that tends to show a defendant did or did not have the mental state for a charged offense should be admissible. Such an approach is probably constitutionally required. Several state courts have held that principles of fairness and due process require that defendants be permitted to introduce any competent relevant evidence, including psychiatric testimony, in their defense.[5] It could also be argued that since

---

Vermont) have ruled that evidence concerning a defendant's mental condition at the time of an offense is admissible to prove that the defendant did or did not have a "specific intent" required for conviction. Massachusetts restricts such evidence to homicide cases. About an equal number of states (Arizona, Delaware, Florida, Georgia, Indiana, Iowa, Louisiana, Maryland, Minnesota, North Carolina, Ohio, Oklahoma, Tennessee, West Virginia, Wisconsin, Wyoming) have refused to admit such evidence and eight (Alabama, Illinois, Mississippi, New Hampshire, North Dakota, South Carolina, South Dakota, Virginia) have not addressed the issue directly or clearly. Three states (Idaho, Montana, and Utah) have abolished the insanity defense, replacing it with the *mens rea* rule. *See* commentary to standard 7-6.1, note 36 and accompanying text. Courts in Alaska, Arkansas, and Missouri have limited the rule to specific intent crimes.

3. The Model Penal Code provides that evidence concerning a defendant's mental condition should be admissible at a criminal trial whenever it is relevant to prove that a defendant did or did not have the state of mind required for conviction. ALI Model Penal Code §4.01(1) (Permanent ed. with revised commentary 1985).

4. In the Comprehensive Crime Control Act of 1984, Congress adopted language in 18 U.S.C.A. §20(a) (Supp. 1986) that "mental disease or defect does not otherwise constitute a defense" beyond the complete defense of mental nonresponsibility [insanity]. *See* commentary to standard 7-6.1, notes 18-22 and accompanying text. It further amended Fed. R. Crim. P. 12.2 and Fed. R. Evid. 704(b) to disallow expert opinion other than on the complete defense. Pub. L. No. 98-596, §§402, 404, 406, 98 Stat. 3134 (Oct. 12, 1984).

5. *See* State v. Hines, 187 Conn. 199, 445 A.2d 314 (1982); People v. Wetmore, 22 Cal. 3d 318, 583 P.2d 1308, 149 Cal. Rptr. 265 (1978); Commonwealth v. Walzack, 468 Pa. 210, 360 A.2d 914 (1976); State v. Edmon, 28 Wash. App. 98, 621 P.2d 1310 (1981). *Cf.* Terry v. State, 465 N.E.2d 1085, 1087-1088 (Ind. 1984) (court invalidated state legislation limiting the use of evidence of voluntary intoxication to offenses containing a culpability element of "with intent to" or "with an intention to").

The general principle has been set forth by the United States Supreme Court in Green v. Georgia, 442 U.S. 95 (1979) (capital penalty hearing); Davis v. Alaska, 415 U.S. 308 (1974) (defense had constitutional right to impeach a key prosecution witness on the basis of otherwise privileged juvenile court records); Chambers v. Mississippi, 410 U.S. 284 (1973) (state could not invoke limited concept of declaration against interest to exclude defense evidence from apparently credible sources that someone else had admitted the killing with which Chambers stood charged).

prosecuting attorneys are entitled to a permissive inference that defendants intend the natural consequences of their acts,[6] to deny to defendants an opportunity to present competent clinical evidence that is the only means of overcoming the inference in effect permits the prosecution to convict accused persons despite a reasonable doubt as to their guilt.[7]

States that limit expert evidence to specific intent crimes do not necessarily run afoul of this principle. "Specific intent" refers only to an offender's subjective purpose or belief, while "general intent" is often determined by objective rather than subjective standards. In those jurisdictions, evidence concerning subjective mental state would not be logically relevant in cases involving general intent crimes, because liability will turn not on what a defendant actually perceived, believed, or intended but on what an ordinary person in the same situation would or should have perceived, believed, or intended.

In the great majority of cases, evidence concerning a defendant's abnormal mental condition as it relates to *mens rea* will, if believed, do no more than reduce the grade of the offense. Even if defendants lacked the requisite purpose or knowledge (or "specific intent" in common law jurisdictions), they remain convictable of lesser included offenses requiring only recklessness or negligence (or "general intent" in common law jurisdictions). However, in some cases, mentally abnormal defendants may be entitled to acquittal because they lacked the *mens rea* for *any* offense. In these rare cases, there is a tension between a defendant's right to negate subjective criteria of *mens rea* (by evidence of mental abnormality) and the societal interest in control of possibly dangerous persons. This has led some courts to exclude even relevant evidence of mental abnormality if the effect would be an outright acquittal;[8] it has led others to restrict such evidence to cases in which defendants are charged with some form of intentional homicide.[9]

For the evidentiary and constitutional reasons recounted above, standard 7-6.2 does not recognize any exception to the rule of logical rel-

---

6. *See* Sandstrom v. Montana, 442 U.S. 510 (1979).

7. *Cf.* Hughes v. Mathews, 576 F.2d 1250, 1254-1255 (7th Cir.), *cert. dismissed sub nom.* Israel v. Hughes, 439 U.S. 801 (1978) (invalidating statutory presumption of intent that could not be rebutted by defense psychiatric evidence; effect was to relieve prosecution of burden of persuasion beyond a reasonable doubt on the culpability element of the charged crime).

8. *See, e.g.,* State v. Schantz, 98 Ariz. 200, 403 P.2d 521 (1965), *cert. denied,* 382 U.S. 1015 (1966); Ohio v. Wilcox, 70 Oh. St. 2d 182, 436 N.E.2d 523 (1982).

9. Comm'r v. Gould, 380 Mass. 672, 405 N.E.2d 927 (1980); McClure v. State, 575 S.W.2d 564 (Tex. Crim. App. 1979).

evance. Yet, on the subject of disposition, it should be noted that the special concerns presented when defendants are acquitted for lack of requisite *mens rea* because of mental disability are similar to those presented by defendants acquitted on grounds of mental nonresponsibility [insanity]. The special commitment procedures of part VII governing the latter group could be applied, with some modifications, to defendants acquitted of all charged offenses because of abnormal mental condition at the time the acts constituting the objective elements of those offenses were performed.[10] Of course, general civil commitment procedures are also available to subject such individuals to ongoing noncriminal controls. This standard takes no explicit position on the dispositional issue, however.

The standard contemplates that evidence relevant to *mens rea* may often come in the form of expert testimony. The only limitation on such testimony "should be relevance and the normal requirements for expert opinion."[11] Some courts, perhaps fearful that a rule of logical relevance will open the door to unstructured clinical opinion in a wide array of cases, have misguidedly placed other restrictions on expert opinion. Thus, one finds decisions forbidding expert testimony in cases not involving a severe mental disease or limiting such testimony to the issue of whether defendants possessed a capacity to form the requisite mental state.[12] Once more, based on fundamental evidentiary and constitutional principles and the assumption that courts adequately can monitor the qualifications of expert witnesses, the standard does not adopt these artifices. It should also be remembered in this regard that the narrow scope of *mens rea* testimony involves no inquiry into the often problematic area of volitional impairment,[13] nor does it concern the affective component of

---

10. *See* in particular standard 7-7.4 and commentary.

11. Bonnie & Slobogin, *The Role of Mental Health Professionals in the Criminal Process: The Case for Informed Speculation*, 66 Va. L. Rev. 427, 477 (1980). Standard 7-3.10 summarizes those requirements, which include appropriate educational credentials and evaluation techniques and a showing that the opinion is based on "specialized knowledge which can assist the factfinder." Thus, as discussed more fully in the commentary to standard 7-6.6, an expert should not be permitted to testify that a defendant "premeditated" the crime or committed a homicide with "malice aforethought." Such terms have no clinical content; they are legally defined and should not be used by clinicians. If this testimonial restriction is observed and the other requirements in standard 7-3.10 are met, however, mental health professionals should be allowed to address the *mens rea* issue.

12. *See, e.g.*, United States v. Bright, 517 F.2d 584 (2d Cir. 1975); Bradshaw v. State, 353 So. 2d 188 (Fla. Dist. Ct. App. 1978); Johnson v. State, 292 Md. 405, 439 A.2d 542 (1982); Waye v. Comm'r, 219 Va. 683, 251 S.E.2d 202, *cert. denied*, 442 U.S. 924 (1979).

13. *See* commentary to standard 7-6.1, notes 45-50 and accompanying text.

personality encompassed by the "appreciation" test for mental nonresponsibility.

The standard takes no position on two other issues closely related to this point. The first is the admissibility of evidence of so-called diminished responsibility at the adjudication stage of a criminal case. The term *diminished responsibility* most often is used to refer to grading or sentencing rules that accord mitigating impact to mental abnormality falling short of mental nonresponsibility [insanity] and not negating *mens rea.* No American court has applied the concept explicitly at the guilt determination stage, although criteria for diminished responsibility have been listed specifically in most capital sentencing statutes and, increasingly, in structured sentencing schemes specifying mitigating factors.[14] Given the lack of historical precedent for applying it at trial, and the fact that it usually involves volitional impairment, evidence of diminished responsibility is probably best relegated to posttrial determinations, dealt with in part IX of this chapter.

The standard also is silent on the admissibility of expert testimony concerning a defendant's "character" which, unlike diminished responsibility evidence, has found increasing acceptance in American courts. This development is an outgrowth of the traditional rule that opinion evidence of a "pertinent" trait of an accused's character is admissible if proferred for the purpose of proving that the defendant acted in conformity with that trait.[15] This standard takes no position on whether this type of testimony should be limited in any fashion.[16]

One final definitional point should be noted. The term *diminished capacity* has often been employed in discussions about evidence of abnormal mental condition as it relates to *mens rea.* However, this standard and its commentary have eschewed the use of the phrase because it is mislead-

14. *See, e.g.,* Va. Code §19.2-264.4(B) (1983); standards 18-5.1(d)(ii)(E), 18-6.5(a) and commentary; Nat'l Conf. of Comm'rs on Uniform State Laws, Model Sentencing and Corrections Act §3-108 (Approved Draft 1978).

15. *See* Fed. R. Evid. 404, 405. In United States v. Staggs, 553 F.2d 1073, 1075 (7th Cir. 1977), for instance, testimony by a psychologist that the defendant was more likely to hurt himself than others was admissible to show he could not have formed the intent to assault another with a deadly weapon. Similarly, the court in O'Kon v. Roland, 247 F. Supp. 743 (S.D.N.Y. 1965), permitted psychiatric testimony that the defendant, charged with murder, was a passive person and unlikely to commit a violent act. The problem with such evidence of "character" is that, as *Staggs* and *O'Kon* demonstrate, it tends to resemble a mere assessment of whether a defendant is "good" or "bad." It is thus much broader in scope than testimony about criminal responsibility or *mens rea,* and more subject to abuse.

16. *See* G. Melton, J. Petrila, N. Poythress & C. Slobogin, Psychological Evaluations for the Courts: A Handbook for Mental Health Professionals and Lawyers §6.03(b) (1986).

ing. To apply the term *diminished capacity* connotes the existence of an intermediate criterion of partial culpability — a capacity somewhat impaired but not so fully impaired as to establish a nonresponsibility defense. *Mens rea* testimony does not bear such a linear relationship to the defense of mental nonresponsibility [insanity]: Defendants may have had the requisite *mens rea* in a technical sense, and nonetheless be exculpated under the nonresponsibility defense; conversely, evidence concerning mental condition or functioning may be relevant to the *mens rea* question even though it does not establish a mental disease of a kind or severity required as a predicate for the nonresponsibility defense. Whether evidence of mental condition should be admitted if it is relevant to the existence of a state of mind required for conviction is purely an evidentiary question, not an issue of substantive criminal law doctrine.[17]

Standard 7-6.3. Notice of defense based on mental condition

(a) If a defendant intends to rely upon the defense of mental nonresponsibility [insanity] or to introduce expert testimony relating to mental condition at the time of the offense charged, the defendant should, within the time provided for the filing of pretrial motions or at such later time as the court may direct, notify the prosecuting attorney in writing of such intention and file a copy of such notice with the clerk. The court may, for cause shown, allow late filing of the notice or grant additional time to the parties to prepare for trial or make such other order as may be appropriate. If notice is not given in compliance with the requirements of this standard, the court may impose such sanctions as are provided by law.

(b) Neither the court nor the prosecution should assert a defense based on abnormal mental condition over the objection of a defendant who is competent to make a decision about raising the defense.

Commentary Introduction

The standard recommends a statutory or rule requirement that defendants who intend to assert a defense of mental nonresponsibility [insan-

17. For a full discussion of the issues outlined in the commentary text, *see* P. Low, J. Jeffries & R. Bonnie, Criminal Law: Cases and Materials 312-313, 742-759, 808-815, 831-833 (1982).

ity] or to introduce expert evidence relating to *mens rea* or culpability submit advance written notice of that intent. Courts should be able to impose appropriate sanctions in instances of noncompliance. The standard stresses that the decision to assert a defense based on abnormal mental condition is exclusively that of a competent defendant; neither a court nor a prosecuting attorney can advance it over defense objection.

Related Standards

ABA, Standards for Criminal Justice 4-5.2, 7-3.4, 7-3.8(b), 7-6.1, 7-6.4(a), 7-6.5
ALI, Model Penal Code §4.03
Federal Rules of Criminal Procedure 12.2
NCCUSL, Defense of Insanity Act, art. 3, §5 (April 1984 draft)

Commentary

Virtually all jurisdictions require defendants to submit a written notice of an intent to assert a defense of mental nonresponsibility [insanity] as a means of avoiding surprise at or delay of trial.[1] A failure to comply with notice requirements often results in harsh sanctions. Under the Federal Rules of Criminal Procedure, for example, a failure to notify may lead to disallowance of the mental nonresponsibility [insanity] defense if no sufficient explanation is forthcoming for the omission of notice.[2]

Paragraph (a) of the standard incorporates an Association recommendation that statutes or court rules provide that defendants must give advance written notice of a purpose either to rely on the defense of mental nonresponsibility [insanity][3] or to introduce expert testimony relating to culpability or *mens rea.*[4] This notice provision must be read in conjunction with several other standards contained in this chapter. Most importantly, standard 7-3.4 endorses a legislative or rule requirement

1. *See, e.g.,* United States v. Veatch, 647 F.2d 995, 1002 (9th Cir.), *rereported,* 674 F.2d 1217 (9th Cir. 1981), *cert. denied,* 456 U.S. 946 (1982); Thomas v. State, 420 N.E.2d 1216, 1218 (Ind. 1981); Commonwealth v. Mattson, 377 Mass. 638, 644, 387 N.E.2d 546, 550 (1979); State v. Ingram, 607 S.W.2d 438, 440 (Mo. 1980); Schaffer v. State, 590 S.W.2d 490, 491 (Tex. Crim. App. 1979). *See generally* Weiner, *Mental Disability and the Criminal Law,* in The Mentally Disabled and the Law 693, 720 (S. Brakel, J. Parry & B. Weiner eds., 3d ed. 1985) [hereinafter cited as Weiner].
2. *See, e.g.,* Fed. R. Crim. P. 12.2.
3. *See* standard 7-6.1 and commentary.
4. *See* standard 7-6.2 and commentary.

that defendants apprise the prosecution of a defense-initiated evaluation within a recommended forty-eight hours after that evaluation has begun. After receipt of such notice, the prosecution is entitled to seek its own expert evaluation, the results of which are sealed until the defendant gives notice of an intent to raise a defense under this standard. The notice of evaluation provision is designed primarily to assure the prosecution an opportunity to obtain an assessment as fresh as that achieved by defense experts.[5] Its relevance in the present context, however, is that it serves to inform the prosecution that a defendant is considering a factual defense based on mental abnormality, which is distinct from the legal defense of mental nonresponsibility [insanity].

Assuming this preliminary notice is required, many problems traditionally associated with notice of defense provisions should disappear. The principal problem has been the lack of adequate time to secure rebuttal evidence once notice has been given. Very often, existing provisions do not require a defense notice to the prosecution until shortly before trial.[6] Under paragraph (a), notice of a defense based on mental condition generally will be tendered much earlier, *viz.*, at the time pretrial motions are made. Nevertheless, such a rule, standing alone, may not allow the prosecution sufficient time to prepare an expert rebuttal. The prosecution still might be forced either to seek a continuance to assemble its evidence or to try to ascertain the defendant's intentions at an earlier date through more informal and perhaps less desirable means. On the other hand, a requirement of defense notice imposed far enough in advance to avoid significant inconvenience to prosecuting attorneys could inhibit significantly the defense ability to gauge intelligently its strategic options. The dilemma is resolved by the dual notice scheme of the standards: The defense should have ample time to assess its strategy before it is required to give formal notice under this standard and, even if this notice is given shortly before trial, the prosecution will not be seriously prejudiced because it will already have its own expert evaluation and may have collected other evidence as well in anticipation of a possible defense.

---

5. *See* commentary to standard 7-3.4, notes 1-2 and accompanying text.

6. *See, e.g.*, Ariz. R. Crim. Proc. 15.2 (fifteen days after arraignment); Del. Com. P. Ct. Crim. R. 12.1 (1981) (thirty days before trial); Mo. Ann. Stat. §552-030(2) (Vernon Supp. 1986) (within ten days after entry of plea); Tex. Code Crim. Proc. art. 46.03, §2 (Vernon 1983) (at least ten days before trial date); Va. Code §19.2-168 (1982) (at least ten days before trial).

The following discussion assumes that defendants will use expert testimony to support a defense. *See* commentary to standard 7-6.4, note 8 and accompanying text.

Because, in light of the notice provision of 7-3.4, even a delayed notice of a defense under this standard should not hinder prosecution efforts in most cases, harsh sanctions are not warranted, especially if, as paragraph (a) states, a defendant can show cause for late filing and a continuance can be granted by a trial court. Of course, if defense counsel purposely waits until the last moment to initiate an expert evaluation and give notice of the defense, or gives no notice at all, and a continuance is not feasible or just, some sanction may be appropriate. The most just sanction in such instances appears to be an order excluding defense expert testimony. Excluding *all* evidence of mental condition, as the Federal Rules authorize, is not appropriate. The principal prejudice to the prosecution from delayed or nonexistent notice is an inability to marshal expert assistance to rebut the defense case. A prosecuting attorney still enjoys an ability, unimpaired by the want of a defense notice, to identify and call lay witnesses and to present other evidence in rebuttal. Thus, a sanctionable defendant also should retain the ability to call lay witnesses. Accordingly, no broader sanction is appropriate than an exclusion of defense expert evidence.

The foregoing should not imply that the notice provision of paragraph (a) is irrelevant in jurisdictions that also adopt the notice requirement recommended in standard 7-3.4. Formal notice of an intent to raise a defense obviously is important as a means of telling the prosecution definitively that the defense will be asserted. Moreover, several other provisions in chapter 7 are triggered only if the notice required in this standard has been given. As already mentioned, under standard 7-3.4(b), the notice permits prosecution access to the results of expert evaluations that it commissioned following the defense's notice of its own evaluation. Under standard 7-3.8(b), notice of an intent to raise a defense requires a defendant to provide the prosecution with copies of all written reports prepared by mental health or mental retardation professionals whom the defense intends to call as expert witnesses. Finally, under that standard and standard 7-6.5, after notice has been given under paragraph (a), the prosecution must disclose to defense counsel all materials and information within the prosecutor's possession or control bearing on the defendant's mental condition at issue.

The notice provision in paragraph (a) is likewise a necessary means of informing the prosecution about the form of the defense (mental nonresponsibility [insanity] or *mens rea*) a defense counsel plans to advance at trial. The prosecution, of course, always is on notice that all elements of a charged offense are open to factual challenge. But if the defense intends to call experts on the *mens rea* or culpability issue, the prosecution should be given an opportunity before trial to tailor its expert testimony accordingly.

Given the important functions served by notice of an intent to raise a defense within the scheme of these standards, paragraph (a) recommends a requirement that it be in writing and submitted not only to the prosecutor but to the clerk of the trial court as well. This requirement should ensure that defense counsel, the prosecuting attorney, and the court all have copies of the notice in their possession.

Paragraph (b) rests on the Association's policy position that a competent defendant should control the decision whether or not to raise a defense based on mental nonresponsibility [insanity] or a lack of culpability or *mens rea.* This policy is in accord with standard 4-5.2, which provides that plea decisions are to be made by accused persons after full consultation with counsel. Only if a defendant is not competent to assess adequately the benefits and risks of asserting such a defense should a court be empowered to inject the issue into a criminal prosecution at its own initiative or at the suggestion of the prosecuting attorney.

This has been a matter over which the courts have divided. Some have taken the position that justice is not served by the conviction of defendants who are mentally nonresponsible [insane], even though their competent judgment, concurred in by defense counsel, is that the consequences of a conviction are less onerous than those flowing from an acquittal by reason of mental nonresponsibility [insanity].[7] Others forbid *sua sponte* motions unless a trial court determines on the record that a defendant's decision not to forgo the mental nonresponsibility [insanity] defense was not reached voluntarily and intelligently.[8]

The Association prefers the second approach. It is true, as the commentary to standard 7-6.1 stresses,[9] that there is a strong moral basis

7. *See, e.g.,* Whalem v. United States, 346 F.2d 812 (D.C. Cir.), *cert. denied,* 382 U.S. 862, *reh'g denied,* 382 U.S. 912 (1965), which permitted a trial court to raise the defense over a defendant's objection after assessing several factors, including the defendant's opposition to the defense, the quality of the defendant's reasoning, the viability of the defense, and the court's personal observation of the defendant.

8. *See* Frendak v. United States, 408 A.2d 364 (D.C. 1979), which disallowed *sua sponte* motions unless a court finds a defendant's waiver of the nonresponsibility defense not to be voluntary and intelligent. *See also* Labor v. Gibson, 195 Colo. 416, 419, 578 P.2d 1059, 1060 (1978); State v. Jones, 99 Wash. 2d 735, 664 P.2d 1216 (1983). The *Frendak* court reasoned that since a defendant must be competent to stand trial (and therefore presumably able to assess strategic choices) to be triable on nonresponsibility grounds, the decision to assert the defense is that of a defendant in virtually all cases. *See generally* Weiner, *supra* note 1, at 723-724.

9. *See* commentary to standard 7-6.1, notes 48-50 and accompanying text.

underlying the mental nonresponsibility [insanity] defense.[10] Nevertheless, a competent defendant may find the consequences of a successful assertion of the defense distasteful because, for example, confinement in a mental hospital is less desirable than in a prison, the stigma of the label "insane" is greater than that of "felon" or "misdemeanant," or assertion of the defense carries with it an admission that the defendant committed the *actus reus* or objective elements of a charged offense.[11] All such considerations can be overridden by a court under the first approach.

The Association's position in paragraph (b) also accords a proper recognition to the policies underlying the constitutional right of competent defendants to exercise the right of self-representation.[12] That right expressly extends to an ability to control all significant tactical and strategic decisions, particularly in the course of jury trial.[13] Other factual or legal defenses that destroy blameworthiness, like entrapment or duress, cannot be forced on defendants even though from an objective viewpoint the consequences of a successful assertion are more favorable than a conviction. The same should be true of defenses based on mental nonresponsibility [insanity] or lack of culpability or *mens rea.* A concern that mentally disabled defendants, if acquitted, may be returned to the community without legal controls is simply answered: They can be subjected either to civil commitment or an analogous application of procedures following acquittal on grounds of mental nonresponsibility [insanity].[14] If they are convicted, they can be subjected to the special procedures outlined in part IX. The fact that in practice prosecuting attorneys often call the matter of possible nonresponsibility to judicial attention is all the more reason to deny trial courts the power to interpose a nonresponsibility defense over the objection of competent defendants.[15]

---

10. The *Whalem* court held that this moral basis authorizes the trial judge to impose the defense over the defendant's objection in cases where it is necessary to "withhold punishment of someone not blameworthy." Whalem v. United States, 346 F.2d at 818.

11. *See* Frendak v. United States, 408 A.2d at 376-377.

12. *See* Faretta v. California, 422 U.S. 806 (1975) (competent defendants may waive the right to counsel); *cf.* North Carolina v. Alford, 400 U.S. 25 (1970) (a guilty plea that represents a "voluntary and intelligent choice among known alternatives" waives the alternatives not chosen).

13. *See* McKaskle v. Wiggins, 465 U.S. 168, 174, *reh'g denied,* 465 U.S. 1112 (1984) (a pro se defendant "must be allowed to control the organization and content of his own defense, to make motions . . .").

14. *See* commentary to standard 7-6.2, note 10 and accompanying text.

15. The standard does not address three other important related issues: (1) What should defense counsel's response be to a defendant's refusal, against counsel's professional advice, to assert a mental nonresponsibility [insanity] defense if counsel concludes that not to

The Association position in this regard extends to assertions of a want of culpability or *mens rea,* as distinct from the defense of mental nonresponsibility [insanity]. If anything, the policy decision is easier to reach in this context because a culpability or *mens rea* defense raises none of the unique moral questions about societal obligations inherent in the nonresponsibility defense. In practice, in the absence of statutory provisions authorizing the special commitment of persons acquitted for want of a required culpability or *mens rea* element in a charged offense, neither a court nor a prosecuting attorney is likely to inject the issue if the defense chooses not to.

Paragraph (b), however, requires that a defendant be "competent to make a decision about raising the defense." Generally speaking, defendants competent to stand trial will be competent to waive a nonresponsibility defense. However, some defendants with the rudimentary knowledge of procedural matters required under the constitutional criteria for competence[16] may find it difficult to comprehend the strategical nuances of asserting a particular defense. Paragraph (b) should make it clear that the competency envisioned in this context is that affecting the specific function of deciding, in consultation with defense counsel, whether or not to advance a mental nonresponsibility [insanity] or *mens rea* defense, not competency to participate in trial proceedings as a whole.

Standard 7-6.4. Prosecution-initiated evaluation to determine mental condition

(a) Upon the defendant's giving of notice as provided in standard 7-3.4(a), or, if such notice is not required in the jurisdiction, upon the defendant's giving of notice as provided in standard 7-6.3 and a

---

be a competent decision? The answer to an analogous issue in standard 7-4.2 is that counsel may override a client's objection and move for a competence evaluation and that, in any event, counsel should bring the issue to the court's attention. (2) May a defense attorney override a competent defendant's decision not to assert the defense? Under standard 4-5.2, the decision about what plea to enter should be left entirely to the defendant. (3) May a criminal trial court override defense counsel's decision not to assert the defense on behalf of an incompetent defendant? Frendak v. United States, 408 A.2d 364 (D.C. 1979), *discussed supra* note 8, suggests an affirmative answer. Because these complex issues are not at the moment addressed in parts V and VI, the Standing Committee currently is considering the development of a new standard on competency to plead a mental nonresponsibility [insanity] defense for presentation to the Association House of Delegates.

16. *See* commentary to standard 7-4, notes 7-14 and accompanying text.

finding that the defendant intends to rely upon expert testimony, the court may, on motion of the prosecuting attorney, order the defendant to be examined by an expert designated in the order, for the purpose of determining the mental condition which is being put in issue by the defendant. Should the court find that the defendant has refused to comply with such order, the court may prohibit the defendant from introducing expert testimony on the issue at trial pursuant to the provisions of standard 7-3.4(c).

(b) As provided in standard 7-3.6(c)(ii), a defense attorney may attend the mental examination only with the evaluator's prior approval and may participate actively only if requested to do so by the examiner.

(c) The court should not on its own motion order a mental evaluation of the defendant to determine mental condition at the time of the offense.

(d) As provided in standard 7-3.5(c), the defendant's mental condition at the time of the offense charged should not be combined in any evaluation ordered to determine competency to stand trial, unless the defendant should so request or for good cause shown.

(e) Provisions for recording court-ordered evaluations are set forth within standard 7-3.6(d).

(f) As provided in standard 7-3.2, except as otherwise provided by law no statement made by a defendant during the course of a court-ordered mental evaluation and no evidence obtained as result of such statement should be admissible in evidence against that person in any criminal proceeding on any issue other than an issue of mental condition raised by the defendant.

Commentary Introduction

The standard brings together in one place various principles found in part III of this chapter governing prosecution-initiated evaluations of mental state at the time of an alleged offense. Paragraph (a) summarizes the provisions of standard 7-3.4 concerning prosecution-initiated evaluations after defendants have given notice that a defense evaluation has been initiated, with the added proviso that if a jurisdiction does not require such a notice, prosecuting authorities should be allowed to obtain their own evaluation of defendants who have given notice of an intent to assert a defense based on mental abnormality and to offer expert testimony in support. It recommends as the sanction for a defendant's noncooperation in a prosecution-initiated examination the widely recognized device[1] of excluding defense expert testimony. Paragraph (b) embodies the gist of standard 7-3.6(c)(ii) which, in line with the majority stance on the subject,[2] permits defense counsel to be present at a prosecution-initiated evaluation of mental state at the time of an alleged offense only with an evaluator's prior approval.

Paragraph (c) states in more explicit fashion the implication of standards 7-3.5(b) and 7-6.3(b) that only defense counsel and prosecuting attorneys may request an evaluation of mental state at the time of an alleged offense. Paragraph (d) refers to standard 7-3.5(c), which expresses a preference for single-purpose evaluations whenever possible. Paragraph (e) incorporates by reference standard 7-3.6(d), which provides for the recording of court-ordered evaluations interviews, whether defense- or prosecution-requested. Finally, paragraph (f) repeats the provision in standard 7-3.2 setting forth the currently favored view[3] that no statements by defendants, or evidence or opinions obtained from them, should be admissible on any issue other than a defense of mental condition.

Related Standards

ABA, Standards for Criminal Justice 7-3.4, 7-3.5(b), 7-3.6(d), 7-3.8, 7-3.9, 7-3.12(b), 7-6.3

ALI, Model Penal Code §4.09

Federal Rules of Criminal Procedure 12.2

NCCUSL, Defense of Insanity Act, art. 2, §6; art. 3, §§8, 9, 10; art. 4, §16 (April 1984 draft)

---

1. *See, e.g.,* Karstetter v. Cardwell, 526 F.2d 1144, 1145 (9th Cir. 1975); United States v. Handy, 454 F.2d 885 (9th Cir.), *cert. denied,* 409 U.S. 846 (1971); Ott v. Cushing, 289 Or. 705, 617 P.2d 610, 615 (1980); VA. CODE §19.2-168.1(BN) (1983); WIS. STAT. ANN. §971-16(3) (West 1985).

2. *See* Hollis v. Smith, 571 F.2d 685 (2d Cir. 1978); United States v. Cohen, 530 F.2d 43 (5th Cir.), *cert. denied,* 429 U.S. 855 (1976); United States v. Greene, 497 F.2d 1068 (7th Cir. 1974), *cert. denied,* 420 U.S. 909 (1975); Houston v. State, 602 P.2d 784 (Alaska 1979); People v. Martin, 386 Mich. 407, 192 N.W.2d 215 (1971), *cert. denied,* 408 U.S. 929 (1972).

3. *See, e.g.,* Gibson v. Zahradnick, 581 F.2d 75, 78-79 (4th Cir.), *cert. denied,* 439 U.S. 996 (1978); United States v. Reifsteck, 535 F.2d 1030, 1034 n.1 (8th Cir. 1976); ILL. ANN. STAT. ch. 38, §115-6 (Smith-Hurd Supp. 1985); VA. CODE §19.2-169.7 (1983); MODEL PENAL CODE §4.09 (Permanent ed. with revised commentary 1985).

Commentary

Each of the provisions in this standard attempts to balance the state's need for information about a defendant who is considering a defense based on mental abnormality against a defendant's constitutional prerogatives, specifically, the fifth amendment privilege against self-incrimination and the sixth amendment interest in effective representation. The commentary to this standard will present only the major considerations raised by each paragraph; more detailed discussion may be found in the commentary to the parallel standards in part III.

Judicial precedent recognizes that defendants may be compelled to undergo examination by mental health or mental retardation professionals after defense counsel has given notice of an intent to rely on expert testimony to support a defense of mental nonresponsibility.[4] On the other hand, only a few courts have addressed, with mixed results, whether the prosecution may compel evaluations of defendants who expect only to rely on expert testimony in support of a *mens rea* defense.[5] Paragraph (a) reflects the premise that defendants should have no right to remain silent in either situation. Even if the results of a state-initiated examination will be used to prove *mens rea* or culpability, an element of an offense the prosecution must prove beyond a reasonable doubt, privilege against self-incrimination should not govern. If it did, defendants would be free to rely on unrebuttable expert testimony. The Supreme Court has held that defendants may not invoke the privilege against self-incrimination after they have taken the stand and testified on direct examination.[6] There is no greater justification for permitting them to make self-serving statements through the medium of expert witnesses unless prosecution experts also have been allowed to evaluate them.[7] Accord-

4. *See* Estelle v. Smith, 451 U.S. 454, 465 (1981) (dictum); United States v. Albright, 388 F.2d 719 (4th Cir. 1968); Alexander v. United States, 380 F.2d 33, 39 (8th Cir. 1967); State v. Swinburne, 324 S.W.2d 746 (Mo. 1959).

5. At least one court has held that defendants may not be compelled to undergo a prosecution-requested evaluation if the defense intends only to use expert testimony to negate *mens rea*. State v. Vosler, 216 Neb. 461, 345 N.W.2d 806 (1984). However, two other courts have reached a contrary conclusion. State *ex rel.* Jorgenson v. District Court, 289 N.W.2d 211 (N.D. 1980); State *ex rel.* Westfall v. Crandell, 610 S.W.2d 45 (Mo. App. 1980).

6. *See* Brown v. United States, 356 U.S. 148 (1958); Fitzpatrick v. United States, 178 U.S. 304 (1900).

7. *See* Slobogin, Estelle v. Smith: *The Constitutional Contours of the Forensic Evaluation*, 31 Emory L.J. 71, 95-103 (1982) [hereinafter cited as Slobogin].

ingly, once requisite notice has been given of an intent to assert either defense, the prosecution should be able to compel an evaluation.

This reasoning is valid even if a prosecution evaluation is pursued under standard 7-3.4, because of the protection of a defendant's fifth amendment interests achieved by the standard. Under standard 7-3.4(b), once a defense notice has been given within a recommended forty-eight hours that an evaluation has been obtained or is under way, the prosecution is able, if it wishes, to seek a prompt evaluation of a defendant's mental condition at the time of an alleged criminal act. Only in that way can the prosecution be afforded an opportunity to obtain its own expert assessment of a defendant contemporaneously with the defense evaluation, rather than weeks or months later after written notice has been served of defense counsel's expectation of raising a defense based on mental condition.[8] At the same time, however, standard 7-3.4(b) limits the prosecution to a summary of the results of the evaluation until notice has been given under standard 7-6.3. This achieves a functional protection against compelled self-incrimination at the same time that it safeguards the prosecution interest in fresh data for the benefit of prosecution expert witnesses.

The Association's position preserves as well a maximum scope for defense attorneys, in discharging sixth amendment based responsibilities to provide competent representation, to explore strategic and tactical alternatives without unnecessary pressure from courts or prosecuting attorneys. This is possible before committing themselves to a specific defense theory.

Paragraph (a) also addresses the matter of sanctions for noncooperation on a defendant's part in the course of a prosecution-initiated examination. Among the several alternative sanctions (complete exclusion of all defense evidence in support of a mental condition defense; approval of prosecuting attorney comment on a failure to cooperate; limitation of the defense presentation to matters revealed by a defendant to prosecution experts; and exclusion of all defense expert testimony),[9] the Association in this standard and standard 7-3.4(c) has selected only the latter (exclu-

---

8. It should be noted that in the rare instances in which defendants intend to rely solely on lay testimony to support a defense, the standards envision only the notice described in standard 7-6.3. But that is unlikely to frustrate prosecution efforts to secure rebuttal evidence because continuances are available and, in many instances, expert rebuttal testimony will not be sought. *See* commentary to standard 7-6.3, notes 4-5 and accompanying text.

9. *See* note 1 and accompanying text.

sion of defense expert testimony) as the fairest to both parties.[10] Courts should invoke even that sanction, however, only after they have ascertained that a defendant's noncooperation reflects a deliberate effort to frustrate the prosecution and not an abnormal mental condition that itself may be germane to the nonresponsibility or *mens rea* issue.

Assertions might be made that the sixth amendment right to counsel should include defense counsel's right to attend and observe prosecution-initiated mental examinations for the purpose of reconstructing at trial confrontations otherwise witnessed only by prosecution experts and possibly severely disturbed defendants.[11] The Association's position reflected in paragraphs (b) and (e) and standard 7-3.6(d) is that the ability of defense counsel to prepare adequately is sufficiently protected through the audio or video recording of evaluation interviews,[12] and that a rule mandating counsel attendance is likely to promote disruption of evaluation processes by zealous attorneys. Accordingly, under paragraph (b) and standard 7-3.6(c)(ii), defense counsel may attend mental examinations only if evaluators approve in advance, and must confine themselves to passive observation unless evaluators invite them to discharge a more active role, *e.g.*, to encourage defendants to cooperate and in that way to avoid the paragraph (a) sanctions for noncooperation. An authorizing court might also allow a defense expert to observe a prosecution evaluator's interview with a defendant, in lieu of personal attendance by defense counsel.[13]

The premise of paragraph (c) is that only defense counsel or a prosecuting attorney should be authorized by statute or rule to obtain an evaluation of a defendant's mental state at the time of an alleged offense. A trial judge is not a party to the adversarial process. Just as under standard 7-6.3(b) a court should not be allowed to inject a mental condition defense *sua sponte* into a criminal case, so it should be barred from seeking independent expert mental assessments of defendants who do not pursue an apparently meritorious defense. If a court suspects that incompetence or laxness of defense counsel underlies the failure to advance a nonresponsibility or *mens rea* defense, the appropriate judicial

10. *See* Slobogin, *supra* note 7, at 104-106.

11. *See id.* at 114-127.

12. *See supra* note 2 and accompanying text.

13. *See* Aronson, *Should the Privilege Against Self-Incrimination Apply to Compelled Psychiatric Examinations?*, 26 STAN. L. REV. 55, 91 (1973).

response is discipline or removal of defense counsel, not an order subjecting a defendant to a perhaps unwanted evaluation.[14]

To allow court-generated evaluations also may affect the fairness of trial. Juries may be led to believe that a "court's experts" are more credible or impartial than defense or prosecution experts because of the judicial imprimatur implicit in judicial appointments. Given the vagaries of psychiatric assessments, no expert witnesses are inherently superior to any others,[15] and the legal system should not foster a contrary conclusion.

The general premise in standard 7-3.5(c) that single-purpose and not multiple-purpose evaluations should be the norm is confirmed in paragraph (d), which provides that professional evaluations of mental state at the time of an alleged crime should not be performed in tandem with evaluations bearing on competency to undergo criminal proceedings. The lamentable confusion on the part of some mental health and mental retardation professionals and attorneys concerning competency and nonresponsibility criteria can be guarded against by forbidding dual-purpose examinations unless the defense requests them or the prosecution makes a strong showing that overriding considerations of efficiency support them. The risk of damage to self-incrimination interests is less as well, because material relevant to competence but potentially damaging to a defense based on mental condition at the time of an alleged offense cannot seep from a competency-related evaluator report into another bearing on a substantive penal law defense.[16]

Paragraph (e) rests on the premise that prosecution-initiated evaluation interviews should be recorded on audio or video tape, as provided more generally in standard 7-3.6(d). In that way, defense attorneys can learn during preparation for trial of their clients' statements and reactions in the context in which they appeared.[17] The recordings also should be admissible in evidence, according to standard 7-3.6(d), if defense counsel has given advance notice to the prosecution of an intent to introduce them and if their contents meet jurisdiction evidence rules governing relevancy.[18]

---

14. *See* United States *ex rel.* Laudan v. Turnuld, 423 F. Supp. 1210 (S.D.N.Y. 1976); Model Penal Code §4.02 comment (Tent. Draft No. 4, 1955).

15. *See* Diamond, *The Fallacy of the Impartial Expert*, 3 Archives Crim. Psychodynamics 221 (1959).

16. *See* Slobogin, *supra* note 7, at 94 n.98.

17. *See* Thornton v. Corcoran, 407 F.2d 695, 702 (D.C. Cir. 1969).

18. *See* Fed. R. Evid. 403.

Paragraph (f) confirms the rigid bar in standard 7-3.2 against the use of a defendant's statements in the course of court-ordered evaluations other than in relation to an issue of mental condition asserted by that defendant.[19] That restriction protects both the privilege against self-incrimination[20] and the sixth amendment right to control the character of the defense presentation.[21] Moreover, as a pragmatic consideration, defendants should be less reticent in talking with prosecution experts if they know the prosecution is legally unable to use any of the information so communicated until a defense notice has been submitted under standard 7-6.3; even after that notice has been tendered, the information can be used only in relation to the specific issues contained in the notice, and thus only in the course of the prosecution's rebuttal case, not its case-in-chief.[22]

Standard 7-6.5. Prosecution's duty to disclose

Upon notice that the defendant intends to rely upon an insanity defense [a defense of mental nonresponsibility] or to introduce expert testimony relating to mental condition, the prosecutor should timely disclose to defense counsel all materials and information within the prosecutor's possession or control which bear on the defendant's mental condition at issue, including but not limited to:

(a) any reports or statements made by experts, including the results of mental evaluations and tests;

(b) any written or recorded statements and the substance of any oral statements made by the defendant bearing on the issue;

(c) any information that tends to rebut the factual data upon which the experts called by the defendant are relying; this should include documents, names and addresses of witnesses and their relevant written or recorded statements, and the substance of any oral statements;

(d) the names, addresses, and statements of any experts whom the

19. *See supra* note 3 and accompanying text.

20. *See* United States v. Stockwell, 743 F.2d 123, 127 (2d Cir. 1984) (self-incrimination turns on the use made by the government of information obtained by a government attorney through recordings or personal attendance at a psychiatric examination of a defendant).

21. *See also* commentary to standard 7-6.3, notes 12-14 and accompanying text.

22. Other provisions relating to use and derivative use of evaluation results include standards 7-3.4, 7-3.6(d), 7-3.7, 7-3.8, 7-3.9, and 7-3.12.

prosecutor intends to call for the purpose of discrediting the mental nonresponsibility [insanity] defense or evidence of mental condition.

Commentary Introduction

This standard endorses an express prosecution duty to disclose information bearing on a defendant's mental condition after the defendant has formally put that condition at issue by filing notice of an intent to raise a mental condition defense. The duty to disclose is self-executing; the prosecution must provide the information whether the defense has formally requested discovery.

Standard 7-6.5, like standard 7-6.4, for the most part summarizes the thrust of several part III standards in the setting of part VI, but it imposes certain additional obligations on prosecuting attorneys. Paragraphs (a) and (b) delineate the data, particularly expert reports and statements and statements by defendants, that the prosecution should be required to disclose.[1] Paragraph (c) covers information in the possession or control of prosecuting authorities useable to rebut factual data to be relied on by defense experts, including (1) the identity of and statements made by lay witnesses who observed a defendant's mental condition, (2) medical and psychiatric records, and (3) court and police documents. Paragraph (d) lists discoverable information (names, addresses, and statements) about expert witnesses whom the prosecution intends to call to contest or impeach the testimony of defense expert witnesses in support of defense issues embodied in a standard 7-6.3 notice.

Related Standards

ABA, Standards for Criminal Justice 7-3.1(d), 7-3.4(b), 7-3.6(d), 7-3.8(b), 7-6.3, 11-2.1, 11-3.2
Federal Rules of Criminal Procedure 16
NCCUSL, Defense of Insanity Act, art. 4, §13 (April 1984 draft)

Commentary

This standard endorses a recognition in procedural statutes and rules of an obligation on the part of prosecuting attorneys to disclose information critical or useful to the defense, reciprocal to the defense duty of

1. *See* standards 7-3.1(d), 7-3.4(b), 7-3.6(d), 7-3.8(b)(i) and commentary.

disclosure embodied in standard 7-3.8(b). The latter standard states that after written notice of an intent to raise a defense has been filed, defense counsel should provide the prosecuting attorney with written reports prepared by defense experts who will testify on the issue of mental condition at the time of a charged offense. Both provisions are self-executing; the duty of disclosure is not dependent upon receipt of a motion or request for disclosure by the side for whose benefit the duty to discover exists. This automatic exchange of information, once notice has been given, should promote the fair, straightforward litigation of mental disability issues delineated in standard 7-6.3 notices, forestall unwarranted surprise evidence, and protect defendants' constitutional rights at trial.[2] It should be emphasized that the information listed in the standard as appropriate for prosecution discovery to the defense is not meant to be exhaustive. The intent of the standard is to require the prosecution to reveal all material in its possession or control that might prove relevant to mental state issues raised by a defendant.

Both this standard and standard 7-3.8(b) address discovery before trial, which also is dealt with in detail in chapter 11 of the standards, Discovery and Procedure Before Trial. The interrelationship between chapter 7 and chapter 11 discovery provisions merits further comment.

Under standard 11-2.1, defendants are entitled upon request to an array of information within prosecution possession or control, including names and addresses of witnesses, statements by defendants, reports or statements of experts, and documents the prosecution intends to use at hearing or trial. The defense may seek discovery of these items at any time before trial, in many instances well before notice of an intent to raise a mental condition defense is required under standard 7-6.3. None of standards in chapter 7 is meant to disturb this aspect of chapter 11. Much of the data discoverable under standard 11-2.1 should be provided to defense counsel as early as possible; such information may facilitate counsel's decision whether to obtain a mental evaluation of their clients or to assert a defense turning on mental condition. Standard 7-6.5 simply requires the prosecution, after notice has been given under standard 7-6.3, to disclose statements made by experts, lay witnesses, and the de-

2. *See* Blake v. Kemp, 758 F.2d 523, 532-533, *reh'g denied en banc,* 763 F.2d 419 (11th Cir. 1985) (prosecution withholding of evidence bearing on issue of mental nonresponsibility [insanity] raises a presumption of defense counsel's inability to provide the effective assistance of counsel required by the sixth and fourteenth amendments).

fendant if it has not made them available earlier in response to a defense request under standard 11-2.1.

However, under standard 11-3.2(a), defendants who have requested and received discovery under standard 11-2.1 must, upon a request by a prosecuting attorney, disclose "any reports or statements (including results of physical or mental examinations and of scientific tests, experiments, or comparison) which were made by experts in connection with the particular case and which the defense intends to use at a hearing or trial." Although paragraph (b) of that standard incorporates an exception governing defense work product, that term is narrowly defined to include only research and opinions by defense legal staff and communications by defendants to counsel. Under standard 11-3.2, therefore, a prosecution request could impel defense counsel to reveal expert psychiatric reports (presumably with statements of the defendant deleted) whenever a defense request embraced information listed in standard 11-2.1, even though the defense request has been submitted well before formal notice is required under standard 7-6.3. Such a result would both (1) discourage early defense discovery and (2) run counter to standard 7-3.8(b), which precludes discovery of defense reports before submission of a standard 7-6.3 notice, in order to protect a defendant's fifth and sixth amendment interests and to encourage candor in the evaluation process.[3] Therefore, these latter two standards should be read as creating a narrow exception to standard 11-3.2(a) covering expert opinion and expert-generated facts relevant to a defendant's mental condition, obtained before submission of notice under standard 7-6.3. The prosecution may not gain access to those data until standard 7-6.3 has been complied with, even if the defense has used standard 11-2.1 at an earlier time to obtain information in the prosecution's possession or control.

Standard 11-3.2(c) opposes introduction in evidence of "the fact that the defendant has indicated an intention to offer specified evidence or to call a specified witness." It also states that "information obtained as a result of disclosure pursuant to this standard is not admissible in evidence at trial except to refute the matter disclosed." These two provisions are designed to prevent the defense from being penalized if it changes strategy and decides not to rely at trial upon disclosures made to the prosecution at some earlier time.[4] This principle should apply in the present context as well.

---

3. *See* commentary to standard 7-3.8.
4. *See* commentary to standard 11-3.2.

Standard 7-6.6. Limitation on opinion testimony concerning mental condition

Expert opinion testimony as to how the development, adaptation, and functioning of the defendant's mental processes may have influenced the defendant's conduct at the time of the offense charged should be admissible. Opinion testimony, whether expert or lay, as to whether or not the defendant was criminally responsible at the time of the offense charged should not be admissible.

Commentary Introduction

The standard incorporates Association policy that expert witnesses should be qualified to testify concerning defendants' mental processes at the time of charged offenses, but that neither expert nor lay witnesses should be allowed to express opinions on the ultimate issue of criminal responsibility.

Related Standards

ABA, Standards for Criminal Justice 7-3.9(a), 7-6.1, 7-6.2
ALI, Model Penal Code §4.07
APA, Statement on the Insanity Defense 13-14 (December 1982)
Federal Rules of Evidence 702, 704
NMHA, Myths and Realities, recommendation 9

Commentary

Traditionally neither lay nor expert witnesses have been permitted to address ultimate issues of fact that factfinders must decide. This is still the law in many jurisdictions.[1] Standard 7-6.6 endorses a retention of that rule, which Congress has enacted as well in the Comprehensive Crime Control Act of 1984,[2] through amendments to the Federal Rules of

1. *See, e.g.,* Ibn-Tamas v. United States, 407 A.2d 626, 632 (D.C. 1979); State v. Ellingwood, 409 A.2d 641, 645 (Me. 1979); Waye v. Comm'r, 219 Va. 683, 696, 251 S.E.2d 202, 210, *cert. denied,* 442 U.S. 924 (1982). *See generally* Weiner, *Mental Disability and the Criminal Law,* in The Mentally Disabled and the Law 693, 721 (S. Brakel, J. Parry & B. Weiner eds., 3d ed. 1985).
2. Pub. L. No. 98-596, §406, 98 Stat. 3134 (approved Oct. 12, 1984).

Evidence.[3] The Association's view is shared by the American Psychiatric Association[4] and the National Mental Health Association's Commission on the Insanity Defense.[5] The standard by design does not identify precisely what language beyond "responsible" or "not responsible," or "sane" or "insane" should be prohibited in implementing statutes or rules.

The theoretical rationale for the common law prohibition against ultimate issue testimony was that it usurped the province of the jury. Its practical basis was a fear that jurors would be swayed unduly by the authority of expert witnesses on issues a jury alone was to decide. To these concerns could be added a third, *viz.*, that ultimate issue testimony might tempt witnesses to confine themselves to mere conclusions rather than to describe the bases for them, to the detriment of the factfinding process.[6]

Admittedly, several devices can temper these hazards, including cross-examination, testimony by rebuttal witnesses, and arguments of counsel. Courts always can instruct juries that they are the sole judges of credibility, the sole finders of fact, and the sole determiners of inferences properly to be drawn from credible facts. Admonitions of this nature can be reinforced by reminders that jurors can believe the basic facts on which witness testimony rests without sharing a witness's opinions or inferences. It must be conceded as well that a ban on ultimate issue testimony can be artificial, because clever witnesses, or cleverly coached witnesses, can always find ways to paraphrase forbidden language. That premise no doubt powerfully reinforces state evidentiary rules allowing ultimate opinion evidence.[7]

---

3. Fed. R. Evid. 704 (as amended). Congress intended to eliminate "the confusing spectacle of competing expert witnesses testifying to directly contradictory conclusions as to the ultimate legal issue to be found by the trier of fact." Report of the Committee on the Judiciary, United States Senate, on the Comprehensive Crime Control Act of 1983, S. 1762, Report No. 98-225, 98th Cong., 1st Sess. (1983), at 230. The provision does not affect crime, punishment, and the quantum of proof necessary to sustain a conviction, and so may be applied retroactively without impairing the *ex post facto* clause. United States v. Prickett, 604 F. Supp. 407 (S.D. Ohio 1985).

4. American Psychiatric Association, Statement on the Insanity Defense 13-14 (1982) [hereinafter cited as APA Statement].

5. Nat'l Mental Health Ass'n, Myths and Realities: A Report of the National Commission on the Insanity Defense 41-42 (1983).

6. For a discussion of the ban on ultimate issue testimony, *see* Washington v. United States, 390 F.2d 444 (D.C. Cir. 1967); A. Goldstein, The Insanity Defense 96-105 (1967).

7. *See, e.g.*, Mich. Evid. R. 704.

Nevertheless, these arguments are unpersuasive in the context of expert testimony about criminal responsibility. The gap between legal conclusions and expert opinions may be negligible in the context of some issues, for example, competence to undergo criminal trial proceedings. But the same cannot be said of mental nonresponsibility [insanity], which ultimately is entirely a matter of moral blameworthiness, not medical or psychological inquiry. Thus, more so than in other areas, proferred expert conclusions on criminal responsibility are likely to reflect personal conjecture rather than professional judgments based on the specialized knowledge required to qualify witnesses as experts.[8] The legal defect in such purportedly expert opinion evidence is compounded by the aura of authority surrounding mental health and mental retardation professionals as witnesses that easily may lead jurors to place special credence in their opinions, particularly when presented credibly and not vigorously challenged.[9]

The ban on ultimate issue testimony recommended in standard 7-6.6 is not meant to minimize the importance of expert testimony on issues of

---

8. Even under the Federal Rules of Evidence before their amendment by Congress, *see supra* note 3, "ultimate" conclusions about mental nonresponsibility [insanity] arguably were excludable because they did not meet the "specialized knowledge" predicate for expert opinion testimony under rule 702.

9. Similar sentiments have been expressed by the American Psychiatric Association:

> The American Psychiatric Association is not opposed to legislatures restricting psychiatric testimony about the . . . ultimate legal issues concerning the insanity defense. We adopt this position because it is clear that psychiatrists are experts in medicine, not the law. As such, the psychiatrist's first obligation and expertise in the courtroom is to "do psychiatry," i.e., to present medical information and opinion about the defendant's mental state and motivation and to explain in detail the reason for his medical-psychiatric conclusions. When, however, "ultimate issue" questions are formulated by the law and put to the expert witness who must then say "yea" or "nay," then the expert witness is required to make a leap in logic. He no longer addresses himself to medical concepts but instead must infer or intuit what is in fact unspeakable, namely, the *probable relationship* between medical concepts and legal or moral constructs such as free will. These impermissible leaps in logic made by expert witnesses confuse the jury. Juries thus find themselves listening to conclusory and seemingly contradictory psychiatric testimony that defendants are either "sane" or "insane" or that they do or do not meet the relevant legal test for insanity. . . .
>
> Psychiatrists, of course, must be permitted to testify fully about the defendant's psychiatric diagnosis, mental state and motivation (in clinical and commonsense terms) at the time of the alleged act so as to permit the jury or judge to reach the ultimate conclusion about which they, and only they, are expert. Determining whether a criminal defendant was legally insane is a matter for legal factfinders, not for experts.

APA STATEMENT, *supra* note 4, at 14 (emphasis in original).

mental condition; in fact, it should enhance its usefulness.[10] Expert witnesses are needed to shed light on the inner workings of defendants' minds at the time of alleged criminal offenses. Thus, although experts may not offer opinions whether defendants were criminally responsible, they may explain the mental or emotional processes that may have influenced defendants' perceptions, judgments, and conduct. If, for example, they are persuaded from the data that defendants were suffering an acute phase of a schizophrenic disorder at the time of a charged offense, they might express opinions that defendants' perceptions or understandings of reality were quite likely disturbed by hallucinations or delusions. Opposing expert witnesses may believe that the data do not support those inferences and that hallucinations reflect convenient rationalizations by malingerers, and testify accordingly. Whatever the content of professional expert opinion evidence, to shift the focus of psychiatric testimony from stark conclusions of law toward descriptions of psychic functioning and the data supporting them cannot help but provide triers of fact with enhanced information upon which to reach the ultimate conclusions required of them.

Problems will naturally arise in administering a ban against ultimate issue testimony. Although experts have no clinical basis to use terms like *sane* and *insane*, or *responsible* and *not responsible*, other terms like *appreciate* have clinical content because they refer to mental and emotional phenomena. Critics of the approach recommended in standard 7-6.6 are correct when they predict that expert witnesses barred from using such terms merely will paraphrase the language of legal tests for mental nonresponsibility [insanity] or culpability to convey the same conclusion, for example, by using the term *understanding*. To allow experts to couch their professional opinions in legal language is too facile a solution to this problem, however. The proper limits to so-called ultimate issue testimony cannot be determined fully in the abstract. In the context of specific testimony (such as use of the word *appreciate*), courts must choose between the two important principles reflected in standard 7-3.9(a): (1) that expert opinion testimony should be admitted whenever it is based on a witness's specialized knowledge and will assist the trier of fact; and (2) that expert witnesses should not be permitted to express opinions on

10. It should be noted that the exclusion of qualified defense mental health or mental retardation expert witnesses on the issue of mental nonresponsibility [insanity] or a *mens rea* defense denies due process of law. *See* Boykins v. Wainwright, 737 F.2d 1539, 1544 (11th Cir.), *reh'g denied*, 744 F.2d 97 (11th Cir. 1984), *cert. denied*, 105 S. Ct. 1775 (1985).

"any question requiring a conclusion of law or a moral or social value judgment properly reserved to the court or to the jury." It is for this reason that standard 7-6.6 does not address issues of the admissibility of specific types of "penultimate" testimony, which must be resolved on an individual basis.

The principal governing factor in determining the propriety of expert witness use of particular language under standard 7-3.9(a) should be the specificity of the statutory language defining the mental nonresponsibility [insanity] defense or the judicial glosses on it. The more technical and specific the meaning of a statutory term, the stronger the arguments become for barring its use by expert witnesses. If, for example, "appreciation" has been well defined through appellate opinions, clinicians should not be asked to testify in terms of appreciation. If, on the other hand, it has been given no legal meaning beyond its inclusion in statutory language, witness use of it might be permissible. A second concern in such instances is a jurisdiction's general rule of practice governing ultimate issue testimony. If such testimony is barred, the use of penultimate language should be proscribed as well, regardless of the extent to which it has assumed a legal nuance. However, in jurisdictions that allow ultimate-issue opinions, the technical nature of the language should prove the paramount concern.

A similar analysis should determine the admissibility of expert testimony concerning other issues bearing on criminal responsibility, most significantly, whether or not defendants had a mental disease or defect. Because "mental disease or defect" purposely has been given a legal and not a medical or scientific meaning in standard 7-6.1(b), the case for excluding expert opinion phrased in such terms is strong. Such a bar would not have an unduly restrictive effect on the expression of clinical opinions because experts remain free to use the clinical concept of "mental disorder" as well as the specific diagnostic nomenclature on which they rely. Once again, however, counsel predictably will ask expert witnesses to express opinions that simply paraphrase the definition of mental disease or defect found in standard 7-6.1[11] Jurors, counsel, and expert witnesses should be cautioned that such language is not necessarily congruent with the legal test and is merely additional evidence to be considered on the issue by the trier of fact.

---

11. *See* standard 7-6.1(b) ("impairment of mind . . . which substantially affects mental or emotional processes").

Although the standard does not address the matter directly, the ultimate issue limitation quite appropriately may govern expert opinion evidence bearing on culpability or *mens rea.*[12] Terms like *premeditation, malice,* and *provocation* have technical legal meanings concerning which mental health or mental retardation professionals can pretend no expertise. Expert testimony in such cases should focus on facts and the inferences to be drawn from them relating to cognitive impairment experienced by defendants at the time of charged offenses; they should be expressed in comprehensible, nonlegal language.

Standard 7-6.7. A unitary trial

The defense of mental nonresponsibility [insanity] and all other evidence pertaining to the defendant's responsibility for the acts charged should be heard in a unitary trial unless, upon the defendant's request, the court determines that trying the issue of guilt separately from the issue of responsibility is necessary to prevent substantial prejudice to the defendant.

Commentary Introduction

The standard expresses a preference for a single proceeding embracing both objective guilt and mental nonresponsibility [insanity] issues, although some circumstances may justify bifurcated proceedings.

Related Standards

ABA, Standards for Criminal Justice 7-6.2
NCCUSL, Defense of Insanity Act, art. 7, §§14, 19 (April 1984 draft)

Commentary

At one time, eight states required by statute that prosecutions involving a defense of mental nonresponsibility [insanity] be tried in two stages, the second of which was devoted to resolution of the responsibil-

12. *See* standard 7-6.2 and commentary.

ity issue.[1] Today, only three of them retain mandatory bifurcation statutes,[2] and one other state by judicial decision has held that defendants have a constitutional right to request a bifurcated trial.[3] Most states leave bifurcation to judicial discretion once defendants have moved for it.[4] In contrast, at least nine states require a unitary trial.[5]

Under typical bifurcation statutes, the issue of objective or factual guilt is tried first; a determination of criminal responsibility follows for defendants who are found at the conclusion of the first stage to have committed the objective elements of charged offenses.[6] By deferring psychiatric testimony on nonresponsibility until after the first determination, bifurcation promises to (1) avoid jury confusion that might result from superimposing such testimony on other issues arising at trial; (2) eliminate a risk that juries may return compromise verdicts of mental nonresponsibility [insanity]; (3) save judicial resources in cases where defendants are acquitted at the first stage; and (4) protect defendants' fifth amendment privilege against self-incrimination.[7]

Despite these apparent advantages, however, most state courts that

---

1. Arizona, California, Colorado, Florida, Louisiana, Texas, Wisconsin, Wyoming.

2. Cal. Penal Code §1026 (West Supp. 1986); Colo. Rev. Stat. §16-8-104 (1978); Wis. Stat. Ann. §971-175 (West 1985).

3. Novosel v. Helgemoe, 118 N.H. 115, 384 A.2d 124 (1978).

4. *See* Pa. Stat. Ann. tit. 50, §7404(c) (Purdon Supp. 1985); United States v. Greene, 489 F.2d 1145 (D.C. Cir.), *cert. denied,* 419 U.S. 977 (1973), *reh'g denied,* 419 U.S. 1041 (1973); Nielsen v. State, 623 P.2d 304 (Alaska 1981); Garret v. State, 320 A.2d 745 (Del. 1974); State v. Armstrong, 344 A.2d 42 (Me. 1975); People v. Newbury, 53 Ill. 2d 228, 290 N.E.2d 592 (1972); Montague v. State, 266 Ind. 51, 360 N.E.2d 181 (1977); Commonwealth v. Haas, 373 Mass. 545, 369 N.E.2d 692 (1972); People v. Meatte, 98 Mich. App. 74, 296 N.W.2d 190 (1980); State v. Ward, 301 N.C. 469, 272 S.E.2d 84 (1980); State v. Helms, 284 N.C. 508, 201 S.E.2d 850, *cert. denied,* 419 U.S. 977 (1974); State v. Kahn, 175 N.J. Super. 72, 417 A.2d 585 (1980); State v. Hohman, 138 Vt. 502, 420 A.2d 852 (1980); State v. Jones, 32 Wash. App. 359, 647 P.2d 1039 (1982), *vacated on other grounds,* 99 Wash. 2d 635, 664 P.2d 1216 (1983); State v. Boyd, 280 S.E.2d 669 (W. Va. 1981).

5. Simpson v. State, 275 A.2d 794 (Del. 1970); People v. Newbury, 53 Ill. 2d 228, 290 N.E.2d 592 (1972); State v. Levier, 226 Kan. 461, 601 P.2d 6 (1979); State v. Gray, 351 So. 2d 448 (La. 1977); Langworthy v. State, 284 Md. 588, 399 A.2d 578 (1979); Bremer v. State, 18 Md. App. 291, 307 A.2d 503, *cert. denied,* 415 U.S. 930 (1973); Commonwealth v. Bumpes, 362 Mass. 672, 290 N.E.2d 167 (1972), *vacated on other grounds,* 411 U.S. 945 (1973); State v. Olson, 156 Mont. 339, 480 P.2d 822 (1971); State v. Luna, 93 N.M. 773, 606 P.2d 183 (1980); State *ex rel.* Johnson v. Dale, 277 Or. 359, 560 P.2d 650 (1977); Stone v. State, 521 S.W.2d 597 (Tenn. 1974); Jackson v. State, 548 S.W.2d 685 (Tex. Crim. App. 1975).

6. In Colorado the hearing on the criminal responsibility issue is held first. Only if the finding is adverse to a defendant does trial proceed to the second issue. Colo. Rev. Stat. §16-8-104 (1978).

7. A unitary trial threatens to impair that right because psychiatric testimony on mental state at the time of a charged offense often rests heavily on a defendant's own statements,

have considered the issue have held that mandatory bifurcation violates due process.[8] They reason that the prosecution is responsible to prove all elements of a charged offense. To exclude at the guilt determination phase evidence of mental abnormality that tends to negate the requisite state of mind (as evidence of mental nonresponsibility sometimes does) in effect permits convictions in cases in which the prosecution might not be able to meet its burden of persuasion. It can also be argued that persons should not be found "guilty" at the first stage if in fact they are not criminally responsible.[9]

The practical result of the majority stance is that mandatory bifurcation loses its allure. To comply with due process, relevant evidence of mental abnormality must be allowed at the first stage as well as the second, which uselessly duplicates evidence and nullifies many of the supposed advantages of bifurcation.[10]

Nevertheless, to conclude that mandatory bifurcation is constitutionally infirm and inefficient in application does not necessarily mean that the procedure is never appropriate. As several courts have indicated, there may be circumstances in which a two-stage procedure is appropriate, especially if defendants do not intend to present evidence of mental abnormality on the *mens rea* or culpability issue. In such cases, if defendants have a colorable defense on the merits, as well as a tenable defense

---

which might be revealed to the jury on direct or cross-examination of an expert. Bifurcation enables defendants to force the prosecution to prove its case without their help before they need produce potentially incriminating evidence of mental nonresponsibility [insanity].

8. *See* State v. Shaw, 106 Ariz. 103, 471 P.2d 715 (1970), *cert. denied sub nom.* Arizona v. Shaw, 400 U.S. 1009 (1971); State *ex rel.* Boyd v. Green, 355 So. 2d 789 (Fla. 1978); Sanchez v. State, 562 P.2d 270 (Wyo. 1977).

9. The Wyoming legislature attempted to avoid this dilemma through a statute providing for a first stage hearing restricted to "whether the defendant in fact committed the acts charged in the alleged criminal offense." Wyo. Stat. §11-305(a) (1977) (repealed); the current statute is *ibid.* (Supp. 1985). In other words, both the mental nonresponsibility and *mens rea* issues were relegated to the second stage; the jury's chore at the first stage was merely to determine whether the *actus reus* was committed, not to make a determination of "guilt." The Wyoming Supreme Court found this scheme deficient because juries might in fact determine guilt at the first stage, which would prejudice defendants at a later hearing. Sanchez v. State, 467 P.2d 270 (Wyo. 1977).

Only the Wisconsin Supreme Court has ruled that evidence of mental abnormality relevant to *mens rea* issues may be excluded at the first stage of a mandatorily bifurcated procedure. Steele v. State, 97 Wis. 2d 72, 294 N.W.2d 2 (1980). As the commentary to standard 7-6.2, note 14 and accompanying text, makes clear, both the evidentiary principle of logical relevance and due process concerns dictate the opposite conclusion.

10. In view of this, the California Supreme Court recommended that the legislature repeal the bifurcation statute in favor of a unified trial system. People v. Wetmore, 22 Cal. 3d 318, 331, 583 P.2d 1308, 1317, 149 Cal. Rptr. 265, 274 (1978).

of mental nonresponsibility [insanity], and can show that to permit expert testimony on the latter issue at a unitary trial would jeopardize a defense on the merits because incriminating or otherwise prejudicial information might be revealed to a jury, courts have been willing to allow bifurcation.[11]

Although standard 7-6.7 expresses the Association's preference for unitary trials, it recognizes the appropriateness of bifurcation in cases of the above sort. Defendants should not have to waive their fifth amendment rights as the price of asserting a mental nonresponsibility [insanity] defense. Instructing juries to consider expert testimony about a defendant's mental state only when deciding the issue of criminal responsibility, and to disregard it when deliberating on other issues,[12] does not alleviate the prejudice inherent in the sorts of cases described above.[13] On the other hand, if an assertion of a nonresponsibility defense amounts in essence to "confession and avoidance," admitting an offense but alleging it was excusable, or if defendants also present expert testimony bearing on *mens rea,* bifurcation would not appear to be justified even in cases in which psychiatric testimony might prove incriminating.

Standard 7-6.8. Instruction to the jury

The court should instruct the jury as to the dispositional consequences of a verdict of not guilty by reason of mental nonresponsibility [insanity].

Commentary Introduction

The standard recommends the adoption of procedural statutes or rules allowing juries to be instructed about the dispositional consequences of acquittals based on mental nonresponsibility [insanity].

---

11. *See, e.g.,* United States v. Greene, 489 F.2d 1145 (D.C. Cir. 1973), *cert. denied,* 419 U.S. 977 (1974); United States v. Bennett, 460 F.2d 872 (D.C. Cir. 1972); State v. Armstrong, 344 A.2d 42 (Me. 1975). *See also* Garrett v. State, 320 A.2d 745 (Del. 1974); People v. Donaldson, 65 Mich. App. 588, 237 N.W.2d 570 (1975); State *ex rel.* Johnson v. Dale, 277 Or. 359, 560 P.2d 650 (1977).

12. *See, e.g.,* Gibson v. Zahradnick, 581 F.2d 75, 79 (4th Cir.), *cert. denied sub nom.* Mitchell v. Gibson, 439 U.S. 996 (1978); State v. Whitlow, 45 N.J. 3, 21, 210 A.2d 763, 772 (1965).

13. *See* Bruton v. United States, 391 U.S. 123, 135-137 (1968); Jackson v. Denno, 378 U.S. 368, 388-389 at n.15 (1964); Krulewitch v. United States, 336 U.S. 440, 453 (1949) (Jackson, J., concurring).

Related Standards

ABA, Standards for Criminal Justice 7-6.1, 7-6.9, 7-6.10(a), 7-7.1 through 7-7.9

NCCUSL, Defense of Insanity Act, art. 7, §18 (April 1984 draft)

Commentary

In most states, persons acquitted by reason of mental nonresponsibility [insanity] are automatically committed to mental hospitals for evaluation and observation, after which they may become respondents in commitment hearings that apply either normal civil commitment criteria or similar criteria designed to confine mentally disabled persons who are dangerous.[1] Under the standards in part VII, acquittees who at trial were found beyond a reasonable doubt to have committed the *actus reus* elements of felonies involving serious bodily harm may be confined for evaluation up to a recommended maximum of thirty days or longer, if cause is shown.[2] After evaluation, they may be committed for a time not to exceed the maximum term associated with the predicate felony, subject to periodic review.[3] In order to commit acquittees initially and to continue confinement, courts must find by clear and convincing evidence that acquittees (1) are mentally ill or mentally retarded, (2) pose a substantial threat of serious bodily harm to others, or (3) do not meet the first two criteria solely because they are undergoing treatment or habilitation that is not likely to continue unless they are confined in a secure facility.[4] Standard 7-6.8 proposes that trial juries be told of these dispositional consequences, at least in general terms, before they retire to deliberate on a verdict.

At the present time at least twenty-three states[5] and several federal

---

1. *See generally* Note, *Commitment Following an Insanity Acquittal,* 94 Harv. L. Rev. 605, 605-607 (1981).
2. *See* standard 7-7.2 and commentary.
3. *See* standards 7-7.3(a), 7-7.7(a), 7-7.8(a)-(b) and commentary.
4. *See* standards 7-7.4(b), (d), 7-7.8(b) and commentary.
5. Arizona, Arkansas, Connecticut, Delaware, Georgia, Illinois, Iowa, Maine, Michigan (People v. Goad, 421 Mich. 20, 32, 364 N.W.2d 584, 590 (1984)), Minnesota, Montana, Nebraska, New Mexico, New York, North Dakota (State v. Huber, 361 N.W.2d 236, 238 (N.D.), *cert. denied,* 105 S. Ct. 2339 (1985)), Ohio, Oklahoma, Rhode Island, South Dakota, Texas, Virginia, Washington, and Wyoming. In State v. McDonald, 472 A.2d 424, 426 (Me. 1984), the court reversed a conviction on grounds of prosecutorial misconduct when the prosecutor had commented that the defense claim of insanity was merely a subterfuge employed by the defendant to evade responsibility for his acts.

circuits[6] have ruled it is not error to refuse a dispositional instruction; other states have prohibited such instructions altogether.[7] Two states allow a trial court to give an instruction *sua sponte.*[8] Roughly eight states and at least one federal court allow such an instruction at defense request.[9] Only about six states hold, in line with the Association's recommended position, that defendants are entitled to have juries learn the consequences of a nonresponsibility verdict.[10]

The principal argument against informing juries about the disposition of persons found mentally nonresponsible [insane] is that it may distort the decisionmaking process. Jurors are not told of possible sentencing alternatives on the grounds that their decision about guilt might then be based on irrelevant considerations. Similarly, the argument goes, jurors should not be told that defendants acquitted by reason of mental nonresponsibility [insanity] will be confined in hospitals; otherwise, they may

6. *See, e.g.,* Government of the Virgin Islands v. Fredericks, 578 F.2d 927 (3d Cir. 1978) (harmless error to refuse to give instruction; information communicated during voir dire); United States v. Greene, 497 F.2d 1068, 1076 (7th Cir. 1974), *cert. denied,* 420 U.S. 909 (1975) (instruction need not be given; Congress should decide whether such an instruction is appropriate); Pope v. United States, 298 F.2d 507 (5th Cir. 1962) (same); Lyles v. United States, 254 F.2d 725, 728-729 (D.C. Cir. 1957), *cert. denied,* 356 U.S. 961 (1958), 362 U.S. 943 (1960), 368 U.S. 992 (1962), *modified on other grounds,* United States v. Brawner, 471 F.2d 969 (D.C. Cir. 1972) (instruction should be given), *and see* United States v. Hinckley, Crim. Case No. 81-306 (D.C. Cir. 1982) (jury should be instructed of consequences that the court would commit an acquitted defendant to St. Elizabeth's Hospital, from which he would be released should the court find by a preponderance of the evidence that he is not likely to injure himself or other persons due to mental disease). *See also infra* note 14.

7. *See, e.g.,* Payne v. Commonwealth, 623 S.W.2d 867 (Ky. 1981), *cert. denied sub nom.* Payne v. Kentucky, 456 U.S. 909 (1982); State v. Huiett, 271 S.C. 205, 246 S.E.2d 862 (1978); State v. Smith, 136 Vt. 520, 396 A.2d 126 (1978) ("should" not be instructed).

8. *See* Commonwealth v. Callahan, 380 Mass. 821, 406 N.E.2d 385 (1980); State v. Shaffner, 31 Wis. 2d 412, 143 N.W.2d 458 (1966).

9. *See* Lyles v. United States, 254 F.2d 725 (D.C. Cir. 1957), *cert. denied,* 356 U.S. 961 (1958), 362 U.S. 943 (1960), 368 U.S. 992 (1962), *modified on other grounds,* United States v. Brawner, 471 F.2d 969 (D.C. Cir. 1972); People v. Thomson, 197 Colo. 299, 592 P.2d 803 (1979); Isley v. State, 354 So. 2d 457, 458 (Fla. 1978); State v. Amorin, 58 Haw. 623, 627-628, 574 P.2d 895, 897-899 (1978); People v. Boyd, 222 Kan. 155, 563 P.2d 446 (1977) (absent a showing of prejudice); State v. Babin, 319 So. 2d 367 (La. 1975); People v. Rone, 109 Mich. App. 702, 311 N.W.2d 835 (1981); State v. Pike, 512 S.W.2d 505 (Mo. App. 1974); State v. Lister, 122 N.H. 603, 448 A.2d 395 (1982).

10. *See* State v. Hamilton, 216 Kan. 559, 534 P.2d 226 (1975); Williams v. Page, 160 N.J. Super. 354, 389 A.2d 1012 (1978); State v. Taylor, 290 N.C. 220, 226 S.E.2d 23 (1976); Commonwealth v. Mulgrew, 475 Pa. 271, 380 A.2d 349 (1977); Mothershed v. State, 578 S.W.2d 96 (Tenn. Crim. App. 1978); Glasscock v. State, 570 S.W.2d 354 (Tenn. Crim. App. 1978), *cert. denied,* 441 U.S. 943 (1979); State v. Boyd, 280 S.E.2d 669 (W. Va. 1981).

be more willing to find defendants insane as a compromise between prison and a return to the community.[11] Juries that remain unaware of the consequences of a mental nonresponsibility [insanity] finding are more likely to base their decisions solely on the evidence before them than if they are aware of the disposition to be made of defendants whom they acquit.

The position taken in the standard reflects a contrary view that, despite instructions cautioning them to consider only the evidence they have heard, jurors who are not informed about dispositional consequences will speculate about the practical results of a nonresponsibility verdict and, in ignorance of reality, will convict persons who are not criminally responsible in order to protect society. Jurors surely know, without being told, what happens to most convicted offenders, as well as defendants who are acquitted outright; the proposed instruction provides the same level of knowledge with respect to the fate of persons acquitted by reason of mental nonresponsibility [insanity].

Both stances are based on assumptions about jury knowledge and the effects of instructions. Given the absence of solid empirical data supporting either view,[12] common sense and policy considerations must provide guidance. Providing for an instruction seems the most sensible approach given the potential for prejudice to defendants when the alternative course is followed. Particularly in cases in which defendants are charged with violent crimes (which is usually the case if the nonresponsibility issue is tried to a jury, as opposed to a judge), juries need to be told about the effect of a finding of mental nonresponsibility [insanity] if the possibility of a serious injustice is to be avoided. The fear of compromise verdicts is misplaced. Jurors frequently are given instructions about lesser-included offenses which theoretically could as easily soften jury decisions but do not seem to do so in practice. Moreover, most jurors are

11. *See* United States v. Portis, 542 F.2d 414, 420-421 (7th Cir. 1976).

12. One study relevant to the topic found that the overwhelming majority of jurors are aware that dangerous persons are not released upon acquittal by reason of mental nonresponsibility. R. Simon, The Jury and the Defense of Insanity 38 (1967). However, the methodology of this research has been criticized, and the author of the study herself has expressed ambivalence about its conclusions. *See* Schwartz, *Should Juries Be Informed of the Consequences of the Insanity Verdict?*, 8 J. Psychiatry & L. 167, 173-174 (1980) [hereinafter cited as Schwartz]. Another study found that although there is some correlation between verdicts of guilty and the fear that a nonresponsibility acquittal will lead to release, overall jurors had inconsistent perceptions about disposition. Morris, *Whither Thou Goest?: An Inquiry into Jurors' Perceptions of the Consequences of a Successful Insanity Defense*, 14 San Diego L. Rev. 1058 (1977).

aware of the fact that maximum security mental institutions can be at least as grim as prisons.[13]

Thus, the standard recommends that juries be advised of dispositional consequences. The form of a suitable instruction should be left to legislative and rule drafters.[14]

If dispositional instructions are authorized, they should not entitle defendants to submit evidence tending to show they would benefit more from hospitalization than imprisonment. A dispositional instruction seeks only to place a nonresponsibility plea on an equal footing with other pleas in terms of jury knowledge about posttrial consequences. In contrast, evidence showing benefit of acquittal to defendants is intended to influence juries in the direction of a verdict of mental nonresponsibility [insanity]. Evidence of that sort not only is irrelevant to issues prop-

---

13. *See* Schwartz, *supra* note 12, at 174-175.

14. To illustrate, the instruction given in federal courts in the District of Columbia states,

> If the defendant is found "not guilty by reason of insanity," it becomes the duty of the Court to commit him to St. Elizabeth's Hospital. There will be a hearing within 50 days to determine whether the defendant is entitled to be released. In that hearing the defendant has the burden of proof. The defendant will remain in custody and will be entitled to release from custody only if the Court finds by a preponderance of the evidence that he is not likely to injure himself or other persons due to a mental disease.

United States v. Hinckley, Crim. Case No. 81-306 (D.C. Cir. 1982) (jury instruction).

In a jurisdiction that adopts the standards in this chapter, in particular standards 7-6.1, 7-6.9, 7-6.10(a), and 7-7.1 through 7-7.9, an appropriate instruction might be as follows:

> If the defendant is found "not guilty by reason of mental nonresponsibility," the defendant will be committed for evaluation for approximately thirty days, after which this court will hold a hearing to consider evidence about the defendant's current mental condition. If, as a result of this hearing, the court finds that the defendant is mentally ill or mentally retarded and that he poses a substantial threat of bodily harm to others, or that he does not meet these criteria solely because he is undergoing treatment that is not likely to continue unless he is committed to a secure facility, then the defendant will be confined in a secure facility for a term not to exceed the maximum term of confinement he would have received had you found him guilty of the offense charged. He may be released before this term is expired if a court finds either that he is no longer disordered or that he no longer poses a threat of bodily harm to others and that he does not require continued confinement in order to ensure that he will remain in this improved condition.

In the Comprehensive Crime Control Act of 1984, Pub. L. No. 98-596, §403(a), 98 Stat. 3134 (approved Oct. 12, 1984), Congress enacted a new provision governing the disposition of federal defendants acquitted on grounds of mental nonresponsibility [insanity]. 18 U.S.C.A. §§4243, 4247 (Supp. 1986). Presumably, the statutory language can form the basis for the sort of instruction envisioned in the standard.

erly tendered for jury resolution but is likely to distort jury resolution of those issues — a result that standard 7-6.8 is drawn to forestall.

Standard 7-6.9. Burden of production and burden of persuasion

(a) The defendant should have the burden of ensuring that evidence of mental nonresponsibility [insanity] is introduced.

(b) Once evidence of mental nonresponsibility [insanity] has been introduced at trial, the burden of persuasion should be allocated as follows:

(i) In jurisdictions utilizing any test for mental nonresponsibility [insanity] which focuses solely on whether the defendant, as a result of mental disease or defect, was unable to know, understand, or appreciate the wrongfulness of his or her conduct at the time of the offense charged, the prosecution should have the burden of disproving the defendant's claim of mental nonresponsibility [insanity] beyond a reasonable doubt;

(ii) In jurisdictions utilizing the ALI Model Penal Code test for mental nonresponsibility [insanity], the defendant should have the burden of proving the claim of mental nonresponsibility [insanity] by a preponderance of the evidence.

(c) Nothing contained in paragraph (b) above relieves the prosecution of its burden of proving beyond a reasonable doubt all elements of the offense charged including the mental state required for the offense charged.

Commentary Introduction

The standard places on the defense the responsibility of going forward with evidence in support of a mental nonresponsibility [insanity] defense. Thereafter, the burden of persuasion should be allocated according to the nature of the substantive criminal law definition of mental nonresponsibility [insanity]. In jurisdictions using an equivalent test to that recommended for adoption in standard 7-6.1(a), the prosecution should be required to disprove the defense claim of nonresponsibility beyond a reasonable doubt. In jurisdictions with the ALI Model Penal Code test, the defense should have the burden to establish nonresponsibility by a preponderance of the evidence. The standard does not affect the constitutional requirement that the prosecution prove beyond a reasonable doubt all elements of charged offenses, including *mens rea* or culpability.

Related Standards

ABA, Standards for Criminal Justice 7-6.1, 7-6.2
ALI, Model Penal Code §4.03
APA, Statement on the Insanity Defense 12-13
NCCUSL, Defense of Insanity Act, art. 7, §15 (April 1984 draft)
NMHA, Myths & Realities, recommendation 4

Commentary

In virtually all states, criminal defendants are presumed responsible.[1] Therefore, they bear the burden of pleading the defense (if that is required by statute or court rule) and of going forward with evidence in support of the claim. Paragraph (a) restates this fundamental evidentiary proposition.

The standard takes no position on the quantum of evidence required to overcome the presumption that a defendant is criminally responsible. Traditionally, very little evidence is needed to satisfy the production burden. No jurisdiction requires psychiatric testimony and lay testimony is regarded as sufficient even when cast in the "broadest generalizations."[2] These decisions reflect the reluctance of judges to take away the responsibility determination from juries if there is any indication of mental dysfunction at the time of a charged offense. The standard is phrased to permit the presumption to be met by either defense evidence or evidence admitted as part of the prosecution case-in-chief. Defense counsel, therefore, is responsible to see that prosecution evidence tending to show mental nonresponsibility [insanity] is properly introduced.

The burden of persuasion is a matter separate from burden of production. Jurisdictions that retain a defense of mental nonresponsibility [insanity] are divided on the matter.[3] Congress has denominated the matter an affirmative defense that defendants must establish by clear and con-

1. *See* A. Goldstein, The Insanity Defense 111-112 (1967).
2. *Id.* at 113.
3. Thirty states and the District of Columbia place the burden of proving nonresponsibility on defendants by a preponderance of the evidence, and one (Arizona) places the burden on defendants by clear and convincing evidence. In contrast, sixteen states require the prosecution to prove the defendant criminally responsible beyond a reasonable doubt. *See* 7 Mental Disability L. Rptr. 140 (1983) for a chart showing the burden of proof in each state.

vincing evidence.[4] Paragraph (b), which restates the policy approved by the ABA House of Delegates in 1983, takes a compromise position on the burden of persuasion issue.[5] In states using a test focusing exclusively on a defendant's knowledge or appreciation of criminal conduct,[6] the standard recommends placement of the burden on the prosecution to disprove a claim of mental nonresponsibility [insanity]. In jurisdictions utilizing the full ALI test for mental nonresponsibility [insanity], it takes the position that defendants should be expected to establish the defense by a preponderance of the evidence. Logically, paragraph (b) also would require defendants to bear the burden of persuasion in jurisdictions employing a combination of the *M'Naghten* and irresistible impulse[7] tests.

Since the *Hinckley* trial,[8] much has been said about the proper allocation of the burden of persuasion in cases involving criminal responsibility. Although burdens and standards of proof may have little practical impact in some contexts, they are of much more than symbolic importance when criminal responsibility is involved.[9] In light of this problem,

---

4. Pub. L. No. 98-596, §402(a), 98 Stat. 3134 (Oct. 12, 1984), enacting 18 U.S.C.A. §20(b) (Supp. 1986).

5. The resolution stated,

> That in jurisdictions utilizing any test for insanity which focuses solely on whether the defendant, as a result of mental disease or defect, was unable to know, understand or appreciate the wrongfulness of his or her conduct at the time of the offense charged, the prosecution should have the burden of disproving the defendant's claim of insanity beyond a reasonable doubt; and, secondly, that in jurisdictions utilizing the ALI-Model Penal Code test for insanity the defendant should have the burden of proving by a preponderance of the evidence his or her claim of insanity.

American Bar Association, *Summary of Action of the House of Delegates*, 1983 Midyear Meeting 3.

6. *E.g., M'Naghten*, the first prong of the ALI test and the test endorsed in standard 7-6.1.

7. *See* commentary to standard 7-6.1, notes 8-9 and accompanying text.

8. *See* United States v. Hinckley, 525 F. Supp. 1342 (D.D.C. 1981), *clarified*, 529 F. Supp. 520, *aff'd*, 672 F.2d 115 (D.C. Cir. 1982); Crim. Case No. 81-306 (D.C. Cir. 1982) (jury instruction); L. Caplan, The Insanity Defense and the Trial of John W. Hinckley, Jr. 33-47, 59-100 (1984).

9. As the American Psychiatric Association has stated,

> Given the inherent uncertainties involved in psychiatric testimony regarding the defense and the ever-present problems relating abstract legal principles to controversies of such emotion, who bears the burden of proof in insanity trials may be quite important. This is particularly so when what must be proved must also be proved "beyond a reasonable doubt." As suggested by the U.S. Supreme Court in the *Addington* case [Addington v. Texas, 441 U.S. 418 (1979)], usually psychiatric evidence is not sufficiently clear-cut to prove or disprove many legal facts "beyond a reasonable doubt."

American Psychiatric Association, Statement on the Insanity Defense 13 (1982).

many have advocated placing the burden of persuasion with respect to mental responsibility [insanity] on defendants. It is clear that there is no constitutional impediment to placing the burden of persuasion in that way.[10]

In the absence of constitutional prerequisites, allocation of the burden of persuasion on mental nonresponsibility [insanity] issues is exclusively a matter of public policy. The Association recommends allocation of the burden on the basis of the underlying nonresponsibility test. A narrow test, such as that recommended in standard 7-6.1, should be treated differently from an expanded combined cognitive-volition norm.

The specific choices represented by this standard — placing the burden on the prosecution beyond a reasonable doubt when the first test is used and on defendants by a preponderance of the evidence when the second is employed — are based on an analysis of these tests as they relate to the proof structure of the criminal justice system and the risk of error associated with each. The prosecution generally should bear the burden of persuading a factfinder beyond a reasonable doubt of all facts necessary to establish an adequate predicate for criminal liability.[11] In the context of affirmative defenses like mental nonresponsibility [insanity], duress, or entrapment, the issue is whether a just penal law can fail to give exculpatory effect to the claimed defense.[12] If, as argued in the commentary to standard 7-6.1,[13] exculpation is morally required when a significant cognitive-affective dysfunction existed at the time of the offense, then the argument is strong that the prosecution should be required to negate the existence of this fact beyond a reasonable doubt. The argument is enhanced further by the narrow nature of the cognitive-affective

10. The Supreme Court held in Leland v. Oregon, 343 U.S. 790, *reh'g denied*, 344 U.S. 848 (1952), that a state may shift the burden of establishing nonresponsibility claims to the defense. *Leland* has been reaffirmed by the Court in Rivera v. Delaware. Rivera v. State, 351 A.2d 561 (Del. 1975), *appeal dismissed sub nom.* Rivera v. Delaware, 429 U.S. 877 (1976). *See also* Vardas v. Estelle, 715 F.2d 106 (5th Cir. 1983), *cert. denied sub nom.* Vardas v. McKaskle, 465 U.S. 1104 (1984) (state law allocating burden of persuasion on insanity issue to defense did not violate due process).

11. *In re* Winship, 397 U.S. 358 (1970); Underwood, *The Thumb on the Scales of Justice: Burdens of Persuasion in Criminal Cases,* 86 Yale L.J. 1229 (1977).

12. From this premise, some commentators have argued that if the law need not recognize a defense at all, it is entirely proper to recognize the defense if and only if the defendant bears the risk of nonpersuasion. Jeffries & Stephan, *Defenses, Presumptions, and Burden of Proof in the Criminal Law,* 88 Yale L.J. 1325 (1979). This may be the correct approach in cases involving claims of duress or entrapment, for example.

13. *See* commentary to standard 7-6.1, notes 37-39 and accompanying text.

test, which reduces the difficulties inherent in meeting this burden when reliance must be placed on imprecise psychiatric testimony.

The same cannot be said, however, of other tests of mental nonresponsibility [insanity] like the ALI standard. The position taken in the commentary to standard 7-6.1 is that the volitional criterion within the ALI test is not an ethically essential predicate for liability when a broadly phrased appreciation test is available. Even if it is, special considerations warrant a departure from the general rule disfavoring burden-shifting when such predicates are involved. It is the Association's view that mistakes in the administration of the nonresponsibility [insanity] defense occur primarily when the volitional or control tests are employed.[14] The volitional criterion is more likely than the cognitive-affective test alone to produce expert speculation and jury confusion. On that premise, there is ample moral and public policy justification for placing the burden on defendants if the volitional test is to be applied.[15]

However, the rationale for shifting the burden in that way under the ALI test does not support an increase in the quantitative burden to the clear-and-convincing-proof level. This is especially true when the test is cognitive-affective alone. Defendants do not bear such a heavy burden with respect to any other defense; to make an exception in cases involving mental nonresponsibility [insanity] and in the process to denigrate the defense is an unjustifiable step, particularly when the substantive standard does not incorporate a volitional prong.

Nor does the reasoning supporting the Association's recommended allocation of the burden of persuasion necessarily mean that defendants need to bear the burden of proving mental nonresponsibility [insanity] in jurisdictions that combine cognitive and volitional criteria. Subparagraph (b)(ii) of the standard recommends placement of the burden on defendants if the ALI test is followed because of the impossibility of determining accurately which of its two prongs juries relied upon in finding defendants nonresponsible. Courts may be willing to permit defendants to elect the prong under which they prefer to proceed, with concomitant jury instructions. Such an approach should be taken with caution, however, since it in effect overrides a legislative determination of a preferred test for mental nonresponsibility [insanity].

---

14. *See id.* at notes 46-47 and accompanying text.

15. Much of this analysis is drawn from Professor Bonnie's discussion of the issue in Bonnie, *The Moral Basis of the Insanity Defense,* 69 A.B.A.J. 194-197 (1983). However, Professor Bonnie concluded that "the burden of persuasion should be borne by defendants under an exclusively cognitive" test as well as under a test which includes a volitional criterion.

A final word of explanation is necessary with respect to the specific language in subparagraph (b)(i). The standard states that the prosecution should have "the burden of disproving the defendant's claim of mental nonresponsibility [insanity]," rather than "the burden of proving the defendant's criminal responsibility" beyond a reasonable doubt. This language was chosen intentionally to convey the notion that the prosecution's responsibility is not to prove defendants are mentally "healthy" persons, but rather that they are not responsible under the appropriate test. There is not, and probably cannot be, a clear definition of "sanity" or "criminal responsibility" for purposes of the criminal law; the standard reaffirms the proposition that juries are to determine that defendants meet the legislative standard for mental nonresponsibility [insanity], not some amorphous concept of its converse.

Paragraph (c) recognizes the well-settled proposition[16] that the prosecution always has the burden of proving all elements of a crime, no matter which side has the burden with respect to the mental nonresponsibility [insanity] defense. The standard emphasizes that the prosecution must bear the burden of proving all elements of charged crimes beyond a reasonable doubt, including *mens rea.* Thus, under legislative proposals that would abolish the defense of mental nonresponsibility [insanity] and replace it with the *mens rea* approach,[17] the allocation issue does not and should not arise. In the same way, in jurisdictions that permit testimony on both mental nonresponsibility [insanity] and *mens rea,* the burden of persuasion on the latter issue must rest on the prosecution and not the defense, no matter which side bears the burden on the nonresponsibility issue and irrespective of whether the issues are tried together in a unitary trial or separately in a bifurcated procedure.[18]

Standard 7-6.10. Forms of verdict

(a) When the defense of mental nonresponsibility [insanity] has been properly raised, the verdict returned should be in the form of either guilty, not guilty, or not guilty by reason of mental nonresponsibility [insanity]. The jury should be instructed that it may consider the verdict of not guilty by reason of mental nonresponsi-

16. *See In re* Winship, 397 U.S. 358 (1970).

17. *See* commentary to standard 7-6.1, notes 38-39 and accompanying text.

18. Admissibility of evidence of mental condition short of a nonresponsibility defense is covered in standard 7-6.2 and commentary.

bility [insanity] only after finding, beyond a reasonable doubt, that the defendant committed the conduct charged.

(b) Statutes which supplant or supplement the verdict of not guilty by reason of mental nonresponsibility [insanity] with a verdict of guilty but mentally ill should not be enacted.

Commentary Introduction

The standard recommends that juries should be allowed to return only verdicts of guilty, not guilty, and not guilty by reason of mental nonresponsibility [insanity]. It rests on Association policy opposing a fourth alternative of a guilty-but-mentally-ill verdict. Juries should be cautioned to find that defendants committed the *actus reus* elements of charged offenses before considering mental nonresponsibility [insanity].

Related Standards

ABA, Standards for Criminal Justice 7-6.1, 7-7.4, 7-9.6
ALI, Model Penal Code §4.03(3)
APA, Statement on the Insanity Defense 9-10
NMHA, Myths & Realities, recommendations 2, 3

Commentary

As noted in the introduction to this part,[1] the term *insanity* has been replaced by the term *mental nonresponsibility*. Accordingly, paragraph (a) provides that jury instructions, like the form of the verdict itself, should be couched in terms of mental nonresponsibility rather than insanity. Aside from this desirable change in nomenclature, paragraph (a) limits verdicts to the three forms traditionally provided in criminal cases: guilty, not guilty, and not guilty by reason of mental nonresponsibility [insanity].[2]

1. *See* the asterisk footnote and accompanying text, introduction to part VI.

2. Although the Standing Committee considered a verdict form eliminating the words *not guilty* and simply stating that a defendant was "not mentally responsible," the committee rejected it because it implied a defendant who was mentally nonresponsible [insane] at the time of the offense could at the same time be "guilty" of the offense. In fact, however, a person who is found nonresponsible at the time of the act charged is not criminally culpable. Thus, the committee recommended the retention of the three traditional forms of jury verdicts, with the substitution, of course, of "mental nonresponsibility" for "insanity."

The requirement endorsed in paragraph (a) that juries determine beyond a reasonable doubt that defendants committed the *actus reus* element of charged offenses before determining nonresponsibility is necessary to implement the dispositional provisions of part VII of this chapter. To be constitutionally acceptable, commitment hearings affecting persons found nonresponsible, conducted under the provisions of standard 7-7.4, must be predicated on such a finding by either a trial judge or a committing judge. In addition, the fact that defendants almost certainly committed otherwise criminal acts generally will be highly material evidence on the issue of a threat of harm to others if they are not civilly or specially committed,[3] one of the two criteria addressed at the commitment proceeding (the other being current mental condition).

Paragraph (b) of the standard reinforces paragraph (a) by banning alternative "quasi-insanity" verdicts. It reflects policy endorsed by the Association House of Delegates in 1983 in response to a wave of guilty-but-mentally-ill statutes adopted in recent years. Since 1975, when Michigan enacted the first such statute,[4] eleven other states have enacted guilty-but-mentally-ill legislation;[5] at least ten more[6] have considered comparable laws in the wake of the *Hinckley* trial.

---

3. *See generally* J. Monahan, The Clinical Prediction of Violent Behavior 71-72 (1981).

4. Mich. Comp. Laws Ann. §§768.29a(2), 768.36 (1982).

5. *See, e.g.*, Alaska Stat. §12.47.020(c) (1984); Del. Code Ann. tit. 11, §§401, 408 (Supp. 1984); Ga. Code Ann. §17-7-131 (Supp. 1985); Ill. Ann. Stat. ch. 38, §§6-2, 6-4, 113-4, 113-5, 115-2, 115-3, 115-4 (as amended by 1985 PA 84-413 (approved Sept. 16, 1985) (West Supp. 1986); Ind. Code Ann. §35-36-2-5 (West 1985); Ky. Rev. Stat. Ann. §504.130 (1985); N.M. Stat. Ann. §31-9-3 (Supp. 1985); 18 Pa. Cons. Stat. Ann. §314 (Purdon 1983); S.D. Codified Laws Ann. §§23A-7-2, 23A-25-13, 23A-7-16, 23A-26-3, 23A-26-14 (Supp. 1985); Utah Code Ann. §§77-13-1, 77-35-21.5 (Supp. 1985).

See generally Hermann & Sor, *Convicting or Confining?: Alternative Directions in Insanity Law Reform: Guilty But Mentally Ill Versus New Rules for Release of Insanity Acquittees*, 1983 B.Y.U. L. Rev. 499; LaGrone & Combs, *Alternatives to the Insanity Defense*, 12 J. Psychiatry & L. 93 (1984); McGraw, Farthing-Capowich & Keilitz, *The "Guilty But Mentally Ill" Plea and Verdict: Current State of the Knowledge*, 30 Villanova L. Rev. 117 (1985); Slovenko, *Commentaries on Psychiatry and Law: "Guilty but Mentally Ill,"* 10 J. Psychiatry & L. 541 (1982); Note, *Guilty But Mentally Ill: An Impractical Alternative to the Insanity Defense*, 14 Sw. L. Rev. 544 (1984); Weiner, *Mental Disability and the Criminal Law*, in The Mentally Disabled and the Law 693, 714-716 (S. Brakel, J. Parry & B. Weiner eds., 3d ed. 1985) [hereinafter cited as Weiner]. Statutory provisions as of October 1982 are gathered in Weiner, *supra*, at 778-785, Table 12.6.

6. *See, e.g.*, Florida, S. 323 (1980), H. 710 (1980); Hawaii, H. 86 (1981), S. 2073-80 (1980); Maryland, S. 806 (1980), S. 1284 (1978); New Hampshire, S. 126 (1979), S. 51 (1981); New York, S. 11765 (1980), S. 4013 (1979), S. 7185 (1978), H.9705 (1978); Ohio, S. 297 (1979).

Under the Michigan statute,[7] which is representative of most such formulations, defendants who file a notice of an intent to rely on the insanity defense may be found guilty, not guilty, not guilty by reason of insanity, or guilty but mentally ill at the time of a charged offense. The latter finding is required if a factfinder concludes beyond a reasonable doubt that a defendant committed the act charged, was mentally ill at the time of the offense, and was not criminally responsible at the time of the offense. If a guilty-but-mentally-ill verdict is returned, a defendant is sentenced to any term appropriate for the offense and subjected to treatment in a mental hospital as needed. The constitutionality of the Michigan statute has been upheld by Michigan state courts on several occasions[8] and proponents of this alternative look upon it as a successful compromise necessary for the survival of the insanity defense.

A second pattern of reform legislation, not yet legislatively adopted by any state but apparently sanctioned by one court,[9] would supplant rather than supplement the verdict of mental nonresponsibility [insanity] with a verdict of guilty but mentally ill or guilty but insane. This alternative appears to allow mental abnormality no mitigating effect at trial, but instead merely accords juries a means to indicate their belief that defendants are sick as well as guilty.

Paragraph (b) disapproves of any type of guilty-but-mentally-ill (GBMI) verdict. This policy, adopted by the ABA House of Delegates in 1983, is also supported by the American Psychiatric Association,[10] the National Mental Health Association Commission on the Insanity Defense,[11] and virtually all commentators who have analyzed the subject.[12] Indeed, legislation that supplants the mental nonresponsibility [insanity] verdict arguably may be unconstitutional on its face, since it does not

---

7. MICH. COMP. LAWS ANN. §§768.29a(2), 768.36 (1982).

8. People v. McLeod, 407 Mich. 632, 288 N.W.2d 909 (1980); People v. Ramsey, 89 Mich. App. 468, 280 N.W.2d 565 (1979); People v. Soma, 88 Mich. App. 351, 276 N.W.2d 892 (1979). *See also* People v. Smith, 124 Ill. App. 3d 805, 811-812, 465 N.E.2d 101, 104-105 (1984) (sustaining constitutionality of Illinois legislation).

9. *See* Pouncey v. State, 297 Md. 264, 465 A.2d 475 (1983).

10. AMERICAN PSYCHIATRIC ASSOCIATION, STATEMENT ON THE INSANITY DEFENSE 9-10 (1982).

11. NAT'L MENTAL HEALTH ASS'N, MYTHS AND REALITIES: A REPORT OF THE NATIONAL COMMISSION ON THE INSANITY DEFENSE, recommendation 2 (1983).

12. *See* Bonnie, *The Moral Basis of the Insanity Defense,* 69 A.B.A.J. 194 (1983); Note, *The Constitutionality of Michigan's Guilty But Mentally Ill Verdict,* 12 U. MICH. J.L. REF. 188 (1978). For a discussion of GBMI as it relates to mentally retarded defendants, *see* Ellis & Luckasson, *Mentally Retarded Criminal Defendants,* 53 GEO. WASH. L. REV. 414, 442-444 (1985).

accord exculpatory significance to even the type of gross psychosis that would preclude requisite *mens rea.* Even if, as a result of judicial interpretation, such statutes should allow the introduction of evidence of mental abnormality relevant to *mens rea,* the fact that they abolish the defense of mental nonresponsibility [insanity] would, as discussed in the commentary to standard 7-6.1,[13] run counter to the moral imperative of the criminal law.

Guilty-but-mentally-ill statutes that make the verdict an option in lieu of, rather than a substitute, for the nonresponsibility verdict are also unwarranted on both functional and theoretical grounds. The new verdict fails on its own terms and at the same time introduces a conceptually alien element into the criminal justice system.

Proponents of the GBMI statute argue that increasing numbers of violent crimes committed by persons prematurely released from mental institutions, after having been found not guilty by reason of mental nonresponsibility [insanity], necessitate this alternative verdict form. By offering jurors a compromise verdict between a guilty finding and a finding of mental nonresponsibility [insanity], they hope both to reduce acquittals by reason of mental nonresponsibility [insanity] and to provide greater protection to the public.

In fact, the verdict appears to accomplish neither goal. With respect to the first objective, for instance, the number of nonresponsibility acquittals in Michigan since passage of the 1975 GBMI statute has actually increased.[14] Ironically, it is likely that one reason for this increase has been the GBMI verdict itself. Defendants who ordinarily would not have pleaded mental nonresponsibility [insanity] may now do so, on the theory that even if they are unsuccessful on the responsibility issue they may avoid outright conviction and imprisonment through a GBMI finding[15] which, as an alternative to imprisonment, allows placement in mental institutions. Data from other jurisdictions amply support the proposition that introduction of the GBMI verdict has a negligible effect on insanity acquittals.[16]

Even assuming that a GBMI verdict effectively replaces nonresponsibility acquittals with guilty-but-mentally-ill findings, the degree of extra

13. *See* commentary to standard 7-6.1, notes 38-39 and accompanying text.

14. Smith & Hall, *Evaluating Michigan's Guilty But Mentally Ill Verdict: An Empirical Study,* 16 U. MICH. J.L. REF. 77, 101 (1982).

15. *Id.* at 102.

16. *See* Slobogin, *The Guilty But Mentally Ill Verdict: An Idea Whose Time Should Not Have Come,* 53 GEO. WASH. L. REV. 494, 506-508 (1985) [hereinafter cited as Slobogin].

security it affords the public is probably negligible. A person found GBMI must be considered for parole just like any other convicted offender.[17] Once the minimum period of confinement necessary to establish eligibility for parole has passed, the primary criterion governing the release of defendants found GBMI is the same as that ruling the release of those found not guilty by reason of mental nonresponsibility [insanity], namely, dangerousness. As a result, the duration of a given individual's confinement is likely to be roughly similar under either the traditional system or one which employs the GBMI verdict. Indeed, research indicates that the duration of confinement for felons and acquittees charged with the same crime is roughly equivalent.[18]

Accepting for the sake of argument that the GBMI verdict tends both to reduce acquittals by reason of mental nonresponsibility [insanity] and to lead to longer confinement for mentally ill offenders, it is still highly debatable whether the manner in which GBMI statutes achieve this result is acceptable. Under the typical GBMI scheme, jury instructions directing when defendants should be found "insane" as opposed to merely "mentally ill" are at best confusing and at worst extremely prejudicial.[19] There is a strong possibility that jurors, seeing little distinction between these competing terminologies, will choose the guilty-but-mentally-ill verdict solely because it appears to result in longer confinement. Persons with a valid nonresponsibility defense may, therefore, be convicted instead of acquitted on mental nonresponsibility [insanity] grounds. Unfortunately, there is probably no way to define mental illness to avoid this result and still distinguish in a meaningful way between nonresponsible disturbed offenders and normal ones.

Finally, the GBMI verdict is deficient for an important theoretical reason: It is not a proper verdict at all. Rather it is a dispositional mechanism transferred to the guilt determination phase of the criminal process. The

---

17. *See, e.g.,* People v. McLeod, 407 Mich. 632, 288 N.W.2d 909 (1980); MICH. COMP. LAWS ANN. §768.36(4) (1982). To the extent parole is denied those found GBMI, a violation of equal protection may occur.

18. *See* Slobogin, *supra* note 16, at 500-501.

19. For example, in Kentucky, a nonresponsible person is one whose mental disease causes a lack of "substantial capacity to appreciate the criminality of (the offense) or to conform his conduct to the requirements of the law," KY. REV. STAT. ANN. §504.020 (1985), while mental illness for purposes of the state's GBMI statute is defined as the "substantially impaired capacity to use self-control, judgment, or discretion in the conduct of one's affairs and social relations, associated with maladaptive behavior or recognized emotional symptoms." *Id.* at §504.060. *See also* State v. Page, 100 N.M. 788, 791, 676 P.2d 1353, 1356 (1984) (form of instruction under New Mexico statute).

hybrid nature of the verdict is demonstrated by the fact that a jury determination of mental illness at the time of a charged offense is relevant not to criminal responsibility or culpability but to whether accused persons *might* receive treatment after they have been sentenced, a finding best made and acted upon after trial when information about various dispositional alternatives can be obtained and qualified experts consulted. Even if the GBMI verdict accurately identified offenders needing psychiatric treatment, which it apparently fails to do,[20] it would not be a particularly useful innovation because virtually every state already provides for the hospitalization of prisoners requiring inpatient care.

If the goal is to reduce acquittals by reason of mental nonresponsibility [insanity], attention should be deflected to the proper scope of the nonresponsibility defense. If it is instituted to prevent premature release of persons found nonresponsible, criteria for committing and releasing them should be reexamined. If, instead, the concern is the proper treatment of mentally ill or mentally retarded offenders, sentencing and prison transfer provisions should be evaluated.[21] The guilty-but-mentally-ill verdict fails to address any of these problems adequately. Instead, it adds a confusing and conceptually unjustifiable element to the criminal justice system.

---

20. In Michigan, 75 percent of defendants found GBMI are not mentally ill. Statement of Bill Meyer, Director of the Forensic Psychiatry Center in Ann Arbor, Michigan, at State Mental Health Forensic Directors Third Annual Conference (Sept. 1982). Of the forty-five defendants found GBMI in Illinois over a thirteen-month period, all have gone directly to the custody of the department of corrections. Statement of Terry Brelje, Coordinator for the Forensic Psychiatry Program at Chester Mental Health Center, Illinois, at Mental Health Forensic Directors Third Annual Conference (Sept. 1982).

21. Parts VI, VII, IX, and X of this chapter cover these functions.

Part VII

Commitment of Nonresponsibility Acquittees

William H. Erickson, *Chairman*
Standing Committee on Association Standards for Criminal Justice

Steven H. Goldberg
Task Force Chairman

James W. Ellis
Reporter

Task Force

Steven H. Goldberg, *Chairman*
Associate Dean, University of Minnesota School of Law, Minneapolis, Minnesota

David L. Armstrong
Attorney General, State of Kentucky, Louisville, Kentucky (representing ABA Section of Criminal Justice)

Janet L. Coye
State of Hawaii Department of Health, Mental Health Division, Honolulu, Hawaii

Thomas G. Gutheil, M.D.
Psychiatrist, Brookline, Massachusetts (representing American Psychiatric Association)

Howard Janssen
Private practitioner, Crosby, Heafey, Roach & May, Oakland, California

Carl P. Malmquist, M.D.
Psychiatrist, Professor, Department of Sociology, University of Minnesota, Minneapolis, Minnesota

Karl Menninger II
Deputy Chief Counsel, Illinois Department of Mental Health/Developmental Disabilities, Springfield, Illinois

John T. Monahan, Ph.D.
Psychologist, Professor of Law, Psychology & Legal Medicine, University of Virginia School of Law, Charlottesville, Virginia (representing American Psychological Association)

J. William Savage
Private practitioner, Rieke, Geil & Savage, P.C., Portland, Oregon (representing ABA Young Lawyers Division)

Leslie J. Scallet
Private practitioner, Scallet, Zweig and Associates, Washington, D.C.

Henry J. Steadman, Ph.D.
Director, Special Project Research Unit, New York Office of Mental Health, Albany, New York

David B. Wexler
Professor of Law, College of Law, University of Arizona, Tucson, Arizona

JAMES W. ELLIS, *Reporter*
Professor of Law, School of Law, University of New Mexico

INTRODUCTION

The controversy surrounding the mental nonresponsibility [insanity] defense has two major components. The first involves the appropriateness of assigning criminal responsibility and blame to individuals whose functioning was substantially impaired by severe mental disease or defect. This issue, nonresponsibility for crime based on mental condition, is addressed within part VI of these standards. The second component of the controversy relates to the disposition of defendants whose claim of mental nonresponsibility [insanity] results in acquittal. Confinement and treatment of these acquittees form the subject of this part.

The dilemmas that present themselves are both theoretical and practical. The willingness of the public to support or at least tolerate the mental nonresponsibility [insanity] defense may depend upon some form of reassurance that persons who have committed acts of violence will not be freed automatically to return to society. On the other hand, special statutory provisions that treat mental nonresponsibility [insanity] acquittees in a substantially different manner from other persons whose civil commitment is proposed raise serious constitutional and public policy questions. To be acceptable, such laws must afford acquittees due process, and differences from ordinary civil commitment must not offend the equal protection clause. The United States Supreme Court has ruled on some of the constitutional issues involved in special commitment. In *Jones v. United States,*[1] it rejected challenges to the District of Columbia system of special commitment for insanity acquittees. The petitioner had been acquitted by reason of insanity of attempted petit larceny and sought release from subsequent commitment because it had exceeded the length of time during which he could have been incarcerated had he been con-

1. 463 U.S. 354 (1983).

victed of the criminal charge. The Court rejected this challenge, holding that "when a criminal defendant establishes by a preponderance of the evidence that he is not guilty of a crime by reason of insanity, the Constitution permits the Government, on the basis of the insanity judgment, to confine him to a mental institution until such time as he has regained his sanity or is no longer a danger to himself or society."[2]

The standards in this part afford greater procedural protections to mental nonresponsibility [insanity] acquittees than those afforded by the District of Columbia's system upheld in *Jones.* It should be noted that the *Jones* decision does not preclude jurisdictions from adopting more rigorous procedures than the federal Constitution requires; the Court found only that the District of Columbia system was within constitutional limits. The standards within this part reflect a judgment that substantial deprivations of liberty require equally substantial procedural protections. Whenever a black letter standard in this part proposes higher levels of procedural protection than the minimum procedures upheld in *Jones,* the commentary to that standard will discuss the specific policy issues at stake.

While differences between these standards and the system in the District of Columbia are grounded primarily in public policy concerns, it should be noted that the system approved in *Jones* might be subject to constitutional challenges in other jurisdictions. The *Jones* holding is premised upon the allocation of burdens on the issue of mental nonresponsibility [insanity] in criminal trials in the District of Columbia.[3] If the burden of persuasion (proof) regarding the nonresponsibility [insanity] defense is placed on the prosecution, as recommended elsewhere in these standards,[4] the *Jones* holding is not directly applicable and the rationale for that decision is weakened. It should be noted as well that even if a particular system of committing acquittees does not violate the due process or equal protection clause of the fourteenth amendment, it may be subjected to stricter scrutiny under provisions of a state constitution.[5]

---

2. *Id.* at 370.
3. *Id.* at 369.
4. Standard 7-6.9 recommends that the burden be placed on the prosecution in jurisdictions adopting the definition of mental nonresponsibility [insanity] recommended in standard 7-6.1, but it endorses placement of the burden on the defendant in jurisdictions that use the ALI Model Penal Code definition of insanity.
5. *See* Meisel, *The Rights of the Mentally Ill Under State Constitutions,* 43 Law & Contemp. Probs. 7 (1982).

The principal purpose of the standards within this part is to balance a legitimate concern for public safety against the need for fair and consistent treatment of mental nonresponsibility [insanity] acquittees.[6] To that end, the standards reflect the current state of empirical research regarding the characteristics of such acquittees.[7] Striking a necessary and appropriate balance between policy concerns for public safety and fair treatment requires careful consideration of the current state of scientific knowledge and the reconciliation of often conflicting principles.

Standard 7-7.1. Commitment hearing following mental nonresponsibility [insanity] acquittal

(a) Criminal defendants found not guilty by reason of mental nonresponsibility [insanity] are referred to within part VII as mental nonresponsibility [insanity] acquittees or acquittees.

(b) Mental nonresponsibility [insanity] acquittees may be involuntarily confined following acquittal only if their commitment is sought in subsequent proceedings which satisfy the requirements of due process of law. States should have authority to conduct mental evaluations of acquittees. Statutes which authorize automatic commitment for a period longer than necessary to accomplish an evaluation of the acquittee's current mental status should be repealed.

(c) If the commitment of a mental nonresponsibility [insanity] acquittee is not sought, or if the commitment is sought but the court declines to order such commitment, the acquittee should be entitled to release.

---

6. *See generally* Ellis, *Commitment of Insanity Acquittees*, in Mental Health Law in the 1980's (A. Brooks & B. Winick eds., in press); Margulies, *The "Pandemonium Between the Mad and the Bad": Procedures for the Commitment and Release of Insanity Acquittees After* Jones v. United States, 36 Rutgers L. Rev. 793 (1984); Weiner, *Mental Disability and the Criminal Law*, in The Mentally Disabled and the Law 693, 725-729 (S. Brakel, J. Parry & B. Weiner eds., 3d ed. 1985); Zenoff, *Controlling the Dangers of Dangerousness: The ABA Standards and Beyond*, 53 Geo. Wash. L. Rev. 562, 581-587 (1985); Note, *Rules for an Exceptional Class: The Commitment and Release of Persons Acquitted of Violent Offenses by Reason of Insanity*, 57 N.Y.U.L. Rev. 281 (1982); Note, *Commitment Following an Insanity Acquittal*, 94 Harv. L. Rev. 605 (1981).

7. For an overview of the research, *see* Steadman & Braff, *Defendants Not Guilty by Reason of Insanity*, in Mentally Disordered Offenders: Perspectives from Law and Social Science 109-129 (J. Monahan & H. Steadman eds. 1983); Monahan, *The Prediction of Violent Behavior: Toward a Second Generation of Theory and Policy*, 141 Am. J. Psychiatry 10 (1984).

Commentary Introduction

Standard 7-7.1 provides for commitment of criminal defendants who have been found not guilty by reason of mental nonresponsibility [insanity]; however, it precludes automatic commitment for periods longer than necessary to conduct an examination of an acquittee's current mental condition.

Related Standards

MHLP Model Statute: Insanity Defense, §4

Commentary

It has long been recognized that the most appropriate disposition for a majority of mental nonresponsibility [insanity] acquittees is confinement in a mental hospital or similar facility for treatment or habilitation that may ameliorate or cure the mental disability that underlay the acquittal.[1] The incentive for such placements often has been the confinement itself rather than the treatment or habilitation that will follow. Some states have been so concerned about the certainty of confinement that they have mandated the automatic commitment of acquittees without any form of hearing.[2] Paragraph (b), however, although not heedless of legitimate concerns for public safety, rests on an overriding policy position that long-term confinement without a commitment hearing is not warranted.

Several rationales have been offered to support legislation requiring automatic commitment. The argument most frequently advanced asserts that the general presumption of a person's continued abnormal mental condition, once established, supports automatic confinement.[3] Under this

1. One court has traced back to 1854 the system of special commitments of insanity acquittees. State v. Blubaugh, 80 Wash. 2d 28, 491 P.2d 646, 648 (1971). *See also* Gleason v. West Boylston, 136 Mass. 489 (1884).

2. *See* B. Sales *et al.*, Disabled Persons and the Law: State Legislative Issues 709-713 (1982) (chart of state statutes); Weiner, *Mental Disability and the Criminal Law*, in The Mentally Disabled and the Law 693, 725-729 (S. Brakel, J. Parry & B. Weiner eds., 3d ed. 1985) [hereinafter cited as Weiner]; Note, *Commitment Following an Insanity Acquittal*, 94 Harv. L. Rev. 605, 605 n.4 (1981); Note, *Automatic and Indefinite Commitment of Insanity Acquittees: A Procedural Straitjacket*, 37 Vand. L. Rev. 1233 (1984).

3. The United States Supreme Court found this rationale sufficiently persuasive to support the constitutionality of a statute when a defendant had borne the burden of the criminal nonresponsibility [insanity] defense at criminal trial. Jones v. United States, 463 U.S.

theory, criminal verdicts of mental nonresponsibility [insanity] establish that acquitted defendants were mentally disabled; habeas corpus offers them a sufficient opportunity to rebut the presumption that their mental condition has not changed since the commission of the criminal acts for which they were tried. There are several problems with this argument. In some jurisdictions, the form of the criminal verdict on the mental nonresponsibility [insanity] issue provides no assurance that factfinders were persuaded that defendants were in fact mentally ill or mentally retarded at the time of their actions; a reasonable doubt as to sanity will suffice in many states.[4] Even if a verdict embodies a more authoritative finding on a defendant's previous mental state, the different tests of mental condition (criminal responsibility *versus* committability) and the passage of time between a criminal act and a verdict of acquittal deprive this presumption of the degree of accuracy necessary to support the "massive curtailment of liberty"[5] that civil commitment represents. Indeed, it has been observed that the implied or actual finding that a defendant was competent to stand trial supports at least as persuasive a presumption concerning the defendant's postacquittal mental condition as the fact of a mental nonresponsibility [insanity] acquittal.[6] A similar response can be made to the argument that it is undesirable to require prosecutors to assert an acquittee's mental disability as a basis for commitment immediately after they have contested a mental nonresponsibility [insanity] defense.

Other rationales supporting an automatic long-term commitment system are also inadequate. One holds that defendants should be estopped from denying mental disability after they have advanced it as a defense at a criminal trial. As with the previous argument, however, this is weakened by the fact that two quite different periods of time are in question: The actions on which criminal charges rested are likely to have preceded by many months or years the entry of a mental nonresponsibility [insanity] judgment of acquittal.

Perhaps the rationale that comes closest to expressing the true motivation for automatic commitment views it as a disincentive to fraudulent pleas of mental nonresponsibility [insanity]. There is reason to assume

---

354, 366 (1983). As indicated in the commentary to standard 7-7.3 at notes 3-8 and accompanying text, the standards reflect the view that this rationale is unpersuasive as a matter of policy even in jurisdictions where defendants bear the burden of persuasion at trial.

4. *See* People v. McQuillan, 392 Mich. 511, 531, 221 N.W.2d 569, 578 (1974).
5. Humphrey v. Cady, 405 U.S. 504, 509 (1972).
6. *See* G. Morris, The Insanity Defense: A Blueprint for Legislative Reform 61 (1975).

that the prospect of long-term confinement in mental institutions may affect the frequency with which the mental nonresponsibility [insanity] defense is asserted. It often has been observed that the likelihood of indeterminate commitment has made the defense unattractive to defendants facing trial for crimes the punishment for which is a relatively short period of imprisonment.[7] Nevertheless, there is no reason to think that commitment is a more potent deterrent to fraudulent mental nonresponsibility [insanity] defenses than it is an unwarranted but effective barrier to legitimate assertions of the defense.[8] In other words, the deterrent impact of automatic commitments is not confined to abusive assertions of the mental nonresponsibility [insanity] defense. In fact, the factor most likely to deter defendants from advancing the defense is the probable length of confinement that ensues, not the availability of a civil commitment hearing immediately following acquittal.

In summary, the position of the Association is that automatic commitment is undesirable because it fails to take into account possible changes in an acquittee's mental condition between the commission of an otherwise criminal act and the verdict. A hearing is indispensable to determine whether a mental nonresponsibility [insanity] acquittee currently meets the criteria for civil commitment. Subsequent standards address the timing and nature of that hearing.

Finally, it should be noted that a measure of confusion may surround use of the term *automatic commitment*. The standard precludes automatic commitment that is indeterminate in length or lasts for an unreasonable length of time. Statutory provisions that condition civil commitment hearings following acquittal on a mandatory mental examination necessitating a transient period of confinement do not represent an unwarranted restriction on an acquittee's liberty.[9]

Standard 7-7.2. Evaluation

(a) After issuance of a verdict of not guilty by reason of mental nonresponsibility [insanity], the criminal trial court, upon motion by

7. *See* Morris, *Mental Illness and Criminal Commitment in Michigan*, 5 U. Mich. J.L. Reform 1, 35 (1971).

8. *See* Note, *Rules for an Exceptional Class: The Commitment and Release of Persons Acquitted of Violent Offenses by Reason of Insanity*, 57 N.Y.U.L. Rev. 281, 307 (1982).

9. *See* commentary to standard 7-7.2, notes 1-4 and accompanying text.

the prosecution, should order an evaluation of the acquittee's current mental condition. The evaluation should not exceed [thirty] calendar days except, when for good cause shown, the court extends the period for a short time. This evaluation is for the sole purpose of assisting the court in determining whether the acquittee should be committed.

(b) The court may order that the evaluation be conducted while the mental nonresponsibility [insanity] acquittee is either an outpatient or is placed within a mental health or mental retardation facility, a general hospital, or, when security considerations so dictate, within another appropriate facility. In choosing the location of the evaluation, the court should be guided by the least restrictive alternative principle and by concern for public safety. The evaluation should be conducted by mental health or mental retardation professionals possessing the qualifications required by standard 7-3.10.

(c) Consistent with the requirements of institutional and community safety, mental nonresponsibility [insanity] acquittees should have the same rights regarding treatment and habilitation as do ordinary civil patients during evaluation for possible involuntary civil commitment.

(d) The evaluation should be completed and an evaluation report should be submitted to the court and to all parties within [thirty] calendar days of the issuance of the verdict. Upon submission of the evaluation report the prosecuting attorney may move for a commitment hearing. If the prosecuting attorney decides to seek commitment, a motion for a hearing must be filed within [five] days. That hearing must be held within [fifteen] days from the court's receipt of the evaluation report.

(e) If the prosecuting attorney does not file a timely motion seeking commitment, an acquittee in custody should be entitled to release.

Commentary Introduction

The standard provides for an evaluation of an acquittee's current mental condition, because the only finding inherent in a mental nonresponsibility [insanity] acquittal is related to past mental condition at the time of a charged offense. The standard covers the procedures before and after evaluations and the time periods that should govern them.

Related Standards

ABA, Standards for Criminal Justice 7-3.10, 7-3.11, 7-3.12, 7-6.10, 10-1.1

APA, Model Statute §4.6

MHLP Model Statute: Insanity Defense, §4

MHLP Model Statute: Civil Commitment, §§2, 6

Commentary

Although a verdict of not guilty by reason of mental nonresponsibility [insanity] is insufficient to justify automatic long-term commitment for either treatment or habilitation or public protection, it does justify a mandatory evaluation of an acquittee's current mental condition. Such an evaluation is indispensable to ensuing civil commitment hearings because a commitment court will need current information that was not relevant and thus not presented during the earlier criminal trial.

Courts that have struck down provisions for long-term automatic commitment following an acquittal have accepted mandatory confinement for purposes of evaluation.[1] While an acquittal by reason of mental nonresponsibility [insanity] does not provide sufficient information to justify an extended commitment for treatment or habilitation, it evidences a sufficient likelihood of committability to legitimate the loss of liberty inherent in the evaluation envisioned in this standard. As provided in standard 7-6.10, an acquittal verdict should contain a finding that a defendant committed the act on which criminal charges rested; that finding coupled with an inference based on an unchanged mental condition warrants an investigation into the appropriateness of commitment. A concern for public safety is sufficient to support a procedure that should ensure current and reliable information about an acquittee for the benefit of a court conducting civil commitment hearings.

Paragraph (a) of the standard recommends that an evaluation order be initiated by a prosecution motion; a trial court should not have discretion to release an acquittee without an evaluation if the prosecuting attorney

---

1. *See, e.g.,* Powell v. Florida, 579 F.2d 324 (5th Cir. 1978); Bolton v. Harris, 395 F.2d 642 (D.C. Cir. 1968); State v. Clemons, 110 Ariz. 79, 515 P.2d 324 (1973); People v. McQuillan, 392 Mich. 511, 221 N.W.2d 569, 586 (1974). *See also In re* Franklin, 7 Cal. 3d 126, 496 P.2d 465, 101 Cal. Rptr. 553 (1972); People v. Lally, 191 N.Y.2d 27, 224 N.E.2d 87, 277 N.Y.S.2d 654 (1966).

has requested one. On the other hand, paragraph (e) envisions an automatic discharge from custody if a prosecution motion for an evaluation is not forthcoming. Thus, a mandatory evaluation will be authorized unless it is so indisputably clear an acquittee is not currently committable that the prosecution sees no reason for an evaluation. Such cases will be rare, but they include instances in which both parties and all experts agree that the only mental disability asserted at criminal trial was transient and no longer present by the time of trial. If such a consensus is present, no purpose is served by an evaluation of an acquittee's current mental condition, and immediate release is appropriate.[2]

The duration of a postacquittal evaluation is a matter on which legislatures and courts have disagreed. The standard suggests thirty days as a period that allows for a substantial inquiry but does not extend beyond what is needed for the evaluation. Some courts have accepted longer periods.[3] One reason for rejecting substantially longer periods of time is congruence with evaluation commitments for regular civil commitments which, by statute, tend to be brief, particularly if no probable cause hearing has preceded an evaluation.[4] Nonetheless, within limits, the duration of evaluation commitments for mental nonresponsibility [insanity] acquittees may exceed somewhat those in the context of civil commitments: The state may be concerned that acquittees pose a greater danger

---

2. *Compare In re* Lewis, 403 A.2d 1115, 1119 (Del. 1979), which held that although a trial court, on the basis of a motion by the state attorney general, should order an acquittee committed for evaluation, the statute did not preclude it from ordering an evaluation on its own motion.

3. The United States Supreme Court has accepted a fifty-day delay as constitutional after the acquittee was found affirmatively by the criminal trial court to have been insane. Jones v. United States, 463 U.S. 354 (1983). Other courts have accepted sixty days. *See, e.g.,* State v. Krol, 68 N.J. 236, 256, 344 A.2d 289, 300 (1975). One court which accepted a period of ninety days relied in part upon a presumption of continuing insanity, which these standards reject. *See* commentary to standard 7-7.1. *In re* Franklin, 7 Cal. 3d 126, 142 n.10, 496 P.2d 465, 475 n.10, 101 Cal. Rptr. 553, 563 n.10 (1972). The period of six months, accepted as constitutional by another court, seems longer than necessary to accomplish an evaluation. People v. Chavez, 629 P.2d 1040 (Colo. 1981). Even if such a period is within constitutional limits, public policy considerations dictate a shorter time limit for evaluation.

4. *See* Stromberg & Stone, *A Model State Law on Civil Commitment of the Mentally Ill,* 20 Harv. J. on Legis. 275, 324 (1983) [hereinafter cited as Stromberg & Stone] (American Psychiatric Association model statute recommending 14 days); *Legal Issues in State Mental Health Care: Proposals for Change — Civil Commitment,* 2 Mental Disability L. Rep. 73, 137, 141 (1977) (72 hours for emergency treatment; 14 days for evaluation following a probable cause hearing).

to public safety than respondents in civil commitment proceedings and thus may demand a more thorough examination requiring an extended period of time. In addition, a verdict of acquittal may serve some of the purposes of a probable cause hearing in ordinary civil commitment proceedings; the criminal court disposition assures that the person facing evaluation has not been randomly or mistakenly selected from the general population. On the other hand, an acquittee is not an unknown quantity to the evaluators, as a general commitment patient brought in from the community may be. Although the data at hand are not dispositive on the issue of subsequent commitment, they may contain relevant information that will assist the evaluation process, particularly if a recent inquiry into competence to stand trial had been conducted. Therefore, while some differences may be tolerable and even warranted, a radical departure from the evaluation time limits provided for general commitment patients is not justified. In particular, an evaluation period must not be allowed to serve as a partial surrogate for the punishment an acquittee has escaped by virtue of a verdict of mental nonresponsibility [insanity].

Paragraph (b) of the standard envisions an evaluation competently performed by mental health or mental retardation professionals possessing the educational, clinical, and forensic knowledge required under the provisions of standard 7-3.10. If these evaluators are to serve as expert witnesses at a commitment hearing they should also meet the qualifications set forth in standard 7-3.11. Finally, it should be noted that standard 7-3.12 recommends that every jurisdiction establish by statute, regulation, or court rule minimum education and training requirements for mental health and mental retardation evaluators and expert witnesses.[5]

Paragraph (b) also provides that evaluations can be conducted in a variety of settings rather than invariably at a particular institution. The standard suggests that the choice of location should be guided by the least restrictive alternative principle: Mental health and mental retarda-

5. In this regard, standard 7-3.12(c)(ii) recommends that when an evaluation is conducted as part of a special commitment proceeding the evaluator or expert witness should be either (1) a licensed physician who has completed postdoctoral specialty training in a psychiatric residency program approved by the American Board of Psychiatry and Neurology or (2) a clinical or counseling psychologist who has received a doctoral degree in psychology from an educational institution accredited by an organization recognized by the Council of Post-secondary Accreditation and who is licensed or certified as a psychologist if the jurisdiction requires such licensure or certification.

tion services should be supplied in a location that does not infringe unnecessarily upon an individual client's liberty.[6] The standard accepts the relevance of this principle to the selection of a location for evaluation but also acknowledges that a concern for public safety also must be taken into account in the decision. Therefore, the location and conditions of an acquittee's interim confinement during the evaluation period should not be more restrictive of liberty than necessary, but a committing court should be authorized to subject an acquittee to a level of custodial restraint appropriate to protect the community.

Paragraph (c) adopts the premise, recognized in the law of some but not all jurisdictions, that mental nonresponsibility [insanity] acquittees should enjoy the same rights as persons awaiting general civil commitment proceedings to receive or to refuse treatment or habilitation services. There is nothing distinctive about mental nonresponsibility [insanity] acquittees to warrant treating them differently from other patients undergoing a compelled mental examination. Note, however, that paragraph (c) provides for treatment parity that takes institutional and community safety factors into account.

After an evaluation report has been submitted, paragraph (d) provides that a commitment hearing should be conducted promptly. Setting time limits for such a hearing is a matter of some delicacy. The state's legal representative must be given adequate time to read the report and consider whether to seek the acquittee's commitment. If the interval between the submission of a report and the convening of a hearing is insufficient to allow proper deliberation and preparation, unnecessary hearings may be held in some cases, counsel on both sides may be poorly prepared for the hearing, and a dangerous acquittee possibly could be released through inadvertence. However, all this must be weighed against an individual's right to a prompt adjudication of the continuing need for con-

---

6. *See* Wyatt v. Aderholt, 503 F.2d 1305 (5th Cir. 1974); Lake v. Cameron, 267 F. Supp. 155 (D.D.C. 1967); American Association on Mental Deficiency, The Least Restrictive Alternative: Principles and Practices (H. Turnbull ed. 1981); Chambers, *Alternatives to Civil Commitment of the Mentally Ill: Practical Guides and Constitutional Imperatives,* 70 Mich. L. Rev. 1108 (1972); Weiner, *Rights of Institutionalized Persons,* in The Mentally Disabled and the Law 251, 262-267 (S. Brakel, J. Parry & B. Weiner eds., 3d ed. 1985). The principle has found widespread acceptance in state statutes, sometimes under the label of "the least drastic means principle." *See, e.g.,* N.M. Stat. Ann. §43-1-3(D) (1984 repl.); *Legal Issues in State Mental Health Care: Suggested Statute on Civil Commitment,* 1 Mental Disability L. Rep. 127, 131 (1977); *see also* Stromberg & Stone, *supra* note 4, at 291.

finement and treatment or habilitation. The standard strikes a balance by recommending a period of five days within which to move for a hearing and a limit of fifteen days within which a hearing should be held. Thus, the recommended maximum period between an NGRI verdict and the completion of a commitment hearing is forty-five days.

This standard presumes that a jurisdiction has instituted a special verdict of not guilty by reason of mental nonresponsibility [insanity], as recommended in standard 7-6.10. Jurisdictions that allow only two verdicts, guilty and not guilty, with the latter subsuming acquittals by reason of mental nonresponsibility [insanity], will need a device of some sort to trigger an automatic commitment for purpose of evaluation. One approach is to employ the procedures embodied in this standard for defendants found not guilty after they have asserted the defense of mental nonresponsibility [insanity]. However, that approach is uncomfortably imprecise because it will sweep within its coverage some defendants juries believed did not commit the objective elements of charged offenses, along with others who committed harmful acts for which they were not criminally responsible. In such a jurisdiction, the standard might appropriately be modified to require trial courts, before ordering an evaluation, to find probable cause to believe that a respondent meets statutory commitment criteria as of the time of an acquittal.

Standard 7-7.3. Commitment procedures; general and special

(a) Each state should adopt a separate set of special procedures ("special commitment") for seeking the civil commitment of those acquittees who were acquitted by reason of mental nonresponsibility [insanity] of felonies involving acts causing, threatening, or creating a substantial risk of death or serious bodily harm.

(b) States may seek the civil commitment of mental nonresponsibility [insanity] acquittees who were acquitted of felonies which did not involve acts causing, threatening, or creating a substantial risk of death or serious bodily harm, or of misdemeanors, only by using those procedures ("general commitment") used for the civil commitment of persons outside the criminal justice system, provided that those procedures satisfy the requirements of due process of law.

Commentary Introduction

Standard 7-7.3 recommends that special commitment procedures be enacted for the subsequent confinement of acquittees, the criminal charges against whom involved personal violence. Persons acquitted of misdemeanors and other felonies should be commitable only pursuant to general commitment procedures.

Related Standards

ABA, Standards for Criminal Justice 7-4.13, 7-6.8
DD Model Statute: DD Offenders Act §10(6)
MHLP Model Statute: Insanity Defense §4

Commentary

The Need for Special Commitment Procedures

The coverage of a standard governing special commitment procedures for mental nonresponsibility [insanity] acquittees poses a difficult choice. One alternative is to propose that jurisdictions choose between committing all acquittees under the general commitment procedures employed for patients outside the criminal justice system and enacting special provisions for acquittees who were tried for crimes involving threats of serious bodily harm. A proposal offering alternative choices is attractive because it allows jurisdictions that currently find it satisfactory to commit all patients under general procedures to continue doing so. However, the Association through this standard has rejected such a "choice doctrine" and has concluded there are compelling reasons to recommend that all jurisdictions adopt special procedures governing the disposition of violent mental nonresponsibility [insanity] acquittees. The special commitment procedures recommended in this standard do not differ radically from general commitment under the law of most jurisdictions. Nevertheless, the differences are substantial enough and so specifically tailored to the circumstances of acquittees to warrant their adoption by all jurisdictions.

It is undisputed that the public feels threatened by the potential release of mental nonresponsibility [insanity] acquittees. Although some of that fear is undoubtedly exaggerated, it is important that agencies responsible for protecting public safety be able to monitor the location and condition of dangerous acquittees. Increasingly, general commitment statutes have been amended to reduce unnecessary institutionalization; the procedures they authorize are structured to facilitate the release of patients as swiftly as possible. This objective is accomplished, among other means, through frequent, rigorous periodic review and discretionary, liberal release procedures. Though these provisions are appropriate and arguably constitutionally mandated by due process for patients who pose relatively little danger to others, they may protect the public safety insufficiently in instances involving patients who have committed violent acts in the past.

It is also a matter of concern that the public's apprehension about the possible release of violent acquittees may skew the character of procedures for all patients in a jurisdiction that provides a single commitment system for all involuntarily committed patients. Hence, reforms in a civil commitment system, desirable from the aspect of a vast majority of civil patients, may be jeopardized because of public concern over the dangers posed by a small minority of patients who are violent acquittees.[1] The existence of a special commitment system should allow jurisdictions to devise general commitment procedures to meet the need for facilitated community placement manifested by the majority of patients who present little or no danger to others.[2]

A secondary benefit from adopting a special commitment system for violent acquittees is the promotion of more accurate criminal jury verdicts concerning the defense of mental nonresponsibility [insanity]. If juries know (as they could be instructed under standard 7-6.8) that upon acquittal a defendant is subject to procedures designed to prevent inappropriate release into the community, they might be less hesitant to bring in verdicts of mental nonresponsibility [insanity] warranted by the facts of a case.

1. *See* Burt, *Of Mad Dogs and Scientists: The Perils of the "Criminal-Insane,"* 123 U. Pa. L. Rev. 258, 292 (1974); Wexler, *The Structure of Civil Commitment: Patterns, Pressures, and Interactions in Mental Health Legislation*, 7 Law & Human Behav. 1, 15 (1983); Note, *Rules for an Exceptional Class: The Commitment and Release of Persons Acquitted of Violent Offenses by Reason of Insanity*, 57 N.Y.U.L. Rev. 281, 283 (1982) [hereinafter cited as N.Y.U.L. Note]. *See generally* McGraw, Fitch, Buckley & Marvell, *Civil Commitment in New York City: An Analysis of Practice*, 5 Pace L. Rev. 259 (1985).

2. States that currently have a single commitment system for all patients should reevaluate their general commitment procedures after they adopt special procedures governing violent mental nonresponsibility [insanity] acquittees. They may find that restrictions necessary to protect the public against the dangerous minority of this previously undifferentiated class are no longer needed for patients who have not evidenced dangerousness by the commission of a violent, otherwise criminal act.

Constitutional and Policy Issues

The United States Supreme Court has sustained the constitutionality of special commitment procedures governing defendants acquitted by reason of mental nonresponsibility [insanity] and has recognized considerable latitude for jurisdictions to devise different practices and procedures governing general civil commitment.[3] The standards in this part reflect the Association's view that legislatures should exercise considerable caution in fashioning a system of special commitment. Even if the equal protection clause permits wholesale departures from general commitment practices, public policy considerations require that any such deviations be supported by identifiable differences between the classes of general commitment patients and special commitment acquittees. Policy concerns about fairness and equality require that disparate treatment of the two groups be justified in each particular by empirically verifiable data.

The different procedures affecting the two groups recommended in these standards reflect the fact that violent acquittees have been found to have committed an otherwise criminal act dangerous to others; consequently, the public is justified in its apprehension that dangerous conduct will recur if an acquittee is released prematurely.[4] This dimension of the problem is both real and relevant, but should not be exaggerated. General commitment usually covers persons who are dangerous to themselves and others. Some among the latter have manifested their hazardous potential through earlier dangerous conduct. Indeed, it is increasingly true that a general police power commitment requires a showing of some overt act or threat evidencing the likelihood of future dangerous behavior.[5] In some instances, such an overt act might be proscribed by the criminal law; in other instances it will not be. In any event, rarely will the commission of overt dangerous activity have been proven beyond a reasonable doubt, as is recommended in this standard as a prerequisite to special commitment procedures.

The same circumspection required in describing differences between civil committees and violent acquittees must extend to conclusions about future dangerous or violent conduct if their members are allowed to

3. Jones v. United States, 463 U.S. 354, 370 (1983).

4. A difference "between acquittees and committees, which might be thought to justify different treatment of the two classes, is that the former have already unhappily manifested the reality of anti-social conduct." Waite v. Jacobs, 475 F.2d 392, 396 (D.C. Cir. 1973).

5. *See, e.g.*, N.M. Stat. Ann. §43-1(M) (1984 repl.).

remain at liberty. In practice, differentiation in treatment and disposition must stem from comparative predictions of the future violent behavior of members of these two groups. It has been well established that the ability of psychiatrists and other mental disability professionals to predict future dangerous behavior accurately is quite low.[6] However, current studies also reveal that the accuracy of predictions rises when the subjects are habitually violent persons and the predictions are short range rather than long term.[7] Both for these reasons and for the want of a practical alternative, courts have been willing to accept predictions of dangerousness as a basis for the civil commitment of acquittees and other mental patients.[8] The Association's position is that, although myriad problems attend attempts to predict future violent behavior, the factual predicate of a mental nonresponsibility [insanity] acquittal provides adequate information to support the limited departures from general commitment procedures embodied in these standards.

Scope of Special Commitment

Paragraph (a) makes clear that the special commitment procedures proposed by the Association should govern only cases involving acquittees who were charged with felonies involving acts or threats of serious bodily harm to others. Criminal trial courts learn nothing about the propensities for future violent behavior on the part of defendants acquitted of crimes like embezzlement that involve no violent conduct. Because

6. *See* J. MONAHAN, THE CLINICAL PREDICTION OF VIOLENT BEHAVIOR (1981) and sources cited therein [hereinafter cited as J. MONAHAN]; H. STEADMAN & J. COCOZZA, CAREERS OF THE CRIMINALLY INSANE (1974); T. THORNBERRY & J. JACOBY, THE CRIMINALLY INSANE: A COMMUNITY FOLLOW-UP OF MENTALLY ILL OFFENDERS (1979); Monahan, *The Prediction of Violent Behavior: Toward a Second Generation of Theory and Policy,* 141 AM. J. PSYCHIATRY 10 (1984) [hereinafter cited as Monahan]; Zenoff, *Controlling the Dangers of Dangerousness: The ABA Standards and Beyond,* 53 GEO. WASH. L. REV. 562, 565-567, 595-607 (1985). *See also* Mullen & Reinher, *The Mentally Ill Offender: A Comparison of Prison Inmates, Forensic Psychiatric Patients, and General Psychiatric Patients,* 9 J. PSYCHIATRY & L. 203 (1981); PASEWARK, *Insanity Plea: A Review of the Research Literature,* 9 J. PSYCHIATRY & L. 357 (1981); Steadman & Morrissey, *Measuring the Costs of a Public Protectionist Versus a Civil Libertarian Model,* 5 LAW & HUMAN BEHAV. 263 (1981) Weiner, *Mental Disability and the Criminal Law,* in THE MENTALLY DISABLED AND THE LAW 683, 735-736 (S. Brakel, J. Parry & B. Weiner eds., 3d ed. 1985). For a fuller discussion of the dilemmas caused by professional inability to predict dangerousness accurately, *see* standard 7-3.9 and commentary.

7. J. MONAHAN, *supra* note 6, at 14-15.

8. *See* Monahan, *supra* note 6, *passim;* N.Y.U.L. Note, *supra* note 1, at 314-321.

nothing distinctive has been learned about nonviolent acquittees, there is no justification for employing procedures more restrictive than those governing general commitment patients.[9]

The standard does not attempt to specify crimes that involve acts or threats of serious bodily harm. The taxonomy of crimes in the states varies widely, and the task of classifying crimes meriting special commitment is appropriately left to individual legislatures.[10] State legislatures have listed crimes of violence for other purposes, for example, in defining the scope of the felony-murder rule, thus delineating aggravating circumstances warranting augmented sentences and multiple-offender legislation. Such experience may prove helpful in defining the scope of special commitment procedures governing violent acquittees.

Paragraph (b) of the standard directly envisions that government representatives will retain the authority to seek the civil commitment of mental nonresponsibility [insanity] acquittees, the criminal charges against whom did not embrace felonies involving personal violence. The general civil commitment procedures ordinarily employed for persons not charged with crime and for criminal defendants found permanently incompetent to stand trial[11] remain available. The standard assumes that acquittees in nonviolent criminal prosecutions are sufficiently similar in

---

9. In Jones v. United States, 463 U.S. 354, 365 (1983), the Supreme Court held that a distinction between violent and nonviolent crimes is not constitutionally required. The *Jones* majority observed that "crimes of theft frequently may result in violence from the efforts of the criminal to escape or the victim to protect property or the police to apprehend the fleeing criminal." *Id.* at 365 n.14. One noted scholar has characterized this argument as "Pickwickian." Monahan, *supra* note 6, at 13. More importantly, the Court's holding in *Jones* is based on a conclusion that the Constitution does not require that special commitment laws be tailored to a scientific understanding of the validity of predictions of future dangerous conduct. "We do not agree with the suggestion that Congress' power to legislate in this area depends on the research conducted by the psychiatric community." 463 U.S. at 364-365 n.13. In contrast, the standards reflect a judgment that when a fundamental right like personal liberty is at stake, public policy dictates that legislation should rest on the substantial available body of empirical knowledge which strongly suggests that predictions of future violent conduct are not reliable if based solely upon earlier nonviolent activity caused by mental disability. *See* the authorities cited in note 6.

10. The federal Insanity Defense Reform Act of 1984, 18 U.S.C.A. §4243(d) (Supp. 1986), exceeds the scope of coverage recommended in the standards by including offenses involving serious damage or a substantial risk of serious damage to the property of another person, as well as bodily injury or a substantial risk of bodily injury to another person. *See infra* notes 25-27 and accompanying text.

11. *See* Jackson v. Indiana, 406 U.S. 715 (1972).

relevant characteristics to general commitment patients that the same procedures for commitment and periodic review hearings and release will prove appropriate.

The language of the standard carefully endorses the use of general commitment procedures only if they satisfy the requirements of due process of law. The standard, in limiting the scope of special commitment for acquittees, should not be interpreted to imply an endorsement of the constitutionality or appropriateness of all general commitment procedures now employed by the states. This poses no major problems in the context of civil commitment of mentally ill persons, however. Since the early 1970s, almost all states have adopted procedures that afford prospective mental patients a hearing, counsel, the right to expert testimony, and other procedural due process rights.[12] In contrast, the constitutionality of general commitment statutes governing mentally retarded persons is much less clear. Many existing statutes in this area have failed to provide even the rudiments of procedural due process and have not kept pace with constitutional developments in the area of mental health law generally.[13] States with deficient statutes in the mental retardation area should revise them, but the appropriate contours of general commitment procedures affecting retarded persons is beyond the scope of these standards.[14]

The standard, in designing a special commitment system, departs in only a few respects from general commitment practices; those departures directly meet special concerns about the prospect of violent behavior by acquittees who are specially committed. Therefore, the special commitment procedures outlined in the subsequent standards in this part recognize the substantial public apprehension about premature release of violent acquittees and address it through modified periodic review and

12. These statutes follow the rough outlines of a series of constitutional cases mandating such procedures. The leading case was Lessard v. Schmidt, 349 F. Supp. 1078 (E.D. Wis. 1972) (three-judge court), *vacated on other grounds*, 414 U.S. 473, *reinstated and enforced*, 379 F. Supp. 1376 (E.D. Wis. 1974), *vacated on other grounds*, 421 U.S. 957 (1975), *reinstated*, 413 F. Supp. 1318 (E.D. Wis. 1978). For a model statute codifying these procedures, *see Legal Issues in State Mental Health Care: Civil Commitment*, 2 Mental Disability L. Rep. 73-159 (1977).

13. B. Sales *et al.*, Disabled Persons and the Law: State Legislative Issues 416-21 (1982) [hereinafter cited as B. Sales *et al.*]. *See also* Dybwad & Herr, *Unnecessary Coercion: An End to Involuntary Civil Commitment of Retarded Persons*, 31 Stan. L. Rev. 753 (1979).

14. *See Model Statute: An Act to Guarantee the Right of Developmentally Disabled Persons to Receive Appropriate Services and to Establish Consent Procedures to Allow the Provision of Those Services*, *in* B. Sales *et al.*, *supra* note 13, at 409-452.

discharge procedures designed to protect against ill-considered or inadvertent release.

Federal Acquittees

The standards in this part are all cast in terms of recommendations to the states. Mental nonresponsibility [insanity] acquittees in federal courts present different dispositional issues that have been dealt with through the Insanity Defense Reform Act of 1984.[15] Under that legislation, federal defendants acquitted on grounds of mental nonresponsibility [insanity] are committed to a suitable facility until released on the basis of a later proceeding.[16] The Attorney General may contract with a state or local or privately operated facility for hospitalization, care, and treatment,[17] and is to consider the suitability of the facility's rehabilitation programs to meet the individual's needs.[18]

A judicial hearing is held concerning the validity of a committed former defendant's continued hospitalization not later than forty days following the jury NGRI verdict.[19] However, the hearing may be delayed beyond that time if the district court orders a psychiatric or psychological examination.[20] An initial diagnostic commitment can extend for a reasonable time not to exceed forty-five days, but the director of a facility to

15. Comprehensive Crime Control Act of 1984, Pub. Law No. 98-473, 98 Stat. 1976, §§401-403 (approved Oct. 30, 1984). *See generally* B. George, A Practical Guide to the Comprehensive Crime Control Act of 1984, 108-123 (1986); Mental Health Law in the 1980's (A. Brooks & B. Winick eds., in press).

16. 18 U.S.C.A. §4243(a) (Supp. 1986). A suitable facility is one appropriate "to provide care and treatment given the nature of the offense and the characteristics of the defendant." *Id.* §4247(a)(2).

17. *Id.* §4247(*i*)(A).

18. *Id.* §4247(*i*)(C). The Department of Health and Human Services is to be consulted in establishing standards for facilities used to hospitalize former federal criminal defendants. *Id.* §4247(*i*)(D).

The director of a facility in which an NGRI patient has been received is required to inform the patient about the rehabilitation programs available in the facility. *Id.* §4247(e)(2). Rehabilitation programs include: (1) basic educational training to assist the patient in understanding the society to which he or she will return and the magnitude of his or her offense and its impact on society; (2) vocational training to assist the individual in contributing to and participating in the society to which he or she will return; (3) drug, alcohol, and other treatment programs to assist the individual in overcoming psychological or physical dependence; and (4) organized physical sports and recreation programs. *Id.* §4247(a)(1).

19. *Id.* §4243(c).

20. *Id.* §4243(b).

which a person has been committed may, upon a showing of good cause that the additional time is necessary to observe and evaluate the patient,[21] apply to the committing court for a reasonable extension not to exceed thirty days. Accordingly, as much as two and one-half months conceivably might elapse between entry of a jury verdict of acquittal based on mental nonresponsibility [insanity] and the commencement of a forty-day hearing.

The forty-day hearing procedures are governed by federal law.[22] Respondents have the right to counsel, including appointment of counsel if they are financially unable,[23] and must be given an opportunity to testify, to present evidence, to subpoena witnesses on their behalf, and to confront and cross-examine witnesses who appear at the hearing.[24] All procedures are civil in character, unaffected by the constitutional provisions regulating the trial of criminal cases.

The standard for continued hospitalization is that a respondent suffers from a mental disease or defect and that release would create a substantial risk of bodily injury to another person or serious damage to the property of another.[25] In the latter respect, Congress has differed from the Association's recommended criterion reflected in the instant standard. The burden of persuasion rests on former defendants to establish that they pose no risk of bodily injury to another person or serious damage to the property of another. The measure of the burden turns on the crime for which a former defendant was tried and concerning which the defendant was found not guilty solely because of mental nonresponsibility [insanity]. If the predicate offense involved (1) bodily injury to (including, presumably, the death of) another person, (2) a substantial risk of such injury, (3) serious damage to the property of another person, or (4) a substantial risk of such property damage, then the burden is at

21. *Ibid.*
22. *Id.* §4243(c).
23. *Id.* §4247(d).
24. *Ibid.*
25. *Id.* §§4243(d)-(f), 4247(c)(4)(C). Congress interpreted Jones v. United States, 463 U.S. 354, 364-365 (1983), to imply that danger to property can be a constitutionally valid consideration underlying compulsory post-NGRI commitments. *See* Report of the Committee on the Judiciary, United States Senate, on the Comprehensive Crime Control Act of 1983, S. 1762, Report No. 98-225, 98th Cong., 1st Sess. at 243 and n.77 (1983). For a state decision including damage to property within a statutory criterion of "danger to self or others," *see* State v. Lafferty, 192 Conn. 571, 472 A.2d 1275 (1984).

the level of clear and convincing proof.[26] If any other category of federal offense was involved, the level is at the preponderance of the evidence.[27]

Respondents who fail to meet that burden of persuasion are to be committed to the custody of the Attorney General.[28] The ensuing responsibilities on the Attorney General are three-fold: (1) The Attorney General first is to make reasonable efforts to have the authorities of the state in which the former defendant is domiciled or was tried assume the responsibility for custody, care, and treatment. If that succeeds, the Attorney General may initiate state commitment proceedings if otherwise authorized by state law.[29] (2) If, despite the Attorney General's reasonable efforts, the appropriate state authorities will not carry through civil commitment proceedings, the Attorney General is to hospitalize the person for treatment in a suitable facility as defined in the statute.[30] (3) If the respondent is hospitalized under federal sponsorship, the Attorney General is to continue to exert all reasonable efforts to bring about state commitment proceedings in the respondent's state of domicile or trial.[31]

If a state accepts responsibility for an acquitted former federal defendant through civil commitment proceedings eventuating in a commitment order, the duration and termination of that hospitalization will turn on state law. If the Attorney General fails to achieve state placement, release from hospital or outpatient status requires additional federal administrative and judicial activity under the statute.[32] This embraces three forms of review. One is a motion for discharge lodged by the counsel for or legal guardian of a hospitalized former criminal defendant at any time during a period of hospitalization, at 180-day minimum intervals.[33] A hearing must be held on the motion. The second is a certification by a facility director that the former defendant has been treated or habilitated to the extent that release or conditional release no longer poses the requisite threat of bodily injury or serious property damage.[34] The third is a re-

26. 18 U.S.C.A. §4243(d) (Supp. 1986).

27. *Ibid.*

28. *Id.* §4243(e).

29. *Id.* §4247(*i*) (B).

30. *Id.* §4247(a)(2). This could mean a state or local hospital or a privately operated facility, *id.* §4247(*i*)(A), if its rehabilitation programs are suitable to the respondent's needs. *Id.* §4247(*i*)(C). *See supra* note 17.

31. 18 U.S.C.A. §4243(e) (Supp. 1986).

32. *Id.* §4243(e)(2).

33. *Id.* §4247(h).

34. *Id.* §4243(f).

quired annual report of a facility director covering a patient's condition, including the need for continued hospitalization.[35] A certification may permit an immediate discharge without a hearing, but a hearing will be held if counsel for the government moves for it or the court so decides on its own motion. Hearing procedure is identical to that in a forty-day review.[36] At the conclusion of the hearing, the district court can order immediate discharge[37] or conditional discharge,[38] or continue a respondent in compelled institutional status if he or she has not met the burden of persuasion that the substantial risk of bodily injury to another person or serious damage to the property of another has dissipated.

Standard 7-7.4. Special procedures; commitment criteria

(a) Special commitment procedures for mental nonresponsibility [insanity] acquittees acquitted of felonies involving acts causing or creating a substantial risk of death or threatening serious bodily harm should afford every such acquittee with the right to a commitment hearing which meets the requirements set forth in standard 7-7.5.

(b) At the conclusion of the commitment hearing, the court may order the acquittee to be committed if it finds by clear and convincing evidence that the acquittee:

(i) is currently mentally ill or mentally retarded; and, as a result,

(ii) poses a substantial risk of serious bodily harm to others.

(c) The court may not commit the acquittee unless it finds, beyond a reasonable doubt, that the acquittee committed the criminal act for which he or she was acquitted by reason of mental nonresponsibility [insanity], or unless the trier of fact made such a finding at the acquittee's criminal trial. The commitment court should evaluate the

---

35. *Id.* §4247(e)(1)(B). Counsel for a hospitalized respondent can request in writing that the individual's "testimony" or the interview(s) upon which a periodic report is based be videotaped and a copy submitted to the court along with the periodic report. *Id.* §4247(f). Copies in turn can be transmitted to others, including counsel for the respondent, as the recipient district court directs. *Ibid.*

36. *See* notes 21-23 and accompanying text. Nothing in 18 U.S.C.A. §4243 (Supp. 1986) is to be construed to prevent a patient from using federal habeas corpus to attack the legality of continued hospitalization. *Id.* §4247(g).

37. 18 U.S.C.A. §4243(f)(1) (Supp. 1986).

38. *Id.* §4243(f)(2).

relevance of the criminal act to the proposed commitment in light of the amount of time which has passed since its occurrence and the possibility that the acquittee's confinement may have prevented the commission of other overt acts posing a serious threat of bodily harm to others.

(d) If the court concludes that the only reason the acquittee does not meet the standard for commitment set forth in paragraph (b) is the effect of treatment or habilitation currently being received, the acquittee may be committed unless the court is persuaded by a preponderance of the evidence that the acquittee will continue to receive such treatment or habilitation following release for as long as the treatment or habilitation is required. If the court is persuaded that acquittee will continue to receive the needed treatment or habilitation, it may order either that acquittee be released or, in the alternative, that acquittee be released upon condition that acquittee continue to receive the treatment or habilitation. If acquittee does not continue to receive the treatment or habilitation, the conditional release may be revoked pursuant to standard 7-7.11.

Commentary Introduction

Standard 7-7.4 recommends that special commitment procedures for acquittees allow commitment upon a finding by clear and convincing evidence that an acquittee is mentally disabled and poses a substantial risk of danger to others. This parallels the standard of proof utilized in civil commitment cases and represents a modest departure from the substantive criteria for commitment common in state civil commitment statutes. Departures from general commitment procedures are warranted only when the personal characteristics of acquittees differ from those of ordinary civil committees.

Related Standards

ABA, Standards for Criminal Justice 7-4.14, 7-6.9, 7-6.10, 18-7.5
APA, Model Statute §6.C
DD Model Statute: DD Offenders Act §10(6)
DD Model Statute: Right/Consent to Services §§8, 9
MHLP Model Statute: Insanity Defense §4
MHLP Model Statute: Civil Commitment §17

Commentary

Substantive Criteria for Commitment

Paragraphs (a) and (b) embody the Association's position that a committing court, after considering an evaluation report and hearing the evidence adduced at a hearing conforming to the recommendations set forth in standard 7-7.5, should order special commitment only on the basis of findings that an acquittee is currently mentally ill or mentally retarded and, as a result, poses a danger of serious bodily harm to others. This approximates the substantive standard for commitment now found in most state statutes for the general commitment of mentally ill persons;[1] it is, however, narrower than the federal criteria enacted in 1984.[2] In a few respects, however, the standard may differ from general commitment criteria in ways warranted by the personal characteristics of violent mental nonresponsibility [insanity] acquittees.

The first point of departure is that the special commitment procedures are limited to acquittees who pose a perceived threat of harm to other persons. In contrast, civil commitment statutes generally include the factor of danger to respondents themselves. Although an acquittal on mental nonresponsibility [insanity] grounds may suggest a likelihood that the acquittee might harm other persons, it reflects not at all on the potential for suicide or other self-injurious behavior. Accordingly, acquittees dangerous to themselves cannot be distinguished from respondents in general civil commitment proceedings who present a similar danger, so that there is no justification for applying to them the more restrictive release procedures governing specially committed acquittees.[3] If the latter are to be committed because they endanger their own safety, general commitment procedures should be utilized.

---

1. *See generally* S. Brakel *et al.*, The Mentally Disabled and the Law (3d ed. 1986).

2. A substantial risk of serious damage to the property of another is an alternative basis for continued commitment under the Insanity Defense Reform Act of 1984. *See* commentary to standard 7-7.3, note 25 and accompanying text.

3. The holding in Jones v. United States, 463 U.S. 354, 370 (1983), is couched in terms of dangerousness to self or society. The inclusion of danger to self is arguably dictum and is not discussed in the Court's opinion.

In Hickey v. Morris, 722 F.2d 543, 547 (9th Cir. 1983), the court rejected equal protection attacks on special commitment legislation based on a requirement of proof of dangerous acts for civil commitment but not for post-mental nonresponsibility [insanity] commitments. It noted that defendants have injected the insanity issue at criminal trial, which in turn has generated special commitment proceedings following such verdicts.

A similar conclusion follows in jurisdictions that permit civil commitments on the basis of the likelihood of threat to property.[4] Special commitment of acquittees who threaten only property interests is inappropriate because the restrictive release provisions governing special committees are justifiable solely on the basis of protecting human life and safety.

The standard endorses a statutory requirement that acquittees be found both mentally disabled and a threat to others.[5] Some jurisdictions allow special commitment upon a finding of only one of these criteria.[6] Such provisions cannot be justified on the basis of any identifiable differences between acquittees and general commitment patients. To allow special commitment on the basis of a prediction of dangerousness in the absence of current mental disability ignores an essential element of civil commitment and converts special commitment into a form of imprisonment despite an acquittal based on mental nonresponsibility [insanity]. Moreover, the continued confinement of nondangerous acquittees until they become free of mental disability cannot be justified on the basis of any characteristic peculiar to mental nonresponsibility [insanity] acquittees.[7]

The standard does not provide a definition of mental illness or mental retardation. However, legislation should embody a legal definition consistent with the therapeutic and rehabilitative goals of civil commitment. Thus, special commitment statutes should not incorporate the legal definition of "insanity" governing criminal responsibility; the statutory focus should be on the relationship between the disability and future dangerous behavior and not an acquittee's ability, for example, to distinguish right from wrong.[8] Many states may use the definitions of mental illness

---

4. *See, e.g.*, Suzuki v. Yuen, 617 F.2d 173 (9th Cir. 1980); *In re* Herman, 30 Wash. App. 321, 634 P.2d 310 (1981) (involving threats to a particular statue in a cemetery).

5. *See, e.g.*, MICH. COMP. L. ANN. §§330.1400a, 330.1401, 330.1500(g), 330.1500(h), 330.1515, 330.2050 (1980).

6. *See, e.g.*, Harris v. Ballone, 681 F.2d 225 (4th Cir. 1982) (requiring a showing of dangerousness but not mental illness); State v. Krol, 68 N.J. 236, 344 A.2d 289 (1975) (striking down a provision that justified continued confinement of acquittees so long as their "insanity" continued); State v. Gebarski, 90 Wis. 2d 754, 280 N.W.2d 672 (1979) (requiring a showing of dangerousness but not mental illness).

7. *See In re* Torsney, 47 N.Y.2d 667, 394 N.E.2d 262; 420 N.Y.S.2d 192 (1979).

8. *See In re* Franklin, 7 Cal. 3d 126, 145, 496 P.2d 465, 477, 101 Cal. Rptr. 553, 565 (1972). *See also* United States v. Shorter, 343 A.2d 569 (D.C. 1975) (statutory provision for commitment of insanity acquittees applied to a person acquitted by reason of mental retardation, because it falls within the definition of insanity, but mental retardation differs from mental illness in respect to the nature of subsequent treatment).

and mental retardation contained in their general civil commitment statute. Other states, however, might prefer a broader definition for special commitment purposes, especially if the general commitment definition of mental illness is limited to severely psychotic individuals. These states may decide that the narrower definition for general commitment purposes will limit the scope of state intervention into the lives of individuals who have not been involved in the criminal justice system, while the broader definition for purposes of special commitment procedures will subject dangerous acquittees to more rigorous release procedures whatever the exact nature of their mental disabilities.[9]

Although the standard does not address the issue directly, constitutional and public policy problems are evident if government seeks to use special commitment procedures against dangerous acquittees whose current mental disability is unrelated to the mental conditions from which they suffered at the time of the dangerous activity underlying the earlier criminal charges.[10] In such cases, governmental authorities in fact have relevant information about the possibility of future violence based on past activity, but the fact that current mental condition is unrelated to an acquittee's mental condition at an earlier time may diminish the relevance of that information.

The standard also does not require specifically that a mental disability constituting a basis for special commitment be amenable to treatment.[11] If state legislation includes this factor among the requirements for general commitment, an equal protection issue arises if the same element is not required for special commitment. Acquittees are not less dangerous because they suffer mental disabilities that cannot be treated effectively; indeed, release under such circumstances may prove especially hazard-

---

9. It is less clear whether a state could include "psychopathy" in its special commitment definition, thereby allowing the committment of acquittees even though the only evidence of mental disability is a pattern of repeated criminal behavior.

10. *See* Lee v. Kolb, 449 F. Supp. 1368, 1382 (W.D.N.Y. 1978) (approving special commitment under such circumstances). This issue may be of particular interest if evidence becomes available later that a defendant feigned mental disability at a criminal trial in order to obtain acquittal. *See generally* United States v. Carter, 415 F. Supp. 15 (D.D.C. 1975) (holding that an acquittee was entitled to release when it was shown that he was not currently suffering from any mental disability, even though there were indications that he had feigned mental illness at his criminal trial).

11. *See generally* People v. Goff, 127 Cal. App. 3d 1039, 179 Cal. Rptr. 190 (1982) (approving such commitments as a matter of statutory interpretation). *But see* Stromberg & Stone, *A Model State Law on Civil Commitment of the Mentally Ill*, 20 HARV. J. ON LEGIS. 275, 330 (1983) (requirement of a "reasonable prospect that [the] disorder is treatable").

ous to the public. However, whether this is a sufficient justification for treating special committees differently than general civil committees is an issue on which the Association takes no position.

The criterion of potential future harm recommended in the standard, like that of mental illness or mental retardation, has substantial consequences. Subparagraph (b)(ii) endorses a requirement that committing courts find that an acquittee "poses a substantial threat of serious bodily harm to others." As noted earlier, this approximates the standard now employed by a substantial number of jurisdictions for general commitment.[12] Courts correctly have noted that this is a more precise formulation than "dangerousness."[13] This precision may also mitigate some of the difficulties inherent in the prediction of future violent behavior.[14] How substantial the threat must be in an individual case is a matter for a court to decide. Accordingly, conclusory testimony bearing on this issue should be avoided.

The standard includes no specific provision regarding the imminence of the threat that an acquittee must pose. This issue does not lend itself easily to formulae or limitations. But it is clear that a commitment based on predictions of remote future behavior should be considered inappropriate. There are two difficulties with such long-range predictions. The first is that the limited reliability of predictions relating to the immediate future is attenuated even further as the time lengthens between prediction and the realization or nonrealization of that prediction. In addition, the justification for depriving acquittees of liberty weakens if the predicate is an event not predicted to occur for a substantial period of time. Therefore, the Association's position, embodied in the standard, is that a valid commitment must be based upon a belief that an acquittee poses a substantial threat of harm within a reasonably short period of time.

Burden of Persuasion (Proof)

Paragraph (b) assigns the burden of persuasion to the state. In that way, a hearing conducted after an evaluation becomes a true commitment hearing rather than a form of habeas corpus. The state must dem-

---

12. *See* commentary to standard 7-7.3, note 1 and accompanying text.

13. *See* Hill v. State, 358 So. 2d 190, 195 (Fla. Dist. Ct. App. 1978); State v. Olson, 181 Mont. 323, 593 P.2d 724, 731 (1979).

14. *See* commentary to standard 7-7.3, notes 6-8 and accompanying text; J. MONAHAN, THE CLINICAL PREDICTION OF VIOLENT BEHAVIOR 4-5 (1981). *See generally* D. WEXLER, MENTAL HEALTH LAW: MAJOR ISSUES 59-68 (1981).

onstrate that an acquittee meets the commitment criteria. The allocation of the burden of persuasion in that way reflects the Association's belief that there are no relevant differences between acquittees and general commitment patients. In general commitment cases, the Supreme Court has held that the state must bear the burden of persuasion.[15] But in *Jones v. United States,* it distinguished cases involving mental nonresponsibility [insanity] acquittees.[16] In contrast to the policy enunciated in these standards, the *Jones* majority believed that defendants who have established successfully an affirmative defense of mental nonresponsibility [insanity] — the establishment of which, in the *Jones* view, could support a presumption of continuing mental disability and dangerousness — cannot insist on the protection of constitutional requirements governing civil commitment cases. It must be stressed that the *Jones* holding does not address the allocation of burdens in special commitment hearings if, as in standard 7-6.9(b)(i), defendants may be acquitted when juries entertain a reasonable doubt as to their mental responsibility [sanity] at the time of a charged offense. Whatever the persuasiveness of a presumption of committability flowing from an affirmative finding of mental disability, certainly much less should be distilled from a mere finding of a reasonable doubt about mental condition.

Beyond the constitutional questions, however, the issue of burdens presents important public policy questions. Principles of fairness and equity require that departures from general commitment procedures be justified by relevant characteristics that distinguish acquittees from civil patients. A finding, at whatever level of certainty, that an acquittee was mentally disabled at the time of an alleged offense reveals little or nothing about mental condition at the time of acquittal. Months or even years may have intervened between the two events. The passage of time and, in many cases, the provision of treatment or habilitation in the interim generate a serious possibility that an acquittee's mental condition will not have remained constant from activity through acquittal. To draw inferences from such stale information may well be seriously unfair if the consequences of the presumption of continuing dangerousness affect something as important as personal liberty.[17]

---

15. Addington v. Texas, 441 U.S. 418 (1979).
16. 463 U.S. 354 (1983).
17. The Supreme Court in *Jones* did not discuss the issue of the significance to commitment of an intervening passage of time.

Standard of Proof

The standard of proof endorsed by the Association, like the burden of persuasion, is comparable to that governing civil commitment hearings, and the grounds for preferring parity with the civil commitment system are parallel. This portion of the standard also recommends a higher standard of proof than the constitutional minimum approved in *Jones v. United States.*[18] The *Jones* majority concluded that legislatures constitutionally might allow inferences of continuing dangerousness to be drawn from proof of a criminal *actus reus* even though the available body of scientific knowledge indicates that such wholesale predictions regarding future conduct are unreliable.[19] In contrast, standard 7-7.4 accurately reflects the current consensus of empirical studies on point, which offer no support for the view that the state's interest in allowing a lower standard of proof can be justified by relevant shared characteristics of acquittees whose mental condition has not been ascertained since the occurrence of an alleged crime. In the absence of an empirical justification, public policy considerations demand that acquittees be treated comparably to civil patients.

The Criminal Act

Paragraph (c) recommends a requirement that the criminal *actus reus* be demonstrated beyond a reasonable doubt, either at criminal trial or, if a verdict of acquittal is ambiguous, at a subsequent commitment hearing.[20] Special commitment procedures are acceptable as a matter of constitutional law and public policy only if they rest on a clear finding that the *actus reus* occurred. Such a finding also is highly relevant to a determination under subparagraph (b)(ii) regarding a prospective threat of harm to others. The more recently the harmful, otherwise criminal activity has occurred, the greater its probative value. In addition, however, committing courts are admonished through paragraph (c) to consider that an

18. 463 U.S. 354 (1983). As noted above, *Jones* is not directly applicable in jurisdictions that adopt the preferred standard 7-6.9(b)(i) on the allocation of burdens at criminal trial. However, the present standard reflects the Association's judgment that a standard of clear and convincing evidence is appropriate even in jurisdictions where defendants bear the burden of persuasion at trial.

19. *See* commentary to standard 7-7.3, notes 6-8 and accompanying text.

20. *See* standards 7-6.9 and 7-6.10 and commentary.

acquittee's nonviolent recent past may have been a product of incarceration and incapacitation rather than a changed mental condition.[21]

Effects of Treatment or Habilitation

Paragraph (d) addresses a difficult issue, sometimes erroneously labeled *synthetic sanity,* but more accurately to be described as "treatment-contingent noncommittability."[22] The legal relevance of currently effective treatment has arisen in a number of settings.[23] Although committing courts should not ignore issues concerning the effectiveness of treatment or habilitation, they ought not ignore the possibility that acquittees might cease taking medication or participating in other forms of treatment. Accordingly, paragraph (d) recommends placement on acquittees, by a preponderance of the evidence, of the burden of persuasion that treatment or habilitation will be continued following release. If a court is persuaded that an acquittee's release is warranted, it may condition release on continued treatment or habilitation. If the condition is breached, an acquittee's conditional release then will be subject to revocation as provided in standard 7-7.11.

Standard 7-7.5. Special commitment hearings

(a) A special commitment system for mental nonresponsibility [insanity] acquittees should provide the procedural protections described in this standard.

(b) The acquittee should be represented by counsel at the commit-

21. *See* People v. Howell, 196 Colo. 408, 586 P.2d 27, 30-31 (1978); Pitts v. State, 151 Ga. App. 691, 261 S.E.2d 435 (1979).

22. *See generally* Gutheil & Appelbaum, *"Mind Control," "Synthetic Sanity," "Artificial Competence," and Genuine Confusion: Legally-Relevant Actions of Anti-Psychotic Medications,* 12 Hofstra L. Rev. 77 (1983).

23. *See, e.g.,* People v. DeAnda, 114 Cal. App. 3d 480, 170 Cal. Rptr. 830 (1980), *cert. denied sub nom.* DeAnda v. California, 451 U.S. 990 (1981) (general commitment); State v. Collins, 381 So. 2d 449 (La. 1980) (effect of medication relevant in special commitment); State v. Hampton, 253 La. 399, 218 So. 2d 311 (1969) (competence to stand trial); Wolonsky v. Balson, 58 Ohio App. 2d 25, 387 N.E.2d 625 (1976) (effect of medication not relevant at special commitment).

ment hearing and is entitled to assistance of counsel during this period. If the acquittee is without counsel, the court should appoint counsel. If the acquittee is financially unable to afford counsel, the cost should be borne by the state. Representation by counsel cannot be waived.

(c) At the hearing, acquittee is entitled to confront and cross-examine adverse witnesses. Acquittee is also entitled to present witnesses, including an independent expert witness or expert witnesses. For financially unable acquittees the reasonable cost of expert witnesses should be borne by the state.

(d) At the hearing, the rules of evidence should apply, including the prohibition against hearsay testimony.

(e) The acquittee cannot be required to testify at the hearing.

(f) Acquittee should have the right to appeal on the record an adverse ruling on the issue of commitment. The appeal should be heard on an expedited basis.

Commentary Introduction

The standard outlines the procedures to be followed at hearings for special commitment of acquittees, including the right to counsel, confrontation and cross-examination, expert witnesses, rules of evidence, and appeals.

Related Standards

ABA, Standards for Criminal Justice 4-1.1, 5-4.1, 5-5.1, 6-3.6, 7-3.9, 7-3.11–7-3.14, 21-1.1, 23-2.2
APA, Model Statute §§6.D, 14.A
DD Model Statute: Right/Consent to Services §16
MHLP Model Statute: Insanity Defense §4
MHLP Model Statute: Civil Commitment §§14, 20

Commentary

The standard outlines the procedural requirements at commitment hearings and, through a cross-reference in standard 7-7.8(b), at periodic review hearings. The recommended procedural protections are generally found in modern general commitment statutes for the mentally ill.[1] There appears to be no persuasive argument for withholding from acquittees any of the procedures afforded to general commitment patients. Indeed, since periodic review may be somewhat less frequent under the special commitment system, rigorous enforcement of procedural requirements may be even more important in special commitments.[2]

The role of counsel is of paramount importance in cases involving mentally disabled persons who are unlikely to receive adequate hearings if they are unrepresented.[3] Paragraph (b), therefore, confirms that acquittees should be afforded a statutory right to the assistance of counsel, including appointed counsel if they are financially unable.[4] The standard also recommends that the assistance of counsel at a special commitment hearing not be waivable. This reflects the Association's belief that the risk of procedural abuses is unacceptably high if an acquittee likely to be suffering from a form of mental disability is without the aid of an attorney. The standard assumes that, because special commitment proceedings against acquitted former criminal defendants are civil in character and not a continuation of criminal prosecutions, the sixth amendment does not govern them; consequently, the holding of *Faretta v. California*,[5] that criminal defendants must be allowed to exercise the right of self-representation under that amendment, does not apply either. Even were that not so, so many acquittees would be unable to meet the constitutional standard for waiver of procedural rights, "an intentional relinquishment or abandonment of a known right or privilege,"[6] that it

1. *But see* commentary to standard 7-7.3, notes 12-13 and accompanying text, regarding commitment statutes for the mentally retarded. *See also* Ellis & Luckasson, *Mentally Retarded Criminal Defendants*, 53 Geo. Wash. L. Rev. 414, 466-470 (1985) [hereinafter cited as Ellis & Luckasson].

2. *See generally* Mathews v. Eldridge, 424 U.S. 319 (1976), for the fourteenth amendment test for procedural due process requirements in the contexts of civil and administrative proceedings. Cases extending the right to counsel and other procedural protections to special committees include Dorsey v. Solomon, 604 F.2d 271 (4th Cir. 1979); Schock v. Thomas, 274 Ark. 493, 625 S.W.2d 521 (1981); Clark v. State, 245 Ga. 629, 266 S.E.2d 466 (1980).

3. *See generally* Herr, *The New Clients: Legal Services for Mentally Retarded Persons*, 31 Stan. L. Rev. 553 (1979).

4. On the right of civil committees to counsel, *see* Weiner, *Rights of Institutionalized Persons*, in The Mentally Disabled and the Law 251, 284-288 (S. Brakel, J. Parry & B. Weiner eds., 3d ed. 1985) [hereinafter cited as Weiner]. Legislation as of October 1982 is summarized in *id.* at 162-165, Table 2.15.

5. 422 U.S. 806 (1975). *See* standard 7-5.3 and commentary.

6. Johnson v. Zerbst, 304 U.S. 458, 464 (1938). On equivalent problems in the context of waiver of rights during interrogation, *see* Ellis & Luckasson, *supra* note 1, at 446-452.

appears preferable to preclude waivers of counsel as a matter of law. The potential for abuse in the form of incompetent or ill-considered waivers of counsel is so great that it outweighs any administrative convenience that might flow from avoiding unnecessary appointments of attorneys to represent acquittees.

Paragraph (c) confirms the claim of acquittees to attend hearings and to confront and cross-examine witnesses testifying in support of commitment. Expert witnesses are especially important in special commitment proceedings. Consequently, the provision confirms the right of acquittee/respondents to present independent expert witnesses, at government expense if respondents are financially unable.[7] Paragraph (d) embodies a policy that the rules of evidence applicable to civil proceedings, including restrictions on the admissibility of hearsay testimony, should govern special commitment hearings. The Association recommends one exception to this policy in paragraph (e), however. Although parties to civil proceedings may be called as witnesses by their opponents, and must respond to specific questions unless they can assert a valid claim of self-incrimination or an evidentiary privilege, acquittees who probably suffer from a present mental disability are less likely than other witnesses to be aware of or understand the legal bases for withholding testimony. Moreover, granted the fairly limited coverage of double jeopardy,[8] it is quite possible that an acquittee's testimony might support the prosecution's affirmative presentation in a related but unbarred criminal proceeding and be admissible on the basis that, by responding, the respondent waived privilege against self-incrimination.[9] To forestall the possibility,

---

7. *See* standards 7-3.9, 7-3.11–7-3.14 and commentary; State *ex rel.* Hoover v. Bloom, 461 S.W.2d 841, 844 (Mo. 1971); Ellis & Luckasson, *supra* note 1, at 490-491. *See also Legal Issues in State Mental Health Care: Civil Commitment,* 2 Mental Disability L. Rep. 73, 104 (1977).

8. The double jeopardy provision, U.S. Const. amend. V, covers only the "same offence." The test utilized to determine identity is "whether each provision requires proof of a fact which the other does not. . . ." Blockburger v. United States, 284 U.S. 299, 304 (1932). *See also* Missouri v. Hunter, 459 U.S. 359 (1983); Albernaz v. United States, 450 U.S. 333 (1981); Simpson v. United States, 435 U.S. 6 (1978); Brown v. Ohio, 432 U.S. 161 (1977).

9. The leading case is McCarthy v. Arndstein, 262 U.S. 355 (1923). The Supreme Court has held in the context of criminal prosecutions that defendants cannot be required to relinquish one set of constitutional rights as the price of exercising another. Simmons v. United States, 390 U.S. 377 (1968) (government used defendant's admissions during a motion to suppress hearing as prosecution evidence, relying on doctrines of waiver of witness privilege; the Court mandated protection of both fourth and fifth amendment rights by continuing the privilege intact and forbidding prosecution use of the defendant's admissions). It is doubtful, however, that federal courts on constitutional grounds would construct an analogous doctrine governing special commitment proceedings.

the standard urges adoption of a statutory privilege protecting acquittees against compelled testimony at special commitment hearings.[10] They would continue, of course, to be competent witnesses should they choose to testify in person.

The standard does not discuss the right to a jury trial at civil commitment hearings, because jury trials are not required by the federal Constitution in that context.[11] Nevertheless, if respondents in general civil commitment proceedings, who cannot be distinguished from acquittee/respondents, are accorded by state constitution or statute the right to request a jury trial, equal protection[12] as well as principles of equity may require that special commitment patients be afforded the same right.

An order for special commitment is a final judicial order that in most if not all jurisdictions will be appealable of right like other civil judgments. Paragraph (f) affirms the desirability of legislation or court rules confirming the right to an appeal on the record by specially committed acquittees. It does not address the counterpart statutory right to appeal by a governmental entity that has failed to achieve a special commitment order, because the standards by design address the procedural rights and claims of respondents. Nevertheless, it may be assumed that forum law will allow all disappointed parties to civil litigation to appeal final adverse rulings of any sort, so that respondents who prevail in a committing court must submit to government appeals. However, because they will have been acquitted of criminal charges, and a hearing court has refused to commit them, they must be allowed to remain free in the community pending appeal, unless independent civil commitment proceedings are begun. If a committed acquittee/respondent appeals, paragraph (f) calls

10. *See* Tyars v. Finner, 709 F.2d 1274 (9th Cir. 1983) (dictum suggesting that fundamental fairness may require the equivalent of the privilege in commitment cases). *See generally* Shuman, *The Road to Bedlam: Evidentiary Guideposts in Civil Commitment Proceedings*, 53 Notre Dame Law. 53, 73 (1979); Wesson, *The Privilege Against Self-Incrimination in Civil Commitment Proceedings*, 1980 Wis. L. Rev. 697; Note, *Application of the Fifth Amendment Privilege Against Self-Incrimination to the Civil Commitment Proceedings*, 1973 Duke L.J. 1729.

11. *See generally* Jones v. United States, 463 U.S. 354, 379 n.10 (1983); People v. Lally, 191 N.Y.2d 27, 224 N.E.2d 87, 277 N.Y.S.2d 654 (1966).

12. *Compare* Jackson v. Indiana, 406 U.S. 715, 727 (1972) (equal protection requires that procedures to determine present mental competency accord substantially with those governing civil commitments), *with* Baxstrom v. Herold, 383 U.S. 107 (1966) (equal protection requires that a mentally disabled convict, at the expiration of a criminal sentence, be hospitalized through usual civil commitment procedures, not an administrative transfer to a mental health facility). *See generally* Weiner, *supra* note 4, at 168-169. Statutes as of October 1982 are summarized *id.* at 122-128, Table 2.7, cols. 9-10.

for an expedited review. Accelerated review, of course, would not be necessary if a state official appeals a hearing court judgment rejecting special commitment of an acquittee/respondent.

Standard 7-7.6. Special commitment; conditions of confinement

Consistent with the requirements of institutional and public safety, persons committed pursuant to special commitment statutes should be confined under comparable conditions and should have the rights of persons committed under general commitment statutes.

Commentary Introduction

The standard recommends that specially committed acquittees be confined under the same conditions governing and have the same rights as civilly committed patients, unless concerns about institutional or public safety dictate variations.

Related Standards

ABA, Standards for Criminal Justice 7-9.11, 7-10.2, chapter 23 (*passim*)
APA, Model Statute §10
MHLP Model Statute: Civil Commitment §38
MHLP Model Statute: Insanity Defense §5
MHLP Model Statute: Mental Health Standards and Human Rights §§4, 5, 6, 7, 8

Commentary

Some mental nonresponsibility [insanity] acquittees who have been specially committed may present special security problems, so that the conditions of their confinement must be more restrictive than those experienced by other committed persons.[1] However, not all specially committed acquittees will require additional security measures; those that do

1. *See, e.g.,* Coley v. Clinton, 479 F. Supp. 1036 (E.D. Ark. 1979), *aff'd in part and modified in part,* 635 F.2d 1364 (8th Cir. 1980) (additional restrictions may be appropriate for insanity acquittees and persons found incompetent to stand trial).

should be treated like civilly committed patients who behave violently while in confinement. Therefore, individual attributes, not commitment status, should govern the imposition of especially restrictive conditions of confinement.

Considerations of public and institutional safety aside, specially committed acquittees should enjoy the same rights and be treated under the same conditions as other similarly situated persons. The standard does not describe the level of desirable conditions or conditions meeting minimal constitutional requirements. Rather, the Association recommends a criterion of equality of specially committed acquittees with other persons confined for treatment or habilitation. In *Youngberg v. Romeo,*[2] the United States Supreme Court held that the due process clause mandates certain minimum levels of care and training, and specifically to treatment at least equal to that required for convicted prisoners.[3] Therefore, even though acquittees are not prisoners and cannot be punished, the Association's Legal Status of Prisoners Standards[4] serve to describe by analogy the minimally adequate conditions to be provided for persons who have been committed involuntarily, whether through general or special procedures.

Many states have enacted statutory guarantees of the rights of institutionalized mentally ill[5] and mentally retarded persons.[6] These rights should apply with equal force to persons committed under the provisions of part VII of these standards. Among the most important of these rights is the right to receive treatment or habilitation according to an individualized treatment or habilitation plan.[7]

---

2. 457 U.S. 307 (1982).

3. *Id.* at 315-316.

4. *See,* in particular, standards 23-5.1–23-5.5 (medical treatment), 23-6.1–23-6.14 (personal integrity and security).

5. *See* Lyon, Levin & Zusman, *Patients' Bill of Rights: A Survey of State Statutes,* 6 Mental Disability L. Rep. 178 (1982); Weiner, *Rights of Institutionalized Persons,* in The Mentally Disabled and the Law 251-288 (S. Brakel, J. Parry & B. Weiner eds., 3d ed. 1985) [hereinafter cited as Weiner].

6. *See Rights of Disabled Persons in Residential Facilities,* in B. Sales *et al.*, Disabled Persons and the Law: State Legislative Issues 849-864 (1982) [hereinafter cited as B. Sales *et al.*].

7. *See, e.g.,* Wyatt v. Stickney, 344 F. Supp. 387, 397 (M.D. Ala. 1972), *aff'd sub nom.* Wyatt v. Aderholt, 503 F.2d 1305 (5th Cir. 1974) (listing six items to be included in each habilitation plan); B. Sales *et al., supra* note 6, at 435-438; Bennett, *Reviewing an Individual Habilitation Plan: A Lawyer's Guide,* 4 U. Ark. Little Rock L.J. 467 (1981). In Marshall v. Kort, 690 P.2d 219, 221 (Colo. 1984), the court approved habeas corpus as a remedy for mental nonresponsibility [insanity] acquittee/patients who were not provided treatment.

States vary in the extent to which they recognize a right of involuntarily committed patients to refuse unwanted treatment or habilitation.[8] The standard does not speak specifically to that issue, but merely mandates that specially committed persons be treated like other patients in that respect.[9] A difficult point of interpretation may arise in states where general commitment patients may be found incompetent to make treatment decisions, one of the criteria for civil commitment. Because incompetence in whatever form is not embraced in the commitment criteria recommended in standard 7-7.4 for specially committed acquittees, the latter should not be deemed automatically incompetent to make personal treatment decisions. Therefore, they might enjoy a more expansive right to refuse treatment than do general committees. However, the standard takes no position on the issue and leaves it for the consideration of state courts and legislatures.

Standard 7-7.7. Special commitment; maximum duration of commitment order

(a) When a court commits a mental nonresponsibility [insanity] acquittee pursuant to standard 7-7.4, it should also issue an order setting the maximum duration of the acquittee's special commitment. The maximum duration set by the court may not exceed the maximum term of incarceration provided by law had the acquittee been found responsible for the crime charged. Upon the expiration of the maximum duration of special commitment, the acquittee may only be confined if subsequently committed under general commitment procedures.

(b) In setting the maximum duration for special commitment, as in other commitment proceedings under this chapter, the court

8. *See generally* Brooks, *The Constitutional Right to Refuse Antipsychotic Medication*, 8 Bull. Am. Acad. Psychiatry & L. 179 (1980); Keilitz, Conn & Giampetro, *Least Restrictive Treatment of Involuntary Patients: Translating Concepts Into Practice*, 29 St. Louis. U.L.J. 691, 695-712 (1985); Kemna, *Current Status of Institutionalized Mental Health Patients' Right to Refuse Psychotropic Drugs*, 6 J. Legal Med. 107 (1985); Weiner, *supra* note 5, at 341-351.

9. Some courts have found in the due process clause a right to refuse treatment. *See, e.g.*, Rogers v. Okin, 738 F.2d 1 (1st Cir. 1984); Rennie v. Klein, 720 F.2d 266 (3d Cir. 1983); Rogers v. Comm'r of Dep't of Mental Health, 390 Mass. 489, 458 N.E.2d 308 (1983) (response to questions certified by First Circuit in Rogers v. Okin, *supra*).

should consider the acquittee's need for treatment or habilitation and its concerns for the public's safety, but it may not consider retributive or punitive factors.

Commentary Introduction

The standard recommends as the outer limit on the duration of confinement based on the special commitment of acquittees the maximum term of imprisonment an acquittee could have received if convicted. Beyond that time, an acquittee must be subjected to civil commitment proceedings to be continued in confinement.

Related Standards

ABA, Standards for Criminal Justice 7-6.7, 18-4.2
DD Model Statute: DD Offender Act §§10(7), 10(8)
MHLP Model Statute: Insanity Defense §7

Commentary

Paragraph (a) calls upon committing courts to establish an outer time limit for each specially committed acquittee, beyond which special commitment may not extend. To allow special commitments to extend beyond the hypothetical maximum prison or jail sentences that acquittees could have received if convicted reflects, in the Association's view, a fundamentally unfair exercise of state powers. After the maximum authorized period of involuntary confinement has expired, acquittees can be retained for an extended period only if regular civil commitment proceedings are commenced, which result in a new commitment order unrelated to the earlier special commitment proceeding and periodic review under standard 7-7.8. Paragraph (b) confirms that the criterion governing maximum duration of special commitments is a legal restriction that cannot be exceeded in the context of part VII proceedings. If a shorter period of treatment or habilitation will suffice, a committing court should elect it. In other words, a lengthy term of imprisonment for a serious violent felony should not routinely or automatically fix the period of special commitment as well. In particular, the provision cautions against a judicial consideration of retributive or punitive factors in determining the duration of an initial commitment; only treatment or habilitation needs are germane.

The United States Supreme Court has ruled that in jurisdictions where defendants bear the burden of persuasion on the issue of mental nonresponsibility [insanity] at the criminal trial, the Constitution sets no outer limits on the duration of special commitments.[1] This, however, fixes only constitutional minimum requirements. Jurisdictions are free to adopt more restrictive limitations; through this standard the Association recommends that they do so. An admittedly arbitrary time limit should be established after which an acquittee's propensity for violence, established through the criminal verdict, no longer can be dispositive.[2] In addition, it seems inherently unjust to allow government to control former defendants for a longer period after an acquittal by reason of mental nonresponsibility [insanity] than would have been permitted had they been convicted.[3] Therefore, for reasons of both convenience and symmetry,[4] the Association has recommended the hypothetical maximum sentence of imprisonment that an acquittee could have received following conviction as the outer limit of special commitment.

It may be argued that such a norm is inappropriate because it creates the appearance that, through special commitment, acquittees are being sanctioned commensurate with the punishment they would have received if convicted. The standard explicitly addresses this concern through paragraph (b), which condemns a judicial consideration of retributive or punitive considerations in assessing the maximum duration of special commitment to be authorized against acquittees.

The identification of a hypothetical maximum prison sentence in any given case is not without difficulty. It can easily be accomplished in states that, like California, bifurcate criminal trials involving mental nonresponsibility [insanity] defenses. Standard 7-6.7, however, incorporates

1. Jones v. United States, 463 U.S. 354, 368-369 (1983).

2. *See* Note, *Rules for an Exceptional Class: The Commitment and Release of Persons Acquitted of Violent Offenses by Reason of Insanity*, 57 N.Y.U.L. Rev. 281, 326-329 (1982).

3. An alternative approach might be to fix by legislation the maximum period for special commitments at two-thirds of a hypothetical maximum sentence, because few prisoners in fact serve the maximum periods of imprisonment allowed under penal statutes; they are paroled or benefit from good-time credits that accelerate the time of ultimate release. Like the full-sentence approach discussed below in the text, however, a prorated standard is subject to abuse through prosecutorial overcharging. Nevertheless, if abuse of prosecutorial charging discretion is suspected, courts can compensate for it by using the power reflected in paragraph (b) to fix a shorter maximum period of confinement than is authorized by law, taking into account both treatment or habilitation needs and the functional maximum period of incarceration that would have flowed from a conviction.

4. Note that the absence of a durational limit may serve as a disincentive to the assertion of a meritorious defense of mental nonresponsibility [insanity].

the Association's position that trials should be unitary unless bifurcation at defense request is required to avoid substantial prejudice to a defendant. In jurisdictions that conform to that recommendation, the appropriate maximum prison term may not be readily apparent. Homicide is a good example. Under paragraph (a), a committing court will have to select between the maximum terms for murder and manslaughter, a selection that will be rendered peculiarly difficult in mental nonresponsibility [insanity] cases if culpability or *mens rea* affects gradation of homicide offenses. Courts also must keep in mind the possibility of prosecutorial overcharging; on occasion, prosecuting attorneys might be tempted, in cases in which a successful assertion of the mental nonresponsibility [insanity] defense is a realistic possibility, to charge a more serious crime than otherwise would be likely, simply to increase the "hypothetical sentence" and thus extend the period during which the defendant, if acquitted, could be specially committed under paragraph (a). Finally, computations of maximum limits on special commitments must turn on criminal charges submitted for consideration by a trier of fact; the fact that plea negotiations might have resulted in a plea to a lesser charge cannot be taken into account in fixing a maximum time of confinement.[5] Nonetheless, despite these practical difficulties, the Association believes that the injustice of ordering special commitments for long periods of time unrelated to treatment or habilitation needs clearly outweighs the transient inconvenience courts may encounter in administering the criterion recommended in the standard.

Standard 7-7.8. Special commitment; periodic judicial review

(a) A specially committed acquittee may petition for a judicial hearing to determine whether the acquittee continues to meet the criteria for special commitment set forth in standard 7-7.4. The acquittee may petition the court for such a hearing [one year] after acquittee's original special commitment, and every [two years] thereafter. At the original commitment hearing, or at subsequent periodic review hearings under this standard, the court may issue an order

5. *See* Rogers, Bloom & Manson, *Insanity Defenses: Contested or Conceded,* 141 Am. J. Psychiatry 885 (1984).

allowing the acquittee to petition for a rehearing sooner than the usual [one year] or [two year] period. The court should issue such an order when it appears that the acquittee's mental condition and other relevant factors warrant a shorter interval between periodic review hearings.

(b) Upon filing of such petition the court should convene a hearing within [thirty] days and that hearing should be conducted in accordance with the procedures set forth in standard 7-7.5. The state should have the burden of proving, by clear and convincing evidence, that the acquittee continues to meet the criteria for special commitment as set forth in standard 7-7.4. Overt acts by the acquittee tending to prove a substantial threat of serious bodily harm to others should be evaluated pursuant to the requirements of standard 7-7.4(c), and any overt acts committed by the acquittee prior to institutionalization may be considered to the extent that they continue to support a finding that the acquittee remains dangerous. Such previous overt acts should be evaluated by the trier of fact in light of the amount of time which has passed since their occurrence and the possibility that acquittee's confinement may have prevented the commission of other overt acts indicative of a substantial threat of serious bodily harm to others.

(c) Legal assistance should be regularly available to all specially committed acquittees at the location of their confinement. To ensure that each acquittee's right to periodic review as set forth in paragraph (a) of this standard is effective, each acquittee should have ready access to counsel, including appointed counsel. When the acquittee is entitled to periodic review, counsel should request a hearing on the acquittee's continuing need for commitment or should notify the court in writing that counsel has conferred with the acquittee and that a hearing is not requested at that time. By declining to request a hearing when the acquittee is entitled to review, the acquittee does not waive the right to any subsequent hearing.

(d) Nothing in this standard should be interpreted as limiting the right of a specially committed acquittee to petition for a writ of habeas corpus at any time.

Commentary Introduction

The standard provides a mechanism for periodic review of a specially committed acquittee's continuing need for commitment. An acquittee may petition for review at specified intervals and is then entitled to a commitment hearing at which the state bears the burden of persuasion by clear and convincing evidence on the need for continued commitment. Legal assistance for specially committed acquittees, at public expense if necessary, is recommended as essential to an exercise of the power to impel periodic review of commitment status.

Related Standards

ABA, Standards for Criminal Justice 4-3.6(a), 4-3.8, 4-3.9, 4-4.1, 4-4.3, 4-4.4, 4-5.1, 4-7.6, 7-10.6
ALI, Model Penal Code §4.08(5)
APA, Model Statute §11
DD Model Statute: DD Offender Act §10(10)
DD Model Statute: Right/Consent to Services §13
MHLP Model Statute: Civil Commitment §§21, 22, 23
MHLP Model Statute: Insanity Defense §6

Commentary

Perhaps the most difficult aspect of designing a special commitment system is formulating procedures for periodic review of an acquittee's continuing need for confinement and treatment or habilitation. In the development of this standard consideration was given to a dual option for periodic review: either automatic initiation by the state or initiation by a specially committed acquittee. However, a dual system can generate confusion and reliance on state-initiated review alone might generate practical difficulties. Accordingly, the standard recommends a single system that incorporates features adapted from both of the above options.

The standard recognizes the importance of regular judicial review of an individual's continuing need for confinement and treatment.[1] Increasingly, state statutes provide periodic review for general commitment patients. But it is even more important to persons confined under special commitment legislation because their commitment otherwise will extend for a fixed period of time[2] and their only other avenue of discharge

1. *See* Fasulo v. Arafeh, 173 Conn. 473, 378 A.2d 553 (1977).
2. *See* standard 7-7.7 and commentary.

requires initiative on the part of a facility superintendent.[3] Therefore, periodic review must be structured in a fashion that allows a full and fair review of a specially committed individual's current condition.

Despite the importance of periodic review to specially committed acquittees, the standard recommends a different form of review procedure than that employed for general commitment. The underlying reasons are the same ones that support more restrictive release procedures for special commitment than govern civil patients.[4] The concern for public safety dictates that procedures that can result in the discharge of specially committed acquittees must be designed and administered with great care.[5]

One major difference between the provisions of this standard and legislation in some states governing periodic review of general civil commitments is that they recommend a limited frequency of review hearings: Paragraph (a) envisions an initial review one year after an original special commitment order and every two years thereafter.[6] Some, but not all, states limit the frequency of client-initiated periodic review in their general commitment statutes. Legislation following the Association's recommended review procedures should withstand equal protection challenge in states that place no limitations on review of general civil commitments because the frequency of review recommended in paragraph (a) is adequate in comparison with civil commitment practice.[7] Moreover, periodic review of special commitments entails substantial preparation in which many persons, including mental health or mental retardation professionals, may participate. Hence, because special commitment review hearings may well be more elaborate than those affecting less dangerous individuals confined under general commitment statutes, a state has a substan-

---

3. *See* standard 7-7.9 and commentary.

4. *See* commentary to standard 7-7.9, notes 3-5 and accompanying text.

5. *See generally* Ellis, *The Consequences of the Insanity Defense: Proposals to Reform Post-Acquittal Commitment Laws*, 35 Cath. U.L. Rev. — (1986) (in press).

6. However, a committing court should retain the power to authorize more frequent review if the facts of a particular case so dictate, and specially committed acquittees should be able to obtain a review of their confinement at any time through habeas corpus proceedings. *Cf.* 18 U.S.C.A. §4247(g) (Supp. 1986), discussed in commentary to standard 7-7.3 at note 36.

7. The review periods under some state statutes are not, however, as frequent as those provided for general commitment patients. *See, e.g.*, N.M. Stat. Ann. §§43-1-12, 13 (1984 repl.) (six months to one year for the mentally ill, six months for the mentally retarded).

Precedent rejecting equal protection attacks on special release procedures include Williams v. Wallis, 734 F.2d 1434, 1437, *reh'g denied*, 704 F.2d 979 (11th Cir. 1984); Hickey v. Morris, 722 F.2d 543, 547 (9th Cir. 1983).

tial interest in preventing acquittees from requesting frequent review proceedings, perhaps for purposes of obstruction and harassment.[8]

Paragraph (a) incorporates a policy recommendation authorizing specially committed acquittees to initiate periodic review proceedings; state authorities may also do so but state initiation is discretionary under standard 7-7.9. Immediate release of generally committed patients is the consequence commonly required or authorized if state authorities have not initiated required periodic review proceedings. The potential for violence on the part of specially committed acquittees, however, which is greater than that usually to be encountered on the part of generally committed patients, prompted the Association to forestall release as an enforcement mechanism against inattentive state officials by recommending that only specially committed acquittees be allowed to initiate review proceedings. The standard rejects a periodic review system that would require a committee's release if the state failed to seek recommitment on a periodic basis.

Placement of the responsibility in this way is not without its own problems.[9] In particular, some confined individuals, because of their mental condition, may not be able to exercise their right to seek periodic review and, therefore, may remain in confinement although they no longer need to be confined. Paragraph (c) addresses the problem by urging that legal assistance be available regularly at public expense for all specially committed acquittees where they are confined.[10] Assistance of counsel is an absolute predicate for a fair and effective implementation of a patient-initiated system of periodic review. Attorneys must be appointed for

8. *See* Harris v. Ballone, 681 F.2d 225, 228-229 (4th Cir. 1982). One court struck down a limitation on special commitment release hearings as violative of equal protection, but the state appears to have limited the frequency of hearings that are analogous to the superintendent-initiated release provided in standard 7-7.9, as well as those that are initiated by an acquittee. Benham v. Edwards, 678 F.2d 511, 542 (5th Cir. 1982), *vacated sub nom.* Ledbetter v. Benham, 463 U.S. 1222 (1983) (for reconsideration in light of Jones v. United States, 463 U.S. 354 (1983)); *see also* Benham v. Ledbetter, 609 F. Supp. 125 (N.D. Ga. 1985) (on remand). Standard 7-7.9 places no limitation on the frequency of superintendent-initiated release hearings.

9. The Supreme Court implicitly has held that it does not violate the Constitution to place the burden of initiating periodic review on an acquittee who has established mental nonresponsibility [insanity] at criminal trial. Jones v. United States, 463 U.S. 354 (1983).

10. *See* Ward v. Kort, 762 F.2d 856, 860-861 (10th Cir. 1985) (constitutional right of access to courts requires either access to legal materials or assistance of counsel for acquittee/patients for purposes of federal habeas corpus or federal Civil Rights Act proceedings under 42 U.S.C. §§1983-1985 (1982)); Marshall v. Kort, 690 P.2d 219, 221 (Colo. 1984) (state habeas corpus is an available remedy for an acquittee/patient denied treatment).

specially committed acquittees and have access to their clients and the institutional records relating to them; only in this way may they assist their clients in deciding whether and when to seek review hearings and prepare adequately for the hearings envisioned in paragraph (b).

Moreover, paragraph (c) offers a mechanism to ensure that clients are not lost within a mental health system: Counsel should be required by statute to request periodic review hearings for which their clients are eligible or to notify committing courts in writing that they have conferred with their clients, who have decided not to seek hearings at the time. A pro tem declination cannot affect a specially committed acquittee's ability to seek habeas corpus review at any time, a point confirmed in paragraph (d), or to seek subsequent periodic review hearings. Counsel's responsibilities under this standard should be viewed as identical to those of criminal defense counsel.[11]

While paragraph (b) confirms that periodic review proceedings must be conducted by courts and not administrative officials or agencies, the psychiatric security review board approach to periodic review is both interesting and important.[12]

Under the standard, the recommended period within which a hearing should be commenced after a petition for a review has been filed is thirty days; the procedure to be followed should be identical to that of an original special commitment hearing.[13] Specially committed acquittees should have only a burden of petitioning for or initiating review proceedings. Thereafter, the state should bear the burden of persuasion at the level of clear and convincing proof that the criteria for special commitment continue to be met. Although the Supreme Court approved the

---

11. *See* standards 4-3.6(a), 4-3.8, 4-3.9, 4-4.1, 4-4.3, 4-4.4, 4-5.1, 4-7.6 and commentary.

12. Oregon has created a special interdisciplinary board to consider the cases of insanity acquittees. *See* Or. Rev. Stat. §161.327 (1979 repl.); Rogers, *1981 Oregon Legislation Relating to the Insanity Defense and the Psychiatric Security Review Board,* 18 Willamette L.J. 23 (1982); Rogers & Bloom, *Characteristics of Persons Committed to Oregon's Psychiatric Security Review Board,* 10 Bull. Am. Acad. Psychiatry & L. 155 (1982); Weiner, *Mental Disability and the Criminal Law,* in The Mentally Disabled and the Law 693, 733-734 (S. Brakel, J. Parry & B. Weiner eds., 3d ed. 1985).

Although the standard leaves these matters to judicial discretion, other provisions of these standards are compatible with a nonjudicial system and thus could be adapted to the needs of a state that has enacted a system like Oregon's. *See generally* Herman & Sor, *Convicting or Confining? Alternative Directions in Insanity Law Reform: Guilty But Mentally Ill Versus New Rules for Release of Insanity Acquittees,* 1983 B.Y.U.L. Rev. 499.

13. *See* standard 7-7.5 and commentary. In *In re* Reyes, 161 Cal. App. 3d 655, 657-658, 207 Cal. Rptr. 763, 765 (1984), the court held that petitioners are entitled to confront and cross-examine witnesses.

constitutionality of a special commitment system in which acquittees bore the burden of persuasion (proof) at periodic review,[14] the Association finds the policy considerations persuasive that support assignment of the burden of persuasion to governmental authorities, policy factors that are even stronger because of the passage of time and the provision of treatment or habilitation than those governing burden allocation at the initial special commitment hearings.[15] Note that the level of the burden of persuasion at review hearings is indicated as clear and convincing proof, which is the standard constitutionally required for civil commitment proceedings.[16]

Paragraph (b) addresses the relevance of the overt acts of dangerousness committed by specially committed acquittees before they were institutionalized, usually the *actus reus* elements of the criminal charges of which the acquittees were found mentally nonresponsible [insane]. The standard recommends that courts conducting periodic review hearings evaluate the earlier dangerous activity in light of the time elapsed (and, presumably, treatment or habilitation results),[17] bearing in mind the possibility that confinement itself may have forestalled more recent overt acts indicative of a substantial threat of serious bodily harm to others.

Although the standard does not address the matter of appellate review, it cross-refers in paragraph (b) to standard 7-7.5 as the source of procedural standards; standard 7-7.5(f) confirms that acquittees should have the right to an expedited review of adverse rulings on the issue of commitment, including continued commitment. Recall that, under paragraph (d), habeas corpus always continues as a mode of reviewing the lawfulness of commitment, a reservation that is constitutionally required.[18] It

---

14. Jones v. United States, 463 U.S. 354 (1983).

15. *See* commentary to standard 7-7.4, notes 15-17 and accompanying text.

16. *See* Addington v. Texas, 441 U.S. 418 (1979).

17. In State v. Robb, 125 N.H. 581, 588-589, 484 A.2d 1130, 1135 (1984), the court invalidated an irrebuttable presumption of dangerousness based on proof at the original criminal trial that the acquittee/patient had caused death or serious bodily injury. A permissive presumption would be acceptable, however, and the state would not have to offer evidence of a more recent overt dangerous act to legitimate continued commitment. *Id.* at 586-587, 484 A.2d at 1135. Rebuttable presumptions of continuing dangerousness based on the harmful acts underlying the earlier criminal charges appear to have been approved by the Supreme Court in Jones v. United States, 463 U.S. 354, 366 (1983); *see also* Benham v. Ledbetter, 609 F. Supp. 125, 127 (N.D. Ga. 1985).

18. Abolition of habeas corpus other than under circumstances of rebellion or invasion violates the Constitution, art. I, §9, cl. 2, unless at least as plenary an alternative remedy is provided by law. *See* United States v. Hayman, 342 U.S. 205 (1942) (sustaining the validity

should be noted as well that the Association does not seek to foreclose the availability of administrative review in intervals between judicial review.[19]

Standard 7-7.9. Special commitment; superintendent's petition for acquittee's release

(a) When the superintendent of the facility in which a specially committed acquittee is confined determines that substantial clinical evidence indicates that the acquittee no longer meets the special commitment criteria, the superintendent may petition the court for the acquittee's release.

(b) The superintendent should have access to counsel for preparing and presenting the petition to the court.

(c) The petition should set forth the clinical findings supporting the conclusion in favor of release and should contain a summary of all pertinent clinical data.

(d) A hearing should be held no later than [fifteen] days after filing the petition and the acquittee should remain confined pending the hearing.

(e) Following the hearing the court should order the acquittee's release if it finds, by a preponderance of the evidence, that the acquittee no longer meets the criteria for special commitment.

(f) The acquittee should receive a copy of the superintendent's petition and should have the right to be present at the hearing, to be represented by counsel, and to present evidence.

---

of 28 U.S.C. §2255 (1982), which federal prisoners are required to use in lieu of habeas corpus under 28 U.S.C. §§2241-2254 (1982)). *See also* Marshall v. Kort, 690 P.2d 219, 221 (Colo. 1984), in which a divided court approved the use of habeas corpus as a device to fashion a remedy short of discharge for acquittee/patients denied adequate treatment. The dissenters preferred mandamus in a committing court as a remedy. *Id.* at 226-227 (Erickson, C.J., dissenting).

In Williams v. Wallis, 734 F.2d 1434, 1440, *reh'g denied,* 740 F.2d 979 (11th Cir. 1984), the court sustained a requirement that patients utilizing state habeas corpus establish their release eligibility by a preponderance of the evidence.

19. A system of interim administrative reviews on a fixed schedule at state initiative might help mitigate the problems encountered in administering a system of judicial periodic review at patient initiative, the mainstay device under standard 7-7.8. *See generally* Government of the Virgin Islands v. Wallace, 679 F.2d 1066 (3d Cir. 1982).

(g) The prosecuting attorney should receive a copy of the superintendent's petition and should have the right to be present at the hearing and to present evidence.

Commentary Introduction

The standard recommends an alternative method for releasing a specially committed acquittee who no longer meets commitment criteria; it is based on a petition for release of an acquittee submitted to a committing court by the superintendent of a facility in which the acquittee is held. A judicial order based on delineated procedures should be required before an acquittee can be released.

Related Standards

ALI, Model Penal Code §4.08(2)
APA, Model Statute §12
DD Model Statute: DD Offender Act §10(11)
MHLP Model Statute: Insanity Defense §6

Commentary

This standard endorses, in addition to patient-initiated periodic review proceedings,[1] review petitions from the superintendent of a facility in which an acquittee is held which assert the belief that an acquittee no longer meets the criteria for special commitment.[2] This represents a substantial departure from the release procedures usually found in general commitment statutes, which allow the staff of a residential facility to release patients without a court order based on a belief that they no longer can benefit from treatment or habilitation or that a less restrictive alternative setting is appropriate. In contrast, under paragraph (e) specially committed acquittees would not be released without a court order. This comports with a growing body of precedent[3] recognizing this as a

1. *See* standard 7-7.8 and commentary.
2. *See* standard 7-7.4(b) and commentary.
3. *See, e.g.*, Powell v. Florida, 579 F.2d 324 (5th Cir. 1978); Clark v. State, 245 Ga. 629, 266 S.E.2d 466 (1980). The Supreme Court in Jones v. United States, 463 U.S. 354, 379 n.11, did not reach the issue of the constitutionality of the District of Columbia release procedures. *See generally* Weiner, *Mental Disability and the Criminal Law*, in The Mentally Disabled and the Law 693, 729-731 (S. Brakel, J. Parry & B. Weiner eds., 3d ed. 1985).

constitutionally acceptable departure from release practices governing generally committed patients.

The Association believes such a distinction is desirable and constitutes a principal reason for enacting a system of special commitment governing violent acquittees. A history of violent conduct, which is the distinguishing characteristic of the class of special acquittees, justifies more restrictive release procedures than govern other committed persons. Judicial review of a superintendent's petition and the clinical data underlying it,[4] which may include information not supporting discharge, should safeguard against inadvertent premature release of still-dangerous persons and reflects a proper regard for public safety.

In addition, a hearing in committing courts ought to ensure that acquittees who no longer meet the special commitment criteria are not retained in custody solely for purposes of incapacitation. Some facility administrators, because of their justifiable fear about public reaction, might be reluctant to discharge acquittee/patients who no longer meet the criteria but would not hesitate to file a petition under this standard because the ultimate authority to release lies elsewhere. Hence, a requirement of judical approval of recommendations for release probably is in the best interest of both acquittee/patients and society.[5]

Paragraph (b) recommends that facility administrators have counsel for purposes of preparing and presenting a petition and of providing representation at the hearing envisioned in paragraph (d). In some states, directors of facilities are not represented at release hearings. A lack of representation may place facility staff members, and ultimately acquittee/patients, at a substantial disadvantage. Access to counsel should ensure that petitions will be properly prepared and presented to committing courts. Note also that under paragraph (f) acquittees and their counsel and, under paragraph (g), the prosecuting attorney in the predicate criminal case should have a right under statute or rule to attend release hearings. Their participation should promote a proper determination of release status.

Under the Insanity Defense Reform Act of 1984, 18 U.S.C.A. §4243(f) (Supp. 1986), facility directors may certify to the clerks of federal district courts which ordered commitment following mental nonresponsibility [insanity] acquittals that former defendants have recovered to the point that release should no longer "create" a substantial risk of bodily injury to another person or serious damage to the property of another.

4. Paragraph (e) recommends adoption of a procedural requirement that a petition state the clinical findings underlying it and summarize all pertinent clinical data.

5. *See* D. Wexler, Mental Health Law: Major Issues 124-127 (1981).

It should be observed that a requirement of judicial approval of the release of specially committed acquittees is not without cost. Committing courts might conceivably reject a superintendent's petition and thereby compel the continued confinement of patient/acquittees whom facility staff members believe no longer to be mentally disabled or dangerous. Admittedly, this poses a substantial ethical dilemma, but the Association nonetheless prefers to err on the side of protecting public safety. The best check against unwarranted confinement in such instances is a sense of judicial restraint in substituting a court's lay opinion for the expert judgment of medical, mental health, or mental retardation professionals.[6] Release decisions properly remain the province of committing courts, but the judicial function should be restricted to an assessment of the validity of professional conclusions and the risk to the public safety posed by premature release. Indeed, courts properly may attach considerably greater weight to the possibility of future dangerous behavior than to the degree of a patient/acquittee's mental disability. Nevertheless, although they may disregard noncredible data, they cannot extend special commitments to protect the public safety in the absence of clear and convincing proof that an acquittee meets the mental disability criterion for commitment.

Under paragraph (e), the petitioning official should bear the burden of persuasion, by a preponderance of the evidence, that the criteria for continued special commitment no longer exist.[7] This lower level of persuasion is appropriate because a government representative has sought release and has submitted clinical data in support of that recommendation.

---

6. *See* DeVeau v. United States, 483 A.2d 307, 315 (D.C. 1984) (trial court is not bound by expert testimony but may not arbitrarily disregard it); Warner v. State, 309 Minn. 333, 336, 244 N.W.2d 640, 643-644 (1976).

7. Under current federal legislation, a facility director in whose custody an acquitted defendant has been placed by the Attorney General under federal court authorization can certify to the committing federal district court a belief that the acquittee/patient no longer meets the statutory criteria for hospitalization. If counsel for the government concurs, the acquittee/patient may be discharged without a hearing. If, however, any attorney for the government moves for a hearing, the burden of persuasion rests on the acquittee/patient to establish eligibility for release by clear and convincing proof if the predicate criminal charges involved bodily injury to or serious damage to the property of another person, or a substantial risk of either, and by a preponderance in all other cases. 18 U.S.C.A. §4243(d), (f) (Supp. 1986). The District of Columbia legislation has been construed to require a judicial finding by a preponderance that release is appropriate. *See* Deveau v. United States, 483 A.2d 307, 314 (D.C. 1984).

Standard 7-7.10. Special commitment; notification of release

When the release of a specially committed acquittee is imminent, the prosecuting attorney should have the authority to notify relevant individuals and agencies.

Commentary Introduction

Standard 7-7.10 recommends the recognition of a power of prosecuting attorneys to notify individuals and officials who have a legitimate interest in the fact of a forthcoming release of an acquittee/patient from confinement.

Related Standards

MHLP Model Statute: Therapeutic Confidentiality §4

Commentary

Some officials and private individuals may be concerned about the release of specially committed acquittees, even under judicial approval. Therefore, the standard endorses a system of notice to them from prosecuting attorneys that release is imminent.[1] It should be stressed that the power to notify rests in the hands of prosecuting authorities under the standard and not with mental disability professionals or facility administrators. This avoids the legal and ethical problems attending release of information in the context of general civil commitment outside the criminal justice system.

Appropriate recipients of notice include persons with whom acquittee/patients may have been involved in the past, *e.g.*, victims of violence or threats of violence, law enforcement authorities responsible for crime prevention in the community, and community representatives who may be concerned that persons who committed or threatened earlier violent acts will be returned to the community.

The notice practice reflected in the standard represents a departure from usual general commitment procedures, which customarily include no notice authorization. Indeed, notification in some jurisdictions might well violate statutory prohibitions against disclosure of confidential infor-

1. *See* Commonwealth v. Killelea, 370 Mass. 638, 351 N.E.2d 509 (1976).

mation concerning patients. Nevertheless, mental nonresponsibility [insanity] acquittees present public safety concerns not ordinarily raised when general commitment patients are discharged into the community. This, in the Association's view, is sufficient justification for authorizing prosecuting authorities to notify public agencies and private individuals about the imminent release of specially committed former criminal defendants who committed violent acts. In utilizing this authority, however, prosecuting attorneys should consider carefully whether adverse consequences might flow from notice, for example, in the form of tensions that might promote rather than forestall further violent activity. It should be stressed that the standard envisions in prosecuting authorities only a power to give notice, not a duty to do so.

Standard 7-7.11. Special commitment; authorized leave

(a) Authorized leave means a temporary absence from the facility without staff supervision. Authorized leave for specially committed acquittees should be permitted only by court order.

(b) When the superintendent of the facility concludes that a specially committed acquittee may be granted authorized leave without posing a danger to the community and that such leave would benefit the acquittee's treatment or habilitation regimen, the superintendent should petition for a court order permitting authorized leave and setting its specific conditions. The petition should include a summary of all pertinent clinical data.

(c) A copy of the petition should be served on the prosecuting attorney who should have the right to respond to the petition.

(d) The court should order authorized leave if it finds, by a preponderance of the evidence, that the petition for leave constitutes treatment or habilitation consistent with the least restrictive alternative principle and that it is consistent with community safety. The court may set any conditions it believes necessary for community safety.

(e) If a specially committed acquittee violates any condition of an authorized leave order, or if the leave is no longer appropriate to the acquittee's treatment or habilitation regimen or is no longer consistent with public safety, the leave may be terminated by the superintendent or the court. An acquittee permitted authorized leave who believes that such leave has been terminated wrongfully by the su-

perintendent may petition the court for its reinstatement. Review of the acquittee's petition should satisfy the requirements of procedural due process. The court should reinstate authorized leave if it finds, by a preponderance of the evidence, that the acquittee complied with the conditions of that leave and that reinstatement would be consistent with acquittee's treatment or habilitation needs and with community safety.

Commentary Introduction

The standard addresses the issue of authorized unsupervised leave from facilities in which acquittee/patients are confined. Accompanied leave may be approved and implemented through administrative action, but all other authorized leaves must be approved by committing courts and must be based on findings that public safety will be protected adequately during interim release.

Related Standards

ABA, Standards for Criminal Justice 18-7.5
ALI, Model Penal Code §4.08(4)
APA, Model Statute §12.F
MHLP Model Statute: Civil Commitment §§29, 30

Commentary

Frequently it is either therapeutically desirable or necessary for acquittee/patients to participate in activities or programs outside facilities to which they have been committed by court order,[1] including educational programs, outpatient therapy or habilitation, work release, sheltered workshops, transitional therapy, and release on specified conditions. Leaves may extend from a few hours to an indefinite period.[2] If acquittee/patients are under constant supervision by facility staff members,

1. *See* standard 7-7.4(c), (d) and commentary.

2. Several states have developed successful outpatient programs for acquittees. *See, e.g.*, Bloom, Rogers & Manson, *After Oregon's Insanity Defense: A Comparison of Conditional Release and Hospitalization*, 5 INT'L J.L. & PSYCHIATRY 391 (1982); Cavanaugh & Wasyliw, *Treating the Not Guilty by Reason of Insanity Outpatient: A Two-Year Study*, 13 BULL. AM. ACAD. PSYCHIATRY & L. 407 (1985).

there is no call for advance judicial authorization. If, however, they are to be placed on authorized leave status, defined in paragraph (a) as a temporary absence from a facility without staff supervision, the position of the Association is that a court order should be obtained before leave[3] and should be based on a judicial determination under paragraph (d) that the change in circumstances constitutes treatment or habilitation consistent with the least restrictive alternative principle and compatible with concerns for public safety. Implementation of the standard may well require a substantial departure from earlier practice allowing temporary release based on informal administrative action, but this departure is warranted because of the legitimate objective of safeguarding the community against even temporary release of persons with a potential for committing further violent acts.

Paragraph (b) recommends that authorized leaves for specially committed persons be granted only on the basis of a written petition to a committing court from the superintendent of a facility in which an acquittee/patient has been confined by court order. Petitions should include a summary of all relevant clinical data. In this way, a recipient court will be able to ascertain that a competent professional judgment underlies a request for authorized leave status. Paragraph (c) envisions a notice to the prosecuting attorney who represented the state in the predicate criminal proceedings, so that that official can respond to the petition.

Paragraph (d) does not require a hearing before a judicial order can issue, although the implication of paragraph (c) is that one might be held on the basis of a prosecuting attorney's response to a petition for approval of an authorized leave. If a hearing is conducted, it need not necessarily be as formal as that for special commitment hearings[4] or periodic judicial reviews of commitment orders[5] (although a court should have discretion to invoke all or most of the procedural safeguards that govern them). The burden of persuasion, which in form rests on a committing court under paragraph (d), is stated at the level of the preponderance of the evidence. The bases for authorization are stated in the standard as compatibility with treatment or habilitation needs consistent

3. Under current federal legislation, 18 U.S.C.A. §4243(f)(2)(A) (Supp. 1986), a federal district court must authorize conditional discharge and order a federal acquittee/patient to comply with the prescribed regimen. *Id.* §4243(f)(2)(B). It can modify or abrogate the treatment regimen at any time, *id.* §4243(f), after a formal hearing. *Id.* §4247(d).

4. *See* standard 7-7.5 and commentary.

5. *See* standard 7-7.8(b) and commentary.

with the least restrictive alternative concept[6] and community protection. Admittedly, the judicial task in deciding whether these criteria are met is difficult and intricate.[7]

Paragraph (d) recommends that authorizing courts be allowed to fix conditions on authorized leaves to protect community safety.[8] Such conditions nevertheless should relate clearly to an acquittee/patient's treatment or habilitation needs and should not simply mirror the conditions typically imposed on convicted defendants placed on probation.[9] The three recommended criteria for authorized leave — treatment or habilitation needs, the least restrictive alternative principle, and community safety — must be balanced or harmonized in individual cases.

Revocation or withdrawal of authorized leave status is an issue of some difficulty. Paragraph (e) envisions that either the facility superintendent or the authorizing court can terminate authorized leave if a judicially imposed condition has been violated or if one or more of the factors found originally to support the leave authorization have ceased to exist.[10] If termination of leave status is based on administrative action, the standard recommends that acquittee/patients be empowered to petition committing courts for reinstatement of leave, a remedy recognized by some courts for general commitment mental patients[11] and mental nonresponsibility [insanity] acquittees.[12] The Association believes that specially

6. *See generally* Keilitz, Conn & Giampetro, *Least Restrictive Treatment of Involuntary Patients: Translating Concepts Into Practice,* 29 St. Louis U.L.J. 691 (1985); Weiner, *Rights of Institutionalized Persons,* in The Mentally Disabled and the Law 251, 262-267 (S. Brakel, J. Parry & B. Weiner eds., 3d ed. 1985).

7. On factors that courts should consider in this context, *see* Hill v. State, 358 So. 2d 190, 209 (Fla. Dist. Ct. App. 1978); State v. Krol, 68 N.J. 236, 262, 344 A.2d 289, 303 (1975).

8. *See generally* Application of Noel, 226 Kan. 536, 601 P.2d 1152, 1166-1167 (1979).

9. *See* 18 U.S.C.A. §3563(b) (Supp. 1986); Scheidt v. Meredith, 307 F. Supp. 63, 66 (D. Colo. 1970); Zion v. Xanthopoulos, 178 Mont. 468, 474-476, 585 P.2d 1084, 1088 (1978). *See generally* Weiner, *Mental Disability and the Criminal Law,* in The Mentally Disabled and the Law 693, 731-732 (S. Brakel, J. Parry & B. Weiner eds., 3d ed. 1985).

10. On grounds for revocation, *see generally* Friend v. United States, 388 F.2d 579 (D.C. Cir. 1967); State v. Thompson, 28 Wash. App. 728, 626 P.2d 51 (1981).

11. *See* Lewis v. Donahue, 437 F. Supp. 112 (W.D. Okla. 1977) (three-judge court); Meisel v. Kremens, 405 F. Supp. 1253 (E.D. Pa. 1975); Application of True, 103 Idaho 151, 645 P.2d 891 (1982); *see also* C.R. v. Adams, 649 F.2d 625 (8th Cir. 1981) (availability of state judicial remedy for wrongful revocation of outpatient status requires federal court to abstain from proceeding with federal Civil Rights Act proceeding under 42 U.S.C. §§1983-1985 (1982)); Note, *The Summary Revocation of an Involuntary Mental Patient's Convalescent Leave — Is It Unconstitutional?,* 33 Okla. L. Rev. 366 (1980). One court held that revocation does not require a hearing. Hooks v. Jaquith, 318 So. 2d 860 (Miss. 1975).

12. *See In re* Anderson, 73 Cal. App. 3d 38, 140 Cal. Rptr. 546 (1977).

committed former defendants should be treated no differently from general commitment patients in this respect.[13] If a court finds by a preponderance of the evidence that an acquittee/patient complied with the conditions and that a continuation of authorized leave status continues to be compatible with treatment or habilitation needs and community safety, under paragraph (e) it can reinstate authorized leave.[14]

13. The standard does not cover arrest or custody of acquittee/patients who violate conditions of authorized leave. *See* 18 U.S.C.A. §4243(g) (Supp. 1986), allowing a facility director to notify the Attorney General and committing federal district court that an outpatient is not complying with the treatment regimen ordered by the court under *id.* §4243(f)(2)(B). The patient/acquittee then can be arrested on the basis of the notice or probable cause to believe that grounds for termination exist. *Ibid.* Nor does the Association either recommend or discourage a legislative differentiation based on the length of authorized leaves. *See* Dietrich v. Brooks, 27 Or. App. 821, 558 P.2d 357 (1976) (no hearing required when the leave had not exceeded 90 days).

14. A federal court can either order renewed hospitalization or modify the circumstances of outpatient treatment. 18 U.S.C.A. §4243(f), (g) (Supp. 1986).

Part VIII

Special Dispositional Statutes

William H. Erickson, *Chairman*
Standing Committee on Association Standards for Criminal Justice

Norman S. Early, Jr.
Task Force Chairman

Elyce H. Zenoff
Reporter

Task Force

Norman S. Early, Jr., *Chairman*
District Attorney, Denver, Colorado

Ann Burgess, R.N., D.N.Sc.
Associate Director of Nursing Research, Department of Health & Hospitals, Boston, Massachusetts (representing American Orthopsychiatric Association)

Louise Centers, Ph.D., J.D.
Sinai Hospital of Detroit, Detroit, Michigan (representing American Psychological Association)

Penelope D. Clute
Private practitioner, Clute, Clute & Thompson, Plattsburgh, New York

Gilbert L. Ingram, Ph.D.
Assistant Director, Correctional Programs, Federal Bureau of Prisons, Washington, D.C. (representing American Correctional Association)

Robert B. Levinson, Ph.D.
Former Deputy Assistant Director, Inmate Program Services, Federal Bureau of Prisons, Washington, D.C.

Frederick M. Miller, M.D.
Psychiatrist, Denver, Colorado

John Roll
Assistant United States Attorney, Tucson, Arizona

Loren H. Roth, M.D., M.P.H.
Director, Law & Psychiatry Program, University of Pittsburgh School of Medicine, Pittsburgh, Pennsylvania (representing American Psychiatric Association)

Miles Santamour
President's Committee on Mental Retardation, Washington, D.C.

Gerard F. Treanor
Private practitioner, Venable, Baetjer & Howard, Arlington, Virginia (representing ABA Section of Criminal Justice)

ELYCE H. ZENOFF, *Reporter*
Professor of Law, National Law Center, George Washington University

INTRODUCTION

The single standard in part VIII addresses only one issue: the repeal of special dispositional statutes providing for the sentencing and treatment of sexual psychopaths, psychopaths, or defective delinquents. The assumptions on which legislation of this sort has rested have largely been rejected in the behavioral sciences, and the experiences that accumulated during the administration of such legislation have been disappointing: (1) the categories of mental disorder the statutes address for the most part are no longer viewed to be clinically valid: (2) treatment for special offenders has been nonexistent or largely ineffective; and (3) some offenders have been held longer than community protection requires while other offenders who have been released as cured have committed new offenses. The premise on which part VIII rests is that parts IX and X of this chapter are sufficient for purposes (1) of identifying convicted offenders and prisoners who suffer from severe mental illness or serious mental retardation and (2) of subjecting them to appropriate custody and treatment or habilitation. Therefore, special dispositional statutes appropriately may be repealed.

Standard 7-8.1. Repeal of psychopath statutes

Statutes which provide for special sentencing and treatment of sexual psychopaths, psychopaths, or defective delinquents should be repealed.

Related Standards

ABA, Standards for Criminal Justice 18-2.5, 18-4.4 through 18-4.6, 18-6.2

Commentary

Sexual psychopath laws first were enacted in the late 1930s,[1] usually in response to high visibility sex crimes[2] resulting in death to their victims.[3] Initial opposition to such legislation was based on charges of vagueness and inadequate procedural safeguards violative of due process and on unreasonable legislative classifications under the fourteenth amendment equal protection clause. But after the United States Supreme Court sustained the constitutionality of the Minnesota statute,[4] several more states enacted similar statutes.[5]

Legislation aimed solely at sex offenders had two objectives. One was to protect the community against sex offenders by incarcerating them for indeterminate sentences ranging from one day to life; in this way, offenders could be detained for longer periods than was possible under predi-

1. For a background discussion of the statutes, *see* GROUP FOR THE ADVANCEMENT OF PSYCHIATRY REPORT, PSYCHIATRY AND SEX PSYCHOPATH LEGISLATION: THE 30S TO THE 80S 842-860 (1977) [hereinafter cited as GAP REPORT].

2. *See* Dix, *Special Dispositional Alternatives for Abnormal Offenders* [hereinafter cited as Dix], in MENTALLY DISORDERED OFFENDERS 135 (J. Monahan & H. Steadman ed. 1983) [hereinafter cited as MENTALLY DISORDERED OFFENDERS]; Sutherland, *The Diffusion of Sexual Psychopath Laws,* 56 AM. J. SOC. 142 (1950); Weiner, *Mental Disability and the Criminal Law,* in THE MENTALLY DISABLED AND THE LAW 693, 739-743 (S. Brakel, J. Parry & B. Weiner eds., 3d ed. 1985) [hereinafter cited as Weiner].

3. *See* CLECKLEY, THE MASK OF SANITY 505 (2d ed. 1950):

> In big letters on the front page of newspapers all over the United States the "BESTIAL SEX-SLAYING" of an eleven-year-old girl by a boy of seventeen is proclaimed. Details of torture and dismemberment follow. The horrible impact of impulses perverted from the aims of Eros and fused with those of hate and brutality arouses disgust and vengefulness in millions upon millions. Additional articles point out that the murderer, now remarkably callous and undisturbed by his act, had, over a period of many years, shown gross maladjustment, indifference to social values, to ordinary aims, to the rights of others. He had on several occasions been placed in a reform school and kept for various periods determined in accordance with the legally estimated seriousness of his antisocial acts, with the amount of punishment these were officially regarded as deserving.

Illinois adopted the first statute of this type in 1938 (sustained by state courts as constitutional), ILL. REV. STAT. ch. 38, §§820.01-825, and other states followed suit almost immediately. California, Massachusetts, Michigan (Michigan enacted the first law of this type in 1937, declared unconstitutional in People v. Frontczak, 286 Mich. 51, 281 N.W. 534 (1938)), Minnesota, Ohio, and Wisconsin.

4. State *ex rel.* Pearson v. Probate Court of Ramsey County, 309 U.S. 270 (1940).

5. By 1949, twelve states and the District of Columbia reportedly had such laws. *See* Sutherland, *The Sexual Psychopath Laws,* 40 J. CRIM. L. 547 (1950) [hereinafter cited as Sutherland].

cate criminal statutes.[6] The second objective was to provide suitable treatment or habilitation for sex offenders. This would benefit sex offenders by curing them in perhaps a shorter time than they would serve as convicted criminals: it would also protect society against premature release of dangerous offenders who had not been cured within the maximum period of incarceration available under a predicate criminal statute.[7] Several state legislatures perceived these objectives as important in the context of crimes other than sex offenses and enacted special commitment statutes aimed at psychopaths or defective delinquents who committed nonsexual offenses.[8]

All such special dispositional legislation rested on six assumptions: (1) there is a specific mental disability called sexual psychopathy, psychopathy, or defective delinquency; (2) persons suffering from such a disability are more likely to commit serious crimes, especially dangerous sex offenses, than normal criminals; (3) such persons are easily identified by mental health professionals;[9] (4) the dangerousness of these offenders can be predicted by mental health professionals; (5) treatment is available

---

6. *E.g.*, the Maryland Legislature's Council on Medico-Legal Procedure reported that the primary objective of the proposed Defective Delinquency Law was "to protect society from this segment of the criminal population who will probably again commit crimes if released in the expiration of fixed sentence." MD. COMM'N TO STUDY MEDICO-LEGAL PSYCHIATRY REPORT 21 (1948).

7. Some commentators have maintained that in fact offenders often were held for a shorter time than they would have been incarcerated on the basis of convictions for predicate offenses. *See* Guthman, *MDSO Law: The Assumptions Challenged*, 4 CRIM. JUST. J. 75, 83 (1980).

8. The most sweeping example of legislation resting on the use of psychiatric knowledge to cure criminality is Maryland's defective delinquent statute for the identification and treatment of mentally disturbed offenders. MD. CODE ANN. art. 31B, §§1-16 (1983 & Supp. 1985). The Maryland legislature funded a new institution at Patuxent for institutionalizing and treating defective delinquents. The statute defined the term *defective delinquent* to embrace any

> individual who, by the demonstration of persistent aggravated antisocial or criminal behavior, evidences a propensity toward criminal activity, and who is found to have either such intellectual deficiency or emotional unbalance, or both, as to clearly demonstrate an actual danger to society so as to require such confinement and treatment. . . .

Id. art. 31B, §5. See Zenoff & Courtless, *Autopsy of an Experiment: The Patuxent Experience*, 5 J. PSYCHIATRY & L. 531, 532 (1977).

9. However, the mental disability addressed by such legislation was not well defined in many jurisdictions, which generated a circular definition, such that offenders were labeled mentally ill because they had committed sex offenses. *See* GAP REPORT, *supra* note 1, at 840. *See also* TENN. CODE ANN. §33-6-302 (1984).

for the condition; and (6) large numbers of persons afflicted with the designated disabilities can be cured.

Although there were few extant data to support these assumptions at the time special legislation of this sort appeared, many legislatures and courts thought them attractive and supported legislative action.[10] Although proponents of such statutes were heartened by reports of success in the form of reduced recidivism rates,[11] strong criticism was voiced from the outset against legislative adoption of special dispositional legislation.[12] During the 1960s and 1970s, litigation attacking the constitutionality of such statutes dramatically increased, despite the Supreme Court decision in *Pearson;*[13] the principal grounds were vagueness and indefiniteness in the criteria for special commitment and unreasonable legislative classifications that meant some offenders could be detained indefinitely under psychopathy laws while equally dangerous persons who committed offenses not comprehended within special statutes were incarcerated for shorter periods of time and could not be forced to participate in unwanted treatment regimens. Considerable support was given to these attacks by the Supreme Court decision in *Specht v. Patterson,*[14] at least as far as procedural due process was concerned.[15]

---

10. Similarly, there were no hard data to support the view of eugenicists that mental illness and mental retardation, criminality, pauperism, and various other defects were hereditary. Nevertheless, a majority of states passed sterilization laws affecting these classes. In Buck v. Bell, 274 U.S. 200 (1925), the United States Supreme Court upheld their constitutionality. *See* Zenoff, *Eliminating the Unfit — Is Sterilization the Answer?,* 27 Ohio St. L.J. 591 (1966). *See generally* Brakel, *Family Laws,* in The Mentally Disabled and the Law 507, 521-531 (S. Brakel, J. Parry & B. Weiner eds., 3d ed. 1985). As of October 1982, eighteen states continued such legislation in force. *See id.* at 552-555, Table 9.5. *See* Ellis & Luckasson, *Mentally Retarded Criminal Defendants,* 53 Geo. Wash. L. Rev. 414, 416-421 (1985).

11. *See, e.g.,* Boslaw & Kohlymeyer, *The Maryland Defective Delinquent Law: An Eight Year Follow-Up,* 120 Am. J. Psychiatry 123-124 (1964); Poeht, Halleck & Ehrmann, *Diagnosis and Treatment of the Sexual Offender: A Nine Year Study,* 118 Am. J. Psychiatry 802 (1962).

12. *See, e.g.,* N. Kittrie, The Right to Be Different 392 (1971); M. Ploscowe, Sex and the Law 235-237 (1951); J. Robitscher, Pursuit of Agreement: Psychiatry and the Law 154-168 (1966); Sutherland, *supra* note 5, at 543-544; Tappan, *Sentences for Sex Criminals,* 42 J. Crim. L. 332 (1951); Wilkins, *Putting Treatment on Trial,* 5 Hastings Center Rep. 35 (1975).

13. State *ex rel.* Pearson v. Probate Court of Ramsey County, 309 U.S. 270 (1940). *See* note 4 and accompanying text.

14. 386 U.S. 605 (1967).

15. The Court held that, before being sentenced as a psychopath, a convicted offender is entitled to a judicial hearing with counsel, an opportunity to be heard, confrontation of prosecution witnesses and an opportunity to cross-examine them, and a chance to offer evidence. *Id.* at 610. It also mandated sufficient factual findings on the record to support a meaningful appeal. *Ibid.* Commentators also have asserted that the array of constitutional

Constitutional litigation aside, a growing body of mental health and mental retardation professionals attacked the scientific validity of special dispositional statutes with the assertion that they had not met and could not fulfill their stated purposes.[16] Dissatisfaction with them also was voiced in the commentary to chapter 18 of the standards,[17] even though that did not embody formal Association policy. Some legislatures came to feel that offenders were being released prematurely under such statutes, with consequent danger to public safety.[18] As a result, in recent

---

rights governing special dispositional hearings should include jury trial, the burden of persuasion (proof) at the level of beyond a reasonable doubt, a claim to treatment, and an ability to refuse treatment. *See* Dix, *supra* note 2, at 170-184.

16. *See* GAP REPORT, *supra* note 1, at 78; Monahan & Davis, *Mentally Disordered Sex Offenders*, in MENTALLY DISORDERED OFFENDERS, *supra* note 2, at 326 [hereinafter cited as Monahan & Davis]; Zenoff, *Controlling the Dangers of Dangerousness: The ABA Standards and Beyond*, 53 GEO. WASH. L. REV. 562, 578-581 (1985). For example, GAP asserted that such laws lack clinical validity, GAP REPORT, *supra* note 1, at 935, and that sexual psychopathy is not a psychiatric diagnostic category. *Id.* at 840. *See also* Dix, *supra* note 2, at 152; Monahan & Davis, *supra*, at 320-321. GAP stated that "sexual psychopathy is a questionable category from a legal standpoint and a meaningless grouping from a diagnostic and treatment standpoint." GAP REPORT, *supra* note 1, at 936. Other GAP concerns included a lack of treatment, or inappropriate or ineffective treatment, *id.* at 858, 873, and the inability of clinicians to predict future criminality on the part of released offenders. GAP concluded that sexual psychopath laws should be repealed. *Id.* at 940. The Task Panel on Legal and Ethical Issues of the President's Commission on Mental Health also called for repeal of sexual psychopath statutes. *See* Monahan & Davis, *supra*, at 313.

The American Psychiatric Association, however, believes that recent research and clinical studies suggest that a small number of offenders can be diagnosed accurately as sexual psychopaths and treated effectively. *See* letter to the Standing Committee Director from Robert Luskin, Esq. (March 29, 1985), on behalf of APA. This is not a justification to retain special legislation, in APA's view, but does suggest that this class of offenders should be given appropriate treatment under procedures and in settings as delineated in parts IX and X of this chapter.

17. *See* 18•130-18•136, commentary to standard 18-2.5: "[A] strong case can be made for their total elimination." *Id.* at 18•136. Because of perceived limitations on its role in preparing the second-edition standards, however, the Standing Committee did not recommend at that time adoption of the Association policy now embodied in standard 7-8.1. *See ibid.*

18. *See* Note, *Repeal of the Wisconsin Sex Crimes Act*, 1980 WIS. L. REV. 944-975. The repeal was seen as a "law and order" measure based on perceptions that offenders might be released too soon. *Id.* at 950-951. Similar perceptions seem to have been responsible for changes in the California law. *See* Dix, *supra* note 2, at 188; Monahan & Davis, *supra* note 16, at 191. There are some data, although soft, to support the assertion that some offenders are released in a shorter period of time when institutionalized than they would have been had they been imprisoned. *Id.* at 200.

years these special statutes for the most part have been either repealed[19] or substantially modified.[20]

Standard 7-8.1 now embodies a formal expression of Association policy condemning all special sentencing statutes governing such categories of convicted offenders as sexual psychopaths, psychopaths, and defective delinquents. Offenders who repeatedly commit new offenses, particularly those who manifest patterns of criminality that endanger society, can be dealt with under habitual offender laws or other statutes providing for sentence enhancement.[21] Under parts IX and X of this chapter, offenders (whether recidivists or not) who need treatment for mental illness or habilitation services because of mental retardation can be sentenced

19. At least fourteen states have repealed their statutes. *See* ALA. CODE tit. 15, §434 (declared unconstitutional in Davy v. Sullivan, 354 F. Supp. 1320 (M.D. Ala. 1973) and apparently dropped from further codifications); FLA. STAT. ANN. §§917.011-917.019 (repealed by LAWS 1979 c.79-341); IND. CODE ANN. §35-11-3.1 (repealed by ACTS 1979, P.L. 294, §1); IOWA CODE ANN. ch. 225A (repealed by ACTS 1976 (66 G.A.) ch. 1245, ch. 4, §526); MICH. COMP. LAWS §§780.501-780.509 (repealed P.A. No. 143, p.203 (1968)); MINN. STAT. ANN. §246.43 (repealed by LAWS 1978, ch. 723, art. 1, §20); MO. ANN. STAT. §§202.700-202.770 (repealed by LAWS 1980 p.H.B. No. 1724, §1); N.H. REV. STAT. ANN. ch. 173-A (repealed 1983, 206:1), *and see* Grindle v. Miller, 119 N.H. 214, 400 A.2d 787 (1979); OHIO REV. CODE ANN. §§2947.24-2947.29 (repealed 137 v. H565 §2, 1978); PA. STAT. ANN. §19-1166 (repealed 1978, P.L. 202, No. 53, §2a [1287]); R.I. GEN. LAWS §§14-2-1-14-2-8 (defective delinquents) (repealed by P.L. 1969 ch. 238, §2; P.L. 1979 ch. 293, §1); VT. STAT. ANN. tit. 18, §8501 (repealed 1977, No. 219 (Adj. Sess.), §1); VA. CODE §19.2-300 (repealed by ACTS 1975, c.593); WIS. STAT. ANN. §975.01 (repealed by LAWS 1979 c.117).

20. At least eleven states have done so. *See* CAL. WELF. & INST. CODE §§6300-6330 (1979 & Supp. 1985); CONN. GEN. STAT. ANN. §§17-238–17-255 (Supp. 1985); KAN. STAT. ANN. §§22-3429–22-3431 (1981); MD. ANN. CODE art. 31B, §§8-13 (1983 & Supp. 1985); NEB. REV. STAT. §§29-2911–29-2921 (1979); N.J. STAT. ANN. §§2C-47-1–2C-47-7 (1982); OR. REV. STAT. §§426.510-426680 (1979); TENN. CODE ANN. §§33-6-301–33-6-306 (Michie 1984 & Supp. 1985); UTAH CODE ANN. §§77-16-1–77-16-55 (1982); WASH. REV. CODE ANN. ch. 71.06 (1975 & Supp. 1986), *and see* State v. Edwards, 93 Wash. 2d 162, 606 P.2d 1224 (1980); WYO. STAT. §§7-13-601–7-13-615 (1977 & Supp. 1985). Thus, the Maryland statute was modified to require that offenders volunteer or consent to remain in the defective delinquency program. Most statutory modifications have restricted the length of commitment to that of the incarceration authorized for a predicate offense.

Only five jurisdictions currently allow indefinite commitment of psychopaths. *See* COLO. REV. STAT. §§17-23-101–17-23-103 (1978 & Supp. 1985); D.C. CODE §§22.3501-22.3511 (1973 & Supp. 1985); ILL. ANN. STAT. ch. 38, §§105-1.01–105.12 (Smith-Hurd 1980 & Supp. 1985); MASS. ANN. LAWS ch. 123A (1969 & Supp. 1985); MINN. STAT. ANN. §§526.09-526.11 (1975 and Supp. 1985).

For a survey of legislation as of October 1982, *see* Weiner, *supra* note 2, at 796-801, Table 12.8.

21. *See* standards 18-4.4–18.4.6, 18-6.2 and commentary.

and dealt with appropriately without the need for special legislation. By taking this stand, the Association hopes that the residue of states that perpetuate special dispositional legislation[22] will join the sizeable body of jurisdictions that have repealed it.

22. *See* note 19.

Part IX

Sentencing Mentally Ill and Mentally Retarded Offenders

William H. Erickson, *Chairman*
Standing Committee on Association Standards for Criminal Justice

Norman S. Early, Jr.
Task Force Chairman

Elyce H. Zenoff
Reporter

Task Force

Norman S. Early, Jr., *Chairman*
District Attorney, Denver, Colorado

Ann Burgess, R.N., D.N.Sc.
Associate Director of Nursing Research, Department of Health & Hospitals, Boston, Massachusetts (representing American Orthopsychiatric Association)

Louise Centers, Ph.D., J.D.
Sinai Hospital of Detroit, Detroit, Michigan (representing American Psychological Association)

Penelope D. Clute
Private practitioner, Clute, Clute & Thompson, Plattsburgh, New York

Gilbert L. Ingram, Ph.D.
Assistant Director, Correctional Programs, Federal Bureau of Prisons, Washington, D.C. (representing American Correctional Association)

Robert B. Levinson, Ph.D.
Former Deputy Assistant Director, Inmate Program Services, Federal Bureau of Prisons, Washington, D.C.

Frederick M. Miller, M.D.
Psychiatrist, Denver, Colorado

John Roll
Assistant United States Attorney, Tucson, Arizona

Loren H. Roth, M.D., M.P.H.
Director, Law & Psychiatry Program, University of Pittsburgh School of Medicine, Pittsburgh, Pennsylvania (representing American Psychiatric Association)

Miles Santamour
President's Committee on Mental Retardation, Washington, D.C.

Gerard F. Treanor
Private practitioner, Venable, Baetjer & Howard, Arlington, Virginia (representing ABA Section of Criminal Justice)

ELYCE H. ZENOFF, *Reporter*
Professor of Law, National Law Center, George Washington University

INTRODUCTION

This part covers appropriate procedures for the sentencing, placement, treatment, and habilitation of mentally ill and mentally retarded offenders. Until recently, problems of mental illness and mental retardation affecting sentencing and disposition of convicted offenders have received considerably less attention from the legal and mental health professions than mental disability affecting the arrest, trial, and conviction phases of the criminal justice process. Part IX endeavors to correct the imbalance.

Certain terms are defined in standard 7-9.1, but others not formally defined there have technical meanings important to the several standards within this Part:

Mental health facility. An inpatient or residential mental health hospital or institutional setting that offers treatment programs for mentally ill offenders, preferably under the jurisdiction of a state department of mental health.

Mental retardation facility. A residential facility offering specific programs of habilitation for mentally retarded offenders, preferably under the jurisdiction of a state department of mental health or mental retardation.

Expert witnesses. Mental health or mental retardation professionals who provide expert data at sentencing hearings and who meet applicable qualifications, including education and training requirements, as delineated in standards 7-3.10 through 7-3.13.

Mental health professionals providing treatment. Mental health professionals who provide therapy and treatment for convicted offenders and who have the requisite qualifications and experience to perform similar functions within the community.

Mental retardation professionals providing habilitation. Mental retardation professionals, including certified special education teachers, speech and language pathologists, audiologists, physical therapists, and occupational therapists as well as professionals qualifying as "mental health professionals," who provide habilitation for mentally retarded persons and who possess experience in the field of mental retardation.

Part IX addresses the impact of mental illness or mental retardation on sentencing and advocates that it have a potentially mitigating impact on penal sanctions. Although under standard 7-9.4, defense counsel should have assistance from qualified mental health or mental retardation professions, evidence based on a competency evaluation is admissible only under the strictures delineated in part IV;[1] expert data resting on pretrial evaluations are admissible only if a defendant places mental condition at issue at a sentencing hearing.[2]

Convicted offenders sentenced to imprisonment should have a claim to needed treatment or habilitation within a correctional facility[3] unless their disabilities are severe enough to warrant care in a mental health or mental retardation facility, preferably under the administrative jurisdiction of a state department of mental health or mental retardation.[4] It should be stressed that the standards have provided, through standard 7-9.7(c), a functional system of treating mentally disabled defendants who are not found mentally nonresponsible [insane]. It is for this reason that the Association has taken a stand opposing the legislative recognition of a guilty-but-mentally-ill alternative to the verdict of guilty by reason of mental nonresponsibility [insanity].[5]

Standard 7-9.8 recommends procedures to be followed before and during the sentencing of severely mentally ill and seriously mentally retarded offenders, and standard 7-9.9 recommends the option of their special commitment to a mental health or mental retardation facility instead of an adult correctional facility.[6] The least-restrictive alternative criterion should govern such placements after a sentencing court has considered a convicted offender's history, the nature of the offense, the penalties authorized by the penal law for that offense, institutional security requirements,[7] and the offender's current mental condition.

Specially committed offenders should have a claim to treatment or habilitation, under standard 7-9.11,[8] and have the same right as civilly

1. Standard 7-9.5, cross-referring to standard 7-4.6.
2. Standard 7-9.6.
3. Standard 7-9.7(a).
4. Standard 7-9.7(b), cross-referring to standards 7-9.8 and 7-9.9.
5. *See* standard 7-6.10 and commentary.
6. However, such offenders are to be sentenced under standard 7-9.10 without regard to the special commitment that otherwise may be ordered.
7. *See* standard 23-1.1 and commentary.
8. However, no release into the community should be made without approval by an authorized correctional official or the sentencing court. Standard 7-9.11.

committed patients and prisoners[9] to decline treatment or habilitation.[10] Commitment to a mental health or mental retardation facility, instead of a correctional facility, should be reviewed periodically on precisely the same basis as civil commitments;[11] if special institutionalization no longer is required, a convict should be transferred to a correctional facility if specified administrative procedures are followed.[12] Offenders whose sentences expire while they are retained in a mental health or mental retardation facility must be either released or civilly committed.[13]

The enactment of legislation embodying the criteria and procedures in part IX will enable appropriate dispositions to be made of convicted offenders who may be denominated sexual psychopaths, psychopaths, defective delinquents, and the like. It is for this reason that the Association has recommended the repeal of all special legislation covering special categories of offenders.[14]

Standard 7-9.1. Definitions

(a) An adult, or a minor under eighteen years of age who was tried as an adult, convicted of a crime and subject to sentencing, is referred to within this part as an offender.

(b) An offender who suffers a substantial disorder of thought, mood, perception, orientation, or memory which grossly impairs judgment, behavior, or the capacity to recognize reality or the ability to meet the demands of life, is referred to within this part as a severely mentally ill offender.

(c) An offender with very significant subaverage general intellectual functioning existing concurrently with substantial deficits in adaptive behavior is referred to within this part as a seriously mentally retarded offender.

---

9. *See* standard 23-5.5 and commentary.

10. Standard 7-9.12.

11. Standard 7-9.13. This class of prisoners is eligible for good-time credits as if incarcerated, standard 7-9.15(a), and should be eligible for parole like other prisoners. Standard 7-9.15(b)-(d).

12. Standard 7-9.14.

13. Standard 7-9.16. This is constitutionally mandated. *See* Baxstrom v. Herold, 383 U.S. 107 (1966).

14. *See* standard 7-8.1 and commentary.

Commentary Introduction

This standard defines severely mentally ill and seriously mentally retarded offenders for purposes of the more detailed coverage by the rest of the part IX standards.

Related Standard

ABA, Standards for Criminal Justice 7-9.7, 7-9.8, 7-9.9, 7-9.10, 7-10.1

Commentary

Paragraph (a) defines the term *offender* to include anyone who is an adult, or a juvenile under age eighteen who has been tried as an adult under the laws of a given jurisdiction, and who has been convicted and is eligible for sentencing. Juvenile offenders who remain within the jurisdiction of a juvenile, family, or probate court, even if adjudicated delinquent on the basis of conduct that would be criminal if committed by an adult, are not subject to these standards.

Paragraph (b) defines the term *severely mentally ill offender,* which is key to the special commitment provisions of this part,[1] in language that parallels the criteria for civil commitment.[2] The proffered definition reflects contemporary behavioral science norms as well.[3]

Paragraph (c) defines a significantly less clear area, that of serious mental retardation. It qualifies the basic definition of mental retardation to require that subaverage intellectual functioning be "very" significant and

---

1. *See* standards 7-9.8, 7-9.9, 7-9.10(b) and commentary.

2. The definition of mental illness in paragraph (b) is adapted from the Wisconsin civil commitment statute, Wis. Stat. Ann. §51.01(13) (Supp. 1985), and is similar to definitions of mental illness found in other state statutes. *See, e.g.,* Mich. Stat. Ann. §14.800(400a) (1980).

3. *See* American Psychiatric Ass'n Committee on Public Information, A Psychiatric Glossary 184 (3d ed. 1969), defining "psychosis" as "a major mental disorder of organic or emotional origin in which the individual's ability to think, respond emotionally, remember, communicate, interpret reality, and behave appropriately is sufficiently impaired so as to interfere grossly in his capacity to meet the ordinary demands of life." The current Diagnostic and Statistical Manual indicates that "psychotic" means "a gross impairment in reality testing where the individual incorrectly evaluates the accuracy of his or her perceptions and thought and makes incorrect inferences about external reality, even in the face of contrary evidence." American Psychiatric Ass'n, Diagnostic and Statistical Manual of Mental Disorders 367 (3d ed. 1980) [hereinafter cited as DSM-III].

that deficits in adaptive behavior be "substantial," before a defendant can be classified as seriously mentally retarded. Moreover, the standard omits any requirement that mental retardation[4] be manifested during the developmental period because a temporal manifestation of retardation is not germane to the process of sentencing convicted offenders in adult criminal courts.

The qualifications imposed on the definition of "seriously mentally retarded offender" in paragraph (c) reflect the fact that the dividing line between those to be dealt with specially at sentencing and other mentally retarded offenders is not as easy to make as the counterpart classification of mentally ill offenders, where the presence of psychosis suffices for the purpose. The paragraph (c) definition excludes the so-called borderline retarded, whose intelligence quotient (I.Q.) scores range from seventy to eighty-five. It does, however, comprehend the categories of "moderate,"[5] "severe,"[6] and "profound"[7] retardation. All are forms of serious mental retardation under paragraph (c).

The more difficult category is "mildly retarded" individuals.[8] The paragraph (c) definition reflects the Association's judgment that seriously retarded offenders should be treated in mental retardation facilities instead of correctional institutions,[9] pursuant to an agreement by all con-

---

4. The current and generally accepted definition of "mental retardation" is as follows: "Mental retardation refers to significantly subaverage general intellectual functioning existing concurrently with deficits in adaptive behavior and manifested during the developmental period." American Ass'n on Mental Deficiency, Classification in Mental Retardation 1 (Rev. ed. 1983). This definition is essentially unchanged from that in the 1973 and 1977 editions of the AAMD Manual on Terminology and Classification, and thus has found its way into a substantial number of statutes and court rules. *See, e.g.*, Fla. Stat. Ann. §393.063(23) (West Supp. 1985); Ga. Code Ann. §37-4-2(12) (1982); N.H. Rev. Stat. Ann. §171-A:2(XIV) (1977); Ky. Rev. Stat. §202B.010(1) (1982). *Cf.* Ellis & Luckasson, *Mentally Retarded Criminal Defendants*, 53 Geo. Wash. L. Rev. 414, 471-479 (1983).

5. Moderately retarded persons have I.Q.s that range from thirty-five to forty-nine. These persons typically have acquired some language but they are very limited in their abilities. They comprise up to 12 percent of the overall retarded population. *See* DSM-III, *supra* note 3, at 39; and AAMD Manual, *supra* note 4.

6. Severely retarded persons have I.Q.s that range from twenty to thirty-four, their level of functioning is very low, and they, together with the profoundly retarded, comprise no more than 8 percent of the overall retarded population. *See* DSM-III, *supra* note 3, at 39.

7. Profoundly retarded persons have I.Q.s below twenty, possess no language, and typically lack basic physical capacities. *See id.* at 39-40.

8. Persons within this class have I.Q.s in the fifty-to-seventy range and comprise about 80 percent of the overall retarded population. Typically, mildly retarded persons will possess language skills and will be capable of learning some other basic skills. *See id.* at 39.

9. *See* standard 7-9.7 and commentary.

cerned that commitment is the most appropriate disposition or a finding by the sentencing tribunal that a defendant is seriously retarded and requires habilitation services not available in a correctional facility.[10] Mildly retarded offenders are neither excluded from nor embraced automatically within the special commitment procedures envisioned in part IX. In fact, almost all convicted offenders who are mentally retarded will be only mildly retarded; it is inconceivable that profoundly retarded individuals will be subjected to criminal prosecution, and moderately and severely retarded offenders also are most likely to be screened out at earlier stages of criminal proceedings. The criteria embodied in paragraph (c) will enable convicted mentally retarded offenders to be screened for purposes of part IX, depending on the range of intellectual functioning and adaptive behavior manifested by each. Consequently, some mildly retarded offenders will be sentenced to regular incarceration while others appropriately will be committed to mental retardation facilities.

A sentencing court should evaluate the totality of circumstances presented by a convicted mentally retarded person before selecting incarceration, commitment, or an alternative sanction. The definition in paragraph (c), if recognized in forum law, will allow sentencing tribunals to incarcerate mentally retarded offenders who, based on intellectual functioning and adaptive behavior established by data adduced at a commitment hearing under standard 7-9.9, fall within the upper range of the mildly retarded class. In contrast, special commitments usually will be in order for offenders within the lower range of that class. But functional assumptions of this sort do not legitimate mathematical divisions based on intelligence quotients, on the basis of which mildly mentally retarded convicted offenders routinely are either incarcerated or specially committed. Judges must consider specific indicia of retardation in individual cases. Their evaluation of an offender's need for habilitation measures in a mental retardation facility rather than in an adult correctional institution must be based on findings that (1) the offender is retarded, with very significant subaverage general intellectual functioning and substantial deficits in adaptive behavior; (2) the offender as a result falls within a given sector of the seriously retarded range; and (3) habilitative services appropriate to the offender are not available within a correctional institution.

---

10. *See* standards 7-9.8 through 7-9.9 and commentary.

Standard 7-9.2. Probation

An offender should not be denied probation solely because the offender requires mental health or mental retardation treatment or habilitation.

Commentary Introduction

This standard adopts Association policy that mental illness requiring treatment or mental retardation necessitating habilitation should not render convicted offenders ineligible for probation that otherwise would be selected as a penal sanction.

Related Standards

ABA, Standards for Criminal Justice 7-9.8, 7-9.9, 7-9.10, 7-9.11, 7-9.12, 7-9.13, 7-10.3 through 7-10.7, 18-2.3(c)-(f), 23-5.1

Commentary

The criteria for use of probation rather than incarceration are governed by chapter 18, Sentencing Alternatives and Procedures.[1] An offender who otherwise is a suitable candidate for the sanction of probation should not be imprisoned simply because of mental illness or mental retardation. Instead, the court should either condition probation on outpatient or voluntary inpatient treatment,[2] or await the institution of regu-

1. *See* standards 18-2.2(a), 18.2.3(a), 18•73-18•78, commentary to standard 18-2.3.

2. *See* United States v. Stine, 675 F.2d 69 (3d Cir.), *cert. denied,* 458 U.S. 1110 (1982) (sentencing court had discretion to require psychological counseling as a condition of probation; no unconstitutional infringement of the right of privacy). *Compare* King v. Neely, 143 Ariz. 329, 331, 693 P.2d 984, 986 (1984) (courts could not interfere with exercise of prosecutorial discretion not to allow a defendant into a special therapy program for child molesters, successful completion of which would qualify the defendant for a plea agreement in which the prosecuting attorney would agree not to oppose probation).

Under the Comprehensive Crime Control Act of 1984, a federal district court may require probationers to undergo available medical, psychiatric, or psychological treatment, and remain in a specified institution if required for that purpose. 18 U.S.C.A. §3563(b)(10) (West 1986). The Senate Judiciary Committee envisioned that

> a court may require a defendant to . . . regularly visit a psychiatrist, participate in a recognized group therapy program, or undergo some other form of treatment for

lar civil commitment procedures if residential treatment is indicated. Naturally, if a convicted offender, were he or she not affected by mental illness or mental retardation, would be sentenced to incarceration, that disposition is appropriate under standard 7-9.2. In that event, however, the sentenced offender, if seriously mentally ill, may be subjected to the special commitment procedures recommended in part IX[3] for legislative adoption. Offenders not specially committed but sentenced to imprisonment in an adult correctional facility are entitled to adequate mental health treatment or mental retardation habilitation services there[4] or, after transfer, at a facility where they can be treated or habilitated properly.[5]

Standard 7-9.3. Sentencing effect of mental illness or mental retardation

Evidence of mental illness or mental retardation should be considered as a possible mitigating factor in sentencing a convicted offender.

Commentary Introduction

This standard provides that evidence of mental illness or mental retardation should be considered as a mitigating factor to ensure individualized sentencing in all sentencing procedures.

Related Standards

ABA, Standards for Criminal Justice 18-2.1(b), 18-2.2(a), 18-3.2(b)(i)(D)

> physical or emotional problems. Because receipt of treatment in an institution rather than on an outpatient basis would involve a deprivation of liberty, the judge would have to assure himself that it was reasonably necessary to a purpose of sentencing set forth in section 3553(a)(2) to require residence at an institution.

S. Rep. No. 225, 98th Cong., 1st Sess. at 97-98, *reprinted in* 1984 U.S. Code Cong. & Ad. News 3182, 3280-3281.

3. *See* standards 7-9.8, 7-9.9, 7-9.10(b) and commentary.
4. *See* standard 23-5.1(a) and commentary.
5. *See ibid.;* standards 7-10.3 through 7-10.7 and commentary.

Commentary

Whether mental illness or mental retardation militates toward the choice of incarceration as a sanction in noncapital cases[1] is a matter of disagreement. Some consider it to be an aggravating factor because it is an index of dangerousness. The Association's position, however, is that mentally ill or mentally retarded convicted offenders as a class cannot and should not be considered dangerous and hence subject to automatic sentences to imprisonment.

Instead, the Association policy embodied in standard 7-9.3 is that, in general, the presence of mental illness or mental retardation should be considered as a mitigating factor, rendering a sentence of probation more appropriate than a sentence of incarceration.[2] In taking that stand, the ABA allies itself with the American Law Institute[3] in urging that sentencing courts make individualized determinations in which mental illness or

---

1. The Association takes no position on the relevance of mental illness or mental retardation to capital sentencing. In constitutional litigation, the United States Supreme Court has noted in dictum that state legislation under attack did not embody references "to conduct that actually should militate in favor of a lesser penalty [than death], such as perhaps the defendant's mental illness." Zant v. Stephens, 462 U.S. 862, 885 (1983). In Eddings v. Oklahoma, 455 U.S. 104 (1982), the Court reversed a death sentence against a sixteen-year-old youth because the sentencing court had refused to consider his childhood environment and emotional disturbance. In Lockett v. Ohio, 438 U.S. 586 (1978), it indicated that due process requires that capital defendants be allowed to advance all possibly mitigating data whether or not they are identified in a statutory list of mitigating factors.

For illustrations of death penalty statutes listing mental disability as a mitigating factor, *see* Fla. Stat. Ann. §921.141(6)(b), (c) (West 1985); Ohio Rev. Code Ann. §2929.04(B)(3), (7) (Page 1982). Under statutes not following that pattern, *e.g.*, Ga. Code Ann. §17-10-30 (1982); Okla. Code Ann. tit. 21, §701.10 (1983), *and see* Eddings v. Oklahoma, 455 U.S. 104 (1982), some courts have given a broad definition of mitigating factors. *See, e.g.*, Rex v. State, 242 Ga. 876, 252 S.E.2d 383, *cert. denied*, 442 U.S. 934 (1979).

On procedures under state law to determine a defendant's competency to be executed, *see* Ford v. Wainwright, 752 F.2d 526, 528 (11th Cir. 1985).

See generally Weiner, *Mental Disability and the Criminal Law*, in The Mentally Disabled and the Law 693, 706-707 (S. Brakel, J. Parry & B. Weiner eds., 3d ed. 1985) [hereinafter cited as Weiner].

2. This reinforces the ABA policy expressed in standards 18-2.1(b) (legislature should provide a full array of alternatives) and 18-2.2(a) (least onerous sanction principle). *See generally*, Ellis & Luckasson, *Mentally Retarded Criminal Defendants*, 53 Geo. Wash. L. Rev. 414, 471-479 (1985).

3. ALI Model Penal Code §210.6(4)(c) (Permanent ed. with revised commentary 1980). *See also* Mont. Code Ann. §46-14-312 (1985) (authorizing special commitments for defendants suffering from mental disease or disorder); State v. Watson, 686 P.2d 879, 886-888 (Mont. 1984).

mental retardation is more likely to prove a mitigating factor than a neutral or aggravating one. This confirms a position already taken by the Association in chapter 18 of the standards.[4]

Standard 7-9.4 Assistance of experts during sentencing

In discharging the duties specified in standard 18-6.3(f), defense counsel may require the assistance of mental health or mental retardation professionals to explore the availability of evidence concerning the defendant's mental condition insofar as it may be relevant to issues of mitigation or disposition. Accordingly, in appropriate cases each jurisdiction should ensure that this form of assistance is available to defendants who are financially unable to obtain such assistance.

Commentary Introduction

This standard expresses Association policy that public funds should be made available to counsel for financially unable defendants so they may engage the services of mental health or mental retardation professionals to assist counsel preparation for sentencing hearings.

Related Standards

ABA, Standards for Criminal Justice 5-5.2, 18-5.1(d), (e), 18-6.3(e), (f)

Commentary

Chapter 18 of the standards, Sentencing Alternatives and Procedures, recognizes that defense attorneys have heavy responsibilities to represent their clients through adequate preparation for sentencing hearings, in-

---

4. *See* standard 18-3.2(b)(i)(D) and commentary. *See generally* Weiner, *supra* note 1, at 734-735. Legislation as of October 1982 may be found in *id.* at 759-768, Tables 12.3 and 12.4.

cluding the investigation and development of dispositional alternatives.[1] If, as the Association recommends,[2] presentence reports have been prepared in felony cases or cases in which a defendant is a first offender or younger than age twenty-one at time of conviction, they should reflect the existence of mental illness or mental retardation on the part of a defendant.[3] A defense counsel who believes the data reported in a presentence report are sufficient for purposes of a sentencing hearing nevertheless is responsible to verify the accuracy and sufficiency of the contents of the report.[4]

If the material contained in a report or already in the hands of defense counsel[5] is insufficient for purposes of representation at a sentencing hearing, counsel is under a responsibility to acquire the needed additional data for presentation to the sentencing court. If a client is funded, no judicial or administrative intervention is indicated; counsel in the exercise of professional responsibilities will make the necessary arrangements for diagnostic evaluations and reports and transmit findings and recommendations to the court, following recommended procedures.[6]

If, however, a client lacks financial resources to retain needed mental health or mental retardation professionals, the present standard embodies Association policy that legal machinery must be in place to provide the needed professional services. This possibly may be a constitutional necessity,[7] but in any event is consonant with the Association's position, expressed elsewhere,[8] that supporting services are imperative if attorneys are to discharge their professional responsibilities to clients.

---

1. *See* standard 18-6.3(f); 18•440-18•447, commentary to standard 18-6.3.
2. *See* standard 18-5.1(b).
3. *See* standard 18-5.1(d)(ii)(E); 18•353-18•354, commentary to standard 18-5.1.
4. *See* standard 18-6.3(f)(ii); 18•445-18•446, commentary to standard 18-6.3.
5. For example, because counsel has invoked the procedures delineated in standards 7-3.2, 7-3.5.
6. *See* standard 18-5.5(b) (notice to prosecuting attorney of an intent to contest or supplement; factual summary to preparer of presentence report in sufficient time for verification).
7. *See* Ake v. Oklahoma, 105 S. Ct. 1087 (1985), *discussed* in the commentary to standard 7-3.3, notes 3-6 and accompanying text; *see* Weiner, *Mental Disability and the Criminal Law*, in THE MENTALLY DISABLED AND THE LAW 693, 722-723 (S. Brakel, J. Parry & B. Weiner eds., 3d ed. 1985). *See also* Walker v. State, 254 Ga. 149, 327 S.E.2d 475, 481-482, *cert. denied sub nom.* Walker v. Georgia, 106 S. Ct. 185 (1985) (predicate facts insufficient to trigger *Ake* requirement of appointment of private psychiatrist in preparation for a capital sentencing hearing). The apparently open issue is *Ake*'s application to a noncapital, nonjury sentencing hearing where data bearing on mental illness or mental retardation do not exculpate or mitigate a noncapital offense, conviction of which is the predicate for sentencing proceedings.
8. *See* standards 5-5.2, 18-6.3(f) and commentary.

Standard 7-9.5. Inadmissibility of expert testimony based on competency evaluation

Testimony of a mental health or mental retardation professional which is based on a competency evaluation is admissible in a sentencing hearing only in accordance with the provisions of standard 7-4.6.

Commentary Introduction

The standard supports the basic premise of standard 7-4.6 that information obtained in the course of competency evaluations cannot be used to support a sentencing decision unless the defense places the defendant's mental status at issue at a sentencing hearing.

Related Standards

ABA, Standards for Criminal Justice 7-1.2, 7-2.3, 7-3.3, 7-3.4, 7-3.6, 7-3.8, 7-3.9, 7-4.2, 7-4.8

ALI, Model Penal Code §4.04

Commentary

It is possible, although not inevitable, that one or more mental evaluations will have been performed on a defendant before conviction to determine competency to undergo trial proceedings[1] or other forms of competency within the context of criminal proceedings.[2] Otherwise, it is entirely possible that a mental evaluation will have been performed in connection with the preparation of a presentence report.[3] Any such evaluation, other than one commissioned exclusively by defense counsel and not revealed in connection with the presentation of a defense case or evidence,[4] may very well contain information adverse to a defendant in the context of a sentencing hearing.

Standard 7-9.5 incorporates the premise that unless a defendant's mental condition has been advanced by defense counsel to support a recommended disposition of the case,[5] the contents of evaluation reports

1. *See* standards 7-4.1, 7-4.2 and commentary.
2. *See* standards 7-5.1 through 7-5.3 and commentary.
3. *See* standard 18-5.1 and commentary; commentary to standard 7-9.4, notes 1-4 and accompanying text.
4. *See* standards 7-3.2(a), 7-6.3, 7-9.4 and commentary.
5. *See* standard 7-9.3 and commentary.

authorized on motion of a prosecuting attorney or by a court *sua sponte,*[6] or conducted at defense request[7] and later made available to the prosecution,[8] cannot be submitted to or utilized by a sentencing court. Conversely, as in the context of information obtained from defendants in the course of competency evaluations,[9] if mental illness or mental retardation has been advanced by defense counsel as a basis for, *e.g.*, probation or a limited term of imprisonment, the contents of existing mental evaluation reports and the testimony of mental health and mental retardation professionals may be used to the extent the contents are relevant to a sentencing determination under a jurisdiction's criminal procedure and evidence statutes and rules. In taking this position, the Association builds on the Supreme Court holding in *Estelle v. Smith*[10] and extends it to non-capital sentencing proceedings and to the results of mental evaluations initiated by the defense during earlier stages of a criminal prosecution.

The standard refers to "testimony of a mental health or mental retardation professional." This is intended to incorporate by reference the restrictions in part III that an expert witness must have performed an evaluation on a defendant that included a personal interview.[11] That position by design exceeds the constitutional minimum established in *Barefoot v. Estelle,*[12] which allows responses to hypothetical questions asked of expert witnesses who have not directly evaluated and personally interviewed the subject of their opinions.[13]

Standard 7-9.6. Inadmissibility of expert testimony based on pretrial evaluation

No testimony of a mental health or mental retardation professional based on a pretrial evaluation is admissible at a sentencing hearing unless the defendant puts mental condition in issue at that hearing.

---

6. *See* standard 7-3.4 and commentary.
7. *See* standard 7-3.3(a) and commentary.
8. *See* standard 7-3.3(b) and commentary.
9. *See* standard 7-4.6(a) and commentary.
10. 451 U.S. 454 (1980). *See* commentary to standard 7-4.6, notes 11-13 and accompanying text. The Court held that a defendant's statements made to a prosecution psychiatrist at a court-ordered competency examination could not be used by the prosecution to establish dangerousness at a death penalty hearing; fifth and sixth amendment concerns are relevant to sentencing proceedings as well as guilt-phase trials. *Id.* at 453.
11. *See* standard 7-3.11 and commentary.
12. 463 U.S. 880, *reh'g denied,* 464 U.S. 874 (1983).
13. *See* commentary to standard 7-3.11, notes 13-17 and accompanying text.

Commentary Introduction

The standard confirms that data acquired in connection with a defense based on mental condition at the time of the commission of an offense cannot be utilized at a sentencing hearing unless a defendant has asserted mental illness or retardation bearing on an appropriate sentencing determination.

Related Standards

ABA, Standards for Criminal Justice 7-3.2(a), 7-3.9(b), 7-3.10, 7-3.11, 7-6.1, 7-6.2, 7-6.3, 7-6.4, 7-9.2, 7-9.3, 7-9.5

Commentary

By court order entered at prosecution request,[1] defendants who earlier asserted the defense of mental nonresponsibility [insanity],[2] or who otherwise advanced mental illness or mental retardation to raise a reasonable doubt about their culpability under the criminal law,[3] probably will have been evaluated to determine their mental condition at the time of their alleged offenses. In this event, they may have made statements to evaluating mental health or mental retardation professionals that the prosecution would like to use in support of a severe sentence. The policy recommended in standard 7-9.6 is that such data should not be available unless defendants have advanced their present mental condition as germane to a proper sentencing disposition. If they do so, then the information may be advanced to the extent it is legally relevant to issues at a sentencing hearing.[4] Although the Supreme Court has not dealt directly with the issue, dictum in its opinion in *Estelle v. Smith*[5] indicates that the assertion of a defense based on mental condition serves as a waiver of fifth and fourteenth amendment privilege against self-incrimination concerns, to the extent incriminating admissions are used solely to support the professional conclusions of prosecution expert witnesses.[6] The same doctrinal premise should be valid if waiver rests not on a substantive

1. *See* standard 7-6.4 and commentary.
2. *See* standards 7-6.1, 7-6.3 and commentary.
3. *See* standards 7-6.2, 7-6.3 and commentary.
4. This is the counterpart to the standard governing the use of information of that sort at trial. *See* standard 7-3.2(a)(ii).
5. 451 U.S. 454 (1980).
6. *Id.* at 468.

penal law defense but on the invocation of abnormal mental condition that affects the contents of a penal sentence.[7]

In this context, like standard 7-9.5, expert professional testimony bearing on future dangerousness should be subject to the general strictures on that form of opinion evidence,[8] and opinion evidence must be based on a personal evaluation that includes a personal interview with the defendant to whom the evidence relates.[9]

Standard 7-9.7. Treatment for mentally ill and mentally retarded offenders sentenced to imprisonment

(a) Mental health and mental retardation services should be available within the adult correctional facility for offenders whose mental illness or retardation is not severe enough to necessitate commitment to a mental health or mental retardation facility.

(b) Severely mentally ill or seriously mentally retarded sentenced offenders should be treated in a mental health or mental retardation facility, preferably under the supervision of the jurisdiction's department of mental health or mental retardation, in accordance with standards 7-9.8 and 7-9.9.

Commentary Introduction

The standard covers treatment and habilitation services for mentally ill and mentally retarded offenders within correctional facilities; it also covers the transfer of severely mentally ill or mentally retarded prisoners to mental health or mental retardation facilities outside correctional administrative jurisdiction.

Related Standards

ABA, Standards for Criminal Justice 7-6.10, 7-8.1, 7-9.1, 7-9.8, 7-9.9, 7-9.10, 7-10.2, 7-10.3, 23-5.1

---

7. *See* standards 7-9.2, 7-9.3 and commentary.
8. *See* standard 7-3.9(b) and commentary.
9. *See* standard 7-3.11; commentary to standard 7-9.5, notes 11-13 and accompanying text.

Commentary

Prisoners have a constitutional right to adequate medical diagnosis and treatment, including psychiatric care.[1] The severity of mental illness or seriousness of mental retardation governs the situs of treatment or habilitation under the standard: Severely mentally ill[2] or seriously mentally retarded[3] prisoners should be treated in mental health or mental retardation facilities, not in correctional facilities.

Offenders whose mental illness or mental retardation can be treated adequately within an adult correctional facility should remain there, according to paragraph (a). The scope of appropriate facilities and treatment or habilitation regimens is, by design, left to judicial implementation.[4] However, if an offender's mental condition is too severe or serious to allow adequate treatment or habilitation within a prison system, paragraph (b) envisions a transfer to a mental health or mental retardation facility, which should be within the administrative jurisdiction of a state department of mental health or mental retardation, not the department of prisons or corrections.[5] The latter preference for nonpenal

---

1. *See* commentary to standard 23-5.1, at n.9. *See also* Weiner, *Mental Disability and the Criminal Law*, in The Mentally Disabled and the Law 693, 737-738 (S. Brakel, J. Parry & B. Weiner eds., 3d ed. 1985).

2. Defined in standard 7-9.1(b). *See* commentary to standard 7-9.1, notes 2-3 and accompanying text.

3. Defined in standard 7-9.1(c). *See* commentary to standard 7-9.1, notes 4-8 and accompanying text.

4. *See* standard 23-5.1 and commentary. Balla v. Idaho State Bd. of Corrections, 595 F. Supp. 1558, 1477 (D. Idaho 1984), and Ruiz v. Estelle, 503 F. Supp. 1265, 1339 (S.D. Tex. 1980), 650 F.2d 555 (5th Cir. 1981), 666 F.2d 854 (5th Cir.), *aff'd in part & vacated in part*, 679 F.2d 1115 (5th Cir.), *amended in part & vacated in part, reh. denied in part*, 688 F.2d 266 (5th Cir. 1982), *cert. denied*, 460 U.S. 1042 (1983), delineated six elements of a constitutionally adequate prison-based mental health treatment program: (1) a systematic program to screen and evaluate prisoners to identify those requiring mental health treatment; (2) treatment transcending mere segregation and close supervision of inmate patients; (3) employment of trained mental health professionals in sufficient numbers to identify and provide individualized treatment for treatable inmates suffering from serious mental disorders; (4) accurate, complete, and confidential records of mental health treatment processes; (5) a ban on prescription and administration of behavior-altering medications in dangerous amounts, by dangerous methods, or without appropriate supervision and periodic evaluation; and (6) a basic program to identify, treat, and supervise inmates with suicidal tendencies.

5. This policy preference is consistent with the views expressed in Project, *Legal Issues in State Mental Health Care — Mental Health Services for Prisoners*, 2 Mental Disability L. Rep. 665, 672 (1978).

administrative responsibility does not rest on an assumption that correctional facility medical staff cannot provide appropriate treatment or habilitation services, but rather on a recognition that the first priority of a department of mental health or human services is treatment or care, while prisons of necessity have a correctional and custodial focus.

The standard assumes that mentally ill and mentally retarded offenders will be either sentenced to prison[6] or specially committed because of severe mental illness or serious mental retardation.[7] Prisoners who are treated or habilitated to a sufficient extent will be transferred or retransferred to adult correctional facilities. Accordingly, the standard rejects special commitment procedures turning on sexual psychopathy, psychopathy, or defective delinquency,[8] statutes providing for direct judicial placement of convicted offenders in mental health or mental retardation facilities,[9] and the guilty-but-mentally-ill (GBMI) verdict that provides for incarceration and perhaps special treatment or habilitation for mentally ill or mentally retarded defendants who are not acquitted by reason of mental nonresponsibility [insanity].[10] At the same time, it should be stressed that the standard provides a more effective device to accomplish the same effect as GBMI verdicts without the disadvantages inherent in GBMI legislation.[11]

For two reasons, paragraph (b) of the standard envisions only residential or inpatient treatment or habilitation services for convicted prisoners placed in mental health or mental retardation facilities. One is that all such prisoners have been convicted of crimes warranting incarceration were it not for their severe mental illness or serious mental retardation; if from a medical viewpoint they could be released into the community as outpatients, they should be returned to prison. The second is that their

---

6. *See* standard 7-9.10(a) and commentary.

7. *See* standards 7-9.8, 7-9.9 and commentary.

8. *See* standard 7-8.1 and commentary for the basic exposition of Association policy on the matter.

9. Occasionally, state legislation provides for the direct placement of convicted offenders (other than under sexual psychopathy, etc. laws or as a consequence of a guilty-but-mentally-ill verdict) in mental health facilities. *See, e.g.*, N.J. STAT. ANN. §30:4-82 (1981); VA. CODE §19.2-176 (1983). These statutes are virtually identical to prisoner transfer laws. Offenders first are sentenced and then are placed in mental health or mental retardation facilities until their sentences expire or they have recovered sufficiently to warrant transfer to correctional control. These statutes are deficient because they neither meet the criteria for commitment nor offer the procedural protections set out in standard 7-9.9.

10. *See* standard 7-6.10 and commentary.

11. *See* commentary to standard 7-6.10, notes 9-19 and accompanying text.

mental impairment, by hypothesis, is grave enough that they would have been committed civilly had they not been convicted of crime, and therefore would not have been released from hospital confinement. Thus, both the public's need for protection and an offender's expectations of continuous care mandate an assignment to an inpatient facility, not outpatient or community-based mental health or mental retardation services.

Standard 7-9.8. Commitment of severely mentally ill and seriously mentally retarded offenders

(a) Initiation of postconviction proceedings. Commitment proceedings may be initiated by the offender or prosecutor subsequent to conviction and prior to or during the sentencing hearing. The party who raises the issue must present evidence showing that the offender meets the criteria for commitment.

(b) Notice. The offender must receive written notice that commitment as a severely mentally ill or seriously mentally retarded offender is sought if the prosecutor initiates the proceedings. The prosecutor should receive written notice if the offender is the initiating party. The notice should be provided sufficiently in advance to allow full preparation for the hearing.

(c) Mental health and mental retardation evaluations. The offender may not be committed as a severely mentally ill or seriously mentally retarded offender unless the offender has been evaluated by a mental health or mental retardation professional within the last [sixty] days and found to be severely mentally ill or seriously mentally retarded. The judge may order a mental evaluation of the offender which may be conducted in the setting where the offender is located, or the offender may be committed for observation and diagnosis. Such commitment period should not exceed [thirty] days, and the offender's sentence should be credited with time spent while confined for observation.

(d) Evaluation reports. Mental evaluation reports of the offender should address the question of whether the offender is severely mentally ill or seriously mentally retarded. All reports should be disclosed to the prosecution and the defense prior to the hearing. In addition to the diagnosis, the reports should describe the specific behavior or other indicators which led to the conclusion that the

offender is or is not severely mentally ill or seriously mentally retarded. An offender may not be committed unless a report from a mental health or mental retardation professional indicates that the offender suffers from severe mental illness or serious mental retardation.

Commentary Introduction

The standard outlines recommended procedures for postconviction proceedings to commit severely mentally ill and seriously mentally retarded offenders to mental health or mental retardation facilities instead of adult correctional facilities.

Related Standards

ABA, Standards for Criminal Justice 7-3.6, 7-3.7, 7-3.12, 7-4.3, 7-4.8(a)(ii), 7-4.15, 7-5.3(b), 7-6.3(a), 7-9.1, 7-10.4, 7-10.11(c), 18-5.3, 18-5.4, 18-6.5(b)(i), 21-2.5(b)

Commentary

Severely mentally ill[1] or seriously mentally retarded[2] convicted offenders should be eligible for special commitment procedures in lieu of incarceration.[3] Standard 7-9.8 covers the procedures preliminary to a determination of eligibility for commitment.

Paragraph (a) incorporates a judgment that special commitment procedures should be available at the instance of either an offender[4] or the prosecuting attorney.[5] Although the standard does not state so expressly, if a sentencing court suspects that an offender is severely mentally ill or

1. Defined in standard 7-9.1(b). *See* commentary to standard 7-9.1, notes 2-3 and accompanying text.

2. Defined in standard 7-9.1(c). *See* commentary to standard 7-9.1, notes 4-8 and accompanying text.

3. *See* standard 7-9.9 and commentary.

4. Usually through defense counsel, who will represent a convicted defendant, *see* standard 7-9.9(a)(ii), unless the right of self-representation has been exercised competently, *see* standard 7-5.3(b) and commentary.

5. It has been suggested that, under sex offender statutes allowing special commitment proceedings to be initiated solely by prosecuting authorities, the selection of offenders for special disposition at times has been made unfairly. *See* Dix, *Special Dispositional Alternatives for Abnormal Offenders*, in MENTALLY DISORDERED OFFENDERS 133, 160-162 (J. Monahan & H. Steadman ed. 1983).

seriously mentally retarded and neither counsel has sought a special commitment proceeding, it may communicate its concerns to either the prosecuting attorney or defense counsel, who then should submit the appropriate notice under paragraph (b). However, a bare assertion of a belief that a convicted offender may be eligible for special commitment is insufficient; the attorney raising the issue is also expected to present evidence showing that the offender is eligible for special commitment.[6] This is intended to forestall frivolous claims of severe mental illness or serious mental retardation motivated, for example, by a desire to postpone sentencing proceedings.

Paragraph (b) sets out a requirement that written notice be given to opposing counsel in sufficient time to allow full preparation for a hearing on a request for special commitment. This corresponds to notice procedures elsewhere in chapter 7.[7]

Current mental status evaluation data are indispensable to a proper resolution of a request for special commitment. Therefore, paragraph (c) urges a requirement that a convicted offender have been evaluated by a mental health or mental retardation professional[8] within a recommended sixty-day period before submission of a request for special commitment and determined to be severely mentally ill or seriously mentally retarded; no special commitment should be lawful without such a recent evaluation report. Presumably, the attorney submitting a request for special commitment, in compliance with paragraph (a), will have provided the sentencing court with copies of existing evaluation reports or called the court's attention to their presence in court records, so that the need for an initial or new evaluation report can be identified without the need for an ancillary hearing on the matter. The standard contemplates only the necessity of a contemporaneous evaluation, but does not require that it be performed in a custodial setting. Accordingly, paragraph (c) acknowledges judicial discretion to select either inpatient or outpatient evaluation.[9] A commitment for evaluation, however, should not extend longer

---

6. *See* standard 7-9.9(d) and commentary.

7. *See, e.g.*, standards 7-4.8(a)(ii) (competency hearing); 7-6.3(a) (notice of mental condition defense); 7-10.11(c) (notice of prospective return of prisoner from mental health facility to correctional control).

8. The requirements of standards 7-3.6 and 7-3.7 govern these evaluations; evaluators should be qualified in accordance with standard 7-3.12.

9. Although conviction alters a defendant's claim to release pending sentencing, *see* standard 21-2.5(b) and commentary, a concern with the least-restrictive alternative perhaps should govern the court's choice in this context as it does pretrial commitments to ascertain competence to undergo trial. *See* commentary to standard 7-4.3, notes 11-15 and accompanying text.

than a recommended maximum period of thirty days and should be for a shorter period if a competent evaluation can be made within that time. Paragraph (c) confirms that time spent in custody for evaluation should be credited against a subsequently imposed term of imprisonment.[10]

Paragraph (d) supplements the basic standards' delineation of the contents of evaluation reports[11] by noting certain contents needed for a proper determination of a request for special commitment: (1) a professional judgment whether the offender is severely mentally ill or seriously mentally retarded; and (2) descriptions of specific behavior or other indicators supporting that professional judgment. Paragraph (d) confirms the thrust of paragraph (c) that no convicted offender may be specially committed unless a qualified mental health or mental retardation professional evaluator has reported that the offender is severely mentally ill or seriously mentally retarded. A report indicating the absence of either condition should serve to bar further proceedings and should lead to a dismissal of the motion or request for special commitment proceedings.

A copy of an evaluation report, under paragraph (d), should be provided to opposing counsel before a special commitment hearing.[12] The scope of disclosure should be governed by provisions applicable to presentence reports[13] because, functionally speaking, evaluation reports under standard 7-9.8 constitute a form of presentencing data.

Standard 7-9.9. Commitment hearing procedures

(a) Procedural protections. The commitment hearing should afford the offender the following minimum procedural protections:

(i) notice as provided in standard 7-9.8(b);

(ii) the right to counsel;

(iii) the right to be present at the hearing and to call witnesses, including independent expert witnesses, and to cross-examine witnesses;

(iv) a judicial hearing officer;

10. Recall that defendants found incompetent to undergo criminal proceedings also receive credit against later incarceration for periods of detention incident to mental evaluation of competence. *See* standard 7-4.15 and commentary.

11. *See* standard 7-3.7(b) and commentary.

12. *Compare* standard 18-6.5(b)(i) (notice requirement governing sentencing data, sufficiently in advance to allow preparation for a defense submission to a sentencing court). *See* 18•477-18•478, commentary to standard 18-6.5.

13. *See* standards 18-5.3, 18-5.4; 18•373-18•377, commentary to standard 18-5.4.

(v) a decision based upon the record;

(vi) written findings of fact by the hearing officer; and

(vii) to be informed of the foregoing rights.

(b) Procedures when neither party objects. If neither the prosecutor nor the offender objects to the offender being committed as a severely mentally ill or seriously mentally retarded offender, a hearing is not required. However, the court must still find, based on at least one report from a mental health or mental retardation professional, that the offender suffers from severe mental illness or serious mental retardation.

(c) Burdens of proof. If either the offender or the prosecutor objects to commitment, the other party must then show by clear and convincing evidence that the offender meets the criteria for commitment.

(d) Criteria for commitment. At the commitment hearing the court must find that the offender is severely mentally ill or seriously mentally retarded and requires treatment or habilitation in a mental health or mental retardation facility rather than an adult correctional facility.

(e) Expert opinion testimony as to whether the offender is severely mentally ill or seriously mentally retarded and requires treatment or habilitation in a mental health or mental retardation facility should be admissible subject to the limitations set forth in standards 7-9.5 and 7-9.6.

Commentary Introduction

The standard sets out hearing procedures that should be followed before special commitments of severely mentally ill and seriously mentally retarded offenders should be ordered. It also sets out the criteria on which such commitments should rest.

Related Standards

ABA, Standards for Criminal Justice 7-3.10, 7-3.11, 7-3.13, 7-3.14, 7-5.3, 7-7.4(b), 7-9.1, 7-9.4, 7-9.5, 7-9.6, 7-9.8, 7-9.9, 7-9.10(a), 7-10.5, 7-10.10, 18-5.5

Commentary

Paragraph (d) establishes the criteria on the basis of which special commitment orders may be entered against convicted offenders: (1) they must be determined to be either severely mentally ill[1] or seriously mentally retarded;[2] and (2) they must be found to require treatment in a mental health facility or habilitation services in a mental retardation facility rather than in an adult correctional facility.

The primary foci of the standard, however, are procedural. The bounds of constitutional regulation turn on whether special dispositional procedures are (1) a form of criminal sentencing, and therefore within the ambit of constitutional criminal guarantees affecting that phase of criminal procedure,[3] or (2) an administrative transfer from correctional to mental health or mental retardation departmental control.[4] In either case, standard 7-9.9 accommodates the issue by treating special commitments as an alternative sentencing procedure[5] and thus governed by the usual array of constitutional guarantees other than jury trial.[6]

The scope and formality of a hearing turn on the extent to which counsel for the prosecution and defense agree with evaluation report findings that an offender is either severely mentally ill or seriously mentally retarded.[7] If both the prosecuting attorney and defense counsel (act-

---

1. Defined in standard 7-9.1(b). *See* commentary to standard 7-9.1, notes 2-3 and accompanying text.

2. Defined in standard 7-9.1(c). *See* commentary to standard 7-9.1, notes 4-8 and accompanying text.

3. In Specht v. Patterson, 386 U.S. 605 (1967), the Supreme Court found that commitment under a state sex offenders act required a separate determination from an adjudication of guilt, according to procedures (whether denominated civil or criminal) consonant with the due process and equal protection clauses of the fourteenth amendment. The Court's rationale, although directed toward a sex offender statute, arguably governs special commitment proceedings against convicted offenders.

4. *See* Vitek v. Jones, 445 U.S. 480 (1980), governing procedures to be followed for transfers from correctional to mental health or mental retardation facilities. These include written notice that a transfer is being considered, a hearing, the opportunity to be heard and to present documentary evidence and testimony, the opportunity to cross-examine prosecution witnesses, an independent decisionmaker, a written statement of the evidence relied upon by the decisionmaker, and at least one level of administrative review. *Id.* at 494-495. *See also* standard 7-10.5 and commentary.

5. *See* standard 7-9.10(a) and commentary (a criminal sentence should be imposed whether or not a convicted offender is specially committed).

6. *See* standard 18-1.1 and commentary (recommending abolition of jury sentencing).

7. Recall that such a finding is a prerequisite to a special commitment under standard 7-9.8(c) and 7-9.8(d). Waiver of a special hearing is consistent with the provision of standard 18-5.5 calling for a presentence conference at which the parties should attempt to agree on disputed facts. If both parties agree that a convicted offender is mentally ill or mentally retarded and should be placed in a mental health or mental retardation facility, there is no need for a formal hearing at which expert witnesses are called to testify concerning the offender's mental condition. In that event, evaluation reports themselves will provide the factual basis specified in paragraph (b) for a special commitment order.

ing for a convicted offender) accept the validity of the findings, paragraph (b) allows the sentencing court to determine the matter on the basis of evaluation reports, although the court must enter formal findings based on at least one evaluation report, that the offender meets the criteria for commitment under paragraph (d). Should either attorney object to the evaluators' conclusion, paragraph (b) envisions that a hearing must be held before a special commitment order may be entered.[8]

Paragraph (a) contains a catalog of procedural protections for respondents in special commitment proceedings:[9]

1. Written notice to opposing counsel that a special commitment has been sought must have been given sufficiently in advance to allow adequate preparation for a special commitment hearing.[10]
2. The right to counsel must have been implemented, including assignment of counsel for financially unable defendants, or a valid exercise of the right of self-representation must have been documented on the record.[11]
3. The defendant must have been afforded the right to be pre-

8. To illustrate, a prosecuting attorney may believe that a convicted offender is motivated by a desire to serve a period of incarceration in a setting perceived as more desirable than an adult correctional facility. Or he or she may fear that the offender will be recommended by mental health or mental retardation administrators for release earlier than an anticipated prison parole date, even though parole release is not supposed to be affected by the fact that a prisoner is receiving mental health treatment or mental retardation habilitation services. *See* standard 7-10.10(b), (d) and commentary. Misgivings of this sort, however, can be expressed under the standard only through a prosecution objection impelling a hearing; prosecuting authorities have no control over the initiation or resolution of special commitment hearings. If, on the basis of a hearing conforming to the procedural requirements of paragraph (a), a court finds by the burden of persuasion (proof) recommended in paragraph (c) that the criteria for special commitment delineated in paragraph (d) have been met, a convicted offender should be specially committed, whatever the prosecuting attorney's reservations about the consequences.

9. Other specific rights may be afforded a respondent in a civil commitment hearing under state laws; those protections should apply to special commitment proceedings under standard 7-9.9 as well.

10. *See* standard 7-9.8(b); commentary to standard 7-9.8, note 7 and accompanying text.

11. *See* standard 7-5.3(b) and commentary. Sentencing proceedings, of which standard 7-9.9 hearings are a form, are clearly a critical phase of the criminal proceeding within the sixth amendment. *See* Coleman v. Alabama, 399 U.S. 1 (1970). Trial counsel also is familiar already with a convicted offender and is best able to provide competent representation at sentencing or special commitment hearings.

sent at the hearing, to call witnesses including independent expert witnesses,[12] and to cross-examine witnesses.

4. The hearing must be conducted by a judicial hearing officer, not an administrative official.
5. A decision must be made by the judge, based on the record and documented by written findings of fact.
6. Advice must have been given to the respondent, in advance of the hearing, of the above procedural guarantees.

A hearing usually is demanded by either or both attorneys so that evaluating professionals can appear as expert witnesses and be subjected to cross-examination. Expert witnesses should have the qualifications recommended in the standards for all such witnesses[13] and should present their expert testimony in acceptable form.[14] Their professional opinions must rest on a personal evaluation that includes a personal interview with the subject of their testimony,[15] according to paragraph (e).

The burdens of going forward with evidence and of persuasion (proof) are placed by paragraph (c) on the party requesting a hearing. Consequently, the burden of persuasion may rest on the defense if defense counsel moved for an evaluation and hearing, and on the prosecuting attorney if the defense moved for an evaluation and is satisfied with the evaluators' findings but the prosecution insists on a hearing. In either event, the burden of persuasion is stated at the level of clear and convincing proof, which is the constitutional criterion for civil commitments[16] and the norm recommended in these standards for commitments following acquittals based on mental nonresponsibility [insanity].[17]

Standard 7-9.10. Disposition of offenders

(a) Sentence. The court should impose the sentence for the criminal offense whether or not the offender is placed in accordance with paragraph (b) of this standard.

(b) Commitment. A severely mentally ill or seriously mentally re-

12. *See* standard 7-9.4 and commentary.
13. *See* standards 7-3.11, 7-3.13 and commentary.
14. *See* standard 7-3.14(b) and commentary.
15. *See* standards 7-9.5, 7-9.6 and commentary.
16. *See* Addington v. Texas, 441 U.S. 418 (1979).
17. *See* standard 7-7.4(b) and commentary.

tarded offender who is committed pursuant to standard 7-9.9 should be placed in a mental health or mental retardation facility. The principle of least-restrictive alternative should apply in the placement of such offenders, but the placement should also take into consideration the offender's history, the offense, the sentence, institutional security requirements, and the offender's current mental condition.

Commentary Introduction

This standard confirms that all convicted offenders should be sentenced but provides for special commitments of those who are severely mentally ill or seriously mentally retarded.

Related Standards

ABA, Standards for Criminal Justice 7-4.13(a)(ii), 7-9.1, 7-9.2, 7-9.5, 7-9.7, 7-9.8, 7-9.9; 7-9.13, 7-9.14, 7-9.16, 7-10.2 through 7-10.5, 7-10.11, 7-10.12, 18-6.4 through 18-6.7

Commentary

Because criminal convictions must precede the disposition of offenders under part IX, and because special commitments are not ordered in lieu of criminal sanctions, paragraph (a) of the standard confirms that courts always should assess sentence against mentally ill or mentally retarded offenders according to the provisions of chapter 18, Sentencing Alternatives and Procedures.[1] Offenders sentenced to probation can be provided needed mental health treatment or habilitation services within the community.[2] Incarcerated convicts can be treated within adult correctional institutions[3] or transferred to mental health or mental retardation facilities under appropriate administrative procedures.[4] Severely mentally ill[5] or seriously mentally retarded[6] offenders can be specially committed.[7]

1. *See* standards 18-6.4 through 18-6.7 and commentary.
2. *See* standard 7-9.2 and commentary.
3. *See* standards 7-9.7, 7-10.2, 23-5.1(a) and commentary.
4. *See* standards 7-10.3 through 7-10.5 and commentary.
5. Defined in standard 7-9.1(b). *See* commentary to standard 7-9.1, notes 2-3 and accompanying text.
6. Defined in standard 7-9.1(c). *See* commentary to standard 7-9.1, notes 4-8 and accompanying text.
7. *See* standards 7-9.8, 7-9.9 and commentary.

Nevertheless, whenever special treatment or habilitation services no longer are necessary, patient/offenders must be returned to prison control.[8] This is possible only if a valid penal sentence to incarceration exists at the time of return or transfer.[9] Consequently, sentencing in accord with paragraph (a) is a legal prerequisite to appropriate procedural disposition of convicted offenders.

Paragraph (b) provides that convicted offenders who are severely mentally ill or seriously mentally retarded and who require treatment in a mental health facility or habilitation services in a mental retardation facility may be specially committed by court order.[10] The standard states that the principle of least-restrictive alternative should be taken into account by sentencing courts, but only as they decide to enter commitment orders for treatment or habilitation. The principle, at this stage, is not the exclusive dispositive factor, however. In addition, sentencing courts are admonished to take into consideration an offender's history, the nature of the criminal conduct on which a criminal conviction is based, the penal sanctions authorized in the underlying criminal provisions, institutional security requirements (including those of both adult correctional institutions and mental health or mental retardation facilities), and an offender's mental condition. It is extremely improbable that a suitable balancing of these factors will support immediate release of persons into the community, as outpatients, who have been convicted of violent felonies and who have been adjudicated, on the basis of clear and convincing proof,[11] severely mentally ill or seriously mentally retarded.

This does not mean, however, that persons who are convicted of nonviolent offenses[12] but who are not currently dangerous must be held indefinitely under maximum security conditions in mental health or mental retardation facilities. Placement within a facility or assignment to a facility should be made by mental health or mental retardation facility administrators in light of each committed convict/patient's treatment or habilitation needs, using the least amount of control consistent with effective treatment or habilitation, on the one hand, and community and institutional security on the other. The greater a convict/patient's history

8. *See* standards 7-9.14, 7-10.11 and commentary.

9. *See* standards 7-9.16, 7-10.12 and commentary.

10. *See* standard 7-9.9(d).

11. *See* standard 7-9.9(c); commentary to standard 7-9.9, notes 18-19 and accompanying text.

12. *Compare* the corollary problem of persons permanently incompetent to undergo criminal proceedings. *See* standard 7-4.13(a)(ii); commentary to standard 7-4.13, note 30.

of or propensity toward violence, of course, the more secure will be the facility or ward to which that convict/patient is assigned. It should be noted, incidentally, that although the initial commitment order should rest on a judicial balancing of the factors set out in paragraph (b), the intent is not to involve the judiciary in either initial classification determinations or ensuing transfers or reclassifications. These are matters exclusively within the control of mental health or mental retardation facility administrators. Later judicial review is restricted to the issue of a continued need *vel non* for mental health treatment or habilitation services for mental retardation.[13]

Standard 7-9.11. Right to treatment and habilitation; limitation on access into community

Once placed in a mental health or mental retardation facility, a mentally ill offender should have the right to treatment described in chapter 23 of these standards and a mentally retarded offender should have a comparable right to habilitation. These offenders should not, however, be permitted access into the community by mental health or mental retardation officials without authorization from appropriate correctional officials or the court.

Commentary Introduction

The standard confirms the claims of mentally ill offenders to treatment and of mentally retarded offenders to habilitation services, with the limitation that mental health or mental retardation facility administrators are not to allow them into the community without advance authorization from either sentencing courts or appropriate correctional administrators.

Related Standards

ABA, Standards for Criminal Justice 7-9.15, 7-10.8, 23-3.1, 23-3.2, 23-5.1 through 23-5.5, 23-6.1 through 23-6.14

---

13. *See* standard 7-9.13 and commentary.

Commentary

Convicted offenders who are severely mentally ill or seriously mentally retarded and who are committed because they cannot be placed safely in the community on a probation/outpatient basis, and yet cannot be treated adequately or habilitated in adult correctional facilities, are prisoners, legally speaking, even though they have been committed to mental health or mental retardation facilities. Therefore, whatever the constitutional claims of civilly committed patients generally to a safe environment and at least minimal treatment or habilitation services,[1] convict/patients have the same claims to adequate diagnosis, treatment, habilitation, and care that prisoners generally must be accorded.[2] Standard 7-9.11 is included to make sure that fact is not overlooked.

Convicts specially committed under standards 7-9.9 and 7-9.10 cannot be affected adversely by the fact of their committee status. Therefore,

---

1. Originally, the right to treatment for civil patients appeared to mean only a right to be treated or released. *See* O'Connor v. Donaldson, 422 U.S. 563 (1975). However, in Youngberg v. Romeo, 457 U.S. 307 (1982), the Supreme Court concluded that there is a constitutional right to provide "minimally adequate training" for mentally retarded patients. *Id.* at 322. Lower courts have sought to expand the minimum constitutional requirements of *Romeo.* For example, the Third Circuit in Scott v. Plante, 691 F.2d 634 (3d Cir. 1982), reiterated the right to adequate treatment, secured by the fourteenth amendment. Lombard v. Eunice Shriver Center for Mentally Retarded, Inc., 556 F. Supp. 677 (D.C. Mass. 1983), explicitly held "that the Fourteenth Amendment imposes an affirmative obligation on the state to provide adequate medical care for involuntarily committed residents of state mental institutions." *Id.* at 678.

Other decisions have indicated that *Romeo* is not limited to involuntarily confined mentally retarded residents. Scott v. Plante, 691 F.2d 634 (3d Cir. 1982), held that a defendant committed as incompetent to stand trial was entitled to treatment for mental illness. In Milonas v. Williams, 691 F.2d 931 (10th Cir. 1982), the Tenth Circuit applied the *Romeo* doctrine for the benefit of adolescents involuntarily confined in a private boys school because of behavioral problems.

Some jurisdictions have established a statutory right to treatment, *e.g.*, D.C. Code §21-562 (Supp. 1985), although whether this right applies to severely mentally ill or seriously mentally retarded offenders is unclear.

See generally Weiner, *Treatment Rights*, in The Mentally Disabled and the Law 327-351 (S. Brakel, J. Parry & B. Weiner eds., 3d ed. 1985) [hereinafter cited as Weiner]; Project, *Legal Issues in State Mental Health Care: Proposals for Change: Suggested Statute on Mental Health Standards and Human Rights*, 2 Mental Disability L. Rep. 305, 308-309 (1978). Legislation as of October 1982 is summarized in Weiner, *supra* at 352-367, Table 6.2.

2. *See* standards 23-5.1 through 23-5.6 and commentary. *See also* Project, *Legal Issues in State Mental Health Care — Proposals for Change: Mental Health Services for Prisoners*, 2 Mental Disability L. Rep. 665 (1978).

they must be afforded all the protections delineated in chapter 23 of the standards, Legal Status of Prisoners.[3] However, if a mental health or mental retardation facility follows practices less restrictive than those of adult correctional institutions, there should be no discrimination within the facility based on the status of convict/patient. All facility residents should be treated alike.[4] That includes ground privileges, if compatible with institutional security needs. In other words, convict/patients as a class should not be denied ground privileges; restrictions should be imposed in individual cases (whatever the original commitment status of an individual) because they are necessary for the protection of staff members and other patients or for maintenance of effective control over the patient, and for no other reason.

The standard confirms that in only one context may convict/patients be treated differently from civilly committed or voluntary patients. Facility administrators usually may release civilly committed patients on furlough or outpatient status without judicial approval;[5] voluntary patients, of course, must be released whenever they wish.[6] In contrast, convict/patients are convicted offenders, whatever their current mental health status. Therefore, facility administrators are precluded under the standard from allowing convict/patients into the community on any basis whatever, unless they have obtained advance approval from the sentencing court or an official of the prison or correctional system in which a convict/patient would have been incarcerated had it not been for the special commitment under standards 7-9.9 and 7-9.10(b). Thus, for example, if a correctional administrator believes that a convict cannot be allowed in the community without risk of repeated dangerous conduct or the generation of community fears about the convict's renewed presence there, and if the convict's mental condition can be treated within an adult

---

3. *See, e.g.*, parts II (access to the judicial process, legal services and legal materials, VI (personal integrity and security). They should be subject to disciplinary sanctions, *id.* standard 23-3.2, if a mental health or mental retardation facility has promulgated the necessary rules of conduct, *id.* standard 23-3.1. *See* Weiner, *Mental Disability and the Criminal Law*, in THE MENTALLY DISABLED AND THE LAW 693, 737-738 (S. Brakel, J. Parry & B. Weiner eds., 3d ed. 1985).

4. Project, *Legal Issues in State Mental Health Care: Proposals for Change: Suggested Statute on Mental Health Standards and Human Rights*, 2 MENTAL DISABILITY L. REP. 305, 306-308 (1978).

5. *See* Project, *Legal Issues in State Mental Health Care — Proposals for Change: Suggested Statute on Zoning for Community Residences*, 2 MENTAL DISABILITY L. REP. 323, 324-325 (1978).

6. *See* Project, *Legal Issues in State Mental Health Care — Proposals for Change: Procedures for Voluntary Treatment*, 2 MENTAL DISABILITY L. REP. 329, 330-331, 335-337 (1978).

correctional facility, the administrator can insist on the convict's return to prison control,[7] whatever the preferences of a mental health or mental retardation facility administrator.

Standard 7-9.12. Right of offender to refuse treatment

An offender who has been placed in a mental health or mental retardation facility has the same right to decline habilitation or mental health treatment as a civilly committed person in that jurisdiction.

Commentary Introduction

The standard restates the general principle that convicted offenders have the right to refuse treatment or habilitation to the same extent as prisoners and civilly committed citizens, measured by the law of the jurisdiction in which they are held.

Related Standards

ABA, Standards for Criminal Justice 7-4.10(c), 7-10.9, 23-5.5, 23-5.8

Commentary

Convicts committed specially under part IX are prisoners even though they are committed to mental health facilities because of severe mental illness or to mental retardation facilities based on severe mental retardation. Accordingly, they enjoy the right to decline medical examination or medical treatment or habilitation unless it is (a) required by court order, (b) reasonably believed by a responsible physician to be necessary to protect the health of other persons, or (c) reasonably believed to be necessary in an emergency to save the prisoner's life or to prevent perma-

7. The correctional system, of course, can release a convict on parole conditioned on mental health outpatient treatment or mental retardation outpatient habilitation services if he or she is parole eligible. Note that special commitment is not to affect the accumulation of good-time credits and parole eligibility. *See* standard 7-9.15 and commentary.

nent and serious damage to the prisoner's health.[1] The claim to reject treatment or habilitation under other than emergency circumstances rests on the fact that treatment or habilitation is primarily, if not exclusively, for the benefit of the convict/patients specially committed under part IX, and not for the benefit of the criminal justice system.[2] It should be noted also that convict/patients cannot be subjected to medical, psychiatric, or pharmaceutical experimentation that is not directly beneficial to them.[3]

There should be complete congruence, therefore, in the ability of convict/patients and civilly committed patients to decline treatment or habilitation services.[4] Standard 7-9.12 is intended to make this clear, however, by noting that specially committed convict/patients have the same right to refuse mental health treatment or mental retardation habilitation services as civilly committed patients, although it does not presume to delineate scope of that right other than to refer to the law of the jurisdiction in which a convict/patient has been hospitalized.[5]

---

1. *See* standard 23-5.5 and commentary.

2. *Compare* the inability of persons committed as incompetent to undergo criminal trial proceedings to refuse treatment or habilitation that may restore or attain competence, because the criminal justice system is concerned that they become competent. *See* standard 7-4.10(c) and commentary.

3. *See* standard 23-5.8 and commentary; Weiner, *Rights of Institutionalized Persons*, in THE MENTALLY DISABLED AND THE LAW 251, 288-294 (S. Brakel, J. Parry & B. Weiner eds., 3d ed. 1985).

4. *See* Weiner, *Treatment Rights*, in THE MENTALLY DISABLED AND THE LAW 327, 341-351 (S. Brakel, J. Parry & B. Weiner eds., 3d ed. 1985); Project, *Legal Issues in State Mental Health Care: Proposals for Change: Civil Commitment*, 2 MENTAL DISABILITY L. REP. 57, 89-93; *Suggested Statute on Zoning for Community Residences*, 2 MENTAL DISABILITY L. REP. 323, 324-326; *Mental Health Services for Prisoners*, 2 MENTAL DISABILITY L. REP. 665, 668-669 (1978).

The American Psychiatric Association comments that even a qualified right to refuse treatment places mental health professionals in a difficult position, *viz.*, they continue to be responsible for patients who as a consequence may receive improper or inadequate treatment unless a court order can be obtained forcing a patient's submission to treatment. The APA believes that it may be economically wasteful to continue to devote scarce resources to patients who refuse treatment and demoralizing to treating professionals and other patients to be in forced contact with severely disturbed patients who reject appropriate care. *See* letter from Robert Luskin, Esq. to Standing Committee Director (March 29, 1985) (presenting the APA view).

5. Project, *Legal Issues in State Mental Health Care: Proposals for Change: Suggested Statute on Civil Commitment*, 2 MENTAL DISABILITY L. REP. 127, 149-150 (1978). *See In re* Guardianship of Richard Roe III, 383 Mass. 415, 434-442, 421 N.E.2d 40, 51-55 (1981), which held that noninstitutionalized mentally incompetent patients have a right to refuse treatment with antipsychotic drugs. In Rennie v. Klein, 720 F.2d 266, 269 (3d Cir. 1983), the Third Circuit reaffirmed its view that involuntarily committed mentally ill patients have a qualified right to refuse antipsychotic drugs.

Standard 7-9.13. Periodic review of the need for commitment

Committed severely mentally ill and seriously mentally retarded offenders should be entitled to the same kind of periodic review by the institution providing treatment or habilitation and by the court as provided for involuntary civil committees. The purpose of this review is solely to determine if treatment or habilitation in a mental health or mental retardation facility is still necessary.

Commentary Introduction

This standard provides for the same periodic review that civilly committed patients enjoy of a convict/patient's continued need for institutional treatment or habilitation.

Related Standards

ABA, Standards for Criminal Justice 7-4.11, 7-7.3(a), 7-7.8, 7-9.7, 7-9.12, 7-9.14, 7-10.6

Commentary

Periodic review of the current need for institutional treatment or habilitation services is a feature under the standards of commitments based on incompetence to undergo trial proceedings[1] and of acquittal on mental nonresponsibility [insanity] grounds of persons charged with dangerous felonies.[2] Standard 7-9.13 provides for the same periodic review of convicted offenders committed on the basis of severe mental illness or seri-

---

A study of the current status of psychiatric patients' rights to refuse psychotropic medication revealed that forty-five states recognize a qualified right to refuse medication. Of these, twenty-five states extend the right to all adult psychiatric patients who are treated in state mental institutions. Callahan & Longmire, *Psychiatric Patients' Right to Refuse Psychotropic Medication: A National Survey*, 7 Mental Disability L. Rep. 494, 495 (1983). For an extensive review of the right of prisoners to refuse treatment, *see* Winick, *Legal Limitations on Correctional Therapy and Research*, 65 Minn. L. Rev. 331, 383-392 (1981).

1. *See* Standard 7-4.11 and commentary.
2. *See* standards 7-7.3(a), 7-7.8 and commentary.

ous mental retardation. In this context, however, because convict/patients are to be treated or accorded habilitation services on substantially the same basis as civilly committed patients,[3] the standard incorporates by reference the review procedures in the jurisdiction governing the latter class of patients;[4] it does not specify administrative and judicial functions. Note that review is limited to the continued need to retain a convict/offender in a mental health or mental retardation facility under the control of a governmental entity rather than a department of prisons or corrections.[5] Convicted offenders who no longer require hospitalizations should be transferred to prison system custody.[6]

Standard 7-9.14. Transfer to correctional facility

When the offender no longer meets the criteria for commitment, the offender should be transferred to a correctional facility. The offender, the correctional facility, and the court should receive written notice of this decision at least [fifteen] days prior to transfer. The notice should include the factual basis for the transfer decision and confirmation that the offender has been advised of the right to object. If the offender objects, that objection must be included in the notice sent to the court. The court should determine whether the return decision reflects a disregard for the offender's reasonable mental health needs and may hold a hearing to determine this issue. The court must hold such a hearing in cases where the mental health or mental retardation facility seeks to return to a correctional facility an offender who has spent [ninety] days or less within the mental health or mental retardation facility.

Commentary Introduction

The standard governs procedures (1) to notify sentencing courts of a pending transfer of institutionalized convict/patients to prison control and (2) to obtain judicial approval of contested transfers.

3. *See* standard 7-9.12 and commentary.
4. *See, e.g.,* Mich. Stat. Ann. §§14.800(472)-14.800(485) (1980 and Supp. 1985); Project, *Legal Issues in State Mental Health Care: Proposals for Change: Civil Commitment,* 2 Mental Disability L. Rep. 57, 96-108 (1978); Note, *Constitutional Standards for Release of the Civilly Committed and Not Guilty by Reason of Insanity: A Strict Scrutiny Analysis,* 20 Ariz. L. Rev. 233 (1978).
5. *See* standard 7-9.7 and commentary.
6. *See* standard 7-9.14 and commentary.

Related Standards

ABA, Standards for Criminal Justice 7-3.7, 7-9.8, 7-9.9, 7-9.16, 7-10.5, 7-10.11, 18-6.8(d)-(e), 23-3.4, 23-5.1(a)

Commentary

Severely mentally ill or seriously mentally retarded convicts who cease to require institutional treatment or habilitation services outside the administrative jurisdiction of a department of prisons or corrections should be transferred promptly to prison control; they do not constitute simply another class of civilly committed patients.[1] Standard 7-9.14 rests on that principle. Convicted offenders sentenced to prison belong there if their treatment and habilitation needs can be met there sufficiently.[2]

However, the standard does not leave the ultimate transfer decision in the hands of mental health or mental retardation administrators, but instead places it under the control of sentencing courts. Accordingly, administrators are to give written notice of a decision to discontinue institution-based treatment or habilitation to the sentencing court and to the department of prisons or corrections;[3] it should be given fifteen days before a transfer decision is implemented through physical removal of a convict/patient. The notice must include the factual basis for the administrative decision on which transfer is based[4] and confirm that the convict/patient affected by the decision has been told specifically about a right to object to the transfer.

Under the standard, a judicial determination of the propriety of transfer should be made under either of the following two circumstances:

1. A convict/patient has been in mental health or mental retardation custody for less than a recommended period of ninety

---

1. *Compare* standard 7-9.16 and commentary (civil commitment of convict/patient after expiration of sentence).

2. *See* standard 23-5.1(a) and commentary.

3. Although the standard refers to "the correctional facility," offenders sentenced to imprisonment are committed to the control of "prison authorities," *see* standard 18-6.8(d)-(e), and their ensuing classification occurs under general correctional administrative control. *See* standard 23-3.4 and commentary. Convict/patients transferred under standard 7-9.14 have not been assigned earlier to a specific correctional facility. Consequently, notice under the standard should be transmitted to a department of prisons or corrections, not to the principal administrator of a particular prison or correctional facility.

4. Normally, this should be in the form of one or more evaluation reports conforming to the criteria enunciated in standard 7-3.7.

days[5] by the time a transfer to prison or correctional control is sought by facility administrators. This is designed to forestall the practice of purging convicted offenders from a mental health or mental retardation facility by a *fiat* decision to transfer control to prison or correctional authorities. The standard embodies a judgment that institution staff members cannot reach a professionally sound judgment about a convict/patient's needs for treatment or habilitation away from prison control with less than three months of observation, and that convict/patients have a valid claim not to be removed from mental health or mental retardation facilities until their condition no longer impels a placement there. Under such circumstances, a judicial hearing[6] always should be held before a judicial order confirming or denying a transfer is entered.

2. The respondent convict/patient has objected to the transfer.[7] The standard does not envision that a judicial hearing always must be conducted under such circumstances; if written evaluation reports are sufficient to support a decision confirming a transfer, a formal hearing is unnecessary.

Standard 7-9.15. Good time credits and parole

(a) An offender in a mental health or mental retardation facility is entitled to earn good time credits on the same terms as offenders in adult correctional facilities.

5. The American Psychiatric Association has commented that most individuals requiring acute hospitalization for mental disorders can be treated and returned to the community (or transferred to prison or correctional control) in much less than ninety days; most require only three to eight weeks' treatment. Adoption of the ninety-day period recommended in the standard usually will ensure that diagnosis and treatment have been completed before convict/patients are turned over to prison or correctional control; that goal will be attained, however, at the cost of prolonged hospitalization for some of them and unnecessary judicial hearings. These factors should be weighed carefully by legislatures establishing specific time limitations in implementing statutes. *See* letter from Robert Luskin, Esq. to Standing Committee Director (March 29, 1985) (presenting the APA view).

6. Although there is no specific cross reference in the standard, hearing procedures should be those governing a contested return of a prisoner/patient to prison control. *See* standards 7-10.5, 7-10.11 and commentary. *See also* Weiner, *Mental Disability and the Criminal Law*, in The Mentally Disabled and the Law 693, 738-739 (S. Brakel, J. Parry & B. Weiner eds., 3d ed. 1985).

7. Under the standard, the fact of an objection is to be included in the written notice transmitted to a sentencing court.

(b) An offender in a mental health or mental retardation facility should be eligible for parole release consideration on the same terms as offenders in adult correctional facilities.

(c) If otherwise qualified for parole, an offender should not be denied parole solely because the offender had or is receiving treatment or habilitation in a mental health or mental retardation facility.

(d) If otherwise qualified for parole, an offender who would benefit from outpatient treatment or habilitation should not be denied parole for that reason.

Commentary Introduction

This standard provides that offenders placed by sentencing courts in mental health or mental retardation facilities should be entitled to the good time and like credits and parole eligibility criteria applicable to offenders in adult correctional facilities.

Related Standards

ABA, Standards for Criminal Justice 7-9.10(b), 7-9.16, 7-10.10

Commentary

Convicted offenders specially committed to mental health facilities because of their treatment needs or to mental retardation facilities for habilitation services are prisoners and should not be in a worse position as a result of their hospitalization than they would have been had they been sentenced directly to incarceration. Standard 7-9.15 confirms this premise by guaranteeing them the same good time and other credits against length of sentence that they would have received had they been placed in an adult correctional institution. Moreover, by hypothesis, every day spent in the custody of mental health or mental retardation officials must be credited against the maximum and any minimum sentence, because convict/patients have been sentenced[1] and as a consequence serve their terms wherever they are held under official control by virtue of a criminal judgment and sentence. If their maximum sentences, less statutory credits, expire, they must be either released immediately or subjected to civil commitment proceedings.[2]

1. *See* standard 7-9.10(b) and commentary.
2. *See* standard 7-9.16 and commentary.

Paragraph (b) confirms that convict/patients must be considered eligible for parole release whenever they would have been given a parole review had they been sentenced initially to an adult correctional institution. In other words, they cannot be placed in a special category of convicts considered ineligible for parole release. Paragraph (c) expresses the corollary to that principle, namely, that convict/patients cannot be denied parole solely because they have received or currently are receiving treatment in a mental health facility or habilitation services in a mental retardation facility.[3]

Paragraph (d) indicates the appropriate resolution of cases involving convict/patients who remain in the custody of a department of mental health or mental retardation when they become parole-eligible: If they cannot be released safely into the community as outpatients, they should not be paroled from prison control and given leave as outpatients.[4] Conversely, however, if they can be furloughed from a mental health or mental retardation facility for treatment or habilitation as outpatients or in community mental health or mental retardation centers, and otherwise are eligible for parole release, paroling authorities should parole them. Parole in this case, however, is presumably conditioned on compliance with whatever treatment regimens or habilitation programs the facility administrators would have expected had the convict/patients been civilly committed patients allowed to leave hospital confines on outpatient or furlough status.

Standard 7-9.16. Procedure when sentence expires

A committed severely mentally ill or seriously mentally retarded offender must either be released or civilly committed pursuant to the state's general civil commitment statute when the sentence expires.

Commentary Introduction

This standard incorporates the constitutional standard that convict/patients must be either released from incarceration or hospitalization or committed civilly when their criminal sentences have expired.

3. This position conforms to the Association's suggested statute on mental health services for prisoners. *See* Project, *Legal Issues in State Mental Health Care — Proposals for Change: Mental Health Services for Prisoners,* 2 Mental Disability L. Rep. 665, 669-670, 674 (1978).

4. *See generally* Barnes & Sibilla, *Figuring Good-Time — The Postconviction Process,* 16 U. Rich. L. Rev. 505 (1982).

Related Standards

ABA, Standards for Criminal Justice 7-9.9, 7-9.10, 7-9.14, 7-10.12

Commentary

Standard 7-9.16 is based on the constitutional doctrine that due process and equal protection require mentally ill convicts to be released from confinement at the end of their terms of imprisonment unless they are civilly committed like other involuntarily hospitalized mentally ill persons; they cannot be transferred from prisons to mental health or mental retardation facilities by administrative action.[1] Moreover, the same criteria of dangerousness that determine eligibility for involuntary hospital commitments must govern the hospitalization of former convicts.[2]

The fact that convict/patients were committed by sentencing courts to mental health or mental retardation facilities[3] at time of sentencing and held there throughout their sentences, or transferred from those facilities to adult correctional institutions with judicial approval,[4] does not resolve the constitutional issue; the critical time in constitutional terms is expiration of a criminal sentence that constitutes the sole legal authority to retain convicts in official custody. Although the standard might have set out judicial procedures to be followed in ordering the involuntary hospitalization of mentally ill or mentally retarded prisoners, the most economical approach, which the standard incorporates, is to require either immediate release or completion of regular civil commitment procedures by the time their sentences expire. In no event can convict/patients be retained in prisons or correctional facilities past the conclusion of their criminal sentences.

1. Baxstrom v. Herold, 383 U.S. 107 (1966).
2. *Id.* at 114-115.
3. *See* standard 7-9.10 and commentary.
4. *See* standard 7-9.14 and commentary.

Part X

Mentally Ill and Mentally Retarded Prisoners

William H. Erickson, *Chairman*
Standing Committee on Association Standards for Criminal Justice

Norman S. Early, Jr.
Task Force Chairman

Elyce H. Zenoff
Reporter

Task Force

Norman S. Early, Jr., *Chairman*
District Attorney, Denver, Colorado

Ann Burgess, R.N., D.N.Sc.
Associate Director of Nursing Research, Department of Health & Hospitals, Boston, Massachusetts (representing American Orthopsychiatric Association)

Louise Centers, Ph.D., J.D.
Sinai Hospital of Detroit, Detroit, Michigan (representing American Psychological Association)

Penelope D. Clute
Private practitioner, Clute, Clute & Thompson, Plattsburgh, New York

Gilbert L. Ingram, Ph.D.
Assistant Director, Correctional Programs, Federal Bureau of Prisons, Washington, D.C. (representing American Correctional Association)

Robert B. Levinson, Ph.D.
Former Deputy Assistant Director, Inmate Program Services, Federal Bureau of Prisons, Washington, D.C.

Frederick M. Miller, M.D.
Psychiatrist, Denver, Colorado

John Roll
Assistant United States Attorney, Tucson, Arizona

Loren H. Roth, M.D., M.P.H.
Director, Law & Psychiatry Program, University of Pittsburgh School of Medicine, Pittsburgh, Pennsylvania (representing American Psychiatric Association)

Miles Santamour
President's Committee on Mental Retardation, Washington, D.C.

Gerard F. Treanor
Private practitioner, Venable, Baetjer & Howard, Arlington, Virginia (representing ABA Section of Criminal Justice)

ELYCE H. ZENOFF, *Reporter*
Professor of Law, National Law Center, George Washington University

INTRODUCTION

This part provides the procedural framework both for voluntary and involuntary transfers of prisoners from correctional to mental health or mental retardation facilities and for their later return to correctional control. Correctional facilities should provide mental health treatment for mentally ill prisoners and mental retardation services to mentally retarded prisoners.[1] Prisoners with severe mental illness or serious mental retardation should be transferred for treatment or habilitation services to appropriate facilities, preferably under the jurisdiction of a state department of mental health or mental retardation.[2] Prisoners with sufficient mental capacity may seek voluntary transfer with the approval of correctional administrators,[3] but otherwise judicial approval is required for transfers to mental health or mental retardation administrative control[4] and for contested returns to correctional administrative control.[5] Transferred prisoners should be returned to prison whenever they no longer require special mental health treatment or mental retardation habilitation services;[6] they should, however, continue to receive good-time credits and to be eligible for parole as if they had remained in adult correctional institutions.[7] They have the correlative rights to receive treatment or habilitation[8] or to refuse it to the same extent civilly committed patients can.[9] If they are in mental health or mental retardation facilities when their maximum sentences of imprisonment expire, they must be either released immediately or committed as a result of regular civil commitment proceedings.[10]

The definitions in part X[11] are substantially like those of part IX,[12] except that they refer to prisoners rather than convicted persons who have not been sentenced to imprisonment before being specially committed because of severe mental illness or serious mental retardation.

1. *See* standard 7-10.2(a) and commentary.
2. *See* standard 7-10.2(b) and commentary.
3. *See* standard 7-10.3 and commentary.
4. *See* standards 7-10.4, 7-10.5 and commentary. Emergency administrative transfers are covered in standard 7-10.7.
5. *See* standard 7-10.11 and commentary.
6. *See* standards 7-10.6 (periodic review), 7-10.11 and commentary.
7. *See* standard 7-10.10 and commentary.
8. *See* standard 7-10.8 and commentary.
9. *See* standard 7-10.9 and commentary.
10. *See* standard 7-10.12 and commentary.
11. *See* standard 7-10.1 and commentary.
12. *See* standard 7-9.1 and commentary.

The following glossary of terms likewise mirrors that in part IX[13] with the substitution of *prisoners* for *offenders*:

Mental health facility An inpatient or residential mental health hospital or institutional setting that offers treatment programs for mentally ill prisoners, preferably under the jurisdiction of a state department of mental health.

Mental retardation facility A residential facility offering specific programs of habilitation for mentally retarded prisoners, preferably under the jurisdiction of a state department of mental health or mental retardation.

Expert witnesses Mental health or mental retardation professionals who provide expert data at transfer hearings for prisoners and who meet applicable qualifications, including education and training requirements as delineated in standards 7-3.10 through 7-3.13.

Mental health professionals providing treatment Mental health professionals who provide therapy and treatment for transferred prisoners and who have the requisite qualifications and experience to perform similar functions within the community.

Mental retardation professionals providing habilitation Mental retardation professionals, including certified special education teachers, speech and language pathologists, audiologists, physical therapists, and occupational therapists, as well as professionals who qualify as "mental health professionals," who provide habilitation for mentally retarded persons and who possess experience in the field of mental retardation.

Standard 7-10.1. Definitions

(a) An adult, or a minor under eighteen years of age who was tried as an adult, convicted of a crime and incarcerated within a correctional facility, is referred to within this part as a prisoner.

(b) A prisoner who suffers a substantial disorder of thought, mood, perception, orientation, or memory which grossly impairs

13. *See* introduction to part IX.

judgment, behavior, or the capacity to recognize reality or the ability to meet the demands of life is referred to within this part as a severely mentally ill prisoner.

(c) A prisoner with very significant subaverage general intellectual functioning existing concurrently with substantial deficits in adaptive behavior is referred to within this part as a seriously mentally retarded prisoner.

Commentary Introduction

This standard defines severely mentally ill and seriously mentally retarded prisoners for purposes of the more detailed coverage of the rest of the part X standards.

Related Standards

ABA, Standards for Criminal Justice 7-9.1

Commentary

Paragraph (a) defines the term *prisoner* to include adults, or juveniles under age eighteen tried as adults, who have been convicted and sentenced to incarceration in an adult correctional institution. It is the exact counterpart to *offender* as used in part IX.[1] The definition excludes from the coverage of part X respondents in juvenile delinquency proceedings who have been committed to juvenile training schools and similar institutions.

The baseline expectation in part X is that mentally ill and mentally retarded prisoners will be provided appropriate care and habilitation services in adult correctional facilities.[2] However, severely mentally ill and seriously mentally retarded prisoners are to be treated or habilitated in mental health and mental retardation facilities. Accordingly, the instant standard incorporates the criteria on the basis of which transfer eligibility is to be determined. Paragraph (b) defines *severely mentally ill prisoners* exactly parallel to the term *severely mentally ill offenders* in part IX[3] and

1. *See* standard 7-9.1(a) and commentary.
2. *See* Standards 7-10.2(a), 23-5.1(a) and commentary.
3. *See* standard 7-9.1(b); Weiner, *Mental Disability and the Criminal Law*, in THE MENTALLY DISABLED AND THE LAW 693, 736-737 (S. Brakel, J. Parry & B. Weiner eds., 3d ed. 1985) [hereinafter cited as Weiner].

reflects civil commitment legislation[4] as well as current psychiatric concepts.[5]

In similar fashion, paragraph (c) uses a definition of *seriously mentally retarded prisoner* that corresponds precisely to that of *seriously mentally retarded offender* in part IX,[6] and it incorporates identical behavioral scientific concepts.[7] As in the context of special commitments of seriously mentally retarded offenders,[8] the purpose underlying paragraph (c) and the several standards in part X is to promote an individualized determination (1) that prisoners are seriously mentally retarded, (2) that appropriate habilitative services are unavailable in facilities administered by a department of prisons or corrections, and (3) that the indicated services can be provided in a mental retardation facility under the administrative control of another department of state government. If all three elements are satisfied, seriously mentally retarded prisoners should be transferred; if one or more cannot be established, they should be retained in adult correctional institutions.

Standard 7-10.2. Mental health or mental retardation care for prisoners

(a) Correctional facilities should provide a range of mental health and mental retardation services for prisoners and should have adequately trained personnel readily available to provide such services.

(b) Prisoners who require mental health treatment or mental retardation habilitation not available in the correctional facility should be transferred to a mental health or mental retardation facility, preferably under the supervision of the jurisdiction's department of mental health or mental retardation, pursuant to procedures set forth in the following standards.

Commentary Introduction

The standard confirms that treatment and habilitation services should be available for mentally ill and mentally retarded prisoners within cor-

4. *See* commentary to standard 7-9.1, note 2 and accompanying text.

5. *See* commentary to standard 7-9.1, note 3 and accompanying text.

6. *See* standard 7-9.1(c).

7. *See* commentary to standard 7-9.1, notes 4-10 and accompanying text. *See also* Ellis & Luckasson, *Mentally Retarded Criminal Defendants*, 53 GEO. WASH. L. REV. 414, 479-484 (1985); Weiner, *supra* note 3, at 737.

8. *See* commentary to standard 7-9.1.

rectional facilities; it enunciates the principle that severely mentally ill or mentally retarded prisoners should be transferred to mental health or mental retardation facilities outside correctional administrative jurisdiction.

Related Standards

ABA, Standards for Criminal Justice 7-1.1(d), 7-3.6(a)-(b), 7-9.7, 7-10.1, 7-10.3, 7-10.12, 23-1.1, 23-5.1, 23-5.2, 23-6.11, 23-7.4

Commentary

The constitutional right of prisoners to adequate medical diagnosis and treatment, including psychiatric care,[1] is restated in chapter 23 of the standards, Legal Status of Prisoners;[2] paragraph (a) of the present standard stresses that departments of prisons or corrections should be staffed with properly trained mental health and mental retardation professionals who can offer appropriate mental health treatment and mental retardation habilitation services.[3]

If, however, prisoners are severely mentally ill or seriously mentally retarded to the extent that they cannot be effectively treated or habilitated in an adult correctional facility, the judgment embodied in paragraph (b) is that they should be transferred to the administrative control of a department of mental health or mental retardation services. This is the exact counterpart to part IX coverage,[4] and the underlying policy and pragmatic grounds are identical.[5] As in part IX, transferred prisoners are to be given only residential treatment or habilitation services and should not be allowed in the community as outpatients or patients at community mental health centers.[6]

---

1. *See* 23•59 note 9, commentary to standard 23-5.1. In Balla v. Idaho State Bd. of Corrections, 595 F. Supp. 1558, 1569, 1578 (D. Idaho 1984), the court held that inmates, who were not legally eligible for parole as sexually dangerous persons until one or more psychiatrists or psychologists had examined and evaluated them as suitable for parole, had a constitutional claim to rehabilitative services to help them achieve parole eligibility.

2. *See* standards 23-5.1(a), 23-5.2 and commentary; Weiner, *Mental Disability and the Criminal Law,* in THE MENTALLY DISABLED AND THE LAW 693, 737-738 (S. Brakel, J. Parry & B. Weiner eds., 3d ed. 1985).

3. *Cf.* standard 23-7.4 and commentary (legislative responsibility to provide sufficient resources to implement the legal rights of prisoners).

4. *See* standard 7-9.7(b).

5. *See* commentary to standard 7-9.7, notes 4-5 and accompanying text.

6. *See* commentary to standard 7-9.7.

Although mental health and mental retardation treating professionals must comply with regulations and procedures bearing on institutional security and order,[7] correctional staff members should not interfere otherwise with therapist or counselor relationships with prisoner/patients. Even though treating professionals are employed by state governmental departments, including departments of prisons or corrections, their relationship to their prisoner/patients is identical to that in any professional treatment or counseling setting.[8] However, to the extent that legitimate institutional needs relating to security and order require a modification of usual confidentiality principles, prisoners should be told in advance of legal limits on confidentiality governing their confidences to treating professionals.[9]

Standard 7-10.3. Voluntary transfer to mental health or mental retardation facility

If a prisoner desires treatment or habilitation in a mental health or mental retardation facility the prisoner may make an application for voluntary admission to a mental health or mental retardation facility. If the correctional institution believes such treatment or habilitation is warranted, the application should be endorsed by the chief executive officer of the correctional institution and accompanied by the report of an evaluation conducted by a mental health or mental retardation professional. The prisoner should be admitted to such facility if it accepts the endorsed application.

---

7. *See* standard 7-1.1(d) and commentary. *Cf.* standard 23-1.1 (basic limitations on prisoners' rights).

8. However, correctional administrators should advise treating professionals of their appropriate roles and the governing limitations on the usual therapist/patient relationship based on concerns of institutional security and order, *see* standard 7-3.7(a) and commentary, so that professionals understand their roles and are not asked to perform outside their professional competence or in an ethically improper manner. In addition, treating professionals, consonant with standard 7-3.6(b), should advise prisoner/patients of the nature of their relationship in a prison setting as a means of ensuring that the legal rights of prisoner/patients are not compromised in the course of therapy.

9. *See* standard 23-6.11(c) and commentary (information given to employees of a correctional authority in a designated counseling relationship under a representation of confidentiality should be privileged unless the information concerns a contemplated crime or disclosure is required by court order).

Commentary Introduction

The standard recognizes that prisoners may request and receive an administrative transfer to mental health or mental retardation facilities, if correctional and mental health or mental retardation authorities concur.

Related Standards

ABA, Standards for Criminal Justice 7-10.4, 7-10.5

Commentary

Mentally ill persons within the community can subject themselves voluntarily to hospitalization for mental health treatment,[1] and parents of mentally retarded minors may commit their children to mental retardation facilities if minimal administrative due process concerns are met.[2] Standard 7-10.3 affords a like opportunity for mentally ill and mentally retarded prisoners in adult correctional facilities, as a means of avoiding the time, expense, and trauma inherent in the judicially approved transfers that otherwise are the norm under part X.[3]

Nevertheless, the standard does not accord prisoners an absolute right to achieve a transfer from correctional to mental health or mental retardation custody. Correctional authorities can refuse to concur in a prisoner application for voluntary transfer if they prefer to meet their constitutional obligations[4] within the corrections or prison system. Moreover,

1. *See, e.g.,* Mich. Stat. Ann. §§14.800(411)-14.800(412) (1980 & Supp. 1985); Brakel, *Voluntary Admissions,* in The Mentally Disabled and the Law 177-201 (S. Brakel, J. Parry & B. Weiner eds., 3d ed. 1985); Project, *Legal Issues in State Mental Health Care — Proposals for Change: Procedures for Voluntary Treatment,* 2 Mental Disability L. Rep. 329, 331-332, 335-336 (1978).

2. *See* Pennsylvania Sec'y of Public Welfare v. Institutionalized Juveniles, 422 U.S. 640 (1979). Parham v. J.R., 442 U.S. 585 (1979). The safeguards are that a "neutral factfinder," who may be a staff physician, has determined that statutory requirements for admission have been satisfied and that a child's mental and emotional condition warrants treatment in a facility. Parham v. J.R., 422 U.S. at 606-607. The Court noted that at least thirty states at the time had statutes allowing "voluntary" admissions at parental request. *Id.* at 612 n.20. *See also* Brakel, *Involuntary Institutionalization,* in The Mentally Disabled and the Law 21, 43-46 (S. Brakel, J. Parry & B. Weiner eds., 3d ed. 1985) [hereinafter cited as Brakel]; Project, *Legal Issues in State Mental Health Care — Proposals for Change: Mental Health Treatment for Minors,* 2 Mental Disability L. Rep. 459, 461-465, 474-477 (1978). Legislation as of October 1982 may be found in Brakel, *supra,* at 146-155, Table 2.11.

3. *See* standards 7-10.4, 7-10.5 and commentary.

4. *See* commentary to standard 23-5.1, notes 2-6, 9 and accompanying text.

mental health or mental retardation facility administrators can refuse to accept a prisoner/patient on the basis of a voluntary transfer approved by correctional administrators; they can insist on a court order approving a transfer.[5] But if all agree, the administratively endorsed transfer application becomes a lawful basis for transferring to and retaining custody of a prisoner/patient in a mental health or mental retardation facility.

Standard 7-10.4. Rejection of voluntary transfer application; court-ordered transfer to mental health or mental retardation facility

(a) Procedures for court-ordered transfer.

(i) If an application for voluntary admission submitted in accordance with the procedures set forth in standard 7-10.3 is rejected by the mental health or mental retardation facility and the correction officials believe that the applicant is a severely mentally ill or seriously mentally retarded prisoner, the chief executive officer of the correctional facility or a designee may file a petition for court-ordered transfer to a mental health or mental retardation facility. Notice of the petition should be sent to the mental health facility when the petition is filed. Such petition should be accompanied by the prisoner's voluntary application and the report of a mental evaluation. The court should set the matter for a prompt hearing.

(ii) The prisoner's mental evaluation reports should address the question of whether the prisoner is mentally ill and/or mentally retarded. In addition to the diagnosis, the report should describe the specific behavior or other indicators which led to the conclusion that the prisoner is or is not mentally ill or mentally retarded. A prisoner may not be transferred unless a report from a mental health or mental retardation professional indicates that the prisoner suffers from a severe mental disability. All mental evaluation reports should be disclosed to all parties prior to the hearing.

(b) Criteria for court-ordered transfer. If the court finds, by clear and convincing evidence, that the prisoner is severely mentally ill or seriously mentally retarded and requires care not available in the

5. *See* standard 7-10.4(a)(i) and commentary.

correctional facility, it should order the prisoner transferred to a mental health or mental retardation facility.

Commentary Introduction

The standard governs procedures to obtain judicial authorization for prisoner/patient transfers if mental health or mental retardation facility administrators reject applications for voluntary transfer endorsed by prison or correctional administrators.

Related Standards

ABA, Standards for Criminal Justice 7-4.9(a)(ii), 7-7.4(b), 7-9.8, 7-9.9, 7-10.1, 7-10.2, 7-10.3, 23-3.4(c), 23-5.1(b)-(c)

Commentary

As noted,[1] voluntary transfers under appropriate procedural safeguards[2] can be in the best interests of mentally ill or mentally retarded prisoners and appropriate prison administration. Nevertheless, the position taken in part X is that mental health or mental retardation facility administrators are under no obligation to accept voluntary admissions of prisoners.[3] Nevertheless, they cannot possess absolute, unreviewable discretion to construct the patient demography in their facilities as they wish. Standard 7-10.4 sets out procedures to resolve the administrative impasse that results when prisoner/patients and correctional administrators, on the one hand, and mental health or mental retardation facility administrators, on the other, cannot resolve their differences concerning transfers of prisoner/patients from prison or correctional institutions to mental health or mental retardation facilities.

Prison or correctional authorities, of course, may be persuaded by mental health or mental retardation administrators that prisoner/patients should not be transferred from adult correctional institutions. In that event, the requisite treatment or habilitation services will be provided

1. *See* standard 7-10.3 and commentary.

2. For an empirical study suggesting that a failure to apply procedural safeguards in the context of transfers to prison operated mental health facilities severely limits their impact, *see* Hardstone, Steadman & Monahan, *Vitek and Beyond: The Empirical Context of Prison to Hospital Transfers.* 45 LAW & CONTEMP. PROBS. 125, 130 (1982).

3. They are not bound to accept voluntary admissions from the community at large.

within a department of prisons or corrections according to constitutional standards.[4] If, however, correctional authorities believe a transfer is indicated despite a reluctance on the part of mental health or mental retardation departmental officials to accept a prisoner/patient on a voluntary transfer basis, subparagraph (a)(i) adopts the premise that the chief executive officer[5] of the correctional facility (or a designee) should be able to petition for a court-authorized transfer of a prisoner/patient to mental health or mental retardation control.[6] However, the belief on the part of correctional administrators that a prisoner/patient should be transferred must be documented by one or more evaluation reports that address the existence of mental illness or mental retardation and describe the specific behavior or other data supporting a diagnostic conclusion that a prisoner/patient is or is not mentally ill or mentally retarded. Unless at least one evaluator concludes that a prisoner/patient is severely mentally ill or seriously mentally retarded, an application for judicial approval of a request for voluntary transfer should be rejected summarily.[7]

If the procedural prerequisites to a judicial order of authorization have been met, and if the requirements of notice of a petition[8] and disclosure of evaluation reports[9] have been met, a recipient court should conduct a hearing on the petition,[10] following appropriate procedures.[11] Although the burden of going forward with evidence is not addressed in the standard, the fact that prisoner/patients and correctional administrators wish

---

4. *See* commentary to standard 23-5.1, notes 2-6, 9 and accompanying text.

5. *See* 23•7, glossary of terms, for the meaning of "chief executive officer."

6. Subparagraph (a)(i) of the standard envisions that a copy of a prisoner/patient's application for a voluntary transfer will be attached to an application for judicial approval of transfer.

7. This is the counterpart to the policy embodied in part IX that convicted offenders cannot be specially committed without at least one evaluation report indicating that they are severely mentally ill or seriously mentally retarded. *See* standard 7-9.8(d) and commentary.

8. *See* subparagraph (a)(i) (providing for notice to a mental health facility). This means either a mental health or mental retardation department or a mental health or mental retardation facility, depending on state law.

9. Evaluation reports must have been made available to the parties under subparagraph (a)(ii).

10. The intent of the standard is that a hearing must be held and that petitions cannot be disposed of on the basis of written evaluation reports. *Cf.* standard 7-9.9(b) and commentary (no hearing is required on a petition for special commitment of severely mentally ill or seriously mentally retarded offenders if neither party objects; by hypothesis, an objection on the part of mental health or mental retardation facility administrators exists whenever standard 7-10.4 proceedings have been commenced).

11. An appropriate parallel is involuntary transfer proceedings. *See* standard 7-10.5 and commentary; *cf.* standard 7-9.9 and commentary (special commitment hearing procedures under part IX).

to achieve a transfer over the objection of mental health or mental retardation administrators warrants a conclusion that the petitioners must bear the burden of adducing data in support of the petition. A judicial order authorizing transfer must rest on findings that a prisoner/patient is either severely mentally ill[12] or seriously mentally retarded[13] and requires treatment or habilitation services unavailable within the jurisdiction of a department of prisons or corrections.[14] If by clear and convincing proof[15] a court finds that these requirements are satisfied, it should enter an order for a prisoner/patient's transfer to mental health or mental retardation facility custody; the order provides a legal basis for both the transfer and subsequent institutional control of the prisoner/patient.

Standard 7-10.5. Involuntary transfer

(a) Procedures for involuntary transfer. If correction officials believe a prisoner is severely mentally ill or seriously mentally retarded and requires treatment in a mental health or mental retardation facility and the prisoner objects to such placement, involuntary transfer proceedings should be instituted. At a minimum, involuntary transfer hearings for prisoners should provide the following procedural protections:

(i) the right to legal counsel, furnished by the state if the prisoner is financially unable to secure counsel;

(ii) the right to be present, to be heard in person, and to produce documentary evidence;

(iii) the right to call and cross-examine witnesses;

12. *See* standard 7-10.1(b) and commentary.
13. *See* standard 7-10.1(c) and commentary.
14. Although the standard refers to treatment or habilitation services not available "in the correctional facility," the intent of the standard is that they must be unavailable within an entire correctional system. If the system has a psychiatric unit properly staffed, *see* standards 7-10.2(a); 23-5.1(b), and equipped, *see* standard 23-5.1(c), to provide needed treatment or habilitation services, the prisoner/patient should be transferred there in accordance with standard 23-3.4(c).
15. That is the burden of persuasion constitutionally required for civil commitments under Addington v. Texas, 441 U.S. 418 (1979). Although arguably *Addington* does not govern this context, *see* Vitek v. Jones, 445 U.S. 480, 485-486 (1980), the *Addington* norm is utilized in all chapter 7 settings. *See* standards 7-4.9(a)(ii) (commitment based on incompetence to undergo criminal proceedings), 7-7.4(b) (commitment following acquittal based on mental nonresponsibility [insanity]), 7-9.9(c) (special commitment of severely mentally ill or seriously mentally retarded offenders).

(iv) the right to review mental evaluation reports; and,

(v) the right to be notified of the foregoing rights.

(b) Evaluation reports. The prisoner's mental evaluation reports should address the question of whether the prisoner is severely mentally ill or seriously mentally retarded. In addition to the diagnosis, the reports should describe the specific behavior or other indicators which led to its conclusions. A prisoner may not be involuntarily transferred unless the evaluation report indicates that the prisoner is severely mentally ill or seriously mentally retarded.

(c) Criteria for involuntary transfer.

(i) In order to commit the prisoner, the judge must find by clear and convincing evidence that the prisoner meets the criteria for involuntary commitment and cannot be given proper treatment or habilitation in prison. Expert opinion testimony as to whether a prisoner is severely mentally ill or seriously mentally retarded and requires treatment or habilitation in a mental health facility should be admissible.

(ii) When the prisoner is a minor involuntary transfer is authorized if there is clear and convincing evidence that the minor is severely mentally ill or seriously mentally retarded and needs treatment or habilitation in a mental health or mental retardation facility.

Commentary Introduction

The standard establishes criteria for and procedures governing involuntary transfers of prisoner/patients under court order from adult correctional institutions to mental health or mental retardation facilities for treatment or habilitation services.

Related Standards

ABA, Standards for Criminal Justice 7-3.6, 7-3.7, 7-4.9(a)(ii), 7-3.10, 7-3.11, 7-3.13, 7-3.14(b), 7-7.4(b), 7-9.8(d), 7-9.9, 7-10.1, 7-10.4, 23-3.2(a)-(b)

Commentary

If prisoner/patients do not seek or acquiesce in a transfer from prison or correctional control to the control of mental health or mental retardation authorities, they have the same liberty interest in remaining free from unnecessary mental treatment or habilitation services as free-world citizens enjoy.[1] However, their objections to necessary treatment or habilitation services can be overridden constitutionally if they are accorded administrative due process;[2] a judicial civil commitment proceeding is not required. Standard 7-10.5 perforce accepts the minimum procedural safeguards dictated by constitutional precedent; subparagraph (a)(ii) ensures the rights to be present, to be heard in person, and to produce documentary evidence. However, it goes beyond them in significant respects. Thus, it provides in paragraph (c) for a judicial, not an administrative, approval of involuntary transfers.[3] Subparagraph (a)(i) provides for legal counsel in all transfer cases[4] including the claim to appointment of counsel for financially unable prisoners. Under subparagraph (a)(iii), the right to call and cross-examine witnesses is unlimited, in contrast to prison disciplinary matters.[5] In all significant respects, the pattern for procedures under the standard is civil commitment proceedings.[6]

1. Parham v. J.R., 442 U.S. 584, 600 (1979).

2. In Vitek v. Jones, 445 U.S. 480 (1980), the Supreme Court mandated certain administrative due process procedures before prisoners can be transferred from a correctional facility to a mental health or mental retardation facility, including written notice that a transfer is being considered, a hearing, an opportunity to be heard and to present documentary evidence, an opportunity to present testimony and cross-examine witnesses, an independent decisionmaker, and a written statement of evidence relied on by the decisionmaker. *Id.* at 494-496. In *Jones,* Justice Powell indicated that a prisoner should be provided qualified independent assistance in preparing and presenting objections to transfer, but not that of an attorney. *Id.* at 499 (Powell, J., concurring). *See generally* Brakel, *Discharge and Transfer,* in The Mentally Disabled and the Law 203-205 (S. Brakel, J. Parry & B. Weiner eds., 3d ed. 1985); Churgin, *The Transfer of Inmates to Mental Health Facilities,* in Mentally Disordered Offenders 207, 221-223 (J. Monahan & H. Steadman eds. 1983) [hereinafter cited as Churgin]; George, *United States Supreme Court 1979-80 Term: Criminal Law Decisions,* 26 N.Y.L. Sch. L. Rev. 99, 178-182 (1981); Hardstone, Steadman & Monahan, Vitek *and Beyond: The Empirical Context of Prison to Hospital Transfers,* 45 Law & Contemp. Probs. 125 (1982) [hereinafter cited as Hardstone, Steadman & Monahan]; Comment, Vitek v. Jones: *A Case for Prisoners' Mental Health Rights, Breakthrough and Compromise,* 30 Am. U.L. Rev. 765 (1981); Weiner, *Mental Disability and the Criminal Law,* in The Mentally Disabled and the Law 693, 738-739 (S. Brakel, J. Parry & B. Weiner eds., 3d ed. 1985).

3. On policies favoring judicial rather than administrative proceedings, *see* Churgin, *supra* note 2, at 221-223.

4. For discussions of the significance of counsel in such proceedings, *see* Churgin, *supra* note 2, at 229-230; Hartstone, Steadman & Monahan, *supra* note 2, at 190-191. Counsel is not envisioned in prison disciplinary proceedings, the pattern for Vitek v. Jones. *See* 455 U.S. at 495-496; *see also* standard 23-3.2(a)-(b) and commentary. Although, as noted, *Jones* reflects the constitutional minimum requirements affecting transfer proceedings, the Association has adopted a weightier array of procedural safeguards in the present standard. *See also* standard 7-9.9, commentary to standard 7-9.9. note 13 and accompanying text.

5. *See* standard 23-3.2(a)-(b) and commentary.

6. *See* standard 7-9.9(a) and commentary. The standard, however, does not provide for jury trial, although many jurisdictions recognize it in civil commitment proceedings.

Precisely as in the setting of special commitments of convicted offenders[7] and judicial approval of applications for voluntary transfer from prisons or correctional institutions to mental health or mental retardation facilities,[8] at least one qualified professional evaluator must conclude that a prisoner/patient is either severely mentally ill[9] or seriously mentally retarded[10] before a court can order an involuntary transfer. In other words, the want of such an evaluator's finding should destroy the jurisdictional basis to hear a petition for transfer. That in turn means, first, that an evaluation must have been performed by qualified mental health or mental retardation professionals[11] in accordance with procedures set out to govern mental evaluations[12] and, second, that evaluation reports should conform to the pattern for such reports generally.[13] Paragraph (b) confirms that evaluation reports should address the question whether a prisoner/patient is severely mentally ill or seriously mentally retarded and should describe the specific behavior or other data on which a professional evaluator's conclusion on the point is based.

The standard does not require that evaluating professionals be called as expert witnesses in all involuntary transfer proceedings. Instead, paragraph (c) allows the admission of expert opinion testimony on the ultimate issues of the existence of serious mental disability and the need for appropriate treatment or habilitation services outside the jurisdiction of a department of prisons or corrections. Nevertheless, expert witnesses should have the qualifications recommended generally in the standards,[14] and should present their expert testimony in acceptable form.[15] Their professional opinions must rest on personal evaluations that include a personal interview with a prisoner/patient.[16]

Under subparagraph (c)(i), a court should be required to determine that a prisoner/patient: (1) is severely mentally ill or seriously mentally retarded; and (2) cannot be given proper treatment or habilitation services within the jurisdiction of a department of prisons or corrections. However, the second branch is somewhat relaxed under subparagraph

7. *See* standard 7-9.8(d) and commentary.
8. *See* standard 7-10.4(a)(ii).
9. *See* standard 7-10.1(b) and commentary.
10. *See* standard 7-10.1(c) and commentary.
11. *See* standard 7-3.10 and commentary.
12. *See* standard 7-3.6 and commentary.
13. *See* standard 7-3.7 and commentary.
14. *See* standards 7-3.11, 7-3.13 and commentary.
15. *See* standard 7-3.14(b) and commentary.
16. *See* standard 7-3.11(a)(iii) and commentary.

(c)(ii) if a patient/prisoner is a minor; in that even the issue is one of need for a transfer on a relative basis. In other words, if better or more effective treatment is available in a mental health or mental retardation facility than in a prison clinic or psychiatric unit, a minor prisoner can be transferred even though constitutionally adequate treatment or habilitation services can be provided within a department of prisons or corrections. In the instance of an adult prisoner/patient, in contrast, transfer is inappropriate unless the court concludes that required treatment or habilitation services simply are unavailable unless a transfer is authorized.

As in proceedings to approve voluntary transfers[17] and to commit convicted offenders who are severely mentally ill or seriously mentally retarded,[18] paragraph (c) utilizes the clear-and-convincing-proof standard set out as the constitutional minimum standard for civil commitment proceedings.[19]

Standard 7-10.6. Periodic review of the need for commitment

Committed severely mentally ill or seriously mentally retarded prisoners should be entitled to the same kind of periodic review by the institution providing treatment or habilitation and by the court as provided for involuntary civil committees. The purpose of this review is solely to determine if treatment or habilitation in a mental health or mental retardation facility is still necessary.

Commentary Introduction

This standard provides for the same periodic review of prisoner/patients that civilly committed patients enjoy as to continued need for institutional treatment or habilitation.

17. *See* standard 7-10.4(b) and commentary.

18. *See* standard 7-9.9 and commentary.

19. Addington v. Texas, 441 U.S. 418 (1979). Although arguably *Addington* does not govern this context, *see* Vitek v. Jones, 445 U.S. 480, 495-496 (1980), the *Addington* norm is utilized in all chapter 7 settings. *See* standards 7-4.9(a)(ii) (commitment based on incompetence to undergo criminal proceedings), 7-7.4(b) (commitment following acquittal based on mental nonresponsibility [insanity]), 7-9.9(c) (special commitment of severely mentally ill or seriously mentally retarded offenders).

Related Standards

ABA, Standards for Criminal Justice 7-4.11, 7-7.3(a), 7-7.7, 7-7.8, 7-9.13, 7-10.1, 7-10.2(b), 7-10.5(c), 7-10.8, 7-10.11

Commentary

A periodic review of the need for continued institutionalized treatment or habilitation services is an aspect under the standards of commitments based on incompetence to undergo criminal trial proceedings,[1] acquittal on grounds of mental nonresponsibility [insanity] of persons charged with dangerous felonies,[2] and convicted offenders specially committed because of severe mental illness or serious mental retardation.[3] The present standard urges an identical protection for prisoner/patients committed involuntarily because of their severe mental illness[4] or serious mental retardation.[5] However, because convict/patients are treated or receive habilitation services exactly as civilly committed patients do,[6] standard 7-10.6 incorporates by reference the review procedures governing civil committees,[7] and it does not delineate special review practices specially governing convict/patients. It should be stressed that review under the standard is limited to the question of a continued need to retain a prisoner/patient under mental health or mental retardation facility control instead of in a prison or adult correctional institution.[8] Prisoners who no longer need to be treated or given habilitation services in a treatment facility administered by a department of mental health or mental retardation[9] should be returned promptly to department of prisons or corrections control.[10]

1. *See* standard 7-4.11 and commentary.
2. *See* standards 7-7.3(a), 7-7.8 and commentary.
3. *See* standard 7-9.13 and commentary.
4. *See* standard 7-10.1(b) and commentary.
5. *See* standard 7-10.1(c) and commentary.
6. *See* standard 7-10.8 and commentary.
7. *See, e.g.,* Mich. Stat. Ann. §§14.800(472)-14.800(485) (1980 & Supp. 1985); Brakel, *Discharge and Transfer,* in The Mentally Disabled and the Law 203, 211-213 (S. Brakel, J. Parry & B. Weiner eds., 3d ed. 1985) [hereinafter cited as Brakel]; Project, *Legal Issues in State Mental Health Care: Proposals for Change — Civil Commitment,* 2 Mental Disability L. Rep. 57, 78-79; *Suggested Statute on Civil Commitment,* 2 Mental Disability L. Rep. 127, 144-147 (1978); Note, *Constitutional Standards for Release of the Civilly Committed and Not Guilty by Reason of Insanity: A Strict Scrutiny Analysis,* 20 Ariz. L. Rev. 233 (1978). Legislation as of October 1982 is gathered in Brakel, *supra,* at 241-245, Table 4.5.
8. *See* standard 7-10.5(c) and commentary.
9. *See* standard 7-10.2(b) and commentary.
10. *See* standard 7-10.11 and commentary.

Standard 7-10.7. Emergency transfer to mental health or mental retardation facility

(a) If in respect to any prisoner a need for emergency intervention exists, the chief executive officer of the prison or that officer's designee may authorize immediate transfer to a mental health or mental retardation facility provided that an involuntary transfer hearing is initiated not later than [forty-eight] hours after the transfer is effected.

(b) An emergency exists when the chief executive officer of the correctional facility, or that officer's designee, reasonably believes that an immediate transfer is necessary to prevent serious injury to the prisoner or to protect the safety of other persons.

Commentary Introduction

The standard recommends the governing criteria and procedures for emergency transfers of severely mentally ill or seriously mentally retarded prisoner/patients from adult correctional institutions to mental health or mental retardation facilities, in contemplation of involuntary transfer proceedings.

Related Standards

ABA, Standards for Criminal Justice 7-2.1(a), 7-2.2(a), 7-2.5(a), 7-10.1(b)-(c), 7-10.5, 23-1.1(c), 23-5.2(a), 23-5.5(c)

Commentary

Prison medical personnel may override prisoner/patients' refusal to accept medical diagnosis and treatment if they believe emergency treatment is necessary to save life or prevent permanent and serious damage to health, including mental health.[1] Adult correctional institutions must be able to provide timely emergency medical care for prisoners consistent with accepted medical practice and standards.[2] Standard 7-10.7 supplements chapter 23 provisions by allowing the chief executive officer[3] of a prison, or a designee, to authorize the immediate transfer of a severely mentally ill or seriously mentally retarded prisoner/patient to the cus-

1. *See* standard 23-5.5(c) and commentary.
2. *See* standard 23-5.2(a) and commentary.
3. *See* 23•7, glossary of terms, for the meaning of "chief executive officer."

tody of a mental health or mental retardation facility to which an involuntary transfer might be made.

Paragraph (b) defines such medical emergencies as instances in which designated correctional officials reasonably believe that immediate transfer is necessary to prevent serious injury to a prisoner/patient or to protect the safety of other persons.[4] They also should believe that a prisoner is severely mentally ill[5] or seriously mentally retarded,[6] because that condition is a prerequisite to an involuntary transfer order.[7]

Nevertheless, to forestall the possibility that a purported emergency transfer might be used to circumvent involuntary transfer proceedings, paragraph (a) recommends a statutory requirement that an involuntary transfer hearing[8] be initiated not later than a recommended forty-eight hours after a transfer to department of mental health or mental retardation control has been effected. This has its counterpart in emergency commitment procedures preliminary to a civil commitment proceeding.[9]

Standard 7-10.8. Rights of transferred or committed prisoners

Once transferred or committed to a mental health or mental retardation facility, mentally ill prisoners should have the right to treatment described in chapter 23 of these standards and mentally retarded prisoners should have a comparable right to habilitation. These prisoners should not be permitted access into the community by mental health or mental retardation officials without authorization from appropriate correction officials or the court.

Commentary Introduction

The standard confirms the claims of mentally ill prisoners to treatment and of mentally retarded prisoners to habilitation services, with the limitation that mental health or mental retardation facility administrators are not to allow them into the community without advance authorization from either courts or appropriate correctional administrators.

4. *See* standards 23-1.1(c), 23-5.5(a) and commentary for counterpart criteria.
5. *See* standard 7-10.1(b) and commentary.
6. *See* standard 7-10.1(c) and commentary.
7. *See* standard 7-10.5(b) and commentary.
8. *See* standard 7-10.5 and commentary.
9. *See, e.g.,* Mich. Stat. Ann. §§14.800(423)-14.800(431) (1980 & Supp. 1985).

Related Standards

ABA, Standards for Criminal Justice 7-9.11, 7-10.2(b), 7-10.5, 23-3.1, 23-3.2, 23-5.1 through 23-5.5, 23-6.1 through 23-6.14

Commentary

Prisoner/patients who have been transferred involuntarily by court order[1] to the custody of mental health or mental retardation facilities under the administrative control of a department of mental health or mental retardation[2] continue to be sentenced convicts and therefore are guaranteed the adequate diagnosis, treatment, habilitation, and care that all prisoners must be accorded.[3] In addition, even though they are confined in mental health or mental retardation facilities they are entitled to all the protections prisoners are to receive under chapter 23 of the standards, Legal Status of Prisoners.[4] However, as in the case of convicted offenders specially committed because of severe mental illness or serious mental retardation,[5] transferred prisoner/patients cannot be allowed to leave treating facility premises on outpatient status or through an assignment to a community mental health center without authorization from appropriate correctional officials or a court. In this context, the latter should be considered the court that authorized the underlying involuntary transfer and not the sentencing court, to the extent they are different under jurisdiction rules of venue and civil procedure. Except for that restriction, prisoner/patients should be treated exactly like civilly committed patients in the same facility, as long as facility conditions, regulations, and practices equal or exceed the criteria established in chapter 23.[6]

1. *See* standard 7-10.5 and commentary.

2. *See* standard 7-10.2(b) and commentary.

3. *See* standards 23-5.1 through 23-5.6 and commentary. On the constitutional claim of civilly committed patients to a safe environment and treatment or habilitation services, *see* commentary to standard 7-9.11, note 1.

4. *See, e.g.,* parts II (access to the judicial process, legal services, and legal materials; VI (personal integrity and security). They should be subject to disciplinary sanctions, *id.* standard 23-3.2, if a mental health or mental retardation facility has promulgated the necessary rules of conduct, *id.* standard 23-3.1.

5. *See* standard 7-9.11; commentary to standard 7-9.11, note 7 and accompanying text.

6. *See* commentary to standard 7-9.11, note 4 and accompanying text; Weiner, *Rights of Institutionalized Persons,* in THE MENTALLY DISABLED AND THE LAW 251-268, 271-276, 279-284 (S. Brakel, J. Parry & B. Weiner eds., 3d ed. 1985).

Standard 7-10.9. Right of prisoner to refuse treatment or habilitation

(a) A prisoner, unless involuntarily transferred to a mental health or mental retardation facility, should be permitted to decline habilitation or mental health treatment except:

(i) when required by order of a court; or

(ii) when reasonably believed to be necessary in an emergency to save the life of the person or to prevent permanent and serious damage to the person's health.

(b) An involuntarily transferred prisoner has the same right to refuse treatment or habilitation as a civilly committed person in that jurisdiction.

Commentary Introduction

The standard restates the general principle that prisoner/patients have the right to refuse treatment or habilitation to the same extent as other prisoners and civilly committed patients, measured by the law of the jurisdiction in which they are held.

Related Standards

ABA, Standards for Criminal Justice 7-9.12, 7-10.2(b), 7-10.5, 7-10.8, 23-5.5, 23-5.8

Commentary

Prisoner/patients transferred involuntarily under court order[1] to mental health or mental retardation facilities outside the administrative jurisdiction of a department of prisons or corrections[2] are still prisoners. The correlative to their claim to adequate treatment and habilitation services,[3] confirmed in paragraph (a), is the same right to refuse medical examination or treatment they would have had they been retained in adult correctional institutions.[4] Although paragraph (a) probably suffices to protect

1. *See* standard 7-10.5 and commentary.
2. *See* standard 7-10.2(b) and commentary.
3. *See* standard 7-10.8 and commentary.
4. *See* standard 23-5.5 and commentary. In Large v. Superior Court, — Ariz. — , 38 Crim. L. Rptr. (BNA) 2378 (Jan. 24, 1986), the court held that due process limits the forced administration of psychotropic substances to inmates held in mental health treatment facili-

prisoner/patients wherever they are held, nevertheless, because they will be hospitalized with civilly committed patients, paragraph (b) states that they also have the same right as the latter to refuse treatment or habilitation services.[5] This should ensure that treating facility professionals and administrators do not discriminate on the basis of the nature of the route through which patients came to their facilities. The scope of the right of refusal will be determined on the basis of constitutional principles and jurisdiction precedent, statutes, rules, and regulations.[6]

Standard 7-10.10. Good time credits and parole

(a) A prisoner transferred to a mental health or mental retardation facility is entitled to earn good time credits on the same terms as prisoners in adult correctional facilities.

(b) A prisoner transferred to a mental health or mental retardation facility should be eligible for parole release consideration on the same terms as prisoners in adult correctional facilities.

(c) If otherwise qualified for parole, a prisoner should not be denied parole solely because the prisoner had or is receiving treatment in a mental health or mental retardation facility.

(d) If otherwise qualified for parole, a prisoner who would benefit from outpatient treatment or habilitation should not be denied parole for that reason.

---

ties to emergencies or as a recognized form of medical treatment authorized for involuntary treatment of civilly committed patients; security considerations are not legally admissible.

It should be noted also that prisoner/patients cannot be subjected to medical, psychiatric, or pharmaceutical experimentation not directly beneficial to them. *See* standard 23-5.8 and commentary. On counterpart problems of medical, psychiatric, and pharmaceutical experimentation on civilly committed patients, *see* Weiner, *Rights of Institutionalized Persons,* in The Mentally Disabled and the Law 251, 288-294 (S. Brakel, J. Parry & B. Weiner eds., 3d ed. 1985); Project, *Legal Issues in State Mental Health Care — Proposals for Change: Civil Commitment,* 2 Mental Disability L. Rep. 57, 126 (1978); *Suggested Statute on Civil Commitment,* 2 Mental Disability L. Rep. 127, 158-159 (1978).

5. *See generally* Weiner, *Treatment Rights,* in The Mentally Disabled and the Law 327, 341-351 (S. Brakel, J. Parry & B. Weiner eds., 3d ed. 1985). On the American Psychiatric Association view concerning the right to refuse treatment, *see* commentary to standard 7-9.12, note 4.

6. *See* commentary to standard 7-9.12, note 5.

Commentary Introduction

This standard provides that prisoners transferred to mental health or mental retardation facilities should be entitled to the good time and like credits and parole eligibility criteria applicable to prisoners in adult correctional facilities.

Related Standards

ABA, Standards for Criminal Justice 7-9.15, 7-10.2(b), 7-10.3, 7-10.4, 7-10.5, 23-3.1, 23-3.2, 23-7.2

Commentary

Prisoner/patients continue in the legal control of a department of prisons or corrections even though they have been transferred voluntarily[1] or involuntarily[2] into the custody of a department of mental health for treatment of severe mental illness or a department of mental health or mental retardation for habilitation services.[3] Therefore, they must be treated exactly like other prisoners with respect to the accrual of good time and other credits against sentence.[4] This principle is restated in paragraph (a).

Paragraph (b) confirms that prisoner/patients must be evaluated for parole release whenever they would have been given a parole review had they been retained continuously in an adult correctional institution. In other words, they cannot be placed in a special category of prisoners considered ineligible for parole release. Paragraph (c) expresses the corollary to that principle, namely, that prisoner/patients cannot be denied parole solely because they have received or currently are receiving treatment in a mental health facility or habilitation services in a mental retardation facility.[5]

---

1. *See* standards 7-10.3, 7-10.4 and commentary.
2. *See* standard 7-10.5 and commentary.
3. *See* standard 7-10.2(b) and commentary. The standard is identical to that governing convicted offenders who have been specially committed because of severe mental illness or serious mental retardation. *See* standard 7-9.15 and commentary.
4. *See generally* Barnes & Sibilla, *Figuring Good-Time — The Postconviction Process*, 16 U. Rich. L. Rev. 505 (1982). Credits could be withdrawn, therefore, only on the basis of disciplinary proceedings conforming to standard 23-3.2, applying substantive disciplinary regulations promulgated consonant with standards 23-3.1 and 23-7.2.
5. This position conforms to the Association's suggested statute on mental health services for prisoners. *See* Project, *Legal Issues in State Mental Health Care — Proposals for Change: Mental Health Services for Prisoners*, 2 Mental Disability L. Rep. 665, 674 (1978).

Paragraph (d) indicates the appropriate resolution of cases involving prisoner/patients who remain in the custody of a department of mental health or mental retardation when they become parole-eligible: If they cannot be released safely into the community as outpatients, they should not be paroled from prison control and given leave as outpatients. Conversely, however, if they can be furloughed from a mental health or mental retardation facility for treatment or habilitation as outpatients or in community mental health or mental retardation centers, and otherwise are eligible for parole release, paroling authorities should parole them. Parole, however, must be conditioned on compliance with treatment regimens or habilitation programs prescribed by treating professionals for civilly committed patients allowed to leave hospital confines on outpatient or furlough status.

Standard 7-10.11. Return to correctional facility

When the prisoner no longer meets criteria for transfer or commitment to a mental health or mental retardation facility, the prisoner should be returned to a correctional facility in accordance with the following procedures:

(a) When the prisoner, the mental health or retardation facility, and the correctional facility agree that the prisoner no longer meets the transfer criteria, the prisoner should be returned promptly to the correctional facility.

(b) When a voluntarily transferred prisoner seeks return to a correctional facility but the mental health or mental retardation facility disagrees that the prisoner currently meets retransfer criteria, the prisoner must be returned to the correctional facility or hearing procedures under standard 7-10.5 must be initiated.

(c) When the mental health or mental retardation facility determines that the prisoner no longer meets the criteria of standard 7-10.5(b) and decides to return the prisoner, then the prisoner, the correctional facility, and the court should receive written notice of this decision at least [fifteen] days prior to the return. The notice should include the factual basis for the return decision and confirmation that the prisoner has been advised of the right to object. If the prisoner objects, that objection must be included in the notice sent to the court. The court should determine whether the return decision reflects a deliberate indifference to the prisoner's mental condition and may hold a hearing to determine this issue. The court must hold

such a hearing in cases where the mental health or mental retardation facility seeks to return to a correctional facility a prisoner who has spent [ninety] days or less within the mental health or mental retardation facility.

Commentary Introduction

This standard provides procedures for returning prisoner/patients to correctional control when the criteria for transfer or commitment to a mental health or mental retardation facility are no longer met.

Related Standards

ABA, Standards for Criminal Justice 7-9.14, 7-10.1(b),(c), 7-10.2(b), 7-10.3, 7-10.4, 7-10.5

Commentary

Prisoner/patients can be transferred voluntarily[1] or involuntarily[2] to the custody of a department of mental health or mental retardation[3] only if they are severely mentally ill[4] or seriously mentally retarded[5] and cannot receive appropriate treatment or habilitation services in a department of prisons or corrections institution.[6] If their condition improves to the point that they no longer need treatment or habilitation services, or treatment or habilitation services can be provided within the jurisdiction of the department of prisons or corrections, they should be returned promptly to the control of the latter. That is the objective of standard 7-10.11.

Just as prisoner/patients may be transferred to mental health or mental retardation facility control if corrections and mental health or mental retardation administrators concur,[7] so under paragraph (a) may they be returned to the department of prisons or corrections by tripartite agreement. Judicial resources need not be expended wastefully in confirming the agreement.

1. *See* standard 7-10.4(a)(iii) and commentary.
2. *See* standard 7-10.5(b) and commentary.
3. *See* standard 7-10.2(b) and commentary.
4. *See* standard 7-10.1(b) and commentary.
5. *See* standard 7-10.1(c) and commentary.
6. *See* standards 7-10.4(b), 7-10.5(c) and commentary.
7. *See* standard 7-10.3 and commentary.

If, however, a voluntarily transferred prisoner/patient wishes to be returned to prison but mental health or mental retardation facility administrators disagree with that decision, under paragraph (b) they must pursue an involuntary transfer (functionally, a commitment) application,[8] just as they would have been required to do had the prisoner/patient not sought and achieved a voluntary transfer at an earlier time. Note that adult correctional administrators have no role to play under paragraph (b): They must reassert custodial responsibility for the patient/prisoner based on the criminal conviction and sentence that underlie prisoner status.

If a prisoner/patient originally was committed involuntarily by court order, the position of paragraph (c) is that a return to correctional custody should be subject to judicial authorization. The procedures specified correspond precisely to those governing the transfer to correctional control of convicted offenders who initially were specially committed to the custody of a department of mental health or mental retardation and who no longer require special treatment or habilitation services.[9] Accordingly, reference appropriately may be made to the commentary to that standard for the underlying policy objectives of paragraph (c).[10]

Standard 7-10.12. Civil commitment at expiration of sentence

A committed severely mentally ill or seriously mentally retarded prisoner must either be released or civilly committed pursuant to the state's general civil commitment statute when the sentence expires.

Commentary Introduction

This standard incorporates the constitutional standard that prisoner/patients must either be released from incarceration or hospitalization or be committed civilly when their criminal sentences have expired.

Related Standards

ABA, Standards for Criminal Justice 7-9.16, 7-10.1, 7-10.3, 7-10.4, 7-10.5, 7-10.11

8. *See* standard 7-10.5 and commentary.
9. *See* standard 7-9.14.
10. *See* commentary to standard 7-9.14, notes 3-7 and accompanying text.

Commentary

Standard 7-10.12, like the corresponding standard in part IX,[1] is mandated by the constitutional precedent forbidding convicts whose maximum terms of imprisonment have expired to be transferred administratively to hospital status under the jurisdiction of a department of mental health or mental retardation; they must be civilly committed if they are to be compulsorily hospitalized.[2] In exactly the same manner, prisoner/patients who were either voluntarily[3] or involuntarily[4] transferred to mental health or mental retardation treating facilities, and who have not been returned to department of prisons or corrections control[5] by the time their prison sentences have been served out, must be released immediately or made the subject of a civil commitment order entered according to valid statutory commitment criteria and on the basis of civil procedures conforming to due process requirements.

1. *See* standard 7-9.16.
2. *See* commentary to standard 7-9.16, notes 1-2 and accompanying text.
3. *See* standards 7-10.3 and 7-10.4 and commentary.
4. *See* standard 7-10.5 and commentary.
5. *See* standard 7-10.11 and commentary.